Diaghilev's Ballets Russes

Serge de Diaghileffs
Ballet Russe

DIAGHILEV'S BALLETS RUSSES

Lynn Garafola

New York · Oxford
OXFORD UNIVERSITY PRESS
1989

Oxford University Press

Oxford   New York   Toronto
Delhi   Bombay   Calcutta   Madras   Karachi
Petaling Jaya   Singapore   Hong Kong   Tokyo
Nairobi   Dar es Salaam   Cape Town
Melbourne   Auckland

and associated companies in
Berlin   Ibadan

Copyright © 1989 by Lynn Garafola

Published by Oxford University Press, Inc.,
200 Madison Avenue, New York, New York 10016

Oxford is a registered trademark of Oxford University Press

Library of Congress Cataloging-in-Publication Data
Garafola, Lynn.
Diaghilev's Ballets russes / Lynn Garafola.
p. cm.   Bibliography: p.   Includes index.
ISBN 0-19-505701-5
1. Ballets russes—History.
2. Diaghilev, Serge, 1872–1929.
3. Impresarios—Russian S.F.S.R.—Biography.
I. Title.
GV1786.B3G37   1989
792.8'0947—dc20   89-9365   CIP

Portions of this manuscript have been published in
Raritan, Dance Research Journal, and the *Proceedings*
of the Society of Dance History Scholars.

Excerpts from Bronislava Nijinska's "Creation of 'Les Noces' "
reprinted courtesy of *Dance Magazine* (December 1974).

Ezra Pound: *Personae.* Copyright 1926 by Ezra Pound.
Reprinted by permission of New Directions Pub. Corp.
and Faber and Faber Ltd.

1 2 3 4 5 6 7 8 9

Printed in the United States of America
on acid-free paper

To my father
and the memory of my mother

PREFACE

I N THE HISTORY OF twentieth-century ballet, no company has had so profound and far-reaching an influence as the Ballets Russes. It existed for only twenty years—from 1909 to 1929—but in those two decades it transformed ballet into a vital, modern art. The Ballets Russes created the first of this century's classics: *Les Sylphides, Firebird, Petrouchka, L'Après-midi d'un Faune, Le Sacre du Printemps, Parade, Les Noces, Les Biches, Apollo,* and *Prodigal Son,* all of which continue to be performed today. It nurtured several of the century's outstanding choreographers—Michel Fokine, Vaslav Nijinsky, Léonide Massine, Bronislava Nijinska, and George Balanchine—and through them influenced the direction of choreography until the 1970s. It brokered the century's most remarkable marriages between dance and the other arts, partnerships involving composers such as Igor Stravinsky, Claude Debussy, Maurice Ravel, and Serge Prokofiev and painters like Pablo Picasso, Natalia Gontcharova, André Derain, and Henri Matisse. From the numerous dancers who passed through its ranks emerged the teachers and ballet masters who continued its work in the metropoles and outposts of the West. And, as if this were not enough, the company also created a following for ballet that anticipated today's popular audiences. Had the Ballets Russes not existed, the history of twentieth-century ballet would have been very different.

The origins of the company lay in Russia, the birthplace of its early dancers and all its choreographers, as well as many of its composers and designers. Yet the Ballets Russes never performed in Russia, and after 1909 had no official ties with the country. Beginning with its name (French for "Russian Ballet"), the company was a creature of the West. Paris was the city of its birth, Vichy of its demise; in between, it made its home on the stages of three continents. This peripatetic existence left a deep mark on the Ballets Russes, redrawing its identity not once, but several times. But even in the company's salad days the works it presented differed from Russian fare at home. At St. Petersburg's Maryinsky Theater, Marius Petipa's ballets held sway—full-length works like *The Sleeping Beauty, Raymonda,* and *La Bayadère.* But at the Ballets Russes, from its inception to 1914, Michel Fokine's one-act dramas and lyric "miniatures" held pride of place— the "new ballet" that existed only on the fringe of Russia's official dance culture.

From the first, then, secession was the cornerstone on which the company built its identity, the *raison d'être* behind the turmoil of its successive revolutions. Through the repertory passed the many expressions of modernism—symbolism, primitivism, cubism, futurism, constructivism, neoclassicism, and any number of other "isms" that flitted across the period's artistic horizon. For twenty years the Ballets Russes seemed engaged in an ongoing experiment, the result of which was to extend the expressive possibilities of ballet. Nothing was left untouched: subject matter, movement idiom, choreographic style, stage space, music, scene design, costuming, even the dancer's physical appearance—all felt the imprint of the quest for new forms. The ideas seeding these experiments often derived from arts other than dance—painting, avant-garde performance, and especially the "new drama," revolutionized by the innovative stagecraft of directors such as Konstantin Stanislavsky and Vsevolod Meyerhold. Not all these experiments bore fruit, and many disappeared after a season. But together, they cast off the burden of the nineteenth century.

Yet Ballets Russes choreographers never fully disowned the past. However iconoclastic, their work nearly always acknowledged its heritage. Throughout twenty years of existence the company's vernacular remained the steps, syntax, and rhetoric of classical ballet. This is what the dancers practiced in daily class and what even the most subversive of the company's choreographers used at least some of the time as their common idiom. Along with the language of the danse d'école, they took something else from the past—the idea that meaning in dance had its source in movement. Unlike many of their contemporaries, then, Ballets Russes choreographers never disavowed the substance of classicism. What they got rid of were the late nineteenth-century conventions that had come to define it. Just as many writers of the period sought to identify a living literary tradition, so these choreographers struggled to redefine the vital inheritance of classicism for the twentieth century. In so doing, they prepared the ground for the mid-century triumph of neoclassicism, a style that first emerged in the 1920s.

But it was not only on choreography that the influence of the Ballets Russes was felt. The 1920s, 1930s, and 1940s witnessed the birth of many new ballet companies, most of which owed their inspiration and at least part of their identity to the Ballets Russes. Among these were the various "Ballet Russe" touring ensembles, which inherited the glamor and repertory of their illustrious forebear and took them to the four corners of the world. In England, the descendants included the Vic-Wells Ballet (which later became the Royal Ballet), Ballet Rambert, and the Markova-Dolin Ballet—all founded by veterans of the Ballets Russes. In the United States, there was Ballet Theatre (today, American Ballet Theatre), in its early days a showcase for major Ballets Russes works, and the New York City Ballet, whose artistic director, George Balanchine, had been the company's last in-house choreographer. Several short-lived companies could be added to the list—Bronislava Nijinska's Théâtre de la Danse, Ida Rubinstein's company, Adolph Bolm's Ballet Intime—as well as established institutions such as the Paris Opéra and the Teatro Colón in Buenos Aires, both reinvigorated by the presence of Ballets Russes alumni. That today ballet thrives from the Antipodes to the Midlands is largely owing to the Ballets Russes.

Throughout its life the company was a meeting ground for the glamorous, talented, and celebrated. But one figure towered above them all—Serge Diaghilev, the impresario *extraordinaire,* who presided over the Ballets Russes from its inception until his death in 1929 brought the company to an end. He was a man of ferocious will and infinitely discerning taste, encyclopedic knowledge and passionate curiosity—a Napoleon of the arts and a Renaissance man in one. He was born in Russia in 1872, and by the age of thirty had already made his mark. He has often been called a dilettante, and certainly, in his youth, he tried his hand at many trades. Yet his early undertakings prompted nothing less than a rejuvenation of Russian art, while serving as a superb apprenticeship for the future.

Diaghilev's father, a military man, had destined his son for the civil service. But although he dutifully went to law school in St. Petersburg, Diaghilev had other plans. He enrolled at the Conservatory, intending to be a composer. But his talent proved unequal to his ambition, and he dropped the idea, never imagining that the experience would be critical to the success of his later career. Beginning in the mid-1890s his interests came to center on the visual arts. He wrote criticism and became a collector, while organizing the first of several exhibitions that defied the era's taste for realism. But his greatest contribution was the St. Petersburg journal he founded in 1898 and edited until its demise in 1904.

Mir iskusstva (The World of Art) was to Russia what *The Yellow Book* was to England—a breath of fresh air in a stagnant art world. The journal was committed to beauty, which made it anathema to Russia's utilitarian-minded critics, and it promoted artists whose work challenged the methods and aims of the dominant school of realist painting. From the first, *Mir iskusstva* looked to the West, with articles and reproductions that introduced the Russian public to painters associated with symbolism and post-impressionism. The journal's taste was nothing if not catholic. Although its slant was toward the contemporary, the art of Russia's distant past received unwonted attention, an interest that culminated in Diaghilev's spectacular 1905 exhibition of eighteenth-century portraits, his last major undertaking in Russia. The journal also had a literary side, and here, too, the accent was on the new, with contributions by prominent symbolist writers and articles that were highly critical of the country's artistic institutions. By the early 1900s *Mir iskusstva* stood at the center of a broad movement pressing for artistic change on nearly every front.

Although Diaghilev was its driving force, the journal was a collaborative effort. At his side were old friends, including several who would later form the artistic nucleus of the Ballets Russes. Chief among them were Alexandre Benois and Léon Bakst, painters who found their true calling as designers and created the company's early signature style in works such as *Cléopâtre, Les Sylphides, Schéhérazade,* and *Petrouchka.* Their friendship with Diaghilev dated to the beginning of the 1890s and over the decade ripened into a close professional association. They worked with him on *Mir iskusstva* and followed him to the Imperial Theaters, where in 1899 he received a plum appointment as special assistant to the director of that state-supported complex. Their first Imperial undertaking—which also happened to be their first theatrical commission—was a production of the ballet *Sylvia.* The work never materialized, but as a project enlisting a half-dozen *Mir iskusstva* artists, *Sylvia* proved to be a forerunner of the collaborative method adopted by Diaghilev in the Ballets Russes.

Although Bakst and Benois received a number of subsequent commissions, Diaghilev remained at his post only two years. His dismissal, a result of bureaucratic intrigue complicated by his own high-handedness, closed the civil service to him. But it was not until the Revolution of 1905 had dashed all hope for a reform of the country's artistic bureaucracy that Diaghilev set his sights abroad. In 1906 he organized a mammouth exhibition of Russian art in Paris, and the following year, in the same city, a concert series of Russian music. In 1908, at the Paris Opéra, he presented the first *Boris Godunov* seen outside Russia, and the following year, the season of opera and ballet that marked the unofficial debut of the Ballets Russes.

Almost always, histories of the Ballets Russes begin with Diaghilev and the designer friends who accompanied him on the journey from Petersburg to Paris. This book also begins in the Russian capital. But it opens with a different set of heroes and a different point of view. The Ballets Russes was first and foremost a dance company, and although choreography may have been the least appreciated ingredient of Diaghilev's recipe, it was the one that gave his enterprise its unique identity. Michel Fokine never belonged to the *Mir iskusstva* circle, and until preparations for the 1909 season were under way he had only a nodding acquaintance with most of the group's personalities. From the start, then, his history followed a different course. His art sprang not from a dissatisfaction with realism, but from what he perceived as the inadequacy of late nineteenth-century ballet to convey a modern sense of beauty and a personal poetic vision. The choreographic secession led by Fokine and his followers within St. Petersburg's Imperial Ballet is the natural starting point of a book that sees the Ballets Russes as the progenitor of modern ballet.

The revolution Fokine initiated was carried forward by his successors in the Diaghilev company. With Nijinsky, ballet crossed the threshold of modernism; with Massine, it formed an alliance with futurism; with Nijinska, it absorbed the abstract method of constructivism; with Balanchine, it mated with neoclassical idealism. Under each of these choreographers, the repertory was remade and the idea of modernity transformed. Yet all responded to the imperatives that had guided Fokine—that ballet take heed of the world around it and express a subjective vision. The chapters that comprise the remainder of this book's opening section examine the work of these choreographers from this dual perspective, probing in each instance the sources of their work and its underlying ideology.

Just as compelling as this story of artistic revolution is the saga of the company's economic survival. The Ballets Russes was a vast theatrical enterprise, a traveling circus of dancers, musicians, composers, designers, scene painters, rehearsal pianists, wigmakers, and publicists. Never easy to keep afloat, several times in its twenty-year history it nearly went under. Unlike the government-subsidized Imperial Theaters, the company was a creature of the marketplace, and from the first it had to scrounge for money. Diaghilev begged and borrowed, drove hard bargains with producers and sold off assets when nothing was in the till. The decisions he made were often stop-gap measures, compromises with circumstance that enabled the company to survive but subtly altered its character. The Ballets Russes assumed many guises during its twenty-year life. Although dance was its bread and butter, it produced nearly twenty operas. In London it appeared on music-hall stages; in Monte Carlo, as a resident of the local opera house. At times, it was purely a touring ensemble; at others, it resembled nothing so much as an experimental studio or laboratory. These changing identities touched nearly every aspect of the company's life. They determined who paid the bills and what the dancers received in their pay packets; they affected the size of the company and where it performed. They also influenced repertory trends and collaborative relationships, the status of the dancer and that of the choreographer. More often than one might suspect, the art of the Ballets Russes reflected its status as a complex economic enterprise. This story, which has never been fully told, is the subject of the book's middle section.

For twenty years the Ballets Russes brought crowds to the theater. Not since the romantic era of the 1830s and 1840s had ballet attracted so huge a following. But even apart from the sheer number of bodies, this audience was remarkable. Before the advent of the Ballets Russes, it was said that ballet was for children and old men. With Diaghilev, however, it became a pastime for the privileged. The rich and famous came to his performances—the royalty of blood and talent chronicled in the era's gossip columns. But there were also writers, painters, composers, and collectors—an intellectual and artistic elite that ballet performances since have rarely attracted. Diaghilev created other select publics as well. But one, at least, included ordinary people who mixed with his intellectual and society followers in postwar London's music-halls. With Diaghilev, too, ballet became a magnet for homosexuals. In numerous ways, today's audience for ballet can be traced to the Ballets Russes.

Diaghilev's audience established the broad cultural context of his company. It defined its social identity and to a large extent its artistic one. At a time when advertising was in its infancy, the enormous vogue for the Ballets Russes rested with social tastemakers who brought friends to performances, hired dancers to entertain at private parties, and wore Diaghilev-inspired costumes to fancy-dress balls. The company was lionized in print, and few were the fashion and general interest magazines that failed to take notice of its personalities. Although the tone was different, the same was true of the era's intellectual journals, even those that rarely covered dance. The Ballets Russes left its mark on fashion, design, and entertainment. But these, in turn, left their imprint on the company, from the costuming of its dancers to the content of its choreography. In a general sense, the identity of the Ballets Russes at any given moment reflected the social composition of its audience. The role of Diaghilev's many publics in shaping the evolving ideology of his enterprise is the theme of my third and concluding section.

The era of the Ballets Russes is probably the most chronicled in dance history. Yet this book is the first to look at the company as a totality—its art, enterprise, and audience. The task has led me to ask new questions of familiar sources and has taken me to archives in Paris, Monte Carlo, New York, Berkeley, Syracuse, and Princeton previously unexamined by Diaghilev scholars. This is also the first book to challenge the premises of what might be called the British school of Ballets Russes history, which came into being in the 1930s. Its writings, above all those of Cyril W. Beaumont and Arnold Haskell, created the basis for modern Diaghilev scholarship, providing first-hand accounts that remain indispensable sources. Over the years, however, little has changed in the school's interpretative framework. In the many works of Richard Buckle, today England's leading Diaghilev expert, the company appears either as the link in an apostolic succession leading from Russia's Imperial Ballet to England's Royal Ballet or as a maverick untouched by the arts and ideas of its era. Buckle has unearthed new facts, but has failed to rethink their significance. And he has assiduously avoided the newer methods of social history, dance criticism, and feminism that have vitalized American dance scholarship, and to which this book is indebted.

The story that follows is a long one. It begins in fin-de-siècle Russia and ends in Western Europe of the Jazz Age. It embraces political and artistic revolutions and a world war. And it includes among the cast of characters men and women from all walks and stations of life—personalities as diverse as Lady Cunard, a leader of London society; Edward Bernays, the father of modern public relations; Anatole Lunacharsky, the Soviet Commissar of Enlightenment; and Otto Kahn, an underwriter of the Allied war effort. The giants of modernism are here—Picasso, Stravinsky, Joyce, and Proust—along with the dancers and choreographers whose names have passed into legend. And there are the people whose lives are mostly unsung—like Vasily Kisselov, an early colleague of Fokine, committed to a psychiatric hospital for his role in the dancers' strike of 1905, and Doris Faithfull, who complained on behalf of a half-dozen dancers about not being able to make ends meet on one of the company's American tours. They, too, make appearances in these pages, adding their prosaic realities to the march of events. As much as it belongs to the luminaries of the era, the history of the Ballets Russes is also theirs.

New York   L. G.
May 1989

ACKNOWLEDGMENTS

To THE MANY archivists and librarians who guided me to material in this country and abroad and to the Social Science Research Council, for a generous grant for research in Europe, I owe a special debt of gratitude. I also wish to thank the friends and colleagues who helped me along what proved to be a long and arduous journey: Mary Pat Kelly, at whose urging I embarked on this study; Parmenia Migel Ekstrom, of the Stravinsky-Diaghilev Foundation, who opened her home, her collection, and her memories to me; Joan Acocella, who indulged my obsession with Diaghilev in endless hours of conversation and gave portions of the manuscript a close and critical reading; Gerald Ackerman, Nancy Baer, Sally Banes, Vicente García-Márquez, Debra Goldman, Millicent Hodson, Elizabeth Kendall, Claire de Robillant, Hamideh Sedghi, and Mary Ann de Vlieg, who shared thoughts, ideas, and research material with me; Elizabeth Souritz and Ilya Zilberstein, both of Moscow, and Melvin Gordon, who directed me to important Russian sources; Dr. Mikaly Cenner, of Budapest, who supplied me with copies of documents relating to Nijinsky; Robert Craft, Nancy Lassalle of Ballet Society, David Leonard of Dance Books Ltd., Robert L.B. Tobin, and George Verdak, who allowed me to reproduce material from their collections; Irene Huntoon, Ellen Scaruffa, and Susan Cook Summer, who translated the Russian material; Frederick McKitrick, who translated the German material incorporated into Appendix A; Paul Kolnik and Pat Brancaccio, who copied some of the illustrations; Robert A. Day and Burton Pike, who supervised the dissertation on which this book is based; Arno Mayer, who read early drafts of certain chapters; Arthur Wang and Geoffrey Field, who read the final manuscript; Rachel Toor, who did everything possible to help produce a handsome book; Sheldon Meyer, my editor, who offered many helpful suggestions and words of encouragement.

〈xv〉

To my husband Eric Foner I owe a debt of gratitude that can never be repaid. Without his unflagging belief in the importance of this book and the inspiration of his own example, *Diaghilev's Ballets Russes* would never have been completed.

NOTE

Many of the Russians who figure in this book made careers in the West under variously transliterated names. As a general rule, the spelling of Russian names follows *The New Grove Encyclopedia of Music and Musicians, The Dance Encyclopedia,* and *The Concise Oxford Dictionary of Ballet.* For individuals not listed in any of these sources, names are given in their most common form or as they appeared in cast lists, reviews, and other documents of the period.

The titles of works staged in Russia have been translated into English, except when the original title was in French. For works produced in the West, titles have been left in the original language, except where the English title is better known or has become the standard form used in revivals.

CONTENTS

I

ART

1 ✎

THE LIBERATING AESTHETIC
OF MICHEL FOKINE

O N JANUARY 9, 1905, striking workers from the outlying districts of
St. Petersburg converged on the Winter Palace with a petition beg-
ging the Tsar, "in the name of all the laboring class of Russia," to end the
war with Japan and "eliminate the tyranny of capital over labor." The
watchwords of the petition, which precipitated the massacre that has passed
into history as "Bloody Sunday," were self-determination, individual freedom, and hostility to the Tsarist bureaucracy.[1]

In the ensuing months the cry of civil liberties and autonomy moved
from the factory districts of St. Petersburg to Tsardom's most privileged
cultural institutions. In February a student strike broke out at the Conservatory of Music. "Some of the students' demands are very sensible,"
wrote the mother of conservatory student Serge Prokofiev:

> They want monthly opera productions with students participating: singers,
> conductors, and a full orchestra, with students playing on the instruments they
> are studying . . . They want a library, a higher level in academic studies, and
> polite treatment from the attendants and the professors. For example, they say
> that [Leopold] Auer hits his students over the head with his bow. The situa-
> tion right now can be compared to an impending storm when the air is heavy
> and it is hard to breathe.[2]

In March, amid a wave of protest, Nikolai Rimsky-Korsakov, a liberal
given to publishing outspoken letters in newspapers, was dismissed from
his post as conservatory director, an action that led Alexander Glazunov
and Alexandre Benois to resign from the faculty. Forty students were ex-
pelled, and after the premiere of Rimsky-Korsakov's *Kostchei the Immortal* at Vera Komissarzhevskaya's theater turned into a political demonstration, the Tsar banned from the Imperial Theaters the works of this
"revolutionary" composer.[3]

The conservatory was not the only artistic institution shaken by the events of 1905. In the autumn a strike broke out at the Imperial Ballet. In the overall panorama of the Revolution, the dancers' strike is certainly a minor footnote. Yet the event had a major impact on the genesis and aesthetics of the early Ballets Russes. In an art where idea takes form only in the performer, the assembling of a human corps sympathetic to a choreographer's vision assumes a vital artistic function. The strike at the Maryinsky Theater had precisely that effect: it transformed the company's dissidents into the makers of a choreographic secession—and Ballets Russes protagonists of 1909. The strikers elected a dozen delegates to press their claims, and of the twelve no fewer than three—Michel Fokine and ballerinas Anna Pavlova and Tamara Karsavina—were future Diaghilev stars. Even the closely guarded pupils of the Imperial Theatrical School were touched by the "endless talk about strikes and risings," as ballerina Yelena Lukom, a student at the time, recalled those troubled days. In October the youngsters staged a mild protest that Vladimir Telyakovsky, the director of the Imperial Theaters, recorded in his diary: they "assembled, without having obtained permission, to discuss their needs." Vaslav Nijinsky was one of the students who attended this unwonted meeting, which demanded improvement of education, instruction in theatrical make-up, and the right for advanced students to wear their own shoes, collars, and cuffs with the school uniform.[4]

The strike articulated grievances intensified by the leadership crisis and artistic malaise that followed the golden age of the Imperial Ballet in the 1890s. This decade had marked the high point of Marius Petipa's long career at the Maryinsky and witnessed the creation of classic works such as *The Sleeping Beauty, The Nutcracker, Raymonda,* and *Swan Lake.* Many of the strikers' demands were economic—higher salaries, a voice in budgetary decisions, and a five-day work week. But as at the conservatory the key issues were artistic. The dancers demanded the right to choose their own regisseurs, company directors who took charge of rehearsals and represented management in day-to-day relations with the dancers, and the return to active duty of Petipa, his assistant Alexander Shiryaev, and teacher Alfred Bekefi, all recently forced out of the company for political reasons. That Petipa, who had ruled the Imperial Ballet for over four decades and given a definitive form to Russian classicism, figured so prominently in the dispute indicates to what degree art and politics were interwoven at the Maryinsky. As Karsavina explained to her disapproving mother, the aim of the dancers "was to raise the standard of art. We were going to ask for autonomy, choose our own Committee to decide artistic questions . . . do away with the methods of bureaucratic organization."[5]

The Revolution of 1905 was carried out in the name of "liberty." It stood for the principle of individual freedom in social and cultural as well as economic life. For the dancers and other personnel of the Imperial Theaters, the strike kindled a feeling of common artistic identity not unlike the bonds uniting the artists grouped around Diaghilev's journal *Mir iskusstva.* "Bear in mind," a striking regisseur reminded the dramatic troupe as he rang down the curtain at the Maryinsky's "sister" Alexandrinsky Theater, "we are striving for an honourable freedom. Not long ago the Russian actor was a serf."[6] Implicit in the assertion of political unity was a transformation of the strikers' artistic and social consciousness.

Karsavina's recollection notwithstanding, life at the Imperial Ballet did not resume its normal course in the aftermath of 1905. A commission of enquiry was set up to investigate the disturbances, and despite an official amnesty, Pyotr Mikhailov and Valentin Presniakov, leaders of the striking dancers, were dismissed, while another activist, Vasily Kisselov, was sent to a psychiatric hospital. (His stay must have had no long-term effect on his dancing, for both he and Presniakov appeared in the early seasons of the Ballets Russes.) Joseph Kchessinsky, the brother of Mathilde Kchessinska, the Maryinsky's *prima ballerina assoluta* and Tsar Nicholas II's former mistress, was also dismissed for his role in the strike, although thanks to his sister's influence within the Imperial Court, he did not lose his pension. Even Pavlova, the brightest star of the younger generation, was warned by Baron Vladimir Fredericks, the all-powerful court minister who controlled the Imperial Theaters, to desist from further trouble or suffer the consequences. "Many of the other artists involved were eventually dismissed without cause," recalled Bronislava Nijinska, "or were not given the chance to dance good roles, or simply were not duly promoted."[7] Mild, to be sure, by tsarist standards, these repressive actions nevertheless deepened the rift between dissidents and management loyalists.

Further polarizing an already divided company, such measures prepared the ground for the exodus of talent that eventually drained the Imperial Ballet of its younger generation. Beginning in 1907 Maryinsky dancers began to sound foreign waters for engagements. Adolph Bolm and Pavlova made a number of forays abroad in 1907–1908, including a Scandinavian tour that ended in Berlin and met with resounding success everywhere. Bolm also partnered Lydia Kyasht on her first appearance at the Empire Theatre in London in 1908, while Karsavina herself danced in the English capital during Lent 1909, anticipating Diaghilev's Paris debut by several months. Other dancers of the company's left wing soon followed: George Kyasht (Lydia's brother), Ludmilla Schollar, and the Bekefi sisters all made London appearances in 1909–1910, as did Olga Preobrajenska, a senior ballerina, who also danced at the Paris Opéra in 1909. (Not to be outdone, the doyenne of the traditionalists, Mathilde Kchessinska, arranged a series of guest performances at the Opéra to coincide with Diaghilev's production of *Boris Godunov* in 1908 at the same house.) If monetary considerations made foreign engagements attractive, even more compelling was the excitement of working outside the bureaucracy and artistic stagnation of the Imperial Theaters. "There are many of us in the theaters of St. Petersburg and Moscow," wrote Bolm, "who are eager to use our art for better purposes. We are helpless, though, because the administration of our theater is strictly reactionary. We dare not criticize them openly. We are not even allowed to make suggestions. Petipa is dead. [He had died in 1910.] The masters still use his creations, but they have forgotten his spirit. Such an atmosphere is stifling after the freedom of travel."[8] Here, Bolm voices the passion for art, and belief in its high purpose, that animated the young idealists of the Ballets Russes.

Like all tsarist institutions, the Maryinsky was a microcosm of society at large, where politics, social relations, and artistic goals were inextricably linked. The revolutionary impulse kindled responses to all these facets of the dancer's experience. It colored attitudes toward the "old classical technique" epitomized by Kchessinska and Nicholas Sergeyev, the Imperial Ballet's chief regisseur, as well as the careerism such traditionalists represented. It politicized "aspirations for new creativity in dancing," while sensitizing Fokine's future ensemble to the creative demands of group effort. And it sharpened criticism of the "parasites of art," as Fokine termed the officeholders who controlled the fortunes of the Imperial Theaters, impelling him and like-minded colleagues to seek work outside the bureaucratic world.[9] The ideals of 1905 not only altered the habits of mind and patterns of behavior among the younger generation of Maryinsky dancers; they also charged the imaginative universe of Fokine's early choreography. In the themes and methods of his first ballets, the aspirations of his fellow strikers reappeared, fused into a statement of liberal ideology.

Michel Fokine's emergence as a choreographer coincided with the Revolution of 1905 and reflected the social and artistic discontents that contributed to the turmoil within the Maryinsky. Like the other strike leaders, he was connected with the Gogol School, a charitable institution founded and supported by the dancers, which became a focal point of the company's left wing.[10] He strongly opposed Alexander Krupensky, the conservative head of the St. Petersburg office of the Imperial Theaters, and at the six-hour meeting on October 15, 1905, when striking dancers and administration supporters met in acrimonious confrontation, he openly denounced Sergeyev as "the Directorate's spy." Sergeyev, who achieved lasting fame in the West for his stagings of *Giselle, Swan Lake,* and *The Sleeping Beauty* in the 1920s and 1930s, played an ugly role in these events. A caricature of the period entitled "Fruits of a Ballet Strike" shows him waving the dancers' petition over a recumbent Olga Preobrajenska, who is being flogged by a skeletal henchman as Krupensky and Telyakovsky look on.[11]

Although Fokine's impatience with the artistic and bureaucratic strictures of the Imperial Ballet anticipated the Revolution, the events of that tumultuous time goaded him to action. Between February 1906 and March 1909 he choreographed at least two dozen ballets and dances, an astonishing output considering that previously he had only three to his credit. Almost without exception, these works were created for organizations other than the Maryinsky, in the freer atmosphere of school performances and charity events, many organized by the choreographer himself. In such surroundings Fokine could pick and choose his collaborators; he could expect what he received—"full co-operation and enthusiasm."[12] His first important commission, *La Vigne,* came at the behest of fellow dancers and was produced for a Gogol School fundraiser early in 1906. Fokine cast the ballet almost exclusively with Maryinsky dissidents: the wines in the tippling scene, for instance, were impersonated by Pavlova, Karsavina, Kyasht, and his wife, Vera Fokina. "Left-wingers" appeared in all his postrevolutionary works created for professional dancers—*The Dying Swan, Eunice, Chopiniana* (and its various successors), *Le Pavillon d'Armide, Une Nuit d'Egypte,* and *Bal Poudré*—with Pavlova and Karsavina dancing in nearly every production. In the original version of *Carnaval,* which brought to an end the cycle of "personal" works opened by the revolution, not only Karsavina but three dissident leaders appeared: Alfred Bekefi (who also danced in *Bal Poudré*), Alexander Shiryaev, and Vasily Kisselov.

Especially close to Fokine in these years was Pyotr Mikhailov. In his memoirs the choreographer describes a gathering at his home in late 1907 attended by Benois and other Mir Iskusstva artists where, at Fokine's request, Mikhailov read a paper "on the subject of the desirability of the union of the world of painters with the ballet, the new road on which the ballet was entering, and the possibilities which the revived ballet presented for the work of painters, musicians, and so forth." The views expressed, adds Fokine, were "in total accord" with his own.[13] The presence of this dissident network bespeaks more than loyalty. On the one hand, it reveals that the genesis of Fokine's artistic secession was inextricably bound up in the political events of 1905; on the other, that Diaghilev's mighty ensemble had its origins in the community of artists formed by those events and knitted together by Fokine's early undertakings. In their "exhilarating" atmosphere, "everyone," the choreographer wrote, "felt that he was pioneering in a new movement and that he was part of the birth of a new form of ballet."[14]

Although Petipa stood high in the esteem of Imperial dancers, for the generation that came of age in the early years of the twentieth century, his artistic accomplishment belonged to the past. "The productions following *Sleeping Beauty* grew larger and larger," recalled Karsavina, Fokine's great interpreter who was equally at home in the Petipa repertory:

> The subject was treated like a peg on which to hang numerous ballabiles. Though his choreographic mastery never deserted Petipa . . . he had lost sight of the . . . inner motivation of the dance . . . *Bluebeard* [for instance] (1896) . . . had several dancing displays with a loosely connected plot. They were the tableaux of the treasure-chambers of Raoul the Bluebeard, visited by his seventh wife, Isora . . . Dancing knives, forks, spoons and platters in one of them furnished a pretext for dancing . . . reducing the classical dancing to absurdity. In fact, this *Bluebeard* had all the features of a pantomime or a French revue . . .[15]

Fokine's qualms about Maryinsky artistic conventions arose early in his career as a professional dancer. "When I played a 'mime' role," he wrote in *Memoirs of a Ballet Master*:

> I represented an authentic image of the period. But when I danced a "classic" part, I portrayed a leading dancer— outside the confines of place or time . . . I felt that, the more historically authentic were the costumes of the mimes, . . . the more idiotic we, the classic dancers, must have appeared in the midst of them . . . in pink tights and short skirts looking like open umbrellas.[16]

In 1904, on the very eve of the Revolution, Fokine submitted the libretto of *Daphnis and Chloë* to Vladimir Telyakovsky. To the draft of his proposed two-act ballet, he attached a prefatory memorandum explaining the principles to be observed in its production. Couched in the form of suggestions, this memorandum stands as Fokine's earliest aesthetic statement. It was time, he wrote:

> [to] make an experiment in producing a Greek ballet in the spirit of the [Hellenic] age . . . No ballet-master could commit the following mistake: arrange dances for Russian peasants in the style of Louis XV or . . . create dances in the manner of the Russian *trepak* to a French theme. Then why permit the constant error in productions based on subjects from Ancient Greece: shall Greeks dance the French way?[17]

Fokine's call for authenticity was both an integral part of his aesthetic and the focus of his many dissatisfactions with the Imperial Theaters. From the start his ideal was that of a naturalist: art must incarnate its *race*, *moment et milieu*—Taine's famous dictum—rather than adhere to classical precepts:

> Just as life differs in different epochs, and gestures differ among human beings, so the dance which expresses life must vary. The Egyptian of the time of the Pharaohs was very different from the Marquis of the eighteenth century. The ardent Spaniard and the phlegmatic dweller in the north not only speak different languages, but use different gestures. These are not invented. They are created by life itself.[18]

Today, naturalism has fallen into disrepute, and when we speak of this scientific offspring of realism, the tone is apt to be disparaging. Yet in its time naturalism was a galvanizing imaginative force that hurtled the artist into the real world of slums, mines, brothels, and vaudeville theaters; taught him the empirical method of the scientist; and impressed upon him that art was a vehicle of social change. Although Fokine eschewed the lower depths, from an early age his inquisitive mind probed beyond Theater Street. As a vacationing student, he cycled daily to the Hermitage to copy statues and canvases from its great collection. During the period of crisis that followed his debut as a dancer, he traversed the length and breadth of St. Petersburg to take art classes, study anatomy, draw in charcoal, paint in oil, and pore over art books. "Admission to the Academy of Arts," he later wrote, "became the goal of my ambition."[19]

In addition to painting, travel and music obsessed him. He spent holidays combing the hinterlands of Russia, far from St. Petersburg. His first trip, in a third-class railway carriage, took him from the Imperial capital to Moscow, Nizhni Novgorod, the Volga, Caspian Sea, and Caucasus; the second, to the land of ancient Rus', now Kiev, and the Crimea; the next, to Budapest, Vienna, and Italy. What he saw gave life to the tales stockpiled in his imagination. By the mighty Volga, Stenka Razin seemed to offer his beloved Persian princess to the waters, while in Bakhchisarai the "fantastic and majestic splendor" of *The Thousand and One Nights* mingled with Pushkin's verses. Before the treasure-troves of Venice, Florence, Rome, and Pompeii, the dancer stood "in awe, in admiration, in a trance."[20] Everywhere he went he found evidence of dance. From the Caucasus he returned home with the memory of the light, proud walk of slippered Circassians; from Italy, with postcards and reproductions of art works depicting dancing that became the basis of a vast collection of ritual and folkloric material.

Back home, Fokine found his way to circles that catered to the growing interest in Russian folk music. He played the mandolin in an orchestra of Maryinsky professionals and the balalaika in factories, and joined groups that performed Russian folk music on authentic national instruments. From what he called "this amateurish venture into music," he learned to handle scores and even to compose—well enough to orchestrate entire works for these amateur ventures. Not only did this apprenticeship deepen his understanding of music, but it also made him keenly aware of the effect music could exert on its listeners. The stylish public that grew misty-eyed at "The Song of the Volga Boatman" impressed on him the power a living art had to speak directly to the emotions. It drove home the lesson of Tolstoi: that the very essence of pure art form was the "projection of feeling, the innoculation of the audience with it."[21] Hitherto, he had understood this only theoretically; now it became an article of his artistic creed. So, too, did another Tolstoian notion: that art belonged to the broad masses of people, not to the "narrow circle of balletomanes" that attended the Maryinsky. Reinforcing this idea were readings of an overtly political nature—Peter Kropotkin, Mikhail Bakunin, August Bebel, and Ferdinand Lassalle—introduced to him by exiled Russian socialists whom he met in Switzerland.[22]

These experiences left a deep imprint on Fokine's imagination. From the start of his choreographic career, an acute historical sense informed his work. He believed that theme, period, and style in ballet must conform to the time and place of the scenic action; that empirical observation and research must accompany the act of creation; that expressiveness stemmed directly from the fidelity of a representation to nature. Under the aegis of history, Fokine mounted his attack on ballet convention.

From the romantic era onward, realism had held an honored place in ballet. It existed, however, as a complement to classicism, within a framework of dualities that permeated every aspect of postromantic style. Dualism was reflected in the narrative structure (mime scenes vs. pure dance ones); in the dance idiom ("character" or folk-derived vs. academic); in the gestural style (pantomimic vs. symbolic); in the costuming (historically accurate vs. tutus); even in the footwear (boots and soft slippers vs. pointe shoes). These dualities, first assembled into an iconographic system in the 1830s, grew increasingly conventionalized as the century progressed. To Fokine they were anathema.

In place of dualism, Fokine sought a complete unity of expression. Two courses lay open to him: he could dispense with realism or do away with classicism. In most instances, he chose the latter course. But even in works conceived in classical style—*Les Sylphides* and its various predecessors, *Les Préludes,* and *Eros*—he contextualized the material, setting it within a framework of history. To Fokine's "warmed sensibilities," in André Levinson's eloquent phrase,[23] classicism did not lie in the creation of timeless images, but in the evocation of a style identified with the romantic era,

the choreographer's paradise of original innocence. The century's later ac-
cretions—virtuosity, acrobatism, and vulgar display—were for him the cause
of ballet's artistic decline.

If realism was the foundation of Fokine's poetic, ethnic material provided the bricks and mortar. In Petipa's works, character dances had fleshed
out the choreography, texturing it with historical particularity, while conveying the dynamic physicality and unbridled emotion so congenial to
Fokine's sensibility. By the century's end, however, stylization had undermined both the vitality and authenticity of the original folk forms. "A
follower of the classic ballets, Petipa went to the character dance from
them, and not from folk dances," wrote Alexander Shiryaev:

> The Saracen dance in *Raymonda* is based on the classic tempos of the pas de
> basque and ballonnée, the Spanish panaderos in the same ballet also on the
> pas de basque, the Indian dance in *La Bayadère* on grand battement and so
> on . . . No matter how externally brilliant and effective the character dances
> of Petipa may have been, it would be more correct to consider them classical
> variations on some national theme than actual national dances, even in a purely
> theatrical sense.[24]

Often pointe was used, along with the jumping techniques of classical
dance. (This was usually the case of Chinese, Japanese, and other "exotic"
styles.) At times, traits of one national dance turned up in another, a confusion to which Spanish and Italian forms were especially prone. Although
Hungarian and Polish dances reached a "high degree of . . . perfection,"
reflecting, in part, the presence in the Imperial troupe of dancers of those
nationalities, others were so distorted, wrote Fokine, "that their origin was
almost unrecognizable."[25] By the turn of the century, character dancing
expressed little more than national stereotypes dressed in sanitized pi-
quancy.

Fokine restored the vitality to these languishing dialects. Drawing on
living sources, he created what came to be known as the *genre nouveau,* a
form independent of the academy and identified exclusively with national
and ethnic styles of movement.[26] Between 1906 and 1918, the year he left
the Maryinsky to settle permanently in the West, he mined this living vein
repeatedly. In *La Vigne,* Marie Petipa danced a rousing czardas as the
spirit of Hungarian wine. 1906 also witnessed the creation of two Spanish-
style works—*Sevillana* and *Spanish Dance,* which had its premiere on the
same program as *La Vigne*. In 1907 he drew for the first time on material
from his travels. Although *Eunice* was set in antiquity, the sheepskin wine
bag that inspired the Dance of the Boordukes was a household item in the
Caucasus. That same year he choreographed the first version of *Chopi-*

niana, a "grand ballet" in miniature, in which the two classical sequences—the Nocturne and the Waltz—were framed by scenes in character style. The ballet opened with a brilliant Polonaise, ballroom dances
created, Fokine wrote, "in the fullest bloom of the Polish nation."[27] The
third tableau, to Chopin's Mazurka, depicted a wedding in a Polish village.
The fifth and concluding scene was a Tarantella in which Fokine sought
"to project the authentic character of the national dances . . . [he had]
studied in detail on the island of Capri."[28] Although eliminated (as were
the other character sequences) from the classical version of the ballet staged
the following year, the Tarantella marked a new stage in Fokine's approach to folk material. For the first time, he "experimented . . . with
'looking around,' "[29] defining his ideal as a symphony created from living
forms. Again and again, Fokine made good his method. In *Thamar,* choreographed in 1912 for the Ballets Russes, he drew on memories of the
Caucasus to create the fierce and thrilling dances of this Georgian legend.
Stenka Razin, which had its premiere at a Maryinsky charity gala in 1915,
opened on the shores of the Volga, again recollecting his first journey to
the Russian heartland. The following year, also at the Maryinsky, he presented *Jota Aragonesa,* a suite of Spanish dances inspired by a trip to Andalusia in 1914. Here, he took pains not only to reproduce the rhythms,
steps, and distinctive line of the Iberian originals, but also to convey "the
gaiety and the joy of life so characteristic of the genuine dances."[30]

In these ballets Fokine worked primarily as an ethnographer, bringing
the methods of the naturalist to the study of living peoples. When dealing
with the past, he adopted an equally empirical course, rummaging libraries
and museums for the shards of lost civilizations. The idea for *Daphnis and
Chloë* came from the Longus pastoral; that for *Eunice* from a libretto
based on Henryk Sienkiewicz's novel *Quo Vadis?;* both *Chopiniana* and
Carnaval were inspired by episodes in the lives of their composers.[31] But
literature was merely a starting point. In the "Dance of the Three Egyptian
Girls" in *Eunice,* he simulated the profile positions and angular lines of
ancient frescoes and bas-reliefs. He garbed the trio in body-hugging tunics
and period wigs, darkened the flesh with paint, and elongated the eye with
make-up after the manner of Egyptian art. This dance was a forerunner of
Une Nuit d'Egypte, choreographed in 1908 and, as *Cléopâtre,* taken to
Paris the following year. Now, the profile positions and flattened palms
were sustained throughout the ballet, while the angularity of the plastique
was further elaborated in the lines of the groupings. When staging the
work, Fokine immersed himself in ancient Egypt, scurrying to the Hermitage in his free moments and surrounding himself with books on the subject. The snake dance he created for Pavlova was inspired by a reproduction he found in his rambles through the museum. In *Le Dieu Bleu,*

choreographed for the Ballets Russes in 1912, study was equally apparent. The angular poses of the limbs, the upturned palms and curved fingers all revealed the influence of Hindu sculpture.

At times, however, imagination supplanted archaeology as his method. *Schéhérazade,* the seraglio tale that thrilled Paris in 1910, was pure orientalist fantasy. "Dancers with bare feet," he later wrote, "performing mostly with their arms and torsos, constituted a concept far removed from the Oriental ballet of the time."[32] Equally inspired and equally fanciful were *The Polovtsian Dances,* staged to the ballet act of Borodin's *Prince Igor* and produced with full opera chorus by Diaghilev in 1909. During the preparations Fokine found himself in a quandary. His researches drew a blank: nothing was known about Borodin's ancient tribe of Tartars. After much soul-searching and considerable embarrassment, he began to compose. "I had faith in the fact that, if the Polovtzy did not actually dance this way to the music of Borodin, that is exactly how they should have danced." Fokine overstated the contribution of his imagination. His *Polovtsian Dances* bore considerable resemblance to an earlier divertissement choreographed by Lev Ivanov, Petipa's long-suffering assistant ballet master. (Nicholas Roerich, who designed the work, dealt with the problem in a somewhat different fashion. His costumes blended features of Yakut and Kirghiz national dress.)[33]

The *genre nouveau* differed from character dance both in its fidelity to historical sources and in its overt emotionalism. But it also departed from its predecessor in another way. Implicit in Fokine's ethnographic method was a respect for human diversity and the multiplicity of cultural expression—the belief that in the best of all possible worlds pluralism would reign. Nineteenth-century Russian ballet, by contrast, exalted a vision that was both Imperial and imperialist. Here, Russia's vast and growing empire, and the Pan-Slavic ideology that supported it, found ready theatrical expression. One of the works that Alexandre Benois saw "with unabated excitement" as a young child was *Roxana, The Beauty of Montenegro.* First performed in 1878, only months after Russian armies had liberated Montenegro from the hated Turk, it was "an indication," he wrote, "of the Russian attitude in favor of freedom for the Slavs in the Balkans."[34] Another popular ballet, *The Humpbacked Horse,* pitted a Russian peasant-turned-prince against a repulsive, lecherous khan. Produced in 1864 as General Chernyaev began his advance on the khanates of Turkestan, it ended with a grandly nationalistic finale. "At the back of the stage," recalled Benois, "rose the Novgorod monument of Russia's thousandth anniversary, and marching past it were all the nations of the Russian Empire come to pay homage to the Simpleton, who had become their master. There were Cossacks and Karelians, Tartars, Little-Russians and Samoyeds."[35]

That Fokine's *genre nouveau* carried its own political overtones is clear from a vicious attack that appeared in 1911 in the right-wing newspaper *Novoye Vremia.* The article, by M.O. Menshikov, denounced Fokine as a Jew (which he was not), and as such, an artist to whom genuine Russian culture was alien. As proof, the author cited the choreographer's *Polovtsian Dances,* which glorified the barbarian Polovtsi rather than their Russian, Christian conquerors.[36]

Prior to his meeting with Alexandre Benois in 1907, Fokine had little intercourse with his future collaborators. Nevertheless, the affinities between his work and theirs were marked. Although symbolism, broadly conceived, was "the rock on which *Mir iskusstva* was built,"[37] the painters clustered around the journal adhered to a program that transcended pure aestheticism. Indeed, even as they rejected the utilitarianism of the realist painters known as the Wanderers, Diaghilev's prewar designers revealed the influence of the earlier school in their fascination with nativist themes and in their zeal to depict subject matter in the full regalia of its time and place.

Like Fokine, these artists came to maturity in the neonationalist tide that swept Russia at the century's end. Virtually all had been touched by the movement to revitalize indigenous art, and several had participated in the art colonies established by Savva Mamontov and Princess Maria Tenisheva in Abramtsevo and Talashkino respectively. At these locales, offshoots of the English Arts and Crafts movement, workshops manufactured furniture, embroidered goods, bibelots, and other items that drew on peasant artisan traditions and were sold in Moscow and St. Petersburg. Both colonies housed vast collections of folk and ancient Slavic art, unique and fascinating assemblages that encouraged artists to study Russia's semihistorical and legendary past. And at both centers, artists impatient with the strictures of the academy found a congenial setting, a community of likeminded peers in which to study and work.

A Petersburger, Princess Tenisheva early cemented relationships with future Diaghilev artists. Between 1895 and 1899 Benois served as curator of her collection of paintings and drawings, while beginning in 1898 Ivan Bilibin studied at her art school under Ilya Repin, the greatest living exponent of Russian realism. After 1893, the year she acquired Talashkino, the estate became a meeting ground for a diverse group of artists and intellectuals: among the summer visitors in the 1890s and early 1900s were Feodor Chaliapin, Alexander Golovin, Konstantin Korovin, Roerich, and Dmitri Stelletsky, all of whom figured in Diaghilev's theatrical enterprises. In 1898 and 1899, moreover, she helped underwrite his journal *Mir iskusstva.*

Important as it was to the prehistory of the Ballets Russes, her contribution was minor compared to Mamontov's, for in the opera troupe that grew out of the amateur theatricals staged at Abramtsevo in the 1870s and early 1880s, one finds the musical and artistic blueprint for Diaghilev's initial "Russian Seasons." Between 1896 and 1899 the Moscow Private Opera (as Mamontov now rebaptized the troupe he founded in 1885 as the Krotkov Private Opera Company) became a proselytizer for lyric nationalism, staging in this brief span no fewer than eleven works by Russian composers. Although the repertory included Tchaikovsky's *Maid of Orleans*, Mikhail Glinka's *Life for the Tsar*, Alexander Serov's *Judith*, and Alexey Vestovsky's *Askold's Tomb*, overwhelmingly it honored the captain of the group of nationalist composers known as "The Five." Nikolai Rimsky-Korsakov was indeed the lion of Mamontov's troupe, not only in Moscow, where its headquarters at the Solodnikov Theater stood directly across from the Bolshoi (an instance of physical position symbolizing an artistic one), but also in St. Petersburg, where it paid frequent visits. Five of Rimsky's works were presented in these years—*Ivan the Terrible* (*The Maid of Pskov*), *Sadko, Snegurochka, May Night*, and *Mozart and Salieri*—in addition to his revised versions of Mussorgsky's *Boris Godunov* and *Khovanshchina*. Except for *Snegurochka* and *Mozart and Salieri*, all these works were subsequently produced by Diaghilev, as were selected scenes from *Judith*.[38] Even when he added to the repertory, Diaghilev followed the path laid out by Mamontov. *Ruslan and Ludmilla* was by Glinka, the father of Russian opera, while *Prince Igor* bore the signature of Borodin, who, like Rimsky, belonged to "The Five." In launching Stravinsky, who composed his first ballet—*Firebird*—in 1910, Diaghilev brought to the fore the successor to Rimsky's neonationalist crown.

Music, however, was not the only realm where Mamontov's policy established a precedent for the Ballets Russes. At Abramtsevo painters had gathered for over twenty years, and from the beginning Mamontov had mined their talents for his theatrical enterprises. The cycle of operas brought to the stage in the late 1890s introduced a number of artists featured among Diaghilev's first generation of designers. Of these, Konstantin Korovin, Mamontov's chief decorator, Alexander Golovin, and Valentin Serov were the most important.[39] Like the Wanderers, they took their distinctive subject matter from Russian themes and the Russian past. But unlike their Realist predecessors, they invested their material with an aura of beauty alien to the utilitarian spirit of their elders. Opening their minds to the West, they employed new techniques, infused their compositions with movement, and conveyed their subjects in virtuoso coloring and brushwork. Between 1896 and 1899, the year Mamontov went to prison for embezzlement, his design studio created sets and costumes for over a dozen operas. Although they generally bore the signature of a principal designer (e.g. Korovin, for *Sadko;* Serov, for *Judith;* Mikhail Vrubel, for *Mozart and Salieri*), these productions were actually collaborative undertakings. Not only did they rest upon a concept elaborated through a collective exchange of ideas, but they also often employed a number of artists both as designers (Vrubel, for instance, created the costume worn by the Sea Queen in *Sadko*) and scene painters, the latter being specifically credited for their work. From the first, this collaborative method was adopted by Diaghilev, as was the use of easel painters rather than professional decorators as designers.

In addition to defining Diaghilev's approach to stagecraft, the contributions of Korovin, Golovin, and Serov defined his enterprise in another way: they established its Russian character. Between 1908 and 1910 the three designed the sets and in some instances also the costumes for *Boris Godunov* (Golovin), *Le Festin* (Korovin), *Judith* (Serov), *Ivan the Terrible* (Golovin), *Ruslan and Ludmilla* (Korovin), *Les Orientales* (Korovin), and *Firebird* (Golovin). In 1911 Serov also designed a front curtain in the style of Persian miniatures that "accompanied" Rimsky's overture to *Schéhérazade,* and two years later Golovin designed the revival of *Ivan the Terrible.* All these endeavors were a logical extension of Abramtsevo neonationalism, as well as a point of connection with the nationalist-minded Petersburgers—Bilibin, Stelletsky, Roerich, Bakst, and Benois—who collaborated on several of these productions as well. From the start, however, "Russianness" defied neat categories; it was tinged with the orientalism that Paris redefined as its common denominator. Even at Abramtsevo a fine line had divided nationalist material and exotica. Indeed, for artists of all kinds in late nineteenth-century Russia, the two inhabited similar compartments of the imagination. In an empire that spanned the Trans-Siberian railway, that included Bukhara, the Muslim holy city of Central Asia, Bakhchisarai, and Odessa, arguably the cultural "other" was not the East, but the West. The conceptualization of Russia as historically and ethnically non-Western—a key element in the ideology of Diaghilev's prewar enterprise—is yet another Mamontov legacy.[40]

For Léon Bakst and Alexandre Benois, Diaghilev's chief prewar designers and sometime artistic directors, the subject of neonationalism was secondary to its method. That is, they rejected its Slavic content, while preserving its empirical and historical method. In the case of Bakst the line of descent from the Wanderers is clear. His connection with the group dated to the mid-1880s, when as a student at the Academy of Arts in St. Petersburg, he met Mikhail Nesterov, Victor Vasnetsov, and Valentin Serov, painters associated with Abramtsevo. Serov, who had studied for a time there with Ilya Repin, became an intimate friend. Bakst's paintings of the late 1880s and early 1890s—with titles like "The Pall Bearer," "Suicide," and "Mismatched Couple"—followed in the Wanderers' tradition of social realism, combining illustrative portrayal and a fascination with life's grimmer aspects. During the 1890s Bakst gradually abandoned his early aesthetic. In part, this reflected knowledge of more advanced tendencies in painting encountered on frequent trips to Paris, where he lived intermittently until 1899. To a greater extent, it grew out of a rapprochement with nature. As Fokine somewhat later, so Bakst in this transitional decade removed himself from the studio, drawing landscapes from nature, making quick sketches of country scenes or the effects of sky and atmosphere, painting the first of many fine portraits. In 1897, after discovering his mistress in the arms of another lover, he escaped to North Africa, a journey that marked the beginning of a fascination with the Middle East, seedbed of the orientalism so closely identified with his work for the Ballets Russes. Ten years later a trip to Greece, then a mixture of Greek, Arab, and Turkic cultures, left an equally indelible impression.

As with Fokine, however, the scaffolding of Bakst's imagination was an intellectual act—the historical reconstruction of time and place. Long before he undertook his first Diaghilev commission, he had turned his encyclopedic knowledge of the artistic past to account in more than a half-dozen productions, mostly for the Imperial Theaters. In *Le Coeur de la Marquise* (1902), his first stage venture, and *Puppenfee* (1903), he drew inspiration from nineteenth-century European styles, including the German Biedermeier used in *Carnaval* (1910), *Le Spectre de la Rose* (1911), and *Papillons* (1914). In *Hippolytus* (1902), *Oedipus at Colonus* (1904), and *Antigone* (1904), Attic tragedies or plays after them, he decided against "accessorizing" contemporary attire with Greek touches—the usual solution to theatrical costume then—in favor of reconstructions of classical dress, his procedure in *Narcisse* (1911), *Daphnis and Chloë* (1912), and *L'Après-midi d'un Faune* (1912). His costumes for Ida Rubinstein's *Salomé* (1908) mined an orientalist vein, anticipating the exoticism of *Cléopâtre* (1909), *Schéhérazade* (1910), *Thamar* (1912), and *Legend of Joseph* (1914). As Charles Mayer has shown, all these productions rested upon solid knowledge—of museum artifacts, architectural reproductions, fashion plates and illustrations, portraits, historical costume studies, design portfolios—enriched, as in 1912, when he spent several weeks in the Caucasus making preparatory studies for *Thamar,* by direct observation.[41] Such historicizing was not an empty academic exercise. To Bakst, as to Fokine, the representation of reality in light of fresh knowledge rather than received convention was an innovative and liberating act. Shorn of its progressivist ideology, naturalism was a step to the future, a way of seeing that was radically new. Like other artists of Europe's periphery, Bakst arrived at the discovery of the real long after those of the Parisian core.

In the case of Alexandre Benois, a similar imperative was at work. But in this child of Petersburg and grandson of Paris the quest for authenticity led backward in time. Benois's obsession with the past centered on three historical moments: the *grand siècle*, embodied in Versailles, that incarnation of French classical civilization; Petrine Petersburg, a Latin vision rising on northern marshlands by an act of monumental will; Mitteleuropa Gothic, exemplified in the tales of E.T.A. Hoffmann. For Benois art was an act of recovery that plumbed the present to relive the past. He painted Versailles and Petersburg obsessively, as if by recreating their monuments he could raise the civilizations that created them—only to find that his melancholic canvases spoke only of their demise. From the first his theatrical work mirrored and enlarged upon his obsessions. In *Cupid's Revenge*, the one-act opera produced at the Hermitage Theater that marked his debut as a designer in 1900, he drew on his authoritative knowledge of the eighteenth century, while in the Maryinsky production of *Götterdämmerung* that followed in 1903 he invoked the medieval cosmos of Wagner's Teutonic mythography. And when in 1907 Nikolai Drizen and Nikolai Evreinov sought to revive the theatrical forms of the Middle Ages and Spanish Golden Age, it was Benois who served as artistic and historical consultant of their Antique Theater. His writings, both scholarly and journalistic, fetishize memory in much the same way, as do his remarkable volumes of reminiscence. Fingered like bibelots, events past set the mind on a journey backward in time. Typically, the journal he edited between 1907 and 1916 bore the Proustian title *Bygone Years*.[42]

Benois, the *passéiste*, found an ideal mate in Fokine, the romanticist. "I immediately felt at ease in his company," wrote the choreographer of their first meeting in the autumn of 1907, an encounter that would culminate in the production of *Le Pavillon d'Armide:*

> We were talking on a subject which was exciting and provoked enthusiasm in both of us: we were wandering into the world of the unreal, into the gardens of the charmer Armide. From our very first meeting, we formed that strong bond of mutual understanding that was destined to lead us to so many artistic joys and so many achievements.
>
> Benois took me up the scaffold right above the scenery. My head was spinning, both from the height and from joy. Under my feet the scenery was spread out: a marvelous pavilion for Armide. What a happy moment that was![43]

With its rococo setting *Le Pavillon d'Armide* lay close to the designer's heart. He fussed endlessly over the costumes, which were in Louis XIV style, pondering the exact color of a braid or piece of lace: effectiveness, in his mind, went hand-in-hand with authenticity. Less than four months later, the two collaborated on *Bal Poudré*, a pantomime in the style of a seventeenth-century harlequinade. *Les Sylphides*, which followed in 1909, struck an emotional chord in both, as did the 1911 *Petrouchka*, their fourth collaboration and the second to exploit the commedia dell'arte theme. Haunted by Proustian detail, both ballets invoke the past—the first, through romantic lithographs, the second, via a prism of memory—to resurrect an age of lost innocence. Like Bakst, Benois discerned in the creation of images faithful to reality a means of conveying emotional and poetic truths.

Fokine's advocacy of scenic realism struck a deep chord in the historically minded artists grouped around *Mir iskusstva*. But it also aligns his work—and more tellingly, I believe—with innovative approaches in the dramatic theater, above all, with the reforms associated with Konstantin Stanislavsky's Moscow Art Theater. In *Russian Theater From the Empire to the Soviets*, Marc Slonim calls the "archaeological-historical . . . realism" made famous by Stanislavsky's celebrated troupe "one of the most important trends" contributing to changes in Russian theatrical production in the early twentieth century. Stanislavsky, he writes:

> applied the same method of research and authenticity to all historical and period plays, whether it was the *Merchant of Venice* or *Julius Caesar*. For the latter, he went with his actors to Rome and reproduced on the Moscow stage the narrow streets, the Forum, and the picturesque southern crowd of Caesar's city. In the same way, the company made an expedition to the island of Cyprus in preparation for *Othello*. In order to make the public understand the seriousness of these efforts, productions of new plays were accompanied with matching exhibitions. The spectators of *Julius Caesar*, for instance, could see in the foyer stalls Russian translations of Shakespeare, as well as genuine objects of the period—coins, armor, and paintings and engravings.[44]

Like Fokine, Stanislavsky viewed style as the creation of historical illusion based on direct observation of reality combined with historical reconstruction.

Founded in 1898, the Moscow Art Theater presented its first season in St. Petersburg three years later. Fokine was in the audience.[45] The revelation of Stanislavsky's earliest productions thus coincided with Fokine's formative years as an artist, a time when by his own admission he was searching for new creative outlets. Fokine's own family had many connections to the theater. His brother Vladimir became a well-known actor; another brother, Alexander, founded the Troitsky Miniature Theater (at which his wife, Maryinsky soloist Alexandra Fedorova, appeared as prima ballerina).[46] Though Fokine does not mention them, Stanislavsky's epoch-making productions of Ibsen and Chekhov surely impressed his youthful imagination. With their artistry and evocative reconstructions of character and place, they must have left suggestions of future possibility, intimations of the high seriousness that art at its best can communicate, and images of stylistic unity, dramatic coherence, and psychological plausibility—all of which found their way into his early work.

A number of links, rarely mentioned in studies of the Ballets Russes, united the Diaghilev group and the Moscow Art Theater. "Benois loved our Theatre [and] knew it well," wrote Vladimir Nemirovich-Danchenko, cofounder with Stanislavsky of the famed ensemble. In 1909, at the height of his collaboration with Diaghilev, Benois became artistic director of the Art Theater, forming "a close association with Stanislavsky." He took a prominent role in the polemic that raged in 1910 around Nemirovich-Danchenko's production of *The Brothers Karamazov* and, at Stanislavsky's behest, helped draft the open reply to the play's severest critic, Maxim Gorky. Two years later Benois joined the troupe as a designer and some-time producer.[47] Another "crossover" figure was Alexander Sanin, who left the Art Theater in 1902. A staff director at the Alexandrinsky Theater, Sanin was among the first Imperial artists to recognize Fokine's talent. In 1905, after seeing *Acis and Galatea,* he asked the choreographer to create a dance for buffoons and jesters in Alexis Tolstoy's *The Death of Ivan the Terrible,* a request turned down by Alexander Krupensky, who told Sanin that "he had no right to select his colleagues without the approval" of management.[48] Furious, Sanin left the Alexandrinsky. In 1908, however, Diaghilev engaged him to direct *Boris Godunov* and the following year to stage his Paris operas—*Ivan the Terrible, Ruslan and Ludmilla, Judith,* and *Prince Igor.* In 1913 and 1914, when Diaghilev returned to opera production, he again called upon Sanin, who directed *Boris Godunov, Khovanshchina,* and *Le Rossignol* (the last with Benois).[49] Another point of contact between the two groups was Savva Mamontov, who emerged from debtors' prison with his energy, if not his fortune, undiminished. In 1905 he joined forces with Stanislavsky as codirector of the Theater-Studio, an experimental ensemble attached to the Moscow Art Theater. Under Mamontov's aegis, designers attuned to new trends were brought in to collaborate—among them, Nikolai Sapunov and Serge Soudeikine, students of Korovin and Serov who moved in World of Art circles. In 1906, at Diaghilev's invitation, Soudeikine traveled to Paris in connection with the exhibition of Russian art organized by the former at the Salon d'Automne. Seven years later he designed *La Tragédie de Salomé* for the Ballets Russes. Another artist close to the World of Art group who designed for Diaghilev after working for Stanislavsky was Mstislav Dobujinsky. He did *Woe for Wit* for the Art Theater in 1906, and three years later, in *A Month in the Country*, turned to the Biedermeier style used so effectively the following year by Bakst in *Carnaval*. (Influence was not entirely a one-way street. In Gerhart Hauptmann's *Schluck and Jau*, staged at the Theater-Studio in 1905, Stanislavsky transferred the setting from medieval Silesia to the periwig age of Louis XIV after visiting Diaghilev's magnificent exhibition of eighteenth-century portraits at St. Petersburg's Tauride Palace.)[50]

Art Theater influence also extended to dance. At the Bolshoi Stanislavsky's influence was far-reaching and started almost simultaneously with the formation of the Art Theater in 1898, the year Alexander Gorsky, a character dancer and aspiring choreographer, arrived from the Maryinsky. His revival of *Don Quixote* in 1900 was "as good as a revolutionary reform in ballet," dance historian Natalia Roslavleva has written:

> The influence of the Art Theatre was particularly evident in the first act of the old Minkus ballet. Instead of the stiff and frozen lines of the corps de ballet, there appeared a living crowd of characters—moving, laughing, selling their wares on the piazza. Instead of make-shift costumes, there were real Spanish ones.[51]

Gorsky formed a whole constellation of dancer-actors—including Mikhail Mordkin, Theodore Koslov, Alexandre Volinine, and Laurent Novikov—all of whom danced for Diaghilev. He discovered Sophia Fedorova, unsurpassed as the Chief Polovtsian Girl in Fokine's *Polovtsian Dances*. Stanislavsky, for his part, invited Mordkin to teach expressive movement to his actors.

Along with scenic realism, Fokine's work embodied another principle of Art Theater practice: both treated the ensemble as a living collective. "The new ballet," he wrote in a letter to the London *Times* in 1914, "advances from the expressiveness of the whole body, and from the expressiveness of the individual body to the expressiveness of a group of bodies and the expressiveness of the combined dancing of a crowd."[52] The word "crowd" is telling here, a key to his formal method and to the liberatory vision charging his work generally. Discarding the diagonals and rectangles of Petipa's regimented formations, Fokine transformed the corps de ballet into what critic Valerian Svetlov described as "a sort of collective artist, imbued with the idea and style of a production, living in it and collaborating."[53] In Petipa's ballets the corps framed the ballerina, inscribing her into an etiquette as strict as that of the Imperial court; she ruled the stage as absolutely as a tsar. Around her, in order of precedence, lesser ranks danced: coryphées, in groups of eight; demi-coryphées, in groups of four; *demi-solistes,* in pairs; soloists and premières danseuses, in lesser principal roles. In the heavenly hierarchical city of *La Bayadère* or *The Sleeping Beauty,* the disposition of dancers onstage reflected their rankings in the Maryinsky bureaucracy.

Fokine, by contrast, abolished the privileges and trappings of rank. He did away with the ballerina as a being apart: in his works she merged with her newly democratized court. Even in *Les Sylphides,* which invoked the classical order of *Giselle* and *Swan Lake,* he integrated the soloists into the ensemble, allowing them only fitfully—and briefly—to claim the stage as individuals. At the same time, he fragmented Petipa's imperial, rectilinear masses, replacing them with small, asymmetrical groupings that wove a filigree of constantly shifting patterns. Fokine's "leveling" was thus two-pronged: in dethroning Petipa's queen, he humanized the drones who supported her.

Fokine's liberated ensemble appeared early and repeatedly in his work. In *La Vigne* the tipplers and the wines they tippled came together for a final Bacchic rout. This ending, a variation on the traditional coda, became the prototype of the frenzied, freewheeling crowds that sent shudders of excitement through Fokine's prewar audiences. "A thrill," wrote Arnold Bennett of *Schéhérazade's* "shocking brutality":

> In the surpassing fury and magnificence of the Russian ballet one saw eunuchs actually at work, scimitar in hand. There was the frantic orgy, and then there was the barbarous punishment, terrible and revolting; certainly one of the most sanguinary sights ever seen on an occidental stage. The eunuchs pursued the fragile and beautiful odalisques with frenzy; in an instant the seraglio was strewn with murdered girls in all the abandoned postures of death. And then silence, save for the hard breathing of the executioners.[54]

Fokine was drawn to the crowd as an antidote to ballet's visual and social hierarchies. But he was also attracted by its volatility, its potential for violence, its transgressive emotionalism, its ability to act and experience collectively. "In nearly every one of Fokine's ballets," wrote André Levinson, "there is a moment where all the participants, irrespective of their earlier roles, join hands and form a long chain . . . which closes up into concentric circles and carries on to an ever accelerating tempo."[55] Amoun's death in *Cléopâtre* took place during an orgy of collective violence, in which the crowd became a single writhing mass. The orgy that preceded the final slaughter in *Schéhérazade* followed a similar convulsive pattern. "The secret feast begins," wrote Levinson:

> Carrying dishes laden with fruit . . . a motley group of Hindu servant boys runs in . . . and circles the stage in a wide arc. Behind them follow, one after

another in a continuous chain, green- and rose-colored almehs in dark veils. Soon the entire stage is enveloped in the whirlwind of a huge round dance, interlacing in every conceivable figure like a coiling, heraldic snake.[56]

In the images of nature rampant, descending like a sudden blight on ordered society, Levinson exposes the subtext of these convulsive orgies, which turned only incidentally upon sex. Fokine's crowds replicated the paroxysm of revolution itself: the fury of masses unchained, the ecstasy of blood, the triumph of instinct over ego, the liberation of the self through collective action. Unlike Levinson, who cast a baleful eye on all change, Fokine welcomed the contest of old and new: as much as revolution destroyed, that much it also created. The legacy of 1905 did not end, then, with Fokine's birth as a choreographer or the creation of a band of artistic followers. It pervaded the very texture of his work. Drawing on the principle of scenic realism made famous by the Moscow Art Theater, he transformed his living crowd into an image of collective political practice: onstage, the spirit of 1905 continued to live.

Fokine's debt to Stanislavsky is nowhere plainer than in *Petrouchka,* probably his greatest work for the Ballets Russes. Here, he depicted a St. Petersburg street carnival of the 1830s, with the richness of detail and fidelity to nature of Stanislavsky's celebrated crowds for the Art Theater. In creating this living social entity, Fokine sought, above all, to mask the hand of its director. "I wanted all the dancers strolling at the fair to dance gaily, freely, as if the dances were not staged but arose spontaneously from an overabundance of emotion and gaiety, arousing the crowd to wild improvisation. There should be nothing in the nature of this spectacle . . . [to] suggest the existence of a choreographer."[57] Fokine worked his material like an impressionist, blurring movement tonalities, then arresting the gaze with a sudden leap or gesture that dissolved almost immediately into the swarming mass. Levinson's description of the fourth tableau captures the stream of images that made this crowd so richly evocative—and lifelike—to a Russian of 1911:

> [The] square swirls in holiday intoxication: beauteous "nursemaids" in *sara-fans* and *kokoshniks* stream by, spreading their arms and waving their hands; coachmen in colorful *poddyovkas* with lace on their hats click their heels with spirit; boisterous young lads leap into a *prisiadka;* mummers wearing dreadful masks mix into the crowd while elegant ladies accompanied by stately officers in three-cornered hats and greatcoats and by dandies in overcoats fastidiously observe the crude amusements of the common folk through their lorgnettes.[58]

Naturalism extended far beyond Fokine's manipulation of masses. His living crowd was, above all, an assemblage of individuals—coachmen, gypsies, street-hawkers, wet nurses, organ grinders, jesters—who arrived onstage with biographies and fully delineated personalities. The score, Stravinsky's second for the Ballets Russes, included themes for dozens of characters. Benois's designs replicated this musical specificity. He carefully studied the fashions of 1830–1840, tailoring them to over one hundred individuals of varied social status and kind. His settings were full of equally realistic detail—a merry-go-round, gingerbread stalls, a table with a steaming samovar where tea was sold. In rehearsal Fokine worked closely with Benois, who supplied many details of the ballet's realistic "business," which added to the impression of the crowd as an aggregate of individuals rather than an impersonal mass.

Such individualizing, part and parcel of Fokine's method, suggests another parallel with Stanislavsky, whose theater was as famed for the realism of its acting as for that of its ensembles. Fokine abolished what Osip Mandelstam called "the currant smiles of the ballerinas" and "vegetable obedience of the corps de ballet."[59] He humanized and individualized his dancers, transforming them into actors and assigning to each a motivated role in the larger drama. Unlike his neoclassical successors, Fokine believed that steps alone did not tell a story. Movement, he felt, was expressive only to the degree that it conveyed emotional and psychological truth, that it approached the condition of nature. In his 1914 letter to the *Times,* he set forth as the new ballet's second "rule" the need for dancing and gesture to be dramatically motivated—a concept fundamental to Stanislavsky's theory of acting. Unlike mime, Fokine's "living hand movements" were not "substitutes for words," but "additions" to speech, enlargements of natural gesture that made audible what had not in fact been uttered. At the same time, extending the gestural principle to the entire instrument, he advocated a "mimetic of the whole body": "Man can . . . and should be expressive from head to foot," he asserted.[60]

Dramatic realism implied a new approach to characterization. Placing function before form, it exalted the meaning rather than the metaphor of movement; its broad strokes spoke the vernacular of the demos, not the coded language of the clerisy. In *Petrouchka* psychology dictated plastique: the naive and guileless hero, an introvert, is turned in; the flamboyant Blackamoor, an extrovert, is turned out; the Ballerina, a flirtatious, empty-headed Columbine, prances on pointe like a mechanical doll. Acting, too, reflected the new "mimetic," and it is hardly surprising that Fokine's dancers infused his ballets with the same living vitality their peers brought to Art Theater productions of Ibsen and Chekhov. Of all the dancers who worked with him, Pavlova embodied his ideal most fully. "In countries abroad, it was said that there was 'something novel' in my dancing," she told critic Valerian Svetlov:

Yet what I had done was merely to subordinate its physical elements to a psychological concept: over the matter-of-fact aspects of dancing—that is, dancing *per se*—I have attempted to throw a spiritual veil of poetry, whose charm might screen the mechanical element. When dancing, it often happens that I extemporise, especially when my part fascinates and inspires me. I borrow from the palette of choreography any colour which happens to suit my fancy, and turn the slightest thing to the best possible account. That is how I may be able to suggest impressions which are considered as fresh. So far as I know, therein lies the only secret of my art.[61]

To be sure, naturalism was only one weapon in the arsenal trained by Fokine on nineteenth-century ballet. But it occupies pride of place here for a number of reasons. As the central tenet of his reform, it opened classicism to a tide of insurrectionary experiment. At the same time, it forged an alliance between ballet and secessionist movements in drama, music, and painting. Lastly, it staked out a liberal position that Fokine found both congenial and imaginatively stimulating.

Nevertheless, from the outset, naturalism was allied to an aesthetic that elsewhere in Europe succeeded it. Symbolism came late to Russia, and even later to Russian theater. Later still, it came to ballet. However tardy its arrival, it had a pervasive and enduring influence on Fokine's work. From symbolism came a broad assortment of ideas: themes of the beleaguered individual and the commedia dell'arte, notions of synaesthesia, suggestiveness, and subjectivity, the cult of beauty, fascination with eroticism, visions of poetic idealism. Announcements of modernity, these fin-de-siècle ideas linked his work to movements in the other arts to reimage reality rather than represent it phenomenologically, and to experiments of choreographic successors who would complete and transcend the modernist revolution he initiated. Above all, Fokine's symbolism staked out ideological terrain: it embodied an individualist ideal that stood as the antithesis to the collectivist thesis of naturalism.

As we have said, Fokine had little contact with the World of Art before 1907. He knew of it, of course, and had visited at least some of its exhibitions; by his own account, he was familiar with its journal as well. Its members, however, belonged to a world apart: an elite from which by class and calling he was excluded. In his memoirs Fokine describes his initial acquaintance—if one can call it that—with Diaghilev:

When I was just beginning my career as a dancer, Diaghilev was an Official for Special Missions in the administration of the Imperial Theaters. I saw him . . . during intermissions . . . standing in a group of officials, with his back to the stage. I knew that there were always young men of privileged families in the administration who would rapidly bypass hundreds of office workers on the staff and be promoted to higher posts in the theater organization. These were the clerks whom Gogol called by the derogatory but appropriate name of "leeches" . . . I classified this man as belonging to the . . . group which gave out many orders and hindered the ballet so much . . . I do not recall ever speaking to him, and our greetings were limited to the same nod of the head as with the other ballet officials.[62]

Although direct influence must be ruled out, Fokine drew on ideas put into circulation by *Mir iskusstva* and other symbolist journals. How their seeds were planted is another, more puzzling story; one can assume—given the dearth of clues in his memoirs—that it took place informally and un-systematically: in conversations with friends, in performances of the "New Drama," in haphazard and eclectic readings. However spotty his education as a symbolist, by 1907 Fokine's outlook roughly paralleled that of the World of Art. "We agreed with each other at once," rhapsodized Benois about his first meeting with the choreographer to plan *Le Pavillon d'Armide*. "No less than I did, [he wished] to save the ballet from cheapening influ-ences and to give his art a new lease on life."[63]

Founded in 1898 by Diaghilev, who served as editor until its demise six years later, *Mir iskusstva* stood to Russia as *The Studio* to England and *La Revue Blanche* to France: a journal aimed at converting the edu-cated public to the aesthetic of symbolism. The "program," notes Joan Ross Acocella, "was made clear from the very beginning, in the four po-lemical essays, all by Diaghilev, that were the featured items of the first two issues."[64] Here Diaghilev set forth the tenets of his creed: his belief in the autonomy and subjectivity of art, his worship of beauty and his iden-tification of this with the revelation of the artist's personality, his vision of art as an act of communion between the personality of the artist and that of the spectator. Lavishly illustrated, *Mir iskusstva* introduced Russian readers to a "full and varied collection" of Western symbolist artists—representatives of the French school, the English Aesthetic Movement, the Glasgow School, the Austrian Secession, the German Symbolist school, in-cluding the "New Idealists" and Jugendstil graphic artists, Art Nouveau. Like any journal, *Mir iskusstva* had its favorites—Aubrey Beardsley, Maurice Denis, and, above all, James Whistler—whose work decorated its pages and was often the subject of essays and "Art Chronicle" notices.[65] With the publication of Valery Briusov's "Unnecessary Truth" in 1902, the jour-nal extended its critique of realism to the theater. Indeed, this essay, by the "master" of the younger symbolist poets and author of one of the first symbolist plays in Russian (*Earth,* 1904), marked a turning point in Rus-sian theatrical history, for it constituted a thoroughgoing attack—the first—

on both the methods and achievements of the Moscow Art Theater. "It is time," Briusov declared, "that the theater stopped counterfeiting reality":

> The subject of art is the soul of the artist, his feelings and his ideas; it is this which is the *content* of a work of art; the plot, the theme are the *form;* the images, colours, sounds are the *materials* . . . An actor on the stage is the same as a sculptor before his clay: he must embody in tangible form the same content as the sculptor—the impulse of his soul, his feelings . . . The theatre's sole task is to help the actor reveal his soul to the audience.[66]

The affinities with Diaghilev are evident.

Although symbolism had been "in the air" since the 1890s, stagings of symbolist plays in Russia dated to the new century. In 1903, in Sevastopol, Vsevolod Meyerhold—recently dismissed from the Art Theater—produced *The Intruder,* by Maurice Maeterlinck. The following year, in Moscow, Stanislavsky himself presented this and two other plays by the Belgian symbolist—an evening that caused the press to endorse unanimously Maeterlinck's own opinion that his plays were unstageable.[67] In 1905, with Briusov as "dramaturg" and Meyerhold as artistic director, Stanislavsky formed the Theater-Studio to meet the challenge of the "New Drama." The venture, which lasted less than six months and never opened its doors to the public, was not a success. In the long run, however, it paid dividends, for in preparing Maeterlinck's *Death of Tintagiles* and Hauptmann's *Schluck and Jau,* Meyerhold stumbled upon the principle of stylization—the basis of his future productions and the solution to the symbolist conundrum. "The lessons learnt at the Studio," Edward Braun has written, "equipped Meyerhold with the experience to achieve the successes which were soon to follow in Petersburg and which led to the establishment of a new tradition in the Russian theatre, a tradition to which the Moscow Art Theatre itself remained committed and to which it was soon to contribute with a series of productions culminating in 1911 with the *Hamlet* of Gordon Craig."[68]

This is not the place to analyze Meyerhold's enormous contribution to symbolist acting and stagecraft. The point, rather, is that theatrical symbolism in Russia issued directly from naturalism, that it did so in the space of three or four years, and that these years coincided with Fokine's birth as a choreographer. In other words, he began to make dances just at the moment when symbolism and naturalism appeared to converge, when the former seemed to supplant its antagonist by a natural process of evolution. Nemirovich-Danchenko once remarked of Chekhov that he "refined his realism to the point where it became symbolic."[69] So Fokine, enamored of reality, subtly altered the forms of nature: into the mold of realism he poured his unique personality. In his mind symbolism and naturalism joined not in battle but in kinship.

Just as naturalism summed up a nexus of ideas about the collective, so symbolism in Fokine's work staked out terrain associated with the individual. Subjectivity, of course, was a major symbolist tenet, as was the autonomy of the artist; equally dear was the theme of Pierrot, the poet beleaguered and betrayed by philistine society. But Fokine's interest in the individual transcended purely formal concerns: his respect for dancers as collaborators, his obsession with personal emotion, his liberating technique and equally liberated attitude toward the body reflect a vision grounded in social reality. This vision, at once egalitarian and antiauthoritarian, sprang, to all appearances, from the circumstances of Fokine's own life—his clashes with Maryinsky bureaucrats, the collaborative atmosphere of his early creations, his admiration for Isadora Duncan, his liberal politics. Equally, it reflected the presence at his side of a band of acolytes—students, partners, friends—who believed in him and rallied to him, first as a political ally, then as an artistic leader. Within this group, he found the mirrors of his many selves and the protagonists of a struggle that persisted in his work to the end: the assertion of the individual's right to be and the denial of that right by society.

Nowhere is this tension so clearly mirrored as in the solos choreographed between 1905 and 1911 for his greatest interpreters—*The Dying Swan* (1905) for Pavlova, the opening of *Firebird* (1910) for Karsavina, and Petrouchka's soliloquy (1911) for Nijinsky. Meditations on individualism, all three enact a drama of awareness; in each the protagonist comes to know the temporality and powerlessness of the human condition. *The Dying Swan* was exemplary in this regard, articulating an emotion as universal as the applause Pavlova won for herself in twenty-six years of performances. "No one who has not seen this dance," wrote Cyril W. Beaumont, who must have witnessed it scores of times, "can imagine the impression it produces on the mind and heart of the spectator":

> The pitiful fluttering of the arms, the slow sinking of the body, the pathetic eyes, and that final pose when all is stilled, arouse an emotion so deep and so overwhelming that some moments elapse before the spectator can voice his appreciation by means of applause.[70]

Fokine's everywoman was hardly the first avian heroine to expire on the ballet stage. However, unlike Odette in *Swan Lake*, she dies fully conscious of her agony; she experiences the gradual ebbing of life, the limits of mortality itself. Although she yields to fate, she does not accede to it;

her flutterings assert a claim to life; they register, so to speak, a hapless protest. Karsavina's *Firebird* solo rests on a similar dichotomy, a similar juxtaposition of entrapment and struggle. The context, however, is political; like Rimsky-Korsakov's opera *Kostchei the Immortal*, the ballet is a fairy tale of tyranny punished. In Ivan Tsarevich, Fokine transforms the traditional huntsman prince into the maker not of the heroine's freedom, but of her unfreedom. The whole ballet, in fact, turns on the conflict of freedom and authority, the latter embodied not only in Ivan, the future king, but in the monster Kostchei, the tyrant tumbled from his throne by a demos of enchanted princesses, *bolebochki,* Indians, and Youths armed with the Firebird's golden feather. Alone, the Firebird gleams with the power of a fully realized being; captive, she reflects the tenuousness of individualism itself. In her twin aspects she incarnates the very drama of 1905—the hopes raised and then dashed, the aspirations voiced but never fulfilled.

In *Petrouchka,* by contrast, Fokine's concern is with the individual as a social and psychological phenomenon. Again he takes his protagonist from the stock of ballet characters, and again he redraws that character as an existential hero. Like Fokine's other victims, Petrouchka comes to know the tragedy of his unfreedom: to understand that his human soul can never escape the cage of its puppet body or throw off the imprisoning yoke of the Showman and attendant mob; that the love stirring his heart is cursed, like his manhood, to exist only as impotent desire—no matter how much he beats the walls of his cell or mortifies his "flesh" in protest. In a contemporary account, Benois analyzed the ballet's "tragic quality" as stemming from "the very collision of Petrushka's solitary soul with the soul of the mass. [Nijinsky's] whole role consists of expressing the pathetic downtroddenness, the powerless attempts to save personal happiness and dignity."[71]

A combination of Punch and Pierrot, Petrouchka spoke directly to a generation reared on fairground entertainments and poeticized images of the commedia. Symbolism celebrated the commedia, as did the World of Art—in paintings like "The Italian Comedy" by Benois and "Harlequin and Lady," one of Konstantin Somov's many canvases of Harlequins and Columbines at play.[72] More important for ballet, however, was the reappearance of the theme on the dramatic stage. *The Fairground Booth,* by Alexander Blok, was not Meyerhold's first encounter with commedia material. (In 1903, in provincial Kherson, he produced Franz von Schönthan's little-known melodrama *The Acrobats.*) But it was the one that made artistic and intellectual history. Mounted for Vera Komissarzhevskaya's theater, the play caused an uproar at the premiere, when, in the words of an eyewitness, "whistles and roars of anger alternated with piercing howls."[73] *The Fairground Booth* prefigured the inner drama of *Petrouchka* in several

ways: in its characters, drawn from the stock of commedia figures; in its
love triangle, which pitted Harlequin against Pierrot for the heart of Columbine; in its juxtaposition of innocence and guile, true love with its
counterfeit, poetic sensibility with superficial emotionalism. Choreographically, moreover, play and ballet revealed close affinities. Meyerhold's direction "restricted" the characters "to their own typical gestures": Pierrot
sighed and flapped his arms the same way every time, much as Petrouchka
would do five years later. Like Nijinsky's puppet, Pierrot, as impersonated
by Meyerhold, was a figure bordering on the grotesque. Sharply angular,
caustic yet heartrending, he was "nothing," wrote one observer, "like those
familiar, falsely sugary, whining Pierrots."[74]

Fokine must have admired Meyerhold's interpretation very much, for
early in 1910 he cast him as Pierrot in *Carnaval*. (In his memoirs Fokine
calls the director's appearance "unexpected," a strange remark as Fokine
had complete freedom to pick and choose his performers. Certainly, among
the dancers enthusiasm for the project ran high. As Bronislava Nijinska
later wrote: "Every one of the Diaghilevtsy-Fokinisty was anxious to par-
ticipate.")[75] *Carnaval* owed several debts to *The Fairground Booth*. Like
the Blok play, it blended real and commedia elements: masked revelers
who drifted among characters of the traditional harlequinade. The ironic
tone was the same, and in both the stage was hung with blue drapes. At
the premiere, a pre-Lenten ball organized by the journal *Satyricon*, the
dancers ended their capers in the audience, a device that fulfilled Meyerhold's dictum of the period to "destroy the footlights." (In a 1908 revival
of Blok's play, Meyerhold had the "Author" voice his protests from the
stalls, while in *Death's Victory*, produced the previous year, the performers in the prologue made their entrances from the rear of the auditorium.)
Above all, what linked the two was Pierrot, the solitary dreamer who drove
home the tragedy of the poet among the philistines. Meyerhold's "stylized
gestures," wrote an actress who appeared in the original production, "were
inspired by the musical conception of the characterization; they were eloquent because . . . they were prompted by the inner rhythm of the role."[76]
Inner rhythm stamped Meyerhold's interpretation in *Carnaval* as well. "He
followed the flight of the butterfly noiselessly, like a whisper," recalled
Nijinska, who created the role of Papillon:

> He ran to hide, from one settee to the other, and then unexpectedly his head
> peeped out, moving from side to side as he watched the flight of the butterfly.
> Suddenly he rushed after me, but I disappeared from his sight, off the stage.
> Thinking the butterfly to be on the ground, he covered it with his white hat,
> and then clapping his hands he jumped with joy. He lay down on the floor
> beside his hat and very carefully lifted the edge so as not to damage the fragile

wings. With his hands the incomparable artist actually imitated the palpitation of a butterfly caught under his hat, while all his being remained full of anxiety in anticipation of at last having a closer look at the butterfly he admired and coveted. There was a look of utter bewilderment and heartbreaking disappointment as he realized that the butterfly had escaped him and was not under the hat. Very sadly he put on his little hat, low down on his forehead, and with his shoulders and his long arms drooping walked away; crossing the width of the *avant-scène* with long slow strides, he finally disappeared from the stage.[77]

The question of Meyerhold's influence on Fokine is not easily answered. There is little information, to begin with. Furthermore, there is the Promethean myth elaborated by Fokine himself: in his memoirs the creation of the "new ballet" belongs to him alone. That the two collaborated is a matter of record. In addition to *Carnaval,* they worked together on Oscar Wilde's *Salomé,* performed in 1908 at the Mikhailovsky Theater, Gluck's *Orpheus and Eurydice,* produced at the Maryinsky in 1911, and Gabriele D'Annunzio's *La Pisanelle,* staged in Paris by Ida Rubinstein in 1913. Moreover, after 1908, when Meyerhold joined the Imperial Theaters as a staff director, the two inhabited the same artistic world, giving each ample opportunity to follow the other's progress. One also suspects that Fokine knew of Meyerhold's private productions, chamber works, often of an experimental nature, staged outside the Imperial Theaters. One, given late in 1908 at a St. Petersburg artists' club, was Peter Potemkin's folk farce *Petrushka;* with designs by Dobujinsky and Bilibin, it must have come to Fokine's attention, if not directly, then through Benois, who not only knew both Dobujinsky and Bilibin, but reviewed any number of Meyerhold's creations in these years.[78]

In his memoirs the choreographer refers to Meyerhold only once. This, significantly, is in connection with *Carnaval* and solely in reference to Meyerhold's skill as a mime, except for an aside intimating that it was *Carnaval* that initiated the director into the mysteries of rhythmic movement.[79] This, as we know, is patently false and, in the context, purely gratuitous, as if Fokine, smarting with decades of accumulated rancor, finally got his chance to cut Meyerhold down to size. The source of that rancor, it appears, was *Orpheus and Eurydice,* a remarkable experiment on which the two worked closely, transforming the stage into a dynamic, multifaceted construction. To eliminate the disharmony between chorus and corps, a decision was made—by whom we will probably never know—to mix the two, with Fokine taking charge of the entire crowd. "My idea [in the Hell scene] was this," he wrote in a letter to Cyril W. Beaumont, reproduced in the Russian edition of his memoirs:

when the curtain rose, the whole stage would be covered with motionless bodies. Groups in the most unnatural poses, as though frozen in spasms, in awful hellish torment clung to high cliffs and hung down into chasms . . . When the chorus sang . . . this entire mass of bodies made a single slow motion, one fearful collective gesture. As if a monster of incredible dimensions had been aroused and was beginning ominously to rise. One gesture for the entire long phrase of the chorus. Then the whole mass, after pausing for a moment in a new configuration, shrivels just as slowly, then begins to crawl. Everything, the depiction of shadows, the whole ballet group, the entire male and female chorus and the whole theater school—all this was crawling, changing places . . . Naturally, no one in the audience could understand where the ballet began and the chorus ended.[80]

Fokine staged or assisted in staging a number of other scenes, and on the program he shared directing credit with Meyerhold. He felt, however, that Meyerhold had belittled his contribution, and later went so far as to claim that he had staged virtually the entire opera. The rivalry surfaced in the press, and although passions cooled after the premiere, Fokine's self-esteem was deeply wounded. More serious than the blow to his ego, however, was the end to his collaboration with Meyerhold. (With Rubinstein doing the hiring, *La Pisanelle* was job work, not a creative association.) The break with Meyerhold was doubly unfortunate. In a single stroke it severed Fokine from a natural ally inside the Maryinsky, while isolating him from the experimentalist impulse that would shortly give rise to modernism. Less than six months later, he suffered another, equally crippling loss. Leaving the Ballets Russes, he abandoned the dance family that had nurtured his choreography since 1905. By 1912, the most creative phase of his career had ended.

Fokine's existential heroes revealed one facet of his individualist theme— the precariousness of freedom and the tragedy of its loss. Other roles celebrated a different kind of hero: the freewheeling individual who lived outside the rules of society. Exotics, for the most part, and usually male, these liberated heroes dressed the fantasy of freedom in the flesh of human possibility. They exalted the potency of men who lived by their instincts, at once fulfilling their true nature and transgressing the bounds of decorum. As danced by Nijinsky, the Golden Slave in *Schéhérazade* was exemplary in this regard: a primitive who from the moment he bolted onstage until the final spasm of his death exalted the fully liberated self and its inevitable clash with society. Today, *Schéhérazade* seems the height of ballet camp. A Shah, suspecting his favorite wife's infidelity, leaves home to test her; he returns to find the harem in the midst of an orgy and Zobéide in the arms of her Golden Slave. Scimitars flash, and the curtain falls on a stage full of corpses. Since Fokine's day sex has left the seraglio. But in 1910 it was still forbidden fruit. *Schéhérazade's* depiction of lust and illicit intercourse only partly concerned the pleasure of adulterous desire. Of greater moment was the subversiveness of an act that reappropriated what the Shah had expropriated—the freedom, bodies, and selves of the lovers. Equally subversive was the image of masculinity embodied in the protagonist. The Golden Slave ravished rather than courted his mistress; flaunted rather than concealed his body; loosed rather than bridled his physical prowess. Sex incarnate, Fokine's erotic primitive did onstage what respectable men could only do in fantasy.

The title role of *Le Spectre de la Rose*, also created by Nijinsky, turned on a similar theme: the illicit possession of a forbidden woman by a non-conformist male. Here, however, the sex has been tamed, idealized as romance. The seraglio has become a boudoir, the harem wife an unmarried daughter, the erotic tiger a she-man in rose petals. As in *Schéhérazade*, invasion is the motor of the action. "At his magic touch," rhapsodized Cyril W. Beaumont, "[the Young Girl] is spirited out of her chair to join him in the ever-quickening, soothing melody of the waltz. How high she leaps, yet so gracefully that it seems as if she, too, had forsaken her mortal body. Together they float through the still air, impelled everywhere by the fairy-like touch of his hand."[81] Young girls of good family were off-limits for casual dalliance, and for that reason all the more desirable as objects of erotic fantasy. Equally off-limits for men, except in the realm of fantasy, was openly effeminate behavior. Men might engage in homosexual acts, but they did so behind closed doors; in drawing rooms or salons, they abided by heterosexual dress codes and manners. Nijinsky openly flouted both. Masculine in the power of his leaps, feminine in the curving delicacy of his arms, he emitted a perfume of sexual strangeness; he seemed a living incarnation of the third sex, a Uranian reveling in the liberation of his true self.

Individualism as a transgressive force was the theme of other male roles, including several created by Adolph Bolm. A magnificent character dancer, second only to Nijinsky in Diaghilev's prewar stable of male talent, Bolm ranged the stage like a force of nature; his performances invoked the beast in man's inner self, the barbarian untamed by civilization. In *Thamar* his dance of seduction as the captive Prince blazed with power and passion. "He springs into the air," wrote Beaumont:

> jerks his head to and fro, and curves his legs under him so that, with every leap, his body is arched like a strung bow. He bounds higher and higher, his feet stamp, twist, and turn, faster and faster, to the frenzied throbbing of the

tambourines. The queen marks with satisfaction his feverish looks, his savage movements. She joins in the dance and their lips meet in a passionate kiss.[82]

Offstage, queen and captive copulate; onstage, she plunges a dagger into his heart. As in *Schéhérazade* the assertion of freedom through forbidden sex ends in death.

Only in *The Polovtsian Dances,* Fokine's first ballet created under Diaghilev's auspices, is this not the case. Here, primitive male virtue reigns: in Bolm, as the Polovtsian Chief, and in his warriors, who multiplied his postures of defiance and heroism. Like Nijinsky, Bolm vaulted onstage, clearing the groups that framed the fantasy area of the stage. "His whole being," wrote Beaumont, "pulsates with a savage exultation in his strength. He continually whirls round, springs upward, spins in the air and crashes to the group. His brows are contorted, his head flung back, his mouth opened wide in a hoarse, gasping shout of triumph."[83] The end of the ballet collectivized this exultation as the lines of warriors crossed and re-crossed, lashing the air with jumps and the ground with bows, inflaming their spirits with hoarse cries, until the stage became a seething tumult of humanity. "There was a moment," wrote a columnist for *Le Temps* in 1909:

> when the entire hall, carried away by the frenzy of the dances of the Oriental slaves and Polovtsian warriors at the end of *Prince Igor,* was ready to stand up and actually rush to arms. That vibrant music, those archers, ardent, wild, and fierce of gesture, all that mixing of humanity, those raised arms, restless hands, the dazzle of the multicolored costumes seemed for a moment to dizzy the Parisian audience, stunned by the fever and madness of movement.[84]

Although dramatic realism was a Fokine byword, his liberated heroes disavowed psychology. From start to finish, they remained the same: fully actualized beings whose roles demarcated a psychic space where id transgressed and triumphed. Visually, this space was also enclosed, marked off from the larger playing area of the stage—a theater of private fantasy. In *Schéhérazade* the Golden Slave burst onstage from behind closed doors; in *Le Spectre de la Rose* the hero flew through the frame of a bedroom window; in the original version of *Carnaval,* the characters entered through folds in the surrounding curtains. In many ballets Bakst hung the stage with massive verticals—columns in *Cléopâtre,* rock temples in *Le Dieu Bleu,* trees in *Daphnis and Chloë*—that both isolated and weighed on the drama. The vast curtain draped across the upper half of the scene in *Schéhérazade* had a similar effect, as did the bold, upward-thrusting diagonals in *Thamar* that culminated in the apex of a monumental triangle. In all these ballets, engulfment loomed like a constraining hand over the transgressive play of the protagonists within. If Bakst's massive and all-encompassing forms invoked a society hostile to personal endeavor, his spaces, yawning with the promise of secret pleasures, and his colors—hot, vivid, intense—heightened the emotionalism of the inner drama. Bakst "used colors symbolically," a critic has written, "to convey emotion, or induce a desired reaction from the audience."[85] He did this consciously: like symbolist painters and poets, he sought to correlate sense impressions with emotional states and mental images. "I have often noticed," he wrote in 1915:

> that in each color of the prism there exists a gradation which sometimes expresses frankness and chastity, sometimes sensuality and even bestiality, sometimes pride, sometimes despair. This can be felt and given over to the public by the effect one makes of the various shadings. This is what I tried to do in "Sheherazade." Against a lugubrious green I put a blue full of despair, paradoxical as it may seem. There are reds which assassinate and there are reds which are triumphal . . . The painter who knows how to make use of this, the director of the orchestra who can put with one movement of his baton all this in motion, without crossing them, . . . can draw from the spectator the exact emotion he wants him to feel.[86]

Like Fokine, then, Bakst heroicized the individual in two ways: by heightening the emotion attached to his person and by presenting his transgression within a framework of social encirclement. Visually and choreographically, the assertion of individuality attained the stature of an epic act.

Fokine never abandoned the language of ballet. But his liberating aesthetic demanded considerable modification of the technique perfected in the classrooms of the Maryinsky. This technique, blending the softness of the French school with the hard-edged virtuosity of the Italian, had been the very stuff of Petipa's art; its inflections stemmed from his choreographic practice and, in turn, inspired it. By 1900 this vital link was broken. As Petipa's creative powers waned, Imperial technique congealed in the habits of his earlier masterworks: it became an academic language that brooked no departures from its laws. The syntax and vocabulary that had been Petipa's means were now ends in themselves, constraints upon expression rather than instruments of it.

From the start Fokine warred against the academicism throttling ballet. He did so in the name of beauty, in the belief that dancing was not a bravura display but an art of poetic images. "The great, the outstanding, feature of the new ballet," he wrote in 1904:

is that in place of acrobatic tricks designed to attract applause, and formal entrances and pauses made solely for effect, there shall be but one thing—the aspiration for beauty. Through the rhythms of the body the ballet can find expression for ideas, sentiments, emotions. The dance bears the same relation to gesture that poetry bears to prose. Dancing is the poetry of motion.[87]

In the name of poetry, Fokine liberated ballet from the imperative of virtuosity and the conventions supporting it. He remade the pas de deux, formalized by Petipa as an adagio, solo variations, and coda, into a duet that was fluid in shape and function. Jettisoning Petipa's structure, he did away with the variations that often served as displays of technical prowess; he deployed steps in new and unusual ways, and significantly enlarged the canon of supports. Above all, he made the relationship of the partners explicitly emotional, transforming Petipa's abstract matings into realistic human encounters. Unlike the nineteenth-century cavalier, who stood behind the ballerina securing her balance at the waist, Fokine's men stepped out from the shadow of their women, supporting them at a variety of contact points. Save for a handful of conventional lifts, partnering in *Les Sylphides* centers on arms and hands, the former twining the couple into an image of community, the latter giving and taking weight in an expression of mutual trust. Although the partners are nearly always in physical touch, they remain, nonetheless, at arm's length; autonomous individuals, they reach out to one another in an act of willed intimacy. In *Le Spectre de la Rose* Fokine eliminated waist supports entirely; in this world of dreams bodies brush as lightly as butterfly wings. Again, hands take most of the weight; wrists, too, come into play, as in the arabesque penchée where the partners first touch; in lifts, hands disappear under armpits as if denying their part in willing the woman to flight. Where Fokine did use the waist to any extent, as in *Firebird*, he made it a locus of manipulation and entrapment. Ivan Tsarevich stands behind his prey, clutching her with the arrogance of a cad; she twists, bends, turns, reaching for his hands, aspiring to the distancing clasp that will return each of them to their separate spheres. In juxtaposing the old partnering and the new, Fokine reveals here the ideological premises of both.

Fokine did not totally eschew the bravura dance. But he used its vocabulary sparingly and unconventionally, seeking at all costs to avoid its becoming an occasion for applause. Tellingly, he recoiled from successive repetitions. In the male solos of *Spectre* and *Les Sylphides,* a single entrechat did service for the series of four or eight or sixteen that Petipa customarily employed in variations. At the same time, Fokine integrated the bravura step with the surrounding dance. In both *Spectre* and *Carnaval,* multiple pirouettes and grands jetés—traditional male bravura steps—are pulses in a continuum of movement; they begin from a minimum of preparation and end in the briefest of pliés; no pause or pose breaks the momentum of the phrase—or cues the audience to applaud. Fokine's loathing of virtuoso conventions, translated into parody, was a major theme of *Petrouchka,* with the female bravura dance receiving the brunt of his animosity. The Ballerina, in fact, stood for everything he most despised: technical trickery (her coy échappés and tiny hops on pointe, passés relevés and whipping fouetté turns were variation staples) and empty display, as well as any number of lesser sins: drawn-out preparations, the extremes of turnout, arms en couronne, segmented phrasing—all of which he refused to countenance in his "straight" choreography. *Petrouchka* contained a second ballerina parody—the Street Dancer, a hoyden who turns tricks for the carnival merrymakers. In *Early Memoirs* Bronislava Nijinska, who created the role, makes clear that its object was none other than Kchessinska, the Maryinsky's *prima ballerina assoluta,* mistress of Grand Dukes, and sworn enemy of Fokine and the "new ballet":

> "Well, what shall I mount for you, Bronislava Fominitchna? The Street Dancer is an acrobat. Do you know any tricks? Can you do the splits and whirl around on one leg while holding the other foot stiffly, high in the air?"
>
> I felt like joking and replied, "If, Mikhail Mikhailovitch, you want to see an acrobat, then I will dance for you the ballerina's *coda* from the ballet *Le Talisman.*"
>
> I started to imitate Mathilda Kchessinska, her *cabrioles* and her *relevés* on toe from the last act of *Le Talisman,* the coda that was always accompanied by thunderous applause in the Maryinsky.
>
> "That is perfect, it is exactly what is needed." Fokine laughed.[88]

Fokine's antiacademicism was strikingly illustrated in his use of the torso and arms, the first liberated from the corset of verticality, the second from the straightjacket of the circle. His aim in both instances was to heighten the expressiveness of the body by extending its lines and enhancing its plasticity and three-dimensionality. His reforms proved revolutionary. In a half-dozen years he changed the look of the female dancer and made her body anew. Although dancing, especially ballet dancing, requires the strength and agility of a gymnast, nineteenth-century dancers routinely cinched their waists. A pedagogue like Enrico Cecchetti (who conducted company class for Diaghilev intermittently through the 1920s) argued for lacing on the grounds that the corset gave support to the back, but other reasons undoubtedly proved more compelling. One was fashion: until World War I most stylish women wore stays. Another was ballet technique itself: while the trunk of the body might incline, it rarely strayed far from the vertical; activity was concentrated in the legs.

Fokine, by contrast, worked boldly and broadly. His "mimetic of the whole body" demanded a torso as pliant and expressive as limbs. Ridding women of corsets, he freed both midriff and back; recoiling from verticality, he celebrated the curve. Fokine's forward bends and backbends, side pulls and waist twists stretched the body into an expansive spiral. Emotionally, they explored virgin territory as well. In *Schéhérazade* seated almehs arched to the floor as if beckoning sensation, while the bacchantes in *Narcisse,* poised over a high skipping knee, made ready for precipitous action. Like the deep backbend, this prance became a Fokine trademark, appearing in numerous ballets. The two movements were not unrelated. In a series of choreographic sketches for *Le Dieu Bleu,* reproduced in the Russian edition of Fokine's memoirs, a naked female figure arches backward, curves forward in a prance, then breaks into a run with her head flung back—a phrase of exultant orgiastic dynamism.[89] Arms enlarged this emancipatory image. Rejecting the circles and quadrants of academic style, Fokine used the arms to extend the span of his movement, to open the upper body, and to heighten the overall impression of spontaneity. "Arms," he told an American student many years later, "are not pictures on the wall, but horizons."[90] Fokine stretched the arms outward and overhead, behind and to the front of the dancer; he used them asymmetrically, not to frame the body, but to sculpt it three-dimensionally, to round rather than flatten it. Above all, he insisted that arms give an appearance of naturalness, that like a window on the soul, they light the recesses of private emotion and make the discovery public.

Costume unfettered the body no less than choreography. Like Fokine, Bakst freed the back and midriff. He dressed his women in tunics and harem pants, soft flowing garments that released the torso from the constricting bodice of the tutu. He exposed unwonted stretches of flesh. In *Cléopâtre* navels showed; in *Schéhérazade* the lower reaches of the spine; in several ballets legs pushed through a slit in the skirt. (Onstage, the breasts that in some designs spilled freely from his tunics were always modestly covered.) These legs were doubly naked, for in exotic and "Greek" ballets, the dancers often performed without tights, disclosing the flesh of the leg, along with its form, to the gaze of the audience. The tutu, of course, also revealed the body: arms and shoulders from above the bodice, knees and lower legs from beneath the layered skirt. Except for the lower appendages, however, the revelations were decorous, no more than those of an evening gown: the cinched waist and billowing skirt kept the middle of the body under wraps. Bakst's genius for artful concealment dramatized precisely this middle. His harem pants followed the curve of the buttocks as did the panels of tunics tacked together high at the thigh. The hourglass figure of the Belle Epoque gave way to the natural unfettered body. That this body moved easily only heightened the impression of nakedness and naturalness. Unlike the tutu, which either straitened the body or bobbed around its circumference, a Bakst costume flowed with the movement, rounding, loosening, and enlarging it. If the Imperial dancer approximated a pictograph of ballet's encircled vertical, her Fokine successor exalted the very idea of motion.

No less heterodoxical than his female dress was Bakst's costuming for men. The danseur, too, had long revealed portions of his anatomy. But, as with the ballerina, the revelations were selective and always decorous; the ballet hero was a man who minded conventions. His leg was sheathed in tights; his thigh modestly concealed under theatricalized versions of a dressing gown. In ballets set in antiquity, Imperial tunics covered up shoulders and collarbones: women might bare them but men could not. Bakst, on the other hand, took astonishing liberties in dressing the danseur, with garments that were either frankly revealing or frankly feminine. In the title role of *Le Spectre de la Rose,* Nijinsky wore a body stocking with decorative overpinnings; as the Golden Slave in *Schéhérazade,* the outfit of a dancing houri. In *Narcisse* and *Le Dieu Bleu,* the dancer's abbreviated skirt, sharply demarcated waist, exposed collarbones and shoulders teased conventions of masculinity. Even Bolm, the company's he-man, appeared as Darkon in *Daphnis and Chloë* in a free-flowing tunic that enveloped the body in an aura of "natural" femininity.

That Bakst dressed so many ballets of the period in Grecian-inspired garments bespeaks the influence of an artist who has been mentioned only in passing, although she was both a catalyst and an inspiration of the "new ballet." Isadora Duncan first danced in St. Petersburg in December 1904. She returned early the following year, in December 1907, and again in April 1909—visits that coincided with Fokine's initial choreographic undertakings. Her debut was a major event: in the prestigious audience at the Hall of Nobles sat the cream of Petersburg's artistic and fashionable society. Her two performances—one, an all-Chopin program, the other entitled *Dance Idylls*—were "tremendous successes, recognized by dancers and amateurs of the dance as sensational, epoch-making events."[91] The World of Art turned out in force, as did a galaxy of Maryinsky stars; Benois took up her cause in print. Fokine, for his part, was conquered. Diaghilev, who later claimed that the two had attended her concerts together, wrote that "Fokine was mad about her, and Duncan's influence on him was the initial basis of his entire creation."[92] Diaghilev's statement should be taken with skepticism, not only because it was written twenty-two years after the fact in a private letter, but also because by 1926 he

had come to regard the choreographer as old hat. (That critical and popular demand had forced him that year to revive several Fokine ballets,
including *Firebird,* may well have sharpened his acerbic tone.)

Nevertheless, the substance of his statement is true. Fokine was smit-
ten, and even in the dark days of the 1930s when bitterness clouded his
judgment, she remained the shining star of his youth. " 'Tis the gift to be
simple," runs a Shaker hymn, and although Duncan grew up in the Bohemian feminist world of San Francisco, nature blessed her with this Shaker
virtue—her gift, in turn, to Fokine. "Duncan," he wrote, in a rare admission of influence, "reminded us of the beauty of simple movements . . .
[She] proved that all the primitive, plain, natural movements—a simple
step, run, turn on both feet, small jump on one foot—are far better than
all the enrichments of the ballet technique, if to this technique must be
sacrificed grace, expressiveness, and beauty."[93] All these movements appeared in Fokine's choreography. In *Les Sylphides* and *Le Spectre de la
Rose* they modified the classical vocabulary, lightening its texture and em-
boldening its outlines. In other ballets they appeared as signature steps,
recorded time and again by the era's photographers. In still other ballets
they were the warp on which Fokine wove entire dances. In *Firebird* the
Tsarevna's girlish court rings the lovers with rhythmic walks; in *The Polovtsian Dances* the captive maidens cross the stage with tremulous glides.
Fokine had long chafed at the acrobatic tricks designed to attract applause.
Duncan's sublime simplicity transcended this negative critique, opening his
mind to a vision of what could be; in her dances he discerned a wealth of
choreographic possibilities.

Duncan's notoriety derived from her feet—bare feet that shocked an
era that held propriety high on the scale of virtue. To Fokine, however,
they suggested new ways of presenting and using a basic instrument of the
dancer's art. Fokine never discarded blocked shoes entirely; in retrospective works and in ballets that invoked the romantic era, they sculpted the
foot to a crescent of formal beauty. But in exotic or Greek ballets, he
abandoned them for boots, soft slippers, sandals—and Duncan's bare feet.
Liberated from the constriction of the toe shoe, the foot broke out of its
traditional hemisphere. In lifts or prances it relaxed, displaying a natural
instep, while in rises it gripped the floor boldly. If, under Duncan's influence, Fokine rediscovered the foot, her Dionysian body revealed the dynamic physicality of the torso. Arched forward or swept back, Duncan's
torso inspired legions of artists, who paid tribute to its exultant freedom
in sketch after sketch. Fokine did not record his impressions on paper, but
in the curvings and twistings of his dancers the thrill of her body is patent.
Arms were another influence. Pavlova, writes Duncan's most recent biographer, "would tell inquirers that she had learned the fluidity of her arm

movements in *The Dying Swan* from Isadora."[94] Certainly, the asymmetry that Fokine favored must have come from her, along with the freedom and breadth that were equally trademarks of his port de bras.

Music was yet another domain where Duncan's influence was palpable. Her first Petersburg concert—an all-Chopin program—left an enduring impression on the young dancer. The composer figured in what appears to have been Fokine's first independent concert, at the Hall of the Assembly of the Nobility in February 1906. The Chopin music of *The Flight of the Butterflies* is not known, but the final score of *Les Sylphides* used two pieces—the Prelude (op. 28, no. 7) and one of the two Mazurkas (op. 33, no. 7)—from Duncan's 1904 program. Today, Chopin epitomizes the very idea of ballet music. In 1900, by contrast, his work belonged exclusively to the concert hall, as did that of virtually every composer of stature. Duncan's hubris in rifling the literature of "high" music was as scandalous as her bare feet. With Duncan's example before him, Fokine abandoned the specialist composers who regularly supplied the Maryinsky with ballet music. From the first, "serious" composers became his stock-in-trade: Saint-Saëns (*The Dying Swan*, 1905); Chopin (*The Flight of the Butterflies*, 1906; *Chopiniana*, 1907; *Danses sur la Musique de Chopin*, 1908; *Rêverie Romantique—Ballet sur la Musique de Chopin*, 1908; *Grand Pas sur la Musique de Chopin*, 1908; *Variations*, 1911; *Prelude*, 1915); Albéniz (*Sevillana*, 1906); Glinka (*Divertissement—The Valse Fantasia*, 1906; *The Dream*, 1915; *Jota Aragonesa*, 1916); Mendelssohn (*A Midsummer Night's Dream*, 1906); Bizet (*Spanish Dance*, 1906); Rubinstein (*La Vigne*, 1906); Brahms (*Czardas*, 1906); Clementi (*Bal Poudré*, 1908); Glazunov ("The Dance of the Seven Veils," 1908; *Bacchanale*, 1910; *Stenka Razin*, 1915); Tchaikovsky (*The Four Seasons*, 1909; *Francesca da Rimini*, 1915; *Romance*, 1915; *Eros*, 1915; *Andantino*, 1916); Schumann (*Carnaval*, 1910; *Papillons*, 1912); Liszt (*Les Préludes*, 1913); Balakirev (*Islamé*, 1912); Dukas (*The Sorcerer's Apprentice*, 1916)—to name only those composers chosen independently of Diaghilev and the administration of the Imperial Theaters.[95]

Not only did Duncan open the field of musical choices, but her rare musicality suggested new ways of linking movement and sound. Traditionally, ballet scores were tuneful, piecemeal compositions—a string, as Fokine wrote in 1904, of "old-time waltzes, polkas, pizzicati, and galops."[96] As a youth, Fokine had looked to musician friends as an escape from the artistic malaise of the Imperial Theaters. But it was in Duncan's mood pieces, where movement seemed to grow organically and inevitably from the music, that he found the principle laid down early in his career: "to invent in each case a new form of movement corresponding to the subject and character of the music."[97] In teaching sections of his ballets, he went phrase by phrase, insisting that movement had to breathe with the musical pauses and fill them out. Well might critic Valerian Svetlov assert in 1912 that "the influence of Duncanism on twentieth-century choreography is much more far-reaching and deeper than one would think at first sight."[98]

Under Duncan's aegis Fokine's attack on academic convention transcended its initial nihilism. It became, instead, a cleansing act. Ridding dance of stock, outmoded frippery, he restored the art to innocence. In lyrical compositions, built for the most part on a handful of steps and harmonious groupings, his defiant simplicity invoked a vision of human civility. Among the steps that recur insistently is the bourrée, where the feet, drawn together on pointe, lightly skim the floor. The step makes no claim to virtuosity. Its effect, so to speak, is psychological; in its weightless driftings the body seems both shorn of volition and afloat in timelessness. In almost every instance the bourrée identifies an altered reality—death in *The Dying Swan,* dream in *Le Spectre de la Rose,* poetry in *Les Sylphides*—where the soul, purged of materiality, can finally murmur its delicate complaint. Another step that plunges us into the heart of Fokine's idealism is the arabesque. This, of course, was a glory of the classical lexicon: a statement of pictorial harmony and balance. Fokine broke the step's containing sphere; no longer the quadrant of a circle, his arabesque leaned gently forward, reaching for infinity. He thus temporalized the static image. Rather than a vision of being, the step now spoke of becoming; it dramatized the ephemerality of appearance and the frailty of feeling.

If the bourrée and arabesque identified a plane of spiritual freedom, hands chained the free spirits into a vision of community. Again and again in Fokine's ballets, his women build bridges and trestles, weave and braid themselves into images of social harmony. Fokine's chaining polity deeply impressed his modernist successors. In *Dance Symphony,* choreographed in Petrograd in 1923, Fedor Lopukhov linked the beings of his cosmic order into a chain of triumphant humanity. The work itself, the first avowedly abstract ballet, claimed descent from *Les Préludes,* choreographed by Fokine a decade earlier.[99] *Joseph the Beautiful,* by Kasian Goleizovsky, another Soviet vanguardist who made the passage to modernism from the symbolist course laid out by Fokine, used chaining devices as well. But Fokine's truest son in this regard was George Balanchine, who gleaned the spirit behind the elder's forms, the eden immanent in the lacework of bodies. For Fokine, as for Balanchine, this filigree was nearly always female, as if only women might cross the divide between reality and the ideal. In the image of chaining vestals, Fokine invoked the promise of social harmony born in 1905.

To a very great extent, Fokine's vision and artistic practice developed independently of the Ballets Russes. This is not to deny the obvious: that under Diaghilev's aegis he created a handful of enduring works and entered into his fame as a choreographer. But it does cast a new light on his experience with the Ballets Russes and the way that organization channeled and used his talent. Indeed, one could argue that the Diaghilev enterprise acted detrimentally on his art, deflecting it from its course and commercializing those deflections. Today, Fokine's name is synonymous with the orientalist extravaganzas that made up the bulk of Diaghilev programming prior to World War I. Certainly, exoticism had made its appearance in Fokine's work before Diaghilev. Until 1910, however, this was only one of the styles fueling his experiments. The success of *Cléopâtre*, as Diaghilev retitled *Une Nuit d'Egypte* for Paris in 1909, changed this. The French wanted exoticism, and Diaghilev, with an eye to the box office, obliged. Each year thereafter exotic ballets—either Eastern or Russian in theme—filled one or, more often, two new repertory slots: *Schéhérazade* and *Firebird* in 1910; *Sadko* and *Petrouchka* in 1911; *Thamar* and *Le Dieu Bleu* in 1912; *Legend of Joseph* and *Le Coq d'Or* in 1914. By contrast, the neoromantic vein was practically closed off. In fact, of the three ballets in this style presented between 1910 and 1914, only *Le Spectre de la Rose* was created by the Ballets Russes; both *Carnaval* and *Papillons* received their premieres in Russia. Nor did Diaghilev choose to exploit the choreographer's Hellenist vein. *Daphnis and Chloë*, which Fokine had longed to produce since 1904, only reached the stage eight years later, after numerous postponements and, in the choreographer's view at least, heavy-handed attempts by Diaghilev to "ruin" the premiere. *Daphnis*, in fact, led Fokine to break with the Ballets Russes entirely. (In 1914, however, he yielded to Diaghilev's exceptional powers of persuasion and returned to the company for its last prewar season.)

That the quality of Fokine's work fell off in the years of his tenure with the Ballets Russes seems not only evident but natural. Forced into a mold only partly of his own making, he fell back on proven formulas. But let there be no mistake. By 1912 exotica itself had turned into a jumble of formulas. Calculated to sate a sensation-loving public, they left the choreographer neither room nor reason to grow. Outside the Diaghilev organization, Fokine did spread his wings. At the Maryinsky *Orpheus and Eurydice* broke new ground, even if *Islamé*, a *Schéhérazade* remake, did not. *Les Préludes*, choreographed early in 1913 for Pavlova's troupe, also ventured afield. Cyril W. Beaumont, who saw the ballet in London, described it as "symbolical of man's eternal struggle between life and death."[100] There were two lovers, a court of Botticelli nymphs, and a cortege of spirits of darkness. The plot, such as it was, functioned subtextually, hovering on the periphery of abstraction. The ballet also recorded Fokine's temporary fascination with eurhythmics, the movement system of Emile Jaques-

Dalcroze that from January 1911 onward was the subject of lectures and demonstrations in the Russian capital. André Levinson, who saw *Les Préludes* at the Maryinsky, where Fokine restaged it in April 1913, dismissed the choreography as a "vain wish to rival Dalcroze":

> In sections dance has been replaced by the beating out of the rhythm with the hands and feet. Energetic stamping corresponds to accented notes and pauses correspond to extended notes. There are even attempts to convey the tempo's acceleration and slowing by an unwitting parody of the "system" so studiously created.[101]

Subject matter was not the only constraint under which Fokine labored in the Ballets Russes. Diaghilev's promotion of Nijinsky demanded the creation of star vehicles tailored to his protégé's talent. Although Fokine was not unhappy choreographing for men, he preferred to create for women. From Pavlova to Tatiana Riabouchinska (a favorite dancer of the 1930s), they called forth his highest poetry. Diaghilev toppled woman from her erstwhile pedestal. Beginning with *Schéhérazade*, Nijinsky took precedence over the ballerina, becoming the muse and focus of nearly every production. Indeed, after *Firebird*, conceived originally for Pavlova, only *Thamar* had a woman as its protagonist. Outside the Diaghilev company, Fokine reverted to type. In *The Seven Daughters of the Mountain King*, another of his ballets for Pavlova, *Les Préludes*, *Eros*, and *Francesca da Rimini* (the last two created at the Maryinsky in 1915 and starring Mathilde Kchessinska and Lubov Egorova respectively), the ballerina returned to the poetic limelight.

Fokine's third "deflection" during the Diaghilev years was longer lasting. Ultimately, its consequences were tragic, for it touched a flaw in Fokine's character that virtually stilled his voice for fifteen years. Sudden fame can spoil an artist; when coupled with money it can corrupt him. Thanks to the Ballets Russes, Fokine's choreographic talent became a premium commodity; overnight its value soared, drawing high returns throughout the West. Fokine was quick to profit and quick to equate talent with money. This greed proved his undoing. It led him to leave Russia in 1918 when the Maryinsky could not meet his salary demands—a decision that left him bereft of the dancers who were the material of his art—and to settle in the United States, where titans of popular entertainment dangled pots of gold. Like most immigrants, he soon discovered that concrete, not gold paved the country's streets. The saga of his American career makes sorry reading—music-hall extravaganzas, one-night stands, movie prologues, a very occasional concert. As an artist of the lyric theater, he idled. Not until

1936, when René Blum invited him to work with the Ballets de Monte Carlo, would Fokine pick up the shards of his broken career.[102]

Common wisdom holds that collaboration—that talismanic word— was the key to Ballets Russes success. Certainly, in his 1914 letter to the *Times,* Fokine had laid down as his fifth and last "rule" the "alliance of dancing with the other arts." In practice, however, this alliance only rarely stemmed from collaboration, if by that one understands an act of joint creation. In fact, of all the works staged by Fokine for the Ballets Russes, only one—*Firebird*—was a genuine collaboration. The others, for the most part, were choreographic job work, with Fokine called in to fill out a concept developed by Diaghilev's inner court. That this job work was sometimes inspired suggests that the appearance of unity in a ballet had its source elsewhere than in collaboration. Between Fokine and the two designers—Bakst and Benois—associated with his happiest achievements flowed a current of artistic understanding, a charge that sparked in each reactions of a similar order. Like Bakst, Fokine reveled in sensory liberation; like Benois, he yearned for a lost Arcadia of the ideal. Far more than collaboration, what held together the pieces of Diaghilev's best works was the community of values to which their contributing artists subscribed.

Wagnerian thought gave this "fusion" a name—*Gesamtkunstwerk*— and a theoretical framework, even if the means and models derived from elsewhere. The "ideas associated with Wagner and his operas were . . . the greatest single influence on the attitude of the *Mir iskusstva* group towards the theatre," art historian Janet Kennedy has written. The *Ring* was performed in St. Petersburg in 1889, and in the early 1890s Diaghilev heard the performance of *Lohengrin* that converted him into a Wagner enthusiast. By the end of the 1890s the group regarded Wagner not simply as a great composer but as a "major influence on recent art in general."[103]

Wagner had envisioned a theater in which the "elemental mixture of visual and aural impressions" would create a "total art work." This ideal of *Gesamtkunstwerk* about which Wagner had "dreamed," Benois argued in a review of the 1910 season, the Diaghilev group had achieved in its productions of the "new ballet."[104] To what extent this was true remains a matter of debate, as does the more perplexing question of whether *Gesamtkunstwerk* itself is theoretically possible without destroying the properties inherent in the individual component arts. André Levinson argued throughout the prewar period that Fokine's attempts to appropriate to ballet procedures derived from music, painting, and drama had ended by subordinating the choreographic element to these other media. (Isadora Duncan reached the same conclusion during her sojourn at Bayreuth. "The Master has made a mistake," she intrepidly announced to Cosima Wagner. "Man must speak, then sing, then dance. But the speaking is the brain, the thinking man. The singing is the emotion. The dancing is the Dionysian ecstasy which carries away all. It is impossible to mix in any way, one with the other. Musik-Drama kann nie sein.")[105] Levinson further argued that all the arts suffered in the attempted fusion:

> Besides Fokine's unnecessary, superficial and jejune attempt to dramatize ballet, another weak spot in his compositions is . . . [the] predominance of the pictorial. If all the action of *Sheherazade* and *Firebird* could have been replaced by a skillfully-arranged series of living pictures, the audience might have been at leisure to discern more freely the extraordinary beauties of the set design and the ornamentation lavished by Bakst and Golovin. Sometimes all the mad moving about on stage seems like nothing more than an annoying commotion and distraction.[106]

Levinson is grossly unfair to Fokine, ascribing to the choreographer a preeminence that, as we have seen, he did not actually enjoy. The ascendancy of painters in Diaghilev's organization explains in part the dominance of visual effects in Fokine's works beginning in 1909. But another impulse was at work as well: the acclamation by Diaghilev's Parisian audience of precisely that note of luxuriant opulence that became a hallmark of his company's style. Comtesse Anna de Noailles, a minor poet and fashionable Ballets Russes enthusiast, recalled the impact of *Cléopâtre*, the model for Diaghilev's exotic extravaganzas:

> When I entered the box to which I had been invited . . . I realized that I was seeing a miracle, something that had never before existed. Everything that could dazzle, intoxicate, seduce, arrest seemed to have been dredged up and brought to the stage to luxuriate there . . . On the stage of the Ballets Russes, the kings of India and China, skillfully clasped to the center of a slender and violent drama, appeared in the enormous luxury of palm trees spreading their greenery against indigo skies. Their costumes, gold with heavy embroideries . . . amplified them in such a way as to make their sovereignty formidable and superhuman. The angel, the genius, the triumpher of the spectacle, the divine dancer Nijinsky took hold of our hearts, filling us with love, while the soft or sharp sonorities of the Asiatic music completed this stupefying and luxuriant work.[107]

To Diaghilev's fashionable audience, works like *Cléopâtre* and *Schéhérazade* marked a radical departure from contemporary practices on the lyric stage. Theatrical reformers, however, did not share this assessment. Gordon Craig's journal *The Mask*, wrote Levinson, correctly "identified the theatrical novelty of the 'Russian plagiarists' as a deceptive recycling of the old, moribund pre-reform theatre. Beneath the luxuriant raiment of exotic decors the principles of staging have remained untouched." The emphasis on material luxury, a major production value up to 1914, indicates imperatives of a quasi-commercial order. "In the ballet conceived as *Gesamtkunstwerk*," theater historian Denis Bablet has written, "painting remains painting and is applauded as such. The stage becomes an exhibition hall."[108]

Firebird or *Schéhérazade* indicated the shortcomings of the Wagnerian method when applied to ballet, yet judged by the prevailing standards of the day, they were models of artistic harmony. To contemporaries, the absence of glaring stylistic incongruities, coupled with Diaghilev's repeated avowals of artistic as opposed to commercial intent, bespoke a practical realization of Wagner's ideal *Gesamtkunstwerk*. But if Wagner provided the theoretical scaffolding of the Ballets Russes's prewar aesthetic while dictating the expectations of knowledgeable members of the audience, the practical achievement of this ideal rested on a social imperative. Diaghilev's organizing committee was shaped by the semifeudal habits of the Tsarist theaters and the informal networks of nonprofit-oriented enterprise. This contradictory experience prepared them to work within a collective framework, while at the same time impelling them toward the creation of democratized structures in which each member functioned essentially as an individual. It was this collective-individualist impulse that enabled the former *miriskusstniki* to achieve the exemplary consistency and high artistic merit that distinguished the company's best works.

An identical impulse, of course, had animated Fokine's Maryinsky followers, who now became the backbone of Diaghilev's celebrated ensemble. In their writings about the Ballets Russes, the early French critics revealed a profound admiration for precisely this ability of the "magnificent and anonymous" troupe of Russians—the phrase is *Figaro* critic Robert Brussel's—to pool individual talents to common artistic purpose. Jacques-Emile Blanche, for example, looked upon the French artistic world as being stifled by excessive individualism. By contrast, the Russian artists demonstrated an ability to subordinate personal values and goals for the benefit of a larger whole born of collaboration.[109] Between choreographer and dancers exists a special kind of intimacy. Each gives to the other; each reveals the other; each needs the other to complete himself as an artist. More than most choreographers, Fokine made the act of creation a collaborative endeavor. Although he might take notes into rehearsal, he created on the living body. He drew material from his dancers and relied on them to divine the imagery embedded in his steps. The Street Dancer's solo in *Petrouchka* grew out of Nijinska's improvised parody of the coda in *Le Talisman*. Her role as Papillon in *Carnaval* made equal demands on her imagination. Here, Fokine had merely sketched out the patterns and steps;

with Nijinsky's help she refined them into the fluttering image of a butter-fly.[110] This living collaboration was not one-sided. For the dancer the jour-ney to artistic "personhood" can be completed only with the aid of the choreographer. Intuitively, Fokine divined the "soul" immanent in a dancer's unripened personality, and this individual essence he distilled in his cho-reography. The flower of her generation at the Maryinsky, Pavlova passed into legend as the Dying Swan, while Petrouchka came to be seen as pres-aging Nijinsky's tragic fate. To artist and audience alike, Fokine revealed the uniqueness of a dancer's individuality.

For a number of reasons, this vital form of collaboration has never received its due. For one thing, murmurings in the studio to "try this" or "keep that" have no life independent of the final work. Unlike a set or costume design, which may exist in a half-dozen versions, all that survives of a dance—when this survives at all—is the incarnation that reaches the stage. For another, the discussion of collaboration is predicated on as-sumptions derived from music and the visual arts. Dance figures in, but only secondarily. Almost always, the perspective is that of composer and/or designer.

There is a third reason for this neglect. Although lip service is paid to Fokine's historical importance, his reputation as a choreographer is at low ebb. In part this reflects the quality of revivals, few of which do honor to the style or spirit of their originals. To a greater extent, however, it reflects Balanchine's tutelage—his emphasis on steps, his de-emphasis of acting, his preference for plotless as opposed to narrative forms. It also reflects—and not well—on those who in their zeal to crown Balanchine with the mantle of Petipa have wiped two decades from the history of twentieth-century ballet.

In those twenty years lay the insurrection of modernism. As in the other arts, modernism in ballet forced a breach with the past: old idols were toppled, commandments broken in a search for new forms. Fokine's 1904 manifesto set this revolution in march, even if his own works, loyal to the inspiriting realism of his youth, stopped short of completing it. His achievements were many and far-reaching. He revamped the ensemble, pas de deux, and solo dance, redefining their function and inventing forms adequate to that new function. He enhanced the expressiveness of the arms and torso. Creating new sequences of steps and new kinds of transitions, he modified academic syntax. In all these aspects of choreographic prac-tice, Fokine laid the foundation for his modernist and neoclassical heirs.

He left them another equally important legacy: the idea that ballet could reimage the world after the promptings of a subjective vision, that no less than painting, music, or drama it could speak personal and histor-ical truth. From the start Fokine's work centered on themes of collective

identity and individual freedom. These concerns were not the subject matter of his ballets, but the dialectic on which their inner content turned—a
vision of social and personal autonomy. This humane ideal wove a common thread into works as different as *Schéhérazade, Petrouchka,* and *Les
Sylphides.* Fokine's obsession with these themes had its source in the experiences of his youth: his rearing as a dancer in the shadow of absolutism,
his searches in the liberal quarters of the arts community and intelligentsia.
Above all, it stemmed from the shock of 1905. The revolution turned the
dreamer into a maker of dances. But its influence did not stop there: its
very dynamic haunted Fokine's work long after the event itself had faded
from consciousness, as if the shock of freedom and the shock of its defeat
had branded his imagination with the vision of a promised land never to
be realized save in art.

2 ✍

THE VANGUARD POETIC

OF VASLAV NIJINSKY

FROM 1909 TO 1912 the "new ballet" embodied in the Ballets Russes was overwhelmingly the creation of Michel Fokine. In sheer numbers, his work dominated the repertory, as it did imaginatively: apart from *Giselle, Swan Lake,* and the divertissements *Le Festin* and *Les Orientales*— all of which epitomized styles of the "old ballet"—the entire corpus of new work bore the choreographic signature of Fokine.

Beginning in 1912 this ceased to be the case. In that year Diaghilev launched a palace revolution—the first of several in the history of the Ballets Russes—that led Fokine to resign from the company. His place was quickly filled; his art, with equal swiftness, superseded. This shake-up involved more than a changing of Diaghilev's Pretorian guard: it revealed a restive impresario anxious to make his mark as an artist. With Fokine's departure, Diaghilev took up the choreographic reins of the Ballets Russes, and with the dancer/protégé who became the instrument of his imagination, set out to conceptualize its new "new ballet."

If Fokine had opened the door to modernism, he himself failed to cross its threshold. That radical step was taken by Vaslav Nijinsky, upon whom Diaghilev now thrust the mantle of the "new ballet's" succession. Unlike Fokine, who had supplied his former master with annual funds of novelties, Nijinsky created only four works for the Ballets Russes: *L'Après-midi d'un Faune* (1912), *Jeux* (1913), *Le Sacre du Printemps* (1913), and *Till Eulenspiegel* (1916). Except for *Till,* which was performed only in the United States and never seen by Diaghilev, all were choreographic milestones: *Faune,* in its movement design; *Jeux,* in its intimation of neoclassicism; *Sacre,* in its creation of primitivist movement and style. *Faune* and *Sacre* brought fame and notoriety to Nijinsky, the former because of the final masturbatory gesture, which outraged the guardians of Parisian morality, the latter because it provoked one of the great *scandales* of French theatrical history. Indeed, no twentieth-century dance work has cast so long a shadow over the popular imagination as *Sacre*—all the more remarkable as the original was almost immediately lost. Recreated in more than sixty versions, the ballet has become synonymous with the very idea of modernity.

Within the Ballets Russes, Nijinsky's works of 1912 and 1913 marked a definitive break with the Maryinsky. Although rarely commissioned by its administration, Fokine's ballets had stocked galas and benefit evenings, entering the general consciousness of the cultivated St. Petersburg public. Nijinsky's works, by contrast, belonged solely to the West. News of them percolated to Russia, but except for the experiments conducted by his sister Bronislava Nijinska in postrevolutionary Kiev, they left no issue there: with Nijinsky, modern ballet history first splits into Russian and Western branches. As a group, Nijinsky's ballets administered the first shock of ballet modernism. But they also laid out, with a symbolism that can only be described as prescient, the larger aesthetic project of the Ballets Russes— a dialectic of rupture and return in relation to the classical past.

Although Nijinsky's stature as a choreographer is no longer in question, the sources of his art remain as mysterious today as they were to his first audiences. In part, this stems from the paucity of evidence: until the Joffrey Ballet's reconstruction of *Sacre*, only *Faune*, handed down from Nijinska's 1922 revival for the Ballets Russes, had survived in its entirety. Another mystery derives from Nijinsky's own testimony: his *Diary*,[1] that fascinating document of a failing mind, offers no cogent explication of his art. Finally, there is Nijinsky's mystique as a dancer and his myth as a man, subjects of enduring, even lurid fascination that have deflected attention from his accomplishment as an artist.

Of all Diaghilev's many renowned performers, Nijinsky alone has become a legend. Born in 1889 to a pair of itinerant Polish dancers, he was the single most brilliant star of the Ballets Russes during its twenty years of life. As a dancer, he transcended the bounds of what seemed humanly possible for even a consummate virtuoso, while as an actor he possessed an uncanny, even pathological ability to submerge his personality in the role at hand. These attributes, inspiring some of Fokine's happiest creations, made him a superb interpreter of the "new ballet," and from 1909 to 1913 Nijinsky thrilled audiences as the Golden Slave, Petrouchka, Harlequin, and the Specter of the Rose. Dancing, however, forms only part of his legend. As Diaghilev's lover, he was a homosexual hero; leaving Diaghilev to marry Romola de Pulszky—the event that occasioned his dismissal from the Ballets Russes late in 1913—he became no less notorious as a homosexual turncoat. Above all, the madness—schizophrenia—that clouded Nijinsky's last thirty-two years has hindered an intelligent under-

standing of his work. Cast as an idiot savant and "clown of god" (a recurring phrase in his *Diary*), Nijinsky has become a symbol of naive and
tragic genius.[2]

The plans for Nijinsky's first ballet were laid in the autumn of 1910
during an extended holiday with Diaghilev and Léon Bakst. By December,
when the trio returned to St. Petersburg, *Faune's* general scheme had been
sketched. The setting, Nijinsky announced to his sister, was to be archaic
Greece, the music, Debussy's "Prélude à l'Après-midi d'un Faune." As to
the choreography, "any sweetly sentimental line in the form or in the
movement will be excluded." In front of the pier glass in the Nijinsky
family living room, where brother molded sister into the poses of Faun
and Nymph, the ballet took shape. Early in 1911 the two showed fragments of the work to Diaghilev and Bakst. By the following spring, *Faune's*
"choreographical outlines" were complete.[3]

Although Nijinska sees her brother as the ballet's sole creator, others
have taken a different view. Arnold Haskell, in his biography of Diaghilev,
attributes the conception, including the all-important two-dimensional design, to Diaghilev and Bakst. Because Haskell's chief source was Walter
Nouvel, a friend and collaborator of the impresario for nearly forty years,
his "true story" of the ballet's inception is worth quoting at length:

> After a trip to Greece, Diaghileff, and still more especially Bakst, were haunted
> by the recent discoveries at Knossus and by Greek archaic art. Bakst dreamed
> of interpreting these things on the stage. They discussed the matter at length,
> searching for a subject and music that would be adequate. Finally, they agreed
> on Mallarmé's *Eclogue*, of the existence of which Nijinsky was not aware till
> the work was completed, and Debussy's music. They decided too that they
> would give Nijinsky his first chance with this work, but they kept the strictest
> supervision of detail in their own hands, and, as far as the central idea was
> concerned, they resolved to make of the ballet a moving bas-relief, all in pro-
> file, a ballet with no dancing but only movement and plastic attitude—the
> inspiration for all this being solely Bakst's.[4]

Bakst's passion for archaic Greek art is a matter of record. It prompted
his trip to Greece in 1907 and the memories and sketches he took back
with him to St. Petersburg. "What interested him most," his biographer
Charles Spencer has written, "were Minoan Greece, Mycenae, Knossos
. . . and early archaic sculpture"—whose images soon appeared in "Terror Antiquus," an apocalyptic vision of ancient Greece that Bakst now
completely repainted.[5] Equally a matter of record is Diaghilev's interest in
Debussy, commissioned by him in 1909 to write the music for *Masques et
Bergamasques,* a ballet that never materialized. On October 26 of the fol-

lowing year, the composer authorized the use of his score in Diaghilev's "choreographic adaptation" of *Faune*.[6] As for the subject of the ballet, there is no question that this originated with either Diaghilev or Bakst.

More problematical is Haskell's attribution of three of the ballet's key choreographic ideas—the frieze-like design, profiled stance, and alternation of movement and plastic pose—to Bakst. Nijinska's remark that her brother "from the very beginning, without any preparation, [was] in complete mastery of the new technique" lends support to Haskell's assertion, for it suggests that when Nijinsky began to choreograph, he already possessed a clear vision of the ballet. If Bakst was indeed the source of some of *Faune's* most innovative ideas, the question of his sources then poses itself. And here, archaic Greece—the usual answer—seems inadequate. Certainly, the vine leaves and geometric motifs that decorate his tunics were staples of preclassical ceramic ware. But they appear with equal frequency on the black and red figure vases of the fifth century, where one also finds the flowing garment, ritual gesture, and profiled stance reproduced in his designs. The vase paintings of this transitional period glow with civilized contentment: many are scenes of music-making in which the players trip lightly, their faces wreathed in smiles. Along with graciousness, these images convey a naturalistic intent: if elbows are angled, the flesh of a surrounding arm softens the angle; if bodies are flattened, a pleated tunic rounds the flatness—as Bakst does in his designs for the Nymphs. Here, no less than in the Greek originals on which he drew, we are far from the totalizing design of *Faune's* identically imaged bodies. We are closer, in fact, to the Arcadian vision of Fokine's *Narcisse* and *Daphnis and Chloë*.[7]

Faune's design, like the idea, which Haskell also attributes to Bakst, of using non-dance movement to link the ballet's "plastic attitudes," suggests another—theatrical—source of inspiration. Meyerhold is no stranger to these pages. But he appears now in a different guise: as inventor of the "static" or "motionless" theater that formed the cornerstone of his method in staging symbolist drama. This style, first employed in *The Death of Tantagiles* (1905) and elaborated in productions of 1906 and 1907 for Vera Komissarzhevskaya's renowned St. Petersburg dramatic troupe, contained the germ of Nijinsky's most innovative ideas in *L'Après-midi d'un Faune*.

Diaghilev's relationship to Meyerhold is a lacuna in the former's biography. Yet from 1906, when the temporarily unemployed director expressed the hope that "perhaps Diaghilev will build a new theater," until 1928, when Diaghilev spoke of "giving a joint season with Meyerhold" the following spring, the two fitfully crossed paths.[8] That their first recorded encounter took place in 1906—that is, when Meyerhold "was in the grip of Symbolist art"[9] and anxious to continue the experiments he had begun at Stanislavsky's Theater-Studio—is significant. Not only does it establish Diaghilev's interest in the theater long before his actual debut as a producer, but it also identifies that interest with the currents of symbolist experiment. Diaghilev's castle in the air came to nought, and he soon shifted his activities to Paris. But he maintained his connection with Meyerhold, who attended the soirees that in 1910 brought to Diaghilev's apartment the painters, composers, and friends of his early Russian seasons. Nijinsky, too, was among that elite throng, the only dance artist (if his sister is to be believed) so privileged. The young man, who had once socialized with the greats of the athletic and sporting world, now discovered the world of art of Diaghilev. Nijinska heard about these "meetings" and observed their influence on her brother. "He soon came to the conclusion that this world of art was where he belonged and that he could live only among artists."[10]

In the years immediately preceding the inception of the Ballets Russes, Bakst worked with Meyerhold on at least two occasions. In autumn 1906 both participated in the organization of Komissarzhevskaya's new theater (for which Bakst painted the season curtain)[11] and two years later in Ida Rubinstein's production of *Salomé,* which Meyerhold directed and Bakst designed. The dates, encompassing the director's symbolist period, equally bracket the era that gave birth to *Faune's* most conspicuous innovations. In works like *Hedda Gabler, Pelléas and Mélisande,* and, above all, *Sister Beatrice,* these innovations—two-dimensionality, stylized posture, foreshortened stage, depersonalized performing style, totalizing design, and slow, "signifying" movement—were all in place. What *Faune* did was transpose to the dance stage the principles of Meyerhold's "static theater."

This style had its source in *The Death of Tantagiles,* one of the 1905 Theater-Studio productions that never reached the stage, although it was presented early the following year in Tiflis. The play, wrote the director, "inspired a method of placing figures on stage in bas-reliefs and frescoes and a means of expressing interior monologue with the help of the music of plastic motion."[12] This was the beginning of what Meyerhold called "static" or "motionless" theater, described by Konstantin Rudnitsky as:

> a theater of slow, significant, profound motions [in which] the plastic form of the acting was intended to give not a . . . rendering of . . . real life (as the Moscow Art Theatre tried to do), but the slow "music" of motion in harmony with the hidden spirit of the play . . . Sometimes . . . the actors suddenly froze. At such moments human faces and bodies became living statues. For the first time a director demanded of the actors sculptural expressiveness. So the living bas-reliefs came to be.[13]

The moving frieze reappeared in several of Meyerhold's productions. In *Sister Beatrice,* one of the few works of the period for which photographs exist, Meyerhold's nuns, like the Nymphs of *Faune,* are rigidly stylized, their bodies flattened into an appearance of two-dimensionality, their gestures angled, planed, and subordinated to a totalizing design. Throughout the play these gestures were synchronized with the poses of the heroine. "The rhythm of the production," wrote Meyerhold,

> was achieved by precisely calculated, extended pauses and clearly articulated gestures. Above all, we tried to purge the primitive tragedy of Romantic fervour. The melodious style of delivery and movements in slow motion were designed to preserve the implicitness of expression, and every phrase was barely more than a whisper, the manifestation of an inner tragic experience.[14]

If the stress on inner rhythm, like the slow and "undancerly" quality of the movement, anticipates *Faune,* so too does the archaic character of the pose, inspired, in the case of *Sister Beatrice,* by pre-Raphaelite and early Renaissance painting. Equally prescient is the depersonalized style of acting, an axiom of the new theater, and the use of the foreshortened stage, which confined the action to a narrow ribbon across the extreme front of the proscenium. Like the use of rhythmical movement, this was one of several techniques gleaned by Meyerhold from the theories of Georg Fuchs.[15]

There is little reason to believe that Nijinsky ever saw Meyerhold's ground-breaking works of this period. Until May 1907 he lived within the cloistered precincts of the Imperial Theatrical School, and even after he graduated, his liaison with Prince Pavel Lvov, a sports patron and aficionado, brought him more often to bicycle races and horse shows than to dramas.[16] What he knew of Meyerhold's "stylized theater," the director's term for his symbolist experiments, must have come secondhand, in talks on the Lido beach, where Bakst painted the dancer's portrait in the summer of 1910, in discussions with Diaghilev that autumn when the music for *Faune* was chosen. There is a story that Bakst arranged to meet Nijinsky in the Greek galleries at the Louvre and that the dancer, lost in admiration of Egyptian reliefs on the floor below, stood his friend up: this, it is implied, accounts for the two-dimensionality of *Faune.* But, as Lincoln Kirstein points out, Nijinsky "had long been familiar with the Maryinsky's 'Egyptian' style," if not from operas like *Aïda,* then certainly from ballets like *La Fille du Pharaon* and *Cléopâtre.*[17] In any event plastique was only a starting point. More crucial to *Faune* was the mating of static images with the cadences of rhythmical movement and the stylized forms of symbolist theater. Under the aegis of his twin mentors, Nijinsky's first steps as a choreographer followed the road laid out by Meyerhold, as if fulfilling one of the director's prophetic claims: that the new theater "anticipate[d] the revival of the dance." [18]

Neither Diaghilev nor Bakst, however, entered the family parlor where Nijinsky began to choreograph. And this is where the ideas sowed by them took on new life, and the translation exercise they had proposed became a radical dance statement infused with Nijinsky's personal vision. Like many a first novel, *Faune* is a work of adolescent sexual awakening. The pretext comes from Mallarmé's famous monologue: a Faun sees, or thinks he has seen a group of nymphs in the distance; he pursues them, loses them, then relives the memory—or is it only a fantasy?—of lust, Lesbian passion, and frustrated desire. Only the barest outlines of the poem survive in the ballet: the Faun, the Nymphs who intrude upon his reverie, the mood of erotic languor. Where the poem blurs the line between dream and reality, the ballet presents the erotic theme as lived experience: the reality of the Nymphs, like the scarf that sates the Faun's desire, is never in question. Nor is his innocence: from the opening stretches, where he tests the sensuality of his own body, to the halting steps with which he pursues his female prey and the wonderment that parries with lust as he contemplates her, all this speaks of sexual discovery.

Of heterosexual discovery, to be precise, for in *Faune* Nijinsky voiced a desire unfulfilled in his life with Diaghilev, save in the realm of fantasy. In her biography, Romola Nijinsky describes the subject of the ballet as "a simple incident from ordinary life which happens to every human being: the initial awakening of emotional and sexual instincts and their reaction." [19] But although the surface shimmers with the simplicity of the work's part-human, part-animal protagonist, the vision of heterosexuality itself is fraught with ambiguities: the seductiveness of the Chief Nymph, who throws off not one but three veils as if by this striptease to pierce the Faun's self-involvement; the sudden violence of their embraces, in which he "captures" her, as Joan Acocella says, "between the rails of his extended arms"; [20] the menace of the returning trios of Nymphs, who taunt him with wrongdoing—and guilt. Among the many obsessions haunting Nijinsky's *Diary* is the figure of the prostitute, or cocotte, as he called her, wandering the streets of Paris with cheap scent and promise of guilty pleasure and scorn for the modestly dressed dancer in her pursuit:

> I liked Paris cocottes when I was with Diaghilev. He thought me stupid, but I used to run to them. I ran about Paris looking for cheap cocottes, but I was afraid people would notice my actions . . . I knew that everything I did was awful, and that if I were found out I would be lost. All young men do silly things. In the streets of Paris I went in search of cocottes. I looked for a long time because I wanted the girl to be healthy and beautiful—sometimes I looked

all day long and found nobody because I was inexperienced. I loved several cocottes every day. . . I used to make use of all sorts of tricks in order to draw their attention, as they paid very little to me because I was simply dressed. I was dressed quietly in order not to be recognized.[21]

Like Nijinsky, his Faun heeds the siren call of the seductress, pursues her in a cat's cradle of steps, and allows her to flee, content to savor the memory of her body, rather than experience the joys of possession. The scarf that he hugs to himself and into which, in the ballet's last spasmodic movement, he spills his seed, is not, however, merely a stand-in for its absent owner. Equally, it symbolizes his triumph over the snares of Woman, his resistance to the temptation of her flesh. In the case of *Faune*, where Nijinsky the overt homosexual declared himself a covert heterosexual, the fetishism of the scarf bespoke a deep-rooted ambivalence toward men and women alike. Torn between the power of his lust and the fear of its consequences, Nijinsky opted for the safe haven of self-gratification.

On a stage where the presentation of sex was highly conventionalized, the directness of Nijinsky's language shocked. Shorn of virtuosity and decorativeness, his movement exposed its subject with the bold, naked forms of a primitive idol. On the dramatic stage, such movement had earned Meyerhold the title of a ballet master. When transferred to the dance stage, it amounted to a declaration of war against the received conventions of ballet. Indeed, into the eight minutes of *Faune* Nijinsky packed the essentials of ballet modernism, completing the revolution initiated by Fokine.

In Nijinsky's hands, movement became an end in itself. He broke it down, took it apart, and put it back together again, at every point purging it of acquired flesh. Fokine had used virtuosity sparingly, subordinating it to expression. Nijinsky, by contrast, abandoned it entirely, along with the classical technique that supported it. *Faune* went back to basics. The dancers walked and pivoted, inclined, knelt, and in a single instance jumped— movements that revealed the phylogeny of ballet in these most primitivized signs of its steps. Fokine had uncased the foot. It was Nijinsky, however, who put that liberated foot to work, pinioning it to the floor and weighting it, and using its component parts—heel, ball, arch—to reflexive purpose. His torso, too, called attention to itself, not only because, like Fokine's, it was a locus of physical expression, but because it displayed the openness traditionally associated with turnout. Fokine had weaned ballet from the axiomatic identification of classical style with the outward rotation of the leg. Nijinsky now seized upon parallel stance, which Fokine had occasionally employed, and by hardening its lines, transformed it into a commentary upon the very aesthetics of turnout.

Although Fokine rarely spoke of design, his choreography celebrated the curve. Nijinsky, by contrast, reimaged the body as an interplay of Euclidean forms—triangles, arcs, and lines—that equally served as the unifying design of his ensemble. These forms, now meshed, now layered, invoked the twin planes and geometrized landscape of a cubist painting; they announced the modernity of *Faune*, while simultaneously compacting into a single gestalt an entire narrative sequence. In the Faun's duet with the Chief Nymph, the seesaw of angled bodies suggests a host of competing desires: lust, fear, acquiescence, timidity, evasion, a will to dominate. But the angles and lines of this Euclidean universe serve another, more important end. Purged of sentimental and romantic padding, the choreography narrows the definition of sex to pure instinct. Nijinsky's Faun is only partly human. Like his classical forebears, he is also half-beast, and it is this aspect of his nature that comes to the fore in his encounter with the Chief Nymph. The partners never touch. They seem to touch, however, and at nearly every point the suggestion of contact is sudden and fraught with violence. Again and again the Faun turns on his prey, locking her in the vise of his powerful arms. Almost always, the throat is the locus of entrapment, as if that exposed column were the gateway to sex itself. At one point, he stands behind her, forming a triangle with his arms that symbolically decapitates her. In this coupling, silence, not rape, is the aim, for if *Faune* speaks of lust, it speaks even more insistently of silencing it, of destroying its claim on the body. This denial of nature is implicit in the very design of the ballet, for if geometry stylizes Nijinsky's protagonists, it also unsexes them, as if form, like some higher morality, were a shield against instinct.

Jeux, Nijinsky's second ballet, also hinges upon sexual ambiguity and desire. But here the barbarism has been tamed, socialized into a vision of modern love. The work was conceived in the heady aftermath of *Faune*, when Nijinsky's confidence was high. Some accounts make Deauville the work's birthplace; others, an outdoor Paris restaurant; the most likely site was Lady Ottoline Morrell's garden in Bedford Square where, in July 1912, Nijinsky, together with Bakst, observed the twilight game of tennis that became the ballet's pretext. To all appearances, the idea for *Jeux* was Nijinsky's own, although as with *Faune*, both Diaghilev and Bakst served as the libretto's midwives. Jacques-Emile Blanche, a fashionable portrait painter and Ballets Russes devotee, described the collective travail, which took place at the Savoy Grill, Diaghilev's favorite London eatery:

Chaliapine was . . . entertaining Lady Ripon to lunch in the large hall of the Savoy, and I was among the guests. A waiter brought me a note from Diaghilev; I opened it and read: "Dear friend, we are in the grill-room with Bakst. Vaslav would like to see you; he wants to talk to you about a mad scheme . . . he wants us to collaborate in a "games" libretto and Debussy is to do the score. Come as soon as you leave the table . . ." Vaslav was drawing on the tablecloth when I reached the grill-room . . . The "cubist" ballet—which became "Jeux"—was a game of tennis in a garden; but in no circumstances was it to have a romantic décor in the Bakst manner! There should be no *corps de ballet*, no ensembles, no variations, no *pas de deux*, only girls and boys in flannels, and rhythmic movements. A group at a certain stage was to depict a fountain, and the game of tennis (with licentious *motifs*) was to be interrupted by the crashing of an aeroplane. What a childish idea![22]

No friend of the avant-garde (the airplane is more a futurist than a cubist touch), Blanche was nevertheless persuaded to convey the idea to Debussy, who dismissed it as "idiotic." Yet when Diaghilev, by return wire, promised to double his fee, the composer managed to produce the score within a matter of weeks—by the end of August.[23]

How much of this was Nijinsky's idea? In an interview published in *Figaro* on the eve of the ballet's premiere, Hector Cahusac quotes some remarks by the dancer the previous spring showing quite plainly that sports were very much on Nijinsky's mind:

The man that I see foremost on the stage is a contemporary man. I imagine the costume, the plastic poses, the movement that would be representative of our time . . . When today one sees a man stroll, read a newspaper or dance the tango, one perceives that his gestures have nothing in common with those, for instance, of an idler under Louis XV, of a gentleman dancing the minuet, or of a thirteenth-century monk studiously reading a manuscript.

The close study I have made of polo, golf, and tennis has convinced me that these sports are not only a healthy form of relaxation but that they are equally creators of plastic beauty. From studying them I derive the hope that in the future our era will be represented by a style just as expressive as those we so gladly admire in the past.[24]

The airplane, on the other hand, seems to have been a pet conceit of Diaghilev. Certainly, in a letter to Debussy, he quickly moves from the first person plural to the first person singular in discussing its appearance in the ballet.

If you do not like the "dirigible" we will delete it. I had evidently understood the aeroplane as a decorative panel, to be painted by Bakst, which would move across the back of the stage, its black wings giving a novel effect. As the action of the ballet takes place in the year 1920—the apparition of this machine will be of no interest whatsoever to the persons onstage. They will only be afraid of being watched from the dirigible. However I shall not insist too strongly on this. Only the "downpour" does not satisfy me either and I think we could quite well finish on the kiss and the disappearance of all three in a final leap.[25]

Diaghilev also mentions an idea that Nijinsky ultimately discarded, but which clearly fascinated Diaghilev: "lots of *pointes* for all THREE. Great secret—because up till the present *never* has a man danced on toe. He would be the *first* to do so and I think it would be very elegant." Diaghilev never underestimated the power of novelty.

As with *Faune,* the choreography was left entirely to Nijinsky. His sister joined him late in September, and with Alexandra Vassilievska, another dancer, he began to sketch the work in Monte Carlo. Like *Faune, Jeux* was an exercise in rhythmic movement. But where the earlier ballet had used this as an instrument of purgative minimalism, its successor made it the starting point of an elaborated construction. The two-dimensional frieze now gave way to the sculpted, three-dimensional mass; the art of Greece to that of Matisse, Cézanne, Gauguin, Modigliani, and Rodin—books of whose work filled Nijinsky's hotel room. Just as the design opened into space, so the vocabulary admitted once-proscribed movements. *Jeux,* Nijinska has written, "was the forerunner of Neoclassical Ballet."[26] Many of the steps came from the academic lexicon. Typically, however, they were performed with the legs in parallel rather than turned-out positions and with the arms bent up in a half circle, with the fingers lightly clenched and the wrists flexed: what Nijinska described as "free movements and positions of the body applied to classical ballet technique." Sports were another influence. The grands jetés that carried brother and sister across the stage were executed with athletic force and roughness, while one of the ballet's signature movements—a sideways and upwards swing of the arms across the body—derived from golf as well as tennis. The latter, however, became an obsession, and often Nijinsky canceled rehearsals to visit nearby tennis courts, where he studied not just the movements of the players, but the positions of the arm and the grip of the hand holding the racquet—sources, perhaps, of the bent elbows and clenched fingers that appear in the few surviving photographs of the ballet.[27]

Another influence seeped into the choreography. The theories of Emile Jaques-Dalcroze were not unknown to Nijinsky, who almost certainly attended the demonstrations by Dalcroze's pupils in St. Petersburg early in 1911. In November 1912, with Diaghilev, he paid the first of two visits to the Dalcroze Institute at Hellerau. Until that time, noted Nijinska, her brother "did not 'graphically' render each musical note by a physical movement, nor did he have recourse to counting the beats aloud, as he did . . . after he had come under the influence of the Dalcroze System."[28] Dalcroze himself never claimed for eurhythmics a role in choreography; his exercises, he said, aspired only to instill rhythm and coordination. Diaghilev, always susceptible to novelty and in late 1912 prey to misgivings about Nijinsky's ability to tackle the rhythmic complexities of *Le Sacre du Printemps,* now invited Marie Rambert, a teacher at the Dalcroze Institute, to join the company as an assistant to Nijinsky. Rambert worked closely with the choreographer throughout 1913 and, unlike Nijinska, was at his side during the final rehearsals of *Jeux,* when much of the ballet was set and when, presumably, the rhythmic oddities that earned Debussy's spleen after the premiere were added. In the Dalcroze system, Percy B. Ingham has written:

> Time is shown by movements of the arms, and time-values, i.e. note-duration, by movements of the feet and body. In the early stages of the training this principle is clearly observed. Later it may be varied in many ingenious ways, for instance, in what is known as plastic counterpoint, where the actual notes played are represented by movements of the arms, while the counterpoint in crotchets, quavers or semiquavers, is given by the feet.[29]

Writing to Robert Godet after seeing the ballet, Debussy roundly condemned its Dalcrozian "mathematics." "This fellow"—by whom he meant Nijinsky—

> adds up demi-semi-quavers with his feet, proves the result with his arms and then, as if suddenly struck with paralysis of one side, listens for a while to the music disapprovingly. This, it appears, is to be called "the stylisation of gesture". How awful! It is in fact Dalcrozian, and this is to tell you that I hold Monsieur Dalcroze to be one of the worst enemies of music! You can imagine what havoc his method has caused in the soul of this wild young Nijinsky![30]

The specificity of Debussy's description makes clear the powerful—and not altogether constructive—influence of Dalcrozian ideas on Nijinsky's choreographic method.

In *Jeux* Nijinsky showed his mettle as a vanguardist. If the design of the ballet owed a debt to contemporary French art, its use of material drawn from the stock of modern, upper-class pastimes anticipated a major trend of the 1920s. So, too, did the use of classical material—a harbinger of that decade's neoclassical revival. In one other regard, *Jeux* also looked forward to *les années folles:* as in many ballets of the 1920s, its theme was explicitly erotic.

"The story," Nijinsky wrote in his *Diary,* "is about three young men making love to each other":

> Diaghilev likes to say that he created the ballet, because he likes to be praised. I do not mind if Diaghilev says that he composed the stories of *Faun* and *Jeux*

because when I created them I was under the influence of "my life" with
Diaghilev. The *Faun* is me, and *Jeux* is the life of which Diaghilev dreamed.
He wanted to have two boys as lovers. He often told me so, but I refused.
Diaghilev wanted to make love to two boys at the same time, and wanted
these boys to make love to him. In the ballet, the two girls represent the two
boys and the young man is Diaghilev. I changed the characters, as love between three men could not be represented on the stage. I wanted people to
feel as disgusted with the idea of evil love as I did, but I could not finish the
ballet.[31]

Audiences were puzzled, not disgusted, by *Jeux*. Bakst's setting of vivid
greens and blues and purples showed a garden near a tennis lawn at dusk.
Electric lanterns shone among the summer foliage. A lost ball rolled across
the stage. A young man appeared, searching for the ball. Two women, in
tennis whites, followed:

> At once the search is forgotten and they flirt, first the youth with one girl, and
> then a change of partners, but this does not suit the other. While the young
> man hesitates, the two girls console each other and begin a flirtation between
> themselves. The young man decides, rather than lose either, to take them both.
> From somewhere another tennis ball is thrown across the garden, and with a
> sudden scared glance they look around and run off merrily. In emotional feel-
> ing Nijinsky made a step forward.[32]

Like *Faune, Jeux* turns on fantasies of seduction. The dancers flirt, embrace, pair off, change partners; they perform for one another, observe
one other; caress themselves. Nijinsky told Debussy that "he imagined an
incident in modern life, athletics and the spirit of modern youth, *'les jeux
de sport, les jeux de l'amour.'* "[33] But *Jeux* is about a great deal more than
love games, or even the sport of love. With its ephemeral matings, voyeur-
istic foreplay, and obsessive self-involvement, the ballet is about the per-
vasiveness of desire and the avoidance of sexual entanglement.

At the center is the Young Man, around whom, like moths circling an
arc-light (one of the images that inspired the ballet), the Young Women
symbolically orbit. Like the hour (dusk) and the setting (a secret garden),
the protagonist exudes erotic expectancy. Yet for a hero he seems curiously diffident: what transpires is almost never the result of his agency.
With one important exception, the action, in fact, is willed by his various
objects: the ball that draws him to the garden; the second ball that puts
an end to his games; the women who follow him, attract him, and insist
upon having their way with him.

Throughout the ballet, detachment follows attachment, each brief encounter giving rise to its solipsistic opposite. Again and again, the action comes back to the desirous, desiring self who stands apart, watching the others couple, while gesturing to one or another of the body's erotic loci—breast, waist, crotch, neck. Even when the pairs—mixed or same sex—and the threesome embrace, the gaze of the individuals is averted, as if sex were not only divorced from feeling, but from awareness of another human presence, as if, under any guise, it were merely a form of self-gratification. In *Faune,* of course, the final gesture had conveyed this with notorious directness. But where the women there were essentially projections of the Faun's erotic fantasies, in *Jeux* they are mirror images of the protagonist's compound sexual identity. One can go further: if his diffidence dresses masculinity in the garb of femaleness, their vigor dresses femininity in the garb of malehood. But these women are "men" of a special kind: their same-sex dalliance marks them as Sapphic or "third sex" males. Their flirtation intrigues the Young Man (in one of Valentine Hugo's pastels, he stands off to the side observing them); at the same time, it arouses his jealousy, and in the one decisive action he takes in the ballet, he puts an end to it. If, before, he had hesitated between the two masculinized women, now, in their guise as feminized men, he chooses them both. But this solution induces even greater anxiety, and as in *Faune,* when the moment of consummation approaches, Nijinsky employs an object to prevent nature from taking its course. In this case, his deus ex machina is a wayward ball. Frightening the Young Man's playmates, it salvages desire by resurrecting a surrogate object—solitary fantasy. *Jeux,* the second installment of Nijinsky's erotic autobiography, reveals, no less urgently than *Faune,* the power of desire, the ambiguity of sexual identity, and his aversion to intercourse itself.

With *Le Sacre du Printemps,* Nijinsky's adolescence ended. No longer would he take the self as his subject or individual fantasy as his theme. Immolating the personal, he moved the social, absent from his previous ballets, into the limelight: *Sacre* was nothing less than a vast human tapestry, a vision of primal man and his primal tribe, and the human sacrifice that ensured the continuity of both. More than any other work produced by Diaghilev, *Sacre* cut deep into the consciousness of its time. It received only nine performances (including the *répétition générale*), but those performances turned the ballet into an overnight legend. The premiere on May 29, 1913, was the occasion of a tumultuous demonstration that recalled the *scandale* of Victor Hugo's *Hernani* nearly a century before and the reception of Wagner's *Tannhäuser* in 1861. One smart lady slapped a hissing neighbor; another called Ravel "a dirty Jew"; whistles hissed; a composer yelled for the "sluts" of the sixteenth arrondissement—where many of Diaghilev's boxholders lived—to "shut up."[34] Musically and choreographically, *Sacre* bid adieu to the Belle Epoque. Few among the era's fashionable public were ready to do the same.

Ironically, the work that has passed into history as an icon of the modern stemmed from a nineteenth-century impulse—the neonationalist fascination with Russia's mythic past. The idea for the ballet came to Stravinsky in the spring of 1910 as he was finishing *Firebird*. "I had dreamed a scene of pagan ritual in which a chosen sacrificial virgin danced herself to death." Almost immediately his thoughts turned to the artist who eventually designed the ballet. "I wanted to compose the libretto with N[icholas] . . . Roerich," he wrote to *Russian Newspaper* editor Nikolai Findeizen in 1912, "because who else could help, who else knows the secret of our ancestors' close feeling for the earth?"[35] Roerich had designed both *The Polovtsian Dances* and *Ivan the Terrible* for Diaghilev in 1909. But long before, he had displayed a keen interest in ethnography and comparative mythology. Beginning in the 1890s he had taken part in archaeological expeditions to Russia's ancient cities and embarked on a scholarly quest centered on the art and religious rites of the ancient Slavs. The knowledge culled from these researches found its way into his paintings: the series "Early Russia" shown at the World of Art exhibition in Moscow in 1902 and the scenes of old Pskov that followed later in the decade combined the illustrative with the totemic—the past recreated as magical realism. In the early 1900s he became a Talashkino familiar, designing peasant-style furniture for Princess Tenisheva's craft center and murals for her neonationalist church. Talashkino housed a large collection of peasant artifacts and folk costumes as well as an embroidery workshop, and these, one imagines, were closely studied by Roerich and Stravinsky in July 1911 when the two met at the estate to compose "the plan of action and the titles of the dances" for the ballet originally known as "The Great Sacrifice." The trip quickened Stravinsky's imagination. On September 26 he wrote to Roerich from Switzerland:

> I have already begun to compose, and, in a state of passion and excitement, have sketched the Introduction for "*dudki*" [reed pipes] as well as the "Divination with Twigs." The music is coming out very fresh and new. The picture of the old woman in a squirrel fur sticks in my mind. She is constantly before my eyes as I compose the "Divination with Twigs." I see her running in front of the group, sometimes stopping it and interrupting the rhythmic flow. I am convinced that the action must be danced, not pantomimed, and for this reason I have connected the "Dance of the Maidens" and the "Divination with Twigs," a smooth jointure with which I am very pleased.[36]

For Stravinsky, no less than Roerich, ethnography marked the path to creation. "It is imperative that we see each other," he wrote to Roerich on the eve of their rendezvous at Talashkino, "and decide about every detail—especially every question of staging—concerning our 'child.'"[37] The libretto stitched together in the course of this visit garbed the composer's dream in the pomp of Slavonic myth. The action, he wrote to Findeizen, "roughly takes the following form":

> *First Part. The Kiss of the Earth.* This contains the ancient Slavic dances. "The Joy of Spring." The orchestral introduction is a swarm of spring pipes.
>
> Later, after the curtain rises, fortune-telling, dance games, the game of abduction, the dance game of the city with the city, all of which is interrupted by the procession of the "Eldest-Wisest," the elder who kisses the earth. The first part ends with the wild dancing-out on the earth, of the people drunk with spring.
>
> *Part Two.* The secret night games of the young maidens on the sacred hill. One of them is condemned by fate to be sacrificed. She enters a stone labyrinth, and the other maidens celebrate her in a wild, martial dance. The elders come, and the chosen one, left alone with them, dances her last Sacred Dance, *The Great Victim,* which is the title of the *Second Part.* The elders are the witnesses of her last dance, which ends with the death of the condemned.[38]

Ethnography textured the music no less than the libretto. Although Stravinsky repeatedly denied it, *Sacre* was "built up," as musicologist Richard Taruskin has written, "out of a multitude of folk melodies."[39] The Augurs of Spring, the Ritual of Abduction, and the Spring Rounds, in addition to the Introduction to Part I, appropriated material from a mammoth anthology of Lithuanian folk songs compiled by a Polish priest named Anton Juszkiewicz. Other tunes derived from Rimsky-Korsakov's *100 Russian Folk Songs,* a collection published in 1877; still others seem to have been recorded directly by Stravinsky either at Talashkino, where he noted down a number of folk tunes from the lips of the singer and gusli player S.P. Kolosov, or at Ustilug, the family estate in the Ukraine where the composer spent his summers until 1914. Most of these melodies, Taruskin notes, belong to the type known by ethnographers as "pesni obryadnye"— ceremonial or ritual songs. Associated with Christian holidays, whose ceremonies they accompanied, they reached back to pagan times and to ancient rituals of sun worship. Thus, the round dance "Nu-ka kumushka, my pokumimsia," from Rimsky-Korsakov's book, was associated with a folk holiday known as "semik" celebrated on the Thursday of the seventh week after the first full moon in springtime. "The customs and ceremonies of Green Week are bound up with the ancient cult of vegetation, and also the cult of ancestors," writes Tatiana Popova, who goes on to relate the melody to the practice of divination and the dancing of the khorovod. As Taruskin notes: "The exact coincidence of all this with the scenario of the first part of *The Rite of Spring,* and particularly that of the Spring Rounds, is self-evident." [40]

Stravinsky, of course, was hardly the first Russian composer to appropriate folk material. But unlike Tchaikovsky or Rimsky-Korsakov, who treated their borrowings in the style of European art music, Stravinsky "sought in folk songs something far more basic to his musical vocabulary and technique, employing them as part of his self-emancipation from that artistic mainstream—and, as things turned out, its downright subversion." [41] In *Sacre,* Stravinsky subjected folk material to a process of abstraction so transformative as to render the source invisible. "The discoveries I have made in Stravinsky's sketchbook," writes Taruskin:

> are particularly interesting because they reveal the underlying presence of folk melodies which . . . are not "displayed" in the finished product, but are absorbed into Stravinsky's musical fabric to such an extent that without the sketchbook their presence could never be suspected. In other words, the sketchbook allows us for the first time actually to witness the . . . *abstraction of stylistic elements from folk music* that marked such a turning point in Stravinsky's development as a composer. [42]

Stravinsky's radical approach to folk material was not echoed in Roerich's designs. These adhered to the principles of scenic naturalism that guided Diaghilev's prewar collaborators generally, invoking a primal world through the shards of antique civilizations and the remnants of old peasant crafts. The costumes were holiday peasant wear—bloused tunics in heavy white or red felt, with designs that recalled the motifs of traditional embroidery. Brilliantly decorative, these designs contained a wealth of esoteric references—which, given both the subject of the ballet and Roerich's lifelong interest in the iconography and systems of ritual signs, is hardly surprising. The presiding deity of *Sacre* is Yarilo, the ancient Slavonic sun god to whom the Chosen Virgin is ultimately sacrificed, and several of the motifs displayed on the costumes seem to have been associated with his worship. Alexander Gavrilov's costume, writes Millicent Hodson, "was notable for the emblems that ran up the border at the hem; the emblems look like ladders surmounted by wheels, and they may represent the wooden wheels that were threaded with dry twigs, placed atop ladders or poles, and set afire to celebrate the return of the sun." [43] The colors chosen by Roerich—orange for the ladder and wheel, dark aqua for the spaces between the spokes—support the interpretation of these emblems as fire-wheels. The same colors, she notes, reappear on the sleeve in the stenciled figure that may well be a totem of Yarilo. Along with the firewheel emblems edging the costume, Roerich placed concentric circles surrounded by arcs and broken circles. This motif, Hodson observes, seems to have carried over into the choreography: in the second act, the girl singled out for sacrifice stands at the center of a circle of young women around whom the elders begin to close. Hodson's research yielded a number of other correspondences between costume and ground pattern, leading her to speculate that Nijinsky, who seems to have awaited Roerich's drawings and costumes before choreographing the ensemble sequences, may have sought to emulate the continuity of design typical of ritual art.

Although, as she admits, "it may well be impossible to prove any relationship between the dancers' garments and the dance,"[44] Roerich's own paintings did contribute to the ballet—if not to the actual choreography, then to the spirit behind it. "Now that I am working on *Sacre*," Nijinsky explained to his sister, for whom he created the role of the Chosen Virgin:

> Roerich's art inspires me as much as does Stravinsky's powerful music—his paintings, *The Idols of Ancient Russia*, *The Daughters of the Earth*, and particularly the painting called, I think, *The Call of the Sun*. Do you remember it, Bronia? . . . the violet and purple colors of the vast barren landscape in the predawn darkness, as a ray of the rising sun shines on a solitary group gathered on top of a hill to greet the arrival of spring. Roerich has talked to me at length about his paintings in this series that he describes as the awakening of the spirit of primeval man. In *Sacre* I want to emulate this spirit of the prehistoric Slavs.[45]

Roerich's two sets for the ballet—the first, a hilly landscape with a lake and birch trees under a cloudy sky; the second, a hilltop—are in the same style of magical realism as this cycle of paintings. The mount that dominates the backdrop in Scene I establishes the visual motif: a hemisphere whose rounded form is repeated in the copses, rocks, and smaller rises surrounding the "sacred hill." A semicircular lake lies at its base, and this is where the tribe gathers to celebrate its spring rites. There is an incantatory quality to the scene—in the repetitions and undifferentiated smoothness of the mounds—coupled with a literalism of detail: here are the sacred stone (a big reddish rock), the sacred birches (white trunks under dark tops), and the sacred mount in all their iconic simplicity. The setting for Scene II reduces this vista even further: now, under the vast Slavic sky lie only "enchanted rocks" and the magic mountain of sacrifice.[46] Neither violence nor modernity disturbs this primal paradise. Innocence reigns, and harmony: at peace with god, tribe, nature, and self, man is restored to spiritual wholeness through recreated ritual. This, of course, is precisely what Stravinsky's score is not—nor Nijinsky's choreography. Roger Fry, the English art critic, was among those struck by the "dissidence" between the "extremely original and formal design of the dance in 'Le Sacre du Printemps' and the rather fusty romanticism of M. Ruhrich's [sic] scenery." It was evident, he wrote, "that both dance and music had outstripped the scenic artists, had arrived at a conception of formal unity which demanded something much more logically conceived than the casual decorative pictorial formula of the scenery."[47] In *Sacre*, Roerich's neonationalist vision was transcended by the primitivism of his two collaborators.

Roerich located his primal scene in a reconstituted past. For Stravinsky, as for Nijinsky, this past was only a metaphor, a vehicle for conveying the tragedy of modern being. *Sacre* exposed the barbarism of human life: the cruelty of nature, the savagery of the tribe, the violence of the soul. It saw community as a Damoclean sword hovering over the individual, and fate—powerful, atavistic, aleatory—as the ruler of a godless universe. Above all, it presented a society governed by instinct, the brute instinct of Eros in his Freudian guise—wedded indissolubly to Thanatos. This tragic vision, exposing the heart's darkness, guided composer and choreographer into the artistic unknown. "I am very pleased with the way everything has turned out," Nijinsky wrote to Stravinsky on January 25, 1913:

> If the work continues like this, Igor, the result will be something great. I know what *Le Sacre du Printemps* will be when everything is as we both want it: new, and, for an ordinary viewer, a jolting impression and emotional experience. For some it will open new horizons flooded with different rays of sun. People will see new and different colors and different lines. All different, new and beautiful.[48]

In Nijinsky's hands, ethnography became the raw material of a grand modernist design. Like Stravinsky, he raided ritual and folk material, then absorbed this into a succession of subversive signs. The dancers trembled, shook, shivered, stamped; jumped crudely and ferociously, circled the stage in wild khorovods. At times the movement approximated the involuntary condition of trance. "In the first scene," wrote Lydia Sokolova, who danced in the ballet, "I remember a group of Ancients with long beards and hair, who stood huddled together, shaking and trembling as if they were dying with fear." At other times "a stampede of humanity" took possession of the stage—anarchy triumphant.[49] *Sacre* completed Fokine's rupture with classicism; it destroyed the equilibrium of his masses and what Lincoln

Kirstein has called "the magic of gracious acrobatics in self-impelled move-ment."[50] In their stead, Nijinsky created a biologic order that designed the body into both an instrument and object of mass oppression.

As in *Faune* and *Jeux*, Nijinsky formed that body anew. In *Sacre*, he trained stance and gesture inward. "The movement," wrote Jacques Ri-vière in the *Nouvelle Revue Française*, "closes over the emotion; it arrests and contains it . . . The body is no longer a means of escape for the soul; on the contrary, it collects and gathers itself around it; it suppresses its outward thrust, and, by the very resistance that it offers to the soul, be-comes completely permeated by it . . ." To this imprisoned soul the tran-scendence of the romantic is denied: chained to the body, spirit becomes mere matter. In *Sacre*, Nijinsky banished idealism from ballet, and with it the individualism bound up in romantic ideology. "He takes his dancers," wrote Rivière, "rearranges their arms, twisting them; he would break them if he dared; he belabors these bodies with a pitiless brutality, as though they were lifeless objects; he forces from them impossible movements, at-titudes that make them seem deformed."[51] In Nijinsky's hands, design thus attained a totalitarian function. Fokine's community now became a society of masses, his aggregate of individuals a collective of programmed ciphers. From the start, Stravinsky had suppressed pantomime. Nijinsky, in turn, reduced the characters to a handful of vignetted figures—elders, virgins, shamans, adolescents—who came to the stage without the armature of history. Significantly, only the Chosen Virgin danced alone. The rest, as Kirstein has said, built "kinetic blocks mortared with intervals of shifting action." At the end of the first tableau, Romola Nijinsky recalled, great circles of women in scarlet ran wildly, while shifting masses within cease-lessly split up into tiny groups revolving on eccentric axes. The second tableau, the sacrifice of the Chosen Virgin, reiterated the themes of collec-tivity and ruptured order. The scene began, wrote Sokolova, "with all the female dancers standing in a large circle facing outward, the Chosen One among them":

> We all had our toes pointing inwards, the right elbow resting on the left fist, and the right fist supporting the head which was leant sideways. As the ring began to move round, at certain counts the whole group would rise on tip-toe, dropping their right hands to their sides and jerking their heads to the left. When one circuit of the stage had been completed, every other girl would leap out of the ring, then back again.[52]

For Rivière, Nijinsky's depersonalized mass was the key to *Sacre's* primitivism:

We find ourselves in the presence of man's movements at a time when he did not yet exist as an individual. Living beings still cling to each other; they exist in groups, in colonies, in shoals; they are lost among the horrible indifference of society . . . Their faces are devoid of any individuality. At no time during the dance does the Chosen Maiden show the personal terror that ought to fill her soul. She carries out a rite; she is absorbed by a social function, and without any sign of comprehension or of interpretation, she moves as dictated by the desires and impulses of a being vaster than herself.[53]

Ruling this primeval universe is Moloch, come back from "the depths of the ages" to devour his children, a god as base as he is devoid of spirit, a relic, like *Sacre* itself, of man at his "most primitive stage" before the birth of thought and conscience. But as much as the ballet looked back to the dawn of human life, so—and this was a leap Rivière did not make—it also looked into the future: to a war that unleashed the accumulated evil in men's souls and to a society ruled by the machine. In this sense, *Sacre* was a harbinger of modernity: of its assembly lines and masses, its war machines and cities of slain innocents. Stripped of their costumes, Nijinsky's masses were both the agents and victims of twentieth-century barbarism.

Although to Paris and London, *Sacre* had no precedent, Nijinsky's manipulation of ensembles displayed certain parallels with Meyerhold's handling of masses at roughly the same period. Two-and-a-half weeks before the dancer's dismissal from the Imperial Theaters in January 1911, the director unveiled his controversial *Boris Godunov*. With Feodor Chaliapin in the title role and designs by Alexander Golovin, the revival took its cue from Diaghilev's Paris production three years earlier. Because Meyerhold had to work quickly, he followed Alexander Sanin's general stage plan—except in the crowd scenes. "Sanin individualizes the crowd in his production," Meyerhold told *The Bourse Chronicler* in an interview:

. . . with me the crowd is divided into groups and not into individuals. There are, for instance, the leaders of the crippled pilgrims: all of them are just one group; the audience must perceive them at once, as something making up a unit . . . Or take, for instance, the crowd of Boyars. Should this be differentiated into a collection of single Boyars unlike each other, while the idea of it is that of a collective whole of groveling menials? No sooner did one rise above the crowd than he became a Tsar; . . . Shuisky and Godunov were by nature rare individuals.[54]

Like Nijinsky, Meyerhold transformed the ensemble into a mass of depersonalized humanity, blocks of generic figures mortared with violence. In the first scene, the Moscow bailiffs flogged the people into submission with a brutality that called forth the "patriotic indignation" of the right-wing

press. "Where did Mr. Meyerhold . . . get all that?" asked M.O. Menshikov in *Novoye Vremia:*

> I believe that Mr. Meyerhold got those bailiffs from his Jewish soul and not
> from Pushkin's "Boris Godunov," which has neither bailiffs nor knouts. Per-
> haps in reality there were bailiffs looking like executioners, and knouts, but
> must an opera . . . transfer this mean reality to the stage? Mr. Meyerhold, or
> that handful of aliens in whose hands the Imperial Theater now lies wanted
> to stress from the very first scene the deep slavery in which ancient Russia was
> presumably immersed, and so in the first scene he brought out the Moscow
> police, waving their many-thonged knouts.[55]

Scurrilous as it is, Menshikov's attack reveals the key to Meyerhold's
subversive politic: the use of masses. In Meyerhold's *Boris* the mass is an
agent of history and its victim, the subject and object of a materialist fate.
Something akin to this seems to be at work in Nijinsky's *Sacre*, where fate,
implacable and omnipresent, has been wrested from an absent god and
delivered into the power of man. In this divine void, the human collective
disposes; in its hand lies the secret of life and the agency of death; above
all, it holds power over the individual. The Chosen Virgin is the axis on
which *Sacre* turns. Although conceived by Stravinsky, the role spoke directly to the choreographer. As Nijinska (who worked with her brother on
the earliest sketches) later wrote, the Chosen Virgin's dance of death was
Nijinsky's "own." Like the Golden Slave in *Schéhérazade*, the Chosen Virgin expires in an ecstasy of self-immolation; like Petrouchka, she takes
upon herself the sins of the artist, the wages of psychic difference. In the
"Danse Sacrale," wrote Nijinska:

> I pictured the calm of nature before . . . a hurricane. As I envisaged the prim-
> itiveness of the tribal rites, where the Chosen Maiden must die to save the
> earth, I felt that my body must draw into itself, must absorb the fury of the
> hurricane. Strong, brusque, spontaneous movements seemed to fight the ele-
> ments as the Chosen Maiden protected the earth against the menacing heav-
> ens. The Chosen Maiden danced as if possessed, as she must until her frenzied
> dance in the primitive sacrificial ritual kills her.[56]

Not only the Chosen Virgin is immolated in *Sacre*. In her dance of
death, Nijinsky's ambisexual youth also met his end, a premonition of the
event that within little more than three months of the ballet's premiere
would end his relationship with Diaghilev: marriage to Romola de Pulszky.
Henceforth, the heroes of his ballets—the prankish iconoclast of *Till Eulenspiegel*, the romantic Faust of *Mephisto Valse*, the grim samurai of an
untitled Japanese ballet, the questing painter of another untitled ballet, this

one set in the Renaissance—would assert conventional masculine identities. On the few occasions where gender lines were blurred—in a ballet to Debussy's *Chansons de Bilitis* and in another set in a *maison tolérée*—the protagonists were women. Of these projects, conceived during the war years, only *Till* reached the stage. Here, as in *Sacre*, the savior of Nijinsky's collective is sacrificed. But unlike the earlier ballet, *Till* spells this out in class terms: in the rabble, streaming up from the alleys of medieval Braunschweig, and the bourgeoisie, descending in state from its mansions. "Night falls," wrote H.T. Parker in the *Boston Evening Transcript:*

> the respectable are at home and abed; only the rabble, fed, happy, elated, intoxicated with the happenings of Till's afternoon, haunt the square . . . they acclaim and enthrone him as their deliverer. On the shoulders of the mob sits Till, enthroned, the sovereign of the wit that brings freedom, of the mockery that sends conventions and hypocrisies toppling down . . . Into the "public place" troop the inquisitors . . . Then and there he is strung up . . . But no sooner are the executioners gone than he springs anew into being, the perpetual being of the humor that bursts sham, the jeer that pricks pretension. Wistfully, prophetically . . . the rabble eyes a perennial miracle.[57]

Ironically, Till, the Flemish folk hero, is closer to the sacrificed gods of ancient myth than the Chosen Virgin. For unlike Attis, Osiris, and the other male divinities slain on the altars of European and Middle Eastern fertility goddesses, the paschal victim in *Sacre* is a girl. Neither ancient tale nor Slavonic lore offers a precedent for female sacrifice. Only in Aztec Mexico, among the slave girls and noble maidens slain by priests of the Maize Goddess, can an ancestor be found—and this bloody ritual *Sacre*'s collaborators nowhere mention.[58] Dreamed up by Stravinsky, archaized by Roerich, and given life by Nijinsky, the Chosen Virgin is a creation of the early twentieth century, cousin to the invented myths of W.B. Yeats, T.S. Eliot, and Sigmund Freud. Indeed, the latter's *Totem and Taboo*, offered to the public in the same year as *Sacre*, also turns on human sacrifice, in this case, the murder of the primal father, rather than the primal daughter. At the heart of the ballet's synthetic myth is the fin-de-siècle obsession with the "feminized" artist, that enervated androgyne of symbolist fiction, painting, and drama. In *Sacre*, however, the image has been tamed; shorn of its subversive sexuality, it assumes the "safe" guise of a young girl, ballet's traditional instrument of redemption. A Giselle reimaged through the primitivism of the golden horde, the Chosen Virgin is, above all, a creation of twentieth-century male sexual anxiety.

If there is irony in *Sacre*'s myth being no older than the fin de siècle, there is also irony in the fact that its primitivism has nothing to do with

African art. African sculpture, of course, was crucial to the development of cubism: it taught the modern artist, Apollinaire said, a "moral lesson."[59] But such a lesson did not derive from Africa per se, but from the perception of differentness: the extent to which such art refuted the values and forms associated with "civilization." In this sense, primitivism reflected a state of mind; defining a psychological rather than physical fact, it posited a mysterious, impenetrable Other. For some, this Other was epitomized by Woman. For others, by the unconscious displayed in children's art or in automatic writing. If for modernized Europe the search led to exotic lands, for Europeans of the periphery this Africa of the mind lay within their own national identity—in archaic Iberian art, if one were a Spaniard, in ancient Slavonic art, if one were a Russian. In these traditions, and in the twentieth-century realities of the countries where they had flourished, the Third World took concrete form, sowing in the mind of the artist memories of underdevelopment. In primitivism the two worlds met and bore modernist fruit. For Nijinsky and his collaborators, the heart of darkness began at Russia's steppes.

With *Le Sacre du Printemps* ballet crossed the threshold of modernism. Yet Diaghilev, having expended untold sums and vast human resources, drew back from the revolution he had set in motion. As early as the summer of 1913, Nijinska writes, Diaghilev appeared "disenchanted with Nijinsky's talent and disappointed in him as a choreographer." That is, even before Nijinsky's departure for South America and his marriage to Romola de Pulszky, Diaghilev "had made it clear . . . that he did not want to entrust him with the choreography of any new ballets." Indeed, the telegram dismissing him from the Ballets Russes reached the dancer even as word sped around St. Petersburg that Diaghilev and Fokine had reached complete agreement regarding the latter's participation in the 1914 season.[60] With their rapprochement, Nijinsky's position within the company became untenable. But one also wonders whether Nijinsky himself had not also retreated from the front lines of experiment represented by *Sacre*. Although Robert Edmond Jones's designs for *Till* ventured far beyond Roerich's "fusty romanticism," the concept of the ballet, courting, as H.T. Parker wrote, a "verity of illusion of time, place and circumstance," seems closer to *Petrouchka* than to *Faune, Jeux,* or *Sacre*. Nor do the sketches in Romola Nijinsky's biography indicate that her husband sought to build upon the innovating abstraction of *Sacre*. If the ballet to Debussy's *Chansons de Bilitis* harked back to *Faune, Mephisto Valse* was "living Dürer," a medieval tale of greedy landlords, ribald peasants, and mismatched lovers, while one of his last creations, about a youth seeking truth, first as an artist, then as a lover, was set in the High Renaissance.[61]

The medieval theme of *Till* and *Mephisto,* both of which incorporated popular material, suggests that Nijinsky was working along lines similar to Doctor Dapertutto, the pseudonym adopted by Meyerhold in his activities outside the Imperial Theaters. The director's experiments of 1912–1914 continued his investigation of the commedia dell'arte and the Spanish theater of the Golden Age. At the same time, he was absorbed by the problem of movement, "the most powerful means of theatrical expression," as he wrote in 1914.[62] Assisting him in these undertakings was Vladimir Solovyov, a member of the Imperial Ballet who taught a class on the commedia at the studio opened by Meyerhold in 1913. In addition to studying the formal discipline of the Italian improvisational theater, students were introduced to the conventions of the Chinese and Japanese theaters. It was at this time that Meyerhold laid the basis for the system of physical exercises codified in the early 1920s as biomechanics. These Etudes derived from a variety of sources—physical culture, dance, acrobatics, eurhythmics, and sports; they inculcated balance, elasticity, and physical awareness.[63] To the student of Nijinsky, photographs of the exercises cannot fail to startle. Many bear an uncanny resemblance to the dancer's poses in *Faune* and to his postures in *Till;* the sense of weight is the same, and the centripetal concentration of force; both artists, it seems, sought to transmit the internal essence of an image through its external form. The question of influence naturally arises, although the facts to trace this are too few to speculate on its transmission or direction. The point to be made is merely the one reiterated throughout this chapter: that Nijinsky's creation, however idiosyncratic it may have seemed to critics in the West, did not spring from an artistic void, but belonged fully to the theatrical culture of its era, and, in particular, to that moment on the eve of World War I when the symbolists of Russia plunged headlong into the adventure of modernism.

Who knows what kind of choreographer Nijinsky might have become had fate treated him differently; if the Ballets Russes had not been the forcing ground of his talent; if schizophrenia had not buried his art in the recesses of a disturbed mind? Such questions lie beyond the power of the historian to answer. In the case of Nijinsky, the facts are clear. By whatever mysterious agency, in *Faune, Jeux,* and *Sacre* Nijinsky crossed the threshold of modernism. He did this by drawing on the raw materials of his personal obsessions and of contemporary experiments in music, dance, and drama, and he did it, amazingly, in two short years: by 1913, the choreographic revolution initiated by Fokine was complete. This, however, was only one of Nijinsky's accomplishments. In *Sacre,* he created a twentieth-century icon, a summation of modernism at its most subversive and visionary. His third legacy was equally important: that ballet could generate styles of expression as powerfully imagined, deeply personal, and vitally contemporary as those of the other arts. By any yardstick, Nijinsky's was no small achievement. How much greater for an artist who had yet to celebrate his twenty-fourth birthday.

With *Sacre* modernism took choreographic and musical root within the Diaghilev enterprise. Yet however much the work promoted the image of the Ballets Russes as a seedbed of experiment, it did not perceptibly alter the company's overall aesthetic. On the contrary, this remained identified with exoticism and the symbolist inheritance of the fin de siècle. Only with World War I and the jolt of Diaghilev's encounter with the futurist avant-garde would the Ballets Russes fully enter the twentieth century.

3 ✍

THE MAKING OF

BALLET MODERNISM

BY FAR DIAGHILEV'S most significant prewar achievement, *Le Sacre du Printemps* had little impact on his company's artistic future. Performed fewer than a dozen times, the work vanished with Nijinsky's dismissal from the Ballets Russes, even if ten years later, in *Les Noces*, his sister briefly invoked its legacy. By then, however, another sort of modernism had taken hold of the Ballets Russes. This new aesthetic also parted ways with Fokine and Diaghilev's World of Art designers. But it did so from a very different vantage point and for very different ends.

By and large, historians have dated this artistic shift to *Parade*. Unveiled in Paris in 1917, three years after Diaghilev's last full-scale season in the French capital, the work served as public notice of the switch in his allegiance to the avant-garde. *Parade* came with impeccable modernist credentials: designs by Pablo Picasso, music by Erik Satie, a libretto by Jean Cocteau, program notes by Guillaume Apollinaire. Only Léonide Massine, the ballet's choreographer, was an unknown quantity, although by the early 1920s, his name, too, would be synonymous with modernism. It is not difficult to understand why historians have identified this work as the cradle of Ballets Russes modernism.

Ironically, *Parade* came at the end rather than the beginning of an extraordinary revolution initiated by Diaghilev in late 1914. Between that year and 1917, the *barin* yielded to the visionary radical, the bellettrist to the creative artist: as Europe warred, Diaghilev moved the Ballets Russes to the forefront of the avant-garde. Although the transformation in his company's identity grew out of Diaghilev's personal restiveness, he did not embark on this undertaking alone. At his side stood a circle of vanguard artists, whose vision of the modern became the foundation of his madeover enterprise. The pillars on which this now rested—futurism, neoprimitivism, and what I call period modernism—sustained the Ballets Russes into the 1920s.

With two notable exceptions (both, significantly, art rather than dance historians), scholars of the Ballets Russes have simply ignored the futurists.[1] Yet Diaghilev's encounter with this dynamic avant-garde in wartime Italy was an event of the first magnitude, a major catalyst of the transition to modernism. Futurism posited new relationships between the performer and a larger stage environment, visualized new ways of filling that space and making it expressive, and urged the vanguardist to comb the modern world, including its popular entertainments, for raw material. Although only one of the several futurist productions planned by Diaghilev came to fruition, futurist ideas, often in tandem with other approaches, lingered in the postwar repertory, becoming, in some instances, key elements of modern ballet style. How deep an imprint they made on Diaghilev's imagination can be judged by that curious intermezzo in his 1926 *Romeo and Juliet,* when the curtain rose a yard above the ground to reveal throughout the scene only the feet and lower legs of the dancers. Eleven years before, Filippo Marinetti, doyen of the futurists, had used an identical device in his play *Feet.*[2]

Although futurists had long since raised eyebrows, only in 1914 did they cross Diaghilev's path. The first encounter may well have been in London, where a "Grand Futurist Concert of Noises" at the Coliseum coincided with Diaghilev's June season in the British capital. Certainly, the months that followed brought him close to the nomadic group and its happenings. In a reminiscence, poet Francesco Cangiullo describes a soiree in Marinetti's "oriental" drawing room in Milan, where Diaghilev, looking like a "vertical hippopotamus," presided over a concert of *intuonarumori*—or "noise-intoners"—and Stravinsky played his "frenzied audacities" for the Italians. The composer was fascinated by the futurists' "bizarre new instruments" and thought he might "interpolate two or three into the already diabolical scores of his ballets." Diaghilev, ever the impresario, wanted to present all thirty in "clamorous concert" in Paris. He had come, moreover, to hear compositions by another futurist, Francesco Pratella, and to reach an understanding with him about setting Cangiullo's poem "Piedigrotta" to music, in a choreographic adaptation.[3]

In February 1915 Stravinsky joined Diaghilev in Rome for a concert of *Petrouchka,* an event, as the composer wrote to his mother, that brought out "all" the futurists, who "greeted me noisily."[4] During this visit, Stravinsky sought out sculptor Umberto Boccioni, who, like nearly all the group, worked in a variety of media, including performance. "I was invited today to a tea," wrote Boccioni on February 13th, "in honor of the Russian musician Stravinsky. He wants to meet me and do something with futurist

. . . color, dance, and costume."[5] Stravinsky was not alone in seeking futurist collaborators. In a telegram dated late January, Diaghilev speaks of "the alliance with Marinetti," while a letter to the composer written in early March describes the futurist leader's "brilliant" idea for a sound score to accompany *Liturgie,* a religious ballet Diaghilev had originally intended to produce to Russkin liturgical music, then in silence.[6]

Although no futurist artist received a formal commission until December 1916, the first steps of Diaghilev's modernist revolution took place under the aegis of futurism. They coincided, moreover, with Léonide Massine's formative years as a choreographer. Plucked by Diaghilev from the Bolshoi corps de ballet in the spring of 1914, he now followed his mentor down the futurist path. Among the poets, painters, sculptors, and composers who tutored the pair, interest in performance was consuming. Enormous energy was expended on it, and the noisy demonstrations that presented futurist work—literary, visual, and theatrical—to the public comprise a telling chapter of the movement's history. Between 1913 and 1917, moreover, performance became a subject of intense theoretical enquiry, the theme of more than a dozen manifestos that touched on all aspects of theater—including dance (the group's least distinguished effort, however)[7]—with unfailing originality. In these provocative and idiosyncratic documents, we find the ideas that erected the aesthetic scaffolding of the wartime and postwar Ballets Russes and permeated Massine's early choreography.

Foremost among these was antinaturalism, a key tenet of futurist performance and of Diaghilev's modernist credo. Marinetti's "Variety Theater" manifesto, published in October/November 1913, opened with a ringing denunciation of naturalism:

> We are deeply disgusted with the contemporary theatre (verse, prose, and musical) because it vacillates stupidly between historical reconstruction (pastiche or plagiarism) and photographic reproduction of our daily life; a finicking, slow, analytic, and diluted theatre worthy, all in all, of the age of the oil lamp.[8]

If Marinetti railed against the fidelity to authentic sources and passion for anchoring subject matter in particularities of time and place so typical of the prewar Ballets Russes, with equal fervor he attacked psychology, that "dirty thing and dirty word" that brought Fokine's heroes and crowds to the stage armed with biographies. In the "Futurist Synthetic Theater," dated January-February 1915, Marinetti, Emilio Settimelli, and Bruno Corra extended this indictment of "passéiste" theater. Now, along with verisimilitude and psychology, the conventions supporting them—plot, dramatic structure, and characterization—were assailed. Against the "prolixity, meticulous analysis, [and] drawn-out preparation"[9] of current dramaturgy, the futurists advocated a theater that was synthetic, atechnical, dynamic, and autonomous—shorthand for (1) brevity and compression (*Parsifal* in forty minutes!), (2) abandonment of narrative, (3) speed and simultaneity, and (4) non-objective forms of representation. All these ideas found their way into Diaghilev's modernist aesthetic.

They were joined by others, the most important of which concerned mechanization, especially as applied to the performer. Simply put: futurist acting and costuming mechanized the performer, subordinating him to the scenic design. In the 1914 "Dynamic and Synoptic Declamation" manifesto, writes Michael Kirby:

> Marinetti transforms, at least in theory, every aspect of the performer: he should wear anonymous clothing . . . his face should be free of personal expression; his voice should make no use of "modulation or nuance"; his movement should be "geometric". In describing the use of gesture, Marinetti suggests a repertoire of "cubes, cones, spirals, ellipses, etc." . . .[10]

Fortunato Depero, whom Diaghilev commissioned to design the condensed version of *Le Chant du Rossignol* scheduled for production in spring 1917, elaborated. The performer, he wrote in his 1916 "Notes on the Theater," must distort his natural appearance by wearing exaggerated makeup; donning wigs, masks, headlight-eyes, megaphone mouths, funnel ears, and mechanical clothes; eliminating, in short, all idiosyncratic and realistic detail. Depero's costume designs for *Rossignol* followed these prescriptions closely, with rigid, geometrized space suits that concealed not only the body, but the hands and face, while geometric protuberances indicated whiskers, eyes, and mouths. All the dancers, announced the French weekly *Opinion* in March 1917, were to be masked. "The dances," Depero explained, "will thus be less episodic in character; interest will center, above all, on the movement of volumes."[11] The setting enlarged upon these themes. A photograph of the artist's studio dated Rome, 1917, shows huge, semiabstract sunflowers (half-discs fitted at right angles to whole ones), triangular solids set on their apex, and metallic rods attached to floor stands. Another photograph, presumably of the completed set, reveals a stylized futurist garden, with fronds, flowers, and shrubs rendered as freestanding cones, arc segments, and discs. Varnish and enamel were used to enhance the brightness of the colors.

Along with the physical appearance of the performer, his movement and gesture were also mechanized. In *Printing Press*, a 1914 "typographical ballet" (the phrase is futurist architect Virgilio Marchi's), Giacomo Balla, who designed Diaghilev's production of *Fireworks,* had twelve robot-actors impersonate parts of the machine. A sketch of Balla's "choreography" survives: two pairs of performers, arms rigidly extended in front, rock forward and back, making what could be a piston driving the "wheels" created by a third pair, who sweep their arms, also rigidly extended with wrists held at right angles, in overlapping circles. Balla's automata also spoke: to be exact, they declaimed "very loudly" pieces of "rumorist onomatopoeia" that, like Luigi Russolo's music, aspired to pure sound.[12] *Printing Press* so intrigued Diaghilev that he considered producing it. One evening, recalled Marchi:

> we all went to Diaghileff and Semenoff's salon to make the decision whether to choose *Fireworks* or the *Printing-Machine Ballet,* a mechanical invention of Balla's. For the second, the author arranged us in geometric patterns and, with the inevitable grey stick, conducted the mechanical movements and gestures we all had to make to represent the soul of the individual pieces of a rotary printing-press. I was told to repeat with violence the syllable 'STA', with one arm raised in gymnastic fashion, so that I felt that I was on the square of a training barracks. Balla, needless to say, had reserved for himself the more delicate syllables, onomatopoetic sounds and verbalizations, which issued from his lips with his unforgettable Piedmontese "neh", while the shameless, bearded Semenoff kept popping the corks of bottles of Frascati, turning the whole performance into a highly intelligent and most amusing grotesque.[13]

Although Diaghilev chose not to produce *Printing Press,* he commissioned its author to create the mise-en-scène for Stravinsky's *Fireworks.* Balla's design for this short piece—a light show played on a setting of geometrical solids—epitomized the brevity, dynamism, and abstraction to which futurist theater aspired. "Balla did his best," Italian critic Maurizio Fagiolo dell'Arco has written, "to harmonize with the composer's pyrotechnical inventions":

> He filled the stage with disturbing crystalline forms, beams of colored light, coral formations, symbols of the infinite (spirals and running light-waves), emblems of light (obelisk, pyramids, rays of sunlight and sickle-moons), aerodynamic symbols (flights of swifts and firebirds). It was all projected onto a black backdrop, illuminated from behind with red rays.[14]

Diaghilev, it is said, designed as well as executed the complicated lighting scheme. But, surely, he took his cue (so to speak) from the futurists, in whose theories lighting occupied a well-nigh mystical place. Enrico Prampolini's "Futurist Scenography," written in April-May 1915, ends with the vision of a new radiant theater. "In the totally realizable epoch of Futurism we shall see the luminous dynamic architectures of the stage emanate from chromatic incandescences that, climbing tragically or showing themselves voluptuously, will inevitably arouse new sensations and emotional values in the spectator."[15] Prampolini's fascination with the "illuminating stage" and Diaghilev's friendship with Stravinsky notwithstanding, the choice of *Fireworks* and the method of its realization probably stemmed from another source: the mixed-media piece—to the same music—presented by Loie Fuller in May 1914 at the Théâtre du Châtelet in Paris. An "orgy of color, light, and sound," Fuller's *Fireworks* received its premiere a week before the opening of Diaghilev's last prewar season.[16]

Futurist performance extended the limits of traditional forms in unusual and often extreme ways. Diaghilev, ever the pragmatist, shied from the group's confrontational tactics, but the idea that inherited categories could be bent, reshaped, combined with others, and injected with new material was one he found highly congenial. Futurism exalted the variety theater, Marinetti wrote, because it was "fed by swift actuality," distracted the public with comic effects and imaginative astonishment, enriched its programs with cinematic visions, and plumbed "abysses of the ridiculous" in lightning-quick transformation scenes that exploited the wonders of modern technology.[17] The impact of these ideas on Diaghilev cannot be overestimated. The postwar trend toward caricature, parody, and alogical structure that, along with popular entertainment material, first appeared in the war years, stemmed directly from futurist theory and practice.

Only one futurist collaboration with the Ballets Russes reached the stage. Yet between late 1914 and spring 1917 the projects involving futurist artists that Diaghilev toyed with producing amounted to more than a half-dozen: the concert of *intuonarumori, Piedigrotta, Liturgie, Printing Press, Fireworks, Le Chant du Rossignol,* and *The Zoo,* a ballet by Francesco Cangiullo for which Ravel agreed to compose the score and Depero to create the designs.[18] Ironically, the work that summed up the years of futurist experiment was *Parade.* Here, as Marianne Martin points out, "it was not just Cubism that was put on stage,"—Gertrude Stein's oft-quoted line notwithstanding—"but a subtle and delightfully humourous confrontation between Cubism and Futurism and their respective ideals."[19] *Parade* embodied any number of futurist ideas: concrete gesture and sound, variety material, alogical structure, mechanistic movement, constructed costume—ideas that had percolated through the Paris avant-garde and been transmogrified by their contact with cubism.

If Diaghilev did not remake the Ballets Russes in the image of futurism, his contact with the movement certainly altered the company's countenance. To naturalism, dramatic narrative, and psychologically motivated characterization, he said good-bye. He cast out the exoticism of Bakst (Prampolini's "Assyrian-Persian-Egyptian-Nordic plagiarist")[20] and the passéism of Benois, and threw over the symbolist thematic of *Mir is-kusstva*. Henceforth, he would hang his stage with backdrops that acknowledged the revolution of cubism. Through his choreographic Galatea, Massine, he would incorporate into ballet the dynamism and angularity advocated by the futurists, along with the impersonal performance style, discontinuous narrative, and studied incongruity that became trademarks of Ballets Russes modernism.

Diaghilev, however, never completely abjured the past, even in these years of modernist experiment. Quite the reverse. In the vast majority of works conceived during World War I, many of which came to fruition only in the post-Armistice years 1919–1921, the stylistic innovations of the avant-garde were married to traditional ballet themes and genres. From this amalgam of old and new emerged the hybrid forms that became the major vehicles of ballet modernism: neoprimitivism and what I have called period modernism. Descendants of prewar exoticism and retrospectivism, these combinations of experimental and received material provided, as *Parade* did not, the aesthetic foundations of Diaghilev's remade repertory.

In the evolution of neoprimitivism, no two artists proved more crucial to Diaghilev than Natalia Gontcharova and Michel Larionov. Life companions, these Russian vanguard painters stood at his side through most of the war and post-Armistice years, living and traveling with him, and assisting at the birth of his new modernist repertory. In 1915, when the couple joined his artistic colony in Switzerland, neither was a stranger to Diaghilev. Paintings by Larionov had hung in the 1906 World of Art Exhibition, Diaghilev's last major show in Russia, and later that year, in the exhibition of Russian art that was his first undertaking in Paris. Gontcharova, for her part, had been signally honored by Diaghilev: her commission to design *Le Coq d'Or*, the high point of the 1914 season, was the first to an artist—and a woman artist, at that—who stood outside the tradition of *Mir iskusstva*. Following close upon the musical and choreographic breakthroughs of *Le Sacre du Printemps*, her appointment bespoke Diaghilev's incipient restiveness with the prevailing decorative aesthetic of the Ballets Russes.

Only thirty-three at the time she received her first Diaghilev commission, Gontcharova was a leading figure of the Moscow avant-garde, a founder of rayonism, and a close associate of the Russian futurists. Her painting in 1913–1914 displayed the broad eclecticism of the prerevolutionary vanguard at its creative zenith: semiabstract rayonist compositions that used the intersection in space of rays emanating from objects to create new forms; cubo-futurist works that blended the futurist obsession with mechanization, speed, and light with a cubist treatment of solids; and a type of neoprimitivism that drew on native Russian folk art, the icon and mediaeval manuscript tradition, and Russian naive painting. In August 1913 Gontcharova staggered Moscow with a mammoth exhibition of 768 works, her entire output of the previous decade. No doubt it was the impression created by this show that led Diaghilev to her studio in the autumn of that year to enlist her collaboration in *Le Coq d'Or*.[21]

Gontcharova stressed the authenticity of her sources, beginning with a childhood spent in the Russian countryside where she had come to know peasant customs and folk traditions firsthand.[22] In a 1959 interview she described other research for the production: visits to archaeological museums where she discovered the rich heritage of peasant costume and "such treasures as the magnificent rings of our Tsars and boyars," and discussions with artisans.[23] Nevertheless, neither Gontcharova nor Larionov, who renewed his acquaintance with Diaghilev at this time, viewed mimesis as the goal of design. "The ballet decor," they wrote in a joint article:

> does not have as its sole purpose the establishment, according to the indications of a libretto, of the time and place of an action; the scrupulously historical reconstruction of this or that style is not the end assigned to it. Decor is above all an independent creation, supporting the spirit of the work to be performed; it is an autonomous art form with its own problems and subject to its own laws . . . If [theatrical] form . . . is not established on an experimental basis, if it does not obey these unformulable but strict artistic laws, served by a sure talent, it is not viable and cannot stand the test of time.[24]

Gontcharova and Larionov returned to Russia after the outbreak of World War I. Larionov was sent to the front and not long after wounded. Gontcharova, meanwhile, overwhelmed with commissions as a result of her Ballets Russes success, designed the sets and costumes for Alexander Tairov's production of Carlo Goldoni's play *The Fan* and began work on Rimsky-Korsakov's opera *Grad Kitezh*. In the summer of 1915, at Diaghilev's invitation, the two artists joined the nucleus of the new troupe he was forming at the Villa Belle Rive in Ouchy, the company's Swiss headquarters from May to December 1915.

Although neither Larionov nor Gontcharova seems to have accompanied Diaghilev to London, their presence at his side in the early months of 1914 helps to explain his startling aesthetic turn the following autumn and his receptiveness to futurist ideas. Now, with plans ripening for the first of the troupe's American tours, they updated the neonationalist approach to Russian peasant art. Under their aegis, the treatment of folklore was profoundly transformed, its content stripped of orientalism and its representation of exotica. Between 1915 and 1917 Larionov and Gontcharova contributed designs and libretti to the half-dozen ballets on Russian themes that had their genesis (or a substantial part thereof) in Diaghilev's traveling studio. Without exception, these works jettisoned the living "oriental" traditions of Fokine's *genre nouveau*. Skipping over the nineteenth century, they turned to preliterate Russian sources: Orthodox ritual in *Liturgie*, performances by folk entertainers known as *skomorokhi* in *Chout* and *Le Renard*, dramatized wedding customs in *Les Noces*, and folk tales in *Midnight Sun* and *Contes Russes*.[25]

Unlike Nijinsky's *Sacre du Printemps*, which linked mythic past and modern present in man's abiding fear of the unknown, the neoprimitivist ballets of Larionov and Gontcharova presented time past and time present as distinct categories of experience. To the first belonged the peasant world of tale and legend; to the second, the modernism that dressed it: uniting the two was a common stylization. Viewed through a prism of artistic forms removed from the naturalist's observed reality, folklore was an artifact to be contemplated, a witty, ironic contrivance of the artist's primitivizing imagination. In the temporal juxtaposition, ironic distancing, and far-ranging stylization of neoprimitivism, one finds not only the key to the transformation of ethnic material in these years, but the modus operandi of Diaghilev's general modernist approach.

With Larionov and Gontcharova, futurism impregnated all aspects of ballet design. Perspective yielded to flat representation, illusion to partial abstraction. Arcs, triangles, and circles—painted and, occasionally, in the form of cutouts—created geometric landscapes and interiors, while color— vivid, bold, pure—worked its symbolic effects by intensity and juxtaposition. Costume was equally transformed. In *Midnight Sun, Contes Russes, Chout,* and *Le Renard*, Larionov dressed the dancers in futurist-inspired constructions: padded, heavy, stiffened with cardboard. Not only did he mask the body, he also concealed the face, with geometric make-up and anthropomorphizing half-masks, the whole crowned with elaborate headdresses. At all times, costume reiterated the motifs and colors of the setting.

Design, in fact, now took the place of music as the center of gravity in a production. Diaghilev, wrote Larionov, came to understand that decor "should be conceived as one of the integral parts" of ballet in tandem with music and movement.[26] Massine, in 1919, put the designer's case more strongly. He believed that in the new ballet's synthesis of movement and form, choreography and plastic art, "the two essentials would be balanced with an inclination toward the plastic element."[27] Beginning in 1915 and continuing throughout the postwar years, design not only supplanted music as the unifying element of Diaghilev's productions, but altered the relationship of choreography to the overall plan of a work. If, before, dance had been an equal, now it became a subordinate of design, with the goal of the choreographer being to enhance the inventions of scene painter and costumer. In his annal for 1921 Cyril W. Beaumont remarked on the overwhelming effect of Larionov's setting for *Chout:*

> The best part of the production was the setting, the rest fell flat. Larionov's settings, inspired as usual by Russian peasant art, interpreted in the spirit of cubism, were brilliantly conceived, but the colour contrasts, accentuated by the angular shapes composing the design, were so vivid and so dazzling that it was almost painful to look at the stage, and the position was not improved when brilliantly clad figures were set in movement against such a background. I would say that the effect on the eyes was almost as irritating as those flickering streaks of coloured light so characteristic of early colour films.[28]

This dramatic shift in the relationship of choreography and visual design coincided with Massine's apprenticeship and ripening artistry as a dance master. Unlike the vast majority of choreographers, who create their maiden works by imitating or reacting against choreographic models, Massine learned the rudiments of his craft from the painter's static images. Indeed, it was during one of many visits with Diaghilev to the Uffizi Gallery in the autumn of 1914 that Massine, observing the "delicate postures" of Simone Martini's Annunciation, first experienced the desire to choreograph.[29] At Diaghilev's suggestion, he began work on *Liturgie,* a series of tableaux in the style of Byzantine mosaics and Italian primitives, devising for the opening scene, an Annunciation, "a succession of angular gestures and stiff open-hand movements inspired by Cimabue's Virgin."[30] Gontcharova's costume sketches led him to conceive the Resurrection. Here, he sought to simulate in movement the Byzantine hand positions, angular, inturned arm movements, and parallel stance of the painter's ikon-inspired cubo-futurist depiction of Christ.

The concept of pose is essential to ballet, and there are well-defined rules governing the presentation of the body, arrested in motion, to the audience. In *Liturgie, Midnight Sun,* and *Contes Russes,* the three apprentice works choreographed by Massine under the supervision of Larionov, pose suggested something quite different from its textbook definition. Rather than a link in a chain of connected movements, in these works it became an isolated picture, a static two-dimensional image. Just as the function of pose reflected a painterly as opposed to kinetic model, so, too, its content derived from visual rather than dance sources. In *Midnight Sun* Larionov stressed the importance of "authentic peasant style," thus initiating Massine's lifelong fascination with genuine ethnic material, the basis of several of his best works. But at the same time, Larionov also insisted on "embel-lishing" the traditional folk dances of the ballet "with suitably primitive, earthy gestures,"[31] a procedure that recapitulated, choreographically, the stylization of authentic material in neoprimitivist painting. Accompanying these additions to the lexicon of the danse d'école were rearrangements of its syntax. As Massine's editor, Larionov not only reviewed but revised works-in-progress. In both *Liturgie* and the Baba-Yaga episode of *Contes Russes,* he pruned steps and movement to achieve "organic simplicity,"[32] yet another choreographic analogue of his modernist practice as a painter.

The influence of neoprimitivism extended far beyond Massine's war-time collaborations with Larionov and Gontcharova. Indeed, the innova-tions of these works, expanded upon and wed to other themes, remained the foundation of his choreography well into the 1920s. Angularity was perhaps the most dramatic sign of the modernist revolution in ballet. Thanks to Massine, wrote French critic Fernand Divoire in the 1930s, "the inven-tion of the later Ballets Russes in the area of dance was the angular angle, the angle more or less deforming, more or less comic and caricaturing."[33] Under the tutelage of Larionov, Gontcharova, and the futurists, Massine hardened ballet's soft and "beautiful" line. He staunched the flow and cramped the openness of classical movement and substituted contorted gestures for the rounded arms of the traditional port de bras. "All that is plastic, graceful, free from angularity is excluded," wrote Valerian Svetlov in one of many critical articles. "The times of 'the choreographic tenor,' M. Fokine, in the smart phrase of Massine, are gone for ever. All the movements of the dancers are short, angular, mechanical."[34]

No less disturbing to many critics was Massine's choreographic dy-namism, a fusion of simultaneous action and pure motion. In his auto-biography Massine attributes the revelation of dynamism to the close study he made in the autumn of 1916 of preromantic dance manuals, a time (although he neglects to mention it) of heightened contact with the futur-ists. In the techniques of Raoul Feuillet and Jean-Philippe Rameau, he wrote:

> I learned the value of concentrating on detail, and giving full significance to even the most minute gesture. I also discovered that the body includes various more or less independent structural systems each answerable only to itself, which must be coordinated according to choreographic harmony. This led me to invent broken, angular movements in the upper part of the body while the lower limbs continued to move in the usual harmonic academic style. Such an opposition of styles, is, in my opinion, possible, and creates an interesting contrast. I used the eighteenth-century notations as a point of departure for my own variations. In this way, I created entirely new body movements in my imagination, profiting largely by the effect of rhythmic forces, and varying, according to the nature of the movement, its rhythmic value as well as its

tempo in order to attain, in the composition of choreographic phrases, the strongest possible effect.[35]

Beginning with *The Good-Humoured Ladies* and the Baba-Yaga episode of *Contes Russes,* both choreographed in the winter of 1916–1917, simultaneity and speed became preeminent features of Massine's choreography. In seeming response to the futurist call for "synthetic" theater, he compressed Goldoni's play into one act, balancing the action simultaneously on both sides of the stage so as to retain all the complications of the plot. At the same time, he shortened the dance gesture, concentrating and accelerating its action; he stressed dynamism through continual movement; he sought to correlate dance rhythm to musical rhythm on a "scientific" basis, to create a choreographic counterpoint to the musical design of the composer.[36] What he did in effect was substitute rhythm for the musical phrase. "One could describe Massine's style," wrote André Levinson:

> as *perpetuum mobile,* a movement falling on each note, a gesture on each semiquaver, a continual fidget to which we owe the breathless and spirited animation of *The Good-Humoured Ladies;* now, this restless style, with its insistence on distorted or broken lines, is bound to the imperative of polyrhythmic musical movement or tyrannical syncopation that a Stravinsky imposes on the orchestra.[37]

Yet another choreographic legacy of Diaghilev's wartime revolution was a pronounced change in performance style. As we have seen, futurist theory exalted depersonalization. So, too, did futurist practice, especially in 1918–1919, when automatons and life-size puppets—children of Gordon Craig's *Übermarionettes*—proliferated on the futurist stage. In Fokine's ballets the dancers had been compelled to "act," in the sense of interpreting their roles and embellishing character with the arabesques of their own personality. In this guise, performance was akin to conversation: both radiated charm, nuance, and feeling. The triumph of mechanistic concepts in movement, design, and characterization called for a new performing style, one that conveyed emotion by abstracting, concentrating, and projecting it from behind a mask of eloquent impassivity. Beginning in the war years, dancers were encouraged to suppress histrionic displays, those telltale flashes of diva personality, and the psychological acuity, inherited from the Moscow Art Theater, that had buttressed Fokine's approach to characterization. They were asked to present themselves, not as interpreters, but as embodiments of their roles, and they had to do so without crossing the wall dividing actor and audience. Modernist performance was thus rife with anomalies: detached yet compelling, impassive yet eloquent, depersonalized yet replete with emotion. These contradictions explain the presence of so many superb acting talents—including Massine himself—within the Ballets Russes at a time when depersonalization had become a company trademark.

Apart from works inspired by Russian peasant art, neoprimitivism gave rise to another wartime thematic. Lying at the westernmost end of the European periphery, Spain was a country similar to Russia not only in its monarchist traditions but also in the vitality of its folk culture. From Diaghilev's encounters with the Spanish world in 1916 and 1917 came another cycle of works that had its genesis in the war years—*Las Meninas* (1916), *Le Tricorne* (1919), *Cuadro Flamenco* (1921), and the unrealized ballets *España* and *Triana*.

Diaghilev "was in ecstasy at the beauty of Spain," his regisseur Serge Grigoriev later wrote. "We were thrilled by Spanish dancing and bullfights, and found that the Spaniards shared our Russian love of spectacle. Our affection was returned. We [became] truly popular in Madrid."[38] King Alfonso rarely missed a performance, and it was to this self-styled "Godfather of the Ballet" as much as to the Velásquez masterpiece hanging in the Prado that *Las Meninas,* Diaghilev's first Spanish ballet, paid tribute. Of far greater inspiration than its Golden Age was the country's folk culture, which, as in Russia, derived from a blending of European and "Eastern" sources and had survived the passage to the modern era nearly intact. In a 1921 article, Stravinsky referred to the "affinities and resemblances . . . between Spanish music . . . and the music of Russia." "Certain Andalusian songs remind me of Russian ones," he wrote, "and I enjoy these atavistic memories."[39] Dance also stirred atavistic memories. Russians haunted Madrid's flamenco cafes, and in Gontcharova's paintings, Spanish themes now replaced Slavic ones. No one was more intrigued by Spanish dancing than Massine, and under the tutelage of Félix Fernández, a brilliant performer from the gypsy quarter of Granada, the choreographer mastered flamenco technique to a degree rivaling the skill of native practitioners. In the transformation of this authentic source into the modernist idiom of *Le Tricorne,* Massine followed the path laid out by Larionov and Gontcharova in the treatment of Russian material.

Just when Manuel de Falla entered Diaghilev's circle is unknown. It seems likely, however, that plans for a Spanish ballet were underway by the early autumn of 1916. October of that year found the two together in Seville, where the composer helped Diaghilev draw up his first contracts employing Spanish dancers in the company. Certainly, Falla's synthesis of classical and folkloric sources would have appealed to Diaghilev. Equally appealing must have been the composer's previous theatrical undertakings with Gregorio Martínez Sierra, a noted poet, dramatist, and producer. Among these was the production in April 1915 of *El amor brujo,* which not only brought together the collaborators of *Le Tricorne* but also anticipated the method of its creation. Falla's score and Martínez Sierra's libretto for *El amor brujo* incorporated real gypsy music as well as the stories and legends told to them by the matriarch of the gypsy clan that actually danced in the production. This use of authentic performers must also have impressed Diaghilev. In 1921 he not only hired María Dalbaicín, who represented the clan's third generation, but the whole company of Spanish dancers that appeared in his *Cuadro Flamenco.*[40]

Like Martínez Sierra, Diaghilev had toyed with the idea of presenting *Nights in the Gardens of Spain* as a ballet. The project was abandoned in favor of *Le Tricorne,* and a contract was drawn up between Diaghilev, Falla, and Martínez Sierra, as librettist. Diaghilev, apparently, was unable to produce the work as quickly as he had originally hoped, and in 1917 a pantomime version of the work was staged with Diaghilev's permission at the Teatro Eslava.[41]

Martínez Sierra adapted his libretto from Pedro Antonio de Alarcón's nineteenth-century novella *El sombrero de tres picos,* itself a reworking of the popular folktale in verse "El corregidor y la molinera." Both in its use of dance rhythms and direct musical quotations, Falla's pantomime version stayed close to folk sources. Recalling his impressions of the initial score, Massine wrote:

> Falla's score, with its pulsating rhythms, played by eleven brass instruments, seemed to us very exciting, and in its blend of violence and passion was similar to much of the music of the local folk-dances . . . When we talked to Falla about it, he seemed . . . ready to collaborate with us, to the extent of omitting some of the pastiche writing in the music for the Corregidor's dance, and expanding the ending into a fuller, more powerful finale in accordance with Diaghilev's suggestions. He said, however, that he would have to spend some time studying native dances and music before he could successfully translate the *jota* or the *farruca* into a modern idiom.[42]

Over the summer of 1917, as Diaghilev, Massine, Falla, and the dancer Félix Fernández traveled in slow stages across Castile, Aragon, and Andalusia, the dialectic of neoprimitivism was reenacted. Tunes recorded at a Granada wayside, dances glimpsed on a moonlit Seville rooftop added to the composer's and choreographer's stock of living material. At the same time, a process of stylization was at work. Blending discrete regional dances into a "super-national" idiom, Massine imposed classical movements on the forms and rhythms he had learned, together with "many twisted and broken gestures of [his] own."[43] Falla's intention of fusing the music from every part of Spain reflected a similar process of abstraction. The few and deliberate quotations that survived in the score remained there for humorous purpose; they emphasized the farcical character of the action rather than the quality of the reference as folklore. As in *Le Sacre du Printemps,* popular material was absorbed into the very structure of the music, an evolution that followed the general movement of neoprimitivism toward increasingly abstract forms.

Diaghilev's sojourn in Italy aligned the Ballets Russes with the futurist avant-garde. Yet simultaneous with his discovery of Italy's artistic present came a second major breakthrough, a revaluation of its preromantic past. Neoprimitivism had shifted emphasis from Russia's recent past to an era that lay beyond the reach of history in legend and popular tradition. Diaghilev's interest in the classical legacy of his wartime country of adoption during the period 1915–1917 represented a similar redefining of the cultural past. Leaping over the nineteenth century, he discerned in the lost music of Domenico Cimarosa, Giambattista Pergolesi, and Domenico Scarlatti, the forgotten choreographies of Raoul Feuillet and Jean-Philippe Rameau, and the popular art of the commedia dell'arte, expressions of Latinity's authentic tradition. From these discoveries came an aesthetic approach that retained its hold over Diaghilev's imagination until the mid-twenties. Period modernism wed the retrospective themes of traditional lyric theater to the styles and techniques of the avant-garde.

Throughout Diaghilev's life two men warred in his complex personality: the *barin,* powerful, privileged, despotic, and the experimentalist, bold, driving, relentlessly seeking. World War I brought the latter to the fore. Along with a stockpile of techniques, the avant-garde gave courage to Diaghilev the artist; it empowered him to go his own creative way, to lead rather than follow his artistic cabinet. Of all the genres that made appearances in his repertory, period modernism was uniquely the offspring of Diaghilev's invention. Its sources, from libraries, auction houses, and private collections, were the fruit of his tenacious research; their reworking and final assembly the labor of his imagination. Far more than Stravinsky, whose *Pulcinella* is regarded by scholars as a turning point in musical modernism's rediscovery of the past, or Massine, who choreographed the "pastiche" ballets of 1917–1920, the move toward period modernism's intriguing blend of tradition and experiment was spearheaded by Diaghilev.

Diaghilev's music library, a treasure-trove that came to light only in 1984 when it was sold at public auction,[44] testifies to the extraordinary researches of 1916–1918 that lay behind the invention of period modernism. Among the most fascinating items are those charting the genesis of *Pulcinella*, Stravinsky's 1920 "remake" of eighteenth-century music by Italian composer Giambattista Pergolesi:

> Diaghilev's music library contains about twenty items of Pergolesi's music, mostly transcriptions of chamber music and arias from various libraries, including the British Museum, the Bibliothèque Nationale and the Conservatorio di Musica, Naples. Almost all are annotated by Diaghilev, most are signed with initials and dated and give details of their provenance; a number contain his ideas and thoughts . . . for the music of *Pulcinella* and also for a projected performing version of *La Serva Padrona*. Among the manuscripts are copies of variations on the Gavotte used in *Pulcinella* . . . and excerpts from *Il Flaminio*, possibly in Diaghilev's hand . . . Other operatic items include printed copies of *Livietta e Tracollo* and an edition of *La Serva Padrona* extensively annotated by Diaghilev. In addition there are Diaghilev's annotated copies of B[enedetto] Croce's *Saggi sulla Letteratura Italiana del Seicento*, the chapter on Pulcinella marked in pencil by Diaghilev, and M. Scherillo's *L'Opera buffa napoletana*, which not only discusses the Pulcinella story, but also the works of Pergolesi and Paisiello; it is these latter sections and not the Pulcinella story itself that Diaghilev marks here.[45]

Diaghilev now picked over his finds, choosing the ingredients of his basic recipe. Only then did he approach the professional composer, who was to combine and orchestrate them for the public. In *Expositions and Developments*, Stravinsky explains:

> The suggestion that was to lead to *Pulcinella* came from Diaghilev one spring afternoon while we were walking together in the Place de la Concorde: "Don't protest at what I am about to say . . . but I have an idea that I think will amuse you . . . I want you to look at some delightful eighteenth-century music with the idea of orchestrating it for a ballet". When he said that the composer was Pergolesi, I thought he must be deranged. I knew Pergolesi only by the *Stabat Mater* and *La Serva Padrona*, and though I had just seen a production of the latter in Barcelona, Diaghilev knew I wasn't in the least excited by it. I did promise to look, however, and to give him my opinion.
>
> I looked, and I fell in love. My ultimate selection of pieces derived only partly from Diaghilev's examples, however, and partly from published editions, but I did play through the whole of the available Pergolesi before making my choice. My first step was to fix a plan of action and an accompanying sequence of pieces. Diaghilev had found a book of Pulcinella stories in Rome. We studied this book together and selected certain episodes. The final construction of the plot and the ordering of the dance numbers was the work of Diaghilev, Leonid [sic] Massine, and myself, all three of us working together.[46]

Diaghilev allowed his "first son" far greater latitude in *Pulcinella* than he permitted either Vincenzo Tommasini or Ottorino Respighi, the Italian composers who prepared the musical texts of the era's other period ballets. For *The Good-Humoured Ladies* (1917) Diaghilev chose from among some five hundred sonatas by Domenico Scarlatti, then little esteemed, the twenty pieces he thought "would . . . enhance the comic situations" of Carlo Goldoni's classic play.[47] Only then, with the creative work behind him, did he call upon Tommasini's technical skills as an orchestrator. Respighi, too, was kept under tight rein. His contract for Domenico Cimarosa's opera-ballet *Le Astuzie Femminili,* produced in 1920, stipulated that he "create all the recitatives in conformity with the themes of the composer and totally change the orchestration, adding the dances agreed upon with Diaghilev." It also commissioned him to "arrange" Giovanni Paisiello's *Serva e Padrona,* an opera that was never performed.[48] The manuscript of *La Boutique Fantasque,* the frothy toyshop ballet that so enchanted London in 1919, reveals Diaghilev's hand even more patently. Indeed, it raises in acute form the question that must be asked of musical period modernism generally. Who was the author? Gioacchino Rossini, who wrote the early nineteenth-century piano pieces on which the score was based? Respighi, the orchestrator, who added a handful of connectives? Or Diaghilev, who assembled the music for the ballet from numerous compositions, pruned bars and passages, changed chords, keys, and tempi, corrected Respighi's additions, and wrote notes to himself like, "Don't forget that all the chords must approximate stylistically the *old* Rossini of *Barber* [*of Seville*]"?[49]

The premiere of *The Good-Humoured Ladies* in April 1917 brought the first of Diaghilev's "time-travelling" ballets (the phrase is Constant Lambert's) to the stage. But although this popular work, which became a postwar signature piece, combined preromantic music with Massine's choreographic fusion of futurist and eighteenth-century styles, Bakst's illusionist setting marked it as a transitional ballet. For the essence of period modernism was temporal dislocation, a radical contrast between past and present among and within each of ballet's contributing texts. Like *Pulcinella, The Good-Humoured Ladies,* and *Le Astuzie Femminili, Boutique* stemmed from an older theatrical source—Joseph Hassreiter's toyshop ballet *Die Puppenfee,* produced at the Court Opera, Vienna, in 1888, restaged by Nicolas and Sergei Legat at the Maryinsky in 1903 and by Ivan Clustine for the Anna Pavlova company in 1914. Just as Diaghilev reworked rather than reproduced musical sources, so he transformed his theatrical and literary models: their plots and characters were dissected and recombined in ballets structured increasingly as divertissements. "How right you are to proscribe literature from the choreographic work," wrote Francis Poulenc to Diaghilev in early 1919. "Calling on great poets only proves the point. Braque, moreover, said to me the other day, 'Isn't it already too much to have three—choreographer, painter, and musician; if you have to add a writer, then all unity is suppressed'."[50] In rejecting the psychological and historicizing underpinnings of nineteenth-century literary convention, a key tenet of futurist performance, period modernism edged ballet narrative down the path of abstraction.

The juxtaposition of modern form and traditional theme appeared most patently in design. André Derain's brilliant, decorative palette and flattened perspective located *La Boutique Fantasque* in a modernized 1830s setting that undercut the nostalgia and sentimentality inherent in the ballet's evocation of a lost bourgeois world. At Diaghilev's behest, Picasso transposed the setting of *Pulcinella* progressively backward in time. In its final form, the Neapolitan street scene blended cubist perspective with traditional eighteenth-century imagery, a visual analogue of Stravinsky's modernized Pergolesi and Massine's "futurized" commedia dell'arte.

Although these works premiered in 1919–1920, the germ and characteristic method of their creation date to the war years. Like the neoprimitivist experiments that immediately preceded them, they indicated a way in which period material might be updated, streamlined, and, most importantly, transposed from a key of neoromantic sentimentality, as exemplified by Fokine's Biedermeier works, to one of ironic detachment.

The obsessive play of past and present, however, betrays more than a quickening of formal imagination. In Diaghilev's willful plumbing of the Latin past may be discerned an attempt to exorcise the loss of Russia by founding his enterprise on a substitute but no less vital tradition, one, moreover, that was framed within the highly structured parameters of classicism. In a journal entry for October 1917, Charles Ricketts linked Russia with Diaghilev's interest in lost Italian music. "Diaghilev," he wrote, "has been delving in Italian libraries for scores of eighteenth-century Italians now forgotten . . . He wants an Italian revival and a Russian propaganda. We quarrelled over German music which he wants to persecute and suppress; he means to scrap *Carnaval, Papillons* and the *Spectre of the Rose*."[51] Russia was present in other, subtler ways. Both Paisiello and Cimarosa had been employed for a time at the Russian court, while Respighi, as a young man, had played in the Maryinsky and Bolshoi orchestras.

Diaghilev's notebook for the period 1918–1920 contains lengthy excerpts from his readings, laboriously copied in his own hand, that relate Cimarosa's appeal as a composer to the discipline of classical form. These notes suggest the train of Diaghilev's ruminations on larger questions of postwar style:

Cimarosa acted on the imagination through long musical phrases that united extreme richness with extreme regularity . . . [Paisiello] does not evoke in the soul of the spectator images that give enjoyment to profound passions; his emotions hardly rise above grace . . . Nothing in the world is more contrary to Cimarosa's style, glittering with comic verve, passion, force, and gaiety.[52]

It is by *manner* that one pleases a blasé public eager for novelty; it is manner, too, that rapidly causes to age the works of these inspired artists [Beethoven and Rossini], themselves dupes of that false novelty they had sought to introduce into art. Then it often happens that the public returns to forgotten masterpieces and looks anew upon the imperishable charm of beauty.[53]

No one, save Cimarosa, has that proportion, that decorum, that expression, that gaiety, that tenderness, and above all, the element that throws all his qualities into relief, that incomparable elegance, elegance in the expression of tender feelings, elegance in the comic, elegance in the pathetic.[54]

Clearly, what appealed to Diaghilev in the work of Cimarosa and other eighteenth-century composers was the supremacy of style. History exists at the intersection of time and place. Only style, with its ability to remake the transitory and circumstantial into the imperishable stuff of art, stands impervious to change. As the touchstones of European life collapsed around him, something akin to classicism joined the constellation of influences reshaping Diaghilev's aesthetic. Crystallizing initially as a compensatory response to the need for an instant, alternative past, "classicism," with its insistence on the primacy of style, offered a formal counterpoint to the nostalgia and sentimentality implicit in retrospective visions of the past. Style thus became the means whereby past and present were formally united but coded as belonging to distinct epistemological realms. As in poetry, music, and painting, modernist style in ballet channeled perception through an intellectual process of ironic distancing.

Period modernism was a response to the radical displacement of war, as, to a somewhat lesser extent, was the cycle of Spanish ballets that emerged at roughly the same time. Comic works, poised between past and present, they charmed a war-weary public cursed with memories of a vanished order. In 1923–1924 period themes reappeared in the repertory. But in contrast to the war-spawned works of high modernism, in *Le Médecin Malgré Lui, La Colombe, Les Tentations de la Bergère, Les Fâcheux,* and *Une Education Manquée* (operas and ballets based on themes of the French eighteenth century), the obsessive play of past and present occurred on a purely formal level: in the musical "rewrites" of Erik Satie, Francis Poulenc, Georges Auric, and Darius Milhaud, in the settings of Juan Gris and Georges Braque, and in the choreography of Bronislava Nijinska. In these later works (discussed in detail in the next chapter), inner tension and implied tragedy vanish.

In the years 1914–1917 lie the origins of Diaghilev's modernist aesthetic. From the interaction of futurism, neoprimitivism, and the rediscovery of Latinity's preromantic artistic heritage emerged the constellation of styles that would distinguish the postwar Ballets Russes and inspire its numerous imitators. No less dramatic than the influence of the avant-garde on dance, however, was Diaghilev's impact on the avant-garde itself. By successfully appropriating the characteristic methods of the era's artistic vanguard and fusing them with ballet's traditional period and ethnic content, Diaghilev significantly broadened the reach of modernist experiment. He did this by demonstrating the ability of these new formal approaches to transcend the limitations imposed by their original medium and by making the avant-garde aesthetic accessible and acceptable to a considerably broadened public.

Diaghilev's extraordinary achievement in these years rested only in part on his willingness to assimilate new formal procedures. Equally, it reflected his ability to remake the company in the image of the avant-garde itself. Throughout this period Diaghilev worked in the intimacy of a small collaborative group united in pursuit of radical theatrical change. At the center of this experimental nucleus were Larionov, Gontcharova, Stravinsky, and Massine. More than collaborators, they lived and traveled with Diaghilev on terms of intimacy and in their letters addressed him familiarly. (For the overwhelming majority of artists who received commissions in the twenties, the impresario remained, by contrast, a distant "cher ami.") Diaghilev's wartime "studio" exhibited the informal collective structure and shared aesthetics of contemporary avant-garde movements.

Habits of intimacy had united the collaborators of Diaghilev's earliest ballet seasons. However, the aim of this wartime nucleus was not solely production. A higher premium was placed on experimentation than at any other time in the company's history, with projects abandoned or laid aside once their innovative elements had been conceptualized. Only after the war, when production again became a commercial necessity, did the most viable of these abandoned ballets move from studio to stage.

Diaghilev's modernist breakthroughs took place outside the constraints of the marketplace. "Of all the years we travelled with Diaghilev," recalled dancer Lydia Sokolova, "those six months in Switzerland were the happiest." There were classes and rehearsals, and with the company "so much smaller than before," the dancers "lived on rather more intimate terms."[55] Intimacy denoted more than a social style; it implied an economic relationship as well. Reorganizing the company along collectivist lines, Diaghilev leveled distinctions in salary. Irrespective of rank, the dancers in his small but growing troupe received four hundred Swiss francs a month. Within his creative circle, too, financial relationships suggested a throwback to Abramtsevo, *Mir iskusstva,* and his earliest seasons in the West. To help Stravinsky support his large and growing family, Diaghilev secured engagements for the composer wherever the traveling studio happened to alight. In the case of Larionov and Gontcharova, payment seems to have taken the form of a stipend rather than remuneration for work performed under a contractual arrangement. In early autumn 1918 Gontcharova wrote Diaghilev on two occasions asking apologetically for "the money you promised to send."[56] With the laws of the market in temporary abeyance, modernism bloomed in an atmosphere of relative social and economic equality.

In appropriating the formal approaches of avant-garde experiment in Russia, Italy, Spain, and France, Diaghilev brought a supranational character to company modernism, something by no means limited to ballet. This internationalist flavor, which marked collaborations throughout the postwar years, was reflected in the wartime troupe itself. By June 1918 Russians comprised only a minority of the dancers who traveled with Diaghilev from Spain to London, and those with roots in the Imperial Theaters were even fewer. Of the thirty-nine dancers, eighteen were Russian (of whom only ten had been trained at the Maryinsky or Bolshoi), twelve were Polish; there were four Italians, two Spaniards, two Englishwomen, and even a Belgian. The company manager Randolfo Barocchi, who was married to Lydia Lopokova, was Italian in origin.[57] This ethnic mix suggests to what degree the company had ceased to be a Russian enterprise. Henceforth, its roots lay fully in the West, embedded in a stateless present.

Modernism and internationalism emerged from the crucible of war as quintessential elements of the company's identity. The trademark of this modernism, as we have said, lay in the fashioning of a style culled from various avant-garde sources and applied to an extended range of balletic contexts. This style, witty, ironic, farcical, and detached, became the point of unity in a work; it harmonized incongruities among the competing texts and tuned disparities of place and era to a single frequency. Above all, it vested the whole of a work with an aura of modernity. Analogous to its role in new theories of design, style became the means of creating a total, aestheticized environment.

The aesthetic that emerged from Diaghilev's encounter with the avant-garde, the experience of forced exile, and the total rethinking of company organization and artistic purpose comprised what may be called his era of "authentic modernism." But as had occurred in the field of design, where the very nature of the artifact rendered it particularly susceptible to marketing pressures, modernist style in ballet became rapidly commercialized.

Shorn of its wartime rigor in the course of its postwar dissemination, it became a series of immediately discernible and easily imitated signs, a commodity that lent character to a performance as steel tubing attested to the modernity of a chair. Easily copied, reproduced, and marketed, the elements of modernist style became various parts on an assembly line of international ballet fashion.

But this takes us beyond the age of discovery that changed the countenance of ballet into a vastly different chapter of Ballets Russes history. Slashing its moorings in the fin de siècle, Diaghilev plunged the Ballets Russes into the mainstream of the avant-garde. To post-Armistice Europe his brilliant synthesis of old and new summed up both the rupture of World War I and the abiding values of civilization. Like modernism, generally, it fused hallowed artistic traditions with radically innovative forms and techniques.

No era draws to a close with the neatness and finality of a novel. Trends and personalities overlap, blurring distinctions between endings and beginnings. Diaghilev's period of authentic modernism is no exception. But, here, history has been kind, providing an encounter that seems in retrospect to frame the period, freezing its diverse elements into a significant snapshot. In May 1922 Sydney Schiff, the British littérateur who wrote novels under the pen name of Stephen Hudson, had the idea for a kind of modernist summit, a party that would bring together the *monstres sacrés* of the new age—Proust and Joyce in literature, Stravinsky in music, Picasso in painting. So, he invited them, not to one of those literary soirees for which Paris is famed, but to a first-night supper party for *Le Renard,* Stravinsky's ballet-burlesque with songs.[58] Although neither novelist had much to say to the other (physical ailments seem to have been the chief topic of conversation), that their sole encounter took place at a Diaghilev event reveals the extraordinary change that had come over the Ballets Russes between 1915 and 1921. Never again in the twentieth century would ballet stand so close to the avant-garde as in the years of Diaghilev's wartime and post-Armistice adventure.

4

THE TWENTIES

I N THE HISTORY of the Ballets Russes, no era is more elusive than the 1920s—a decade of protean appearances and conflicting identities. Amid the apparent chaos, however, three trends seem to unify the period. The first, which I have baptized "lifestyle modernism," was associated with Jean Cocteau's art of the sophisticated commonplace. The second, "retrospective classicism," mirrored the French elite's fascination with the aristocratic culture of the *grand siècle*. The third, "choreographic neoclassicism," was the offspring of Bronislava Nijinska and George Balanchine, émigré representatives of the Soviet dance vanguard. Overlapping, sometimes even in the same work, these trends coexisted uneasily in the Diaghilev repertory—and in ballet at large—during most of the 1920s.

Jean Cocteau has appeared in these pages before. We meet him now, however, not as the *prince frivole* haunting the corridors of Diaghilev's prewar theaters but as an engineer of the rapprochement between Left Bank art and Right Bank ideology that gave rise to lifestyle modernism. The first step in this transformation came in 1913 with *Le Sacre du Printemps,* a work that drove home to the dandy poet the lesson of his own inconsequence. Art, he discovered, must shock rather than please, defy public opinion rather than court it. *Sacre,* he later wrote, was "the revelation of a form of art that broke with the habitual, was anti-conformist":

> It was when I knew Stravinsky, and later, when I knew Picasso, that I understood that rebellion is indispensable in art, and that the creator always rebels against something if only instinctively—in other words, that the spirit of creation is the highest form of the spirit of contradiction.[1]

At last, Cocteau understood what Diaghilev had meant by his famous injunction, "Astound me!"

From the chrysalis of society now emerged the gadfly of modernism. Between 1913 and 1917, the year *Parade* made its first appearance at the Paris Opéra, Cocteau flitted among the avant-garde. He met its minor luminaries, then made the acquaintance of its lions—Picasso, Apollinaire, Satie. But as he wooed these new artist friends, he also courted the right-wing cultural authorities who came to power in France at the start of World War I. In November 1914, with designer Paul Iribe, he founded *Le Mot,* a strongly nationalistic, anti-German magazine that represented, as Kenneth Silver has written, a complete "volte-face" for someone who had stood, until very recently, "at the very center of cosmopolitan Paris." Here, the poet "offered his confreres in the Parisian avant-garde a formula for finessing their way through the stormy waters of wartime public opinion."[2] His solution linked two conservative ideas: that vanguard art had to contain its experimentalism and that it had to shed its aura of foreignness. Cocteau was quick to heed his own advice. In the ballet *Parade* and in *Cock and Harlequin,* a treatise published in 1918, he absorbed, transformed, and tamed key futurist precepts, laying the foundation for lifestyle modernism.

Despite Cocteau's claims of originality, *Parade* owed its most innovative ideas to futurism. The cult of the commonplace that with *Parade* became an article of his artistic faith was a cherished tenet of futurist performance theory. It was also a major theme of two futurist manifestos, well known in France: Marinetti's "Variety Theater" (translated as "Le Music Hall") and Apollinaire's "L'Antitradition futuriste." Both were published in 1913, the year of Cocteau's post-*Sacre* "moulting." Their ideas fell on fertile ground: in *David,* a spectacle conceived in 1913–1914 that never reached the stage, clowns and acrobats made their first appearance in Cocteau's work. *Parade* had no clowns, but like *David,* took place outside a fairground booth; its "turns," however, likened the ballet to a music-hall show—that jumble of animal, dance, magic, tumbling, and "bioscope" numbers that so appealed to the futurists. If *Parade* exalted the variety stage theatrically, *Cock and Harlequin* did so polemically. In fact, this 1918 pamphlet, dedicated to Georges Auric, one of the group of young French composers soon to be known as "Les Six," drew its most provocative ideas—to say nothing of its provocative tone—from the futurists: the idea that high theater, both dramatic and lyric, was corrupt; that popular entertainment was pure; that romanticism and impressionism were démodé; that the serious must bow before the comic, the sublime before the everyday; that cinema, circus, jazz, and music-hall held the keys to a new theatrical poetic.[3]

Although he characteristically never acknowledged it, Cocteau also owed a considerable debt to Apollinaire. Carried off by influenza two days before the Armistice, the poet-critic who had been a leader of avant-garde Paris left a deep mark on Cocteau's work, nowhere more obviously than in *Parade*. Consider the following texts: the first, Apollinaire's prescriptions in "L'Antitradition futuriste" for attaining the ideals of "Purity" and "Variety"; the second, Cocteau's unpublished notes, given to Satie in 1916, for the Little American Girl in *Parade*:

> Free Words Invention of Words/. . . Onomatopoeic Description/Total Music and Art of Noises . . ./Machinism Eiffel Tower Brooklyn and skyscrapers/ Polyglottis/Pure Civilisation/Epic Nomadism urban exploration Art of Voyages and promenades/Antigraceful/Direct quivers at great free spectacles circuses music halls, etc.

> The Titanic—. . . elevators—the sirens of Boulogne . . . radiotelegrams across the sea . . . tar—varnish—the machines of transatlantic steamers —the New York Herald—dynamos—aeroplanes—short circuits—the palace cinemas . . . Walt Whitman—Cowboys in goat pants . . . the express 199—the Sioux . . . the Negroes who pick corn—the prison—reverberations—the beautiful Mrs. Astor—the declarations of President Wilson—torpedo-boat-mines—the Tango . . . arc lights—gramophones—typewriters—Eiffel Towers—Brooklyn Bridge— big automobiles of ripolin and nickel—. . . bars—ice cream—. . . Helen Dodge . . . the gold seekers —posters—advertisements—Charlie Chaplin—Christopher Columbus—metal landscapes—the victims of the Lusitania—the women dressed in ball gowns in the morning—the isle of Mauritius—Paul and Virginia.[4]

Free associative, flitting from the *objets trouvés* of mechanized modernity to those of a mythic America, the imagery of the two passages reveals a startling similarity. Cocteau works in greater detail, to be sure, but always on a landscape sketched by Apollinaire. (How many writers would independently couple Brooklyn and the Eiffel Tower?) In both passages, moreover, the rhythm is staccato, the pace rapid-fire: images spewed from the barrel of a gun. And in the massing of real objects, both approximate the technique of cubist collage.

Cocteau's true genius lay not in the originality of his ideas, but in the ability to appropriate the ideas of the avant-garde for essentially conservative ends. Purged of radicalism, his sanitized art became the stuff of elite entertainment. Nowhere was this more evident than in his treatment of popular material. For the futurists, this had been a powerful weapon in their assault on high culture, as well as a source of fresh theatrical ideas. For Cocteau, on the other hand, variety, circus, cinema, and jazz—the "music of everyday," as he termed them in *Cock*—were the raw material of an art of the sophisticated commonplace. Scholars routinely speak of

Cocteau's appropriation of popular culture. Rarely, however, do they probe the nature of that material or the character of its popularity; nor do they analyze the intent and method of its "gentrification." As it turns out, the "popular resources" that Cocteau claimed to exploit were the pastimes and consumer styles of France's upper class.[5] Where *le tout Paris* slummed, Cocteau, its self-appointed vanguardist, found the material for its rarified entertainments.

As a child, Cocteau knew the circus well; as an adolescent, he discovered the music-hall. (With fellow *lycéens*, he had tossed violets to Mistinguett, a popular music-hall entertainer.) As a young adult, however, he gave himself to "high" theatrical art. The war necessarily changed this. Darkening most Paris theaters and sharply curtailing the activities of others, it renewed interest on the home front in other forms of recreation. When Cocteau failed to enlist Stravinsky's collaboration on *David*, he incorporated several of its ideas into another doomed project, *A Midsummer Night's Dream*. Like *David*, the play was set in a circus ring; it had designs by Albert Gleizes, a minor cubist, and music by Satie. But what heralded the new era was the mating of Cocteau's beau monde with popular entertainment: produced by Gabriel Astruc, Diaghilev's erstwhile impresario, this unlikely benefit for the Theater Managers' Fund for the Wounded was to take place at a real circus—the venerable Cirque Médrano—with real clowns in the parts of Bottom, Flute, and Starveling. *Dream* proved to be another rehearsal for *Parade*. But it was also a harbinger of Cocteau's *Le Boeuf sur le Toit*, a "Spectacle-Concert" financed by Comte Etienne de Beaumont and presented at the Comédie des Champs-Elysées in 1920. Here, before an audience studded with celebrities, the Fratellini brothers and five of their confreres from the Cirque Médrano cycled popular entertainment into a pastime for *le tout Paris*.

Cocteau paid many visits to the Médrano in the war years, as did many chic Parisians. His visits did not cease with the Armistice. If anything, they became a staple of his social life, the night cap, so to speak, of his weekly dinners with the "faithful"—Francis Poulenc, Darius Milhaud, Jean and Valentine Hugo, Lucien Daudet, Arthur Honegger, and Paul Morand. Sometimes, the band went to the Foire de Montmartre—a stretch of boulevard lined with fair booths between the Place Blanche and the Place Pigalle—or to the Foire du Trône, a street fair in the east end of Paris. Here, Jean Hugo later wrote, Cocteau and "his musicians" sought, and sometimes found, inspiration. Hugo, who designed several Cocteau productions beginning with *Boeuf,* could have added visual artists as well to his list.[6]

Movies also fascinated the poet in these years. World War I did not invent the cinema, but it was then that the French elite took it up. With the cut in domestic production, the movies that Cocteau and his friends saw and remembered were American. At the front for most of the war, Jean Hugo had "missed . . . the films everyone always talked about": *Pour sauver sa race* [*The Aryan*], starring William Hart, alias Rio Jim; *Une Aventure à New York*, with Douglas Fairbanks; *Charlot Soldat*, with Charlie Chaplin. Chaplin was "the best," wrote Cocteau in 1919. "He is the modern Punch. He speaks to all ages, to all peoples. The esperanto laugh." Westerns were another favorite of Cocteau and his wartime "group," and in late 1917 he took to describing himself in letters as living in "Texas," or "a corner of the Far West."[7] Beginning with *Parade*, cinema made its appearance in his theatrical work. The Little American Girl was his declaration of faith: here was a character, transported directly from the silver screen, who moved like a cinematic image and incarnated a cinematic myth—Hollywood's innocent American girl. "The United States," he wrote in 1919, "evokes a girl more interested in her health than in her beauty. She swims, boxes, dances, leaps onto moving trains—all without knowing that she is beautiful. It is we who admire her face, on the screen—enormous, like the face of a goddess."[8] Under Cocteau's tutelage, Massine's American girl aspired to the "reality" of her celluloid counterpart. "Wearing a blazer and a short white skirt," the choreographer wrote:

> she bounced on to the stage, crossing it in a succession of convulsive leaps, her arms swinging widely. She then did an imitation of the shuffling walk of Charlie Chaplin, followed by a sequence of mimed actions reminiscent of *The Perils of Pauline*—jumping on to a moving train, swimming across a river, having a running fight at pistol-point, and finally finding herself lost at sea in the tragic sinking of the *Titanic*. All this was ingeniously danced and mimed by Maria Chabelska who interpreted Satie's syncopated ragtime music with great charm and gusto, and brought the dance to a poignant conclusion when, thinking herself a child at the seaside, she ended up playing in the sand.[9]

These three elements—iconography, movement, myth—became central to Cocteau's "cinematized" ballet. In *Le Boeuf sur le Toit* (subtitled, in English, "The Nothing Doing Bar"), the setting is an American saloon, the cast—a cocktail-mixing barman, a cigar-smoking Negro boxer, a pool-playing Negro boy (played by a dwarf), a bookie with gold teeth, a quietly swigging swell, two ladies in red, and a policeman—the types of an exotic Prohibition America. In *Boeuf*, unlike *Parade*, Cocteau had total charge of the choreography. His goal, only partly realized in *Parade*, was the same: living gesture, "amplified and magnified into dance." In *Boeuf*, he explained in the published libretto, the characters "are *moving decor*. They perform the gestures essential to their roles in 'slow motion,' against the music, with the heaviness of divers."[10] Realism, however, remained the foundation of his method:

> The red-headed lady crosses the stage, takes away the smoke rings with her arm, puts them round the barman's neck and winks at the boxer. The boxer leaves his chair to follow her. The bookmaker sees them, becomes angry, quivers with rage, comes up quietly, takes out his pearl tie-pin and hits the Negro over the head with it. The Negro collapses. The Negro boy drops his billiard cue, helps the boxer up, puts him down in the chair, fans him with a towel.[11]

Not all the movement was dumb show. There was a "little triumphal dance" for the bookie, a tango for the women, an Ur-Salomé dance for the redhead. For the policeman, there was a "ballet aimable," which he performed with the "grace of a ballerina," as the barman sent the overhead fan crashing on his head.

This was the first of several instances where Cocteau parodied the danse d'école. In *Les Mariés de la Tour Eiffel,* presented by the Ballets Suédois in 1921, women in sky-blue tutus with stuffed, oversize bosoms formed a tableau reminiscent of *Les Sylphides.* "The ballet," wrote Jean Hugo, who designed the costumes and masks:

> was a caricature of the classical dance . . . that ended with an immobile group, where the dancers, some on pointe, wavered as if losing their balance. The Bathing Beauty was a sort of bacchante solo with ridiculous gambols. [Jean] Borlin, under the incognito of the mask, danced this role himself several times.[12]

Although Borlin, the troupe's star, apparently "arranged" the dance, the idea for this "Waltz of the Telegrams"—and for the movement throughout—was Cocteau's. "Cocteau did everything," wrote Hugo. "All the poses of the characters were dictated by him. Each had to have his own way of walking: the hunter, the manager, the ostrich, the collector. Cocteau mimed it all himself in front of the dancers." Apart from the Waltz of the Telegrams, a quadrille to the music of the Republican Guard, and the Bathing Beauty's dance, the action advanced through pantomime. As in most of his theatrical pieces, Cocteau borrowed the techniques of slow motion and freeze framing from the cinema.[13]

Movement stood at the center of Cocteau's vision of poetic theater. But unlike Fokine or Nijinsky, he did not believe in the power of dance to speak independently, to invoke by the play of rhythm and design an order of meaning as convincing as words—the reason, no doubt, that speech often accompanied his pieces. (In the case of *Parade,* Diaghilev suppressed the spoken text, much to the poet's chagrin.) For Cocteau, dance was never a form of symbolic language. Always, it retained the function of gesture, imitative and referential. It has been said that "Cocteau broadened the concept of ballet, not only through sound and speech but through innovative use of movement" and that "ballet was a far more open art form after Cocteau had cast off the fetters of tradition and shown its possibilities for interpreting our present reality."[14] But is ballet still ballet when silence is routinely exchanged for speech? Symbolic language for mimetic gesture? Classical technique for pedestrian movement? In Cocteau's theater, the danse d'école existed as a servant of the secular.

Along with circus, fair, and cinema, two other ingredients seasoned Cocteau's gentrified populism. One was jazz. In America, this was a vernacular art. In Paris, it initially belonged to society. In 1918, as the Germans bombarded Paris with the shells of their "Big Bertha," Comte Etienne de Beaumont gave a "great Negro fête"—the first private party in Paris to feature American jazz, supplied by black American soldiers. To his disappointment, Cocteau missed the party. But there was jazz aplenty in Paris as the war wound to its close. At the Marigny Theater, wrote composer Noble Sissle, Louis Mitchell's Jazz Kings had "Paris by the balls," and, soon, all the French music-halls had to have their jazz band.[15] In *Cock and Harlequin,* Cocteau described the scene at the Casino de Paris in 1918:

> The accompaniment was an American band with banjos and big nickel tubes. On the right of the little black-coated group there was a barman of sound effects in a gilt pergola full of bells, triangles, boards, and motorcyle horns. With these he mixed cocktails, adding from time to time a dash of cymbals, all the while rising from his seat, posturing and smiling vacuously. Mr. Pilcer, in tails, thin and rouged, and Mlle. Gaby Deslys, like a big ventriloquist's doll, with a porcelain complexion, corn-colored hair, and a gown with ostrich feathers, danced to this hurricane of rhythms and drumbeats a kind of domesticated cataclysm which left them completely drunk and dazzled under the streaming glare of six air-raid searchlights. The house stood and applauded, roused from its torpor by this extraordinary number . . .[16]

This was only one of many references in Cocteau's writings of 1918–1919 to jazz (or, at least, to what he and most of the French mistook for jazz). Another, published in *Paris-Midi,* referred to a show for American soldiers:

> I listen to a jazz band at the Casino de Paris.
>   The Negroes in the air, in a sort of cage, lash about, waddle, tossing to the crowd morsels of raw meat, to blows of trumpet and rattle. A dance tune—broken, sparring, in counterpoint—rises from time to time to the surface.

The hot hall, full of painted girls and American soldiers, is a saloon in movies of the Far West.[17]

However much he reveled in the primitivism, physicality, and emotionalism of jazz (to say nothing of the exoticism of its black performers), Cocteau never regarded jazz as a genuine art. It might stimulate the imagination and, by its "savagery," "virilize" the result, but, on its own, it was merely the "soul" of contemporary disorder. "The music-hall, the circus, American Negro bands—all this is as fertilizing to an artist as life itself," he wrote in *Cock and Harlequin*. "To make use of the emotions aroused by such entertainments is not to revert to making art from art. These entertainments are not art. They excite like machines, animals, landscapes, danger."[18] Today, Cocteau's paternalism leaves an unpleasant taste. The popular turns out to be no more than a sensory charge for his elitist sensibility.

If there was a single form of entertainment that brought together Cocteau's many interests, it was the music-hall. Here, comics, conjurors, and clowns shared the limelight with dancers, as they would in Cocteau's elegant vaudevilles. In the years before World War I the era's most celebrated dancers played the Paris "halls": Natalia Trouhanova, Loie Fuller, Cléo de Mérode, Ruth St. Denis, Mata Hari, La Belle Otero, Maud Allen, Mistinguett, Gaby Deslys, Harry Pilcer. There were troupes of precision dancers bearing such exotic English labels as the Tiller Girls and Les Sparkling Girls. And there was ballet. At the Folies-Bergère and the Olympia, all-female troupes were a house feature. Picture postcards of the time bring these forgotten Parisian ballet girls momentarily to life: Mado Minty, ample of thigh, slim of waist, an unlikely bellhop in her high-heeled boots, fluffy wig, and heart-shaped belt buckle; a pair of platinum blond "danseuses de Marigny," draped in gauzy veils and ropes of pearls; another twosome, the lady in a lacey négligé, her partner, a danseuse *en travesti*, in tights, a tam-o'-shanter, and ribboned ballet slippers with heels. In these images, as coy as the lines of sentimental verse that sometimes accompany them, are the originals of Cocteau's dancing telegrams in *Les Mariés de la Tour Eiffel*.

Although entertainment was Cocteau's main source of vernacular material, popular pictorial traditions also found their way into his work. The most important of these was the *image d'Epinal*—"crude, folkloric, brightly colored broadsides (first woodcut, then after 1850 lithographic), produced since the sixteenth century in Epinal, a town in Lorraine in eastern France." Popularized during the war especially among the right wing, these images, Kenneth E. Silver explains, were "crucial" to Cocteau's artistic development.[19] In *Parade*, *Le Boeuf sur le Toit*, and *Les Mariés de la Tour Eiffel*:

Cocteau presents a conventionalized humanity much as it appears in the *images d'Epinal*. In *Parade* there are no proper names, only descriptions: the Chinese Magician, the Little American Girl, the Acrobats, the Managers; in *Le Boeuf sur le toit*, again no names, but types: the Woman in a Low-Cut Dress, the Red-Headed Woman, the Barman, the Policeman, the Negro Boxer; and again, in *Les Mariés*, an archetypal humanity: "the Bride, sweet as a lamb," "the Father-in-Law, rich as Croesus," the Groom, pretty as a heart," the Mother-in-Law, phoney as a slug," and other characters, such as the Director of the Eiffel Tower and the Bathing Beauty from Trouville.[20]

Boeuf was designed by Raoul Dufy, once a "satellite" of the fauves, who had gone to work during the war for the government propaganda bureau, creating posters, pamphlets, and broadsides for the national cause. "Whether it was his idea, . . . or . . . Cocteau's," Silver writes, the characters of *Boeuf*

> are quotations from the *images d'Epinal* —the enormous heads on tiny bodies almost certainly derive from a stylization that was standard for the 'Cris de Paris,' where the head was emphasized as the embodiment of the peddler's cry.[21]

Through the *image d'Epinal,* Cocteau gave his futurist borrowings a peculiarly French and a distinctly elitist flavor. Like Depero's automatons, the faces of his characters were masked (or heavily made up), their bodies reconstructed through costume, their voices deformed by megaphones. But where the Italian deployed these techniques to "futurize" his characters, to wrest them from historical time and place, Cocteau, via the *image d'Epinal,* did just the opposite: he settled his characters in a Parisian past. In the transfer from broadside to stage, moreover, something happened to the images: they lost both the roughness and popular subject matter of their originals. Instead of peddlers hawking their wares on public streets, Cocteau gives us the types of a privileged world—rich daddies, big game hunters, art collectors, generals who dine with dukes—and entertainers, scrubbed clean and smartened up. Suffused with charm, reborn as innocents, they evoke the romance of a lost world, the idyll of a bourgeois childhood. Borrowing from the artistic left, Cocteau placed his borrowings at the service of the political right.

Cocteau "broke" with Diaghilev in 1917 when the latter eliminated the megaphone effects and "bits of acoustical illusion"—typewriter clicking, Morse code, sirens, an express train—from the sound score of *Parade*. His bitterness ran deep. "The Russians are here," wrote Madame Cocteau in January 1920, "but Jean goes seldom, because of Diaghilev, whom he detests and for good reason." By spring, however, a rapprochement was underway: Cocteau, with Poulenc, Auric, and Lucien Daudet, attended the first-night party for *Pulcinella* given by Prince Firouz, a Persian diplomat and temporary pet of high society. In December, Diaghilev revived *Parade*, and the following year attended the "Spectacle Bouffe," presented by Cocteau and Pierre Bertin at the Théâtre Martin, and one of the first performances of *Les Mariés de la Tour Eiffel*. "I have it from a very good source that Diaghilev was profoundly interested in our piece," Cocteau announced to Rolf de Maré, founder and director of the Ballets Suédois. "He urgently requested music from our musicians for his London intervals." Within weeks of the premiere, compositions by four of Les Six—Arthur Honegger, Darius Milhaud, Francis Poulenc, and Georges Auric—joined those of the group's "chief," Erik Satie, in the symphonic interludes that were a regular feature of Diaghilev's London programming.[22]

By 1922 poet and impresario had made up. Cocteau's influence now made itself felt. Under his aegis, Les Six and the School of Paris went to work for the Ballets Russes. "I get news of you from one and the next," he wrote to Diaghilev in October of that year:

> Satie is so difficult to manage that I lie in wait for *the right moment* . . . You might repay the advance and the trick will be played. S. is only sensible to money. . . . If it vexes you to write, give your commissions to Poulenc or Marie Laurencin—but Poulenc is stricter about terms.[23]

The projects alluded to in this letter—*Le Médecin Malgré Lui* and *Les Biches*—did not immediately come to fruition, as Diaghilev, hard pressed for money, produced only one new work, *Les Noces*, in 1923. But thanks to the bounty of Monte Carlo's Société des Bains de Mer, which ran the famous Casino, by the end of that year more than a half-dozen productions were underway. Several of these were operas—old, French operas—"modernized" by Cocteau's musical protégés: Poulenc (*La Colombe*), Satie (*Le Médecin Malgré Lui*), Auric (*Philémon et Baucis*), Milhaud (*Une Education Manquée*). Two ballets, also unveiled in January 1924, bore the signature of Les Six as well: *Les Fâcheux*, which had music by Auric, and *Les Biches*, with a score by Poulenc. The designers of these ballets, Georges Braque and Marie Laurencin respectively, stood close to the circle: friends, all would collaborate later that year on ballets produced by Comte Etienne de Beaumont for his Soirées de Paris. The artistic direction announced by the Monte Carlo season quickly gained the upper hand in the Diaghilev repertory. In June 1924 *Le Train Bleu* brought together Milhaud, Cocteau (as librettist), and Gabrielle Chanel, the couturière who had designed the costumes for the poet's 1922 theater piece *Antigone*. *Zéphire et Flore*, produced in 1925, had designs by Braque, and *Les Matelots*, another of that year's novelties, a score by Auric. This composer, Cocteau's favorite among Les Six, also supplied the music for *La Pastorale,* a highlight of the 1926 season, while Satie and André Derain, another Beaumont alumnus, pooled their talents in that year's production of *Jack-in-the-Box.* If Diaghilev's wartime troupe had resembled a traveling studio, that of the years 1923–1926 appeared to be a family begotten by Cocteau.[24]

Matching up talent was only one of the services he performed for Diaghilev. As a librettist, Cocteau had a finger in the creation of at least three ballets, although, officially, he received credit only for *Le Train Bleu.* The idea for *Les Biches* came to the poet during his second honeymoon with Diaghilev. By October 1922 the primitive scenario was complete, and Cocteau was proposing both Laurencin and Poulenc as collaborators.[25] With this ballet, which reached the stage in January 1924, lifestyle modernism made its reappearance in the Ballets Russes.

Unlike the vast majority of twenties dance works, *Les Biches* survives in current repertory. Deliciously modern, the ballet takes place among the mannequins and athletes of Cocteau's raffishly fashionable world—frivolous, chic, slightly off-color. The setting is an elegant drawing room; the occasion, a house party; the characters, a hostess and her guests. Costume, no less than setting, struck a modern note: for the women, flapper dresses, headbands, ropes of artificial pearls; for the men, body-hugging trunks that resembled swimsuits. The theme of the ballet came straight from a twenties novel—the charade of modern love, posturing and ironic.

Many of these same elements reappeared in *Le Train Bleu,* Cocteau's last ballet for Diaghilev. Here, the salon has become a fashionable beach; the flappers and athletes, sun-worshipping tarts and gigolos. Beginning with the title, inspired by the train that sped Paris pleasure-seekers from the Gare de Lyon to the resorts of the Azure Coast, *Le Train Bleu* belonged to the folklore of fashion. There was a tennis player à la Suzanne Lenglen, the great French champion of the decade; a golf player in plus-fours modeled on the Prince of Wales; a bathing belle (*la Perlouse*), who emerged from a cabana with yards of pink georgette around her shoulders; a "handsome kid" (Beau Gosse), who performed breathtaking acrobatic stunts. The libretto, in fact, was rife with suggestions of privilege, from the references to physical culture (practised by newly weight-conscious trendsetters) to the details of prop and costume (cigarettes, swimsuits, wrist watches, sunglasses). The costumes, by Chanel, might have come from her customers' wardrobes—hand-knitted swimsuits, rubber slippers (worn by women for bathing), and tight-fitting bathing caps, which soon made their appearance on fashionable beaches. As in *Boeuf* and *Mariés,* Cocteau's libretto juxtaposed details of fashion with images of pastimes and entertainments:

Scene I

Tarts. Gigolos. Sunbathing. Then gigolos run (*in place*) and do rapid physical exercises, while the tarts, scattered in groups, assume the graceful poses of colored postcards. The combination of gestures, and their absurdity, must give the illusion of an operetta chorus when the curtain goes up. (*Do not fear a certain pomp; this will make the style.*) In short, one imagines the characters singing: "We are gigolos, etc. . . ."

Scene II

The door of the cabana opens. A bather [Beau Gosse] (*in a swimsuit*) appears. He poses in the cabana. The tarts group themselves to the right in graceful attitudes. (*One points to her breasts; another puts a finger over her mouth; a third lies down and shakes her legs.*) Think of the groups as they finish the quadrille at the Moulin Rouge. The gigolos come looking for the bather and hoist him up in triumph. (*Look at pictures of boxers carried in triumph after a match.*) They deposit him in the wing and come on again. The tarts recline downstage right. The gigolos line up next to each other facing the audience in front of the cabanas . . . They all turn their faces toward the right wing. Slowly, with long strides, the bather enters; when he nearly reaches the center of the stage, he runs toward the trampoline, springs over it, and disappears into the left wing. His cross and his jump are followed by the faces of the gigolos; after the jump, all the profiles are facing left. Before the music resumes, the orchestra stops, and the dancers, holding the position they had on the final note, form an immobile tableau. (*Between each orchestral ending and reprise, the dancers keep their pose, as in a photograph.*)[26]

Again and again Cocteau stylized the action, casting it in the form of a mechanically reproduced image. His tarts draped themselves into postcard poses; his gigolos hoisted the bather aloft as in pictures of triumphant boxers; his ensemble froze as in a movie. In Scene V he employed a favorite device—slow motion—while in Scene VI he mimicked the action photograph, which had just made its appearance on the sports pages:

Scene VI

The tennis champion enters from the right (*her gait, her poses, her dance, her entire role should take inspiration from magazine snapshots; it should be the same for the golf player*). People racing—photographed with a foot in the air—in front; people talking—photographed with their mouths open; people jumping, tennis: (*reverse, collecting balls, etc. . . .*)[27]

In Scene IX, Cocteau's directions become even more precise:

Fugue . . . for the tennis champion and the golf player. Gesticulation. While one of the two gesticulates, the other crosses his/her arms and listens, eyes in the air. (*The two, side by side, should be almost still, as the man moves the bottom of his foot, while raising an eye to the sky, and the woman shrugs her shoulders, etc. . . .*) Exasperation leads to blows. The one who receives them should stoop, the one who delivers them should be carried away by the gesture into nothingness, turning in place, etc. . . . (*Think of Ch. Chaplin's battles.*) Tarts and gigolos shoot movies, take pictures, wind film, keep score, etc. . . .[28]

Cocteau's libretto makes few allusions to dance. In fact, it contains very few dances. There is a "dance around the cabanas" in Scene V, a "*valse dansée*" in Scene VII, and a handful of duets for the two lead couples, most of which rely heavily on pantomime. The "sports duet" for the tennis champion and the golf player in Scene VI, wrote Cocteau, "should be . . . inspired by the pantomime of singers who move by turns (couplets) and take up the refrain together." Only the "*valse dansée*" had a dance source, and this, typically enough, derived from the music-hall rather than the ballet stage: the acrobatic adagio was a staple of the decade's professional ballroom dancers.

   Le Train Bleu was Cocteau's last venture with the Ballets Russes. Lifestyle modernism, however, outlasted his association with Diaghilev. At the same time, ingredients of Cocteau's recipe—not always through his agency—entered the ballet mainstream. Within the Ballets Russes the mid-twenties witnessed a rash of contemporary-looking works. In *Zéphire et Flore*, the Muses wore flapper dresses and "chic little pork-pie hats" that had far more to do with current fashions than Braque's wispy designs. As the movie star of *La Pastorale*, Felia Doubrovska wore a short fringed skirt that hung from a dropped waist, while the ballet's other women displayed the latest styles in sportswear—pleated skirts and jersey tops. Even ballets with exotic and period themes had contemporary touches. The valet in *Les Fâcheux*, wrote a London critic in 1925, was "clothed like a famous advertisement for tires"; two years later a colleague described the mechanical nightingale in *Le Chant du Rossignol* "as a clown in a red hat and a costume reminiscent of a well-known advertisement for somebody's motor tires." Meanwhile, the production's real nightingale (Alicia Markova) wore the latest craze in trouser fashions—pyjamas. That same year, the transparent mica constructions by Naum Gabo and Anton Pevsner for *La Chatte* reminded the *Sketch* "of a highly stylised kitchen."[29]

   Lifestyle ballet, moreover, figured prominently in repertories other than Diaghilev's. Among the half-dozen dance works presented by Comte Etienne de Beaumont's Soirées de Paris was *Trois Pages Dansées,* mounted (as the program announced) "in collaboration with the magazine *Vogue*." Unlike the season's other works, all choreographed by Massine, *Trois Pages* was staged by Beaumont, making his choreographic debut. The choreography,

⟨1⟩ *Ivan Bilibin, cover for the* Boris Godunov *souvenir program, 1908.*

⟨2⟩ *Feodor Chaliapin in the costume for the 1908 production of* Boris Godunov.

⟨3⟩ *Michel Fokine, ca. 1914.*

⟨4⟩ *Vaslav Nijinsky as the Golden Slave in* Schéhérazade.

⟨5⟩ *Vaslav Nijinsky in the title role of* Petrouchka.

⟨6⟩ *Vaslav Nijinsky as Harlequin in* Carnaval.

⟨7⟩ *Tamara Karsavina in the title role of* Firebird, *London, 1912.*

⟨8⟩ *Valentin Serov, portrait of Tamara Karsavina, 1909.*

⟨9⟩ *Tamara Karsavina as the Queen of Shemakhan in* Le Coq d'Or, *1914.*

⟨10⟩ *Michel Fokine, choreographic notation for* Le Dieu Bleu.

⟨11⟩ *Léon Bakst, costume design for a Bacchante,* Narcisse, *1911.*

⟨12⟩ *Alexandre Benois, costume design for Vicomte René,* Le Pavillon d'Armide.

⟨13⟩ *Robert Montenegro, Vaslav Nijinsky as the Poet in* Les Sylphides.

⟨14⟩ *George Barbier, Vaslav Nijinsky and Tamara Karsavina in* Le Spectre de la Rose.

⟨15⟩ *George Barbier, Vaslav Nijinsky in* L'Après-midi d'un Faune.

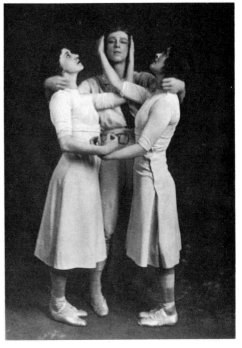

⟨16⟩ *Vaslav Nijinsky in* L'Après-midi d'un Faune, *1912.*

⟨17⟩ *Tamara Karsavina (left), Vaslav Nijinsky, and Ludmilla Schollar in* Jeux, *1913.*

⟨18⟩ *Six women dancers in* Le Sacre du Printemps, *1913.*

⟨19⟩ *Vaslav Nijinsky in the title role of* Till Eulenspiegel, *1916.*

⟨20⟩ *Michel Larionov, costume design for a Young Peasant Girl,* Midnight Sun, *1915.*

⟨21⟩ *Pablo Picasso, the Chinese Conjuror,* Parade, *1917.*

⟨22⟩ *The New York Manager,* Parade, *1917.*

⟨23⟩ *Pablo Picasso, design for the decor of* Le Tricorne, *1919.*

⟨24⟩ *André Derain, design for the backdrop of* La Boutique Fantasque, *1919.*

⟨25⟩ *Léonide Massine as the*
Chinese Conjuror in Parade, *1917.*

⟨26⟩ *Lydia Lopokova in costume*
as the Can-Can Dancer in La Boutique Fantasque.

⟨27⟩ *Léonide Massine as the*
Miller in Le Tricorne, *1919.*

⟨28⟩ *Léon Bakst, "The Queen and Her Pages," design for* The Sleeping Princess, *1921.*

⟨29⟩ *Bronislava Nijinska (left), Lubov Egorova, Lydia Lopokova, Felia Doubrovska, Vera Nemchinova, and Lubov Tchernicheva as the Fairies in* The Sleeping Princess, *1921.*

⟨30⟩ *Ludmilla Schollar (standing, center left) in* Aurora's Wedding, *London, 1924.*

⟨31⟩ *Anatole Vilzak as Eraste and Ludmilla Schollar as a Gossip in* Les Fâcheux, *1924.*

⟨32⟩ *Natalia Gontcharova, sketch for* Les Noces.

⟨33⟩ Les Noces, *Monte Carlo, 1923.*

⟨34⟩ Les Biches, *London, 1924*.

⟨35⟩ Le Train Bleu, *London, 1924*.

⟨36⟩ *Marie Laurencin, design for the drop curtain of* Les Biches, *1924*.

apparently, did not amount to much. But with costumes by Jeanne Lanvin (except for a jockey's outfit, by Hermès) and shoes by Perugia, the ballet was certainly well dressed, as chic as the trio of sexually ambiguous situations of Valentine Hugo's scenario.[30] As early as 1922 the Ballets Suédois, that leading purveyor of ballet experimentalism, had brought to the stage a slice of contemporary Parisian life. *Skating-Rink* had designs by Fernand Léger and music by Arthur Honegger; its setting was a skating rink, its characters, "workers, midinettes, pretty boys with an equivocal allure, and other caricature types."[31] The choreography, by Jean Borlin, drew inspiration from apache dances; the stylized, semiconstructed costumes from colorful skaters' wear. The following year the company produced *Within the Quota*, a piece of Gallicized Americana set to jazz tunes by Cole Porter that parodied the piano music played in silent movie theaters. The striking backdrop, by Gerald Murphy, an American who hovered on the outer edges of the Ballets Russes, was a blow-up of the front page of a Hearst daily, complete with screaming, improbable headlines: "Unknown Banker Buys Atlantic," "Ex-Wife's Heart-Balm Love-Tangle," "Rum Raid Liquor Ban," "Romance Ends in Court." The story, also by Murphy, plotted the mishaps of a newly arrived Swedish immigrant in New York, his encounters with a millionairess, a strutting black vaudevillean, a jazz baby, a cowboy, a social reformer, and, finally, The Sweetheart of the World, a Mary Pickford type who magically transformed the newcomer into a movie star.[32]

Probably the most famous of the Swedish troupe's "contemporary" productions was *Relâche*, which premiered in December 1924 and turned out to be the company's swan song. "*Relâche* is life, life as I love it," wrote Francis Picabia, who wrote the scenario and also designed the ballet:

> life without a morrow, life today, . . . Automobile headlights, ropes of pearls, the slender and rounded forms of women, advertising, music; men in evening dress; movement, play, clear and transparent water, the pleasure of laughter— that's *Relâche* . . . *Relâche* walks through life with a great burst of laughter. *Relâche* is aimless movement. Why think? Why have a convention of beauty and joy?[33]

In the music-halls, dance routinely shared bills with movies. In *Relâche*, with René Clair's *Entr'acte*, film was spliced into the dance work:

> After the cinematic prologue, the curtain rose on a glittering and strange decor . . . There were flashing floodlights that blinded the audience; a fireman who strolled about, smoking non-stop; a woman in an evening dress who made

her entrance through the hall . . . eight men in dinner jackets; games for the woman and several jumping jacks that went on until one of the latter carried her off.[34]

Following Clair's madcap parade of images (in which Picabia and other friends made brief appearances), the authors "trained a cannon at the audience"—posters with such provocative lines as: "Those who are discontent are authorized to clear out" or "There are some—poor imbeciles— who prefer the ballets at the Opéra." The jumping jacks reappeared, stripped, and turned into clowns. The fireman poured water from one bucket to another and then back again. The ballet—if one can call it that—touched off a scandal and the umbrage of most serious critics. Many, one suspects, would have happily traded places with the "imbeciles" at the Opéra.[35]

Rolf de Maré dissolved the Ballets Suédois three months later. Lifestyle modernism continued to flourish, however. The following summer, a highlight of the dance-cum-opera season organized by Marguerite Bériza, a one-time prima donna of the Boston and Chicago operas, was Jean Wiener's jazz ballet *Arc en Ciel*. A concert pianist who took up jazz, Wiener played at Le Boeuf sur le Toit, the celebrated nightspot that took its name from Cocteau's farce, its artistic style from Dada, and its social tone from High Bohemia. Like *Boeuf* and *Within the Quota, Arc en Ciel* exploited the images of a mythic America. "Throughout the ballet, which was stylicized in jazz rhythms," wrote a *Musical America* correspondent, "a Negro banjo player stood in a corner of the stage and strummed jazz, now soft and crooning and again strident in the manner of the vaudeville 'coon shouters.' "[36] Even Bronislava Nijinska, Cocteau's nemesis in the Diaghilev company (their clash will be discussed later), fell victim to the craze. For Theatre Choréographique, the chamber company she organized with the painter Alexandra Exter after leaving Diaghilev early in 1925, Nijinska produced no fewer than three modern-dress ballets: *Touring* (or *The Sports and Touring Ballet Revue*), to Poulenc; *Jazz,* to Stravinsky's *Ragtime*, in which Nijinska donned a hula skirt (along with America, Europe discovered Hawaii in the 1920s); *Holy Etudes,* an abstract work to Bach, in which the dancers, all women, wore dresses with pleated skirts and dropped waists. The following year, for the Teatro Colón in Buenos Aires, she staged *A Orillas del Mar* (At the Seaside), which had costumes "after Chanel," music by Milhaud, and a sporting theme, and sounds suspiciously like a remake of *Le Train Bleu*—without Cocteau. Back in Paris, in 1927, she shocked Opéra audiences with *Impressions de Music-Hall*, featuring chorus girls, "musical clowns," and a cakewalk dancer, impersonated by Carlotta Zambelli, the Opéra's long-reigning *étoile*.[37]

From the start, lifestyle modernism was closely linked to jazz. But with the exception of Darius Milhaud's *La Création du Monde,* which combined jazz elements with a more extended classical form, few ballets exploited jazz with any degree of sophistication. Mostly, jazz served as background; like a Chanel swimsuit, it gave the action of a ballet an aura of chic modernity. This occurred not only on the ballet stage proper, but in the music-halls, where numerous ballet dancers and choreographers went to work in the 1920s. No doubt the massiveness of the invasion induced the anti-jazz backlash that appeared in mid-decade. Reviewing Diaghilev's 1925 *Zéphire et Flore* in the *Nouvelle Revue Française,* Boris de Schloezer made clear his delight that the ballet's composer, Vladimir Dukelsky (who, as Vernon Duke, made a career as a popular American songwriter), had preferred Tchaikovsky to Tin Pan Alley. "One expected jazz band effects; fortunately, the author avoided them, and one finds in *Zéphire* no trace of the Negroid Americanism that has become the very mark of musical modernism, as the whole tone scale was yesterday." Two years later, in a review of the Diaghilev season for the *Christian Science Monitor,* Schloezer's colleague Emile Vuillermoz noted approvingly that "the 'School of Arcueil,' which has dethroned and scattered the group of 'Six,' is returning to a much more harmonious and pleasing musical conception." Of the composer of *La Création du Monde,* he remarked: "And one sees a Darius Milhaud wisely giving up his wild dissonances and polytonality to write a work as sober, pleasant and traditional as his 'Carnaval d'Aix'."[38]

By mid-decade not only were dancers routinely shuttling between concert and variety stage, but also the line demarcating the two was growing increasingly blurred. "It is an established fact," observed Jean Brun-Berty in the French monthly *La Danse,* "that from a choreographic perspective the theater today gives us what formerly the music-hall offered us, and vice versa. Le Train Bleu, presented by the Ballets Russes, confirms this rule."[39] André Levinson echoed the sentiment:

> With *Le Train Bleu* avant-garde ballet gave us notice of its self-willed fall from grace, its solemn abdication to the music-hall. We accepted the portent and abandoned the ballets of Monte Carlo for the attractions of the Olympia . . . Who knows if the music-hall is not destined, before the insolvency and errors of the great lyric stages, to become the refuge of the great tradition of theatrical dance?[40]

Despite its neglect in dance scholarship, the commercial arena was a major locus of ballet activity in the 1920s and a key factor in the rapid dissemination of ballet modernism. Léonide Massine may have achieved his earliest successes with the Ballets Russes, but his artistic personality ripened on the revue stage. *Togo: or The Noble Savage,* his "Amerindian" ballet for *You'd Be Surprised,* a 1923 revue starring George Robey, had all the makings of a Ballets Suédois production: an Afro-Brazilian score by Milhaud, "modern" designs by Duncan Grant, an American setting (the "Wild Cat" Inn in Arizona), and a cast of American exotics—Mexicans, Negroes, an Indian Chief. What *Togo* looked like is anyone's guess. Lydia Sokolova, a longtime Diaghilev dancer who had temporarily left the Ballets Russes, thought the ballet "so poor" that she could hardly remember a thing about it—only the fact that she wore "all-over brown tights with a black wig, had an African make-up and did a war dance." T.S. Eliot, on the other hand, though he had nothing but contempt for the revue itself, waxed eloquent in praise of Massine—"the greatest actor whom we have in London." *Togo* was not the only dance number in this "Jazzaganza" in two acts and fifteen surprises. There was a gramophone number, danced by Ninette de Valois, something called "Trish Trash," to Strauss, performed by Massine and Lydia Lopokova, a "rigaudon from China town," a "ballet," to Chopin, entitled "Les Elégantes," even a variation from *The Sleeping Princess.* (The non-dance line-up was equally a hodge-podge: Little Tich, Marie Leconte in a one-act comedy by Robert de Flers, selections from *The Tales of Hoffmann,* and the Savoy Havana Band, in a "saturnalia of syncopation.")[41]

Two years later Massine went to work for the flamboyant West End producer Charles B. Cochran, contributing three "scenes"—*The Rake, A Hungarian Wedding,* and *Crescendo*—to the revue described by the *Dancing Times* as "the most remarkable 'dance show' . . . ever placed before the London public." *On With the Dance* teamed Massine and Noel Coward, who, as the show's librettist, worked closely with the choreographer on the slice of frenzied modern city life that became *Crescendo.* The ballet, wrote Massine in his memoirs:

> was a real period piece which, in its way, epitomized the whole of the early 1920s. The characters, which included [Alice] Delysia as the Film Star, Eleanora Marra as the Manicure Girl, Pat Kendall as the Mannequin, were very much contemporary types. To counterbalance the women we had a male jazz trio called Three Nifty Nats. I myself was Bobo, the "spirit of the age". My choreography was swift and satirical, in keeping with the score, a composite mixture of popular jazz melodies of which the featured tune was "Pack Up Your Sins."[42]

Unlike Cocteau, Massine packed his "scene" with movement. A photograph, possibly taken in performance, froze the characters *in medias res:* Pat Kendall, in a mannequin's pose; Amelia Allen, in a backbend; Laurie Devine, in a handstand; Eleanora Marra, in a first-position rise in parallel.

The backcloth—angular, abstract forms with the word "café" writ large—was stridently modern, as were the costumes: black tie for the band; flapper dresses for the women. *Crescendo* imitated reality. But it aspired to make that reality the stuff of dance, of movement itself. In an interview with the *Morning Post,* Massine spoke of the need to modernize the danse d'école, to bring classicism in step with the twentieth century:

> Every age has its own way to move and its own dancing modes, and we cannot continue to devise our choreography according to the precepts of the schools of the sixteenth, seventeenth and eighteenth centuries. The so-called classical mode is out of touch with modern life. What we have to do to-day in order to make dancing vital is to learn all we can from the Italo-French School of three hundred years ago, and transpose it into terms of the best in modern jazz. We have to alter the direction of the ancient school, and, by adapting its conventions, its form, and its steps, create a new spirit representative of the spirit of the age.[43]

Lifestyle modernism was born with *Parade,* which joined vanguard form and commercial entertainment for the first time on the ballet stage. The impetus for this alliance came from the futurists; its flowering, however, rested with others. Heading the list was Cocteau, who both Gallicized the futurist formula and blunted its radical edge. Piquant, amusing, replete with accoutrements of modern living, this new brand of modernism was tailored to the palates of *le tout Paris,* or at least to those among it who savored the repasts cooked up by Diaghilev, Rolf de Maré, and Comte Etienne de Beaumont. Beginning with *Parade* and continuing with Cocteau's "Spectacles-Concerts," Maré's Ballet Suédois, Beaumont's Soirées de Paris, and Diaghilev's post-1922 repertory, lifestyle modernism identified the new consumerist chic of the upper class. A theme of these pages has been the transformation of ballet as choreographers strayed ever farther afield of Maryinsky classicism. With lifestyle modernism, the divide widened until the shore from which the first explorers had set sail disappeared from sight. Invented by an avant-garde that despised the past, propagated by artists who scarcely knew it, the genre abjured the twin foundations of classicism: the technique of the danse d'école and the symbolic practice associated with it. Indistinguishable from a host of other entertainments, ballet had lost both its language and its raison d'être.

Although lifestyle modernism is perceived as the style par excellence of twenties ballet, it represented only one trend within the Diaghilev repertory. "Retrospective classicism," on the other hand, has received little attention from scholars. Yet, between 1921, the year of his production of *The Sleeping Princess,* and 1928, when Balanchine created *Apollon Mu-*

sagète, it left its mark on nearly a dozen works that paid homage to the *grand siècle,* the era in French history that roughly dovetailed with the reign of Louis XIV. Just as Picasso discovered Ingrès after the adventure of cubism, so Diaghilev, in the wake of his futurist experiments, rediscovered the glories of the French classical past. In so doing, he allied the Ballets Russes with a deeply conservative phenomenon—the retreat by many postwar artists and intellectuals, especially in France, from the firing lines of avant-garde experiment.

Kenneth E. Silver, in his provocative study of French art from 1914 to 1925,[44] has analyzed this retreat, expressed in a return to figurative styles and nationalist themes, as a response to the reactionary ideology promulgated as part of the war effort. Cocteau, as we have seen, stood at the center of this cultural realignment, articulating the "mediatory" position that had lasting implications for the avant-garde. The conservative turn was felt on the lyric stage as well. The outbreak of hostilities in 1914 closed theaters and opera houses, sending young professionals, from stagehands to premiers danseurs, to the trenches. As the war, which most had thought would end quickly, dragged into its second year, homefront audiences became restive. "Distraction must be had," Paris Opéra director Jacques Rouché told a *Musical America* correspondent, "and none could be morally and psychologically more efficacious than music of the elevating sort."[45] Late in 1915 the Opéra initiated semiweekly matinee performances. At these "concerts," described by Rouché as "an oral history of dramatic music," and the charity benefits that multiplied as the war continued, the ideological foundation of retrospective classicism was laid.

By contrast with the cosmopolitan character of prewar programming, Rouché's wartime entertainments were overwhelmingly French and historical. In a flush of nationalism, German composers were banished from the stage, and in their place audiences heard Lully, Destouches, and Rameau, founders of French opera. Plans were made to produce "the fantastic ballets in which Louis XIV danced in his youth and the so-called 'musical suppers' which diverted him in his old age." But it was not only to masterpieces that Rouché paid tribute. In the historical settings of the concerts he honored the aristocratic and monarchical traditions associated with the *grand siècle,* when France had reigned over European art, manners, and politics:

> It is not only the music of other times that we reproduce but also the settings in which that music was given. The rehearsal of "Esther" by the daughters of the nobility before Mme. Maintenon; a musical soiree at the home of Pouplinière, the protector of Rameau; a session of the French Academy at which

Baif essayed his ingenious coupling of music with the rhythms of Horace and Sappho, and a concert in the Château of Compiègne before the imperial court.[46]

Cultural xenophobia did not end with the Armistice. If anything, the obsession with France's classical and monarchist past increased with the return to normalcy. The Versailles peace conference stirred a flurry of press interest in the architecture, gardens, history, and need for restoration of the château that epitomized more than any other public monument the era of Louis XIV. In 1920 the Musée de Costume opened its doors with a history of French costume, while the following year saw major exhibitions of Fragonard and Watteau and a production of Molière's *Les Fâcheux,* originally devised to fete *le roi soleil.* Interest in seventeenth and eighteenth-century dancing grew, culminating in an exhibition at the prestigious Hôtel Charpentier gallery in January 1923 that featured many prints of ballets presented at the courts of the Sun King and his grandson Louis XV.[47]

The Sleeping Princess (as Diaghilev renamed Petipa's *Sleeping Beauty*) was his first production to acknowledge the new mood. Although the ballet opened in London, it seemed tailor-made for Paris, a fact underscored by the number of French critics who crossed the Channel for the premiere and the number of British critics, especially among the intelligentsia, who looked upon the ballet as a betrayal of Diaghilev's modernist principles. Even before the premiere, moreover, plans were made to bring the work to Paris. On October 8, 1921 Diaghilev and Jacques Rouché signed a contract stipulating that *The Sleeping Beauty* would be produced at the Opéra the following May.[48] This, of course, never happened. The sets and costumes were impounded, and with creditors at his heels Diaghilev beat a hasty retreat across the Channel. Rouché was furious. "In place of *The Sleeping Beauty,*" he wrote to him on April 26:

> you propose to give a fragment of this work, Aurora's Wedding. You understand what difference the substitution of a one-act work . . . for a brilliant . . . and entirely new, full-length one can make at the box office. I had counted on a profitable success, *The Sleeping Beauty* being already known from . . . its numerous performances in London, the magnificence of its staging, its numerous decors and costumes signed by Bakst, and the caliber of its interpreters . . . The solution you propose has nothing but disadvantages: no stars, no decors, no mise-en-scène.[49]

In the end, Rouché took what he could get. *Aurora's Wedding,* a compilation of dances from the court acts of *The Sleeping Beauty,* with additional choreography by Nijinska, received its premiere at France's most prestigious house on May 18, 1922. The accompanying program note—"Classical ballet by Marius Petipa, French choreographer (1822–1910), presented on the occasion of the centenary of his birth"—emphasized the work's Gallic, classical origins.

Diaghilev's attempt to outdo the French at their own game—that is, to resurrect via a masterpiece of the Russian repertory a vision of French monarchical glory—failed. But the imperial theme did not disappear from his repertory. Rather, with the establishment in the autumn of 1922 of Ballets Russes headquarters in Monte Carlo, the winter playground of fashionable Paris, the ancien régime claimed a disproportionate share of his attention. In June 1923, for a fundraising gala sponsored by the "Friends of Versailles," he dazzled the Paris elite with a magnificent spectacle in the Hall of Mirrors—*Aurora's Wedding* "anachronized" by the addition of processionals and vocal interludes. The setting, no less than the format of the "ballet" invoked the entertainments witnessed in that same gallery by the Sun King himself. This "fête merveilleuse" was a foretaste of what now became a staple of Diaghilev's programming. In 1924 and 1925 he produced more than a half-dozen operas and ballets exploiting French classical forms and themes. A few were the genuine article: Michel Pignolet de Montéclair's *Les Tentations de la Bergère,* for instance, actually dated from the period. Others invoked the *grand siècle* via the nineteenth century—Emmanuel Chabrier's *Une Education Manquée* and Charles Gounod's *Philémon et Baucis, La Colombe,* and *Le Médecin Malgré Lui.* Still others—*Les Fâcheux* and *Zéphire et Flore*—were newly minted works with classical themes and titles.

Few of these productions aspired to replicate their originals. Rather, they corresponded to a vision in Diaghilev's mind of a past superficially restyled for the modern palette. To streamline and reorchestrate the existing scores, he called on Darius Milhaud, Francis Poulenc, and Erik Satie. Georges Auric, who had composed incidental music for the 1922 revival of *Les Fâcheux,* was chosen to do the ballet version, while for *Zéphire et Flore,* Diaghilev turned to Vladimir Dukelsky. In visual design, the incongruity between form and content was even more striking. With the exception of *Philémon et Baucis* and *Le Médecin Malgré Lui,* both designed by Alexandre Benois, Diaghilev entrusted this cycle of classical works to modernists. With Juan Gris and Georges Braque receiving the lion's share of Diaghilev's commissions, these tributes to the monarchist past ironically displayed the embellishments of the avant-garde.

Not that these productions were in any way experimental. If anything, they adhered to traditional styles of stagecraft—painted decors, elaborate period costumes, a conventional use of stage space—all of which constructivist and Bauhaus artists had abandoned, and which Diaghilev himself had at least partly abjured during World War I. In fact, about the only thing avant-garde in these productions was the identity of the contributing artists. None of these, however, were collaborators in the true sense of the word. Rather, Gris and Braque were hirelings, taken on for a work previously conceptualized by Diaghilev. For the most part, their designs were strikingly atypical of their painting, with hardly a telltale sign of distortion betraying the authors as one-time makers of cubism. As "visualizers" of a predetermined idea, they found the scope for invention limited, confined in large measure to details and expressed primarily in a tendency toward simplification. Although both Gris and Braque combed seventeenth and eighteenth-century sources for ideas, their designs preferred restraint to retrospectivism. In *Les Tentations de la Bergère,* wrote André Levinson, Gris's

> disdain for trompe l'oeil reduces the decor to a rigid frame. His classical mind, revolted very naturally at the charming and futile liberties of the Regency style—the era of Montéclair—takes Lebrun, rather than Watteau as master. The pink and violet fake marble columns . . . are a reference to Mansard's pilasters in the Hall of Mirrors at Versailles. But here also, Gris reduces the baroque grandiloquence of Mansard, the framing of the cartouches, the profiles of the capitals to simplified formulas. No doubt, Henri Béraud would have accused him of Jansenism.[50]

In *Tentations,* as in Braque's *Zéphire et Flore* and *Les Fâcheux,* costume revealed a similar blend of period and abstract elements. Cuts were simplified; borders edged for dramatic emphasis. Bold geometric motifs appeared as decoration; halos and constructed hemispheres as hats. Elaborate wigs crowned the whole.

At the same time critics noted many allusions to contemporary dress. The Venus depicted on Braque's inner curtain for *Les Fâcheux,* remarked Howard Hannay in the London *Observer,* wore the "dilapidated peignoir" of a goddess *en déshabille.* The designs for *Zéphire et Flore* were "for the most part adaptations of modern fashions," commented the *Sketch.* The *Observer* was more explicit. As Flore, Alice Nikitina was "modishly attired to the waist as for the Champs-Elysées . . . The Muses had chic little pork-pie hats and earrings, quite in keeping with the only Olympus they had ever known—one nearer Deauville than Thessaly."[51] If period costume and contemporary couture more than occasionally overlapped in these ballets, this only emphasized the logic of disjunction central to the genre as a whole.

In all these works, moreover, designer and choreographer labored in isolation, and even to cross purpose. In *Les Tentations de la Bergère* Gris's cumbrous set, with platforms of varying heights, seems to have obstructed rather than enhanced Nijinska's choreographic plan. By the same token, Braque's costumes for *Les Fâcheux* overlooked the dancers who had to wear them. "They were . . . very difficult to dance in," recalled Lydia Sokolova. "They were unbecoming and with heavy flat hats tilted over the eyes, and heavy wigs, they gave an impression of weight."[52] In the absence of collaborative exchange, good ideas came to nought. Among these was Braque's intention of having the dancers disappear from sight by turning the plain brown backs of their costumes to the audience (the fronts were in period style), creating the impression that they had vanished into the brown and ocher backdrop. For whatever reason, Nijinska did not incorporate the device into her choreography, an oversight that led Cocteau to remark that "the true dance in *Les Fâcheux* was the play of [Braque's] beiges, chestnuts, and greys."[53] Rather than collaborations, the ballets of this period were cocktails mixed in Diaghilev's mind, with design, rather than dance providing the outstanding flavor.

Retrospective classicism was hardly a Diaghilev exclusive. Both the Ballets Suédois and the Soirées de Paris exploited French period themes, as did the Paris Opéra—often in tandem with the most blatant modernism. Roland Manuel's scenario for *Le Tournoi Singulier,* produced by the Ballets Suédois in 1924, drew inspiration from Louise Labé's sixteenth-century poem "Débat de folie et d'amour." The work was a piece of modernized mythology: Eros succumbs to Folly while reading a Paris newspaper and daydreaming about a pair of lady golfers in boxer shorts. In keeping with the theme, the dances, by Jean Borlin, and the costumes, by Foujita, juxtaposed "ancient" and modern styles. Earlier that year the Soirées de Paris presented two classical pieces: *Salade,* a commedia ballet set in the eighteenth century that teamed Massine, Braque, and Milhaud, and *Gigue,* which had dances by Massine, designs by Derain, and music by Bach and Handel. Visually and choreographically, *Gigue* sought to recapture the spirit of the *grand siècle.* Derain's setting, a rectangular screen depicting a grove, a statue, and a vase, aspired, wrote André Levinson, to an "ironical summary of royal, 'baroque' display." The choreography also modeled itself after baroque style, with sparkling batterie, quick frappés, and in the climactic pas de trois, ronds de jambe sautés.[54]

At the Paris Opéra, too, dance paid tribute to the French past. In 1921 Fokine mounted *Le Rêve de la Marquise,* a one-act ballet to Mozart set in the eighteenth century. Two years later came *Cydalise et le Chèvre-pied,* which may well have been Rouché's answer to *The Sleeping Princess.* This "charming thing in the manner of Sèvres porcelain," wrote Levinson, "juggles with anachronism and delights in historical paradox. What matters . . . is the grace of faded things, their naughty and melancholic smile; not the vase, but the perfume; not the austere truth, but the imaginary splendor." The choreography, by Opéra ballet master Léo Staats, less inspired than the theme of rustic gallantry, relied chiefly on pantomime. But there were also hints of Nijinsky's *L'Après-midi d'un Faune* in the angular arms and profiled postures of the fauns, Fokine's *Daphnis and Chloë* in the "monologue" danced and mimed by Styrax, and his *Spectre de la Rose* in the delicately sensual "dialogue" for the sly damsel and her ingenuous swain.[55] In 1925 *Le Triomphe de l'Amour,* a court ballet created in 1681 to music by Jean-Baptiste Lully, "reentered" the repertory. With designs by Maxime Dethomas and choreography by Staats, the production invoked the spirit rather than the letter of its distant forebear. As the Opéra paid homage to its classical past, it also attended to a more recent legacy. In 1919 *Sylvia* (in new choreography by Staats) reappeared at the Palais Garnier, followed in 1924 by *Giselle* (staged by Nicholas Sergeyev, the former Maryinsky regisseur) and the next year by a one-act version of *La Source* (choreographed by Staats). Pastiche romanticism also found a place, with *Taglioni chez Musette,* an "evocation" to music of the 1830s, mounted by Staats in 1920, and Ivan Clustine's *Suite de Danses,* a prewar reverie along the lines of *Les Sylphides* revived in 1922.[56]

In the totality of these French period ballets, one discerns an impulse akin to the neoclassicism that emerged in French art and letters in the years immediately following the war. I say impulse, because Diaghilev's obsession with the past did not extend to dance. Only on rare occasions, such as the coda devised by Nijinska for *Les Fâcheux* and some of her dances for *Les Tentations de la Bergère,* did the choreography even distantly evoke period styles. Yet even here, there were stridently modern elements: angular poses, distorted gestures, positions with the legs in parallel. In *Les Fâcheux* Levinson also detected an element of parody: the dance for the shuttlecock players (one of whom was Ninette de Valois) reminded him of Cocteau's mock classical choreography in *Les Mariés de la Tour Eiffel.*[57] Such incongruities probably reflected Nijinska's discomfort with her material. But because they appeared to equally disturbing effect in works by other Diaghilev choreographers of the period, they suggest that by mid-decade Diaghilev had lost faith in the ability of ballet to convey anything more profound than studied inconsequence.

The postwar obsession with classical material had its source in the trauma of the war and its aftermath. In a 1924 article published in the *Nouvelle Revue Française,* Jacques Rivière spoke of the crisis of the romantic concept of literature as young writers, tormented by the yearning for absolutes, labored under a "radical powerlessness to produce something in which they have faith and that stands for something greater than themselves, a creation comparable to the creations of God."[58] In ballet, however, little of that pessimism could be discerned. If anything, frivolity became the touchstone of Diaghilev's art. Trifling with art has a long and respected history. But in the Ballets Russes of the 1920s, the frivolous, however much it seemed to upset the artistic apple cart, went hand in hand with profoundly conservative elements. In the context of postwar France, retrospective classicism implied more than a taste for hallowed masterpieces. It summed up a view of society—ordered, aristocratic, and nationalist—dear to the era's protofascists. The pairing of modernism with social privilege was not the only disturbing union that took place in the twenties repertory. In the trends that appeared and disappeared with the speed of seasonal fashions, ballet was wed to the idea of disposable chic, a new form of market-imposed privilege; it had become "a *magasin de luxe,* an exclusive *salon* designed to exhibit international art at its most *chic* and esoteric."[59]

Yet by some strange dialectical process, the same decade that witnessed the demise of the classical idea in dancing also presided over its rebirth. Until recently, historians traced the origins of neoclassicism to Balanchine's *Apollon Musagète,* produced by Diaghilev in 1928. Since then, a similar claim has been made for Nijinska's *Les Noces* and *Les Biches,* created for the Ballets Russes in 1923 and 1924 respectively. Certainly, these are the oldest surviving works to reveal the intense preoccupation with balletic language and the analytic use of that language identified with neoclassicism. But in Nijinska's case, at least, something akin to neoclassicism had appeared in her work even earlier—simultaneously, in fact, with her first modernist choreography, created in the Soviet Union in the late teens and early twenties. This phenomenon was not unique to Nijinska: it appears in the work of other Soviet choreographers of the period, including both Fedor Lopukhov and Kasian Goleizovsky. For the Russian avantgarde, non-objective modernism, particularly in its constructivist guise, seems to have been a major catalyst of ballet neoclassicism.

Nijinska is no stranger to these pages. Yet only now does the helpmate of earlier chapters appear as a creator in her own right—a transformation all the more remarkable because she was a woman, one of very few to make a career as a ballet choreographer. Of crucial importance were the years she spent in Russia between 1914 and 1921. Separated from her brother, fired by the Revolution's brave new art, she created her first abstract works as early as 1919. Diaghilev had made the transition to modernism via futurism. In Nijinska's case the catalyst seems to have been constructivism. Nijinska first met Alexandra Exter, an experimentalist painter who stood at the forefront of the emerging constructivist movement, in Moscow just after the October Revolution. The two became fast friends, and when Exter opened a studio in Kiev in 1918 (where Nijinska had been living since 1916), close artistic associates. Exter's search in 1919–1920 for a new kind of art that was both non-representational and utilitarian was reflected in Nijinska's own experiments of the period. These were conducted on two fronts: in the choreography of her Ecole de Mouvement, the studio she opened in Kiev in 1919, and in the theoretical speculations that culminated in her treatise *The School of Movement (Theory of Choreography)*, published in 1920. Like the choreography of these years, Nijinska's treatise has been lost. But in a related essay, "On Movement and the School of Movement," its key ideas are recapitulated. Among these is the emphasis on movement:

> Of course, movement is a concept that would not unnaturally spring to the mind of a choreographer. But Nijinska's idea of it seems markedly constructivist in several respects. For one thing, she uses the revealing metaphor of the machine, so dear to the constructivists. For another, she shares with them the idea of movement as a dynamic force pervading every aspect of a work and unifying it. Third, like the constructivists, she analyzes form "objectively"— that is, she examines movement in terms of its temporal and spatial properties. Fourth, she treats her subject as an investigation leading to the discovery of new forms, an experimental approach adopted by the constructivists in the post-Revolutionary "laboratory period." Fifth, she seems implicitly to share the utopianism of the constructivists—to embrace movement as a reflection of the exhilarating momentum of modern life.[60]

Along with movement Nijinska's essay reveals an abiding classical faith. Unlike the traditionalists (among whom Nicolas Legat and critic Akim Volynsky figured prominently), who viewed classicism as unchangeable, she conceived the ballet past as a renewable legacy. "The contemporary school," she wrote:

> must broaden itself, must enlarge its technique, to the same degree that contemporary choreography has by departing from the old classical ballets . . . Today's ballet schools do not give the dancer the necessary training to work with choreographic innovators. Even the Ballets Russes . . . did not create a school to parallel its innovations in the theater. The dancers of this company were always transient, invited from other theaters and schooled by masters of the old style, who trained them in a mechanics too primitive for today's choreographic demands. Such masters preserved intact the style of 1880–1900 . . . The insistent desire of the Ballets Russes school to lead the dancer away from the mechanics of modern ballet, to deprive the choreographer of all his new achievements, seems astounding. At the foundation of the school we see nothing deriving from Fokine, Nijinsky, or others. Yet a choreographer who

worked for Diaghilev was required above all to abjure the old school but nevertheless to expand the artistic possibilities of the classical dance.[61]

In *Les Noces* and *Les Biches,* created by Nijinska for the Ballets Russes in 1923 and 1924 respectively, constructivism and neoclassicism received their first, cogent expression on Diaghilev's stage.

In 1921 word reached Nijinska that her brother had entered a mental institution in Vienna. Turning her studio over to an advanced student, she left Russia with her mother and her two children. In September she rejoined the Ballets Russes in London, where preparations were underway for Diaghilev's revival of *The Sleeping Beauty.* Two years before, at the State Opera Theater in Kiev, she had staged a full-length *Swan Lake* based on the Petipa/Ivanov version she had learned at the Maryinsky. Nevertheless, "Diaghileff's idea in producing the *Sleeping Princess* came . . . as a surprise," she later wrote:

> since it seemed the negation of the fundamental "religion" of the ballet as he conceived it, and of his searching towards the creation of a new ballet . . . I started my first work full of protest against myself. I had just come back from Russia in revolution, and after many a production of my own over there, the revival of the *Sleeping Princess* seemed to me an absurdity, a dropping into the past, mere nonentity. Naturally what I wanted and what I strove for was a return to the former tendencies of Diaghileff's ballet . . . in which I had been brought up from my early youth . . .[62]

In addition to rehearsing the ballet, reconstructed by Nicholas Sergeyev, the Maryinsky regisseur who had left Russia with notated scores of *Beauty* and other Petipa ballets, Nijinska contributed new choreography—according to the program, the "Action-Scenes" and Hunting Dances in Act II, Aurora's Variation in the same act, and the tales of Bluebeard, Scheherazade, and Innocent Ivan and His Brothers (later known as "The Three Ivans") in Act III. She also choreographed a fourth fairytale, "The Porcelain Princesses," and presumably the fairy variation added by Diaghilev in the prologue.[63] Whatever her initial misgivings, she acquitted herself admirably. Cyril W. Beaumont summed up her contribution:

> Several years have passed since Nijinska appeared with the Diaghileff Company. It is earnestly to be hoped that she has come to remain, for she is every whit as great an artist as her brother. She, too, is an excellent *chorégraphe,* as she showed in her arrangement of the additional dances in Act III [known today as Act II] and the tales of *Bluebeard, Schéhérazade* and *Innocent Ivan.*[64]

To Nijinska, however, choreography meant far more than arranging dances. Like her modern-dance sisters and Soviet experimentalist brothers, she regarded the entirety of a production as the choreographer's bailiwick. Overwhelmingly, the look of Diaghilev's ballets in the twenties reflected the vision of their designers. In *Les Noces,* however, things were the other way around: here, the choreographer, seizing the directorial initiative, subordinated the design to the dance. Nijinska had very definite ideas about how the ballet should look, and these clashed head-on with Diaghilev's. In 1922 the two visited the studio of Natalia Gontcharova, the artist he had selected to design the ballet. "There were about 80 sketches," Nijinska later wrote, "admirably drawn, magnificent colors, theatrical and sumptuously Russian":

> Both men and women wore heavy costumes, the long robes of the women trailing on the ground, heads decorated with high kokochnoks, the men with beards, all shod in heavy footwear—boots and shoes on heavy heels . . . The body, the instrument of the dancer, attired in such a costume, its movements concealed, is like a violin enclosed in its case. The sketches of Gontcharova seemed to me to be diametrically opposed to the music of Stravinsky and also to my conception of the choreography of the ballet. Once outside Gontcharova's studio, Serge Pavlovitch turned to me. "Well, Bronia, you are very quiet. I hope the costumes for *Les Noces* delighted you."
>
> "Frankly," I replied, "these costumes, in themselves, are magnificent and may be very good for a performance of a Russian opera, but completely impossible for any ballet and for *Les Noces* most of all. In no way do they respond to the music of Stravinsky as I hear it, nor to the way I already see *Les Noces.*
>
> "Stravinsky and I, however," rejoined Diaghilev, coldly, "have approved Gontcharova's costumes. And so, Bronia, I shall not let you direct *Les Noces* either."
>
> "Fine, Sergei Pavlovitch," was my response, "for that is exactly what I wanted to say—with such costumes I cannot create the choreography for this ballet."[65]

Diaghilev dropped the project until the following spring, when he suddenly announced that he intended to produce the ballet in Paris. Amazingly, he gave Nijinska the upper hand. She reiterated her conditions: "There should not be any colorful ostentation . . . I see the costumes as being of the utmost simplicity and all alike." Diaghilev nodded, and ordered new designs from Gontcharova.[66] Nijinska had conceived the work in strictly functionalist terms. The decor was blue-grey, with only the outline of a window to relieve the monotony. There were benches for the parents and, in the fourth tableau, a platform from which they and the newlyweds gazed down on the revelry of their guests. The costumes were equally functional: for the women, brown pinafores and white blouses; for the men, brown trousers and white peasant shirts—abstractions of everyday country wear. Drab, uniform, impersonal, the costumes, like the men and women who wore them, evoked an anonymous, peasant mass. In fact, the costumes bore a startling resemblance to the proletarian dress adopted by Meyerhold in *The Magnanimous Cuckold,* which officially inaugurated theatrical constructivism in 1922, and by the "Blue Blouse" troupes, which proliferated in the Soviet Union in the first half of the twenties. Nijinska herself preferred blue—the color of worker denims—to brown for the costumes, but acceded to Gontcharova's wishes. Brown, the painter felt, stressed the proximity of the ballet's community to the earth.[67]

In his abrasive review of the ballet, André Levinson referred to Nijinska's choreography as "Marxist." Specifically, he accused her of slighting the individual for the mass: in "swallowing" the dancer, he wrote, she had "leveled" his art.[68] *Les Noces,* in fact, was predicated on the very absence of the individual. The bride and the groom, and their respective sets of parents, exert no control over their destiny; unwilled, they are victims of a higher power. Within the godless universe of the ballet, design is fate: architecture spells out the theme of social determinism. Nijinska masses her ensemble into human pyramids, phalanxes, mounds, and wedges— monoliths as terrible as the peasant customs of old Russia, where girls were torn from their mothers' arms and married off. *Le Sacre du Printemps* had also been a mass, tragic work and, as such, was clearly a forerunner of *Les Noces.* But Nijinska went far beyond her brother's ritual configurations. Fully abstract, her spatial architecture transposed to dance the non-objective forms of the constructivist. Such forms abound in Nijinska's notebooks and diagrams of the period. Worked on graph paper, the diagrams are totally geometric, as if the space of the stage, represented by an enclosing square, encompassed only abstract forms. Often these are circular figures—quadrants, arcs, loops, spheres. At other times they take a linear form: wedges, triangles, and squares that come straight from the canvases of Malevich or Tatlin. Several of these forms reappear in the human massings of *Les Noces.*

These massings reveal constructivist influence in yet another way. Movement had long been an essential ingredient of Russian vanguard theater. In the early Soviet period, directors like Meyerhold freely borrowed from gymnastics, as did the Blue Blouse troupes, which made "acrobatic" and "physical" dancing an important feature of their skits. The pyramid that ends *Les Noces* has a number of Soviet analogues, from the Blue Blouse "oratoria"—dramatic forms at the end of which the actors constructed symmetrical forms or symbols such as a star or a factory complex—to Meyerhold's biomechanical exercise "building the pyramid," which could involve several actors and result in complex towers.[69] Who knows how many of the ballet's other startling configurations had their origin in the movement experiments of early Soviet directors.

Although *Les Noces* was not a narrative work, it did contain narrative elements. "Do you remember the first scene?" Diaghilev had asked. "We are in the home of the bride-to-be, she is sitting in a big Russian armchair, at the side of the stage, her friends are combing her hair and dressing her braids . . ." "No, Serge Pavlovitch, . . . the chair's not necessary, the comb is not necessary and the hair-combing even less so."[70] Ruthlessly, Nijinska purged the ballet of narrative, just as she had purged it of "Russo-Boyar" color. The result was an abstract work, in which the four tableaux—The Blessing of the Bride, The Blessing of the Groom, The Departure of the Bride, and The Wedding Feast—masked a purely choreographic intent. Nijinska later described her conflict with Diaghilev over the libretto:

> In my theatre of 1920 in revolutionary Russia my first works . . . were the *Twelfth Rhapsody,* Liszt's *Mephisto Waltz* and other ballets "without libretti." Diaghileff did not sympathise with the idea . . . "[It] is not a ballet," he used to say, "it is some abstract idea, a symphony. It is foreign to me." He could not readily discard the idea of a literary libretto for the ballet. Yet in spite of this, with great efforts, I was able to carry my ideas of the form of the ballet as I conceived them into my productions with Diaghileff. These ballets of mine . . . carried out the negation of the literary libretto, having a pure dance form for their foundation and moulding this into a new species of composition. *Noces* was the first work where the libretto was a hidden theme for a pure choreography; it was a choreographic concerto.[71]

Les Noces also revealed a new and cogent classicism—the renewable legacy that became Nijinska's credo. Most of the ballet's steps belong to the traditional lexicon. Nearly all, however, have been subtly altered. In the opening tableau, where friends manipulate the ten-foot-long braids that symbolize the bride's virginity, feet cross and recross in a quick pas de bourrée that stresses the toe's downward stab into the floor, not the upward lift of the knee. Her intention, Nijinska has said, was to invoke the action of braiding. But the movement's percussiveness conveys pain and violence as well: intercourse, implied by the bedroom to which the bride and groom repair just before the curtain falls, climaxes the day's festivities. Critic Edwin Denby saw the ballet in 1936, when, under Nijinska's supervision, it was revived by Colonel W. de Basil's Monte Carlo Ballet Russe. "Amazingly few movement-motives are used," he wrote:

> and only the clearest groupings and paths, making the rhythmic subtlety obvious by contrast. That all these movement-motives should be accentuating

the direction into the floor leads to such interesting results as that ballet dancers more familiar with the opposite direction do these movements with a curious freshness; that the leaps seem higher; that further, the "pointes" get a special significance and hardness (almost a form of tapping), . . . and, as a further example, this general downward direction gives the heaped bodies a sense further than decoration and the conventional pyramid at the end, the effect of an heroic extreme, of a real difficulty.[72]

Again and again Nijinska "grounds" the aerial: jumps yield to gravity, rather than appearing to defy it; bodies in huddled clumps bend as if weighted by centuries of toil. Fokine had used arms to open the body. Nijinska, by contrast, used them to hold the body in check. With this unfree body Nijinska gave individual meaning to the ballet's larger social tragedy.

The classicism of *Les Noces* appears most obviously in the use of pointe. Early modernists had tended to eschew pointe. Nijinska, however, chose to keep it. As Denby pointed out, she even gave it "a special significance," a "tapping" and "hardness" that defied conventional usage. But this only scratches the surface of Nijinska's accomplishment. In ballet the metaphor of pointe is at least as important as its technique. In fact, since romanticism, the femininity embodied in pointe has been a central thematic of ballet. *Les Noces* challenged this ideology. Rather than femininity, the ballet spoke of male power and female pain; the stabbing pointes, "masculine" in their violence, enacted, so to speak, the drama of sexual penetration. Throughout the ballet, in fact, the choreography aspires to a "genderless" language. There is no support work, no separate spheres of movement. Men and women dance the same steps and endow these steps with the same quality. In Nijinska's hands sexual difference has no relation to choreographic destiny.

As with her brother, Nijinska's art turned on deeply personal obsessions. In his case, these had reflected the ambiguities of sexual identity; in hers, they expressed a profound unease with established definitions of gender. There is no indication that Nijinska was a feminist. Nevertheless, the pessimism with which she views heterosexual physical relations, to say nothing of marriage, suggests that something akin to a feminist consciousness was at work in *Les Noces*. Consider the circumstances of her life at the time: her lack of physical beauty (for which she was taken to task by critics); her position as a divorcée (she threw out her husband after discovering his mistress was pregnant) supporting two young children and an aging mother; the fact that she was a woman doing a man's job; the misogyny of Diaghilev's immediate circle. In her description of the ballet, gender weighs heavily:

The story of *Les Noces* takes place in a peasant family in old Russia. I saw a dramatic quality in such wedding ceremonies of those times in the fate of the bride and groom, since the choice is made by parents to whom they owe complete obedience—there is no question of *mutuality of feelings.* The young girl knows nothing at all about her future family nor what lies in store for her. Not only will she be subject to her husband, but also to his parents. It is possible that after being loved and cherished by her own kin, she may be nothing more in her new, rough family than a useful extra worker, just another pair of hands. The soul of the innocent is in disarray—she is bidding good-bye to her carefree youth and to her loving mother. For his part, the young groom cannot imagine what life will bring close to this young girl, whom he scarcely knows, if at all. How can such souls rejoice during their wedding ceremonies; they are deep in other thoughts . . . From the very beginning I had this vision of *Les Noces.*[73]

In *Les Biches,* created within six months of *Les Noces,* the sexual theme took an explicitly erotic and analytic form. Here, in fact, Nijinska cracked open the gender codes of classical style, transforming a piece of twenties chic into a critique of sexual mores. The ballet, as we have said, owed its genesis to Cocteau, who wrote the original scenario. There was tuneful music by Poulenc and pastel designs by Marie Laurencin—favorites of Diaghilev's circle. The characters themselves might have hailed from his fashionable milieu: bright young things, who could have doubled as Chanel mannequins; gigolos; a hostess; a pair of teen-aged sapphists; a couple engaged in sex play. The situation—a house party (hence the English title, *The House Party*)—was equally a hallmark of fashionable living.

If the setting for *Les Noces* had been asexual, that of *Les Biches* ("does" or "darlings" in French) was voluptuously feminine. The ballet opened in a flood of pink light. The drop curtain, in Laurencin's signature pastels—greys, blues, salmons, mauves—depicted a woman en déshabille entwined in a circle of pets—horses, does, monkeys: a secluded scene, fraught with erotic possibility. The back cloth added a masculine presence: a blue mound jutted to a phallic point against a pink field. The costumes reiterated the sexualized palette of the decor. The women of the ensemble wore pink; the men and the Garçonne—in French, a bachelor or "mannish" girl—blue. The sofa, locus of the ballet's erotic games, was also blue. Diaghilev, it has been said, chose Laurencin to design *Les Biches* because her art presented "the same ambiguous blend of innocence and corruption" as the ballet.[74] What he could not have anticipated was that the "intemperate and antisocial" Nijinska (his words) would transform it into a work of polymorphous perversity.[75]

Biches explored a host of taboo themes—narcissism, voyeurism, fe-

male sexual power, castration, sapphism—with a directness hitherto un-
paralleled on the ballet stage. Eleven years before, in *Jeux,* the second installment of his erotic autobiography, Nijinsky had opened the subject. But
where this ballet had revealed the anguish of a man uncertain of his sexual
identity, *Biches* expressed the pessimism of a woman soured on relationships with men. For Nijinska sex was a commodity, packaged with care
and paraded in an erotic department store, the chic salon where the ballet
is set. In this all-female seraglio women preen themselves, displaying a
pretty knee, a slim leg, a curvaceous shoulder. Competition is rife. Look
at me, they seem to coo, uselessly, it turns out, for the men they seek to
entice are conspicuously absent. Eventually, of course, they do appear, but
what men—three bicep-flexing look-alikes more enamored of their prowess than of the girls out to snare them. Not that Nijinska's athletes are
totally oblivious to female charm. There is a mysterious girl in blue, whose
very coldness stimulates the passion of the male she allows to seduce her.
And there is the hostess, a commanding figure, who takes her pleasure
with all three. Only the girls in grey—a pair of innocent sapphists—stand
apart from the chase. Alone among the ballet's twosomes and threesomes,
their relationship displays the "mutuality of feelings" that Nijinska postu-
lated as a matrimonial ideal.

To some extent, all ballets are about performing and looking. In *Biches,*
however, Nijinska takes both to their logical extreme, giving us a critique
of the narcissism and voyeurism that make up the business of sex. Again
and again she uses arms to draw attention to the body's erogenous zones.
Her mannequins parade with a hand to one shoulder; her Garçonne with
a hand cupped to the face or, when posed in arabesque, with a hand on
each thigh—emphasizing the crotch between. Her athletes, for their part,
round their arms like champion weight-lifters. Throughout the ballet,
moreover, the dancers eye one another, then train their sights on the audience in attitudes that range from challenging to seductive and vulnera-
ble: rarely has the gaze exposed its sexual intent so nakedly on the dance
stage. That gaze thrusts into relief the erotic character of performance itself and the fact that seduction and voyeurism are built into the very structure of ballet's most canonical forms. In Nijinska's pas de deux, for instance, the partners observe each other's variations, not discretely from the
sidelines—as is usually the case—but in full view of the audience. Here, as
in the Hostess's dalliance with the athletes, Nijinska reveals the bravura
dance as a consumerist display, with sex as the commodity for sale.

Redefining gender boundaries was certainly a theme of twenties fashion, as it was of art in that decade. But Nijinska took this further than any
of her dance contemporaries. Where others merely parodied ballet stereotypes, she exposed the very codes of classical gendering—the conventions

of language, style, and form that defined the art's traditional representation of masculine and feminine. *Les Noces* had used pointe to intimate the violence of the marriage bed. *Les Biches,* by contrast, used pointe ironically, linking familiar conventions of dance behavior to the most stereotypical forms of feminine behavior. For the corps Nijinska devised a strut on full pointe, a balletic equivalent of the mannequin's prance—studied, artful, pretty. But this step, however suggestive in appearance, had a long history, recalling innumerable Petipa variations in which the ballerina ran, hopped, and jumped on toe, displaying, so to speak, the coloratura of her pointes. The artifice of Nijinska's prance, coupled with its narcissism, suggests that the femininity of her women is only skin-deep, a subterfuge applied like make-up, a construction elaborated over time by men, not an innate female property. She treats the male dance in a similar "deconstructive" way. The opening trio for the athletes calls for entrechats-six and double tours en l'air—staples of the male bravura dance. But instead of using these steps, as did Petipa, incrementally, she brought each to a dead stop, thereby exposing their pretentiousness. Men, she seems to say, are peacocks; masculinity, a flatulent pose. And in making her identically dressed musclemen always dance in unison, she portrays them as clones and mindless conformists. What she has done is separate the biological fact of sex from the social reality of gender, a feat all the more remarkable in view of the canonical forms with which she accomplished it.

Unlike most of her dance contemporaries, Nijinska refuted the idea that biology was destiny. In *Biches* at least two of her characters—the Hostess and the Garçonne—transgress gender boundaries: both are women who behave like men. The most intriguing of the two is the Hostess, Nijinska's own role, a vigorous, assertive woman on the prowl. Like a man, Nijinska's queen bee wears soft slippers, not pointe shoes. She also dances like a man: her flying jumps and "beaten" steps are the everyday stuff of male choreography. The contrast between the sophisticated femininity of her accessories—egrets, Chanel pearls, a cigarette holder—and the masculinity of her dancing forms one of the ballet's most subversive images: the Hostess is a man trapped in a female body. Equally provocative is the Garçonne, a boyish seductress who goes through the motions of heterosexual coupling like a practised demimondaine. Her entrance, a manège of bourrées, sets the tone for the duet that follows—icy, deadpan, and mechanical. Nijinska's pas de deux rests on a bedrock of classical convention. There is a supported adagio with promenades and balances in arabesque, a pair of variations, and a coda that climaxes in a triumphant shoulder lift, an echo of the adagio in the Shades scene of *La Bayadère* and the grand pas de deux in *The Nutcracker*. "You put a man and a woman on the stage, already you have a story," Balanchine once said. In the great nineteenth-century ballets, that story was romantic love, the joining of male and female in an image of oneness. *Les Biches,* by contrast, divorces the appearance of love from its reality. For most of the duet, the partners never so much as exchange a glance. They go through the motions of foreplay, but remain totally separate—sex without union. In divorcing love from the formal conventions of romance, Nijinska also exposed the stylized erotics of the ballerina: her cold, triumphant beauty, self-serving technical wizardry, willful personality, and consummate artifice. Rather than a boy, presented for the sake of propriety as a girl, the Garçonne is either an old-style ballerina in ambisexual drag or a fabulous drag queen who happens to be female.

Nijinska's unease with traditional representations of femininity revealed itself time and again in her work. In staging *Petrouchka,* for instance, she shifted the emphasis in the Ballerina role. Where Fokine, in the original, had mocked the display of shallow virtuosity, Nijinska, in her version, conceived the part as a female grotesque. Nijinska's own performing career offers more than a few gender anomalies. In a century that has seen few women perform *en travesti,* Nijinska impersonated any number of male characters, most of her own creation. The first time she did so appears to have been at Diaghilev's insistence. However, the idea of assuming her brother's role in *L'Après-midi d'un Faune,* a role created on her own body, suggests something more: that at the start of her career as a choreographer, she had to possess Nijinsky physically to exorcise him creatively; she had literally to become him to become herself. The *Faune* revival took place in 1922. Two years later, she filled in for Stanislas Idzikowski as Lysandre, the dancing master in *Les Fâcheux.* In the 1930s, long after she had left the Ballets Russes, she created two male roles for herself: Pedrollino in *Les Comédiens Jaloux* (1932) and the title role in *Hamlet* (1934). That decade also saw her cultivate a masculine glamor image: in several portraits she wears Dietrich-style tuxedos. Offstage, no less than on, she mocked gender differences. Ironically, the one unambiguous image of femininity that appears in *Biches* is associated with girlhood. The friendship of the girls in grey is artless, tender, innocent. The end of their duet brings knowledge: in the adult world their affection has a name, and not a nice one. By the time the coda arrives, the two have joined the herd of prancing coquettes. The real trauma of Nijinska's life, one feels, was becoming a woman: exchanging, like the Bride of *Noces,* the cosiness of a mother's arms for the uncertain comforts of a husband's; discovering that what people regarded as feminine—grace, charm, beauty— she lacked. Only a plain woman could have made *Les Biches.*

Nijinska's third major ballet for Diaghilev was *Le Train Bleu.* But here, she was thrown into a collaboration with a man who had rather different views. Cocteau, like Nijinska, was fascinated with gender, as his brilliant essay on Barbette, the American aerialist who performed in female garb, attests. Cocteau, however, took a dim view of women. "In the creator," he wrote in *Cock and Harlequin*, "there is necessarily a man and a woman, and the woman is almost always unendurable."[76] Not unexpectedly, the collaboration of the two artists on *Le Train Bleu* was an unhappy one. In fact, it was fraught with misery on both sides. The backstage drama began with the first rehearsals, which took place in Cocteau's absence. "The best thing," he wrote to Diaghilev in February 1924:

> would be for me to wait for you and go back with you. Ask Nijinska how she's feeling about me. I am not going to make a move unless I am sure she will listen to me, for ridiculous diplomatic games are useless. I do not insist that my name appear on the program as director . . . but, in exchange, I do insist on being listened to.[77]

Nijinska followed some of Cocteau's directions. The dances, dotted with cartwheels and handstands and body-tossing lifts, had the gymnastic flavor he wanted, as did her gestural inventions, which included swimming and other movements derived from sports. But she also made changes. The pas de deux for the tennis players, for instance, changed from a comic flirtation to a love duet, while story elements were added to clarify the libretto. Everything went well until the company arrived in Paris for the final rehearsals. Cocteau, who now saw the ballet for the first time, was in high dudgeon: Nijinska had betrayed his ideas. What happened in the following days will probably never be known. According to Boris Kochno, he intervened again and again, interrupting rehearsals in highhanded fashion and substituting pantomime scenes for dances that Nijinska had created. Anton Dolin, for whom Cocteau had devised the ballet in the first place, insists that Cocteau wanted more dancing, at least for himself. As Dolin sat in his dressing room before the premiere, Nijinska stood in the corridor giving last-minute directions.[78]

Both accounts are probably true. However much Cocteau fancied himself a choreographer, he had no real love of dance. What fascinated him was the spectacle of gesture, movement as unspoken speech. Nijinska, for her part, seems to have had no great love for the male body or, for that matter, for men in general. She choreographed for them, to be sure, but it was never her habit to create vehicles for their talents, as Cocteau— and Diaghilev—routinely did for the handsome youngsters who caught their eye. Students of Cocteau have usually taken the view that *Le Train Bleu*'s acrobatism and ironical treatment of classical forms were exclusively contributions by the poet: neither, they assert, had previously appeared in

Nijinska's work.[79] But this is to overlook the evidence of her choreography—the gymnastic element that appears so clearly in the architectural constructions of *Les Noces* and the classical ironies that mark every aspect of the dancing in *Les Biches*. At one point in *Le Train Bleu*, Dolin did a double pirouette into a cartwheel that ended in a fish dive—a sequence that echoes one of the climactic moments of the wedding pas de deux in *The Sleeping Beauty* (which Cocteau, it should be noted, did not see). In *Le Boeuf sur le Toit* and *Les Mariés de la Tour Eiffel*, he had parodied ballet dancing. But he had done so using its most superficial, telltale signs. Only Nijinska had the technical wherewithal—to say nothing of the analytic mind—to wrest irony from the language and traditions of classicism itself. Only Nijinska could have invented the pirouette-cartwheel-fish dive combination that landed Dolin, like a transsexual Aurora, in the arms of a Désiré costumed as the Prince of Wales.

In the 1920s the neoclassicism of Nijinska's work appeared secondary to its modernism. In part, this reflected the "packaging" of her choreography, a packaging that identified *Les Noces* with neoprimitivism and *Les Biches* and *Le Train Bleu* with lifestyle modernism. To a greater extent, however, the misreading of Nijinska's achievement reflected the limitations of Western critics, unfamiliar with Soviet dance trends. (André Levinson, who left the Soviet Union in 1919, was an exception, but one so unsympathetic to experimentalism that his judgments cannot be fully trusted.) Ignorant of the debates raging in Moscow and Petrograd, few understood the peculiar tension of her work, or the middle ground it staked out between postrevolutionary "futurists," who wanted to do away with ballet entirely, and "reactionaries," who sought to "congeal" it (her phrase) in the forms of the 1890s. Nor did many appreciate her analytic treatment of classical forms: if Westerners knew nothing of Lopukhov and Goleizovsky, with the exception of a handful of British critics they knew little more about Petipa. Only in the past few years has Nijinska's contribution to neoclassicism, unsung for a half-century, gained general recognition.

Nijinska left the Ballets Russes in January 1925. There were a number of reasons for this, including the grief she had experienced with *Le Train Bleu* (Diaghilev had taken Cocteau's part in the eleventh-hour drama) and a desire to form her own troupe. The arrival on the scene of a young choreographer who threatened her position in the company also played a part. George Balanchine was a youngster fresh from Soviet lands when he joined the Ballets Russes in the autumn of 1924. Only twenty, he already had a string of works to his credit. Indeed, by 1923, his experiments had earned him a cover story in *Theater* magazine and the opposition of diehard conservatives like Akim Volynsky. The following year, with a tiny company, impressively styled Principal Dancers of the Russian State Ballet, he embarked on a tour of Germany. The troupe, which included Alexandra Danilova, Nicholas Efimov, and Tamara Geva, decided to stay in the West and eventually secured an engagement in London. Here, at the Empire Theatre, Dolin and Kochno caught their act and alerted Diaghilev, always on the lookout for talent, that there was a choreographer in the group. A telegram from the impresario, which caught up with the dancers in Paris, invited them to audition the next day. Within a week all four members of the Soviet troupe had joined the Ballets Russes.

Today, with Balanchine's name synonymous with neoclassicism, we are apt to forget that he began life as a modernist. Indeed, his work for Diaghilev in the 1920s embodied many of that decade's most distinctive—and highly criticized—trends. From the start of Balanchine's career in the West, critics remarked upon the acrobatism of his work. "References to low music-hall acrobatics abound," wrote André Levinson about *Le Chant du Rossignol* (1925), Balanchine's first ballet for Diaghilev. *La Pastorale*, choreographed in 1926, invited a similar commentary. The story, noted the anonymous reviewer for the *Times:*

> provides an opportunity for one more display of the new gymnastic method which the company has, unfortunately we think, adopted. The exercises have this time been devised by M. Balanchine. It must be admitted that many of them are clever, notably a dance for M. Slavinsky and the duet for M. Lifar (the telegraph-boy) and Mme. Felia Doubrovska (the star). These were amusing and very brilliantly done. It is true that they resembled the acrobatic dancing which has been familiar for some years in music-hall, but there was a relieving touch of burlesque about them, and the technical feats performed, especially by Mme. Doubrovska, were remarkable.[80]

Levinson describes some of these "exercises," noting that they extended the technique of the pas de deux:

> M. Balanchine can pride himself on having added to the heritage. His parody of the classical pas de deux . . . renews the genre. The droll adagio exploits with humor the "hyperbolic" lineaments of . . . Mlle. Felia Doubrovska; the développés, passing over the head of the cavalier like choreographic slaps, and the promenade where the danseur pivoted the star while holding her calf are distortions that amuse.[81]

The source of these "distortions" is a matter of speculation. Certainly, in the aftermath of the Revolution, Soviet choreographers, including Goleizovsky and Lopukhov, both of whom the young Balanchine admired, had used acrobatic elements—high extensions, unusual lifts—to enlarge the stock of choreographic possibilities. In the West, however, experimentation in these areas went forward on the commercial stage. Here, one finds the splits, "ring" poses, and overhead lifts of Lopukhov's experimental ballets; the backbends and handstands of Massine's revue creations; the close supports and high extensions of Balanchine's early duets.

Balanchine's works reflected another prevailing trend of the 1920s. Beginning with *Parade,* critics detected a palpable change in the structure of many ballets. Increasingly, they noted a shift away from dramatic narrative to short sketches and the tendency to divide the dancing into "turns"—typical features of music-hall and revue. "Here again," wrote a critic of Massine's 1924 *Cimarosiana,* "there was no plot, but just a series of detached turns—a pas de trois, a pas de six, a tarantella and so on . . ." *Jack-in-the-Box,* choreographed by Balanchine in 1926 to music by Satie, was "*Parade* all over again," rued Valerian Svetlov, a one-time admirer of the Ballets Russes who found little to praise in its newer works. "It would have been the easiest and most natural thing in the world to have combined the two ballets into one by giving some of the actors of the first a few of the variety turns of the second; 'The Clown,' the 'Black Ballerina,' the two 'White Ballerinas' and two 'Carriers of Clouds.' " Levinson remarked upon the phenomenon as well: the clog dance and burlesque parade of soldiers in Balanchine's *Barabau,* another 1926 work, were the stuff "of a quick sketch by the Chauve-Souris," a reference to the popular émigré cabaret group. Levinson went even further: the whole of a Diaghilev program, he wrote that year, smacked of a "New Year's Eve revue."[82]

Under the aegis of the futurists, Diaghilev had simplifed narrative. But this did not mean that he abjured it. As Bronislava Nijinska wrote in the 1930s, Diaghilev "could not readily discard the idea of a literary libretto." Indeed, all his works of the twenties had plots, however flimsy and unrelated to the choreography they might be. "The story matters little and is not very clearly told," wrote the *Times* critic about *La Pastorale.* Svetlov echoed this in a review of *Les Matelots,* choreographed by Massine in 1925. "The ballet 'Matelots' is not properly speaking a ballet at all but 'scenes from life' or a competition of hornpipe dancing, or even a series of variety turns only slightly connected with the plot. And in fact the plot is difficult to see, if there is any." Balanchine's 1927 *La Chatte,* which took its theme from an Aesop fable about a woman transformed into a cat, was similarly flawed. "The resources of the subject are only poorly utilized," wrote Levinson. "Likewise, the choreography . . . has no obvious relationship to the ideas of the scenario." Boris Kochno, Diaghilev's secretary and production assistant for most of the twenties, contributed the libretti to all three ballets. But the impetus seems to have come from Diaghilev. Certainly, his advice to John Alden Carpenter, an American composer commissioned in 1924 to do a ballet about the modern city, suggests that the impresario had long since given up *Gesamtkunstwerk* as a model of dramatic unity. Write the music, he told Carpenter, without regard to story or action.[83]

In the years Balanchine came of age, Diaghilev seemed torn between two contending forces. Drawn to "pure" dance forms, he remained none-theless committed to the idea of narrative. At this artistic impasse, he adopted a compromise solution, creating suites of dances (as *Cuadro Flamenco* and *Cimarosiana* were actually called), unified by the merest wisp of a plot. In this hybrid form, neither fully abstract nor fully representational, narrative was a pretext, a means of imposing the semblance of a situation upon a string of divertissements. *The Gods Go A-Begging*, wrote the *Times* in 1928:

> is an 18th-century pastoral in which the formal element is naturally the chief feature. There is, however, a slight plot to justify the title and to fertilise with a poetic idea the concerted movements. A *fête champêtre* is in preparation; into the company of noblemen and ladies a shepherd strays; the ladies welcome him to their festivity, but he prefers the simpler charms of a serving-maid; the anger of the company at this rebuff is stilled by the revelation that the two lowly persons are gods disguised as beggars.[84]

Les Matelots, a sailor ballet, and *Barabau*, based on a Tuscan folk song, followed a similar pattern. The scenario for the first, by Kochno, with assistance from Diaghilev, was "exceedingly slight," wrote Serge Grigo-riev, "in accordance with Diaghilev's dictum . . . that the public were bored with plots and only liked dances. *Les Matelots* certainly had plenty of dances and little story. Variety was provided by constant changes of scene . . . and by Massine's choreography, which was lively and admira-bly ingenious." Balanchine's *Barabau*, which, like *Les Matelots*, had its premiere in 1925, was also packed with movement—"bucolic high jinks," as one disapproving London critic put it, "between a passing squad of soldiers and the lassies of the village." If there was one work of the mid-twenties that epitomized the collapse of internal narrative coherence it was *The Triumph of Neptune*, a pantomime in twelve scenes inspired by Vic-torian toy theater. Choreographed by Balanchine, the ballet was replete with "English dance folklore" (in Levinson's happy phrase)—a "weepy" contre-danse, a street dancer's polka, a Scottish reel for the goddess Bri-tannia, a sailor's jig, fling, a hornpipe. There was a fairy ballet (which reminded Svetlov of the snowflakes scene in the old Maryinsky production of *The Nutcracker*), an old-fashioned transformation scene, and a story, patched together by Sacheverell Sitwell, about a pair of intrepid explorers, a journalist, and a British tar. But although *Neptune* delighted British audiences (and even found favor with Svetlov and Levinson), the work was a narrative muddle. "One criticism," wrote *The Queen,* a London magazine, "is that the joke is not worth the trouble it makes with its twelve scenes and its innumerable, confused characters and costumes." But the critic hastened to add, "this ponderousness . . . gives the ballet its true All-British flavour."[85]

Even in Balanchine's initial works for the company, however, there were hints of the neoclassicist to come. In *Barabau,* a work that made Cyril W. Beaumont doubt the wisdom of Diaghilev's choice of Balanchine as a choreographer, Serge Lifar, as the officer, danced a classical solo with a martial accent. Beaumont revised his opinion after *The Triumph of Neptune,* which received its premiere in December 1926. "For this ballet," he wrote:

> Balanchine had temporarily discarded his modernist experiments . . . The dances, always simple and effective, included classical compositions which were poetical in their graceful lines and chaste beauty.
> I am thinking in particular of the scenes called "Cloudland" and "The Frozen Wood," which gave opportunities for dances in the tradition of the pure academic ballet . . . In the Frozen Wood—known to facetious stagehands as Wigan by Night—there was a flying ballet, in which skilled dancers, linked together with floral garlands held in their hands and now indifferent to the laws of gravity, traversed the air to form lovely and ever-changing designs contrived of misty sylphs and loops and knots of garlands.[86]

Here is a Balanchine we recognize. Less familiar is the creator of *La Chatte* (1927), a constructivist fable, taken from Aesop, that glorified the physical beauty of its seven men. "There was something intensely refreshing and exhilarating," wrote Beaumont:

> in the sight of those trained, well formed, lissom brown bodies, . . . leaping, bending, twirling, finally to mass into an impressive group . . . There was one memorable moment when [Serge] Lifar made his entrance carried in a triumphal car formed from his companions. Three youths stood in line abreast, the outer two bending forward, so that Lifar could set one knee on each back; the centre youth rested his elbows on the backs of his companions and locked his forearm about each of Lifar's knees. Three more youths stood in front, the centre one holding his rear arm upright for Lifar to grasp, his other arm being held horizontally forward, and grasped at the wrist by the youth on either side of him. The whole group was held together by the two outer youths in the back row gripping the belts of those immediately in front of them. Lifar, borne

on high in this fantastic car, and seen in the flower of his beauty, seemed to symbolize the Triumph of Youth.[87]

The moment, captured in one of the most frequently reproduced photographs of the ballet, shows Lifar as the glamorous deco god that Balanchine made an integral part of the dancer's artistic persona. But the image also suggests something rarely mentioned in discussions of Balanchine's early choreography—the influence of Nijinska. Not only does the pyramid described by Beaumont recall the final tableau of *Les Noces,* but in the gymnastic element, which he also mentions, and the treatment of groups as architectural blocks, suggested by another photograph, one senses an awareness of Nijinska's ballet.[88] *Les Noces,* in fact, was very much in evidence in the months preceding the creation of *La Chatte.* Revived in Paris for the 1926 season, when it appeared on four of the twelve programs, *Les Noces* was also performed seven times in London. Considering the large cast (nearly forty dancers) and the relatively small size of the company (just over fifty), it is likely that Balanchine himself performed in the ballet. Similar elements also appeared in *Le Fils Prodigue—Prodigal Son*—choreographed in 1929 for what turned out to be Diaghilev's last season. Here, again, the vocabulary incorporated gymnastic and mechanistic elements, while the design, especially in the ensembles, reflected a constructivist sense of mass. A recognizably Balanchinean sensibility appears in the pas de deux, a shocking display of female sexual power.

Of all Balanchine's works for the Ballets Russes, *Apollon Musagète* (later shortened to *Apollo*) was the most important. "The events with which *Apollo* deals," Bernard Taper has written, "are simple, compressed, evocative: Apollo is born, discovers and displays his creative powers, instructs three of the Muses in their arts, and then ascends with them to Parnassus. The theme is creativity itself—Apollonian creativity, vigorous but lucid, untortured, civilizing."[89] A turning point in Balanchine's life—the first time, as he later put it, that he dared "not to use all my ideas"—*Apollon Musagète* stands with *Les Noces* and *Les Biches* as an early masterwork of neoclassicism.

Unlike Nijinska's ballets, however, the Balanchine work fused choreographic neoclassicism with several other "classical" ideas. One of these was idealism: the identification of art with a timeless Parnassus of the spirit. A second was neo-orthodoxy, a major trend of the 1920s, when numerous artists and intellectuals exchanged agnosticism for the verities of religious faith. In *Apollon Musagète,* wrote Henry Prunières, one of the period's most distinguished music critics, Stravinsky's "classicism is no longer a pose as before; one feels that he is responding to an intimate need of his heart and mind."[90] Boris de Schloezer, in the *Dial,* also linked the neo-classicism of the work to a spiritual source:

> Apollo . . . reveals Stravinsky's thirst for renunciation, his need of purity and serenity . . . What this peace and clarity have cost him can be witnessed only by the long series of precedent works whose exasperated dynamism wd. almost seem, by comparison with the Apollo, to be a vain agitation . . . What should we expect from Stravinsky now in the strength of his age and full expansion of his genius? What will his next work be? . . . Logically, after Apollo, he ought to give us a Mass.[91]

Along with idealism and neo-orthodoxy, the ballet expressed the disjunctive logic of retrospective classicism. We tend to forget how different the ballet that audiences saw in 1928 looked from the one we know today—the product of Balanchine's numerous recensions. For one thing, there was a decor. André Bauchant, a naive painter whom Paris art dealers were touting as a successor to Henri Rousseau, was an unlikely choice for the project, and his designs—a huge, festive bouquet of flowers for the birth scene and a craggy rise with a four-horsed chariot for the main one—seem completely at odds with the ballet's transcendent theme. Diaghilev had commissioned Bauchant to avoid, as he said, a false Hellenism. Yet he costumed Apollo in the raiment of a god—a short, girdled tunic and slippers, laced over naked calves, that resembled sandals. But the costuming was far from consistent. The Muses wore tutus with mauve bodices, while in the apotheosis Leto and the goddess attendants at Apollo's birth stood watch in long Duncan-style tunics. Here was "time-travelling" with a vengeance.[92]

Equally jarring were the devices that linked the ballet to traditions of French classicism. The chariot that slowly descended from the skies to bear Apollo and his companions to Parnassus evoked an eighteenth-century *gloire,* noted Cyril W. Beaumont.[93] That century was also present in the allegorical treatment of the theme and the mythological subject matter, both of which recalled conventions of French opera-ballet, to say nothing of devices exploited in Diaghilev's earlier period works. These conventions survive only vestigially in current productions of *Apollo.* But like the music, they stressed the "classicism" of the original, allying Balanchine's return to Petipa with trends extrinsic to the choreography itself.

Unlike *Les Noces* and *Les Biches,* then, *Apollon Musagète* brought together the era's various classicisms. In uniting them, however, the ballet subtly altered their ideologies. Until then, choreographic neoclassicism had been a politically neutral phenomenon. Now, making peace with the idea of social order and religious orthodoxy, it acquired a profoundly conservative aura. Retrospective classicism, for its part, also gained from the marriage: "timeless" form now masked the genre's temporal agenda, nowhere more obviously than in the neoclassical epics created by Serge Lifar at the Paris Opéra in the 1930s. This is not to say that Nijinska's choreography of that decade or Balanchine's of the 1940s and 1950s—above all, in the cycle of "leotard" ballets initiated by *The Four Temperaments*—expunged from their prevailing neoclassicism all trace of radical content. Merely, that the initial subversiveness of the neoclassical idea in choreography—its modernism, so to speak—gave way to an emphasis on artistic and social order. Rather than a vision of the future, neoclassicism came to define an attitude toward the past, the ordered past that had vanished with modernism. In the ideology of apostolic order and idealism that in the decades following *Apollon Musagète* has become identified with neoclassicism, one perceives the continuing legacy of a marriage originally brokered by Diaghilev.

Cataloguing the Diaghilev works produced between 1922 and 1929, one cannot fail to be struck by the transitory character of the vast majority. Few aspired to a place of permanence in the ballet canon, few claimed to offer any critical comment on contemporary life, few evoked the sensation of the abyss. Commenting on the "ultra-modern sauce" in which Cocteau "cooked up" his version of *Antigone,* Gide contrasted his own belief in the immortality of art with the younger man's time-bound vision of the modern:

> Nothing is more foreign to me than this concern for modernism which one feels influencing every thought and every decision of Cocteau. I do not claim that he is wrong to believe that art breathes freely only in its newest manifestation. But, all the same, the only thing that matters to me is what a generation will not carry away with it. I do not seek to be of my epoch; I seek to overflow my epoch.[94]

With the exception of *Les Biches,* where Nijinska, despite the scenario, managed to impose her own vision, Diaghilev's ballet masterpieces of the twenties—*Les Noces, Apollon Musagète,* and *Prodigal Son*—all rejected Cocteau's literal equating of modernism with the transient forms of modernity.

Diaghilev's lesser works, however, exhibited a lack of internal coherence, a failure of belief in the possibility of art to convey meaning at any level. Critics spoke of a cynical misuse of myth and allegory in ballets like *Zéphire et Flore, La Chatte,* and even *Prodigal Son,* where calculated misinterpretations of the letter and spirit of the originals were served up under the guise of extreme modernity. In structure, as we have said, many ballets approximated the sketches typical of contemporary revues. But they were sketches on another level as well. Although they transposed details of modern life, reality itself was evoked only indirectly. Many ballets, in fact, were representations of modern life as perceived through other theatrical forms. *Parade,* which depicts the preview of a performance, rather than the performance itself, anticipated later works such as *Romeo and Juliet, La Pastorale,* and *The Triumph of Neptune.* The first of these showed a ballet rehearsal and dancing class; the second juxtaposed a motion picture runthrough and actual shooting; the third, set in a toy theater of the Victorian period, was a genre piece in the style of a traditional children's pantomime. The play within a play is a time-honored theatrical device that can both shade and intensify dramatic meaning. In these ballets, however, the device is a trick of form resonating within the closed circle of the text, never radiating outward. Like a series of Chinese boxes, these ballets invoke a solipsistic and purely self-reflexive universe untouched by any but the most superficial links to the larger arena of human concern.

Solipsism, however, was implicit in the transformational method of modernism itself, in its obsessive recycling of themes, genres, and typologies. The modernist remade reality not from scratch, but as a pastiche or gloss of existing texts. To some extent, art is always imitative. But traditionally, the artist conceived his task as one of reinterpreting a reality that was directly apprehended even if expressed through received forms. The modernist, on the other hand, fashioned his art within a closed circle of reference that only occasionally opened onto the larger world. Meaning became the transformational process itself, with only the initiate having the keys to its code. At its best, such elitism reflected the modernist's ironic view of the social microcosm, his detachment, chosen or otherwise, from the forces shaping his life. At its worst, however, it constituted a kind of snobbism, as the pale of discourse converged on an ever narrowing public. The first situation characterizes Diaghilev's modernism during and just after World War I, when the artistic product became the sole fact within a universe of uncontrollable flux. The second describes his approach throughout most of the 1920s.

The styles of twenties ballet did not end with Diaghilev's death in 1929. They survived in some of Frederick Ashton's early ballets, in Ida Rubinstein's spectacles, and in Serge Lifar's creations for the Paris Opéra. But the 1930s also witnessed a reaction against Diaghilev's formulas—in the appearance of dream, romance, and fantasy elements, above all in the work of Balanchine and Ashton, in the new importance assigned to dance in the overall ballet spectacle, and in the renewal of interest in the danse d'école. Like *Apollon Musagète, Ode,* choreographed by Massine in 1928, and *Le Bal,* created by Balanchine the following year, anticipated these developments, as did Diaghilev's plan to revive *Giselle* in 1930. But they also recorded a change in artistic mood, brought on in part by the surrealists, in part by a young generation of accomplished classicists, and in part by the rising nationalism of the heirs to Diaghilev's legacy. The times had changed in other ways as well. With fascism on the rise and depression at close hand, the aura of consumer chic that had surrounded the Ballets Russes looked less attractive.

By 1930 the revolution initiated by Fokine twenty-five years before had ended. That revolution, as we have said, took place outside the academy, at the crossroads of the other arts. From these, choreographers enriched their stock of ideas and applied them to dance. If the results were mixed, the experiments themselves were nearly always rewarding. Together, they wrested ballet into the twentieth century. In an art whose history is usually written as a chronicle of institutions, we are apt to think of change as a naturally occurring condition. But in ballet, as in any art whose life is governed by an academy, nothing is more unnatural than change. The history of the Ballets Russes certainly documents this truism. But it also documents its converse: the ability of the academy to absorb change. If modernism at times threatened to destroy ballet, ultimately it renewed it, enabling it to survive as a vital artistic force.

II

ENTERPRISE

5 ✒

RUSSIAN ORIGINS

B Y AND LARGE, historians have given the enterprise of ballet, as opposed to its art, short shrift. They may talk about patrons and occasionally refer to a balance sheet, but they seldom take the matter seriously.
Yet without money, chances are there would be no ballet. Dancers, to be
sure, would still sweat at the barre, and many would find ways of revealing their talent to the public. But as an art of lyric theater, a grand spectacle combining music, dance, and design, ballet would probably vanish.

Historically, ballet has flourished only when men of means—kings,
princes, patrons—lavished fortunes upon it. Undeniably, there were times,
as in the 1830s and 1840s in England, when private enterprise supported
and even furthered the art. But such eras proved rare, and of relatively
short duration. Almost always, ballet in the commercial arena took the
form of pick-up companies, gathered around a touring star, or music-hall
troupes, such as those maintained at the Folies-Bergère in Paris and the
Empire Theatre in London. In both cases, entertainment, rather than art,
was the aim.

The Ballets Russes was unique on several counts, not least of which
was that it was a private enterprise that set itself the task of emulating—
and surpassing artistically—the premier dance institution of its day. To
create a ballet company from scratch is never easy; to create a vital producing organization even harder. To do both in the commercial arena is
almost a miracle. This near miracle Diaghilev performed again and again
for twenty years. How he did so is the subject of these pages.

Money—the dollar and cents tale of keeping a company afloat—lies
at the heart of the story. But by no means is it the whole story. The acquisition of money, like its expenditure, entails choices and relationships.
Rarely are decisions made with only the bottom line in view, and just as
rarely are the consequences of those decisions solely economic. Almost

always, money—how we get it, how we spend it—bears the imprint of social reality. In the case of the Ballets Russes, this reality necessarily intruded on artistic concerns and had artistic consequences. At the simplest level, the interplay of economic and social forces—what might be called the company's political economy—helps explain key developments in its history: shifts in repertory and in collaborative styles, changes in the status of dancers and choreographers, the various strategies by which Diaghilev secured and maintained a position in the Western theatrical world. The political economy of the Ballets Russes, however, has ramifications beyond these specifics. In a larger sense, the history of the Diaghilev enterprise presents a case study of artistic life in the commercial marketplace. Emerging from the "amateur" culture of Russia's Silver Age and the semifeudal world of the Imperial Theaters, the Ballets Russes experienced in twenty years of existence the full impact of capitalism—both its initial freedom and its final uncertainty. If the Ballets Russes gave birth to artistic trends that dominated ballet long after Diaghilev's death, the history of the company as a social and financial entity had repercussions that continue to be felt even today.

Unlike the artistic history of the Ballets Russes, which begins in St. Petersburg, the history of its enterprise opens in Moscow—among the great merchant clans that in the closing years of the nineteenth century used their patronage to redraw the landscape of Russian culture. We have already encountered one of the most colorful of these merchant patrons: Savva Mamontov, the railroad man who founded the art colony at Abramtsevo and Russia's first private opera company.[1] Now, we meet his kinsmen—Morozovs, Tretiakovs, Shchukins, Alexeyevs, Bakhrushins, Botkins, Tereshchenkos, Riabushinskys—who, like him, built empires that steered Russia's semifeudal economy into the modern world.

This native capitalist class has long fascinated scholars.[2] Descended from serfs and religious dissidents—Old Believers, Skoptsy, and Jews—it moved in the course of the nineteenth century from the periphery of Russian society to its economic summit. Merchant capitalists laid the track for Russia's first railroads, built its first textile mills, sugar beet refineries, and tea empires, and founded the banks that underwrote the country's industrial revolution. Such enterprises amassed vast wealth for their owners, who repaid their good fortune by spending its blessings worthily. Entrepreneurs with a civic conscience, they endowed philanthropic institutions, opened hospitals, libraries, schools, and museums. But their greatest contribution to Russian life was as patrons *extraordinaires,* whose passion for art and adventurous taste are reflected to this day in Soviet museums. From merchant ranks emerged the great collectors of late nineteenth- and early twentieth-century Russia: men like Pavel Tretiakov, whose gallery housed Russian paintings and a fabulous collection of fifteenth-century icons; Sergei Shchukin, whose Moscow home had panels by Matisse and master-pieces by Picasso; Mikhail Riabushinsky, who filled his mansion with canvases of Renoir, Degas, and Pissarro; Ivan Morozov, who collected Bonnards, Vuillards, and Cézannes; his brother, Mikhail, who collected Manets, Gauguins, and Van Goghs; Alexis Bakhrushin, who specialized in theatrical material; Dmitri Botkin, who amassed an exquisite collection of Spanish art.

Collecting, however, was only one aspect of merchant patronage. Equally important was the sponsorship of young Russian painters, especially those who attacked the forms and social assumptions of academic and salon art. The first to benefit from merchant largess (in this case, that of Tretiakov and the Tereshchenko family) were the Wanderers, who resigned en masse from the Imperial Academy of Arts in St. Petersburg in 1863. The proper subject of Russian art, they declared, was Russian reality, with all its "accursed problems"—the peasantry, the urban working-class, the corruption of the Church, the status of women—themes that linked Realist painting to the critical thought of social democrats like Nikolai Chernyshevsky and Alexander Herzen. The generation that came to the fore in the late 1870s and 1880s abandoned the idea of art as an agency of political change. Yet, in its way, the interest in peasant crafts that stimulated the neonationalist movement of those decades implied an equally critical view of academic styles and gentry values. Like realism, neonationalism received generous merchant support. Many built homes in Old Russian style; Tretiakov, the gallery that bears his name. Sergei Morozov endowed the Moscow Museum of Handicrafts and gave generous support to village artisans. Mamontov's activities, centered at Abramtsevo, have already been mentioned.

Although merchants traditionally sponsored work with a strong nationalist flavor, in the 1890s and early 1900s they shifted their support to trends associated with Western styles. Mamontov's patronage of painters such as Mikhail Vrubel, Konstantin Korovin, and Valentin Serov exemplified this change in taste. Korovin was also an early favorite of Ivan Morozov, whose vast collection of Russian works included paintings by Vrubel and Isaak Levitan, along with canvases by future modernists such as Michel Larionov, Natalia Gontcharova, and Marc Chagall. Another collector who gave his support to the emerging modernist movement was Nikolai Riabushinsky, a collector who promoted the emerging Moscow avant-garde in exhibitions (including the memorable Golden Fleece show of 1908) and in the pages of *Zolotoye runo,* the journal he had founded two years earlier. Well might Vladimir Nemirovich-Danchenko, cofounder of the Moscow Art Theater, remark: "Merchants flaunted their striving for civilization and culture."[3]

In 1892 Tretiakov had frustrated a plan by Alexander III to purchase his collection for the Russian State Museum in St. Petersburg. Instead, the elderly collector deeded his gallery to the city of Moscow. This dramatic incident, in which a commoner successfully defied the Tsar of All the Russias, exemplifies the ideology of merchant patronage generally. From the first, this had aimed at challenging the cultural hegemony of the state. Progressive and nationalist in outlook, liberal in conviction, and democratic in social style, merchant patronage thus offered a compelling alternative—Russia's first—to the traditional practice of art. No longer was the state the sole source of education (via the Academy), the sole arbiter of quality (via diplomas and competitions), or even the major source of patronage (via commissions). Now, thanks to merchant enterprise, an arena flourished independent of the state and its gentry serviteurs. Into this world, in the late 1890s, stepped Serge Diaghilev.

The young dandy with the streak whitening his thick black hair was already on his way to success when Mamontov, accompanied by his coterie of painters, visited the exhibition of Scandinavian art organized by Diaghilev in St. Petersburg in 1897.[4] At twenty-five, he had a string of accomplishments to his credit—articles, musical compositions, exhibitions, a law degree. But it is safe to say that this meeting marked a turning point in the dilettante's life, setting it firmly on a course of entrepreneurship. Diaghilev, writes his biographer Arnold Haskell, "was full of admiration for Mamontoff."[5] That admiration opened the eyes of the Westward-gazing Petersburger to the artistic riches of Moscow; introduced him to many of the painters who would figure in his activities during the next fifteen years; instilled in him a regard for collaborative relationships; steered him, in fact, toward the theater. Above all, Mamontov turned the dilettante of art into a builder of artistic empires. Beginning in the late 1890s Diaghilev remade his St. Petersburg circle into an Abramtsevo-on-the-Neva, which, like its original, would challenge official tsarist art in the name of free artistic enterprise.

To understand this process, we backtrack to 1890, when Diaghilev arrived in the Russian capital from Perm to make his fortune. Although sent to Petersburg to enroll in the Faculty of Law, entree to the higher echelons of the civil service, the brash, well-connected youth aspired to be a composer. Almost immediately, he met the budding aesthetes—Alexandre Benois, Léon Bakst, Dmitri Filosofov, Walter Nouvel, and Konstantin Somov—who accompanied him on the first stage of his life's journey.

This friendly band, which drank tea together and subscribed to art journals, formed a discussion society (the "Nevsky Pickwickians") and argued about music, painting, and literature, offered a microcosm of the various "cabinets" that would guide the fortunes of the Ballets Russes.

This little group, whose saga has been told many times,[6] was by no means unique, for circles of this kind proliferated among the era's cultivated minority. They enlightened and entertained, fostered intimacy and common habits of thought. They also served an artistic function, providing arenas where privileged amateurs, barred by their status from professional careers, might perform and/or present their work. The soiree that allegedly put an end to Diaghilev's musical ambitions was one such event. Attended en masse by the "Pickwickians," it featured a duet, composed by Diaghilev and sung by him and one of his aunts, that was roundly condemned by his friends.[7] Most circles remained purely social. A few, however, broadened the scope of their activities, transforming themselves into semiprofessional, public enterprises.

In the last decades of the nineteenth century, three "amateur" groups in Russia made this transition. One was the Mamontov circle, which gave birth to the country's first private opera company. Another, associated with Konstantin Stanislavsky, became the Moscow Art Theater. A third was the "Nevsky Pickwickians." Within little more than a decade after Diaghilev's arrival in St. Petersburg, the group stood at the center of a thriving network whose activities touched numerous aspects of Petersburg cultural life. The most important of these undertakings was *Mir iskusstva*, the art journal founded by Diaghilev in 1898 and edited by him until its demise six years later. Other activities included an exhibition society (also known as the World of Art), which remained active until 1910, and a concert society, "Evenings of Contemporary Music," which, beginning in 1901, introduced Russian audiences to modern composers and their works. Seven years later, with Diaghilev's production of *Boris Godunov* at the Paris Opéra, the Pickwickians moved into the theater.

Many bonds united the Mamontov, Stanislavsky, and Diaghilev enterprises. All three grew out of amateur activity and depended on merchant patronage. All professionalized in the commercial marketplace. And all displayed the management styles, organizational structures, and social relationships characteristic of merchant enterprise. In business, merchants clung to the ideological habits of a simpler era. Well into the twentieth century, historian Thomas C. Owen has written, "personal dealings based on mutual trust" were the rule, and many merchants viewed as ideal an economic relation that made no distinction between employer and employee.[8] The business style of this class was thus explicitly antibureaucratic and antihierarchical; it rested on personal exchange, as opposed to a relation mediated by authority, and preferred to view individuals apart from social category or economic function.

In art, as in business, family was the key to merchant enterprise. Mamontov's "folly" (as disparaging Petersburgers termed his opera company) began, literally, as a family affair. One cousin who witnessed (and participated in) the home entertainments initiated by Mamontov in 1879 was Konstantin Alexeyev, the son of a thread manufacturer, who later took the stage name of Stanislavsky. "Oftener than not," he wrote in his autobiography, "the plays were of [Mamontov's] own making or his sons'. Now and then composers of his acquaintance produced . . . an operetta." In the audience sat sympathetic relations and friends who had come from all over Moscow to mix paints, stitch costumes, and work on the props for these "famous productions."[9] In a eulogy written after Mamontov's death, the director recalled the first of these entertainments—a combination of music and tableaux vivants on themes from Russian literature. The evening ended memorably: when his Roman robes snagged on a platform, the god of art took his final pose stark naked. Gradually, these domestic theatricals assumed a more professional character. In 1883, when Mamontov staged his first opera, *The Merry Wives of Windsor* in Russian translation, he hired a small orchestra from the Moscow Conservatory. The following year, he presented an operatic version of his play *The Vermillion Rose*. Although hardly an unqualified success (according to Sergei Tretiakov, it went on for six hours), the production was "a great event for the Moscow musical world": a new opera (by N.S. Krotkov), with young singers (including many Conservatory students), and designs by Victor Vasnetsov and Vasily Polenov, two of the best-known contemporary Russian painters.[10] In 1885 Mamontov invited Krotkov to be his collaborator in a Moscow-based private opera company.

Conceived as a commercial venture (although, to be sure, it never became self-supporting), Mamontov's opera aspired to challenge the Imperial Theaters where their productions were weakest: repertory, casting, and artistic quality. His preference was for Russian works (rarely given on the Imperial stage) performed by young Russian artists (overshadowed by foreigners) in settings that were "artistic" (that is, designed and executed by easel painters rather than by specialist artisans). Few of these goals were met in the troupe's first phase (which ended in 1892), when lack of sustained interest in the Russian repertory and a paucity of experienced young singers forced Mamontov to import performers from France and Italy and to produce such crowd pleasers as *Carmen, Aïda,* and *La Traviata.* In large measure, however, they were realized in the years 1896–

1902 when the entrepreneur-turned-impresario brought to a newly receptive public the "model performances" of the Russian lyric repertory that fired the imagination of Diaghilev and his collaborators and secured Mamontov a place in opera history.[11]

The Moscow Art Theater had a similarly domestic prehistory: it began, in fact, with the ballets, circus turns, and puppet shows "produced" by the Alexeyev children in their Moscow living room. In 1877, Stanislavsky's father built a theater at the family's country house in Lyubimovka, and it was here that the teen-age actor officially made his "debut." In the 1880s Stanislavsky performed exclusively on the amateur stage—at Abramtsevo, at Lyubimovka, at the tiny Secretaryov Theater run by a former tutor. Gradually, however, the character of his work, and its relationship to the public, changed. By the mid-1880s the Alexeyev Circle, as Stanislavsky and his family now called themselves, had ceased to be a purely domestic enterprise. Newspapers reviewed its productions, one of several signs that the Circle was performing a function similar to that of the many amateur groups that, in Moscow at least, "sought to circumvent the monopoly in drama of the Imperial theatres."[12] The Circle collapsed in 1888. It was succeeded by the Society of Art and Literature—like its predecessor, an amateur group. By now, however, Stanislavsky's reputation as an innovator and disciplined professional had captured the attention of the serious theatergoing public. In 1898, with playwright Vladimir Nemirovich-Danchenko, he founded the Moscow Art Theater, his first professional ensemble and a commercial enterprise.

Like Mamontov's Private Opera Company, however, the Art Theater was never self-supporting. From the first, it depended upon merchant patronage to survive as a vital artistic entity. The troupe's "angel" was Savva Morozov, a textile magnate who gave hundreds of thousands of rubles to the Social Democratic Party, sheltered Bolsheviks on his country estate, befriended Maxim Gorky, and shot himself in 1905. Along with radical convictions, Morozov had a genuine love of Russian drama. Unsurprisingly, the play that opened his checkbook—Alexis Tolstoy's *Tsar Fyodor*—was a historical pageant that had been banned by the censor for thirty years. In 1902, through Morozov's generosity, the Art Theater moved to its permanent home, the former Oman Theater, renovated at a cost of 300,000 rubles.[13]

Like Mamontov, Morozov poured more than money into his enterprise. He supervised construction on the new theater personally, moving, as Stanislavsky wrote, into "a little room near the office amid the din and clatter and the clouds of dust raised by the builders." He gave special attention to the revolving stage, a rarity at the time even in the West, and saw to it that the Art Theater had the most up-to-date lighting equipment. As late as 1929 Stanislavsky would point to a ramp that had been "personally made" by Morozov.[14] The "angel" was no aristocratic idler.

The leveling of class distinctions was a major feature of merchant patronage, and many are the testimonials to the friendliness and cooperative spirit of its enterprises. The painter Victor Vasnetsov described the "small, friendly artistic family of Abramtsevo" as a community where "the artistic impulse of creativity of the Renaissance and Middle Ages had come to life again." "I love them so," Valentin Serov wrote to his fiancee in 1884, "and they me . . . I am made to feel exactly as if I were a member of the family." Mikhail Vrubel was another cherished artist. The Mamontov children sat for him, and were taught that any drawing or rough draft that Vrubel threw away had to be saved.[15] At Stanislavsky's temple of art, the actor commanded similar respect. To the producer Mikhail Lentovksy, Stanislavsky once delivered a lecture on stage ethics:

> You are the head of an organization whose duty it is to instruct, educate and enlighten society and the actors are your closest cultural associates. Don't let us forget it, and let us talk to them not as to prostitutes and slaves, but as to people who are worthy of their high calling.[16]

Toward fellow artists Stanislavsky always behaved with exquisite courtesy. This, one of his actors observed "was of tremendous importance to the general tone which was characteristic of our rehearsals and performances."[17] At the Art Theater each actor had his own dressing room, and when, at Morozov's instigation, the troupe was reorganized as a limited company, most of the actors were included in the plan as shareholders.

In their cooperative emphasis, these enterprises offered a striking contrast to the Imperial Theaters. Feodor Chaliapin, who joined Mamontov's opera company in 1898 after an unhappy stint at the Maryinsky, recalled life under the wing of autocracy:

> I hated going to the theatre if only on account of the treatment that was meted out to artists by the administration . . . when the director came backstage, the artists immediately stood to attention, for all the world like soldiers, and enthusiastically shook the two fingers that the director condescended to offer them . . . I can remember an occasion when I was rudely ticked off because I did not go to the director's office on New Year's Day to sign the visitors book. It was degrading to me to have to express my respect to my chief through his doorkeeper . . . There were other irritating trifles, enough to make me lose my pride in being an artist of the Imperial Theatre.[18]

Only when Chaliapin joined the Mamontov troupe did he feel "at home." Here, the "relations between artists were so much simpler, and perhaps even more important, they were sincere." A feeling of equality reigned, and when Madame Winter, the company manager, gave one of her many "interesting and stimulating parties," the entire troupe was invited.[19]

This spirit of friendly collaboration also characterized the Diaghilev circle. The preparations for *Mir iskusstva* involved most of the Pickwickians. "I am now spending all my evenings with Seriozha," wrote Walter Nouvel in the spring of 1898. (Seriozha was the diminutive by which Diaghilev was known among his intimates.):

> We are all keyed up, and excited about his magazine, and working at fever heat. Meanwhile we spend all our time passionately arguing. It absorbs me completely. Perhaps it's all mean and petty (!) but there it is, and I won't, I can't, violate my nature. I shall only move on to better things, when I feel a natural irresistible need to do so.[20]

Alexandre Benois has left another scene of the circle at work—not on *Mir iskusstva,* but on the ballet *Sylvia,* which, in a rare departure from tradition, Prince Serge Volkonsky, director of the Imperial Theaters, had commissioned Diaghilev's "outsiders" to design:

> Diaghilev dashed home, where he found the entire "editorial staff" at his table having the usual five o'clock tea. We were all so convinced that we were actually to create *Sylvia* that we had sat down to tea only after having worked for several hours at sketches for our production. Some of us had taken possession of the dining-room, others were busy in Seriozha's study, while even the back rooms were strewn with drawings and sketches. I . . . had just sketched the plan of the décor for the first act; Lanceray was busy with the third act . . . Korovin was working at the second scene of the second act; Bakst had been entrusted with creating Orion's cave and almost all the costumes; even Serov, carried away by the general enthusiasm, had started on a sketch of the principal satyr . . .[21]

Sylvia never reached the stage. Yet with this commission, the methods of the group's parlor theatricals—a pantomime on the subject of *Daphnis and Chloë* and a musical drama on a theme by Hoffmann are mentioned by Benois[22]—became a professional strategy. *Sylvia* bore all the earmarks of a Mamontov production, from the "homey" atmosphere in which the work went forward to the division of a single assignment among several artists. But the ill-starred project also anticipated the "committee" style of Diaghilev's earliest productions in the West, beginning with *Boris Godunov,* to which no fewer than eight artists—as designers and scene painters—contributed. Valerian Svetlov, who sat on Diaghilev's 1909 "committee," described its inner collective workings in which artists and amateurs alike participated:

> How different things are in the new Diaghilev ballets. Composers, painters, ballet masters, authors and those interested in the arts come together and plan the work to be done. Subjects are proposed, discussed, and then worked out in detail. Each makes his suggestions, which are accepted or rejected by a general consensus of opinion, and thus in the end it is difficult to say which individual was responsible for the libretto, and what was due to the common effort. The real author was, of course, he who first proposed the idea, but the amendments, the working-out, the details, made it the work of all. So too with the music, the dances; all is the result of this collective effort . . . Thus, both artistic unity of design and execution are achieved.[23]

Among the dancers, too, informality reigned. Although everyone worked hard, "the rehearsals," Benois wrote, "were a real enchantment":

> There was, from the start, an atmosphere of friendly and eager collaboration. What a charming picture the theatre hall presented when the young people who were not busy on the stage streamed in to watch the performance . . . In many ways it resembled the memorable first rehearsal of *Le Pavillon* [*d'Armide*] in the Imperial School, but here the atmosphere was different. In the Imperial *école de danse* there was an air of official severity . . . Here . . . there was no trace of red tape or officialdom; our gatherings were very informal and gay.[24]

The atmosphere of quiet professionalism and common purpose suffused the whole troupe. Bronislava Nijinska, a member of the corps de ballet, recalled the "genuine cooperation" that existed among the dancers:

> We all tried to help each other, pointing out mistakes as we noticed them and together finding ways to correct them . . . We younger dancers even suggested to the older artists that the Imperial Theatres' custom of wearing personal jewelry . . . could spoil the artistic details of the performance in Paris. We were so thrilled when they happily agreed.[25]

To artists reared in the shadow of Imperial culture, the appeal of Diaghilev's studio—to borrow Stanislavsky's term for his theater's experimentalist offshoots—was incalculable. As fluid in structure as it was flexible in outlook, it offered a compelling alternative to the bureaucracy and conformism of tsarist artmaking. Benois spent only a few months at the Imperial Academy of Arts, but the experience marked him for life. It left him, he wrote, with a "[loathing for] the bureaucratic world of red tape that seemed to have attached itself to art" and made "any sort of 'state service' [seem] absolutely unbearable."[26] This deep-seated antipathy toward the world of official art, which, he adds, "material considerations" occasionally prompted him to enter, was at least partly shared by Diaghilev. Indeed, as the history of the Ballets Russes makes clear, the studio format was immensely appealing to Diaghilev. At moments of transition—during World War I, for instance—he remade his company from top to bottom, transforming it into a studio in which distinctions were leveled and work went forward collaboratively. That the Ballets Russes collapsed with Diaghilev's death attests to the power of the studio idea on his imagination: never would he yield to pressures to bureaucratize the inner workings of his company.

Under Mamontov and Stanislavsky, the amateur circle gave rise to the quasi-commercial organization of the studio. Among the implications of this transition was a redefining of the notion of professionalism. Traditionally, in Russia, professionalism was defined by the state: in the realm of the visual arts, by the Imperial Academy of Arts, the largest and most prestigious art school in the country. Education, however, was not the Academy's sole function. Along with training, it dispensed patronage and—all-important in a country divided into semifeudal "estates"—legal status. The former enabled students to go abroad; the latter, by leading to a rank in the civil service, to enter the employ of the state.[27] In music, too, an artist's status depended upon his relationship to the state. Indeed, as late as the 1860s (when the Conservatory was founded), a musician had no recognized position in Russian society except insofar as he was attached to a theater or school. Thus, Anton Rubinstein, at the height of his fame as a concert pianist, was legally a "merchant of the second guild," as his father had been.[28]

An artist without rank or the legal standing of a professional, Rubinstein was that anomaly of the estate system—a "free" artist. This, in fact, was the term used by Benois to describe Korovin and Golovin, painters who graduated from the Mamontov circle to jobs in the Imperial Theaters in the late 1890s.[29] Their appearance among the ranks of "professional" artists was an event of magnitude, a sign that the guild, so to speak, had ceased to exercise its once total vetting power. Both Korovin and Golovin were proven talents: their experience, however, lay in the private domain; the record of their accomplishments, in the annals of Abramtsevo and Mamontov's Private Opera Company. As early as the 1860s merchant patronage had made it possible for easel painters to exist independent of the state. But only with the entry of Mamontov's circle into the commercial marketplace via opera production did unofficial artists begin to gain access to official theatrical institutions, a major source of employment. In essence, the private sphere came to be viewed as a professional training ground, where artists tested their mettle and bureaucrats scouted for talent. In so doing, the latter tacitly recognized the existence of the free artist, and, with it, the corollary idea that achievement, rather than rank, defined professional status and the standard for professional work. Freedom also had economic implications. When Chaliapin left the Maryinsky to join Mamontov's troupe, he was earning a modest two hundred rubles per month. Mamontov trebled this salary and agreed to pay the singer's fine for breaking his contract with the Imperial Theaters. Three years and several triumphs later, Chaliapin rejoined his former company as a star.[30] His proven value in the commercial marketplace at home and abroad had effectively breached the Imperial monolith. Thus, free status implied a new set of economic relationships. The artist could now sell his labor, and he could do so at prices determined by the law of supply and demand. For the first time, he became an actor in the capitalist marketplace of art. In this, as in so many instances, Mamontov anticipated relationships that Diaghilev would make commonplace.

Beginning with *Mir iskusstva*, Diaghilev's enterprises revealed the social dynamics of the merchant studio. From the start, however, a tension existed between the pluralism that constituted his circle's official ideology and the overwhelming force of Diaghilev's own personality. This tension was not unique to the Diaghilev circle, nor can it be ascribed solely to the peculiarities of his psychology. Rather, it inhered in the very nature of the studio: on the one hand, because of its organization around a single driving force and, on the other, because of the absence of structures to effect change (leading to constant breakaways). In the hands of a Diaghilev or a Mamontov or a Stanislavsky, the studio was an arena where the impulses of the democrat warred with those of an enlightened despot.

For Diaghilev, as for Stanislavsky, there was a direct connection between such enlightened despotism and modern theatrical practice. In "The Originality of the Moscow Art Theater," one of several articles about that troupe written by him for *Mir iskusstva*, Diaghilev linked Stanislavsky's artistic risk-taking to his authority as a producer:

> The chief prerogative of this group lies in the fact that it can allow itself to take risks which any other daring innovator, enjoying less popularity, less authority, would dearly pay for. Here you have a group to whom everything will be forgiven: more, every effort will be made to give credence to its sincerity and the seriousness of its aims, however outrageous they may seem.[31]

In another article, "More About *Julius Caesar*," Diaghilev hailed the discipline of the troupe, the reason, he says, that Stanislavsky's actors were

able to subordinate their many colors as individuals "into a single picture." "Their great merit," he continued, "lies precisely in what they have
been reproached with, namely 'transferring the center of gravity from the
domain of the actor . . . to that of the mechanics of their art' "[32]—in
other words, to the production itself. His praise of Stanislavsky and the
Art Theater foreshadowed his own achievement as a producer. But it also
suggests that Diaghilev viewed theatrical unity in rather more prosaic terms
than the Wagnerians: that instead of ascribing its achievement to some
quasi-mystical *Gesamtkunstwerk*, he saw it as the work of a "producer-
autocrat," as Stanislavsky referred to himself in recalling his directorial
practice of the 1890s and early 1900s.[33] Although Stanislavsky later rejected this concept of the producer, Diaghilev never did.

If merchant enterprise provided Diaghilev with a social and organizational model for his undertakings, merchant money helped to underwrite
them. In 1898 Mamontov put up five thousand rubles, or about thirty
percent of the capital, to launch *Mir iskusstva*. With the collapse of his
financial empire the following year and the withdrawal in 1900 of Princess
Tenisheva's patronage (an action prompted by a caricature showing her as
a cow being milked by Diaghilev), the journal faced a serious financial
crisis. Into the breach stepped two other merchant patrons: Ilya Ostrukhov, a collector who sat on the Tretiakov Gallery's board of trustees and
was an intimate of the Mamontov circle, and Sergei Botkin, another collector, who was Pavel Tretiakov's son-in-law, Bakst's brother-in-law, one
of Sergei Shchukin's first cousins, and a close friend of the former Pickwickians. Both Ostrukhov and Botkin collected *Mir iskusstva* artists and
contributed to the Exhibition of Russian Art organized by Diaghilev in
Paris in 1906. Botkin, moreover, sat on Diaghilev's 1909 "organizing committee."[34]

Although the Paris show enjoyed government backing, this did not
suffice to pay all the bills. According to Nouvel, Diaghilev raised thirty
thousand rubles in Moscow. Presumably, a sizeable portion of this came
from Vladimir Hirschmann and his wife, Moscow nouveaux riches temporarily installed in the French capital, whom Benois called the "Maecenas" of the Exhibition. Hirschmann, a "clean shaven red-mustachioed
banker," lent fourteen items to the show, most of them by World of Art
painters. He also sat on the patronage committee, as did a number of other
contributors—Botkin, Ivan Morozov, Alexis de Hitroff, Baron Vladimir
von Meck, R. Vostriakov, Prince Vladimir Argutinsky-Dolgurakov, Count
Dmitri Benckendorf, and Benois, who wrote the catalogue essay. In the
invitation to the opening, Comtesse Greffuhle, one of the exhibition's three
honorary chairmen, described the group as "comprising the principal collectors of St. Petersburg, Moscow, and Kiev." And, indeed, along with the

familiar Muscovite names, one finds the network of Petersburg collectors associated with *Mir iskusstva:* Argutinsky, described by Benois as a "friend and comrade" of the circle; Benckendorf, a long-time patron and former pupil of Bakst; von Meck, a founder and principal underwriter of Contemporary Art, a short-lived exhibition society that specialized in interior design. Presumably, like Hirschmann, most of these lenders added to the exhibition kitty.[35]

Many of them, too, continued to help Diaghilev, even though the exhibition hall ceased to be the center of his activities. In 1908 Benckendorf, Hitroff, and one of the Morozovs sat on the patronage committee of *Boris Godunov*. Argutinsky personally guaranteed the last-minute loan from an English bank that enabled Diaghilev to complete preparations for the 1909 season. He came to Diaghilev's rescue again in the spring of 1910, countersigning a three-month bill for one thousand pounds borrowed from a friend of Nouvel's mother. Shortly thereafter, when the promised government subsidy was suddenly withdrawn, Argutinsky and A.N. Ratkoff-Rognoff, another lender to the 1906 exhibition and the husband of Diaghilev's first cousin Zina Filosofov, cosigned a short-term bill for the requisite sum.[36]

However incomplete, this account makes one thing clear: by 1906, Diaghilev stood at the center of a national patronage network. Traditionally, artistic relations between Moscow and St. Petersburg were cool. Neither had much contact with the other or much interest in the home-grown style of its counterpart: refined and Westward-gazing, in the case of Petersburg; vigorous and Russian, in that of Moscow. One of the goals of *Mir iskusstva* had been to heal this rift: to unify the two schools under a single national banner. Thanks to Diaghilev's catholic taste and eye for excellence, the journal largely succeeded. Not that the two schools ceased to display striking differences. (If anything, they drew farther apart in these years.) But each now came to national attention and found collectors outside its home city. Unlike Moscow's traditional patrons, collectors like Hirschmann and Mikhail Riabushinsky opened their pocketbooks to Petersburg artists. Both purchased work by Bakst and Somov (Hirschmann paintings by Dobujinsky and Eugene Lanceray as well), and among their loans to the 1906 exhibition were canvases from both cities. "The significance of *Mir iskusstva*," art historian Janet Kennedy has written, "was not simply the introduction of Western art and ideas into Russia, but the cross-fertilization of ideas within the country, that is between St. Petersburg and Moscow."[37] This is patent in the case of collecting, where the journal (and its exhibitions) helped erode the regional parochialism of earlier years. The national network created by Diaghilev appears in exemplary light in a volume by Benois published in 1904. Entitled *The Russian School of Painting*, the book reproduces works in the collections of Hirschmann, von Meck,

Ostrukhov, Botkin, Grand Duke Vladimir (who chaired Diaghilev's patronage committees in 1906–1908), Baron Gunzburg (Diaghilev's "angel"
in the years before World War I), and Diaghilev himself.[38] Here is the
nucleus of the collecting network that supported Diaghilev's earliest activities in the West.

The Russian concert series, produced by Diaghilev at the Paris Opéra
in 1907, brought new patrons to the fore. Not surprisingly, one of them
was the rich St. Petersburg music lover, Nikolai van Gilse van der Pals, a
backer of the Siloti concerts and the author of at least two volumes on
Rimsky-Korsakov. According to Arnold Haskell, Gilse put up ten thousand rubles for the 1907 series. The following year he contributed to the
production of *Boris Godunov,* and in both years sat on Diaghilev's patronage committee.[39] Gilse was not the only director of the Russian-American
Rubber Manufacturing Company to open his checkbook to Diaghilev. Two
others—G. Geize and one Neuscheller—did so as well, the latter earning a
place on the *Boris* committee. Another contributor to the 1908 season,
although not similarly honored, was the famous millionaire grocer Eli-
seyev, whose emporium on the Nevsky Prospekt was the St. Petersburg
equivalent of Fortnum and Mason.[40] Gabriel Astruc, Diaghilev's Paris impresario, claimed that the 1909 enterprise rested on the latter's promise to
raise 300,000 francs from "Russian capitalists." Some of that money—ten
thousand pounds, it is said—came from a mysterious Mr. K, the head of
a galoshes business, whose dream of ennobling himself, wrote Benois, "Diaghilev's clever but unscrupulous financial adviser, D," had "guessed." (With
pressure from the powerful—someone like Diaghilev's benefactor, Grand
Duke Vladimir, say—the head of a commercial house established for over
a century could apply for a patent of nobility.)[41]

The grocers and galoshes manufacturers who helped finance Diaghilev's initial activities in the West signaled a change in the character of private patronage. Connoisseurs, the great Moscow barons had worshipped
art; some were artists in their own right; as patrons, they sought to share
the very act of creation with their beneficiaries. Morozov, it is said, took
charge of lighting Art Theater productions, astonishing experts with his
technical know-how. (In this, he anticipated Diaghilev, another "amateur"
lighting man.) Mamontov had a finger in every aspect of his company's
productions. He spent hours with Chaliapin, remolding his taste, shaping
his artistic views, helping him find the key to a role—as Diaghilev would
do with his own protégés.[42] Some of Diaghilev's own patrons were inti-
mately involved in his enterprises. At the Catherine Hall, where Fokine
rehearsed his dancers for the 1909 season, Argutinsky and Botkin watched
them work and shared their modest meals during breaks.[43] Unlike these
longstanding supporters, Diaghilev's new patrons were conspicuous by their

absence. With the possible exception of Gilse van der Pals (introduced to Diaghilev by Nouvel), all stood outside the network of friends and artistic comrades that accompanied Diaghilev on the journey that ended in the Ballets Russes. The patronage of the newcomers was impersonal. It was also interested, that is, the gold of Diaghilev's grocers and galoshes manufacturers was expected to earn some kind of return: a notice in the press, a patent of nobility, a place in large type on a gala program. Such gold was an investment, defining an economic relationship between benefactor and beneficiary. With Diaghilev's plunge into the Western capitalist marketplace, relationships of this kind became commonplace.

For all they contributed to Russian art in the late nineteenth and early twentieth centuries, merchants did not fundamentally alter the structure of Russian high culture. In part, this reflected the origins of merchant patronage in the philanthropic impulses of the Old Believers. In a recollection of Mamontov, Stanislavsky mentioned the latter's habit of startling visitors with "the thought that religion is declining and art ought to fill its place." There was a populist edge to Mamontov's gospel as well. He sometimes referred to his company as a "People's Opera," and in 1897 organized a Sunday morning performance of Gluck's *Orpheus and Eurydice* that was free for the school children who made up most of the audience. "The stage," he once said, "is not an amusement for the rich . . . but a school, from which art—pure and noble—goes to the people."[44] Merchant philanthropy gave away what merchant enterprise had accumulated. But this was not the only sign of merchant guilt. In the never-ending stream of money, loyalty, and advice poured by merchant patrons on Russian artists, one thing seemed absent—the business acumen that had built the factories, banks, mills, and railroads that made such generosity possible. There is more than a touch of irony in the fact that the class that laid the foundation of Russian capitalism failed to apply its financial genius to art. As we have said, neither the Moscow Art Theater nor Mamontov's Private Opera Company were ever fully self-supporting. Nor were they ever fully commercial. To be sure, they sold tickets and paid performers, but their continued existence depended on their patrons' largess: they teetered on the market's edge. Thus, their creations and personnel were eventually absorbed by the state, which, in the cultural realm at least, enjoyed virtually unlimited resources. Historians have spoken of the "firm alliance" that existed "between the autocracy and capitalism" in the declining years of the Imperial régime. In artistic as in many other respects, the private sector proved to be a "satrap" of the state rather than its equal.[45]

The failure of the merchant class to develop viable institutions capable of producing high culture on a permanent and self-sustaining basis left artists, especially those with an interest in theater, little recourse outside the sphere of official art. For Benois, "state service" was "unbearable," but like many of his friends, he often found employment there. For Diaghilev, an "animateur" without the means of a patron, an even greater dearth of opportunities awaited in the constricted private sphere. Inevitably, he had to look elsewhere for the prestige, political protection, and economic resources to work on a grand scale. For want of an alternative, he—and his colleagues—turned to the only institutions that could provide them, those of the Imperial state.

Autocracy in Russia was not only sovereign, it was everywhere. Like an octopus, it spread its tentacles into preserves long since appropriated in Western Europe by the private sector or given over to professionals. In the realm of cultural activity, particularly, state and tsar were synonymous. Institutions like the Imperial Academy of Arts and the Imperial Theaters existed as departments under the jurisdiction of the Imperial court. They were funded by the Imperial Chancellery, which is to say, out of the tsar's own purse, and headed by relatives of the emperor or aristocrats personally appointed and responsible to him. To all intents and purposes, Imperial training academies and Imperial performance halls existed as fiefdoms of the Tsar of All the Russias.

Even if they did not enjoy entree into court circles, Diaghilev and his friends grew up in the shadow of the state. Benois was from a family of court architects; his brother, Leonti, also an architect, became rector of the Academy of Arts. Bakst and Somov, whose father was curator of the department of painting at the Hermitage, studied for several years at the Academy of Arts, which Benois also attended in 1887–1888. Both Diaghilev and his cousin "Dima" Filosofov took law degrees at St. Petersburg University (higher education was another government bailiwick), and in 1898 Diaghilev finished the course at the Conservatory of Music. The Diaghilev-Filosofov clans, moreover, had a history of state service. Diaghilev's father was for many years an officer in the most exclusive cavalry regiment of the guards, and his stepbrothers entered the cadet corps. The Filosofovs enjoyed even closer ties to the government. Dima's father had occupied the post of Military Prosecutor, while a cousin, Dmitri Filosofov, became the Minister of Commerce and Industry in 1906.[46]

The artistic education of the circle began at home, in the musicales, puppet shows, and poetry readings that were staples of family life among the era's leisured classes. When Diaghilev arrived in St. Petersburg in 1890, he brought as "baggage" (the word is Benois's) a real knowledge of music. "Seriozha's stepmother," wrote Benois:

> was especially devoted to music. She was Elena Valerianovna, *née* Panaev, the
> sister of the well-known singer and daughter of the queer, extravagant old

gentleman who ruined himself in building an extremely ugly theatre for private opera in St. Petersburg. Seriozha's father was also said to be a fine singer and used to sing in the circle of his friends and relations . . .[47]

Sophisticated as private music-making might be, it paled before the spectacle of Imperial lyric theater. Here, luxury ruled, dazzling the eye with sumptuous sets, magical stage effects, armies of singers, dancers, and supernumeraries. "Unforgettable matinee!" rhapsodized Bakst in 1921 about his first glimpse of *The Sleeping Beauty,* unveiled at the Maryinsky thirty-one years before:

> I lived in a magic dream for three hours, intoxicated with fairies and princesses, splendid palaces flowing with gold, in the enchantment of the old tale. My whole being was as if swayed in cadence to the rhythms, the radiant flow of refreshing and beautiful melodies . . . That evening, I believe, my vocation was determined.[48]

To a remarkable degree, the Maryinsky audience mirrored the state that underwrote its entertainments. Bakst, who saw the Petipa masterpiece thanks to a complimentary ticket from a stage manager friend, remembered that assemblage well: the "brightly clad officers of the Guard," the "ladies in evening dress, bejewelled and radiant," the "red coats and white stockings of the Court, so bedizened with Imperial eagles." Anatole Chujoy, a balcony balletomane in the years before World War I, has described the Maryinsky public in less glowing terms. "The same people attended the ballet, performance after performance. If any audience ever became what is often referred to as 'one big family,' it was the ballet audience at the Maryinsky Theatre." Indeed, few were those unconnected with the Imperial court. That court, Chujoy explains:

> was a rather big institution. At the beginning of our century there were nineteen separate courts in St. Petersburg: the Czar's, the dowager Czarina's and seventeen grand-ducal courts. With the families of the Czar and the grand dukes, courtiers . . . and gentlemen-in-waiting, relatives of these dignitaries, the well-staffed Ministry of the Court, etc., etc., the courts comprised several thousand people. In addition, there were his Majesty's Convoy, the Guard Regiments . . . and the naval Guard Equipage. Foreign embassies with their large staffs . . . were also close to the Court and finally there were the aristocratic clubs . . . Now if we consider that of all the theatres in and around St. Petersburg ballet was given regularly only at the Maryinsky, with a seating capacity of some twenty-five hundred, and that the entire ballet season consisted of fifty performances of which forty were by subscription, it fol-

lows that there was not much room left for people who . . . were not connected with the Court, the Guard, the Government, the press or the theatre
itself.[49]

However much they may have inveighed against Maryinsky artistic
policies (especially after Vladimir Telyakovsky's appointment as director
in 1902), the theater left a permanent mark on Diaghilev and his colleagues. The high standard of professionalism that from the first distinguished Ballets Russes productions was an enduring Maryinsky legacy.
Another was the conviction that ballet belonged in the opera house, that
it was an art of high lyric theater. This meant that so long as Diaghilev
had the means (and even when he did not), the scale of production was
lavish, the setting the most prestigious he could muster: always he aspired
to elevate the Ballets Russes to the status of a major operatic attraction.
At the Maryinsky, ballet was inseparable from the substance and form of
hereditary aristocracy. In the West, Diaghilev summoned a different, but
no less powerful elite to the side of ballet—an aristocracy of money and
taste. A fourth legacy of the Maryinsky was the myth of Imperial succession, consciously nurtured by Diaghilev long after his company had severed all but the most tenuous connection with the Imperial Theaters.

In September 1899, that is, less than a year after the launching of
Mir iskusstva, Diaghilev entered state service. His appointment as special
assistant to the director of the Imperial Theaters, a post he held for two
years, was a critical event in his life. For the first time he found an arena
equal to his talent, energy, and burning ambition. But he also discovered
there a bureaucracy mired in routine and fraught with intrigue that looked
askance upon all three qualities. Initially, however, the scene was bright.
Prince Serge Volkonsky, appointed director in July (when he succeeded his
uncle, Ivan Vsevolojsky), was both an acquaintance and a contributor to
Mir iskusstva; whatever his weaknesses as an administrator, Volkonsky's
artistic sympathies clearly lay with his new assistant. In 1900 Diaghilev
received his first assignment: editing the yearbook of the Imperial Theaters. Previously, this had been a modest record of the previous year's events.
Under Diaghilev, it became a monumental *édition de luxe* that was outstanding as much for the variety and abundance of its contents, as for the
quality of the reproductions and the technical perfection of the printing.
The *Annual* put most of the *miriskusstniki* to work. Benois contributed an
article on the Alexandrinsky Theater; Bakst retouched the photographs;
Lanceray drew lettering for the titles. Among the supplements were programs by Somov and an original lithograph by Serov. "Every page," wrote
Benois, "seemed to present a treat for the eye":

It even gave one pleasure to see the type, the lay-out of the page, the way the illustrations were distributed. The illustrations themselves were all chosen with taste and excellently reproduced from faultless plates.[50]

The *Annual* created a sensation (as Diaghilev had hoped it would) among a public that had looked upon *Mir iskusstva* as "the fad of impertinent, 'decadent' youngsters." Its appearance, Benois observed, "produced . . . a change of public opinion in favor of Diaghilev":

> Here at last was something in which there was nothing to criticise; even Seriozha's bitterest enemies were obliged to agree that this edition was the first of its kind in Russia—never before had such a book been published, and, what is more, by a government institution, where official routine had always reigned supreme.[51]

The *Annual* was not the only activity that revealed the influence of *Mir iskusstva*. Under Volkonsky, "free" artists received their first theatrical assignments: Apollinaire Vasnetsov, *Sadko* and *Eugene Onegin;* Bakst, *Le Coeur de la Marquise;* Benois, *Cupid's Revenge.* For Bakst and Benois these productions marked the first of several Imperial commissions. Between 1902 (when *Le Coeur de la Marquise* had its premiere at the Hermitage Theater) and 1908, Bakst designed no fewer than three productions (*Hippolytus*, 1902; *Puppenfee*, 1903; *Oedipus at Colonus*, 1904), in addition to contributing costumes, curtains, and programs to several others.[52] Benois, less favored by the management, designed *Götterdämmerung* (1902) and *Le Pavillon d'Armide* (1907). With the appointment late in 1901 of Vladimir Telyakovsky to Volkonsky's post, both Golovin and Korovin joined the growing number of "free" artists among the corps of Imperial designers.

If the *Annual* was a triumph, Diaghilev's next Imperial "mission" was a catastrophe. The circumstances surrounding the ill-fated *Sylvia* deserve more than passing mention, not only because they ended Diaghilev's career at the Imperial Theaters, but also because the response they triggered would be repeated in later dealings with authority—and with equally detrimental results. Léo Delibes had long been a Pickwickian favorite, and, now that Diaghilev had gained a foothold in the Maryinsky, the group yearned to mount one of his ballets. As *Coppélia* was already in repertory, it chose *Sylvia*. In January 1901, Volkonsky gave Diaghilev carte blanche to stage a "model" production of the work. "The news," wrote Benois:

> was received with great joy and we started on the spot to distribute the work. It was decided to invite the two brothers Legat to be our ballet-masters, for

they were the most prominent of all the young dancers; the part of Sylvia we assigned to O.O. [Olga] Preobrazhenskaya, for whom we had the greatest admiration . . . The question as to whether such a combination of unofficial people, working independently in an institution so bound by red tape, would be possible, never entered anybody's head.[53]

Although Volkonsky may well have given Diaghilev full power, within days he took this away. The project was fine: what Volkonsky's colleagues objected to was entrusting an entire production to someone outside the regular management. Volkonsky went to Diaghilev and asked him, as a gesture of friendship, to remove himself officially from the production: he could do all the work, but the administration of the theater had to be credited for it. "At that point," says Benois:

> Diaghilev took the bit between his teeth. He insisted, very decidedly, on re-taining the powers already given him and very soon the conversation . . . developed a distinctly unpleasant tone. Losing his self-control, Diaghilev even resorted to a kind of blackmail. He announced to Volkonsky that, should *Sylvia* be taken from him, he would refuse to publish the next *Annual* . . . Volkonsky naturally became indignant . . . taking the tone and attitude of a superior, . . . *ordered* Diaghilev to proceed with the *Annual,* and if Diaghilev did not agree to obey him, he would ask him to resign.[54]

Suddenly, the corridors were abuzz. Letters circulated. Mediators tried to reconcile the parties. Grand Duke Sergei Mikhailovitch, who aspired to Volkonsky's post, urged Diaghilev to stand firm, promising, as a last re-sort, to go to the emperor. When he did, Nicholas II pronounced the some-what puzzling words: "In Diaghilev's place I would not have resigned." Meanwhile, General Rydzevsky, acting Minister of the Court and a per-sonal enemy of Diaghilev, slipped before the tsar an order for Diaghilev's summary dismissal. The tsar signed, then had second thoughts. But the mischief had been done. Under Article 3 of the Civil Service Contract, Diaghilev received what was known as a "wolf's passport": he was de-prived forever of the right to enter the government service. Although he eventually received a nominal post in the Ministry of the Court and a salary that continued to be paid until 1917, his career had ended. Hence-forth, he would have to make his own way.[55]

This reverse did not prevent Diaghilev from cultivating powerful alli-ances within the Imperial family, or even retaining the favor of the tsar himself. Although the latter's pen had sealed Diaghilev's fate in the *Sylvia* affaire, Nicholas continued to subsidize *Mir iskusstva*. In fact, from 1900, when, upon petition from Serov (who was then painting his portrait), he agreed to contribute ten thousand rubles a year, until 1904, when the Russo-

Japanese War caused him to discontinue the subsidy, the journal owed its existence to the tsar's bounty. Alexander Taneyev was not a member of the Imperial family, but his position within the Imperial household made him a useful ally. Taneyev was a composer—"lackluster" and "mediocre" are the usual epithets applied to his music (Benois claimed that he "was absolutely devoid of talent"). But he enjoyed personal access to the tsar: as head of the Imperial Chancellery (through which all the tsar's personal correspondence passed) and as the father-in-law of Anna Vyrubova, the lady-in-waiting who introduced the tsarina to Rasputin. It was through Taneyev's good offices that Diaghilev obtained the sinecure that took some of the sting out of his dismissal from the Imperial Theaters. Taneyev contributed financial support (along with his Second Symphony) to the 1907 season of historical concerts, and at Diaghilev's insistence his name appeared on the posters, circulars, and programs for that event.[56]

Diaghilev's most important Imperial patron was not the tsar but his uncle. Grand Duke Vladimir was an old and loyal friend of the *miriskus-stniki*. He had confided the artistic education of his children to Bakst, made frequent purchases at World of Art exhibitions, and openly championed Diaghilev's "decadents"—to the disgust of conservatives. President of the Imperial Academy of Arts, Grand Duke Vladimir was a powerful ally, in Diaghilev's own words:

> a highly cultivated man who thought no sacrifice too great in the cause of art, and he played a very important part in the development of Russian culture. All the artistic institutions of the country were placed under his control and he directed, inspired, and encouraged art in a great variety of forms.[57]

He bore Diaghilev great personal affection and shared, as few Romanovs did, his admiration for the national lyric repertory. (In his autobiographical notes, Diaghilev recalled that when the tsarina learned that he was mounting *Boris Godunov,* all she could say was: "Couldn't you have found anything less boring?")[58] Grand Duke Vladimir, by contrast, was "truly happy and proud that the idea that he, almost alone, had welcomed with so much confidence and done so much to make a reality, obtained so exceptional a success."[59] Encouragement was not all he gave Diaghilev. In 1901 he opened the doors of the Academy to the third World of Art exhibition and seven years later, those of the Hermitage to an exhibition of *Boris Godunov* costumes prior to the opera's premiere in Paris. He allowed his name to head patronage lists and to be used in the corridors of power. He also gave Diaghilev money: indeed, Grand Duke Alexander Mikhailovitch described his cousin as Diaghilev's "original financial backer."[60] With Grand Duke Vladimir's death in the spring of 1909, Diaghilev lost both a friend and a protector in high places.

A third Grand Duke added to the web of influence spun by Diaghilev in the years after his dismissal from the Imperial Theaters. Nikolai Mikhailovitch was the most scholarly and historically minded of the Romanovs and a logical choice to preside over the exhibition that was the crowning achievement of Diaghilev's career in Russia. Arnold Haskell has called the Exhibition of Russian Historical Portraits at the Tauride Palace in 1905 "the great summing up": the culmination of Diaghilev's plunges into the forgotten art of Russia's eighteenth century. In 1902 Diaghilev brought out the first of three projected volumes on the painting of that era—a masterly study of Dmitri Levitsky that won its author the Uvarov Prize, awarded by the Academy of Sciences. Diaghilev never wrote the other two volumes. But on the walls of the Tauride Palace he spelled out their contents in thousands of portraits, statues, busts, watercolors, miniatures, and drawings collected from every corner of Russia. Benois, who assisted him, marveled at the fury that drove him, the energy, patience, and firmness he displayed. This exhibition, wrote Igor Grabar, an artist and critic, "inaugurated a new era in the study of Russian and European art of the eighteenth and first half of the nineteenth century":

> In place of conflicting data and vague facts, it became possible, for the first time, using the gigantic quantities of material gathered from all over Russia, to establish fresh data, and throw new light on interlocking sources, relations and influences, unsuspected before. One result was a whole series of drastic, and at times unexpected, revaluations of the work of many artists; much that was obscure before now became plainer, and new and tempting vistas for deeper investigation were thrown open.[61]

The tsar gave his "Most August Protection" to the exhibition, and surrounded by his family and suite paid a formal visit to the opening. This took place in the aftermath of "Bloody Sunday," when the dynasty, so proudly displayed on the walls, was tottering in the streets. To many in St. Petersburg, the Tauride Palace became a retreat from the turmoil of those troubled days. One who visited it often was Diaghilev's aunt. "You, no doubt, too, must be feeling the same terrible anxiety and depression we all feel here," she wrote to his stepmother:

> But my thoughts are often with you, and I write now, because I have just undergone a complete spiritual metamorphosis—alas, temporary, no doubt—which has raised me to the skies. I have been to the exhibition in the Tauride Palace, and you cannot imagine—not the liveliest imagination could picture

it—the superhuman grandeur of what I saw. I was transported into a world that seems infinitely nearer than our own.[62]

Yet for all the crowds that flocked to his exhibition, Diaghilev's larger goal eluded him. That goal, now that the Imperial Theaters lay beyond his grasp, was a museum. As early as 1901, he had laid out his ideas for a national gallery in an article in *Mir iskusstva*. Four years later, he had laid the foundation for such a museum in the neglected Tauride Palace. For a time, luck seemed to run in his favor. Change is the essence of revolution, even one as moderate as that of 1905. Although *Mir iskusstva* had led many charges against the citadels of Imperial culture, only in the turmoil of that year did the possibility of taking them finally arise. On September 15, Diaghilev launched a major attack on Vladimir Telyakovsky and his management of the Imperial Theaters in the newspaper *Rus'*. Telyakovsky had complained of the lack of interesting new plays and operas. Diaghilev replied that Telyakovsky had only himself to blame: having no artistic policy, he could hardly expect new talent to flourish:

> Before the rise of the Moscow Art Theater we had no dramatists like Chekhov and Gorky . . . Without Vsevolojsky we would not have had *The Sleeping Beauty* [and] *The Queen of Spades* . . . What would we have missed without the current administration? *The Magic Mirror?*[63]

Two months later, with the country still in the throes of revolution, Diaghilev submitted a report to the Minister of Education that proposed major changes in the organization of artistic life. Advocating the transfer of the Academy of Arts and the Imperial Theaters from the Ministry of the Court to the Ministry of Education, he called upon the new government to undertake a sweeping program of reform:

> In a time of forthcoming reforms and reorganization of Departments and Ministries, the question of the artistic life of the country and the distribution of responsibility to art-administrative organs is extremely important. This question, apparently at first glance not sufficiently substantive in comparison with the major reforms of government structure, nonetheless ought of necessity to arise at one of the first meetings of the State Duma . . . Those reforms that were carried out decades ago in the West—reforms of art education, theatrical institutions, museums and storehouses, organization of exhibition pavilions, preservation of monuments of the past, and, finally, the material position of people working in the field of the arts—have not touched Russia.[64]

Unfortunately, for Diaghilev, his salvo misfired. Within months of his report, reaction set in. Formally, the country became a constitutional monarchy; behind the scenes, the autocracy dug in its heels. Diaghilev's plan had represented a direct attack on Baron Vladimir Fredericks, the all-powerful Minister of the Imperial Court. Far from curtailing his power, the revanche that gained momentum in 1906 and 1907 only strengthened Fredericks's position, as it also did Telyakovsky's. For the latter was a Fredericks protégé, by some accounts, his "adopted nephew," and one of numerous guardsmen appointed by the former aide-de-camp to posts in the cultural bureaucracy. Diaghilev's political maneuvers in the autumn of 1905 can only have earned the Minister's enmity.[65]

Nevertheless, from 1906 to 1908, Diaghilev's star continued to rise. Intrigue failed to dam the flow of Imperial patronage. Late in life Diaghilev insisted that he had "never received a single kopek from the Russian government." It turns out that he received not just kopeks, but rubles—thousands of them. Crown monies, for instance, covered the huge deficit between the cost of the 1906 show at the Salon d'Automne (300,000 rubles) and the income it produced (a scant 25,000). The concert season at the Paris Opéra the following year and the production there in 1908 of *Boris Godunov* received Crown subsidy as well, the contribution to *Boris* being, in the words of Diaghilev's second-in-command, M.D. Calvocoressi, "a huge one." Gabriel Astruc's breakdown of capital for the 1909 season lists a figure of fifty thousand francs under the rubric of government subsidy, while in their memoirs Prince Peter Lieven and Mathilde Kchessinska mention sums ranging from thirty thousand to seventy-one thousand francs.[66] The planning for *Boris* found Diaghilev scuttling from one government office to another. "Don't forget," he had admonished Rimsky-Korsakov on May 2, 1907:

> I have to convince the Grand Duke Vladimir that our undertaking is useful from the national point of view; the Minister of Finance—that it is profitable from the economic point of view; and even the Director of Theaters that it will be of benefit for the Imperial Theaters. And how many others![67]

Imperial bounty enriched these enterprises in still other ways. Many of the priceless works of art exhibited in 1906 came from Imperial Palaces: that is, they were on loan from the Emperor himself. For *Boris Godunov*, the management of the Imperial Theaters lent Diaghilev "all the assistance one might wish." (Considering the strong mutual antipathy that existed between him and Telyakovsky, the cooperation must have been exceptional.) "The chorus," he wrote:

> was borrowed from the Bolshoi Theater in Moscow and the artists invited [to participate] were the best . . . For the backstage part, a team of carpenter-

stagehands, under the direction of K.F. Waltz, the era's conjurer of theatrical illusion, was brought from Moscow. The orchestra was conducted by F.M. Blumenfeld, today director of the Kiev Conservatory of Music.[68]

Diaghilev forgot two things in his recollections: the orchestra and the dancers who appeared in the Polish scene. These, too, came from the Imperial Theaters. The following year, through the influence of Grand Duke Vladimir, Diaghilev obtained "the necessary permission from the Czar . . . to select a troupe from the Imperial Ballet." In 1908 and 1909 rehearsals took place at the tsar's own theater in the Hermitage, another gift arranged by Diaghilev's protector. Indeed, Grand Duke Alexander Mikhailovitch's later assertion that through the generosity of his brother-in-law, Nicholas II, Diaghilev "joined the list of the subsidized theaters," is not far from the mark. Infusions of private capital notwithstanding, Diaghilev's exports had all the earmarks of an Imperial enterprise.[69]

Support of this magnitude was more than a sign of personal favor or Diaghilev's high standing with the emperor. The flow of patronage bespoke a larger design, a game of international cultural politics in which Diaghilev (like today's Bolshoi Ballet) was but one among a host of financial and foreign-office players. On April 16, 1906, an international banking consortium comprising mostly French and British capital negotiated the largest loan ever made to the government of Nicholas II. This transaction not only saved Russia from financial collapse, but enabled the régime to reestablish its authority after the disastrous war with Japan and the Revolution of 1905. Despite liberal opposition to the loan in France, diplomatic pressure forced it through: the country needed an ally on Germany's eastern flank. Terrified of a Russo-German rapprochement and anxious for a convention between Russia and Britain (one was signed in 1907), the French foreign office happily exploited Russia's dire need for cash. The Ministry of Finance, for its part, passed out liberal bribes among the Paris press.[70]

Diaghilev's early ventures abroad thus coincided with a critical moment in Russian financial and political diplomacy. Blessed by the tsar, they graciously acknowledged the rescue of his régime from economic and dynastic collapse. They testified to the renewal of commitment between the two allies, and the enduring quality of their friendship. To the cultivated, they announced the vitality of Russian art and the existence of a national patrimony on a par with that of any European state. Above all, Diaghilev's symbolic gestures confirmed Russia's status as a major power: the slumbering giant of the north, as represented on the walls of the Grand Palais or on the stage of the Opéra, was fully the equal of its Western ally.

From the start Diaghilev's missions enjoyed high favor in Paris diplomatic and official circles. In 1906 two of the three honorary chairmen of his patronage committee held government positions: A.J. Nelidov, the Russian ambassador to France, and Dujardin-Beaumetz, the French Under-Secretary of Fine Arts. Nelidov was not the only Russian diplomat to link his name publicly with Diaghilev's. The exhibition, noted Benois, had the "strong and solid support" of the Embassy, as did all of Diaghilev's enterprises up to 1910.[71] The Embassy also used its prestige to influence the press. In April 1909, for instance, "a gentleman," acting "on behalf of the Embassy," asked the editor of the newspaper *Le Temps* to insert a favorable notice about the forthcoming ballet season. The mysterious caller added that such a notice "would be very agreeable to the Grand Dukes."[72] Moreover, it was from among the banking and financial connections of Arthur Raffalovich, the Russian Government's powerful financial agent in Paris, that significant amounts of guaranty capital for the 1909 season were raised. The subscribers included Baron Henri de Rothschild, whose banking firm had a history of investments in Russia; André Bénac, managing director of the Banque de Paris et des Pays-Bas, the leader of the so-called "Christian" group of banks that had participated in the 1906 loan (the Rothschilds had refused to because of the recent wave of pogroms in Russia); Basil Zaharoff, a Turkish-born financier of Russian parentage whose shipbuilding, oil, and munitions enterprises made him one of the world's richest men. Other subscribers from the Raffalovich circle were Comte Isaac de Camondo and Henri Deutsch de la Meurthe. Such support within Embassy circles attests to a close—and public—link between Diaghilev's enterprises and the Russian government, a link that remained in effect until the spring of 1910, when "the Tsar," Lieven tells us, "was persuaded to command all Russian embassies to refuse any support to the Diaghileff enterprise." The title Diaghilev used in signing contracts through 1909— "Attaché in the Personal Chancellery of His Majesty, the Emperor of Russia"—conveyed to the French, including his own impresario, that he was conducting business under an official mandate.[73]

Diaghilev's successive triumphs proved the value of a policy of cultural export. But Diaghilev did not reap the fruits of his Imperial labors for long. As early as June 1909, Pierre Gheusi, a highly placed Paris Opéra official whom Diaghilev had approached for support, was writing privately: "There will be no *official* Russian season next year in Paris. This is the *express* will of the Russian court and the Grand Dukes." The following spring, Diaghilev met open hostility and contempt in Embassy circles.[74]

As an exporter of Imperial culture, Diaghilev enjoyed a virtual monopoly in the fields of exhibition and musical activities. In ballet, however, a rival had appeared, a star who could garner Imperial prestige without treading on bureaucratic toes. Anna Pavlova's triumphant tours of Northern and Central Europe in 1908 and 1909 were sponsored by the Maryin-sky management, which bore most of the costs, provided most of the costumes, and allowed its name to be used: in 1908 the group of twenty dancers traveled as "The Imperial Ballet from the Maryinsky Theater."[75] More than her extraordinary talent explained the Imperial favor Pavlova enjoyed. For several years, she had lived under the protection of Baron Victor Dandré, a man of wealth who owned considerable property in the Baltic and a vast estate in Poltava. The Baltic connection, like Dandré's business instinct and conservative artistic taste, endeared him to Baron Fredericks who considered appointing him to a post in the Imperial theaters at the time Diaghilev served as Volkonsky's assistant. The claim has been made that Diaghilev broached to Dandré the possibility of organizing a ballet organization around Pavlova. It has also been suggested that Fredericks and Dandré secretly planned Pavlova's 1908 tour with the backing of the tsar and the Council of Grand Dukes as a ballet link in the chain of "politico-cultural gestures" cementing the Entente Cordiale.[76]

How much truth there is to this is a matter of conjecture. Nevertheless, there exists sufficient circumstantial evidence to lend credence to the argument that with the death of Grand Duke Vladimir in the spring of 1909, Baron Fredericks gained the upper hand in an intrigue designed to blacklist Diaghilev and sever the connection between his foreign enterprises and the court. Diaghilev had many enemies in court circles, from Kchessinska's protector, Grand Duke Sergei Mikhailovitch (who allegedly "kept an historic record" of Pavlova's first tours), to the tsar himself. (Apparently, Nicholas told one of Diaghilev's Filosofov cousins "that he was afraid one day or other [Diaghilev] might play him some scurvy trick.") Volkonsky has written of the ill-feeling created in the Imperial Theaters by Diaghilev's high-handed ways, and there are suggestions that Diaghilev's homosexuality played a role not only in his dismissal but also in Fredericks's active dislike of him. Diaghilev's fundraising strategies raised eyebrows as well. Grand Duke Vladimir may not have minded pulling strings to ennoble a generous galoshes manufacturer, but his widow balked at the very idea of it—and declined to help Diaghilev after her husband's death. "It was largely due to Diaghileff's methods of obtaining money," Joseph Paget-Fredericks later claimed to have been told by his great-uncle, "that government support was not forthcoming."[77]

In personnel and artistic orientation, the company assembled by Diaghilev for his first Paris dance season reflected the aspirations of the Maryinsky's left wing. Diaghilev, too, may well have been viewed as a liberal after 1905, especially in court circles. His chief patron that year—Grand Duke Nikolai Mikhailovitch—enjoyed the reputation of a radical and was known among the elite guard units as "Philippe Egalité." The Minister of

Education to whom Diaghilev addressed his 1905 report was Count Ivan Tolstoi, a well-meaning idealist who lost his post when Count Witte's government fell from power in 1906. Sympathetic to Diaghilev's ideas, the liberal Tolstoi allowed his name to be added to the patronage committee of the Paris exhibition.[78] To the arch-conservative Minister of the Court, political differences could easily have compounded personal dislike.

Theoretically, Pavlova was the star around whom the 1909 company revolved. In reality, however, this was far from being the case. The *Wunderkind* of the season turned out to be Nijinsky. The new Vestris created by Diaghilev's publicity not only undermined Pavlova's position, but as a public symbol of Diaghilev's sexual proclivities caused no little consternation in court circles.[79] (A typical instance of Diaghilev's favoritism was the last-minute substitution of *Les Sylphides* and *Le Festin* for *Giselle*, with the ballerina in the title role, at the Paris Opéra gala on June 19, 1909.)[80] Except for a handful of guest appearances in London in 1911, Pavlova abandoned the Diaghilev enterprise. To her withdrawal, Paget-Fredericks claims, Diaghilev later "attributed his lack of success in obtaining from Fredericks further subsidies from the Czar."[81]

Certainly, unlike Diaghilev, Pavlova continued to enjoy the blessing of the Imperial Theaters. She returned periodically to dance on the Maryinsky stage. In 1910 the Imperial government "loaned" to the Max Rabinoff producing organization (upon receipt of a $250,000 bond) the troupe that danced on her first American tour. Indeed, as late as November 1915 there was talk in the American press about a "project of co-operation" between the "Russian Imperial Opera Company" and the Boston Grand Opera, with which Pavlova and her troupe were then performing.[82] After 1912, when legal difficulties, exacerbated in some way by Diaghilev, caused Dandré to flee Russia, he linked his life with Pavlova's, becoming her manager and consort. Whatever "hopes of rehabilitation in the highest circles" Diaghilev may have continued to harbor found no hearing within the Imperial court.[83]

By 1909 the Imperial régime had rightly discerned in the success of Diaghilev's foreign enterprises an explicit challenge to its cultural monopoly. The effort to destroy him failed, however, because by then he had found the contacts, wherewithal, and expertise to survive in the international marketplace even without government backing. Capital from bankers, financiers, and private patrons flowed into his coffers; artists, disenchanted with the Imperial Theaters, eagerly followed him; in Paris an audience awaited new creations. By 1909 Diaghilev had amassed the means for an independent ballet company.

The ensemble that so dazzled Paris audiences in 1909 did more than export the art of the Maryinsky's balletic secession. Drawing on the dual legacy of state and merchant artmaking, this troupe *d'occasion* gave birth to a new and vital form of enterprise. With Diaghilev's first *saison de danse* at the Châtelet Theater, Russian ballet entered the modern marketplace.

6 ✍

INTO THE MARKETPLACE

W HEN DIAGHILEV LED his company of dancers to Paris, no one could have predicted its success. Nor could anyone have foretold the sequence of events that would culminate in the birth of the Ballets Russes two years later. In retrospect, however, the founding of the company and the character it assumed as an enterprise were not entirely fortuitous. Rather, both appear as logical responses to a marketplace for ballet that Diaghilev himself partly created. Between 1909 and 1914 his troupe ceased to be an appendage of the Imperial Theaters or the protégé of merchant godfathers. It became, instead, a vast commercial undertaking, whose complex organization and even more complex finances answered to the laws of supply and demand.

Unlike Russia, the West offered a home to such an enterprise—in the operatic marketplace. Here Diaghilev found the impresarios who promoted his seasons, underwrote at least some of his productions, and brought to them the influential public of opera's Golden Age. Guiding Diaghilev's plunge into this world was one of the era's most remarkable impresarios. Producer, publisher, talent manager, and founder of the Théâtre des Champs-Elysées, Gabriel Astruc stood at the Paris crossroads of the international music world, a major figure in its rapidly expanding trade in properties and attractions. His papers at the New York Public Library and Archives Nationales in Paris disclose the astonishing range of his activities in the decade from 1903–1913, when his star blazed over the City of Lights, then darkened under the shadow of bankruptcy. His correspondents included the greatest singers, composers, and impresarios of the day, while the musical and theatrical projects he brought to fruition made history. Among these was his 1907 production—the first in France—of Richard Strauss's *Salomé,* with a German cast and the composer himself on the podium; the triumphant maiden visit of the Metropolitan Opera three years later; Mozart, Beethoven, and Berlioz festivals; and beginning in 1907, nearly all of Diaghilev's Russian seasons. The claim that between 1905 and 1913 this dynamic producer had a finger in nearly every musical and theatrical event of importance in Paris is scarcely an exaggeration.[1]

Although the 1909 season represented a blazing artistic triumph, it was also a financial disaster. Box office receipts failed to recoup the difference between production costs and capital raised from Russian sources, leaving Diaghilev with a huge Frs. 86,000 debt to Astruc. Through the latter's good offices, one of the season's French guarantors contributed Frs. 10,000. A less altruistic transaction, also negotiated by Astruc, reveals that concerns other than monetary ones were uppermost in his mind. At the bargain price of Frs. 20,000, the sale of Diaghilev's entire stock of matériel to impresario Raoul Gunsbourg aimed to eliminate Diaghilev as an artistic rival. The longtime director of the Monte Carlo Opéra, for his part, quickly brought to the stage his own version of *Ivan the Terrible* using the costumes and settings acquired from the Russian upstart.[2]

As a capitalist of art, Astruc was hardly unaware of the new opportunities for profit created by Diaghilev's success. Indeed, in the months immediately following the 1909 season, he sought to corner the market and appropriate to himself the exclusive role of presenting Russian ballet in the West. During this period, he sounded connections in St. Petersburg for clues to Diaghilev's position. On August 2, 1909, he wrote to ballerina Mathilde Kchessinska, whose relations with Diaghilev were particularly strained, asking when she would be free to review the events of the previous season. "I have learned," he added, "that Monsieur Diaghilev has just negotiated a season at the Paris Opéra for the coming year. Are you aware of this and does it interest you?"[3]

With Russians playing the Opéra on the same nights he offered the Metropolitan Opera at the Châtelet, Diaghilev's engagement seriously jeopardized Astruc's plans to produce the stellar event of the 1910 season. "One small detail worries me," he wrote with ill-concealed fury to Emile Enoch. "The Russian with whom I conducted my business last year has the nerve to return to Paris this year and try to compete with me." By late fall Astruc had embarked on a vendetta aimed at discrediting Diaghilev among potential backers of a 1910 season and challenging his exclusive access to Imperial dancers. In mid-November he called on Grand Duke André, Kchessinska's lover and a sworn enemy of Diaghilev and his enterprise. The day after their interview, Astruc wrote to Baron Fredericks, requesting permission to submit a report of Diaghilev's activities during the previous Russian season. This self-serving document detailed Diaghilev's repeated failures to live up to his contractual obligations and insisted that his behavior had "compromised in France the good name of the administration of the Imperial Theaters." He ended by suggesting that in the future the Minister of the Imperial Court withhold his "official authorization" of an " 'amateur impresario' whose credit in Paris has been so severely damaged."[4] In his eagerness to quash competition in the marketing of Russian ballet talent abroad, Astruc's ruthlessness knew no bounds.

At the same time, Astruc was deep in correspondence with a St. Petersburg impresario about an alternative ballet enterprise for the summer of 1910. His co-conspirator was Boris Schidlovsky, ballet critic for a small St. Petersburg newspaper and husband of Julie Sedova, a première danseuse of the Imperial Ballet whom Diaghilev had failed to engage in 1909. Counting on a campaign in the Russian press to discredit Diaghilev and thus prevent him from raising production money for a 1910 season, Schidlovsky proposed the organization of a troupe headed by Sedova and Pavlova's one-time partner Adolph Bolm (whose ambitions as both a performer and choreographer Diaghilev was unwilling to further), and including other artists "unhappy" with the "small roles" allotted to them in Diaghilev ballets. He suggested that this company be engaged to dance in the opera ballets and divertissements during the Metropolitan season and that if the Diaghilev enterprise should fall through at the last minute (as he thought likely), the two companies could merge and programs of Russian ballet alternate with Italian opera at the Châtelet.[5]

On December 24 Diaghilev signed a Frs. 100,000 contract with the Paris Opéra. By mid-February 1910 he had liquidated his debt to Astruc and also repurchased at least some of the costumes and scenery sold to Gunsbourg the previous summer.[6] An accommodation was reached with Astruc whereby Diaghilev agreed to alternate Ballets Russes performances with those of the Metropolitan. He also agreed to let Astruc's Société Musicale handle advertising and publicity for the forthcoming season. Although the schemes to destroy Diaghilev's monopoly over what had suddenly become a desirable commodity ultimately failed, they attest to what degree the competitive market had intruded by late 1909 into the enterprise of Russian ballet.

The 1910 season at the Paris Opéra established Diaghilev's bargaining position among his fellow impresarios. With a repertory of seven ballets, he again proved his mettle as an organizer. Not only did he repeat the artistic success of the previous season, but he also demonstrated that he could do so without running afoul of creditors. As Astruc had predicted, receipts fell off from the previous season—from Frs. 522,000 to Frs. 398,887. Yet despite the drop in income, Diaghilev managed to cover the Frs. 1,210,000 that by his own estimate represented the cost of the entire 1910 enterprise.[7]

Part of the deficit was made up by seasons in Berlin and Brussels before and toward the end of the Paris engagement. Other sums came from backers in Russia. These included Savva Morozov, M.A. Kalashnikova, Baron Dmitri Gunzburg, and Nikolai Bezobrazov. Bezobrazov, "a friend of the Minister of Trade," and Victor Dandré, moreover, guaranteed loans from the Russian Bank and Société Mutuel Crédit, respectively. On the French end, the names of the Comtesse de Chévigné, Comtesse de Béarn, and above all, the Marquise de Ganay were touted in St. Petersburg as Diaghilev's "grand appui financier."[8]

Yet no matter how many patrons Diaghilev could muster, the sheer economics of ballet necessitated the organization of finances on a more systematic basis. In the Western artistic marketplace, a private company aspiring to the grandeur of the Imperial stage could survive only as an enterprise servicing the international opera network.

Diaghilev's negotiations with major opera house directors and impresarios during the period April–December 1910 marked a crucial step in the creation of the Ballets Russes. Ending in a series of draft contracts, they offered the economic foundation for a permanent troupe. In late July and early August, tentative agreements were reached with Giulio Gatti-Casazza, managing director of New York's Metropolitan Opera, and Thomas Quinlan, manager of the Thomas Beecham Opera Company of London. Five months later, a similar contract was drafted with Messrs. Paradossi and Cansegli of the Teatro Colón in Buenos Aires.[9] Together, these three documents, for which Astruc acted as Diaghilev's intermediary, provided long-term engagements for the 1911–1912 and 1912–1913 seasons. These agreements represented more than bookings at a particular "house." Organizations like the Metropolitan wielded influence over broad spheres of musical enterprise. As producers, they molded public taste, while as theatrical agents they held the key to profitable touring circuits. If Beecham controlled the most prestigious theaters of London's musical world, the Teatro Colón set the standard for Brazil and the River Plate region of South America. Most awesome of all was the power of the Metropolitan, which opened the doors of opera houses and legitimate theaters not only across the vast expanse of the United States, but Canada, Cuba, and Mexico as well. The launching of Diaghilev's independent company rested on his alliance with the powerbrokers of the operatic marketplace.

Although all these contracts were eventually renegotiated, they offered the requisite base for a permanent organization. In the autumn of 1910 Diaghilev signed up the first dancers for his troupe. During these same months, he received permission from Claude Debussy for a "choreographic adaptation" of "Prélude à l'après-midi d'un faune" and commissioned the score of *Le Dieu Bleu* from Reynaldo Hahn. In December, just as Diaghilev advised the Metropolitan via Astruc, "troupe excellente est formée," Nijinsky began the earliest sketches of *L'Après-midi d'un Faune.*[10]

In the years preceding World War I, Diaghilev enjoyed cordial relations with the managements of Europe's established opera houses. His company made regular appearances on the subsidized stages of Paris, Brussels, Berlin, and Monte Carlo, where, beginning in 1911, he set up headquarters for the troupe's winter rehearsal period. Reversing Italy's half-century long tradition of exporting ballet masters and dancers, in early 1911 La Scala mounted both *Schéhérazade* and *Cléopâtre* with Fokine and Ida Rubinstein being specially engaged for the premieres, one of many signs of the rapid internationalization of the Diaghilev repertory.[11] Despite these connections, however, established houses did not so much shape company direction as provide a venue for performances. Catering to traditional tastes and audiences, they were unlikely to identify with and promote Diaghilev's brand of artistic innovation. These houses, moreover, all possessed resident ballet troupes which, though artistically inferior, precluded long-term association with a visiting rival.

To a large degree, Diaghilev's success in integrating his company into the era's operatic marketplace relied upon impresarios who operated outside the subsidized mainstream. Newcomers to a world ruled by tradition, men like Gabriel Astruc and Sir Thomas Beecham, the one a rabbi's son and the other the grandson of a manufacturer of patent medicine, or Oscar Hammerstein and Max Rabinoff in the United States,[12] made their mark by creating alternative organizations that catered to the desire for novelty and innovation among a growing segment of the musical public. Cosmopolitan in taste and outlook, they were entrepreneurs imbued with the religion of high culture who found in the upstart tribe from Russia's steppes the perfect complement of their innovation-minded artistic ideals, a reflection of their status as outsiders, and a means of gaining social and professional legitimacy. With its unusual combination of opulence and artistry, innovation (except for Nijinsky's works) within the acceptable bounds of symbolism and Art Nouveau, and traditional standards of professionalism, the prewar Ballets Russes held enormous appeal for their knowledgeable audience of followers.

Diaghilev's connection with these independent mavericks of the musical world was a marriage of convenience serving both parties. For impresarios like Astruc and Beecham, who produced most of Diaghilev's prewar seasons in the French and English capitals, a touring company that replicated the producing function of the West's class opera houses had become a financial necessity. As Beecham discovered at the end of 1910 when his first twelve-month venture in opera production at Covent Garden had ended, such efforts were "courting disaster," even with considerable financial backing (in his case that of Beecham senior).[13] "It began to be all too clear to me what I had suspected for some time," he wrote with the hindsight of nearly a decade of production experience, "namely, that without assistance from the state or municipality, a first-rate operatic organization could never be maintained on a permanent basis":

> Individual seasons might now and then be run at a trifling loss . . . But an institution that employs the services of the best available singers, musicians, dancers, mechanicians, producers, and scene painters, is a commercial impossibility and beyond the means of one man, unless he be a multi-millionaire. Modern history, alas, has not yet furnished the refreshing phenomenon of a multi-millionaire who has taken a really serious interest in music.[14]

The prospects for survival of a permanent theater were equally grim, a lesson Astruc learned the hard way when he built and quickly lost the magnificent Théâtre des Champs-Elysées. The splendid inaugural season, which included ballet, French and Russian opera, the premiere of Nijinsky's *Sacre du Printemps* and Ida Rubinstein's *La Pisanelle*, ended in bankruptcy. In an age when seventy- or eighty-piece orchestras were de rigueur (*Sacre* called for over ninety instruments), when ballet, like opera, filled the grand stage with huge companies and richly costumed armies of extras, costs precluded production on a regular basis outside subsidized institutions.

Hence the appeal of Diaghilev's prepackaged repertory and company for hire. For a stipulated fee, one reaped the fruits of someone else's investment while counting on a vastly expanded public to cover operating and overhead costs. The uniqueness of the Diaghilev enterprise, however, cost impresarios dear, reportedly £1,000 per night during the 1911 Coronation season, when the company made its London debut with a cast of 100 dancers and 200 supernumeraries.[15] Diaghilev drove a hard bargain, and in this prewar period, when he could write his own ticket, he did not have to answer to the box office. Unlike his postwar contracts, where payment was often calculated as a percentage of box office receipts with a guaranteed performance minimum, Diaghilev's prewar agreements generally stipulated a flat performance fee—£400 in the case of Beecham's initial contract and Frs. 24,000 for the Champs-Elysées season in 1913.[16] Like the international divas who by 1900 had displaced home-grown talent on the opera circuits, the Diaghilev company traveled from theater to theater, the star ballet attraction and touring arm of the era's leading opera brokers.

Touring was the price Diaghilev paid for independence. An imperative

of the marketplace, it set the twentieth-century pattern for ballet companies that did not enjoy government backing. It was a course, moreover,
that had aesthetic consequences, both favorable and unfavorable, for the
company's overall development. In his June 25, 1911, "Art Letter" for
Rech', Benois spelled them out for the St. Petersburg audience:

> But can one expect further systematic . . . development under the conditions
> in which the Diaghilev enterprise exists, the conditions of a touring company?
> Theaters of the greatest genius, it is true, arose amidst wandering actors and,
> in fact, in many respects the special psychology of the itinerant theater is even
> conducive to the special effervescence of creation; such companies are forced
> to learn simplicity and consequently strength of means. This is a miraculous
> gymnastic. But all the same . . . only a settled way of life can now move the
> Diaghilev enterprise further along the path to perfection, having released it
> from accidental conditions with which it must now be reconciled. In a settled
> routine, with an abundance of time, the possibilities of rechecking the crea-
> tions can be freed of compromise—especially the creation itself on stage, the
> realization of the theater action. In an itinerant theater you risk something
> fundamental each minute, and thus somehow never get to the point of polish-
> ing your work.[17]

In an interview published in the Montevideo newspaper *El Día*, Nijinsky
spoke at length about the emotional toll of life on the road: the faceless
impersonality of hotels, the sadness of a new theater glimpsed for the first
time in shadowy work lights. "Always in a hurry, we live the life of a
'wandering Jew' . . . a wandering Jew who travels in a sleeping car."[18]

   Neither Astruc nor Beecham limited their participation in the Diaghilev enterprise to bookings. In 1912 Diaghilev engaged the Beecham
orchestra, which after two seasons at Covent Garden had the company's
repertory at its fingertips, to play a two-month engagement at Berlin's Kroll
Theater. For Beecham's fledgling English orchestra, a debut in the German
music capital under such auspicious circumstances was most advanta-
geous. That same year, Beecham advanced Diaghilev £950; in lieu of his
usual performance fee, Diaghilev agreed to accept twenty-five percent of
the gross receipts after orchestra, lighting, publicity, and other expenses
had been deducted.[19] In 1913–1914, moreover, both impresarios underwrote several company productions. Significantly, their investment was
concentrated in opera. "I was convinced," wrote Beecham in his memoirs,
"that what was vital to the operatic situation in London was some new
visitation of striking originality":

> It was impossible to overlook the undiminished popularity of the Ballet, and
> it was at least imaginable that another one hundred per cent Russian institu-

tion might be the solution of the problem. I accordingly resigned my position at Covent Garden, requested Diaghileff to negotiate the visit of a company from the Imperial Opera of St. Petersburg to include singers, chorus, new scenery and costumes, indeed everything except the orchestra, and took a lease of Drury Lane Theatre. Thus I found myself for the summer of 1913 in the same position of rivalry to the house across the street that I should have occupied two years earlier had I carried out my old program as first intended.[20]

Although Diaghilev's fame rests on the Ballets Russes, his prewar seasons took place against a background of opera. Not only was this the medium in which he had scored his first theatrical triumph, but scarcely a season passed when his troupe did not share venues and even bills with its sister art. In 1913–1914, however, opera became far more than a setting: it occupied a place in the repertory that outweighed even the prominent role it had played in 1909. Coinciding with a period of economic uncertainty, the phenomenon reflected Diaghilev's increasing reliance on musical impresarios for large infusions of capital.

Although Beecham took sole credit for bringing Russian opera to London in 1913, Astruc actually footed the bill. For the revival of *Boris Godunov* and the Paris premiere of *Khovanshchina*, stellar events of the Théâtre des Champs-Elysées inaugural season, Astruc, by his own account, spent "700,000 francs in the land of the Tsars." "The Court mantles of the boyars alone cost 150,000 francs!"—an act of wanton extravagance or utter madness for a producer close to bankruptcy. Astruc then loaned the costumes and scenery to Diaghilev. Under the aegis of the Beecham organization, the operas received their London premiere in tandem with the Ballets Russes summer season at the Theatre Royal, Drury Lane. When Astruc declared bankruptcy, Beecham acquired both productions for Frs. 40,000, subsequently selling *Boris* to the Paris Opéra. The trade in operatic properties benefited everyone except the man who had paid for them.[21]

With Astruc's empire in shambles, Beecham stepped into the breach. More sagacious than his French counterpart, the conductor exploited Diaghilev's impecuniousness to build up the stock of his own enterprise. Under an agreement signed in mid-March 1914, he loaned Diaghilev the amount of the advance the latter had agreed to pay Richard Strauss— whose operas Beecham had long promoted—and librettist Hugo von Hofmannsthal for sole performance rights to *Legend of Joseph*. The magnitude of the sum (Frs. 100,000) and the date of the transaction (barely two months before the premiere) bespeak Diaghilev's plight, while the terms (repayment in installments within forty-eight hours of each performance) reveal Beecham's interest in recouping his investment in money or in kind. *Legend of Joseph* vanished from Diaghilev's repertory without a trace, leading one to suspect that the debt remained unpaid and that the production became the property of the Beecham organization. Still another item of the agreement supports this view: Diaghilev's promise to deliver by May 28, 1914, "free of all charge" and guaranteeing "that they [Diaghilev and his associate Baron Dmitri Gunzburg] are the absolute owners," the "whole of the scenery . . . necessary for the performance of the Opera known as 'Ivan the Terrible'."[22]

For this 1914 Drury Lane season, which opened with Strauss's *Der Rosenkavalier* and Mozart's *Magic Flute,* Diaghilev "had promised to show" four new operas in London. This arrangement, noted Serge Grigoriev, had been worked out the previous year with Sir Joseph Beecham, the conductor's father and underwriter of his musical ventures. By the winter of 1914 preparations for the operatic side of the program, which in addition to Rimsky-Korsakov's *Ivan the Terrible,* included his *May Night,* Borodin's *Prince Igor,* Stravinsky's *Le Rossignol,* and a revival of *Boris Godunov,* were well advanced, suggesting the infusion of large sums into Diaghilev's coffers. By contrast, the ballet repertory presented serious problems. Even with the expensive and prestigious *Legend of Joseph,* the programming was weak, Fokine's *Papillons* and *Midas* being little more than rehashes of existing works. (*Papillons* had actually been done two years before in Russia.) Only *Le Coq d'Or,* a work by Rimsky-Korsakov staged as an *opéra dansé,* quickened the pulse of its collaborators while pointing the way out of the "predicament over the subject for a new ballet."[23]

This creative impasse, suggesting a shift of imaginative resources from ballet to opera, indicates a crisis in the overall direction of the Diaghilev organization. Where did the future of the Ballets Russes lie—in opera, dance, or a combination of the two? If the focus were to be ballet, how was the company to pay for new works? Of the new productions mounted for the 1914 season, the vast majority were never again performed by Diaghilev. This was due not only to the aesthetic shift that took place during the war years, but to the fact that several of these productions became the outright property of the Beecham organization. We have already noted the acquisition of *Boris Godunov* and *Khovanshchina* from Astruc and the contract stipulation vis-à-vis *Ivan the Terrible.* Indeed, the war and immediate postwar years saw Beecham revivals of all three works, along with *Prince Igor* for his own company. That the Benois costumes and scenery for *Le Rossignol* passed to Beecham can also be documented.[24] It is not unlikely that *Le Coq d'Or,* staged by dancer Serafima Astafieva for the Beecham organization in 1918, *May Night,* and *Midas* did so as well. Under the terms of the *Legend of Joseph* loan agreement, Beecham reserved the right of "combining with the Borrowers . . . in productions" of Russian opera or ballet throughout the English-speaking world. The nature of the 1914 season, combined with the record of Diaghilev's indebtedness, suggests that had the war not intervened, the Diaghilev enterprise might well have become a joint venture with "Sir Thomas Beecham Opera Seasons."

By no means did impresarios provide all of Diaghilev's financing. Prewar funding came from other sources as well: private patronage, which traditionally subsidized work outside the public sector, and banks, which provided short-term capital. The juxtaposition of these two sources underscores yet again the contradiction between public image and actual practice in the Diaghilev enterprise. As company mythmakers exploited titled patrons to resurrect a by now tenuous connection with the Imperial Theaters and tsarist court, company finances rested in the rather more prosaic hands of financial powerbrokers.

To what extent private patrons lent Diaghilev material support can probably never be ascertained. Caginess about money is a trademark of the very rich, and when it came to their checkbooks, Diaghilev's patrons were models of discretion. According to her biographer, Princesse Edmond de Polignac was "one of his main patrons and she remained his most dependable supporter until his death in 1929," although the extent of her largess is impossible to determine. "In the first decade she was content to make large donations to his funds and leave all the artistic direction in his hands. Later on she began to finance the production of specific works in addition to continuing her general subsidies. So involved financially, she made sure that she never missed a work presented by him." Misia Sert, another friend of long standing, came up with the odd thousand-franc note when irate costumers and other creditors demanded payment at the eleventh hour, just as the curtain was about to rise.[25] By and large, however, the Aga Khans, Comtesse Greffuhles, Lady Cunards, and other elite patrons whose generosity is taken as a matter of course labored in the social realm—prevailing on friends to take season boxes, organizing prestigious charity benefits, giving parties after premieres or arranging spectacular fetes at which company stars entertained.

The Marchioness of Ripon, and to a lesser degree, Comtesse Greffuhle, rendered Diaghilev an even greater service as influence brokers at the uppermost reaches of the musical world. The company's "most devoted English supporter," Lady Ripon was a power at Covent Garden, of whose board her husband was a member of long standing. Comtesse Greffuhle also pressured behind the scenes. During her 1910 sojourn in the United States, she brought her influence to bear on Otto Kahn, chairman of the Metropolitan Opera board, when negotiations between Diaghilev and Gatti-Casazza had reached a standstill.[26] Even if her efforts came to naught, they point to a dramatic shift in the role of patronage in the years prior to the war. With private donors unable or unwilling to sustain entire enterprises, patronage became a means of generating social aura and access to powerful artistic institutions and moneybrokers.

The trend toward financial brokerage as a leading function of patronage was underscored by Diaghilev's appointment of Baron Dmitri Gunzburg in 1910 as the company's co-administrator. A prominent collector and artistic dilettante, Gunzburg was heir to the largest Jewish banking fortune of the Russian empire. With a branch in Paris and connections in Hamburg, Berlin, and Frankfurt, the House of Gunzburg ranked among Europe's major banks. Gunzburg had invested at least 2,000 rubles in Diaghilev's 1909 season, and throughout the years of his tenure as company administrator wrote checks for out-of-pocket and other expenses. In 1913 he appears as one of the troupe's major creditors, with some Frs. 12,500 outstanding as of May 25. His chief value at Diaghilev's side, however, lay in the financial standing and reputation of his family. With Baron Gunzburg cosigning contracts, creditors received a guarantee that loans and advances would be repaid.[27]

Patrons and impresarios notwithstanding, 1912–1914 were years of acute financial difficulty for the Ballets Russes. Successful seasons sent cash flowing into Diaghilev's coffers, but production capital for new ballets, as opposed to operas, largely failed to materialize. Within a year of the independent company's debut, the cash flow situation became acute, and Diaghilev, hard pressed for money to produce the 1912 season, had recourse once again to short-term bank loans. These, it will be recalled, saved the day in 1909. In 1912 they provided the capital for the season that marked Nijinsky's debut as a choreographer.

Precisely how much Diaghilev borrowed from Brandeis et Cie. in early 1912 remains unclear. The sum, however, was considerable—in the neighborhood of Frs. 300,000 at the very least or three times the French guarantee capital raised in 1909. Negotiated through a firm with offices a few doors from Astruc's headquarters in the rue de Hanovre, the loan was earmarked for expenses incurred in connection with the Paris and Berlin seasons. The debt fell due on August 3, 1912, and from the outset Diaghilev failed to meet the scheduled repayments.[28] It was still outstanding when the company returned to Paris in 1913. During that spectacularly successful season at the Théâtre des Champs-Elysées, nearly twenty percent of the company's gross income went to repay the previous year's "advance." According to documents in the Astruc papers, Diaghilev was paid Frs. 528,000 for the engagement (22 performances at Frs. 24,000 each), of which Brandeis received a total of Frs. 104,000 (Frs. 8,000 for each of thirteen performances). The debt was far from being liquidated, however. In June 1914, Frs. 176,595 remained outstanding, and on June 4 several items, including costume trunks and the Venetian Palace scenery for *Leg-*

end of Joseph, were seized in the corridors of the Paris Opéra just prior to their removal to England for the company's London season. Other creditors took similar action: the art printers Messrs. Balincourt et Dupont, Monsieur Jallot of the Maison Belloir-Jumeau, which had supplied ivy garlands and flats back in 1910, and the Léon Jue et Cie. theatrical agency.[29] Presumably, accounts were settled to the satisfaction of the plaintiffs, as there is no evidence that London saw truncated versions of the season's productions. How Diaghilev raised Frs. 188,606.25 at the eleventh hour remains a mystery, and one is tempted to see Beecham's hand in the affaire. If Beecham did indeed bail Diaghilev out, the productions of *Le Rossignol, Le Coq d'Or,* and *Legend of Joseph* may well have been the price of his generosity.

Whatever the exact amount of Diaghilev's indebtedness, the magnitude of the sum threw open the question of the company's ability to survive. To his confidantes, Lady Ripon and Addie Kahn, Diaghilev expressed the fear that the troupe was close to collapse. "Have had several interviews Lady Ripon Diaghileff about Ballet for New York," Addie Kahn wired her husband, Otto, from London on July 18, 1914. "Are most insistent troupe should go America this winter for urgent reasons too complicated to cable upon which largely depend continuance of organization. Diaghileff willing to go even for 10 New York Brooklyn performances of which several matinees and some in Philadelphia, Boston, Chicago simply to keep company together." A month later, as war rumbled in Central Europe, Gunzburg offered to sail to New York to arrange the details of a tour of both Russian grand opera and ballet, an indication of how desperate Diaghilev was at that point for a quick transfusion of American dollars.[30]

Between 1909 and 1914 Diaghilev transformed ballet from a disparaged form of entertainment to an art prized for its beauty and expressiveness. Did even his admirers in 1909 suspect the indomitable will that lay behind his dandified facade, a will that in the short space of five years would produce nearly two dozen ballets and nearly a dozen operas? Against nearly insuperable odds, Diaghilev resurrected his enterprise from the financial disaster of its inaugural season, creating a company unique in the annals of European dance history, a massive entrepreneurial undertaking carried out in the name of beauty, imagination, and taste. Many sought to usurp his place at the forefront of the Russian movement. They failed, however, because Diaghilev alone harbored in his complex personality the artist's urge to create and the impresario's sense of the marketplace. In his teaming of art and enterprise and his intuitive understanding of how the marketplace might be exploited to serve the traditional ends of high art lay his extraordinary genius.

Nonetheless, even Diaghilev could not escape the changes wrought by the marketplace. Within the company itself the market revamped hierarchies of status and attitudes toward artistic work, transforming both the artist and his creation into prized commodities. It brought a new division of labor to the ranks of company dancers, one that rested, like the newly consolidated operatic star system, on money rather than rank. And by "fetishizing" relationships among artists, it destroyed the studio atmosphere on which the company's early collaborative approach had rested.

The spectacular success of the Ballets Russes whetted appetites throughout the West for the new art of Russian ballet. Overnight, a market for dance sprang into existence in which demand vastly outstripped supply. Suddenly, artists of no great repute at the Maryinsky found themselves besieged by moguls of popular entertainment.

Except for the privileged few who attained ballerina status (in 1909 only Mathilde Kchessinska, Olga Preobrajenska, Anna Pavlova, and Vera Trefilova occupied that exalted rank), salaries at the Maryinsky were low. If Pavlova's salary rose to 3,000 rubles a year with her promotion to ballerina in 1906, the vast majority of her colleagues were paid a fraction of that amount. Nor did dancers, again with the exception of ballerinas and premiers danseurs, have much choice in determining what, where, and how often they danced. Transfers between Moscow and St. Petersburg came at the whim of an Imperial bureaucrat, and casting could be just as arbitrary. Opportunities to dance, moreover, were few. In her journal for 1911 Nijinska compared this aspect of Maryinsky life with the challenges of the Diaghilev company: "In the Imperial Theaters I seldom performed more than ten times in a season, but now in Monte-Carlo I am to dance in all the ballets, four times a week. In the Imperial Theaters I was able to dance everything I was given, but in the ballets of Fokine there is still much that is new for me . . ."[31]

Although the aftermath of the Revolution of 1905 saw the first wave of defections to the West, dancers by and large remained loyal to the Imperial Theaters. Even if many had to teach social dancing to the wealthy to supplement an income that often supported an entire family, the perquisites of being an Artist of the Imperial Theaters more than compensated for its drawbacks. Once accepted as a boarder at the Imperial Theatrical School, even the child of modest gifts could look forward to a respected position in life. Graduation brought automatic admission to the Imperial Ballet and a year-round salary until the age of thirty-five, when the artist drew a pension for life. There were other advantages as well, including the preference given to children or other relatives who applied for entry to the school. Indeed, by 1900 Imperial artists had become a distinct, if unofficial caste in the tsarist scheme of things. With marriages among dancers and other theatrical personnel commonplace, numerous Diaghilev dancers came

from families bred within the tightly knit worlds of the Bolshoi and Maryinsky.

The very existence of the Diaghilev company was itself a form of competition that affected the dancer's economic, social, and artistic status. But
with the spectacular triumph of 1909, repeated the following year, the
Diaghilev troupe became the hunting ground of theater managers anxious
to exploit the newfound revelation of Russian ballet and willing to pay
dearly for the privilege of presenting it. "*Stupendous offers* are being made
to these people," wrote C. Ercole, a Paris theater agent, to Alfred Moul,
general manager of London's Alhambra Theatre, on July 23, 1910. "They
are therefore tempted by these different offers and their terms are naturally
very much bigger than they would have been even a year ago." Producers
Eric Wollheim and Oswald Stoll, Ercole wrote five days later, "ought to
be put for some time in strait jackets and have ice put on their heads—
they are rendering the market *impossible*. It is very evident that as everything in life like the Stock Exchange is based on offer and demand these
people who are kneeling down to the Russian dancers and offering them
engagements on golden trays are causing them to ask unheard of salaries
. . ." Unable to secure either the Diaghilev ballet or a company headed
by Fokine, the Alhambra engaged a Moscow troupe. Diaghilev's second-
season alumna Yekaterina Geltzer headed the ensemble at a salary of £90
a week, more than twice the £40 offered Lydia Kyasht when she became
prima ballerina of the Empire Theatre in 1908.[32]

London's music-halls were not the only commercial stages to dangle
pots of gold before Diaghilev's artists. The end of the 1910 season saw a
thinning of the ranks with the departure of several dancers for the untried
vaudeville circuits of America. Among these was eighteen-year-old Lydia
Lopokova, the company's "baby ballerina," whose successes in Paris and
Berlin had brought several tempting offers from across the Atlantic. Her
letter of July 22, 1910, to Alexander Krupensky, head of the St. Petersburg
office of the Imperial Theaters, requesting a two-month leave of absence,
evokes the atmosphere of theatrical siege:

> Much respected Aleksandr Dmitrievich!
>   Your benevolence toward me provides the reason to narrate what has
> happened to me: thanks to my success in Berlin and Paris, different agents
> began to approach me, inviting me to various cities and various countries; the
> propositions were very tempting, but I refused all of them, remembering that
> after all I have attained, I should be thankful to the School and to you, whom
> I still have not thanked for promoting me to coryphée . . . And now, imagine
> what has been done to me. Surrounded and prevailed upon on all sides, I
> signed a contract for New York. The next day I changed my mind; I cried;
> God knows what I would give for this not to have happened; grief gnaws at

me; I do not want to go *anywhere*, but the agents are like Cerberuses to my soul and the consequences of not fulfilling the contract would be horrible to me . . . I beg of you to give me a leave of absence.[33]

Krupensky granted the young coryphée her leave and a raise in salary as well. Neither sufficed to keep her at the Maryinsky. That fall, in the company of her brother Fedor Lopukhov (the future choreographer) and Anna Pavlova's future partner Alexandre Volinine, she set out on the first of several cross-country tours that kept her in America for six years. For the dancer whom the *Petersburg Gazette* described as "entirely unknown" four thousand rubles a month was an offer she could hardly afford to refuse.[34]

Like Lopokova, many Russian dancers eschewed Diaghilev and Europe. Impresarios plundered the seemingly endless talent of the Imperial Theaters during the annual march of Diaghilev's front-line organization from Petersburg to Paris. By 1911–1912 no fewer than three competing ensembles toured America alone. These loosely knit groups, which coalesced around Anna Pavlova, her one-time partner Mikhail Mordkin, and Broadway's first woman dance producer Gertrude Hoffmann, consisted overwhelmingly of Imperial dancers who had passed through Diaghilev's ranks—a turnstile to the burgeoning world market for ballet. Like their counterparts in Europe, they exploited such Diaghilev-inspired titles as "Saison russe" and "Imperial Ballet Russe," while dancers wore as badges of honor their identity as "Artists of the Imperial Ballet," even when this was no longer the case.[35]

With the partial exception of Pavlova, who made her American debut at the Metropolitan Opera in New York, these Russians adapted their art to the commercial stage. Rather than opening new channels for the presentation of ballet, they became "class acts" among the acrobatic, singing, and magic attractions that formed staple vaudeville and music-hall fare. Taking Diaghilev's one-act and divertissement ballets as their model, they extracted discrete dances from the classical and modern repertory and recast them as concentrated distillations of a dramatic situation. Popular success, as Pavlova's career amply demonstrated, reflected the skill of the dancer in establishing instant rapport with an audience regardless of the artistic framing of the performance.

By 1911, the year his company made its debut as an independent entity, Diaghilev faced an acute shortage of manpower. The loss of dancers to the commercial stage threatened to undermine the company's strength, as did the return each autumn of seasoned performers to the Maryinsky. For the first time, Diaghilev had to recruit large numbers of dancers from outside the Imperial Theaters. Warsaw's Wielki Theater, the private Moscow studio of Lydia Nelidova, Yevgenia Sokolova's studio in St. Peters-

burg, and London's theatrical schools all helped fill the company's de-
pleted ranks. To maintain technical standards and assure stylistic consistency,
Diaghilev engaged the respected St. Petersburg teacher Enrico Cecchetti.
Despite these measures, however, the labor shortage remained a problem,
and in 1911 Diaghilev took the extreme step of literally renting an itinerant group of Russian dancers. For the ten men and two women of the
Molotzoff troupe, Diaghilev agreed to pay Frs. 88,000 a year to the troupe's
impresario—a hefty and continuing drain on his finances. During the 1913
Paris season, Diaghilev paid out no less than Frs. 60,000, or nearly one-
tenth of the season's projected gross income. During the same season, it
will be recalled, he repaid Frs. 104,000 on the long-overdue Brandeis loan.[36]

Like Mamontov, Diaghilev paid his artists well. He did this initially
to woo them from the Imperial Theaters and compensate for loss of job
security, and subsequently, to compete with the upward spiral of salaries
in the commercial realm. With few exceptions, the documentary record of
Diaghilev's prewar pay scales is sketchy. Many contracts, especially those
of principals, remain hidden from the perusal of researchers in private hands,
a result of the mounting speculation in Ballets Russes memorabilia since
the 1960s.[37] Nevertheless, from the entries in Diaghilev's notebook for
1910 and the odd contract that has strayed into public view, a rough idea
of company salaries may be sketched and comparisons drawn with both
the Maryinsky and commercial stage.

In the spring of 1909, Nijinska recalled, Imperial dancers could talk
of "nothing else but [Diaghilev's] remarkable project . . . The recompense
for the *corps de ballet* was to start at one thousand francs (three hundred
seventy-five rubles, more than many earned in half a year at the Imperial
Theaters). Several Artists came to . . . ask that I mention them to Vaslav
and ask him to recommend them to Diaghilev."[38] In 1910, salaries mounted
substantially. For an engagement that began with rehearsals in April and
ended with the last of the company's Paris performances in mid-July, dancers
received more than their total yearly salary at the Maryinsky. Below are
sample comparisons:[39]

	Yearly Salary at Imperial Theaters (*in rubles and equivalent in francs*)		Season Salary Indicated in Diaghilev's Notebook (*in francs*)
Lydia Lopokova	720 rubles	(Frs. 1,872)	Frs. 2,000
Georgi Rosai	960 "	(Frs. 2,496)	Frs. 3,000
Alexander Orlov	960 "	(Frs. 2,496)	Frs. 2,800
Bronislava Nijinska	900 "	(Frs. 2,340)	Frs. 2,200/2,500
Vera Fokina	900 "	(Frs. 2,340)	Frs. 2,800

Diaghilev's move from seasonal to permanent activity, and increased dependence on money to command the loyalty of his troupe, accelerated the trend toward higher salaries. A contract signed on February 10, 1911, with the inexperienced dancer M.V. Guliuk stipulated a yearly salary of Frs. 8,000 for the period 1911–1912 and Frs. 10,000 for 1912–1913. On December 15, 1912, Hilda Bewicke, the first of Diaghilev's English dancers, was hired for a two-and-a-half month trial period at Frs. 750 a month, with the company management reserving the right to prolong her engagement for a year. In early 1913 Hilda Munnings, whom Diaghilev subsequently renamed Lydia Sokolova, joined the company upon similar terms. These base salaries, which amounted to Frs. 9,000 over the course of a year, represented more than twice the stipend of a corps de ballet dancer at the Paris Opéra.[40]

In casting their lot with Diaghilev, artists forfeited the job security, pension rights, and other privileges of the Imperial Theaters. Yet the full precariousness of their position did not become apparent until the war years. If anything, Diaghilev's prewar dancers enjoyed the best of the subsidized and commercial ballet worlds. Diaghilev could not compete with salaries in the music-halls, at least for top performers. He nevertheless offered his dancers a modicum of short-term security: a year-round contract with full pay for summer holidays and rehearsal periods, and the assurance that, unlike the Mordkin troupe (which folded on tour in the American South), his artists would not be left stranded in the middle of a season. Nor in this prewar era did Diaghilev periodically weed dancers from his payroll, as occurred in the 1920s, when performers bore the heaviest brunt of pressures to streamline the company and economize.

The prewar years brought more than high salaries to Imperial dancers in the West. Overnight, the market leveled distinctions in rank elaborated during the previous two centuries. Balletomanes, friends in high places, and precedent-minded bureaucrats suddenly counted for nothing. In the range of choices it opened, the market thus spelled freedom—the freedom to travel and perform at will, the freedom to make dances after the promptings of an inner vision, the freedom to enjoy the enhanced social prestige of an artist outside a caste-ridden institution. If Russia's first ballet troupes were serf companies, it was in the twentieth-century marketplace that the Russian dancer gained his freedom as an artist and individual.[41]

In the studio atmosphere of the company's earliest seasons, Diaghilev largely disavowed the Maryinsky hierarchy of rank. He passed over Mathilde Kchessinska, the reigning *prima ballerina assoluta,* in favor of Pavlova when assembling his 1909 troupe, and heavily weighted the company with followers of Fokine rather than strict adherents to Maryinsky tradition.

He brought talented artists to the fore and gave solo roles to dancers in the corps de ballet. Again and again, he preferred talent to rank, hard work to political favoritism.

Talent, however, does not exist in a social vacuum. In the marketplace, it was increasingly equated with cash value. The box office became the yardstick of success, the dancer's trump card in dealings with theatrical managements, but also the way managements evaluated the dancer. The market created its own hierarchy of success; abolishing titles, it created classes of dancers with divisions expressed purely in monetary terms. By 1910, a new division of labor had begun to crystallize within the troupe, an alternative ranking to the Imperial system that victimized as many dancers as it exalted. Diaghilev's company lists for 1910 make no allusion to coryphés, *demi-solistes* or premiers danseurs. Names of dancers appear in tandem with their price, a figure most often in the Frs. 2,000–2,500 range with a sprinkling of salaries between Frs. 3,000 and Frs. 5,500. Nijinsky, Pavlova, Karsavina, and Fokine, however, stand apart. With payment ranging from Frs. 10,000 to Frs. 25,000, they formed the nucleus of Diaghilev's new star system while suggesting the growing disparity between highest and lowest paid dancers.[42]

This new star system was more than a response to laws of supply and demand. It was an imperative of Diaghilev's integration into the operatic marketplace, where divas of both sexes commanded huge single performance fees as international guest artists. As early as 1906 Chaliapin had received Frs. 6,000 for each performance of *Mephistopheles* at the Paris Opéra. Three years later Diaghilev paid him Frs. 55,000 for his participation in the 1909 *saison russe,* 15,000 francs more than the combined salaries of all the season's ballet soloists, and only 5,000 francs less than the entire corps de ballet. By 1913 his fee for six performances of *Boris Godunov* had risen to Frs. 50,000, which Diaghilev had to deposit in full to his account six months prior to the Champs-Elysées season.[43]

Like Chaliapin, Nijinsky and Karsavina became international drawing cards, their presence stipulated by contract. They danced on nearly every program, often in as many as three ballets a performance, and Diaghilev had works created around their particular gifts. Their names, like their photographs, became commonplaces of the fashion and theatrical press. As the Chaliapin and Nellie Melba of the dance, they socialized in the highest circles and received astronomical sums when they performed outside the aegis of the company. For a private appearance in July 1912 of Nijinsky and Karsavina in *Le Spectre de la Rose* and a pas de trois with Nijinsky's sister, Bronislava, Diaghilev asked no less than Frs. 12,000, or one-half the average fee for a performance by his full company.[44] In May

1914, only months after his relationship with Diaghilev had ended, Nijinsky negotiated a three-year contract with Jacques Rouché, newly appointed director of the Paris Opéra. For a four-month season during which he would dance no more than thirty times, Nijinsky was to receive Frs. 90,000 or Frs. 3,000 per performance. He was also given a "consultative vote" in the choice of the new ballet to be produced each year.[45]

If none of Diaghilev's stars, including Nijinsky, ever approached Chaliapin's earning power, the star system nevertheless contributed appreciably to the upward spiral of production costs. Not only did Diaghilev pay in-house stars handsomely (in Nijinsky's case, remuneration took the form of a luxurious lifestyle), but he frequently engaged guest artists such as Pavlova, Kchessinska, and Carlotta Zambelli, *étoile* of the Paris Opéra, at fees that rivaled those of top-notch singers. For the projected 1912 St. Petersburg season (canceled because of a fire at the Narodny Dom Theater), Diaghilev agreed to pay Zambelli Frs. 20,000 for seven performances in a repertory including *Giselle, Le Spectre de la Rose, Firebird*, and an unspecified fourth ballet. This compared favorably with his engagement the following year of Maria Kuznetsova, the noted Russian lyric artist, to sing a minimum of seven performances of *Boris Godunov* and *Ivan the Terrible* at Frs. 1,500 and Frs. 2,000 per performance respectively.[46]

The reliance on stars, moreover, increased with the cementing of relations with the Beecham organization in 1911. For the autumn follow-up to the Coronation season at Covent Garden, Diaghilev added Kchessinska and Pavlova to his roster of ballerinas. The following year, which coincided with the huge Brandeis loan, found the company's repertory weighted heavily toward star French composers: Debussy, Ravel, and Reynaldo Hahn, a salon favorite if not a creative giant. With Diaghilev's return to opera production in 1913–1914 and the engagement of Chaliapin and other high-priced talent, company finances signally worsened.

If the person of the dancer assumed cash value in the marketplace, the art of presenting him did so as well. For the first time, the dances themselves became a unique and valued property that theater directors vied for the privilege of acquiring. With the transformation of choreographic originality into a marketable commodity, the dancemaker found his own position dramatically altered.

Traditionally, the ballet master had woven his talents into the institutional fabric of the opera house, where he not only staged ballets and the danced interludes of operas but also performed a host of other functions as well—dancing, teaching, coaching, rehearsing, and administration. Now with the whole world opening as a potential market for his skills as a dancemaker, he could sell his creative talents under conditions of his own choice, independently of his other skills. From the trial by cash of the marketplace emerged the modern-day ballet choreographer, a "free" artist on a par with the independent painter, poet, singer, or composer.

Fokine's meteoric rise from obscurity to fame between 1909 and 1914 marked the transition from ballet master to choreographer. A Maryinsky "radical," he moved within two years from being an eager collaborator in Diaghilev's "studio" to a celebrity fully cognizant of his financial and artistic worth. For Diaghilev, the triumph of the 1910 season demonstrated the viability of a permanent company. For Fokine, success that year spelled the opening of a brilliant and many-faceted career. From 1910 to 1914 the dancer who only a few years before had staged graduation exercises with costumes rummaged from the Maryinsky's storage bins assumed the many guises of a successful dancemaker. Thanks in large measure to his Western triumphs, the Maryinsky promoted him to the position of staff ballet master. As maître de ballet, premier danseur, and choreographic director, he served Diaghilev up to the war, save for the brief interlude of Nijinsky's ascendancy in 1912–1913. He also branched out into other fields. In the summer of 1910 there was talk of his upstaging Diaghilev by bringing a company of thirty-three (with his wife Vera Fokina as ballerina) to London for a month-long season. In early 1911 he staged Schéhérazade and Cléopâtre for La Scala, and in July of the following year Otto Kahn and Max Rabinoff were exchanging letters about bringing him to New York for a joint season with Max Reinhardt. His career as a free-lance choreographer blossomed in 1912 and 1913, when Pavlova and Ida Rubinstein commissioned him to create ballets and dances for their respective enterprises.[47]

For all these efforts Fokine demanded and usually received "top dollar." His asking price for the month-long London season was £5,000 (Frs. 126,000). The engagement at La Scala paid Frs. 18,000 plus travel expenses. Fokine's monetary demands in no way lessened when they came to the man who had "made" him in the West. In Diaghilev's notes, Fokine heads the list of company principals with a salary of Frs. 25,000.[48] The overnight change in fortune plainly went to his head. Complaints of Fokine's "exaggerated pretensions," as Gatti-Casazza called his demand in 1910 for $30,000 as ballet master of Diaghilev's projected American tour, extended to non-economic demands such as his insistence that his wife, a mediocre classicist, be given ballerina roles. By 1911, too, he had acquired the uncharitable habit of claiming as his own inventions that were the fruit of collaboration. In the case of the Maryinsky's 1911 production of Orpheus and Eurydice, he publicly disparaged Meyerhold's role in the staging, precipitating a conflict with the director that surfaced in the press. "It is generally difficult to speak with Fokin these days," noted Telyakovsky in his diary. "He has become so conceited that he fails to recognize that if there is anything new or developing in ballet, it is thanks only to Golovin and Korovin."[49] Given the history of Telyakovsky's relations with Diaghilev, it is hardly surprising that the director of the Imperial Theaters omits all mention of the rival enterprise. Nevertheless, his observation points to the streak of arrogance that henceforth marked Fokine's character and colored his remarks about competitors.

Fokine's monetary demands, like his jockeying for title and the perquisites of power, reveal a dramatic change in attitude toward his work. In the brief space of two years, pride in creation had yielded to pride of ownership: Fokine now regarded his work with the possessive eye of the man of property. His proprietary attitude, however, did not square with reality. For unlike Diaghilev's composers, Fokine did not own his work. *Carnaval, Le Spectre de la Rose, Firebird, Schéhérazade,* and Fokine's other creations for the Ballets Russes were the personal property of Diaghilev alone, and no matter how often they were performed, the choreographer, unlike the composer, had no legal claim to copyright protection or royalties.[50] Fokine's bitterness at being cheated of what he regarded as rightfully his is a refrain sounded time and again in his memoirs. The equation of copyright protection with monetary return testifies to what degree choreographic originality had assumed in his mind the value of a marketable commodity.

Although Diaghilev held personal title to Fokine's ballets with the implicit right to alter the choreography (as he did costumes and decor), he generally respected their integrity. If dancers inadvertently changed a movement here and there or if economics precluded armies of extras, Diaghilev took pains to keep style and steps intact. In reviving productions, moreover, he rejected the traditional solution to the problem of failing memory and lack of choreographic notation. However strained the relations between the two men, Diaghilev never remounted ballets "after Fokine." In December 1923 he wrote the following to Jacques Rouché, director of the Paris Opéra, about a proposed revival of the choreographer's *Daphnis and Chloë:*

I hereby confirm and guarantee that I hold absolute title, which has never, moreover, been disputed, to perform all the Ballets which Monsieur Fokine has mounted for me; and in the present instance, it is not a question of remounting "Daphnis", but of recalling certain passages which certain artists of my troupe no longer remember.

As Monsieur Aveline was the last to work on this Ballet with Monsieur Fokine, I thought it appropriate to address myself to you and to him in order to present the choreography in a perfect state so as to safeguard the interests of Monsieur Fokine himself, for it is his name that will appear on the program as the author of the aforesaid choreography.[51]

If Diaghilev no longer subscribed to Fokine's choreographic methods, he recognized in authenticity and faithfulness to the original a selling point unique to the art market in the twentieth century. This concern for exactness in reproduction, analogous to the value of "original" prints pulled from the negative of a master photographer, suggests not simply Diaghilev's artistic integrity, but also the extent to which authenticity had become an issue in an era of mechanical reproduction. Fokine, in the tradition of ballet masters of previous centuries, restaged variants of his works throughout his career; it was Diaghilev who prefigured the obsession with authenticity so characteristic of the modern artistic marketplace.

In its naked equation of money and art, Fokine's property-mindedness signified a necessary condition in the making of ballet's modern choreographer. But an additional ingredient was necessary. The dancemaking art itself had to be assimilated into the new ballet star system. Beginning with Nijinsky, and in a pattern repeated again and again (although not always with equal success), Diaghilev molded choreographers from among his roster of company-created stars. In so doing, he appropriated to both the talent and person of the dancemaker the commodity value of the performer. Thanks to Diaghilev, the ballet master became the choreographic diva of the marketplace, whose specialized, expert skills enabled him to transcend allegiance to a specific institution.

The liberation of choreographer from ballet master lies at the root of another equally important development of the Diaghilev era—a radical shift in the concept of style. Traditionally, style in ballet suggested the distinctive manner bred by a school or system of training. It represented, above all, the triumph of the institution at the expense of the individual, objective utterance over subjective expression. Nijinsky's *L'Après-midi d'un Faune* and *Le Sacre du Printemps*, however, radically altered this relationship. From the choreographer's imagination came the total vision of these works, a vision that determined not only their theme, structure, and floor pattern, but also elements such as technique, body posture, and presentation traditionally belonging to a "school." This vision, at once subjective in origin and universal in application, is the pivot on which the modern concept of style turns, whether in poetry or painting, fiction or music. The fact that Nijinsky's earliest sketches for *L'Après-midi d'un Faune* in the autumn of 1910 occurred simultaneously with Diaghilev's negotiations to launch an independent company cannot, therefore, be dismissed as mere coincidence. The radical innovation such works represented could not take form within the bureaucratic structure of the Imperial Theaters. They needed the luxury of time, faith, and finance that only Diaghilev could provide. The rise of the modern choreographer took place within the context of capitalism.

The marketplace cast a long shadow over all Diaghilev's artists, not only dancers and choreographers. Competition drove a wedge between collaborators, alienating friends of long standing as they now jockeyed for title, power, and position within the company's inner circle. Differences in outlook and sensibility had often divided the former *miriskusstniki*. But where in the past the bond of friendship had sufficed to calm a ruffled ego, now with so much money at stake, the habits of friendship weakened. Opportunities and rewards no longer derived from the informal support system of Russia's amateur networks. Success and failure were proclaimed at the box office with public acclaim promising lucrative commissions for the future. The collaborative eden of Diaghilev's first and second ballet seasons did not collapse because of the impresario's sudden penchant for manipulation or sadistic delight in promoting one artist at the expense of a colleague, even if they helped it along. It was shattered by the inner logic of a marketplace that had created a new set of conditions of artistic validation. Bakst's promotion to company artistic director over Benois in 1910 suggests the beginning of a new division of labor within the collaborative group, as squabbles over crediting ideas arrived at in the course of collaboration indicate a new proprietary attitude toward artistic work. The transformation of Stravinsky's relationship with Diaghilev over the years from friendship to financial bickering brings full circle the dramatic change in collaboration instigated by the newly charged economic climate. From a relationship based on shared attitudes and ideas, cemented by ties of kinship and friendship, collaboration had become a contractual arrangement.

To view the prewar history of the Ballets Russes in terms of the marketplace is in no way to denigrate the splendid artistic achievements of those years. If anything, it enhances them by enabling us to appreciate the background of enterprise against which they flourished. Competition, like the new star system and the "commodization" of the various aspects of the dancer's art, appeared within the Ballets Russes in response to the socio-economic climate of the West. Diaghilev did not invent or will them into existence. Like his financial arrangements with musical impresarios and banks, they answered needs of the moment rather than conforming to some premeditated design. But they also established precedents, and these, in turn, influenced the course of his company's subsequent history.

By all reasonable expectations, the Diaghilev company should have foundered in transplanting Russia's secessionist ballet to the very different soil of the West. Luck or fate do not suffice to explain why it did not. The success of the Ballets Russes rested on Diaghilev's intuitive sense of the marketplace, his feeling for its liberating possibilities, and, above all, his grasp of how it might be manipulated to serve the traditional ends of high art.

7

UNDERWRITING MODERNISM:
AMERICAN INTERMEZZO

THE ARMIES that moved across Belgium and northern France in the summer of 1914 severed Europe from its immediate cultural past. Overnight, the cosmopolitan edifice of Belle Epoque society, amusement, manners, and art collapsed. Princes of finance plowed their capital into munitions; grandes dames organized charities for the orphaned and wounded. War rang down the curtain of the Opéra and a score of Paris theaters, sending performers to trenches, prisoner-of-war camps, and cemeteries. For Diaghilev and his Ballets Russes, London, Paris, Brussels, Berlin, Vienna, and Monte Carlo became memories of tours that had ceased to exist.

Between 1915 and 1917 Diaghilev relaid the aesthetic foundations of the Ballets Russes. But art was not the only aspect of his enterprise transformed in these years. World war and revolution in Russia had economic consequences that touched every aspect of company life. Up to 1914 Diaghilev spent and overspent on the assumption that "angels" would opportunely present themselves, that cash and credit would materialize at the eleventh hour. Although not a rich man, Diaghilev was by no means poor, and one may assume that into the company kitty flowed the personal income that up to 1915 regularly came from Russia.[1] As long as wealth continued to grow—as it did unabatedly in the years before 1914—the economic outlook of the Ballets Russes was never totally bleak.

Along with crowns, World War I and the Russian Revolution toppled the financial pillars on which Diaghilev's enterprise had rested. They brought an end to tours of Europe's belligerent nations, staunched the flow of capital from Russia, and cut off contact with patrons and producers. A lesser man would have bowed before the inevitable. But in these years of relentless artistic experiment, a demon of survival no less than a genie of creation seemed to drive Diaghilev. Against all odds, he rebuilt his troupe from scratch, whipped it into performance shape, then dispatched it to lands that in balmier days he had scorned to conquer. Paradoxically, the lion's share of capital that enabled Diaghilev to resurrect his company and re-make its repertory came from New York's Metropolitan Opera. No less paradoxical in hindsight was the impact of the two Metropolitan tours on the troupe itself. Under the aegis of this operatic dowager, the economic and social dynamics of the Ballets Russes succumbed to the logic of the market. The precariousness to which these years gave rise persisted long after the troupe left American shores, as did another phenomenon of the era—the exploitation of the company's human matériel. Both launched the troupe along a path remote from the communitarian spirit of Diaghilev's creative studio. Dancers of the Ballets Russes paid dearly for the privilege of underwriting modernism.

Plans for the first American tour, a fifteen-week engagement that be-gan in January and ended in April 1916, were laid, ironically, at the time of Diaghilev's initial encounter with the futurists in Milan. Here, on Oc-tober 10, he signed the contract with managing director Giulio Gatti-Cas-azza that underwrote the experimental colony in Ouchy. By Article 24 of that document, Diaghilev received a $30,000 advance, payable in seven monthly installments, the first of which fell due around the time of his arrival in Switzerland on May 1. Augmented by an additional $15,000 to cover the months of November, December, and January when the com-pany went into rehearsal, these cash payments allowed Diaghilev several months of creative freedom unhampered by the necessity of performing. For the duration of the tour, moreover, the Metropolitan agreed to pay Diaghilev $13,500 a week (from which he had to meet all payroll expenses and pay back the full amount of the advance) as well as travel and trans-portation costs for the company of fifty dancers and its trunkloads of cos-tumes, scenery, and effects.[2]

In the ensuing months, the Metropolitan's obligations grew. The weekly payment increased to $15,750 a week, and an additional clause was in-serted into the contract assigning Diaghilev "one-half of the net profits of the engagement." As departure neared, anxious cables from Henry Russell, the Metropolitan's agent charged with handling the company's European send-off, begged for new advances: "Cable Diaghilev's January payment instantly," he wired on December 15th, "or authorize me advance him money. Cash payments due tomorrow. Otherwise Diaghilev collapse." On Christmas Day Russell appealed for an additional Frs. 40,000, needed in part to cover the Frs. 15,000 Diaghilev owed his Paris dressmaker for delivery of the new *Schéhérazade* and *Firebird* costumes ordered for the American tour.[3]

The Metropolitan performed a further service for Diaghilev. Calling on its immense prestige, and with Comtesse Greffuhle, Lady Ripon, the Duke of Alba, and even the King of Spain pulling strings behind the scenes, the Met negotiated the release of Nijinsky and his family from house arrest in Budapest. Otto Kahn, the chairman of the Metropolitan's board of directors and a major underwriter of the Allied war effort, played a crucial role in this endeavor, thanks to his influence at the highest levels of government. "From Vienna," began the telegram he received from Robert Lansing, the American Secretary of State, on February 7, 1916, "Quote. Have succeeded getting promise government permit Nijinsky and wife start immediately New York provided you cable personal guarantee that they will return this monarchy immediately conclusion engagement Metropolitan Opera. Nijinskys can start soon as I transmit your agreement to government. End quote." By February 28 Nijinsky was free at Bern.[4]

But rather than ending the Metropolitan's troubles, the dancer's release began a new round of parleys, with Nijinsky demanding large sums of money that the opera house duly relayed through Henry Russell.[5] Upon landing, moreover, Nijinsky placed the Metropolitan in the awkward position of mediating between him and his former lover, with John Brown, the Metropolitan's business manager, guaranteeing a letter contract whereby Diaghilev agreed to pay Nijinsky the balance of Frs. 75,000 (or $13,000) owing under the terms of a "compromise" made in London in May 1914 through Sir George Lewis. Diaghilev also agreed to pay $1,000 for each of the eleven performances Nijinsky was to dance in New York, a sum far exceeding the Frs. 3,000 he would have received at the Paris Opéra had the war not intervened.[6]

Securing Nijinsky's release was hardly an act of altruism on the part of the Metropolitan nor a good deed to curry favor with Diaghilev. For Otto Kahn the presence of the superstar was essential not only to strengthen the company artistically, but also to justify the expectations aroused by the remarkable publicity campaign launched in the months preceding the tour. In yet another of those amazing coincidences that make the history of the Ballets Russes so fascinating, the young man responsible for this campaign was none other than Edward L. Bernays, a nephew of Sigmund Freud and the future father of modern public relations. For the inexperienced press agent this was truly an eye-opening experience:

I learned a lot working with the Metropolitan Musical Bureau; but never more than when I handled Diaghileff's Russian Ballet in 1915, 1916 and 1917. These three years taught me more about life than I have learned from politics, books, romance, marriage and fatherhood in the years since. I had never imagined that the interpersonal relations of the members of a group could be so involved and complex, full of medieval intrigue, illicit love, misdirected passion and aggression. But while it happened, I took it all for granted as part of a stimulating job. Nevertheless, my experience had a life-long effect on me, for it prepared me to understand and cope with the vagaries of men and women who lived in special worlds of their own.[7]

Unable to promote a large-scale operation like the Ballets Russes, the Metropolitan had turned the task over to its Musical Bureau, which, in a stroke of genius, appointed Bernays general press representative. "No project was ever better prepared for in the matter of publicity and promotion," wrote Adella Prentiss Hughes thirty years later.[8] Relying on what he called "hunch and intuition," Bernays mounted a sophisticated campaign that publicized the ballet, first "as a novelty in art forms, a unifying of several arts; second, in terms of its appeal to special groups of the public; third, in terms of its direct impact on American life, on design and color in American products; and fourth, through its personalities." Bombarding magazines, Sunday supplements, the music and women's page departments of daily newspapers with "reams of stories and photographs angled to their various reader groups," persuading "manufacturers to make products inspired by the color and design of Bakst decors and costumes and [arranging] for their advertising and display in department and other retail stores through the country,"[9] Bernays stimulated public interest in the initial tour beyond all expectation.

Much of this "ballyhoo," as he called the months of intense, nationwide publicity, centered on the company's principals: Nijinsky, Karsavina, and Diaghilev. Of these only Diaghilev steamed into New York harbor on January 12, 1916. Undaunted by news of Karsavina's pregnancy and Nijinsky's continued internment, Bernays set about preparing the ground for their replacements, on the theory that "glowing descriptions of one Russian-named dancer . . . could be applied to any other."[10] He draped a snake from the Bronx zoo around Flore Revalles in her *Schéhérazade* costume, a stunt that brought pictures of this unknown dancer to America's breakfast tables; he planted interviews and glowing accounts of "stars" who had never performed with the Ballets Russes in Europe. Diaghilev must have been struck by the contrast between the genteel character of promotion in Europe and the way the modern mass media in America made commerce of artists, images, and ideas.

Although this first Metropolitan tour enabled Diaghilev to reconstruct his company, certain aspects of the contract presaged the more sharply competitive atmosphere of the post-Armistice period. With Russian ballet somewhat shorn of its novelty, Diaghilev in 1914 agreed to provide a company over twice the size of the troupe specified under the terms of the Metropolitan's 1910 draft agreement, in exchange for a weekly performance fee of only $270 more. Diaghilev's weakened bargaining position was reflected in other ways as well. The 1910 contract had stipulated fifty performances spread out over a two-and-a-half-month period, with no more than six performances a week; by contrast, the 1914 agreement, as modified in August 1915, required the troupe to give seven performances a week throughout the fifteen-week engagement, and at least once a week, to dance both a matinee and evening performance. If during the prewar years, the status of the Ballets Russes had enabled Diaghilev to appropriate the terms of the opera world as the basis for his agreements, now, the emphasis lay on a quantitative increase in the sheer volume of production.

Economics impinged on production in other ways. By today's standards a troupe of fifty ranks as large. With fifty dancers, however, the ensemble that crossed the Atlantic in 1915–1916 was but a shadow of its former self, a version in miniature of the huge Slavic cavalcades Diaghilev had earlier led to the West. For the gala Coronation season at the Royal Opera House—Diaghilev's first in the British capital—a cast of hundreds entrained for London: 100 dancers, 200 supernumeraries, plus singers. In 1914 the numbers were just as staggering. For the Paris season Diaghilev headed a company of twenty principal dancers, eleven principal singers, a corps de ballet of one hundred, and the chorus of the Bolshoi Opera.[11]

Now, the sheer scale of production changed. Old standbys were pared down. Comparing the New York production of *Schéhérazade* with its Parisian original, photographer Baron de Meyer spoke of the artistic effect of such cost cutting:

> "Sheherazade," as shown in New York . . . was but an interpretation, in a minor and reduced key of the amazing and bewildering orgy which we saw in Paris in former days when a multitude of dancers seemed to whirl in a frenzy. Now the multitude is reduced to eight bayadères, eight negroes, six fruit-bearers and a half-dozen or so principals.
>
> There is no doubt that a certain spirit and atmosphere remains in the performances of the present company. The thing in itself is too good, the music too fine, not to produce a most excellent impression, but to anyone like myself who actually was present at the première in Paris, "Sheherazade"— except for the fact that Nijinsky still occasionally dances his original part of the slave—is a poor performance and, at times, far from enjoyable.[12]

Pressures continued to mount during the second American tour, when for the first time in its history the troupe was reconceived in purely monetary terms as an income-producing asset that would provide the wherewithal for Diaghilev and his circle of collaborators to experiment. The 1914 contract had stipulated Diaghilev's presence in the United States; the document negotiated in 1916 did not.[13] Eventually, Otto Kahn, intent at all costs on pacifying the company's star, banned Diaghilev altogether. In response, Diaghilev divided the Ballets Russes into a skeleton troupe that remained with him in Europe and a large ensemble that returned to America under the auspices of the Metropolitan Ballet Company, a subsidiary of the parent opera house set up to handle the financing, management, and travel arrangements of the tour.[14] A similar division took place in the summer of 1917, when Diaghilev entrusted the company to Serge Grigoriev and Randolfo Barocchi, Henry Russell's former assistant now married to Lydia Lopokova, for a four-month tour of Brazil, Uruguay, and Argentina. As a solution to the problem of funding experimentation, this strategy held strong appeal for Diaghilev. Indeed, an illusion he harbored about the 1921 *Sleeping Princess* was that it would prove a long-running money-maker that would keep the greater part of his troupe employed while giving an intimate circle the means to experiment.

"Diaghilev was not really sorry at the prospect of being thus quit of the company for a time," wrote Grigoriev of the second Metropolitan tour. "He realized that the perpetual travelling entailed by an American tour would . . . have prevented him from working during the next winter on any new productions. On the other hand, by remaining in Europe with Massine and a few other dancers, he would be able to plan a whole new repertoire in peace. When telling me of this arrangement, . . . he . . . felt quite happy."[15]

Diaghilev had reason for optimism, as the contract guaranteed him, in addition to the $20,000 advance he received prior to the company's departure for America on September 8, 1916, $9,000 for each week of the twenty-week engagement and half the net profits of the tour. The Metropolitan assumed responsibility for all administrative, travel, and orchestra costs, along with Nijinsky's $60,000 salary and the cost of two new productions, *Till Eulenspiegel* and *Mephisto Valse,* both to be choreographed by the star. Diaghilev's financial commitment was limited to salaries of the dancers, conductor, chief machinist, and company managers Stanislaw Drobecki and Barocchi.[16]

Unfortunately for Diaghilev, the tour was a fiasco. Despite generally good notices and occasionally good houses, the Metropolitan lost a quarter of a million dollars. Its goal of taking "between $6,000 and $7,000 a performance" proved illusory. In Fort Worth, receipts fell as low as $767; during the first week of December alone losses amounted to nearly $15,000. Much of the responsibility for this disaster lay with the Metropolitan's management: the high ticket schedule it had insisted on, incompetent advance men who alienated local newspaper editors, and a failure generally to assess what the market would bear in Wichita and Tacoma. But part of

⟨37⟩ *Serge Lifar as Romeo in* Romeo and Juliet, *1926.*

⟨38⟩ *Pedro Pruna, front curtain* /or Les Matelots, *1925.*

⟨39⟩ *Stanislas Idzikowski as the Puppet and Alexandra Danilova as the Black Dancer in* Jack-in-the-Box, *1926.*

⟨40⟩ La Chatte, *1927*.

⟨41⟩ *Serge Lifar as the
Young Man in* La Chatte,
1927.

⟨42⟩ *Alexandra Danilova in* Ode, *1928.*

⟨43⟩ Ode, *1928.*

⟨44⟩ *Serge Lifar in the title role of* Prodigal Son, *1929.*

⟨45⟩ Apollon Musagète, *London, 1928.*

⟨46⟩ *Giorgio de Chirico, cover design for the Ballets Russes souvenir program, 1929.*

⟨47⟩ *Anton Dolin as the Young Man and Alexandra Danilova as the Lady in* Le Bal, *1929.*

⟨48⟩ *"Fruits of a Ballet Strike," caricature by Miguel, St. Petersburg, 1905.*

⟨49⟩ *"Diaghilev Triumphant," prewar Russian caricature.*

⟨50⟩ *"Monsieur Gabriel Astruc," caricature by Jean Gast, 1912.*

⟨51⟩ *"At the Châtelet (Russian Season)—L'Après-midi d'un Faune,"* caricature by Losques, Figaro, *30 May 1912.*

⟨52⟩ *" 'Le Spectre du Vert': Danced by the Mikst Foursomz Ballet,"* caricature by E. M. Shepard, Sketch, *2 July 1913.*

⟨53⟩ *Michel Georges-Michel, "The Opening of Parade,"* 1917. *From left: Paul Rosenberg, Marie Laurencin, Serge Diaghilev, Misia Sert, Erik Satie, Georges-Michel, Pablo Picasso, and Jean Cocteau.*

⟨54⟩ *"The Can Can in 'La Boutique Fantasque,'"* caricature of Léonide Massine by Ethelbert White, Dancing Times, *July 1919.*

⟨55⟩ *"The Good Fairy Bakst Leads Prince Charming Diaghileff to the Shrine of the Sleeping Princess,"* caricature by Edmund Dulac, Sketch, *28 December 1921.*

⟨56⟩ *Jean Cocteau, caricature of Bronislava Nijinska, March 1924.*

⟨57⟩ *"Mrs. Maynard Keynes sits in a box at the ballet and watches Nikitina, Doubrovska, Tchernicheva and Lifar dancing in Stravinsky's ballet 'Apollo Musagetes,' " caricature by Cecil Beaton, British Vogue, 11 July 1928.*

⟨58⟩ *" 'Le Train Bleu' at the Ballets Russes," caricature by Jean Gast,* Femina, *August 1924.*

Mars 929
M. L
Grand Hotel Paris

⟨59⟩ *Michel Larionov, drawing of Serge Diaghilev, 1929.*

⟨60⟩ *Lady Ripon, early 1900s.* ⟨61⟩ *Lady Cunard, late 1920s.*

⟨62⟩ *Outside the Riviera Palace Hotel, Monte Carlo, 16 April 1911. Standing, from left: Lydia Botkin, Pavel Koribut-Kubitovich, Tamara Karsavina, Vaslav Nijinsky, Igor Stravinsky, Alexandre Benois, Serge Diaghilev, and Sonia Botkin.*

⟨63⟩ *Alexandre Benois (left) and Igor Stravinsky in Tivoli, May 1911.*

⟨64⟩ *"Russian Opera: The Greatest Bass as a Director." Feodor Chaliapin (third from right) conducting a rehearsal at the Theatre Royal, Drury Lane, 1913.*

⟨65⟩ *Serge Diaghilev (right) and Léonide Massine (second from right) in* Granada, *1917.*

⟨66⟩ *Pablo Picasso (second from right) and assistants painting the curtain for* Parade, *1917.*

⟨67⟩ *Bronislava Nijinska (center) conducting a rehearsal in London, 1924. Alice Nikitina and Anton Dolin are on the extreme left.*

⟨68⟩ *George Balanchine (left), with Tatiana Chamié, Nina Nikitina, and Michel Pavloff, clowning on the beach at Monte Carlo, ca. 1925.*

⟨69⟩ *Rehearsal break in Monte Carlo, ca. 1925. Seated, from left: Irina Zarina, Tamara Geva, Vera Nemchinova, Alicia Markova, Dorothy Coxon, Nathalie Miklachevska, Lubov Soumarokova; standing, from left: unidentified woman, Helen Komarova, Vera Savina, Lydia Sokolova, and Tatiana Chamié.*

⟨70⟩ *Randolph Schwabe,
lithograph of Enrico Cecchetti,
ca. 1922.*

⟨71⟩ *Jean Cocteau and "Les Six," 1931. From left: Francis
Poulenc, Germaine Tailleferre, Louis Durey, Cocteau, Darius
Milhaud, Arthur Honegger.*

the blame rested with Nijinsky, who dithered over programs until press deadlines were missed and whose failure to dance as scheduled entitled ticketholders on a number of occasions to refunds. To the chagrin of local managements, he often refused to appear more than once on a program, no more than ten minutes if the scheduled ballet happened to be *Le Spectre de la Rose.* "Just think," Will L. Greenbaum, the manager of San Francisco's Valencia Theater, complained to the Metropolitan Musical Bureau, "of asking $5.00 for a show such as you are giving us certain nights and think what Pavlowa gave us for $2.50 and how that wonderful little woman used to work. Nine times a week and on the stage all the time." And, of course, Nijinsky's *Mephisto Valse,* which as late as November was scheduled to enter the repertory in San Francisco, failed to materialize.[17]

Nijinsky was not the only "prima donna" to cause difficulty. True to its policy of promoting European "stars" at the expense of native talent,[18] the Metropolitan went to great lengths in the months of July, August, and September 1916 to engage a ballerina from Russia. Acting through Captain Philip Lydig, an Allied munitions agent who headed the American Ambulance in Petrograd and served as a special assistant at the Embassy, it engaged Margarita Frohman and Olga Spessivtzeva for a ten-week season at a total salary each of Frs. 30,000 (equivalent to more than $500 a week) plus transportation.[19] Although the Metropolitan apparently conceded Spessivtzeva the privilege of dancing only four performances a week, neither Russian was prepared for the rigors of a cross-country tour. (Typical of the grueling schedule were the company's dates for the week beginning November 13: Monday, Worcester; Tuesday, Hartford; Wednesday, Bridgeport; Thursday, Atlantic City; Friday and Saturday, Baltimore.) Frohman began missing performances, and by the time the company reached Wichita on December 8, Ernest Henkel, the New York–based business manager of the tour, thought there was "very little use in carrying these two girls around the country" and that they should "leave at the end of the week of December 16 in Omaha." Frohman and Spessivtzeva left the company in San Francisco; their dismissal, however, was only one sign of a general belt-tightening by which the Metropolitan hoped to stave off the worst of what was obviously a disaster. In late November Henkel proposed eliminating one of the company's railroad cars; a few weeks later he spoke of dropping two musicians and charging to Drobecki the fares of two Russian women traveling with the company as chaperones.[20]

In addition to trimming expenses, the Metropolitan also cut back its remittances to Diaghilev. By early January he claimed that the Metropolitan owed him $37,500 of the $108,000 due to date. On February 11 he wired both Henkel and Rawlins L. Cottenet, a Metropolitan board member then in Paris, to cable $47,000 immediately to his bank. "Delay in payment inexcusable. Have urgent bank drafts." Later that month he brought consular pressure to bear on the Metropolitan through the Russian Embassy in Rome; by this time, he claimed, the outstanding balance had mounted to $75,000.[21]

The records show that between December 22, 1916, and February 19, 1917, the Metropolitan ordered the Foreign Trade Department of the Wall Street branch of the National City Bank to wire Diaghilev directly or through Drobecki $51,500. Obviously, some of this went to pay the troupe ($22,500 was forwarded to Drobecki on tour), and doubtless, a fair amount ended up in the pockets of Diaghilev's creditors. But surely there was another reason behind the January-February panic: the commitments he had just made to produce *Fireworks, Parade,* and *Le Chant du Rossignol,* which were to be the lynchpins of his spring seasons in Rome and Paris. In November and early December Diaghilev formalized agreements with Giacomo Balla (for *Fireworks*) and Fortunato Depero (for *Le Chant du Rossignol*); on January 11 and 12 he signed letter contracts with Picasso and Satie (for *Parade*). Also on January 12 Maurice Ravel agreed to undertake an untitled ballet with Francesco Cangiullo. Other works went into production at the same time: *The Good-Humoured Ladies* and the mini-ballets *Baba Yaga* and *Kikimora.* A factor in dropping *Le Chant du Rossignol* and the Ravel project may well have been the unanticipated loss of revenue from the American tour.[22]

Theoretically, the Metropolitan's remittances should have covered expenses on both sides of the Atlantic. In practice, however, they did not. Indeed, as Diaghilev signed up artists in Rome, his company virtually starved in America. On December 4 R.G. Herndon, the Metropolitan touring manager, reported from Houston:

> Well, the Diaghileff faction is not leaving a stone unturned to keep going until Diaghileff has instructed the bank to pay over the money . . . The corps de Ballet have had barely enough to keep alive, most of them haven't a cent to eat with. I have been giving those few small amounts out of my own pocket. Drobecki and Barocchi have sent Diaghileff some stinging cables, as they explained to me they asked him if it is his desire to see his company starve and stranded if not to wire immediately to the bank and release the cash . . . I don't know what they will do tonight, I learned they called up Gest to wire them [a] thousand dollars or it would mean end of tour.[23]

By the time the company reached Tulsa on December 11, the situation had worsened. Herndon wrote:

> The company are on their last dollars as Lopokova, Monteux, Revalles, Bolm have given up all the money they have at their command, and unless money is forthcoming at Kansas City, I don't think they can go further.[24]

Money must have come through as the company limped to the end of the tour. The episode, however, underscored how the encounter with America prefigured trends that would dominate the company's social history in the 1920s. In America, which fascinated contemporary European thinkers as the birthplace of "Fordism" and scientific management, "proletarianization" and its implications for the Ballets Russes first became evident. Not only did the company approach the level of productivity of entertainers in the popular theater, but the very labor of the dancers first became a source of Diaghilev's production capital. This was not a matter of isolated payless paydays. Subsistence wages allowed Diaghilev to syphon off funds to finance the development of new productions in Europe. But even when salaries were paid, they barely sufficed to cover living expenses in costly America. In November, from New England, Doris Faithfull wrote to Otto Kahn on behalf of herself and six other dancers in the corps de ballet. All were earning thirty-three and thirty-four dollars a week:

> I am writing this on some of the girls' behalf, also my own. It is concerning our salaries—we wondered if you could intercede with Mr. Diaghileff on the matter. It is absolutely impossible for us to live on the salary we receive—let alone some who have parents to support. When we arrive in a town we have to go hunting about for cheap rooms (carrying heavy suitcases) because we can't afford to stay at the better hotels. We are very sorry to have to trouble you with our private affairs but we are not in communication with Diaghileff. It seems so futile to think that every penny we earn and work hard for has to go in expenses—so cannot save anything in case of illness etc. A list of the salaries are beneath.[25]

Perhaps the democratic air of the United States gave them courage to appeal to the man whose investment house had just loaned fifty million dollars to the French government. Perhaps it was simply that with every stop along the company's New England tour the suitcases of practice clothes and pointe shoes had grown heavier. In any event, the downward slide of wages alongside the upward spiral of living costs anticipated a situation Diaghilev's dancers would encounter with distressing frequency after the war.

If the losses of this second tour dashed hopes that the Metropolitan would prove an ongoing source of capital (needless to say, the opera house chose not to exercise its option for a 1917–1918 tour), Diaghilev's intentions are clear: to finance avant-garde experiment from his company's traditional audiences and institutions, now expanded beyond the geographical borders of the prewar marketplace. The distinction between "elite" and "popular" in defining both the character of productions and the quality of audiences was a new one for Diaghilev.

Prior to the war, coteries had played little role in shaping company ideology. They defined neither the content or style of a work nor the core audience toward which it was directed. These, instead, were provided by the opera house, which linked Diaghilev's Western product to the social and cultural aspirations of the *haute bourgeoisie.* The transition to modernism altered this prewar alignment, shifting the company's ideological center to the Paris art world. From here now came most of Diaghilev's collaborators and the spectators who made up his core audience. Outside lay the *grand public,* which bought tickets, applauded, and criticized, but whose opinions counted for little. The split between Diaghilev's appointed elite and his larger audience was quickly noted, particularly in England, where as early as 1919 Leigh Henry spoke of the "ooze of cult-pretension which . . . has welled up about the Diaghileff company."[26] This redefining of Diaghilev's elite as one of taste rather than material substance (even if the two were frequently allied), like the division between the company's "elite" and "popular" works, had its origins in Diaghilev's recasting of the purposes, structure, and financing of his wartime Ballets Russes.

By early 1918, as the war dragged into its fourth year, not even Diaghilev's fabled inventiveness could find work for the company. "We were in Lisbon just over three months and for the last part of this time we had no money coming in at all: Diaghilev had none to give us," wrote Lydia Sokolova of those desperate days. "What money there was in the company circulated, but in the end we were all living on credit." For the first time in its history, the Ballets Russes was stranded, a predicament from which only an opportunely scheduled tour of Spain's cities and provincial towns rescued it. But all tours come to an end, and spring 1918 found Diaghilev at low ebb. In Madrid, Sokolova, desperate that her sick baby daughter might die, ran to Diaghilev's hotel room; taking a little leather bag from his wardrobe trunk, he emptied on the bed a heap of copper and silver coins from various countries, "all the money he had left."[27] He gave her the silver coins; she found a doctor; the baby lived. Not long afterwards a cable arrived, permitting the company to ship its scenery and effects through France to England, where an engagement at the London Coliseum awaited.

With this, the company's most desperate chapter came to an end. Artistically, the war years moved the Ballets Russes fully into the twentieth century. Financially, they did so as well, even if, in one of the grander ironies of Diaghilev's history, modernization came at the hands of an institution as mindful of the past as the Metropolitan.

8

ERA OF THE DANCE BOOM

ON SEPTEMBER 5, 1918, after an absence of more than four years, the Ballets Russes returned to London, headlining a variety bill at the Coliseum. For Diaghilev, who had previously refused all offers to play the "halls," no matter how celebrated or prestigious the house, the Coliseum engagement was a comedown, a sign of a sea change—and not one for the better—in the theatrical climate of his company's second city. Enthusiasts welcomed the returning prodigal, but so too did a wave of activity that challenged the primacy of the Ballets Russes as a purveyor of dance entertainment. The war years had been hard, but the post-Armistice era, which opened in 1918 and closed in 1922, ultimately proved no easier. After an initial breathing space, in which Diaghilev managed to recoup some of his losses, competition undermined the company's once impregnable bargaining position and brought it to the edge of collapse. On both sides of the Channel, the explosion in dance activity expanded the horizons of performance to once taboo locales. But for Diaghilev's dancers, who sometimes profited from this, it also created a pool of new talent that threatened their claim to the limelight. Initially, few had the schooling or experience to step into the shoes of Diaghilev's veterans. However, as the twenties progressed and jobs grew scarcer, the newcomers added to the precarious atmosphere within the company. With the return of the Ballets Russes to the European mainstream, capitalism doffed its liberating mask. To Diaghilev and his dancers lay revealed a marketplace, implacable in its logic, that they could neither control nor rely upon for their economic and artistic well-being.

"London has saved me," Diaghilev told conductor, Ernest Ansermet in 1919.[1] The impresario hardly exaggerated. From September 1918 to December 1919, his enterprise played sixteen months in London, the longest stretch ever in a single city. This was not the first—or last—time that change in locale would work a restorative miracle on Diaghilev's finances.

It was, however, the only occasion such a miracle was wrought in a popular setting. Between 1918 and 1922 West End music-halls laid out a welcome mat for the Ballets Russes. In the commercial theater Diaghilev found the production capital and popular audience that softened the economic shocks of 1917–1918.

In these years, Raymond Mortimer told *Dial* readers in 1922, "all London became *balletomane*."[2] But one Londoner, above all, headed this ballet rescue operation. Sir Oswald Stoll was a self-made captain of popular entertainment, a maverick risen through the provincial music-hall combines to the summit of a national empire. In 1904 he erected the theater that became the flagship of his operation. The lavishly appointed Coliseum, home today of the English National Opera, brought clerics and suburbanites to St. Martin's Lane, for many, their first excursion to one of London's numerous "halls." Onstage, as in the house, Stoll aspired to high tone. Off-color language was banned; ribaldry frowned upon. And, always, among the acrobats, animal acts, and ventriloquists were to be found elevating attractions from the legitimate theater and concert hall: Max Reinhardt's *Sumurun,* played by its original German cast; the Beecham Opera Company's *Hansel and Gretel;* a "grand futurist concert of noises" accompanied by a discourse in Italian by Marinetti; and Stoll's greatest coup, Sarah Bernhardt, who, beginning in 1910, made numerous appearances in selections from her repertory. Nor did the "cathedral of the Stoll diocese," in the words of a local wag, spurn ballet.[3] Long before 1918, dancers, including sometime Diaghilev ones, appeared on its boards—Tamara Karsavina in 1909 and 1910 (when she gave an abbreviated version of *Giselle*); Theodore and Alexis Koslov in 1912 (in a version of *Schéhérazade*); Adeline Genée (in *La Camargo*) in 1912, and with Alexandre Volinine (in *Robert le Diable*) two years later.

Stoll was not the only prewar showman to act upon the conviction that properly presented, good art was good business, even at popular prices. Both Alfred Butt and Alfred Moul vied with him in importing Russian talent: the former bringing Anna Pavlova and Mikhail Mordkin to the Palace in 1910; the latter, Yekaterina Geltzer, Vasily Tikhomirov, and Alexander Gorsky (who choreographed *The Dance Dream*) in 1912. Lydia Kyasht, partnered by Adolph Bolm, made her debut in 1908 at the Empire, the home of Victorian ballet. Yet another historic event was the full-length *Swan Lake* given at the Hippodrome in 1910 by a company of Imperial dancers led by Olga Preobrajenska. On the eve of World War I, Coliseum programming thus epitomized a growing trend: the gentrification of the Victorian variety palace into a locale at least partly associated with high theatrical art.

Under the management of the self-effacing Stoll, the Ballets Russes plunged into this popular world—first at the Coliseum (September 5, 1918–March 29, 1919), then at the Alhambra (April 30–July 30, 1919). Stoll's enterprise was emulated by other West End showmen: Butt, who presented the troupe at the Empire Theatre (September 29–December 30, 1919), and Charles B. Cochran, a newer-style producer (of whom more later) who brought it to the Princes Theatre (May 26–July 30, 1921). The opening of *The Sleeping Princess* at the Alhambra on November 2, 1921, found Stoll again at Diaghilev's side. This time, however, the producer had far less cause for gratification. Unlike Diaghilev's earlier season at the house, where *La Boutique Fantasque* had sent London "off its head with delight,"[4] the Petipa classic ended in failure. The ballet closed on February 4, 1922, as Diaghilev, a trail of debts in his wake, beat a retreat across the Channel.

Thus, except for a run at Covent Garden in the summer of 1920, Diaghilev's post-Armistice venues and producers belonged exclusively to popular entertainment. This phenomenon, a sign of Diaghilev's straitened circumstances, reflected no less sweeping changes in the economies of his host countries. These changes, eliminating forms of support that had periodically intervened between the demands of the marketplace and his company's survival, exposed Diaghilev as never before to the perils of commercial life. World War I had bled Europe's financial resources as well as its manhood. It "forced sudden and direct economic changes," historian Paul Thompson has written, "which not only altered individual lives . . . but also determined the whole post-war standard of living." Britain was not the only victor to emerge from the conflict "a rather less rich country."[5] France, too, showed signs of relative impoverishment, which the inflation, recession, new tax demands, and social unrest that accompanied peace only exacerbated. Although touching all social classes, these changes eroded to a considerable degree the income and savings of the banking and financial clans to which Diaghilev's traditional patrons belonged. In France "inheritances that were passed on in 1925 had only twice the nominal value of those in 1913, despite the franc's three- to fivefold loss of value between those years."[6] Economic pressures also imposed new constraints on state-subsidized institutions like the Paris Opéra, forcing them to streamline operations, cut costs, and find new ways of increasing revenues. In Russia, moreover, the Bolshevik victory eliminated at a single stroke the sources of income, employment, and patronage that had indirectly subsidized Diaghilev and his collaborators since the Ballets Russes's inception. "My fortune is gone," Diaghilev told Ansermet. "Before the war, I could lose 120,000 *francs* in London in a season, knowing that I would be able to find new sources in Russia . . . Now there are no more excellencies, no more Grand Dukes. In one year I find myself with a million in debts. London has saved me, but I am not rich and I have all I can do to meet my obligations."[7] The buffers that once had shielded the Ballets Russes from the extremes of market caprice belonged to the past.

Nor could Diaghilev in making his postwar comeback rely on the musical impresarios who had promoted and subsidized his earlier undertakings. Astruc's empire, as we have said, had collapsed on the eve of World War I. By 1921 his Théâtre des Champs-Elysées was in liquidation, and the erstwhile maverick, who continued to produce gala events, including prestigious film premieres, had become director of administrative services of the daily financial and economic bulletin "Radio."[8] Beecham, for his part, now abandoned the colleague he had long since picked clean, even though Russian opera—in productions originally mounted by Diaghilev—formed the lynchpin of his autumn 1919 season of "Grand Opera in English" at Covent Garden. The following year the two briefly joined forces in the "International Grand Opera Season" that marked Diaghilev's lone post-Armistice appearance at the Royal Opera House. Ill feeling, rather than glory, covered the season. Listings carefully noted that the ballet programs were "organised by Serge de Diaghilew," a sign of the bad blood between the erstwhile partners that Diaghilev's eleventh-hour cancellation of the last performance did nothing to ameliorate.

The consequences of the season, however, far transcended personal rivalry. In 1913 the Ballets Russes had been the rock on which the theatrical empire of Gabriel Astruc foundered. In 1920 the "heavy losses sustained during the . . . grand season of foreign opera and Russian ballet" drove the Sir Thomas Beecham Opera Company out of business.[9] No matter how deep the rancor he bore his former "angel," surely Diaghilev must have realized the implications of Beecham's failure: in Europe the old system of private operatic enterprise was dead.

Still another phenomenon heightened the company's vulnerability in this period: the dramatic increase in dance activity that undercut Diaghilev's prewar advantage in the competition for audiences and artistic influence. This explosion in the sheer number of troupes, attractions, venues, styles, and performers—which took place within the context of a veritable "craze" for social dancing precipitated by the mass commercialization of jazz—vastly expanded the market for dance, particularly in London and Paris, the era's twin dance capitals. For the Diaghilev company, however, the "boom" turned out to be a mixed blessing. Certainly, it enhanced public awareness of ballet. But at the same time, it destroyed the uniqueness to which the prewar troupe had laid claim. The Ballets Russes now found its artists, aesthetic practices, and institutions appropriated by a score of competing enterprises.

Challenging Diaghilev's preeminence as the leading theatrical patron of the avant-garde were two wealthy "amateurs" whose enterprises in the years 1920–1924 imitated with varying degrees of success the modernist approach and collaborative method of the Ballets Russes. The most important of these undertakings was Rolf de Maré's Ballets Suédois, which from its first performances at the Théâtre des Champs-Elysées in October 1920 until disbanding four years later, aspired, with considerable success, to displace the Ballets Russes from the vanguard of the Paris artistic world. The "Spectacles-Concerts" presented by Comte Etienne de Beaumont in 1920 (the first included Jean Cocteau's *Le Boeuf sur le Toit*) and his short-lived 1924 "Soirées de Paris" similarly aimed at duplicating Diaghilev's modernist "recipe," while adding a strongly Gallic flavor to its eclectic offerings of dance and theater pieces. Like the Ballets Russes, these enterprises were "collaborative" undertakings. Their stars, as in *Parade,* were the composers and painters of the Parisian avant-garde, and in the relationship of Maecenas and choreographer, they recapitulated the Diaghilev company's homosexual archetype. If in repertory, collaborators, and style of operation these enterprises bore a "Russian" stamp, so too did their audiences. Both the Ballets Suédois and the Soirées de Paris appropriated the advanced, coterie public first brought into the orbit of ballet by *Parade.*[10]

If these Paris-based undertakings challenged Diaghilev's commanding role as a purveyor of ballet modernism, various émigré ventures exploited features of his prewar aesthetic to secure a niche for themselves on the postwar landscape. No less a survivor than Diaghilev, Pavlova returned to Europe in late 1919 with a troupe of over forty dancers, and a repertory that continued to exploit the inheritance of the Maryinsky and the neoromantic and exotic styles popularized by Fokine. Pavlova's company, which rivaled the Ballets Russes as the era's longest-running dance enterprise, certainly fell short of its competitor in technical polish and overall artistic quality. Yet in her productions could be discerned a classical vision, absent from Massine's sophisticated choreography, that continued to bring audiences to the theater.

The October Revolution and ensuing civil war led many Russian artists to seek haven in the West. In this emigration dancers were heavily represented: at the Maryinsky in 1919–1920, the ballet ranks thinned from over two hundred, the troupe's normal complement, to only 134. The result was a proliferation throughout the following decade of theatrical enterprises that mined with varying degrees of success the exotic and neo-primitivist vein of Diaghilev's repertory. Early in 1920 a Swiss-based impresario, Naoum Mitnik, approached Jacques Rouché, director of the Paris Opéra, for the 1.5 million francs needed to underwrite an opera and ballet company of Russian émigré talent. Mitnik's proposal never went beyond the letter-writing stage, but it anticipated such émigré undertakings as Boris Romanov's Russian Romantic Ballet, which toured Central and Western Europe in the early and mid-twenties, Maria Kuznetsova's "Russian Seasons" at the Théâtre Femina, and the Chauve-Souris, the transplanted Moscow cabaret directed by Nikita Balieff that became the largest competitor to the Ballets Russes in employing émigré talent. Another troupe that appeared on the horizon was organized by Ida Rubinstein, Diaghilev's original Cleopatra and Zobéide, who, beginning in 1918, mounted a string of exotic productions, including several designed by Bakst, at the Paris Opéra. Her Ballets Ida Rubinstein, which made its first appearance in 1928, had several Diaghilev "graduates," beginning with choreographer Bronislava Nijinska, who had herself formed a short-lived avant-garde ensemble, Theatre Choréographique, after leaving the Ballets Russes in 1925.[11]

Organized ensembles, however, represented only a fraction of émigré dance activity. As newspaper theatrical columns and the pages of the *Dancing Times* make plain, Russian dancers had become a staple of popular entertainment, with the London Coliseum taking the lead in securing their talent. Here, Lydia Kyasht danced a one-act version of *La Fille Mal Gardée* in 1917 and Karsavina the leading mime role in Sir James Barrie's *The Truth About the Russian Dancers* three years later. Over the years Karsavina made frequent appearances on the Coliseum boards, as did Massine, Lydia Lopokova, Nicolas Legat, Stanislas Idzikowski, and a score of Diaghilev alumni when they parted ways with "Big Serge," as occurred with increasing frequency as the decade progressed.[12]

Other music-halls vied in presenting foreign and native ballet talent to the London public. So, too, did revues, especially those that bore the sophisticated trademark of Charles B. Cochran. In these lavish productions, compendia of dancing in all its many contemporary forms, miniballets by choreographic stars such as Massine appeared in the line-up of production numbers. On both sides of the Channel, revues featured dancers of the first order who exploited the vogue for Russian, Spanish, and modernist styles introduced by Diaghilev. By July 1922 the anonymous author of the *Dancing Times* "Paris Notes" column could write: "Laura de Santelmo is the latest, and not least, of a long list of Spanish dancers imported by [the] Olympia. And Russian dancers are as common as blackberries in a good season."[13]

The European dance "boom" of the 1920s did not so much aim at creating new institutions as converting existing ones to new purposes. In England this phenomenon occurred primarily in the commercial arena, where the upscaling of music-hall attractions and proliferation of revues vastly expanded opportunities for classical dancers. Here, ballet even became a feature of cabaret, with Cochran offering supper club patrons at the Trocadero a miniature *Coppélia* in late 1924.[14]

Across the Channel a rather different situation prevailed. Under the leadership of Jacques Rouché, the ballet company at the government-subsidized Opéra embarked on a period of long-overdue reform.[15] Technical standards improved; new works, several of which bore a Russian stamp, entered the repertory, and Russian *étoiles* were engaged. In an era of government austerity, this "Russification" policy represented one of a number of efforts on the part of the Opéra management to enhance revenues and restore the theater's tarnished reputation. Another was the refurbishing of the national repertory, symbolized by the mounting of a festival of French ballet in 1922 and the revival of *Giselle* (with Olga Spessivtzeva in the title role) two years later. If classical dancing remained, for the most part, confined to subsidized institutions, other kinds of dance proliferated on the concert and commercial stage. Indeed, throughout the twenties Paris became a mecca for exotic and interpretative performers of all kinds who flocked to the triple-theater complex on the avenue Matignon where *Le Sacre du Printemps* had premiered in 1913. Like the Coliseum, the Théâtre des Champs-Elysées became a major dance center. Here, in October 1920 the Ballets Suédois made its debut, reopening the theater that had been dark since 1914. Subsequently, the large stage was host to Pavlova and the Ballets Russes, as well as Maré's Franco-Swedish enterprise, while the smaller halls offered concert-style performances and even a Friday dance series. (In 1924 the municipally controlled Théâtre de la Gaîté-Lyrique inaugurated its own "séance des danses," another sign of Terpsichore's popularity in the French capital.) Beginning in November 1923 the Comédie des Champs-Elysées was also the setting for public lecture-demonstrations by André Levinson, the Russian-born doyen of Paris dance critics. Levinson's *La Danse d'aujourdhui,* a reflection of his wide-ranging interests and catholic taste, chronicles the rich dance culture that emerged in Paris during *les années folles.*[16]

Like the expansion in dance activity, the conflating of artistic categories within a wide range of theatrical institutions proved a mixed blessing for the Ballets Russes. Until 1918 Diaghilev's characteristic venues were those that legitimated the high status of his company while shielding it from competition with enterprises of "lesser" artistic value. The post-Armistice years directly challenged this selective segregation, witnessing a trend toward homogeneity in programming that sharpened competition at both the elite and popular ends of the theatrical spectrum. If before the war, only the Pavlova company had shuttled between opera house and music-hall, now many ensembles did so, beginning with the Ballets Russes itself. From 1918 to 1922 the Diaghilev company performed at a broad range of theaters on both sides of the Channel, from such popular houses as the Coliseum and Gaîté-Lyrique to such elite stages as Covent Garden, the

Paris Opéra, and the Théâtre des Champs-Elysées. Loie Fuller's company, the Ballets Suédois, and a score of other attractions followed suit, including Cocteau's *Le Boeuf sur le Toit,* which Stoll imported from the Champs-Elysées for a Coliseum engagement in 1920. All these institutions, moreover, underwent a radical change in image over the course of the twenties. The Opéra, increasingly strapped for funds, enlarged the scope of its activities so as to cater to what was regarded as "popular taste":[17] among these efforts were productions by Ida Rubinstein and Loie Fuller, by now fixtures of the Paris social and artistic scene, premieres of prestigious French films (including Abel Gance's *Napoleon*), and the French dance festival in 1922. An even greater accommodation with prevailing taste took place at London's Royal Opera House. Leased in 1922 by Walter Wanger, Hollywood head of United Artists, it became a "super-cinema," presenting such film classics as *The Three Musketeers* and *L'Atlantide* to the accompaniment of the London Symphony Orchestra. Conductor Eugene Goossens was not the only Diaghilev alumnus recruited by Wanger. To "bolster up the drawing power of the show," Wanger engaged Massine, Lopokova, and other out-of-work Diaghilev stars for a curtain raiser that anticipated the subsequent switch in house policy to revue. The Théâtre des Champs-Elysées underwent a similar metamorphosis: "the home of grand ballet and of the highest artistic productions generally" in the early twenties, by mid-decade it had become a stylish music-hall under the management of Rolf de Maré. Here, ironically, the erstwhile director of the Ballets Suédois presented the 1925 *Revue Nègre* that made Josephine Baker the toast of Paris.[18]

Thus, as music-halls upgraded their programming to encompass high art attractions, elite institutions borrowed from the music-halls. This phenomenon, which paralleled changes in the very substance of theatrical form, challenged distinctions of caste associated with individual artistic styles. In 1914 Diaghilev had stood at the apex of the commercial pyramid. Now, his company took its place alongside numerous competing enterprises on a theatrical continuum broadened and reshaped by the post-Armistice marketplace.

The extent to which the new economic climate straitened company finances may be judged by the provisions of Diaghilev's contracts with the Paris Opéra between 1919 and 1921. These documents, which specified a per performance fee of Frs. 12,000 for engagements in 1919 and 1920 and Frs. 14,000 for the summer 1922 season, suggest that even without taking inflation into account, since 1913 the company's earning power had declined by approximately one-half. With the sharp fall of the franc in 1919–1920 and the quadrupling of prices between 1913 and 1919, the drop in real income was far more dramatic. The adoption of a piecework system of payment represented a significant departure from prewar Opéra policy. Under the terms of his previous agreements, Diaghilev had simply rented the house and its facilities for a fee—Frs. 100,000 for the ten performances of the spring 1914 season.[19] With box office receipts going *in toto* to the producer (after deduction of taxes), the arrangement obviously favored Diaghilev. Under the new system all takings over and above the performance fee remained in the hands of the Opéra. Although the company never performed as frequently in Paris (where a performance every other day remained the norm) as in the United States or even England, Rouché's goal of increasing Opéra productivity was reflected in a number of ways. Not only did the draft April 1919 contract specify two thousand francs less per performance than the final version (necessity had taught Diaghilev the fine art of bargaining), but in the course of negotiations the number of orchestra rehearsals dropped from twenty-two to fifteen and the chorus was eliminated entirely. The October 1921 contract, which stipulated the premieres of *The Sleeping Princess* and Stravinsky's *Mavra* and *Les Noces* the following spring, laid an even heavier financial burden on Diaghilev. Although he received an additional two thousand francs per performance, he had to provide all the singers for the engagement as well as the considerably augmented troupe needed to dance the Petipa classic.

To what extent Diaghilev's position had declined relative to competing ventures may be appreciated by comparing these terms with Loie Fuller's July 1922 Opéra contract. Where Diaghilev was to receive Frs. 14,000 for a full evening of grand ballet, including singers, stars, premieres, and an entire professional organization, Fuller was paid Frs. 4,000 for a troupe of twenty amateur dancers, lighting personnel, and a forty-five minute "ballet fantastique."[20] As it turned out, neither *The Sleeping Princess* nor *Les Noces* was presented in 1922, much to Rouché's annoyance. "In place of *The Sleeping Princess*," he wrote to Diaghilev in April 1922, "a grand, evening-long ballet, you propose to give a fragment of this work, *Aurora's Wedding*":

You understand what difference the substitution of a one-act work . . . [for] an entirely new work can make at the box office. I had counted on a profitable success, *The Sleeping Princess* being already known from . . . its numerous performances in London, the magnificence of its staging, its numerous decors and costumes signed by Bakst, and the caliber of its interpreters . . . The solution you propose has nothing but disadvantages: no stars, no decors, no mise-en-scène . . . Apart from *Petrouchka*, we have no grand ballet: neither *Schéhérazade* nor *Firebird*, only very short works demanding numerous rehearsals and appealing solely to an audience of artists . . . The enormous expense of these performances demands the certainty of very considerable receipts at very high ticket prices. Hence, you will understand my concern at a program change that involves on the commercial side a change whose implications I seek to appreciate.[21]

Other signs of declining income are suggested by the sharp reduction in actual receipts for those few independent seasons in this period for which information survives. At the Gaîté-Lyrique in May 1921, takings at the box office averaged Frs. 26,921 per performance. On opening night, when Prokofiev's *Chout* and *Cuadro Flamenco* received their premiere, receipts amounted to a respectable Frs. 36,462. A few days later they fell to a low of Frs. 14,258, no doubt reflecting competition from the Ballets Suédois, then performing at the Théâtre des Champs-Elysées. In real terms, these figures meant a substantial decline from the Frs. 40,670 average recorded for the 1914 Opéra season.[22] Offsetting this loss, however, was a sharp increase in company productivity. Following the practice of the commercial stage (in the music-halls the company gave twelve performances a week), Diaghilev compressed the brief eight-performance season into seven days, thereby raising the troupe's gross weekly earnings to over Frs. 215,000.

From the Gaîté, the company moved to London's Princes Theatre. For this two-month season, a producer very different from Stoll stood at Diaghilev's side. In Charles B. Cochran, that flamboyant self-styled "showman," the Ballets Russes found a mentor who combined a brilliant sense of the market with a genius for promotion—qualities that made his stylish revues the talk of the 1920s. Unlike Diaghilev, Cochran did not stand on ceremony with social notables, nor did he appeal to snobbery to garner an audience. His tack was that of the populist and the publicist. Like Stoll, Cochran kept ticket prices reasonable; unlike him, he marketed ballet as a trendy event. For the first time, one discerns in the company's European advertising the pen of the modern copywriter. Gone are the sober notices of repertory and casts. From the five-inch column of press clips that followed the premiere of *Cuadro Flamenco* to blurbs announcing *Le Sacre du Printemps* as the "highest achievement of the Russian Ballet,"[23] "hype" made its debut in the company's London advertising. Under Cochran's management every other performance became an event: advertisements announced the presence of composers on the podium (and Stravinsky in the audience); Lydia Lopokova's "reappearance" (she had "vanished" from the company two years before); the London debut of the "famous Russian tenor" Dmitri Smirnov, who sang in the intervals; and the season's first performances of familiar ballets and even pieces of music played during the symphonic interludes.

Socially, "hype" paid off, with items about the Ballets Russes appearing in the *Times* "Court Circular" for the first time since 1914. But as statements for the period July 21–29 reveal, financially it did not. Not only do these documents record a surprising drop in gross receipts (£284 or Frs. 17,324 per performance) as compared to the Gaîté figures, but they also indicate how little of this money found its way into Diaghilev's pocket. Of the £1,752 collected for the first seven performances, no less than £1,250 represented Cochran's "share." For the last two, the producer's share was fifty percent. After deducting the sums advanced as cash on account, Diaghilev received a grand total of £514 or £57 a performance, too little even to cover his payroll. In his memoirs Cochran states that he lost £5,007 on the season. Added to the "share" presumably repaid during the nine-week season, this brings Cochran's advance to £16,257. If few could plow sums of this magnitude into a theatrical venture, fewer still could stand to lose thirty percent of their investment. The Ballets Russes had helped put Astruc and Beecham out of business. With so much red ink splattering his books, Cochran, too, now retired from the field.[24]

What the figures demonstrate, above all, is the precarious thread on which survival of the post-Armistice Ballets Russes hung. Throughout these years Diaghilev walked a fine line between bankruptcy and self-sufficiency, an acrobatic feat that left little margin for experiment and no cushion for failure. Of the ballets that left their mark on the post-Armistice imagination, none laid claim to new aesthetic ground. From *Parade* to *Chout*, virtually all of Diaghilev's new productions coasted on the breakthroughs of the war years. In part, this phenomenon pays tribute to the immense creativity of that era. On the other hand, it suggests the paucity of means that kept Diaghilev from venturing once again into the artistic unknown.

Diaghilev's financial bind can be appreciated from the underwriting of the most ambitious of his post-Armistice productions—the revival of *Le Sacre du Printemps* in 1920 and *The Sleeping Princess* a year later. Although Massine's new version of the 1913 masterpiece used Roerich's original sets and costumes, the ballet's large cast and ninety-seven piece orchestra (more than double the size of the ensemble that had accompanied the troupe in America) entailed an outlay beyond Diaghilev's now straitened means. The revival was made possible by couturière Gabrielle Chanel, whose timely gift of Frs. 300,000[25] not only saved the day, but signaled the emergence of a new kind of ballet patron—the self-made, style-minded entrepreneur.

Ironically, both the idea of mounting *The Sleeping Princess* and the financing of this full-length ballet came from the popular stage. Diaghilev was "amazed," wrote Grigoriev, at the long-running success of *Chu Chin Chow*, the musical extravaganza billed as "The Most Wonderful Entertainment London Has Ever Seen," whose impending "death" was announced and consummated during the company's 1921 season. "One day he said to me half jokingly how much he wished he could discover a ballet that would run for ever . . . I replied that not only was such a thing quite impossible, but that it would bore him to death. 'Not at all,' he retorted. 'You'd run it and I'd do something else!" Rejecting Grigoriev's suggestion of *Coppélia,* the comic ballet in which Adeline Genée had scored her greatest triumph and that was revived in abbreviated form on at least two occasions in the twenties, Diaghilev chose instead to mount *The Sleeping Princess.* Behind the decision to stage this grand classical spectacle lay yet another attempt to fund artistic experiment. Whereas in 1916–1917 the Metropolitan had unwittingly financed his modernist ventures, now Diaghilev proposed to underwrite a creative laboratory from the profits of a West End "hit." [26]

If musical comedy had suggested the idea, a music-hall enterprise footed the bill. For the scenery and costumes the Alhambra Company advanced Diaghilev £10,000, repayable against box office receipts, and twice acceded to his request for additional sums of £5,000. Diaghilev spent lavishly on the production—the second in the West (Giorgio Savocco's 1896 *Beauty* at La Scala, with Carlotta Brianza in the title role, anticipated *The Sleeping Princess* by twenty-five years)—of what has since become the signature work of England's Royal Ballet. Making peace with Bakst, then estranged from his former mentor, Diaghilev entrusted the mise-en-scène to the *miriskusstnik* who had enthused with him over the St. Petersburg original. Bakst's services alone cost Diaghilev Frs. 28,000—Frs. 5,000 for each of the ballet's five scenes plus expenses. "The dresses," rhapsodized Cyril W. Beaumont, who had entree to the company at this time, "were made of the finest materials and in some instances cost from forty to fifty pounds apiece, a large sum at this period." [27] Costuming was not the only aspect of the production to recall Imperial splendor. To dance the role of Aurora Diaghilev scoured Europe for Maryinsky ballerinas, and in the months following the premiere on November 2, 1921, London audiences witnessed in the ballet's title role three brilliant exponents of Russian classicism—Vera Trefilova, Olga Spessivtzeva, and Lubov Egorova. Carlotta Brianza, Petipa's first Aurora, took the part of the Wicked Fairy, which she ceded to Enrico Cecchetti, Petipa's first Blue Bird, on the fiftieth anniversary of his first appearance before the public. Nicholas Sergeyev, the former Maryinsky regisseur who had left the Soviet Union with notated scores of Petipa's ballets, was engaged to reconstruct the choreography. "I can still see that magnificent first scene of the Christening," wrote Beaumont:

> the rich stonework and marble walls and columns lined with gorgeous negro guards in white and gold, and black and silver, the Marshal of the Court greeting the guests—lords and ladies, and fairies with their pages bearing

charming gifts for the baby Princess. The aristocracy bore themselves with distinction, while the fairies invested their movements with an austere nobility which set them apart from the most honoured mortals. So life moved at a stately pace until suddenly interrupted by the appearance of the Wicked Fairy, who arrived in her coach drawn by rats. But she, too, had dignity. She was majestic even in her wrath.[28]

Diaghilev's "gorgeous calamity," as one reviewer called the production, closed on February 4, 1922, in the midst of "a slump of extraordinary severity." One hundred five consecutive performances had been given, probably an all-time record for a full-length Petipa ballet. However, the run fell short of the six months necessary to repay Stoll's advance. The work was withdrawn; Stoll sequestered the scenery and costumes against the remaining debt of £11,000, and Diaghilev left England with five hundred pounds borrowed from the mother of dancer Hilda Bewicke in his pocket.[29] The ballet's seventy artists scattered. Stoll, for his part, abandoned ballet production. Henceforth, the works that appeared on his stage were imports first proven elsewhere.

The immediate consequences of this episode were disastrous. At a single stroke, Diaghilev saw his short-term plans thrown into jeopardy, his troupe weakened by defections, and his London base of operations destroyed. For the second time in less than a decade, the company collapsed: the force majeure of the marketplace proved as implacable as that of war. The threat of legal action, moreover, barred Diaghilev from performing in England until late 1924. When he returned, he faced still another consequence of the fiasco—the fragmentation of the broad-based audience that had grown up around the "Russian Ballet" between 1918 and 1922. A later chapter will analyze in detail the nature of this public and the implications of its dispersal.

Most significantly, the economic failure of *The Sleeping Princess* made very plain the inadequacy of "free enterprise" as a system of artistic production. In the summer of 1922 Diaghilev explored various ways to stabilize the company on a new financial basis. One such plan called for its legal incorporation as the "Société des Ballets Russes." With permanent headquarters in Paris, the new entity was to be organized as a public company with stockholders, who stood to gain a share in the troupe's "continuing accomplishments and unique publicity," if not sizeable dividends, and a board of directors to oversee its financial management.[30] Had the scheme materialized, no doubt the same faithful patrons who now came to Diaghilev's aid would have lent their support to the fledgling enterprise. As it turned out, Princesse Edmond de Polignac placed a "sum at Diaghilev's disposal that enabled him to save the company and proceed with the strictest economy,"[31] while through her good offices, the Ballets Russes became a resident dance troupe of Monaco's Théâtre de Monte-Carlo. In light of subsequent company history, however, the drafting of such a prospectus is significant. It suggests not only Diaghilev's implicit recognition that high art enterprises could no longer survive in the private sector without large and regular infusions of cash, but that with costs and risks so high no single individual could be expected to assume the role of a permanent Maecenas.

Between 1918 and 1922 competition toppled the Ballets Russes from its place at the apex of the prewar dance pyramid. Diaghilev's artists suffered a similar fate. The war wrought major changes in public attitudes toward dancing, accelerating trends catalyzed by the advent of "the Russians" while destroying the social and moral taboos that had previously kept women from entering the job market. In England, where the "boom" touched every aspect of dance activity, the results were dramatic. For the first time, vast numbers of middle-class girls took up dancing as a career, thanks to a plethora of new training and employment opportunities. These newcomers, along with émigrés from the Russian Revolution and a "lost generation" of American dance talent that streamed across the Atlantic, challenged the commanding position of Diaghilev's "free artists" before the war. It is against this background of supply outstripping demand that the "proletarianizing" phenomenon first discernible during the American tours quickened in tempo. For the dancer "aristocracy" of the Ballets Russes, the post-Armistice years brought lower wages and worsening conditions, while intensifying the precariousness of lives spent outside the security of a state-subsidized system.

The postwar dance "boom" vastly expanded opportunities for dancers. Even before 1914 Pavlova and the Ballets Russes had sent numerous enthusiasts to the barre. "It is astonishing," a London teacher told the *Dancing Times* in 1912, "what a lot of ladies and children have taken up fancy and operatic dancing since the advent of the Russian Ballet." Rather than diminishing the numbers of pupils, the war swelled their ranks. Ruby Ginner, a popular teacher of "interpretative" dancing, noted "an increased demand for good dancing." "Personally," she wrote in 1917, "my own school has more than doubled its numbers and its work." The growth of an aspiring corps of professionals between 1912 and 1918 is reflected in the pages of the *Dancing Times*. School advertising grew by leaps and bounds; pictures traced budding careers from the classroom to the professional stage; coverage of theatrical dance spilled well beyond the bounds of concert performance. By early 1918 Ruby Ginner's anticipation of a "time when the dance shall come into her own again," seemed to be realized. As P.J.S. Richardson wrote under his editorial pseudonym "The Sitter

Out," "One has only to glance through the programmes of the various musical comedies, revues and music-halls to find that there never was such a demand for dancers as there is at the present moment."[32]

As the magazine's expanding pages of features, advertisements, and personal columns vividly attest, this phenomenon increased dramatically over the coming decade, and not only at home. The 1920s saw England become a major exporter of dance talent to the cabarets and music-halls of the Continent. The rise of social dancing as a mass pastime, moreover, created an array of opportunities for paid employment in the supper clubs, dance halls, and enormous *palais de danse*—dance palaces—that sprang up throughout England. Even the cinema took to hiring dancers. By 1920 a noted dance writer could rhapsodize that "in the whole history of the dance there has never been any period so rich in various forms of dancing as to-day,"[33] a diversity reflected in the scores of exhibition, operatic, interpretative, acrobatic, grotesque, step, precision, and exotic dancers (to say nothing of paid partners) whose art lent an eclectic flavor to the theatrical and ballroom climate of the 1920s.

Reflecting these new professional opportunities was the proliferation of studios that offered training for stage and ballroom dancing as well as teaching. Within the context of British ballet history, the most important of these was the school opened in 1914 by Serafima Astafieva, a Maryinsky-trained graduate of the Ballets Russes, where most of the younger generation of Diaghilev's British dancers, including Anton Dolin and Alicia Markova, received their early training. Other Russians migrated to London in the wake of the post-Armistice Ballets Russes, and like Astafieva, Nicolas Legat, Laurent Novikoff, and Enrico Cecchetti set up studios that became meccas for advanced students and ambitious young professionals. At the same time, the recognition that "operatic" dancing (as ballet was then called) had become a necessity to meet the higher technical standards of theatrical dancing generally led to the widespread introduction of ballet into the curriculum of schools and academies, including those that catered largely to social dancing. This alliance of ballet, stage, and ballroom dancing, a phenomenon that had no parallel in France, where the categories of amateur and professional remained strictly separate, created a large new pool of enthusiasts with the minimum skills required to turn professional in an era of high demand.[34]

This eclecticism, which many observers feared as "a tendency to formlessness"[35] in standards of taste and technique, differed markedly from the prewar situation. Before 1914 dance education took place largely within the confines of theatrical schools. Here, the pupil studied elocution, acting, and singing as well as dancing in preparation for a stage career. The professional character of these institutions was reflected in the dual role of their principal teachers, who were often attached to London theaters as ballet mistresses or "dance composers," and their function of providing youngsters for musical shows and pantomimes, both in London and on the road. Although they survived into the 1920s, the power of these academies now declined. Not only had the requirements of theatrical training changed, but by the early 1920s a new and competitive teaching market had come into existence, where literally anyone with a notion to do so could declare himself or more frequently herself a teacher. "Just think of it!!!" read an advertisement for the Park Lane Dancing School and Galleries in 1922:

> One Year's Training, and you are ready to take your place as prominent people in the Dancing World. With a Diploma bearing the signatures of the universally famous Mme. Lydia Kyasht and Mr. Henry Cooper, you should get a post anywhere in the world, or set up as a Teacher for yourself. No one-sided restrictions. You are free to open your own School wherever you like. There's no career like a Dancing career for anybody, girl or man, who has the *enthusiasm* and the *determination* to succeed. The work is interesting, lucrative, pleasant and healthy.[36]

Appropriating the claims of health and career training, such schools came as a response to the steep rise in "amateur" demand that the older, professional institutions could not meet.

A striking phenomenon of the post-Armistice years in England was the change in social status of the dancer. Suddenly, the "ballet girl" had become respectable, a remarkable change from the mid-nineteenth century when ballet was "a very favourite amusement with the people who go to cheap penny theatres," and the chief distinction of its "young ladies" was thought to be their "short petticoats."[37] With the establishment in the 1880s of permanent companies at the Empire and Alhambra Theatres, the quality of ballet entertainments improved. Nevertheless, the stigmas of low social class and sexual impropriety remained associated with both the practitioners of choreographic art and its music-hall venues up to World War I.

The advent of Pavlova and Diaghilev's "Russian Ballet" gave a jolt to both prejudices. By contrast to the usual run of London's "ballet girls," the children whom Pavlova accepted for training in 1911 came from "good families." They were daughters of shopkeepers and businessmen, recruited from London dancing classes where they had been sent to acquire grace and deportment for the ballroom and salon. "Hilda Boot," wrote *The Dance Magazine* somewhat tongue-in-cheek in 1926, "like all nice English girls, went to dancing school. She played 'The Spirit of the Oyster' in an underseas ballet, and became Butsova, second to Pavlowa in the famous Russian troupe."[38] Similarly, the men who joined Pavlova's company (aside from her classical partners who hailed from the Maryinsky or, more typically, from the Bolshoi) stood several cuts above their predecessors. Serge Oukrainsky, for instance, was a Russian aristocrat, while Hubert Stowitts, an American who joined the troupe in 1915, was a graduate in economics from the University of California. Pavlova took pains to "protect" her girls, shepherding them like a duenna across oceans and continents, exhorting them to be hard-working, diligent, and lady-like. And no matter what off-color associations had touched her name in Russia, once in the West no hint of scandal was allowed to tarnish her reputation.

In program notes, essays, and interviews, Diaghilev's dancers and publicists emphasized a similar theme of "respectability." Pages were given over to descriptions of the Imperial school, and stress was laid on the "long and arduous training," as Ellen Terry wrote, that "has reformed the ballet on such refined and spiritual lines." In a slim volume produced in tandem with the 1912 Covent Garden season, *Sunday Times* editor and music critic Leonard Rees likewise extolled the "vigorous curriculum of the present day Imperial School" whose "pupils tread no primrose path to artistic distinction, but have all through their career to submit themselves to a stern discipline of body and mind."[39] Rees compared Russian ballet training to an enlightened system of military advancement:

> Having passed through the school stage successfully the pupils are placed 'on the strength' of the *corps de ballet,* and like the conscripts of Napoleon's army have the possibilities of the highest distinction before them. Talent and discipline alone will decide whether they will remain in the rank and file, or climb through the various grades to the eminence of premier place as danseur, mime, or artiste classique. In dancing as in all the arts, the price of high accomplishment is continual striving.[40]

In a series of interviews with Serafima Astafieva, the *Dancing Times* offered a more intimate view of Imperial dance education. Here, the accent lay (as it would in Karsavina's memoir *Theatre Street* published in 1930) on the school's convent-like atmosphere, the rigid separation of boys and girls not only from each other but also from the world at large, and the high standards of physical and moral hygiene enforced by a staff of stiff-lipped governesses.[41]

Another stock refrain of these early commentaries concerned the high social standing of Russian ballet on its native grounds. By contrast with its degenerate counterpart in the West, noted Rees, ballet in Russia provided "an admirable example of the true aristocratic institution, that which is placed above the necessity of justifying itself to every wind of popular favor, and is free to cultivate a lofty idealism and to care for the long results of time rather than immediate and ephemeral success." Astafieva, again anticipating memoirs and statements by her Imperial confreres, emphasized the students' physical proximity to the person of the tsar:

> The pupils are allowed to go home for three days at Christmas and Easter and after the yearly visit of the Emperor, who gives a few days' holidays. In the summer the school is removed to Tsarkoe Selo, to a building in the Palace, where the children spend their holidays playing in the beautiful park of the Imperial Palace . . . Sometimes . . . the rehearsals take place in the theatre, to which the children are taken in government carriages under the protection of class mistresses, and porters in red liveries. This is always a great treat for the pupils . . . Should the Emperor be present at any performance in which the children take part, he invariably invites them to his box, where the Empress personally distributes sweets.[42]

The reiteration of aristocracy and personal morality in these early writings helped wean the image of ballet away from its traditional associations. At the same time it created a new social standard toward which the promoters of a native British ballet self-consciously aspired. Besides offering pupils at leading schools the opportunity to dance for an appreciative audience, the annual "Sunshine Matinees," inaugurated by the *Dancing Times* in 1919, were organized with a view to lending a genteel aura to early all-British concert efforts. Arranged as charity events with distinguished patronage, these matinees anticipated a current that would figure significantly in the future development of British ballet.

Although public estimation of the dancer had begun to rise by 1914, the war made dancing respectable as a career. In part, this reflected new attitudes toward female employment; for the first time, many upper- and middle-class women took jobs that liberated them from a life of tea cups and domestic idleness while enabling them to earn a living. Still another reason lay in the "apparently widespread collapse of sexual caution" that altered moral parameters and expectations. Lastly, the middle-class trend away from private entertaining (owing in part to smaller houses and the postwar scarcity of domestic help) enhanced the respectability of dancing as a public activity. Indeed, in 1919 dancing found a paladin in no less a churchman than the Dean of Manchester, who defended it in the pages of the *Daily Mail* as "a natural outlet from the drabness of surroundings and the monotony of modern industrial processes." Although newspapers continued to titillate readers with headlines like "Is Jazz an Orgy of Immorality?," by 1920 the social and moral stigma that had barred middle-class girls from the profession had largely disappeared.[43] Coupled with the vast expansion of opportunities for novices, dancing became a respectable way for young women to earn their livelihood.

By 1923 the *Dancing Times* had added to its pages a regular feature by "Button Box," the nom de plume of a "ballet mother." Under the title "Chats With Young Dancers," the series counseled youngsters and their generally anxious mothers about careers in teaching and on the stage. Amid answers to queries about "practice" skirts ("I never remember seeing any of our great dancers showing 'ribbons and laces' ") and leg warmers ("cut the feet off a pair of long woolen stockings and wear the legs over your thin tights"),[44] "Button Box" extolled time and again the advantages of dancing as a career. "The life of a dancer alone is a great education," she replied to a mother in a quandary about whether her daughter, an aspiring professional, should attend secondary school:

A dancer has the tremendous advantage of meeting well-educated and much-travelled people, in far greater numbers than the stay-at-home girl. I know one girl who had the good fortune to have as 'dresser' a French gentle-woman who could . . . carry on conversation [in] English, French and German . . . The girl of whom I speak picked up quite good French, and later on, from working with the Russians, sufficient of that language also, for all practical purposes.[45]

Apart from training in languages and the opportunity of meeting "nice" people, traditional aims of middle-class schooling, "Button Box" stressed the economic advantages of a career in teaching, an equally traditional end of female education:

To your question, 'What is an articled pupil?' It means, simply, a pupil who has an agreement drawn up, signed and stamped (to make it legal and binding) between a teacher and herself. The details of the agreement may vary considerably. For instance, a parent may deposit a hundred guineas with a teacher on the understanding that the pupil receives a lesson a day for one or two years, at the end of which, if proficient, the pupil commences to receive a small salary and to assist in teaching.

Another typical arrangement in that pre-scholarship age provided free training to talented but impecunious girls with repayment taking the form of a percentage of the pupil's earnings when she began to dance professionally.[46] Many schools, it should be noted, advertised vacancies for "articled" pupils, and one may be sure that despite "Button Box's" praise of the arrangement, it was regarded by the unscrupulous as a source of cheap labor.

Economic self-sufficiency was also the theme of the dance writer Mark Perugini in a 1925 article that assessed among other things the "remarkable change in one generation" of the "practical possibilities" of the profession. Noting that before the war "a young dancer was glad enough to appear in ballet, or in one of the annual pantomimes, as the unpaid, or practically unpaid, apprentice of a teacher who farmed out the talents of her school," and "when *out* of her apprenticeship, she was glad to earn one portion of her income in business during the day, and another by appearing in some production at night for a salary of a pound a week," Perugini suggested to what extent the situation had changed:

> To-day things are different. *Then* theatres were fewer, the form of entertainment less varied, the opportunities less, and tuition . . . 'sketchy' . . . Now, though a girl may have to pay from thirty to seventy guineas a year for tuition for, say, a couple of years, she is certain of adequate and *standardised* tuition; and, owing to the dearth of well-trained dancers, she is sure of a salary of three pounds or more a week, with opportunities for advancement such as were seldom enjoyed by her forerunners.[47]

Recognizing that 150 guineas represented a hefty sum for most family budgets, Perugini adopted a line calculated to appeal to middle-class parents concerned for their daughters' future. Assuming the cost of study to be recoverable within the first year of a dancer's career, tuition should not be regarded as "mere outlay," but as an "investment, yielding, with fair luck, considerable future returns on expenditure." Clearly, the newfound respectability and status of the post-Armistice dancer rested on her ability to earn a "decent" living.

Two popular novels by Compton MacKenzie registered the metamorphosis of the ballet girl on the contemporary imagination. The first, *Carnival,* appeared on the eve of Diaghilev's first engagement in London. The story of Jenny Pearl, a second-line ballet girl at the Orient Palace of Varieties, the novel recorded, with the fatalism of an earlier generation of naturalists, the tragedy of circumstance that made low birth, loose morals, and lost ambition the inevitable accompaniments of the dancer's profession. A sequel, *Coral,* followed in 1925. In the fifteen-year span between the publication of the two novels, the Orient, now a "theater," has upgraded more than its name. Ballet has given way to revue, while peers and well-heeled families have replaced the Bohemians and provincials of yesteryear in the stalls. Class differences remain, of course, but no longer do they pose insuperable barriers to work and romance. Jenny's son marries the daughter of Maurice, the "wealthy gentleman at large," who years before as a stage-door Johnnie had wooed and abandoned the pretty ballet girl, a decision he naturally regrets. And, typically, when Coral, a "jazz baby" who before her elopement went dancing five nights a week, thinks of getting a job, her first idea is to open a dance studio. Contrived and sentimental as these novels are, they indicate to what degree the English dancer's rise in status had permeated the consciousness of the popular reading public.

In England and to a lesser degree on the Continent, waves of new professionals had totally restructured the labor market. For the novice, riding the crest of rising demand, the era held promise of opportunity. For the old-timer, however, the bright young things who crowded casting offices and studios meant competition, and it is against the struggle for jobs and a shot at the public limelight that the social drama of Diaghilev's postwar dancers must be set.

Ironically, at the very time that the status of dancers, generally, was so markedly improving, members of the Ballets Russes found their conditions of work rapidly deteriorating. Before 1914 Diaghilev's dancers had been the "aristocrats" of the profession. In a market that placed a premium on their talent, they had enjoyed the luxury of choosing among a range of lucrative opportunities, and to win their services Diaghilev had had to pay them well. Beginning in 1915, the enviable position of the Diaghilev dancer began to decline. By 1918 the downward trend had accelerated. Now, in a pattern that became the postwar norm, salaries plummeted and conditions deteriorated. The era of plenitude was over.

In Switzerland, we have already noted, all the dancers had received equal pay. This egalitarian strategy, which enabled Diaghilev to rebuild the company, ended with the ballet's reappearance on the American marketplace. The return to a conventional wage structure, however, did not mean a return to previous levels of pay. In 1916–1917 salaries for the corps de ballet fell substantially, with the dancers in America being the first to feel the pinch.

Nor did salaries rise once the company found a safe berth in London. A contract dated October 20, 1918, engaged one Mlle. Yvonne André at Frs. 750 a month, with the company's two-month rehearsal period and four-week annual holiday being calculated at half-pay. A year later Vera Clark, subsequently rebaptized by Diaghilev as Vera Savina, joined the troupe at a monthly salary of Frs. 800 in France and £4 a week in London, far less than the guinea a day paid a musical accompanist. These entry-level salaries, which over the course of a year ranged from Frs. 7,800 to Frs. 8,400, suggest to what extent wages had declined from the early years of Diaghilev's independent enterprise when a novice could expect an annual salary of Frs. 8,000–10,000. Even veterans like Anatole Bourman, Nijinsky's classmate at the Imperial Ballet School who rejoined the company in London, suffered in the postwar climate of dancer "givebacks." Under the terms of the twelve-month contract signed in August 1921, he received the remarkably low base monthly salary of Frs. 1,275 and even less than the usual half-pay arrangement for rehearsal time and vacations.[48]

Absolute comparisons, however, do not give a true picture of the decline in real income. Camouflaged beneath the statistics is the era's spiraling inflation, when price levels in France more than quadrupled between 1913 and 1919, and the franc dropped in relation to the pound from 25 in 1914 to 61 in 1921. (With the rapid and unpredictable fluctuations in exchange rates, Diaghilev's post-Armistice contracts frequently spelled out wages in the currencies of the countries where the troupe was scheduled to perform.) In early 1924 the Paris daily *Le Gaulois* compared the cost of foodstuffs with prices in 1914 and pronounced the result "frightening." In 1914, five francs had bought seven kilos of sugar; in 1924, only one. Butter had jumped from three to twenty francs, sausage from one franc to seven francs.[49] England did not lag far behind, even if the pound remained strong on the foreign exchange markets. In 1916 alone prices rose by an average of eighty percent.

Other signs of declining economic position accompanied this fall in real income. An earlier chapter alluded to the increase in productivity that enabled Diaghilev to make up in part for the decrease in post-Armistice revenues. For the dancers, the tougher schedule represented more than a reduction in "piece rates." Built into the grueling round of classes, rehearsals, performances, and touring was a life of overwork, which the management did nothing to lessen. Notwithstanding the "stamina" of the Russians "for the hardship of the life," as Ninette de Valois, who joined the Ballets Russes in 1923, put it,[50] the physical instrument suffered, with the constant strain heightening the danger of injury to the dancer's most precious yet ephemeral asset. Lydia Lopokova, one of the most outspoken of Diaghilev's ballerinas and an old company trouper, spoke of this in an interview with a London journalist in 1933. "In Russia dancers used to have to dance once a week, and sometimes now (as Russia is a 'sweated country') they have to dance twice a week! But in the Diaghilev days he sometimes made us dance six times a week—and hence our knees trouble us when we are middle-aged . . . !" (At the time, Lopokova was laid up at home with a sprained knee.)[51]

With no company provisions for medical attention, illness and injury reduced dancers literally to charity. Lord Rothermere, the London newspaper magnate, paid for an operation Lydia Sokolova had in 1926, and a variety of wealthy friends came to her aid in 1928 when ill health plagued her again.[52] (As one of the oldest and ablest company stalwarts, she received some help from Diaghilev, but this was a matter of personal kindness, not company policy.) Other factors contributed to the growing precariousness of the dancer's life. Salaries were often delayed, and not always paid in full. Sometimes, they were not paid at all, as at the close of *The Sleeping Princess* engagement when, according to his associate Walter Nouvel, Diaghilev's total resources amounted to "£1,000, borrowed from an eccentric millionaire, who was clamouring for repayment." With the impresario off in Paris, "some of the artists who had not been given their full pay threatened to ruin the last performance by a general strike," Nouvel recalled. A strike was averted, but the willingness of the dancers to contemplate so extreme an action indicates how close to the edge payless paydays had brought them. (Leon Woizikovsky and his unofficial wife, Lydia Sokolova, who had a child by a previous marriage to support, actually sued Diaghilev for back pay. They won their case, as did Messrs. Thadée Slavinsky and Jalmuzynski.)[53]

Threats of industrial action had become a theatrical reality by the time the curtain fell on the last performance of *The Sleeping Princess*. The year 1920 had witnessed strikes in several Paris theaters, and on two separate occasions, dancers along with musicians and backstage personnel had walked off the job at the Opéra, demanding higher salaries, better working conditions, and a greater voice in management decision-making. In early 1922 unrest spread to London, and in the face of massive unemployment the Actors Association successfully negotiated the so-called "Valentine Contract," guaranteeing a minimum of three pounds per week to every artist. A few months later, the Association debated instituting a "closed shop" to protect its membership from "unfair competition." "The stage suffers," said one of its spokesmen, "more than any other profession, from the influx of incompetents and *dilettanti*. The livelihood of thousands and the standard of dramatic art are thus very seriously threatened." Another proposal to deal with the crisis called for a German-style system of entrance examinations.[54]

Diaghilev's dancers were hardly in a position to organize. Even as they threatened to strike, the company itself fell apart, with dancers seeking whatever employment they could find. Needless to say, provisions for job security did not exist, nor did the itinerant artists qualify for unemployment benefits or the dole. What suggests an analogy with London's thespians, beyond the general economic climate, is the background of competition against which the drama of impoverishment was enacted. Whereas in 1910 or 1911 Russian dancers could write their own tickets, now seasoned hands like Sokolova found themselves knocking on doors for a job. Emigration from Russia, which stepped up in the period of Lenin's New Economic Policy, offered another source of competition, particularly as many of the newcomers were veterans of Diaghilev's prewar seasons. Later in the decade, émigré children, often from families that prior to the Revolution would never have countenanced a stage career for their offspring, joined the scramble for jobs.

Top company stars could and did hold their own against the onslaught of competition. Lydia Lopokova, who earned £100 a week with Diaghilev in 1921, commanded similar fees on the music-hall stage. Karsavina, too, weathered the 1920s in style, thanks to guest appearances with the Ballets Russes, independent touring, and music-hall engagements. "For Tamara, money was then easy to come by," mused her husband H.J. Bruce after the Second World War:

> and never for a moment did it enter either of our heads that, in the comparatively ephemeral career of a dancer, salary should be treated not as income but as capital. So we proceeded first to hire an enormous car and then to take a large furnished house at a rent which I know now to have been for those days fabulous, but which appeared to be a drop in the flood-tide of Tamara's earnings.[55]

For most dancers, life was not so prodigal. Lopokova, who reduced her fee by more than one-half in 1924 for the chance to appear with the Soirées de Paris, alluded to the hand-to-mouth existence of the majority in letters to her future husband, the economist John Maynard Keynes. "[Nicolas] Legat . . . accepts 10 pounds from me . . . with a pride of the Old Regime," she wrote in 1924. "For tea I had [Mikhail] Mordkin, his wife, his child, her dancing partner and his classical dancing partner. *Oh,* Life is difficult . . . I understand they go to America without positive engagement. Of course they have good material . . . and Mordkin is a name . . . but all is tinged with melancholy." Everywhere Lopokova saw the same "awful lack of work and hunger"—and competition.[56] Recording her impressions of a young Russian dancer, she wrote:

> The Russian girl danced full of temperament, nice body and head, but did not know how to dance. Fourteen [years old], accompanied by a 'mother'. I spoke with her, she [had] danced in Paris at Clemenceau and Rothschilds! She was asked to dance [at] Ciro's club, but was it not degrading. I said the competition is so great that it did not matter whether she danced at [the] Alhambra or Ciro's or [the] Coliseum or any other dancing place, to study was the most important thing of all![57]

Economic hardship, coupled with the lack of job security and the stateless condition of so many of Diaghilev's postwar artists, created inordinate dependence on an organism that became for the Russians and other displaced talents an instant, surrogate family, a haven in the cruel world of emigration. "To understand fully the Russian ballet theatre life," Ninette de Valois has written:

> one has to remember that the artists had lived cloistered lives in the Russian State Schools; now they were further bound together by the *emigre* spirit, cut off as they were from the land of their birth, and served with passports issued from Geneva . . . They seemed to carry their lives on their backs, a mental and emotional knapsack, stuffed with memories of the past, anxiety about the present, and hopes for the future.[58]

Over this "family" hovered the beneficent yet distant figure of Diaghilev, a sovereign who ruled through the janissaries of his court, an "uncle" to whom one could appeal in times of trouble. "Please arrange my departure from Vienna immediately," wired Bronislava Nijinska on her arrival in the West with a hungry family to feed. "I want to work with you." On numerous occasions, Diaghilev went out of his way to help and encourage individuals in his troupe, as Sokolova's memoirs movingly attest. Kindness, however, was of a piece with Diaghilev's postwar image as an imperious *barin* ruling all and sundry with the paternalism of another era. If in 1909–1910 and again in 1915 the troupe revealed the stamp of a collective enterprise, by the early twenties it suggested a throwback to tsarist social styles. This atavism shocked Serge Lifar, a youngster "from Soviet lands," on his arrival in the "free city . . . of the *Ballets Russes*." "Customs borrowed from the days of serfdom still prevailed," he recalled. "The leading dancers made the boys of the *corps de ballet* run their errands for them!"[59] Diaghilev's paternalism toward his dancers, an attitude that viewed them as children and chattels, may be appreciated from a letter written to Charles B. Cochran in 1926 following Vera Nemchinova's "defection" to the revue stage:

> You knew, of course, that Mme. Nemchinova was my pupil and that it was with me that she learned to dance in the past ten years . . . Allow me to add in a friendly spirit that I very much regret . . . the way you exploit the Russian artists whom I have discovered and trained. Dukelsky writing bad foxtrots for musicals is not doing what he is destined to do; Massine dancing in supper clubs and composing choreographies in the style of "Pompei à la Massine" dangerously compromises himself; likewise, Nemchinova is not made for revues . . . I take the liberty of telling you this in view of our longstanding friendship. One must create works and artists and not exploit those created by others for purposes very different from yours and in an atmosphere having nothing in common with what you do, and what you often do very well.[60]

Diaghilev's avuncular posture, sustained by the internal configuration of his troupe and the skewed nature of the dance market, masked a larger economic agenda. Beginning in the war years, Diaghilev's stock-in-trade came increasingly to rest on the shoulders of his dancers. From their payless or partial paydays, their tireless efforts, and precarious lives came the means that enabled his company to survive. Before 1914 Diaghilev had been lucky to command the loyalty of his dancers. Now, in the postwar world where supply vastly outstripped demand, his dancers poured the surplus value of their labor into his enterprise.

Thus, from 1918 to 1922 the logic of the marketplace completed the process, set in motion in 1909, of transforming the Ballets Russes into a modern business enterprise. Now, to an ever greater degree, fluctuations in the business cycle, competition, and the forces of supply and demand held the company as surety in the scramble for profits. The transformation of the dancer from "free artist" to wage worker betrays yet another sign of this "modernization," as the dance boom, through its reserve army of competitors, toppled Diaghilev's dancers from their erstwhile position of privilege. From 1918 to 1922 Diaghilev revealed ballet modernism to Europe's war-weary audiences. But he also revealed the limits of the commercial marketplace as a haven for artistic enterprise. The crisis precipitated by the failure of *The Sleeping Princess* drove home a lesson Diaghilev never forgot. Henceforth, government largess would underwrite at least some portion of his Ballets Russes.

9

PROTEAN IDENTITIES

IN THE HISTORY of the Ballets Russes, no era displays such striking inconsistencies or apparent artistic aimlessness as the years 1922–1929. A frenzy of creation seemed to grip the company, as work after work revealed briefly the many facets of twenties' modernism. For a number of contemporaries this succession of "isms" was a sign, not of artistic health, but decadence. But another explanation for the era's protean character is possible, one that reflects the distinctive features of the company's newest backers. Between 1922 and 1929 an unlikely troika presided over Diaghilev's fortunes, a triple cast of paymasters who exacted from the Ballets Russes works tailored to diverse tastes and often rival purposes. From the prevailing instability of these years emerged one certainty. No creative enterprise of the magnitude of the Ballets Russes could sustain itself indefinitely and with complete artistic independence, free of public subsidy.

Diaghilev's arrangement with the Théâtre de Monte-Carlo in the autumn of 1922 was nothing short of providential. Engineered by the Princesse Edmond de Polignac, a relation through marriage of the principality's ruling family, and by the Société des Bains de Mer, which ran the famous Casino, it launched the Ballets Russes on the last and longest phase of its history. For the first time since the inception of Diaghilev's independent enterprise, the company enjoyed the luxury of working at least part of the year in a subsidized environment.

The Ballets Russes was no stranger to the diminutive principality. Its court theater, a replica in miniature of the Palais Garnier built in the 1890s, had welcomed the company as early as 1911. Here, the company danced the *Giselle* that marked its debut as a permanent organization, or, as Diaghilev later inscribed a program for that performance, the first appearance "of my troupe."[1] With the regularity of homing pigeons, the dancers returned to the Mediterranean resort each winter, and in the months preceding the Paris and London seasons, as the company rehearsed new works and refurbished old ones, the theater's exclusive clientele witnessed such gala rarities as the first two-act version of *Swan Lake* ever produced in France, with Mathilde Kchessinska and Nijinsky in the principal roles.[2] World War I and Diaghilev's sojourn in London's music-halls interrupted this arrangement: Monte Carlo became a brief stop in the round of more important seasons. In 1922, however, as the company reeled from its latest brush with disaster, the theater that lay just steps from the adjoining Casino became the hub of Diaghilev's operations. For the next seven years, the jewel of the Azure Coast served as his ballet's winter capital and workshop. Well might Serge Grigoriev, the company's regisseur throughout the whole of its peripatetic existence, heave a sigh of relief. "And so the Ballet at last acquired a permanent base."[3]

Just how much of the Casino's profits reached Diaghilev's pockets in the honeymoon years of his sojourn will probably never be known. Little correspondence survives, even in the archives of the Société des Bains de Mer, which houses a superb, nearly complete run of programs for Diaghilev's seasons at the theater and other Monte Carlo venues. But judging from his record of accomplishment and the evidence of later contracts, one may safely say that at no time since the Beecham era had he enjoyed means on so vast a scale.

Although many terms were subsequently rescinded, Diaghilev's agreements in April 1924 with S.B.M. managing director René Léon reveal the magnitude and many facets of the Casino's subsidy. Over 1.4 million francs were allocated: Frs. 885,000 by way of a general grant; Frs. 30,000 for transportation and travel expenses; Frs. 300,000 to stage Glinka's *Ruslan and Ludmilla,* a new Stravinsky ballet, and *Les Noces, Les Biches,* and *Pulcinella* with their full complement of singers; Frs. 200,000 to provide choreography and dancers for the theater's opera productions.[4] Glinka's opera never reached the stage, nor did the new Stravinsky ballet materialize, and one assumes the subsidy was reduced accordingly. But even at a million francs, the tally was substantial.

At the Café de Paris, where Diaghilev held court, a rival potentate eyed the newcomer with misgiving. Monte Carlo had never wanted for colorful characters, but in Raoul Gunsbourg, the half-French, half-Rumanian Moscow theater producer who had ruled the local opera house for thirty years, it boasted an original whose flair, ambition, and showmanship matched Diaghilev's.

1924 was not a good year for this Monte Carlo veteran. At Lanvin's, a letter penned in a moment of indiscretion slipped from Comtesse Greffuhle's handbag. Quick fingers retrieved it, opened it, then sent it anonymously to Monaco's reigning monarch, Prince Pierre. Whatever its contents, the Prince was so incensed that in January 1925 he rescinded Gunsbourg's contract.[5] For the first time since 1905, Diaghilev's long-thwarted ambition for an opera house of his own seemed close to fulfillment.

Despite the cancellation of *Ruslan* and the new Stravinsky work, Diaghilev moved to consolidate his position. That winter, he wedged into the interval between his January and April seasons an ambitious series of chamber performances at the Casino's Nouvelle Salle de Musique. Most writers have passed lightly over this episode. But these dozen or so concerts comprised full-dress evenings of repertory, even if scenery was not used. No fewer than nine ballets were given—*Les Sylphides, Pulcinella, Cimarosiana, Carnaval, L'Après-midi d'un Faune, Le Spectre de la Rose, The Good-Humoured Ladies, Las Meninas,* and *Papillons*—and four divertissement-style works—*Le Festin, Les Contes des Fées* (the fairy tales from *Aurora's Wedding*), *L'Assemblée,* and *Le Bal du "Lac des Cygnes."* Like Pavlova's programs, each "Concert-Performance" included two or three ballets and a concluding divertissement.[6]

Throughout the winter Gunsbourg prowled the theater, awaiting the infraction that would prove his rival's undoing. (After filing suit against Prince Pierre for five million francs, Gunsbourg suddenly looked more attractive in his post than out.) The unenviable task of keeping peace fell to René Léon, who, as Diaghilev's self-appointed middleman, passed on changes in rehearsal dates and performance schedules, and the demand that Nijinska, as ballet mistress, personally call on Gunsbourg to discuss the opera repertory. (Diaghilev wanted her to do this by correspondence!) Léon also saw to arrangements for the "extra-contractual" chamber series, including details about musicians and stagehands. Again and again, he cautioned Diaghilev: "If the difficulties begin again, it will be very awkward in the future."[7] When the rival powers clashed in what became known as the "affaire Ravel," not even Léon could protect his protégé.

Diaghilev's relationship with France's greatest living composer of the 1920s is another of those recurring puzzles of the impresario's history. That he respected Ravel is beyond dispute; indeed, long after the premiere of *Daphnis and Chloë,* Diaghilev sought his collaboration on other projects. Yet beginning in 1920, when he rejected the score for *La Valse*—"it's a masterpiece," he told the composer, "not a ballet"[8]—one also detects that streak of cruelty that tinged so many of Diaghilev's relationships with "disloyal" or discarded artists. For *La Valse* was very much a ballet, as Nijinska, in a version choreographed in 1929 for Ida Rubinstein's company, and Balanchine, in his 1951 work for the New York City Ballet, made clear. But Diaghilev may well have viewed the piece as a "remake" of the "valses nobles et sentimentales," which, as *Adélaïde ou le Langage des Fleurs,* had long since entered the dance repertory: first, at the Châtelet, where, in choreography by Ivan Clustine, they premiered only weeks before *Daphnis*'s appearance on the same stage; and subsequently at the Paris Opéra, where Jacques Rouché mounted *Adélaïde* in 1917.[9] (Four years later, *Daphnis,* restaged by Fokine, entered the Opéra repertory as well.)

In March 1925 came another "betrayal." Gunsbourg staged the premiere of Ravel's *L'Enfant et les Sortilèges,* a "lyric fantasy" with a libretto by Colette. (The choreography, by Balanchine, was his first major assignment for the Ballets Russes.) Eight days before the opening, Diaghilev bared his claws. Wrote Léon:

> I have just received a complaint from the Director of the Opéra. Your *régisseur,* Mr. Grigorieff, has removed, on your order, the music for Mr. Ravel's opera . . . Mr. Grigorieff states that your artists will not dance in this opera. Whatever your reasons for this decision, I must, in a friendly spirit, warn you of the seriousness of your refusal.[10]

Vindictiveness, alone, does not explain Diaghilev's behavior. Nor does the hubris that often marred his relations with authority. In a fit of what can only be termed hysteria, Diaghilev lost his head. "I was surprised this morning by a visit from your attorney," Léon wrote a day later:

> He came to ask me to look for Mr. Ravel in order to induce him to collaborate with you on the dance parts of [his] opera *L'Enfant* . . .
>
> Then, I had another surprise. As I left the restaurant of the Hôtel de Paris, a steward (!) handed me a letter in which you advise that you decline all responsibility for the perfect execution of the dance parts that your contract obliges you to provide for the operas in general, and Mr. Ravel's opera, in particular . . .
>
> As to your statement that the ballet piano parts . . . were sent to you too late and that Mr. Ravel's music seems very complicated, it is truly curious that these difficulties only became apparent some hours after an incident you seem to have had with Mr. Ravel in the lobby of the Hôtel de Paris, and after which you were heard by several witnesses to declare, "I will never let them dance in his opera."[11]

Léon closed with a threat that temporarily brought Diaghilev to his senses. "You understand that if I receive a formal complaint from the Director of the Opéra . . . I will find it absolutely impossible to ask the Board of Directors to renew your contract." On March 21 the premiere took place, to all appearances without mishap. But the *affaire* had not ended. At a later performance five of the ten dancers in the first-act pastorale failed to appear, and when Gunsbourg, incensed, demanded an explanation, Nicolas Kremnev, the regisseur, told him to talk to Diaghilev. "This organization," Gunsbourg declared to Léon, "is a veritable hindrance to my immense labors." Léon now wrote to Diaghilev saying that he could not, in good conscience, support his candidacy for the following year.[12] One can only imagine what Balanchine, the choreographer, thought of this power play.

Diaghilev was not dismissed, but the unsavory episode brought to a close the honeymoon so auspiciously begun. The contract negotiated on April 30 reveals all too clearly the magnitude of the débâcle and its economic consequences. The Ballets Russes was engaged for a mere four performances in January 1926 and a season of twenty performances in spring. No provisions were made for the Société des Bains de Mer to underwrite new productions, and there was even a nasty aside to the effect that storage space was limited to "materiel employed for and during the season."[13] Diaghilev's fees were reduced accordingly. The basic subsidy amounted to Frs. 420,000 or less than half that of the previous year. His travel and transportation allowances were reduced. As before, the Opéra rented the troupe during the winter months for a sum of Frs. 200,000.[14] The years 1926–1927 and 1927–1928 followed much the same pattern.

The spring of 1925, then, found Diaghilev at yet another financial crossroads. Again he faced the dilemma that had so often challenged his ingenuity in the past. Where was to be found the money to stage new productions, commission new artists, fund new experiment?

Box office receipts could hardly solve the problem. Engagements were often brief—two weeks at most in Turin and Barcelona, fewer than a handful of performances at La Scala[15]—and the takings disappointingly meager, as during the 1925 Christmas season in Berlin when "hardly a soul," as Grigoriev wrote, "came to see us" after opening night.[16] Nor was Paris enamored of Diaghilev in mid-decade. Seasons had grown progressively shorter, and engagements there "under almost any circumstance [meant] certain loss."[17] At the Paris Opéra, where Diaghilev returned in 1927 and 1928, a complicated formula benefiting the house replaced the flat-fee system: Diaghilev retained a percentage of the receipts only after deduction of taxes and payment of a sizable sum to the theater. For the performance given on December 27, 1927, gross receipts amounted to Frs. 90,445, of which Diaghilev retained just under Frs. 41,000. In December of the following year the fixed deduction doubled to Frs. 50,000 for each of three performances.[18] Even London, where the company returned in November 1924 for its first season since *The Sleeping Princess* debacle, could not generate the requisite cash. Although the Ballets Russes remained popular, its earnings, only £1,200 a week in 1925 for two performances a day on a variety bill, were further reduced by payments to the Stoll organization until the company's debt was liquidated.[19] Repaying Stoll, however, made little dent in Diaghilev's overall indebtedness. His habit of borrowing from Peter to pay Paul returned to haunt him, and his correspondence with solicitors in 1925–1926 tells a sorry tale of unpaid debts and lawsuits: Diaghilev vs. Bewicke, and numerous others—Gulbenkian, Polignac, even Nijinsky, on whose behalf his wife Romola resurrected documents from the 1918 South American tour to sue the impresario.[20] And as always, Diaghilev put off royalty payments to composers and music publishers until the latter threatened to bring legal action.

In 1918 London had "saved" Diaghilev. Eight years later England came once more to Diaghilev's rescue, in the person of a tycoon of big business. With Lord Rothermere an unsavory whiff of new money and sexual politics entered the studios of the Ballets Russes.

"One day," recounted Grigoriev, "Diaghilev came to a rehearsal accompanied by a tall, burly man with quite a pleasant English-looking face":

> It was the custom on such occasions for the rehearsal to stop . . . Diaghilev would bow to the company and then shake hands with the *regisseur*, the choreographer, and the leading dancers . . . This ritual was performed . . . except that Diaghilev also introduced us to the visitor, saying that Lord Rothermere was an ardent admirer of our Ballet and was always, when possible, present at our performances; he had been following our progress for years and would be much interested in seeing a ballet in the process of creation. Diaghilev and Lord Rothermere then sat down, and the latter, we observed, watched the rehearsal with the closest attention.[21]

Lord Rothermere's visit to the Monte Carlo studio took place early in 1926. By March he had become the company's "angel."

Unlike the financial elite that formed Diaghilev's early circle of supporters, Harold Sidney Harmsworth, Viscount Rothermere, was a relative newcomer to the genteel world of art. Chief proprietor of the *Daily Mail* and a string of other London newspapers, he commanded vast wealth and influence through an empire consolidated as recently as the war years. The Ballets Russes was not his first act of theatrical patronage. Earlier in the decade he had given his support to *The Beggars' Opera* and, for a brief spell, to Pavlova's troupe. Lady Rothermere, whom Diaghilev also wooed, favored enterprises of a more highbrow sort. From 1923 to 1925 her largess financed T.S. Eliot's *Criterion*.[22]

Despite his millions, Lord Rothermere was a businessman, and his backing, predictably, took the form of guarantees rather than outright grants. In March 1926 Diaghilev received the magnate's first pledge: a "two thou-

sand pounds guarantee" to underwrite an independent London season the
following summer. (Diaghilev's gratitude may be surmised from his thank-
you note, written in English rather than his usual French.) This arrangement, with Rothermere putting up all or part of the guarantee—one thousand pounds in 1927 and 1928—remained in effect for the rest of the
decade. Rescuing the company from the music-hall's single-slot appearances and twelve weekly performances, guarantees enabled Diaghilev to
bypass theatrical middlemen, dictate ticket policy, and retain the lion's
share of receipts at a large West End theater. As Diaghilev's London agent
Eric Wollheim told the press after the impresario's death, the company
"could never do without guarantees."[23]

By the late 1920s Diaghilev was a past master of the fine art of manipulation. In Lord Rothermere, however, he met not merely his match,
but a hand more practised than his own. Dangling the promise of money,
the newspaper magnate demanded his pound of flesh; abjuring interest, he
played a game of power and sexual politics that deepened the era's prevailing uncertainty.

Rothermere's liaison with Alice Nikitina, the company dancer who
became his "adopted daughter"—her phrase—or mistress, is an unsavory
episode that has been told elsewhere. That she was a dancer of talent
is beyond dispute; that she deserved the place in the Ballets Russes he
felt his money could buy is not. In the winter of 1928 her ambitions provoked a crisis that nearly destroyed the jerry-built edifice of Diaghilev's
finance:

> Eric [Wollheim] traveled with patron and Alice. Patron did not want arrival
> on Riviera known . . . Forbids her from taking any but leading roles . . .
> Will do absolutely nothing without her. She complains of sharing "Chatte"
> and receiving only one of three [new] roles, *Apollo* not interesting enough.
> Eric knows for a fact that a word from Alice would arrange London season
> and all financial terms.[24]

Patrons like Rothermere did not materialize upon request, even in Diaghilev's privileged world. The Maecenas belonged to a vanishing breed; World
War I had made him even rarer. Thus, when Rothermere suddenly withdrew his support, Diaghilev faced another period of acute uncertainty. In
an effort to raise cash, he chopped up Picasso's curtain for *Le Tricorne*
and sold it together with portions of the *Cuadro Flamenco* backdrop through
the artist's dealer Paul Rosenberg.[25] It was at this time as well that arrangements for an American tour in the late autumn of 1928 came close
to materializing—a sure measure of Diaghilev's desperation, given the odium
in which he held both sea travel and the United States. Like the American

tours contemplated in 1925–1926, another period of financial anxiety, this one never took place.[26]

A colorful Broadway figure who had his hand in many theatrical pies, E. Ray Goetz first broached the idea of an American engagement while summering on the Lido in 1927. Within months a preliminary agreement was reached, although, given Diaghilev's track record, this by no means guaranteed that a tour was in the offing. With the withdrawal of Rothermere's backing and ensuing financial crisis, however, the tenor of the bargaining changed. Demonstrating an unwonted willingness to compromise on issues of personnel, venues, and film rights, Diaghilev now pressed for a rapid end to negotiations. The last week of May found the parties close to agreement, with Goetz even wiring Diaghilev about mounting the "orchestral ballet" by the producer's former collaborator George Gershwin that became "An American in Paris." A few weeks later, discussions began with Oliver Sayler about publicity, including an exhibition of "[Serge] Lifar's collections of paintings by designers for the ballet."[27]

Between the opening of the season at His Majesty's Theatre on June 25 and the July 28 deadline specified in the letter contract,[28] the project fell through. Writing to Otto Kahn, one of Goetz's U.S. backers, the producer described a sequence of events that must have had a familiar ring to the sponsor of Diaghilev's Metropolitan tours:

> I want you to know that my reason for abandoning the plan was simply due to the fact that Diaghileff became . . . quite unreasonable during the final negotiations I carried on with him in London over a period of about ten days. Contrary to a preliminary agreement . . . he did not guarantee the artists whom I demanded to be included in his troupe and in addition, did not consent to my selection of the repertoire of ballets to be given nor would he allow me to select the numbers to be given for the opening performance.[29]

The decision to break off negotiations, however, involved more than principles. Only days before the contract deadline, Lord Rothermere again opened his checkbook to the impresario. Between April and July, moreover, patronage of a stamp dear to the old school *barin* had materialized. In Paris Diaghilev had struck a mother lode, true-blue English partisans of the ballet who had pieced together the necessary guarantee. With this discovery, Lady Juliet Duff, the daughter of Diaghilev's prewar patron Lady Ripon, entered the offstage chronicle of the Ballets Russes. Now, to this "chère et bonne amie," whose "hereditary energy," as Diaghilev wrote, "was destined once again . . . to save" his enterprise, fell the thankless task of fundraising.[30]

In 1928 and again in 1929 Lady Juliet went cap in hand to London's ladies of culture. One can only pity her good heart, prodded, on the one hand, by Diaghilev, put off by his devotees on the other. In 1929 reticules were slow to open, and when they did, small change was what trickled out: three hundred pounds from the Courtaulds, textile millionaires and bountiful underwriters of the new Courtauld-Sargent Concerts; a couple of hundred guineas from Lady Cunard, subscriber of five thousand pounds a year to the Imperial League of Opera. Was it ballet, in general, or Diaghilev, in particular, the old mercantile elite was snubbing? Or was it simply that the character of patronage had changed and that the old elite, like the new, now demanded a return in public recognition? Lady Juliet failed to muster the £2,000 Diaghilev needed for his last Covent Garden season. Again, Lord Rothermere's support was essential, even if his five hundred pounds and free advertising were contingent upon Nikitina's rejoining the troupe, "receiving a salary equal to that of the Premiere Ballerina and being given every possible opportunity in the principal parts."[31]

From 1923 to 1929 Diaghilev relaid the economic foundation of the Ballets Russes on the twin supports of the Société des Bains de Mer and the company's British guarantors. The new financial arrangements, as fortuitous as they were providential, shifted the center of company gravity. Discarding the "populist" guise of its music-hall days, the Ballets Russes assumed the ideological coloring of its newest patrons. Artmaking and its financing has been the theme of these pages; time and again, this relationship, complex and fluid, shaped the parameters of company activity and altered the content, fashioning, and reception of its work. Up to World War I the demands of art, audience, and finance had coexisted in relative harmony. Modernism, however, profoundly altered this equation. Its aesthetic challenged the conventional artistic taste of both elite and popular audiences, even as its financing and diffusion depended on the resources of the operatic and music-hall stage. Yet despite these fundamental incongruities, modernism flourished because of Diaghilev's remarkable ability to "package" it in works and programs accessible to a broad theatrical public. Between 1918 and 1921 Diaghilev's conflicting loyalties remained, nonetheless, clear. The man of art pledged fealty to the avant-garde while the man of business allied his enterprise with *le tout Paris* and London's popular stage.

Beginning in 1923, however, clarity vanished from the pattern. No single tendency rallied the company to its banner, no single current provided the lodestone around which its identity might coalesce. On the contrary, in this last and most problematic era of its history, the Ballets Russes seemed to founder in a pursuit of artistic novelty as frantic as Diaghilev's search for artistic capital.

In previous periods aesthetic coherence was linked to consistency in the social and economic structure of production. Between 1923 and 1929, however, the stabilizing presences that had guided Diaghilev in negotiating first the musical world and subsequently the popular stage gave way to a plurality of interests. Now, instead of a network of like-minded enterprises, a troika of forces vied for ascendancy in directing his company's passage through the remaining years of the 1920s. From the juxtaposition of Monte Carlo's aristocratic traditions, the artistic conservatism of London's powerbrokers, and the market ethos of the Paris art world emerged the aesthetic contradictions of the Ballets Russes in this, its most protean era.

Diaghilev's agreements with the Société des Bains de Mer offered the Ballets Russes a modicum of security that lasted throughout the twenties. But during the honeymoon of his sojourn in Monte Carlo, they promised something more than a fresh financial start. On the coast where yachts idled under villas that climbed upward from the azure sea, mimosa brought back the fragrance of the Belle Epoque, and hotels with names like the Hermitage resurrected dreams of Imperial grandeur. In the diminutive domain grown rich from roulette, Diaghilev made his last play for the portfolio of fine arts denied him in Russia.

His notes for 1922–1923, preserved at the Opéra library in Paris,[32] record the ambitious sweep of his vision: the plans for festivals and exhibitions, operas and ballets he saw as transforming the staid landscape of the resort into one of artistic ferment and discovery. At various moments of his life Diaghilev yielded to the passion for listmaking. But unlike the Black Notebook of 1910 or the "workbook" he kept in 1918–1919,[33] his Monte Carlo jottings make no reference to casting, cost, or repertory. Rather they trace the amblings of Diaghilev's mind down forgotten byways of the musical past.

During the years of wartime experiment, the present no less than the past had exercised its power over Diaghilev's imagination. Now, the past dominated his thought. But the past, like the present, has many faces: the one Diaghilev chose to reveal was that of the opera house's courtly origins. Donning the guise of the courtier, the self-described charlatan who had revealed Russian art to the West and modern art to the philistines now fashioned a paean to an aristocratic ideal embodied, albeit on an absurdly diminutive scale, by Monaco's ruling Grimaldis.

Diaghilev failed in his ambition of transforming Monte Carlo into an advanced art center. Yet, after so many years in the marketplace, the resurrection of the Ballets Russes within an arena gilded by the traditions of opera house and court had repercussions discernible throughout the rest of the decade. These echoes of the past, often in concert with the most blatant modernism, strike a major chord in the aesthetic dissonance of the period. They account for the prominence of eighteenth-century themes in new ballets such as *Les Tentations de la Bergère, Les Fâcheux,* and *Zéphire et Flore* and in the comic operas that formed the lynchpin of the 1923–1924 French music festival. Classical mythology, a favorite subject of court ballet of the *grand siècle,* reappeared in several works of these years: *Zéphire et Flore, Philémon et Baucis, La Chatte,* and *Apollon Musagète* among the company's new productions, *Daphnis and Chloë, Narcisse,* and *L'Après-midi d'un Faune* among its revivals. Other ballets paid homage to court traditions as well: *Las Meninas,* resurrected from the storage bins in 1924; *Swan Lake,* staged in a two-act version for the great Maryinsky classicist Vera Trefilova; *Aurora's Wedding,* the one-act reduction of *The Sleeping Princess* that became a company moneymaker; and *Ode,* a cantata celebrating Catherine the Great. At one point Diaghilev even considered reviving *Le Pavillon d'Armide.* (He did not actually do so, but a version of the work's Buffoon dance was included among the divertissements presented at the Nouvelle Salle de Musique under the title *Le Festin.*) And in the era's calendar of galas, the magnificent spectacle presented in the Hall of Mirrors at the Palace of Versailles—*Aurora's Wedding* "anachronized" by the addition of processionals and vocal interludes—recalled the *grandes fêtes* witnessed in that same gallery by *le roi soleil* himself.

Still another element heightened this aura of aristocracy: the wave of titled Russian refugees that poured into France after 1920 and gravitated to Diaghilev's Slavic beachhead. By blood and social ties, Diaghilev belonged to this émigré world. He shared its joy at welcoming friends and family to safety in the West and its anxiety about the fate of relations left behind.[34] Remarkably, in view of his close association with this milieu, Diaghilev never turned against the Soviet Union. His feelings about its regime, however, like his political sentiments, are masked in ambiguity. Diaghilev left no diaries, and few letters revealing his personal sentiments have come to light. It seems clear, however, that beginning in 1922 Diaghilev's interest in Soviet artistic life quickened. While on holiday that August in Venice, he dined with Isadora Duncan, fresh from a ten-month visit to the Soviet Union, and her husband, poet Sergei Esenin.[35] November found Diaghilev in Berlin, the largest Russian publishing and cultural center outside the Soviet Union, where he met another poet allied with the Soviet avant-garde. As he would do again two years later, Vladimir Mayakovsky urged Diaghilev to visit Russia.[36]

Other events fanned Diaghilev's interest in his homeland: the visit of Alexander Tairov's Kamerny Theater to the French capital in March 1923 and the growing number of exhibitions that gained Soviet artists a following among the Parisian avant-garde. These exchanges, in which painter

Michel Larionov played an important role, hinted at the extraordinary vitality of postrevolutionary art, something that could not fail to excite Diaghilev, and suggested the high esteem he continued to enjoy in Soviet artistic circles.[37]

In the interim between his meeting with Mayakovsky in 1922 and his encounter with the poet-playwright in 1924, Diaghilev's situation had altered. Disillusioned with Monte Carlo, he now heeded Mayakovsky's urgings to visit Russia. Thanks to Mayakovsky's intervention with Anatoly Lunacharsky, the Soviet Commissar of Education and Culture (an old friend who had reviewed Diaghilev's Paris seasons in 1912–1914 and whose last article on the company, published in June 1927, included an account of a conversation with the impresario), Diaghilev received a two-way exit visa to the Soviet Union. Because the authorities refused a similar visa to his secretary Boris Kochno, who was of military age, Diaghilev abandoned his plans.[38]

Within months, however, preparations were underway to produce an all-Soviet ballet. In June 1925, as the architectural modernism of the Russian Pavilion at the Exposition Internationale des Arts Décoratifs stirred excitement among the avant-garde, Diaghilev approached Prokofiev, his "second son" and a sympathizer with the Revolution, for a ballet depicting life in Soviet Russia. Georgi Yakulov, a Soviet scenic designer whose collaborations with Tairov had stirred controversy in 1923 and whose paintings were now on exhibit in Paris, was invited to write the libretto.[39]

Between the completion of the piano score in the autumn of 1925 and the premiere of *Le Pas d'Acier* in June 1927, Prokofiev paid a three-month visit to the U.S.S.R. He renewed contacts with musical colleagues, acquainted himself with the works of young Leningrad composers, and saw Meyerhold's "brilliant production" of his opera *Love for Three Oranges*.[40] In Monte Carlo that spring, Diaghilev pressed the composer for "news . . . of artistic and cultural developments in Russia, [which] *Le Pas d'Acier* brought him closer to understanding. Once again a terrible nostalgia for Russia overcame him, and he pined to go back." Prokofiev wrote to friends in Moscow and, like Mayakovsky in 1924, to Lunacharsky. He was assured that Diaghilev would be cordially received.[41]

Diaghilev made efforts to engage Tairov and Meyerhold to direct the production. He had hopes as well of bringing Kasian Goleizovsky from Moscow to choreograph, but these faded, depriving Europe of the chance to see the innovative choreographer so admired by the young Balanchine.[42] Eventually, Diaghilev entrusted the ambitious project to Massine, who rejoined the company in 1925 and up to 1928 shared choreographic assignments with the junior ballet master.

In late 1928 Diaghilev contemplated a last Soviet project, a joint Paris season with Meyerhold's renowned dramatic troupe. Like his earlier "flirtations" with Soviet art and artists, this one scandalized the company's inner circle of émigrés. Nouvel was "against it body and soul," Diaghilev wrote. "That can't be helped, however! People such as he and Pavka [Pavel Koribut-Kubitovich, a cousin of Diaghilev's] are very pleasant, but if one took their advice one might as well go straight to the cemetery."[43]

Le Pas d'Acier stands out as one of the few ballets of the middle and late twenties that fully commanded Diaghilev's interest. Yet where *Apollon Musagète* and *Prodigal Son,* ballets that likewise drew the tired impresario to the studio, garnered praise from their earliest performances, reactions to *Le Pas d'Acier* dramatized the conflicting interests that shaped the identity of the Ballets Russes in its final days as well as the political considerations that now intruded on all things "Soviet."

"England wants no more of Russians," wrote Diaghilev to Lady Juliet Duff about French reaction to the syndics' decision to close Covent Garden for repairs in 1928 rather than allow his company to perform there. "Some are even saying it is because 'Pas d'Acier' 'over' pleased the Duke of Connaught."[44] Whatever this grandson of Queen Victoria, who bore a striking resemblance to Nicholas II, may have thought about the ballet, English critical reaction was decidedly mixed. "Many will dislike it," warned the *Daily Express* while the *Observer* spoke of the dancers attired "as for a grim but impromptu charade." Most reviewers found the pistons, apaches, and hammering machine rhythms of the ballet disturbing. But there may well have been other reasons for their discomfiture. In 1927 England was very "anti-Bolshie," and with the previous year's general strike fresh in the minds of its ruling class, one is tempted to see politics in Lady Courtauld's categoric refusal to "join" Diaghilev in "any plan" for the coming year.[45]

In these years modernism tried the patience of even the most faithful company devotees. "I hear the King is going to the ballet next Friday," wrote Lady Cunard in 1926:

> I am *so* glad but I hope you will change the performance and [do] the Boutique, Sylphides and the Carnaval. Otherwise I fear His Majesty will not really *love* the ballet as we all feel he would if he *first* saw the classical ballets of some years ago . . .
>
> Thomas Beecham did *not* like Pastorale and thought it unworthy of your genius as a whole. There is much that is fine and interesting in it and *very new* too, but *as a whole* it lacks beauty and interest I feel. But I know your mind is different.[46]

Other influential Londoners shared her prejudices. In 1928 Diaghilev invited Lady Diana Cooper, one of the brightest of the era's "Young Things" to play the mime role of Nature in *Ode*.[47] But the socialite-turned-actress, the exquisite Madonna of Max Reinhardt's *Miracle,* rejected his proposal. "Dear, dear M. Diaghilew," she wrote:

> All my advisors say that the first time I appear in London must be in the Miracle, which they hope to do this autumn. It is quite true, as they tell me— that I might have been very bad in Ode—and that it is better to appear for the first time in London in something you can do, rather than in something experimental.[48]

Lady Diana's unwillingness to risk a professional debut in an "experimental" work suggests how little esteem modernism enjoyed even in quarters sympathetic to the company. Diaghilev's chief backer of the period, Lord Rothermere, was equally put off by "advanced" productions, and in March 1927 went so far as to express the hope that there would be no "eccentric" ones in the program for the coming season. *Dancing Times* editor P.J.S. Richardson voiced similar prejudices in his monthly ruminations as the "Sitter Out." "Now that we have seen 'Barabau,' 'Les Matelots,' 'The House Party,' and 'Les Facheux,' " he wrote in January 1926, "I think that we have had enough of this sort of thing, and that it is time that M. Diaghileff set out once more in search of the beautiful instead of the grotesque."[49]

Richardson's mid-decade screeds reveal a distinctly British taste in the making and the gradual refining of an aesthetic favoring genteel rather than experimental values. His musings, voiced in the middlebrow guise of the "layman," branded dance with the immutable stamp of neoromanticism:

> It is a little difficult for the ordinary mortal who has been brought up in the fond belief that dancing is the poetry of motion, to appreciate some of the modern Diaghileff choreography, which seems to go out of its way to search for the grotesque and to avoid the beautiful . . . As a mere layman I cannot conceive how it could be humanly possible to evolve anything approaching the "poetry of motion," to the cross rhythms of Stravinsky's "Les Noces," to name but one of the ultra-modern works now being presented to the public.[50]

Richardson went on to compare Diaghilev's *Romeo and Juliet* with a "charming number" by English dancers Anton Dolin and Phyllis Bedells presented at the Coliseum during the Ballets Russes season at His Majesty's. Set to Percy Grainger's "Shepherd's Hey," Dolin's ballet *Exercises,* he wrote, "was invested with a charm of beauty not in evidence in the 'barre' scene in . . . 'Romeo and Juliet.' " It marked a welcome return to "more healthy methods—to a choreography that is modern without being eccentric and ugly." Reiterating a favorite theme, Richardson praised the "sincerity" of the dancers, adding his belief that "it is impossible to be sincere in one's dancing if it is merely the interpretation of 'trick choreography'."[51]

"Sincerity," "charm," "beauty," and "expressiveness," peppered with a dash of native subject matter, were Richardson's ingredients for ballet in Britain. Distasteful as they might have been to the experimentalist in Diaghilev, they added up to a recipe that became a staple of his English programming. Much to Richardson's delight, Fokine's ballets assumed a prominent place in the mid-decade repertory. In 1926 alone Diaghilev presented *Carnaval, Les Sylphides, Thamar, Firebird* (in a new production by Natalia Gontcharova), *Petrouchka,* and *The Polovtsian Dances.* Tamara Karsavina and Lydia Lopokova, dancers identified with Fokine-era ballets and Massine's most popular post-Armistice works, returned from time to time to perform their earlier roles. The year 1926 also witnessed the staging of Diaghilev's first "British" works: *Romeo and Juliet,* which had music by Constant Lambert,[52] and *The Triumph of Neptune,* an all-British production with a libretto by Sacheverell Sitwell, music by Lord Berners, and a setting inspired by Victorian prints. Two years later *The Gods Go A-Begging* united Handel (regarded for all intents and purposes as a British composer) and the dean of British conductors, Sir Thomas Beecham, to score an unexpected success.

Diaghilev harkened to the "knell of romanticism," music critic Edwin Evans noted after the impresario's death, "before most people were ready to speed its parting."[53] In England "most people" embraced the circle closest to Diaghilev and those, like Richardson, who served the cause of ballet as propagandists.

Ballet was not the only art where England gazed willfully backward. Retreating from vorticist abstractions of speed and factory, British painters of the 1920s returned to traditional styles of representation—landscapes, portraits, and still lifes—to evoke a world of rustic peace and domestic tranquility. Literature, too, shied from images of modernity, with the "children of the sun," as Martin Green has called the generation that came of age in mid-decade, cultivating a latter-day pose of Wildean aestheticism. In ballet the reaction against modernism coincided with mounting efforts to contain the dance "free for all" of the early 1920s. With Richardson at the helm, the *Dancing Times* embarked on a campaign aimed at raising standards within the profession. Examinations formed the lynchpin of "standardisation," the beginnings of a system that remains a characteristic feature of British dance training. Under their impact, teaching and technique certainly improved, but with ballet now canonized as the theatrical and concert standard, they did so at the cost of vitality. Indeed, by 1929 Richardson felt obliged to answer complaints that English dancing had "drifted into a backwater" and that England "as a creative force in the world of dance" had become "a negligible quantity." "I am a firm believer," he wrote, "that if the ballet and the spectacular dance are to live and to be in harmony with the times they must be modernised, but I am also a firm believer that only chaos will result if modernisation is attempted at the expense of technique."[54]

If the "standardisation" campaign of the 1920s laid the technical foundation for English ballet, its aesthetic foundation rested on the harnessing of Fokine-style retrospectivism to British popular and middlebrow taste. Fokine's Columbines and sylphs, debutantes and dolls appealed far beyond the circle of socialites and propagandists like Richardson. They spoke directly to an audience reared on the old music-hall ballets and the genteel art of Adeline Genée, who reigned from 1897 to 1909 at the Empire. They defined a middle ground between highbrow "artiness" and kitsch. But this process of definition did not take place in a social vacuum. It is no coincidence that Lord Rothermere, that Hearst-style molder of popular opinion, urged on Diaghilev the low-priced season he gave in December 1926 at the Lyceum Theatre and a repertory calculated to appeal to "the great mob [that] associates the ballet with beauty and are correspondingly disappointed when they see something which is at variance with their impression of what the ballet should be."[55] Like Richardson, Rothermere aspired to seize hold of the "anarchy" of a culture in the critical moment of its transition to mass consumption. Together with Diaghilev's other supporters, they sought to exercise traditional prerogatives of class leadership over a potentially uncontainable movement at the grassroots. Along with the mantle of Diaghilev, British ballet has inherited the taste and claim to hegemony of the company's last British patrons.

Monégasque and English patronage edged the Ballets Russes down a conservative path. Diaghilev followed, but his heart lay elsewhere. In this last era, Paris and its burgeoning trade in modern art set the tone and tempo of company life.

Even in the music-hall days, Diaghilev looked on Paris as his artistic home. From its ateliers Picasso, Matisse, and Derain crossed the Channel to add final touches to their work before a London opening, and in the City of Lights lived friends like Stravinsky, Cocteau, and Misia Sert, whose artistic judgments Diaghilev solicited and esteemed. Although no farther in travel time from Paris than London, Monte Carlo transformed relations with the French capital. No longer on the periphery of its art world, the Ballets Russes became its southern outpost, only a night's ride from the Gare de Lyon on the legendary Blue Train.[56] Splendid, grand, and luxurious, it sped to Diaghilev's side the youthful talent that fueled the company in this last era of its creative life.

Between 1923 and 1926, the years of their closest collaboration with Diaghilev, composers of the group Les Six traveled the Blue Train often. Protégés of Rolf de Maré and the Ballets Suédois, they brought their art, if not their loyalty, to the Russians, and the studied inconsequence of an aesthetic derived from jazz palace and music-hall rather than the grand tradition of symphonic music. In 1924, the banner year of their attendance on Diaghilev, they contributed scores to no fewer than three ballets: *Les Biches* (Francis Poulenc), *Les Fâcheux* (Georges Auric), and *Le Train Bleu* (Darius Milhaud), which had a special fanfare by Auric for Picasso's front curtain.[57] In addition, Diaghilev invited all three composers along with Erik Satie, the self-described "mascot" of the group, to create music for the recitatives of the operas mounted earlier in the season.[58] The years 1925 and 1926 added two other Auric ballets to the repertory—*Les Matelots* and *La Pastorale*. The latter year also saw the production of Satie's *Jack-in-the-Box* as part of a festival honoring the recently deceased composer. In 1927, in an abrupt departure from his standard practice, Diaghilev revived Satie's *Mercure*, a work created not for the Ballets Russes but Comte Etienne de Beaumont's Soirées de Paris in 1924.

As early as 1917 Picasso had joined forces with Diaghilev, contributing in the space of four years designs for *Parade, Le Tricorne, Pulcinella*, and *Cuadro Flamenco*. During this same period, André Derain and Henri Matisse, senior painters of the School of Paris, designed for the Ballets Russes as well. After 1923 Picasso and Derain performed only the odd commission for Diaghilev. Apart from *Mercure*, undertaken at Beaumont's behest rather than Diaghilev's, the front curtain for *Le Train Bleu* represented Picasso's sole contribution to the later repertory even if the numerous sketches reproduced in company programs proclaimed his allegiance to its aesthetic. Although *La Boutique Fantasque* retained its place as an audience favorite, *Jack-in-the-Box* was the only work of the twenties that bore the signature of Derain. Whether the decision to collaborate at such sparse intervals rested with Diaghilev or these artists will probably never be known. No cajolery, however, could induce Matisse to work again for the impresario. "What Diaghilev wants is my name," he told Michel Georges-Michel in early 1929. "Diaghilev is very nice when he needs us."[59]

Need painters Diaghilev certainly did between 1923 and 1929, when he brought to life four new works a year and sometimes more. If history has consigned most of these productions to the ballet dustbin, Diaghilev's painters sounded the roll call of international modernism's rising luminaries—Juan Gris, Georges Braque, Pedro Pruna, Joán Miró, Giorgio de Chirico, Georges Rouault, Max Ernst, Henri Laurens, Naum Gabo, Anton Pevsner, and Marie Laurencin. Easel painters, in the main, with little or no experience in theatrical design, they brought, like Les Six and the newest generation of Diaghilev-bred ballet stars, the unmistakable whiff of youth, malleable and on the make.

In the wake of Montmartre and Montparnasse came, to borrow a phrase from Wyndham Lewis, "the 'revolutionary' High Bohemia of the Ritzes and Rivieras" and the writers and journalists who extended its pale to "the majority of educated people."[60] At the head of this band stood those arbiters of Parisian taste, Misia Sert and "Coco" Chanel, priestesses who tended the Parisian flame of the Ballets Russes. At their homes gathered company intimates, and it was Misia, "the Ballets Russes incarnate" (in the words of her biographers), who stood at Diaghilev's side in 1923, welcoming cabinet ministers and le tout Paris to the gala in the Hall of Mirrors. Artistically, the mid-twenties saw the height of her influence. In 1924 alone the season included revivals of two ballets designed by her husband José-María Sert, and the first works by three of her young protégés from Les Six. That year, too, Diaghilev commissioned Marie Laurencin, "one of Misia's great enthusiasms," to design Les Biches and asked her great friend Chanel to do the costumes for Le Train Bleu. The couturière also seems to have invested in this ballet and persuaded the Princesse de Polignac to do the same.[61] Throughout the period, moreover, the route to public launching of Diaghilev's youthful "discoveries" lay through the drawing rooms of Misia and Chanel.

Diaghilev's invitation brought other intimates to Monte Carlo—Picasso and his wife Olga,[62] and Jean Cocteau. Cocteau was a good deal more than a friend at this time. Reconciled with Diaghilev after their break over Parade, he hovered behind the scenes, giving a powerful impetus to the aesthetic direction that gained ascendancy during the initial period in Monte Carlo. Along with Misia Sert, Cocteau promoted Les Six to the drawing rooms of Parisian fashion and Diaghilev's charmed circle.[63] In June 1921 his Les Mariés de la Tour Eiffel revealed to audiences of the Ballets Suédois the talents of five of the group's composers. Diaghilev was in London when the curtain rose on this collective effort, but he did see the "Spectacle Bouffe" featuring many of the same artists that Cocteau had presented a few weeks earlier.[64] As the tide of company fortunes turned toward France, plans for the first of Diaghilev's "Parisian" works crystallized around the poet's "family" of artists. By October 1922 Cocteau had completed a draft of the scenario for Les Biches and was proposing Poulenc and Marie Laurencin as collaborators.[65] His draft of Les Fâcheux dates from this time as well. Cocteau collaborated on yet a third ballet presented in 1924, his last dance venture until Plein Chant in 1943, and of his Diaghilev works the one that came closest to realizing his theatrical ideas.

This was *Le Train Bleu,* for which he not only wrote a detailed libretto, but also chose Milhaud as his collaborator.[66]

Cocteau served Diaghilev in yet another capacity. A master publicist, he wrote articles and essays hailing the new turn in Diaghilev's repertory, as earlier he had done for Dada and Les Six. On March 1, 1924, the *Nouvelle Revue Française,* France's leading intellectual journal, carried his praise of *Les Biches* and *Les Fâcheux* well in advance of the Paris premiere. Similar "appreciations" appeared in the inaugural volumes of a series on Diaghilev's theater, to which Braque, Auric, Milhaud, Poulenc, and Marie Laurencin also contributed.[67] Satie, too, doubled as a collaborator and journalist that winter, contributing articles to *Paris-Journal, Création,* and the *Transatlantic Review.*[68] Louis Laloy, the influential music critic of *Comoedia* who was also secretary-general of the Paris Opéra, spent the early weeks of the year in Monte Carlo, and like the others readied audiences on the Paris home front.[69] Grist for Diaghilev's publicity mill, their stories ranged far beyond the Right Bank, even crossing the Atlantic. "A new ballet, Les Biches, . . . was given with brilliant success at Monte Carlo," Paul Morand told readers of *The Dial* in July 1924. "Everyone returning from the Midi pronounces [it] a delight." The novelist added a "plug" for *Les Fâcheux.* "After years of shameful farce and opera of incredible ugliness and vulgarity, at last the stage of Monte Carlo returns to authentic art with Les Fâcheux by Auric."[70] In the many roles of collaborator, critic, publicist, and denizen of High Bohemia, Cocteau epitomized, more than any other figure around Diaghilev, the relationship in these years between the production and merchandizing of ballet.

In his 1935 biography, which erected the interpretative scaffolding of this period, Arnold Haskell called the chapter devoted to the last seven years of Diaghilev's life "In Search of Lost Youth." The impresario, he wrote, "felt only too keenly that the distance that separated him from the younger generations was growing with the years. This did not merely worry him, it terrified him . . ."[71] Diaghilev did indeed assume the guise of an aging Charlus in these years. With false teeth and dyed hair, he sought to counter the ravages of time, and in the twenty-year-olds who surrounded him, he drank as much at a fountain of youth as a spring of creation. But there is another way of viewing the often handsome ephebes who briefly entered his circle, one that has little to do with sublimated instinct and surrogate paternity. Boys, whether beautiful or not, cost far less than their elders.

The correspondence and memoir literature paint an unflattering portrait of Diaghilev in these years. No longer the open-handed Maecenas of yore, he drove a hard and high-handed bargain with his tribe of "fledglings." Like Nicolas Nabokov, composer of the 1928 *Ode,* most of Diaghilev's "discoveries" spun dreams of glory in the squeeze of a second-class compartment, and when the *rapide* discharged them in Monte Carlo, some, like composer Vladimir Dukelsky, had to beg Diaghilev for pocket money. And in the months following a premiere, almost all had to badger him for long overdue royalties.[72]

Youngsters came cheap, far cheaper than experienced artists. In 1917 Diaghilev had paid Picasso five thousand francs to design *Parade*.[73] Two years later he had offered Matisse ten thousand francs to design *Le Chant du Rossignol*. This was also the amount he agreed to pay Larionov in 1921 for *Chout* and Derain five years later for *Jack-in-the-Box*. Alexandre Benois, too, enjoyed the bounty Diaghilev reserved for senior collaborators, receiving Frs. 25,000 for *Le Médecin Malgré Lui*, the Gounod opera produced in Monte Carlo in 1923–1924. By contrast, the mid-twenties "fledgling" commanded a fee averaging no more than six thousand francs, a rate that applied to composers as well as painters.[74]

Youthful collaborators rarely protested such terms. A Diaghilev commission enhanced both the value and demand for their services, even within the Ballets Russes itself. For *Les Matelots,* his second project for Diaghilev, Auric proposed a fee of Frs. 6,000. "I feel sure," he wrote to the impresario, "that I am not asking too much of you. With prices being what they are . . . I think I'm being very reasonable . . . And I feel sure you will agree!" The breezy tone of his letter, written even before the Paris premiere of *Les Fâcheux*, suggests the confidence of a young man whose fortunes—and fees—are on the rise. By the time he negotiated his third Diaghilev commission in 1925, Auric's fee had jumped fifty percent to Frs. 9,000.[75]

Did Diaghilev feel that he had been used? There is reason to suspect that he did, as it is hard to believe that his deputy, Boris Kochno, would have demanded a "kickback" amounting to one-third of Auric's royalties (in addition to the one-third share he received as librettist) without the impresario's tacit approval.[76] Only three weeks after commissioning *La Pastorale*, Diaghilev received an outraged letter from the composer:

> Boris is a charming lad . . . but he needs to be taught a lesson or two. He is concerned, so he writes, to advise me that "*the royalty for ballets of which he is the author is fifty-five francs,*" and that in fixing these terms, he "*sacrifices a large share of what he should be getting . . . (SIC!!!!).*" Now, the royalties for *Les Matelots* are split three ways . . . In all fairness, the two people who should be involved in this division are Massine and myself, our work and effort being, in all sincerity totally different from Boris's . . . It is *without precedent* for a music publisher to pay for a *ballet* scenario. Ask Edition Russe, Durand, Heugel . . . or someone like Jean Cocteau who has never received and, moreover, would never dream of receiving anything from the publisher

of *Parade* or *Train bleu* . . . I might add that [Boris] is lucky to be dealing with someone like me. Prokofiev or Stravinsky would take this a lot worse.

I had asked *nine thousand* francs to write this new ballet. If you decide I have to pay a thousand francs for the right to collaborate with Boris on *Les Matelots* and this third ballet, I . . . for my part will only work for *ten thousand francs*. Otherwise, I will pay Boris the sum of 500 francs for *Les Matelots*. I will, however, be compelled to give up the idea of ever working for the Ballet again—to my great regret . . . There is a question of *principle* here on which I cannot compromise, especially as all your musical collaborators, I know, share my view.[77]

By 1925 Auric had priced himself beyond Diaghilev's slender means. After *La Pastorale* he never worked again for the company. Nor, for that matter, did the vast majority of collaborators who emerged from the baptism of even a single Diaghilev assignment as highly visible, marketable commodities. Given Diaghilev's financial plight and the spiraling cost of talent, the era's pace of aesthetic change rested as much on imperatives of an economic order as on psychosexual or artistic considerations.

Exploitation, however, was not a one-way street. If kickbacks, low piece rates, and tardy royalties denied collaborators the just fruits of their labor, most artists who passed through Diaghilev's ballet assembly line proved all too willing to accept his conditions. "Although the terms proposed by Mr. Diaghilev are hardly favorable to us," wrote Vittorio Rieti's music publisher to the young composer of *Barabau* with unusual explicitness, "I accept them, because I am convinced that it will be of the greatest importance for you as a young composer to have your name appear on Mr. Diaghilev's programs." For composers setting out on a professional career, the promise of long-term gain offset the inconvenience of short-term loss. A similar trade-off occurred with visual artists, for whom a Diaghilev commission brought the art market to the doorstep of the atelier. Juan Gris put it succinctly: "A ballet will help to make me known and bring me admirers."[78]

Diaghilev's role in the creation of the market for modern art is a neglected aspect of his multifaceted career. Yet there is evidence suggesting that his intervention at this time was crucial, not so much as the catalyst of a phenomenon that was well under way, but in expanding the market and accelerating the commercialization of work by younger artists.

The case of Picasso is particularly instructive. Between 1917 and 1921 Picasso acquired a new public for his work. His collaboration on *Parade*, followed in short order by *Le Tricorne* (1919), *Pulcinella* (1920), and *Cuadro Flamenco* (1921), opened what Max Jacob called the painter's "*époque des duchesses*." By the year 1920, when Paris saw *Le Tricorne*, *Pulcinella*, and *Parade* in Diaghilev's first seasons in the French capital since the war,

Picasso became "one of the most talked-about and sought-after men in Paris." The artist who before 1917 had rarely ventured beyond Montmartre was "to be seen looking elegant at every cocktail-party and first night, and he dined out continually, accompanied by [his wife] Olga in dresses from Chanel."[79] Like Cocteau and Les Six, Picasso had joined the circle of Diaghilev intimates in the drawing rooms of Misia and Chanel.

Between 1921 and 1923 hundreds of cubist paintings, confiscated during the war as alien property from the dealer Daniel-Henry Kahnweiler, came up for sale by the French government. No market could withstand such an "avalanche," and after the first sale prices dropped steadily. Among Kahnweiler's prewar stable of painters, Picasso alone did not suffer. By 1920, the dealer recalled, the artist's "classical period [had] developed, that is, a kind of painting that addressed itself to a different audience."[80] But surely the fact that, through his association with Diaghilev, Picasso had acquired a new, fashionable public for his work, also enabled him to withstand the temporary collapse of the cubist market.

Up-and-coming artists vied to imitate this exemplary progress. Arriving in Paris in 1921, Christopher Wood trod the byzantine path of introductions that led the unknown painter to the outer ring of Diaghilev's acquaintance. By 1925 his circle came to include Picasso and Cocteau, and through them he met Diaghilev. In March 1926 the "whole of Paris," as he wrote to his mother, was "talking about" his commission for *Romeo and Juliet*. Picasso brought other unknowns into the social world of the Ballets Russes. "As I am now speaking of painting," Paul Morand told *Dial* readers in September 1924, "I want to say a word about a new painter who has been much discussed in Paris for some weeks. At the Boeuf sur le Toit or at the Jockey the first words one hears are always: 'You know Picasso has just discovered a new painter. He is twenty years old; he comes from Barcelona; his name is Pruna.'"[81] The following June, Pedro Pruna made his Diaghilev debut in *Les Matelots*. No wonder Roger Fry found the crassness of the Paris artscape so disturbing. "Mon dieu," he wrote to Helen Anrep in 1925, "the arrivism, the mercantilism, of the art world here! It has fallen very low and it seems to me all the young are given over to the determination to arrive and attract attention."[82]

Competition for Diaghilev's favor on the part of young easel painters indicates to what degree his commissions had become a means of establishing commercial value. But the grand stage of the Ballets Russes offered by no means the only link between Diaghilev's artist and buyer. Undertakings outside the arena of performance enhanced the value of an artist's work by presenting it under the guise of a "collectible" and using it to create new types of artifacts.

Throughout his years as an impresario, Diaghilev promoted company artists and art works through exhibitions organized in tandem with his seasons. In some instances these displays took place within the corridors of the theater itself. At other times galleries scheduled exhibitions to coincide with Ballets Russes performances, including one-man shows of designers contributing new productions to the season's repertory. In 1912 and 1913 major Bakst exhibitions took place at London's Fine Art Society; Gontcharova's exhibition at the Galérie Paul-Guillaume (for which Apollinaire wrote the catalogue preface) opened just after Diaghilev unveiled *Le Coq d'Or* at the Paris Opéra in 1914; Pruna's show at Claridge's in 1925 coincided with the London premiere of *Les Matelots,* while Gontcharova's exhibition there the following year overlapped with the first English performance of *Les Noces* and her new production of *Firebird.*[83] Ballets Russes artists and artifacts figured prominently in many other events over the years—the Russian Arts and Crafts Show (London, 1921), International Theatre Exhibition (London, 1922), shows at the Omega Workshop (London, 1919) and Redfern Gallery (London, 1925), to mention only a few. In 1928 London's Literary Book Club presented an exhibition devoted exclusively to the Ballets Russes.[84]

Beginning with the war years, Diaghilev collected as he commissioned. In Italy he acquired a small but choice selection of futurist art, which was shown along with recent works by Larionov, Gontcharova, Picasso, Juan Gris, Fernand Léger, and other Paris-based vanguardists in tandem with the 1917 season in Rome.[85] Over the years collaborators added to this "Massine collection," as they did later in the 1920s, when Serge Lifar and Boris Kochno became the objects of Diaghilev's affections and the beneficiaries of his collecting mania. Like his predecessor's collection, Lifar's miscellany of ballet designs and paintings by company designers was exhibited in short order upon acquisition.[86]

In the late 1910s Diaghilev also began treating scenery and front curtains as works of art whose value rested not solely on their theatrical function, but on the fact of their creation by a particular artist. Thus, his 1919 contract with Matisse stipulated that the artist himself paint the drop curtain, as opposed to the usual practice of having scene painters copy the original design. Diaghilev wrote a similar provision into his contract with Larionov for the scenery of *Chout* and into agreements with at least some of the artists commissioned later in the decade. In effect, Diaghilev was creating a new kind of signed artifact, exemplified by the curtain identified in the 1924 Paris program as being "by PICASSO." Harnessing to the anonymous and reproducible curtain or backdrop the value of the unique, hand-fabricated painting, he transformed these into marketable commodities. Even with the franc's declining value between 1919 and 1928, Diaghilev profited many times over when he sold portions of Picasso's hand-brushed curtain for *Le Tricorne* to a German collector for Frs. 175,000.[87]

Diaghilev negotiated this sale through Paul Rosenberg. This was by no means Diaghilev's first contact with one of the period's leading dealers in modern art. A sketch by Michel Georges-Michel, entitled "The Opening of 'La Parade'," shows Rosenberg in the company of the critic, Diaghilev, Marie Laurencin, Misia Sert, Satie, Picasso, and Cocteau at the premiere of that epoch-making 1917 ballet. Three years later Rosenberg, who had become Picasso's dealer in 1918, brought out a limited edition of the artist's designs for *Le Tricorne*. Connections with another influential dealer are also a matter of record. In 1921, when Diaghilev considered publishing lithographs by Juan Gris in the company's programs, he also proposed to bring out a "de luxe" issue for Kahnweiler's Galerie Simon. Two years later, at the height of his collaboration with the Ballets Russes, the painter suggested that Diaghilev ask Kahnweiler to lend material for the Monte Carlo souvenir program.[88] Presumably, arrangements of this kind represented a common practice in the 1920s, when unpublished art works vied with photographs of featured dancers in company programs. With Diaghilev, the ephemera of an artist's passage through the dance world, the portraits, figures, and caricatures sketched in the intimacy of collaboration, acquired social and commercial standing by the very act of reproduction.

Diaghilev's programs, produced since 1909 by de Brunoff, a leading art and fine book house and until 1922 publisher of *Comoedia Illustré*, illustrate yet another aspect of the impresario's "packaging" of modern art. The postwar period saw a brisk trade in fine editions about Ballets Russes artists and works, further evidence of the tie, cemented in these years, between the company and the art market. This was particularly true in France, where from the beginning programs and special inserts in *Comoedia Illustré* were aimed at both a collecting and a dance public.[89] *La Danse*, a monthly that began publication in late 1919, similarly appealed to a public of "dance lovers, artists, and bibliophiles."[90]

Even before World War I the Ballets Russes had inspired a dozen or so rare volumes on the era's stars and most popular ballets. In the postwar period ballet publishing came into its own, although high prices, as the *Dancing Times* regretted in the case of Valerian Svetlov's book on Karsavina, placed most volumes beyond the means of dance professionals.[91] Two presses led the way: de Brunoff, which published major works by Svetlov, one of the leading émigré dance writers, an important collection of Diaghilev programs, and Bakst's designs for *The Sleeping Princess*;[92] and C. W. Beaumont, the firm of the London bookseller, ballet critic, and publisher, which brought out over a score of books on Diaghilev's dancers and repertory between 1919 and 1929. Virtually all these volumes were numbered; many were printed on rare vellum; most featured specially commissioned artwork. Like the volumes of symbolist poetry that comprised Beaumont's other specialty line as a publisher, the tone, format, and content of his dance books appealed as much to the collector as the balletomane.[93] As these and other fine art presses added dance titles to their lists, ballet books as a genre took form within the tradition of the "beau livre."[94]

Diaghilev's association with modern art prompted to a large degree the reputation of the Ballets Russes as standing at the cutting edge of avant-garde experiment. This debt was not one-sided. The rapid dissemination of the School of Paris beyond professional and collecting milieux after 1917 owed much to its "advertising" by the Ballets Russes. "There has been established," wrote Paul Morand in 1927, "an arbitration of exchange whereby an economic 'good' becomes immediately negotiable everywhere. Painters or writers have a value which I shall call a gold value which subjects them to universal quotation . . ."[95] Morand neither mentions the Ballets Russes nor poses the question of agency. He cites as examples, however, several painters from the Diaghilev fold, artists like Picasso and Derain, whose work became a medium of exchange at least in part because of their success as designers. To the remarkable list of Diaghilev's postwar achievements, perhaps another should be added: his assistance at the birth of the market for twentieth-century art.

Some artists profited from their connection with Diaghilev. Others suffered. For dancers, these last years of Ballets Russes history saw a gradual ebb in status and earning power, a hardening of paternalist styles of management, and the arbitrary pitting of artist against artist whereby Diaghilev divided and conquered. From this era comes the legacy of labor relations and attitudes that still colors management policies within the private sphere of ballet enterprise.

Even in 1923–1924, when subsidies materialized at regular intervals and in relatively ample amounts, dancers were the "fat" Diaghilev periodically trimmed from his budget. The first such "trimming" occurred in the autumn of 1922, when Diaghilev slashed the troupe to barely half its size of only a year before. In reducing the company to thirty, claimed Grigoriev, Diaghilev's "chief aim" was to eliminate "some of the weaker dancers."[96] One may question whether quality was indeed the concern uppermost in the impresario's mind. Surely, a company of thirty cost less to maintain than one of fifty-five, and in late 1922 Diaghilev was cutting corners wherever he could.

As in 1926, when Diaghilev's hatchet fell once again, the company did not remain a skeleton ensemble for long. Within months of his 1922 pruning, its payroll had climbed to fifty, while in 1926 newcomers immediately took the places of those who had been dismissed.[97] More than any other policy, these "purges," to borrow Grigoriev's term, brought home to the dancers the economic reality of working for Diaghilev in the 1920s. Diaghilev could hire and fire at will, and at the snap of his fingers scores of applicants would materialize. In this buyer's market "purges" became a strategy for reducing wages and enhancing management's control of its "workers."

Terms like cost-effectiveness and productivity rarely enter discussions of ballet history. Yet they formed the cornerstone of Diaghilev's labor policy in the twenties, the framework within which the decline in wages and conditions, arbitrary changes in personnel, and new-style star system must be understood. They suggest the reasons underlying periodic outbreaks of "militancy" in the ranks and help explain the development of a management style that harnessed autocracy to the service of business.

When Nikitina joined the Ballets Russes in 1923, the "usual salary" for dancers in the corps de ballet ranged from Frs. 800 to Frs. 1,000 per month. Like Ninette de Valois, who entered the company in the autumn of the same year, Nikitina herself earned Frs. 1,500, the going rate for a soloist of reasonable experience and competence. By contrast with their counterparts at the Paris Opéra, where as late as 1926 étoiles and premières danseuses received no more than Frs. 1,500 a month,[98] Diaghilev's dancers fared well. But even if salaries compared favorably with those of dancers in the employ of the French government or working on the Paris music-hall stage,[99] the fact remains that pay scales continued the downward spiral that began in the war years. In absolute terms starting salaries in 1923 were little better than what they had been ten years earlier. In real terms they were considerably worse. By 1926 a soloist's pay barely sufficed "to keep body and soul together."[100]

The depreciation of the franc between 1923 and 1926 caused havoc well beyond the financial markets. In France the cost of living rose with the fall in value of its currency. By January 1926 the decline had become so precipitous that the Paris correspondent of the *Dancing Times* felt it necessary to warn dancers signing "long term engagements for France . . . [to] be on their guard," as "the money they stipulate . . . may be worth considerably less six months hence." Among "certain troupes of English dancers in Paris," he noted, dissatisfaction was rampant. "Their expenses are increasing in all directions, and what seemed a satisfactory salary when the contract was signed is no longer so." For Diaghilev's troupe of six-month gypsies, crossing national borders compounded these difficulties. During the autumn 1924 German tour, exchange rates precipitated a crisis when, as Ninette de Valois recalled, the dancers "found to our extreme agitation that a cup of coffee had to be drunk to the tune of seven francs, only a little less than a meal cost, at that time, in Paris. A meeting was held after we had been there a couple of days, presided over by Grigorieff; he informed us that the matter would be adjusted in forty-eight hours, but very naturally he could do nothing until that time had expired. I had eighteen marks in my possession, and Dorothy Coxon, another English girl, two."[101]

The 1923–1924 season marked a hiatus in the era's prevailing economic insecurity. Over a million francs flowed into Diaghilev's coffers from the Casino alone, in addition to earnings on tour. The Monte Carlo portion of the season, moreover, took place under a sign of aristocracy wedded to the artistic and social brilliance of High Bohemia. Privilege, however, existed only at the uppermost reaches of the company hierarchy, and it was the contrast, perhaps, between the aura of wealth and the reality of growing impoverishment that induced the dancers to raise once again the specter of a strike. The particulars of this action remain obscure, but included the demand for a twenty-five percent increase in salaries. "In the end," wrote Diaghilev to René Léon, "I had to raise the entire corps de ballet nearly twenty percent."[102]

A twenty percent raise eased but did not solve the problem of making ends meet. In the winter months when they participated in the operas presented at the Théâtre de Monte Carlo, dancers found ingenious ways of supplementing their income, as Ninette de Valois described in *Invitation to the Ballet:*

> The other excitement . . . was the question of compensation offered for various discomforts endured in certain operas. In *Damnation of Faust* there was a scene laid in hell where five of the ballet were hurled into a fire and burnt. We had to stand on a long grating, to which were tied hundreds of flame-coloured ribbons, a terrific blast of air was turned on, whirling the ribbons up and around us; but the thoughtful Monaco management regarded the ensuing draught as a form of discomfort to the ladies of the ballet, and deemed it right to compensate them to the tune of 50 francs for each performance. The scramble among the Russian *corps de ballet* to get burnt was terrific. Stage flying was even more popular, although compensation for this rather suspiciously soared to 150 francs for each performance.[103]

High-wire supplements notwithstanding, economic conditions worsened signally by 1925. That January forty-two dancers petitioned Diaghilev to raise salaries, citing in their appeal the sharp increase—in some instances, as much as one hundred percent—in rents and hotel prices in

Monte Carlo.[104] A meeting was held, presided over by soloists Ludmilla Schollar and her husband Anatole Vilzak, and the dancers resolved that if Diaghilev refused to give them "a definite promise to raise their salaries," they would not perform the following night. At Grigoriev's urging Diaghilev spoke to the dancers before the performance. The regisseur's summary of his remarks suggests how businessman and *barin* joined forces in Diaghilev's management style:

> "I'm very much astonished at your behaviour," he began. "You've already been told that I intend considering my budget and seeing what I can do for you. What more can you expect? You each of you have a separate contract with me. Very well—if you refuse to perform this evening I shall regard your non-attendance as a breach of contract and shall sue you for damages—which I should in fact have suffered, by having been forced to cancel the performance." On which, turning his back on them, he left the room.[105]

Diaghilev's peroration had the anticipated effect. The dancers turned up for the performance although accounts differ as to whether Schollar and Vilzak did so as well.[106] In any event, Diaghilev took a hard line with the "ringleaders." Advised that they had broken their contracts, both Schollar and Vilzak were dismissed. "As for the malcontents who had launched the protest," wrote Grigoriev, "their grievances were duly redressed, as soon as Diaghilev found he could afford it." In her account of these events, Ninette de Valois suggests the powerlessness of the dancers in their dealings with management:

> That we lost goes without saying, perhaps not so much through lack of a certain justification of fundamental grievance, but through stupidity and knowing so very much less about Diaghileff than Diaghileff knew about us. That he and Grigorieff dealt firmly and forcefully with the matter, and that neither of them showed any attempt or inclination to humiliate any of the more prominent offenders once the matter ended, impressed me in spite of my indignation and disappointment at the "Government win". But the years have shown there was no absolute right or wrong on either side, only a stupid misunderstanding perhaps handled at the beginning too hastily by the dancers and in an unnecessarily autocratic manner by the direction.[107]

The measured pragmatism of these reflections discloses a liberal view of management based on compromise. Compromise, however, was a term that did not exist in Diaghilev's vocabulary. Generous he might be, even to a fault, and as a realist he bowed before a fait accompli. But on the issue of his authority, his right to exercise undisputed power over the lives of his dancers, he brooked no challenge. His authority touched every aspect of company existence.

Although de Valois has contended that "the company . . . was on the whole treated very fairly,"[108] Diaghilev betrayed an often arbitrary hand in his dealings with individuals. This was not mere capriciousness on his part, but a style of management that exploited personal weakness as a means of upholding his authority. Salary negotiations offer a good example of this tactic. Because Diaghilev signed individual agreements with dancers, requests for increases placed the artist in the humiliating position of a petitioner. A letter written by Dorothy Coxon in 1925 illustrates:

I am so sorry to worry you when you are on your holiday but I am writing to ask you if you will raise my salary from 1400 francs to 1500 francs per month. The reason for this is that since my interview with Monsieur Grigorieff I have learned that you have raised Melle Ninette de Valois' salary from 1500 francs to 1800 francs and I am sure you understand that had I known this I would never have agreed to return to the company on the same terms. Although . . . Melle de Valois deserves a rise I do not feel that the difference between her dancing and mine is equal to the difference in our salaries. I feel that it is absolutely just to ask you for 100 francs more as it will just make the difference of 300 francs between our salaries, as it was before, when you engaged her at 1500 francs, and I received 1200 francs. After four years in your Company, I do feel and hope that you will do this for me, especially as Monsieur Grigorieff has promised that I will have much better places next year. I hate to go back on what I said to him, but I am sure you understand that what I have since heard has made a tremendous difference; for I do not feel that it is quite fair that I should receive so much less than other artistes and you cannot think what a big difference the extra 100 francs will make to me. I do hope you will give it to me,—and that you are having a very good holiday.
P.S. I am having Russian lessons![109]

Salaries were not the only sphere where Diaghilev exploited competition as a means of maintaining his hold over the work force. In billing, too, he might favor one dancer at the expense of another, thereby sparking emotional flare-ups that he could turn to his own benefit. Whether Coxon received her one-hundred franc "rise" is unknown. But the following year, she was enraged to find her name removed from company bills in London and Russian "artistes" promoted instead. With typical British forthrightness, she insisted on justice. She found herself without a job, yet another victim that year of Diaghilev's "purge."[110]

In other ways, too, Diaghilev fostered competition among dancers to reduce costs and enhance his authority. Throughout this period no single star shone with the brilliance of a Nijinsky or Karsavina. Nor did any choreographer, including George Balanchine, Diaghilev's in-house ballet master after 1924, enjoy the impresario's total confidence and the luxury of a troupe readied for his command. In dance, as in painting and music, Diaghilev plucked his newest stars from a corps of novices, sacrificing established personalities on the altar of untried youth.

By her own account Tamara Karsavina "broke" with Diaghilev in 1920 for artistic reasons.[111] Among the newer ballets few roles offered scope for dramatic expression or demanded the strong classical technique of the ballerina who had reigned over the Maryinsky no less than the prewar Ballets Russes. Karsavina, moreover, did not need Diaghilev. As a star on whom offers poured from managements all over Europe, she enjoyed both the luxury of independence and a level of monetary reward Diaghilev could afford only at intervals. In 1926 he paid her five thousand francs to dance two performances of *Romeo and Juliet* in Monte Carlo, and £120 per week to do the same in London. By contrast, Nikitina, who danced the role of Juliet in Paris, earned Frs. 1,700 per month, while Balanchine, Diaghilev's in-house choreographer, received a monthly salary of Frs. 2,500 as a soloist and the company's ballet master.[112] More than fifty years later, Balanchine still smarted at the memory of Diaghilev's niggardliness:

> Nobody cared about us dancers . . . We were just ballet people, fools. We did not belong among wise men. And at that time I was so badly paid by Diaghilev, so little—just pennies. You couldn't live on the money. We were always starving. I had several pairs of trousers, and, I remember I went to the Marché aux puces, the Paris flea market, sold a pair, and bought sausages. And we all lived on those sausages.[113]

Thus, for reasons of economy as much as art, Diaghilev turned to youth for his newest stars. Unlike Alexandra Danilova, who had completed the full course of training at the Maryinsky before joining Diaghilev in emigration, Anton Dolin, Nikitina, Serge Lifar, and Constantin Tcherkas lacked the technique of accomplished dancers. They came to Diaghilev almost straight from the classroom. He gave them lessons, roles that displayed their strengths and masked their weaknesses, and publicity buildups that made them instant stars.

In this last era of the Ballets Russes, stardom became a product that rolled off Diaghilev's assembly line with the regularity of a Model T. After 1923 new stars flared in quick succession across the company's firmament: Dolin, Lifar, and Tcherkas among the men; Vera Nemchinova, Nikitina, Danilova, and Doubrovska among the women. Like Massine earlier, this new generation of stars bore Diaghilev's exclusive label of manufacture. None, however, savored the unchallenged ascendancy of their predecessors. Once they had tasted fame, Diaghilev contrived to keep an upper hand, playing off one dancer against another in an elaborate contest for roles, ballets, billings, and sexual favors.

This undercutting of stardom's intrinsic value applied no less to Balanchine, the era's official choreographer, than to its principal dancers. In a radical departure from earlier practice, not a single season between 1925 to 1929 passed without Diaghilev commissioning at least one major ballet from another choreographer. The year 1926 witnessed Nijinska's staging of *Romeo and Juliet,* while Massine choreographed no fewer than four works in this period: *Zéphire et Flore* and *Les Matelots* in 1925, *Le Pas d'Acier* in 1927, and *Ode* in 1928. The following year Lifar made his choreographic debut with the revival of *Le Renard.* In the history of the Ballets Russes, no choreographer worked in so competitive an atmosphere or one so little conducive to artistic collaboration as Balanchine in the years 1925 to 1929.

Along with purges, competition, and lower salaries, overwork had become a permanent feature of company life. "You should see how the ballet works here," Ruth Page wrote to her mother in winter 1925, a time when dancers sometimes gave two performances a day—concert programs in the afternoon and operas in the evening. "They are practically there from 9 in the morning till 12 at night. I think it is terrible, and almost no pay." [114] In both *Come Dance With Me* and *Invitation to the Ballet,* Ninette de Valois also commented on the heavy work load and management's indifference to its effects:

> Viewed in perspective our greatest setback was overwork; at times it was quite inhuman and should not have been permitted. Such a strain on artists is unjust from any angle, and a good deal could have been avoided with a little more carefully planned organisation. It is well to draw attention to this fault, prevalent in all Russian organisations, for they one and and all suffer from the same drawback; so much of this has been alluded to in enthusiastic terms, as if a dancer was a lively species of mosquito with no human feelings or reactions. A great deal of the falling off of the technical standard of the company in the last few years . . . was due to the state of the artists' health and nerves. The collapse of both Lifar's ankles during the dress rehearsal of a new ballet (duration about twenty minutes) and the breakdown of Nikitina's foot after the first performance of the same work and her subsequent enforced rest for four weeks, all point to one thing, over-tired and over-strained youth. [115]

Dancers worked "all day and every day" in that pre-union era except for a one-month summer holiday. Nor did the day necessarily end when the curtain fell on an evening's program. Dancers might be summoned to dance after midnight for Paris *en grand gala*. At such receptions, recalled de Valois, dancers "were never given anything to eat or drink," and there were times when, unable to afford taxi night rates, she had to walk half way across Paris at three o'clock in the morning.[116]

Such conditions aroused the young dancer's "English spirit of justice," although, by her own admission, she was "the only one to express irritation." Her Slavic companions viewed practices like these as part of a natural order, a commonplace of the artist's life on the Continent. As a composer with no social connections and little prestige beyond the avant-garde, Erik Satie also suffered at the hands of snobbish hostesses. Serving a drink to a guest at a soiree where his music was being performed, he was told by a condescending Princesse, "Monsieur Satie, the musicians' buffet is in the other drawing room."[117] Stars like Lifar, Dolin, and Nikitina might circulate among Diaghilev's peers in society. The average dancer, however, remained on the backstairs.

Before 1914 Diaghilev's Russian dancers had assumed a position of equality with Russia's other "free" artists. Beginning in the war years, economic constraints gnawed little by little at the privileges of such freedom. Low salaries succeeded the company's initial premium rates, and conditions deteriorated markedly. Between 1924 and 1928, however, the status of the dancer declined precipitously. Not only did the collapse of the franc erode the dancer's financial position, but the demise of both the Ballets Suédois and Soirées de Paris in 1924 threw numerous performers back on the job market. Not until the formation of Ida Rubinstein's company in 1928, with Bronislava Nijinska as resident choreographer, did an alternative to the Ballets Russes appear on the Parisian horizon. In this buyer's market Diaghilev could hire and fire the human materiel of his enterprise as if it were no more than a collection of interchangeable parts. The status of the "free" artist had rested on the dancer's seizing control of his or her own labor. With the loss of that autonomy, the dancer became a wage-earning proletarian, a second-class citizen of the artistic polity. If this phenomenon did not become the rule in England as it did in France and the United States, one has not only the remarkable talents of Ninette de Valois and British ballet's other founding mothers to thank, but also the "gentrification" of ballet as an art form brought about by the postwar dance boom. Elsewhere, the disenfranchisement of dancers within the larger artistic community formed as much a legacy of this last era as the tradition of creative experiment.

If the years 1923 to 1929 lack the aesthetic coherence of earlier eras, they cannot be dismissed out of hand, an attitude fashionable among the generation of English ballet writers that rose to prominence in the 1930s.

With Nijinska's *Les Noces* and *Les Biches* and Balanchine's *Apollon Musagète* and *Prodigal Son,* Diaghilev brought into the world four ballets whose luster neither changing tastes nor changing casts have dimmed. In painting and music, to say nothing of dance, he launched scores of artists on the journey to fame. And against overwhelming odds, he steered the art of ballet closer to the cutting edge of new artistic trends than anyone since.

The difficulty in assessing this period lies in the complex web of relationships between Diaghilev's art and his enterprise. Enmeshed in overlapping chronicles of personalities, artistic interests, and financial concerns, such relationships make sense of the era's protean and paradoxical character, lifting it above the mere play of chance and genius to an object lesson in twentieth-century cultural economy. For the brutal truth is that by the 1920s, no European enterprise of the magnitude and experimental nature of the Ballets Russes could survive solely within the marketplace. Some form of public subsidy had become essential.

Beginning in 1909 nearly every year had seen Diaghilev make an August pilgrimage to Venice. As favorites romped on the beach, he would sketch out plans for ballets and dine with impresarios anxious to secure his company's services. Artists would be close at hand, and patrons might descend from off-shore yachts to visit. In 1929 Diaghilev made his last journey to the Adriatic's queen city. At his side for most of the way was a new protégé, a composer of seventeen named Igor Markevitch. The two stopped in Baden-Baden to visit Paul Hindemith, who was doing a ballet for the company, and in Munich, where they lunched with Richard Strauss. They went to the opera—*Die Meistersinger, The Magic Flute, Così Fan Tutte.* "My sustenance here is Wagner and Mozart," Diaghilev wrote. "What geniuses and how well performed." At *Tristan,* remembering his first love, he "shed bitter tears."[118] In Salzburg the travelers parted, and the impresario went on to Venice. Although rejuvenated by the trip, Diaghilev was dying. For some time he had been suffering from diabetes; untreated, the disease now took its course. On August 19, 1929, as Serge Lifar, Boris Kochno, and Misia Sert kept vigil, he slipped into a coma and died. Two days later a gondola draped in black carried his body to San Michele, Venice's island cemetery. In the city where Wagner had died and doges had created a monument to beauty from the profits of far-flung trade, Diaghilev's extraordinary chapter in the history of art and enterprise came to an end.

III ✒

AUDIENCE

10 ✒

PARIS: THE CULTIVATED

AUDIENCE

I N HIS TWENTY YEARS at the helm of the Ballets Russes, Diaghilev transformed the art and political economy of ballet, willing to the future a major corpus of works and a range of organizational prototypes. To these legacies must be added a third, equally remarkable one: the public that welcomed and supported his enterprise. Between 1909 and 1929 Diaghilev created a vast new following for ballet. This following was never monolithic, but consisted of fluid configurations that varied from city to city and changed over time. Diaghilev's many audiences laid the foundation for the modern ballet public. But even in their own era, these gatherings of the wealthy, powerful, cultivated, celebrated, and talented were remarkable. They played many roles in the Diaghilev enterprise, from buying tickets to creating publicity, and they gave the Ballets Russes a cachet unique in twentieth-century dance. Their presence in the audience shaped the company's public image, while their influence behind the scenes left an imprint on the repertory: at any given moment, the identity of the Ballets Russes at least partly reflected that of its public. Above all, the audience created by Diaghilev explains the speed with which the Ballets Russes moved to the center of Western theatrical life and the interests that kept it there for the better part of twenty years.

Ballet, of course, was no stranger to the French capital. Even in the years of its decline, it had retained a place of subsidized prominence at the Opéra and, to a somewhat lesser extent, at the Opéra-Comique. Artistically, however, it was at low ebb. Few works of distinction graced its repertory, and even fewer artists of stature deigned to compose for it. The ballet girl, who had long since vanquished her male counterpart, was herself as debased as the art she personified. Pitied, scorned, and desired, she epitomized the dual stigma of low social origins and moral impropriety traditionally associated with ballet. Indeed, for the *abonnés*, that corps of wealthy subscribers with entree to the Foyer de la Danse and access to the theater's management, the Opéra existed as a kind of fiefdom, an all-female preserve for the sexual huntsman. "The Opéra," wrote Arnold Bennett in 1910, "is the splendid prey of the high officers of State. If such a one wants an evening's entertainment, or a mistress, the Opéra is there, at his disposition. The *foyer de la danse* is the most wonderful seraglio in the western world, and it is reserved to the Government and to subscribers."[1] In the early twentieth century, ballet in France was socially and artistically *déclassé*, isolated from the cultural mainstream and patronized by the most philistine stratum of the male upper class. That this was no longer the case in 1914 is a measure of Diaghilev's genius and the extraordinary changes he brought about in the audience for his chosen art.

The forging of a new ballet audience actually began before the fabled season of 1909. Diaghilev's Paris ventures of 1906–1908 usually receive short shrift. Yet from the first these magnificent events—the Exhibition of Russian Art in 1906, the Russian concert series of 1907, and the complete *Boris Godunov* in 1908—captured the city's imagination. In these years, Diaghilev acquired a growing legion of partisans, the embryo of the cultivated elite that formed his most important public up to the War. At the same time, he assembled a band of influential critics, publicists, and patrons who embraced his successive Russian enterprises and ultimately championed his ballet. The sensational triumph of the 1909 *saison russe* stemmed, in part, from the rising tide of enthusiasm for Diaghilev's previous accomplishments and the ever increasing breadth of his audience.

At the center of this following stood the diplomats and high public officials who presided over Diaghilev's early career in the West, underscoring its political character and importance. From the 1906 exhibition (which dovetailed with the State visit of Alexander Izvolsky, Russia's new Minister of Foreign Affairs) to the 1909 *saison russe*, ambassadors, cabinet ministers, political hostesses, entire Russian legations, and even French President Clément-Armand Fallières transformed Diaghilev events into gala assemblies of policymakers. The audience and subscription lists published in *Figaro*, the newspaper par excellence of *le tout Paris*, tell this story in fine print columns. So, too, in glossier form, do Diaghilev's catalogues and programs. Here, we meet the distinguished personalities who lent their names to his 1906, 1907, and 1908 patronage committees: Comtesse Greffuhle, the raven-eyed original of Proust's Duchesse de Guermantes and one of the era's "most charming political women,"[2] who served as chairman; A.J. Nelidov and Anatole Nekludov, Russian Ambassador and Counselor, respectively; embassy intimate Alexis de Hitroff; Count Benckendorf, tsarist minister to the Court of St. James; Grand Dukes Vladimir and Paul; and Aristide Briand, French Minister of Public Education and Religion.

The newly discovered *feuilles de location*—booking sheets—for Diaghilev's production of *Boris Godunov* flesh out the picture. Not only did high tsarist officials, grand dukes, and the cream of the Russian colony turn out in force for this Slavic masterwork, but they did so again and again. In 1909 the web of political and diplomatic interests remained intact, notwithstanding the hostility to Diaghilev in Russian court circles. Indeed, to one observer, the dazzling *répétition générale* that inaugurated Diaghilev's career as a ballet impresario resembled "an official ceremony":

> something like a Russian return to Paris, a new tightening of the alliance. Only this time the Russians have come not with ships and sailors to conquer our sympathy, but with singers, dancers, and decorators to conquer our admiration.
>
> Monsieur Pichon, Minister of Foreign Affairs, and Madame Pichon occupied the center box with Monsieur Nelidov, the Russian Ambassador, and Madame Nelidov . . . If I add that Messrs. Barthou [Minister of Public Works], Doumergue [Minister of Commerce and Industry], Cailloux [Minister of Finance], and Dujardin-Beaumetz [Under-Secretary of Fine Arts] were also present, no will doubt that this was a politico-artistic manifestation of the highest importance.[3]

Four days later the diplomatic corps applauded "the celebrated Russian dancers" from the Châtelet at a brilliant reception given by the Minister of Foreign Affairs.[4] In 1909 ballet fell heir to the influential public that had supported Diaghilev's successive missions in cultural diplomacy.

But diplomats and public officials alone did not suffice to create a self-sustaining audience. The public that took the Russian dancers to heart was, overwhelmingly, a musical one, a community of concert and opera-going professionals and aficionados. The Russian Historical Concerts presented at the Paris Opéra in 1907 stirred enormous interest in that community, as did the production of *Boris Godunov* the following year. The importance of these seasons cannot be overestimated. Not only did they bring together the core public of the Ballets Russes, but as musical and, in the case of *Boris*, decorative preludes to the 1909 enterprise, they set its aesthetic tone. Of the composers represented on the five concert programs, which included both symphonic and operatic selections, most would later figure prominently in ballet. No fewer than four works that year—Balakirev's *Thamar*, Borodin's *Prince Igor*, Liadov's *Baba Yaga*, and Rimsky-Korsakov's *Sadko*—became ballets; other pieces were incorporated into the scores of *Cléopâtre* and *Le Festin*. Between 1909 and 1915, moreover, Diaghilev staged a half-dozen works by Rimsky-Korsakov, the "lion" of that first season—*Ivan the Terrible* (1909; London, 1913 and 1914);

Schéhérazade (1910); *Sadko* (1911), *Le Coq d'Or* (1914); *May Night* (London, 1914); and *Midnight Sun* (1915).

If Diaghilev's concert series prepared the musical ground for the Ballets Russes, *Boris Godunov* anticipated its decorative aesthetic. For his first theatrical venture, Diaghilev called on artists long associated with *Mir Iskusstva*—Alexander Golovin, Alexandre Benois, and Konstantin Yuon, who did the sets, and Ivan Bilibin, Dmitri Stelletsky, Boris Anisfeld, Eugene Lanceray, and Stepan Yaremich, who worked on the costumes. 1909 added others to this roster: major figures like Léon Bakst, Nicholas Roerich, and Konstantin Korovin along with several lesser ones. All these artists contributed to the opera and ballet repertory; in both media, they reiterated the blend of sumptuousness, decorative harmony, and historical veracity so appealing to audiences of *Boris*. Visually as well as musically, Diaghilev aligned his earliest ballet ventures with the aesthetic of his lyric theater.

Diaghilev's initial venues emphasized this connection. Even more, they reinforced the elitist aura that Diaghilev sought to confer on ballet. If this was the stepchild of the Belle Epoque, opera was its favorite son. Divas occupied pedestals once graced by ballerinas, and the themes of marriage, family, and property that fueled so many plots echoed the obsessions of opera's bourgeois, monied public. As the century drew to a close, a powerful draft from *Mitteleuropa* added to opera's prestige. Wagnerism descended upon Paris in the 1880s, penetrating literature, art, and even spheres of religious and intellectual thought in a city where anti-German feeling still ran high in the aftermath of the Franco-Prussian War. Under the banner of the *Revue Wagnérienne,* published between 1885 and 1888, a brilliant constellation of symbolist talents gathered: Edouard Dujardin, Joris-Karl Huysmans, Paul Verlaine, and Stéphane Mallarmé. And in *La Revue Blanche,* founded by the husband of Diaghilev's most loyal and longstanding partisan, Wagnerism sounded a *leitmotif* among the journal's broader themes of symbolism and postimpressionism.

Wagner's lucubrations and innovative productions elevated opera from mere social pleasure to an intellectually compelling art. At the same time, his theater at Bayreuth became the center of a cult, a shrine to which the wealthy, cultivated tastemakers of the Belle Epoque made pilgrimage annually until World War I. Diaghilev himself first visited Bayreuth in the 1890s at the very height of the Master's "enslavement" of the fashionable imagination, as did a host of his future admirers—Princesse de Polignac, Comtesse Greffuhle, Comte Isaac de Camondo, Comte Robert de Montesquiou, Reynaldo Hahn, and Jacques-Emile Blanche, to name only a few.[5] (So popular had the pilgrimage become that between 1897 and 1903 Albert Lavignac's *Le Voyage Artistique à Bayreuth,* a "practical guidebook for the Frenchman in Bayreuth," went through no fewer than five editions.) Here, among the throngs who crowded the Teutonic rituals of Bayreuth in the 1890s and early 1900s was the cultured, cosmopolitan, and knowledgeable audience to which Diaghilev laid claim in his early years in the West. The overnight triumph of the Ballets Russes reflected Diaghilev's success in attracting this sophisticated following to his dance enterprise.

In appropriating this audience for ballet, no one proved more instrumental to Diaghilev than Gabriel Astruc. Publisher, editor, sometime playwright, and impresario of vision, Astruc moved through the many Paris worlds that came together in Diaghilev's public. From 1907 to 1913 he produced virtually all of Diaghilev's seasons, along with a score of other enterprises that successfully located the Ballets Russes on the social and artistic landscape of Paris.

In these years Astruc's trademark was opera, especially in its newer guises, luxuriously packaged, and marketed to an elite public. Under the programming umbrella of his *Grande Saison de Paris,* each spring witnessed a parade of lyric novelties: Richard Strauss's *Salomé* (1907), the Metropolitan Opera (1910), Ida Rubinstein's genre-defying spectacles (1911–1913), to single out only the most celebrated. Like *Salomé,* many of these cosmopolitan extravaganzas wed symbolist theme to secessionist form; they blended exotic color with the perfumed eroticism of the 1890s. Presented in its original German production with Strauss himself on the podium and with Natalia Trouhanova and Aïda Boni alternating in the Dance of the Seven Veils, *Salomé* generated reams of publicity: columns devoted to Oscar Wilde, on whose play the opera was based; Aubrey Beardsley, who illustrated the English translation (an exhibition of his work was reviewed in *Figaro* by Comte Robert de Montesquiou); even the piano score of Strauss's famous dance. Like Diaghilev's first nights, the *répétition générale* at the Théâtre du Châtelet had all the earmarks of a State occasion. A charity gala, it also brought out the wealthiest element of the opera-going public. More than any other enterprise, *Salomé* anticipated the arrival of the Ballets Russes.[6]

As the son of a rabbi whose flock numbered some of the richest and most cultured Jewish families of the French capital, Astruc also stood at the center of yet another network that proved crucial to the survival of the Ballets Russes. Like Comte Isaac de Camondo, the distinguished collector and Turkish banking heir who backed Astruc's Société Musicale, Jews formed an elite opera-going corps to which their coreligionist turned again and again for support. No matter how wealthy and cultivated, however, Jews lacked the prestige to guarantee full-blown social success. For this, Astruc enlisted Comtesse Greffuhle, that blueblood of bluebloods, who presided over the nebulous body that in the social arena "fronted" for the Société Musicale. Under the aegis of the Grandes Auditions Musicales de

France, events like *Salomé* and Diaghilev's Historical Concerts came before the public with the imprimatur of the highest French society. Thanks to Astruc, Diaghilev's lyric theater, including his secessionist ballet, reaped the aura and audiences of the most distinguished musical enterprises of prewar Paris.

Notwithstanding the success of his exhibition of Russian art at the Salon d'Automne in 1906, Diaghilev was a newcomer to Paris. His meeting with Astruc was therefore all the more providential. Guided by this colorful, driving, thoroughly knowledgeable Parisian, the *barin* from Russia gained entree to the prestigious circles of the *haute bourgeoisie* that provided both financial support for his enterprise and the core of his French audience.

In 1909 Diaghilev secured the backing for his first dance season from intimates of the Greffuhles in banking and diplomatic circles. More precisely, Astruc secured this backing for Diaghilev, approaching not only Arthur Raffalovich and André Bénac, key figures, it will be recalled, in the controversial French loan of 1906, but also Nicolas de Bénardaky, Count Nostitz, Basil Zaharoff, and Michael I. Tereshchenko, who occupied positions of prominence in France's Russian community.[7]

More crucial to Diaghilev's enterprise, however, was a second group of investors approached by Astruc in the spring of 1909. French by birth and nationality, this group was mostly Jewish in origin and connections. It included the most distinguished names in Jewish banking circles and many of the era's outstanding patrons, collectors, and artistic dilettantes; by marriage it embraced "regilded" aristocrats who had bartered their threadbare titles for a fortune. There is more than a touch of irony in the outpouring of Jewish wealth and Jewish support for an enterprise aimed at restoring the prestige of a regime so notoriously anti-Semitic as the Russia of Nicholas II.

Astruc's notes listing possible sources for raising the Fr. 100,000 guarantee capital for Diaghilev's 1909 season amply document these overlapping interests. High on his list are bankers and financiers with a passion for the arts: Baron Henri de Rothschild, who wrote plays under the nom de plume of André Pascal; Camondo, who composed as well as collected and presided over the Society of Friends of the Paris Opéra; Otto Kahn, a partner of Goldschmidt, Kahn, and Teutsch and chairman of the board of the Metropolitan Opera; Henri Deutsch de la Meurthe, an international oil magnate and composer (*Icare*, staged at the Paris Opéra in 1912, reflected his passion for aviation), who, like Camondo, had received religious instruction from Astruc's father. Other names are equally revealing. Bardac, Heine, Ganay, Clermont-Tonnerre, Leonino, and Lyon were all prominent names in the arts with links to leading Jewish families and fortunes.[8]

In compiling his list of would-be guarantors of Diaghilev's first ballet season, Astruc called on financial "angels" of long standing. His friendship with both Camondo and Deutsch de la Meurthe dated to childhood. Their names, along with those of Max Lyon and Arthur Raffalovich, appear time and again among subscribers to Astruc's various enterprises.[9] Surely, it was as partisans of Astruc and his cosmopolitan arts programming that they subscribed to Diaghilev's 1909 *saison russe*.

Like his initial backers, the core of Diaghilev's ballet public lay in the *haute bourgeoisie* that supported his own and Astruc's musical undertakings. Thanks to the booking lists (*feuilles de location*) surviving in the Archives Nationales for all seven performances of Diaghilev's 1908 production of *Boris Godunov* at the Paris Opéra, the configuration of this basic audience can now be established.[10] These documents, which indicate the occupants of boxes, loges, and orchestra seats, confirm Diaghilev's overwhelming success in appropriating the serious French musical audience for the Ballets Russes. They also reveal that his public was not primarily an aristocratic one, despite the Proustian-sounding titles reported in the society columns of *Figaro*. Rather, Diaghilev's audience was an amalgam of financiers, bankers, and diplomats, members of the city's foreign and Franco-Jewish communities, and personalities from the worlds of fashion, music, entertainment, and the press.

Prominent among the boxholders was Misia Sert, Diaghilev's future partisan and confidante, who as Madame Edwards attended all seven performances of *Boris*. Russian-born and Paris-raised, this warm, witty, and well-connected Pole epitomized the social, artistic, and financial interests that merged in Diaghilev's audience. A concert pianist *manqué*, she had played for Liszt and studied with Fauré: throughout her life, music remained an enduring passion. For painters, she was a Muse, her face, piano, garden, and voluptuousness enshrined in magnificent canvases by Bonnard, Vuillard, Renoir, and Toulouse-Lautrec. Marriage to Thadée Natanson, son of a Polish-Jewish banker and founder of *La Revue Blanche*, brought her into the artistic and intellectual circles of fin-de-siècle Paris. Through her second husband, Turkish-born railroad magnate Alfred Edwards, who counted the Paris daily *Le Matin* and the Casino de Paris among his holdings, she rubbed shoulders with actresses and demimondaines and the city's racier celebrities. Her brother Cipa Godebski was equally remarkable. Over the years the intimates of his salon included Maurice Ravel, André Gide, Arnold Bennett, Igor Stravinsky, Francis Poulenc, and Paul Valéry. *Boris*, Misia wrote in her memoirs, stirred her "to the point of realizing that something had changed in her life."[11] In the next twenty-one years she stood at Diaghilev's side, a sister, confidante, and adviser, bringing to ballet the passionate commitment and web of connections she had previously reserved for other arts.

Another loyal Diaghilev partisan who attended nearly every performance of *Boris* was the Princesse Edmond de Polignac. Born Winnaretta Singer, this daughter of the American sewing machine inventor, like so many foreign heiresses, had used her fortune to marry into the cash-poor French aristocracy. Even more than Misia, "Tante Winnie," as the Princesse was familiarly styled, devoted her life to art. A Wagnerian who had traveled again and again to Bayreuth in the late 1880s and 1890s, she remained, until World War II, the foremost musical hostess of Paris. In her salon rarely performed antiquities and new compositions, including a number of Diaghilev ballet scores, received a hearing before a socially and artistically influential public. At the time of Diaghilev's earliest seasons, the fin de siècle echoed in many of her entertainments. At one, which Proust attended as a guest, her garden became the setting for a multimedia tribute to Beardsley. Others featured compositions by Camille Saint-Saëns, Gabriel Fauré, Claude Debussy, and Reynaldo Hahn. But she was more than a hostess. The commissions she awarded to Manuel de Falla and Stravinsky showed her to be a patron of generosity and understanding, the very qualities she brought to her support of the Ballets Russes. Indeed, it was at the home of this loyal enthusiast, a patron of the *Boris* season, that Astruc broached the question of a ballet venture to Diaghilev's Imperial patron, Grand Duke Vladimir.[12]

The *feuilles de location* document other links in the chain of financial and cultural interests that meshed in Diaghilev's audience. Like Deutsch de la Meurthe, Camondo, Bardac, and Rothschild, Ephrussi is another name that appears repeatedly among the list of *Boris* boxholders, and it, too, traced that exemplary progress through the social and cultural history of the Belle Epoque that led so many to the Ballets Russes. The Odessa-born son of a Jewish banker, Charles Ephrussi came to Paris in 1871, making a name for himself as an art collector and editor of the *Gazette des Beaux Arts*. He belonged to the Proustian world of the fin de siècle. A friend of Comte Robert de Montesquiou and an intimate of the latter's cousin Comtesse Greffuhle, he was one of Proust's originals for Swann in *Remembrance of Things Past*. Charles was not the only Ephrussi to make pilgrimage to Bayreuth, nor was he the sole musical patron of the clan. His son Maurice gave lavish receptions at which the foremost divas—and in June 1909 two of Diaghilev's singers—entertained. Maurice and his wife, who was born a Rothschild, became ardent balletomanes, inviting Nijinsky and Karsavina to dance at their parties. As was the case with Misia Sert, the

Princesse de Polignac, and most of the stalwarts of Diaghilev's audience, the Ephrussis made the transition to ballet from an initial devotion to opera.[13]

Music, however, was not the only point of contact between Diaghilev's Ballets Russes and Europe's great Jewish clans. In the person of Ida Rubinstein, kinship cemented ties of art. Through the Varshavskys, a Russian-Jewish family of railroad builders, the wealthy, cultured androgyne of *Cléopâtre* and *Schéhérazade* was related to the era's "Jewesses of Art." Rubinstein had two aunts in Paris, Marie Kann and Julia Cahen d'Anvers, and both had glittering artistic salons famous for their wits, socialites, and literati with a passion for novelty in music and art. Julia's husband, an ennobled financier who had made his fortune in the early years of the Third Republic, gloried in *Boris*, to judge from the frequency with which his name appears on the Opéra booking lists. Earlier, both he and his wife had reveled in Wagner at Bayreuth. In the following years the clan gave its patronage to the Ballets Russes, as did the city's other Jewish *salonnières*.[14]

These families are only a few of the names belonging to the international banking aristocracy that patronized the first of Diaghilev's theatrical rituals. Mostly German-Jewish in origin, families like Bischoffsheim, Gunzburg, Oppenheim, Natanson, Lippmann, Schiff, Fould, Lazard, Reinach, Erlanger, Hirsch, Stern, Gugenheim, Pelletier, Haas, Ulmann, Bernheim, and Pourtalès, had risen to social and financial prominence in the tolerant religious climate of the Second Empire and early years of the Third Republic. They had intermarried, formed business and family alliances with the Rothschilds and other financial clans, and by the closing decades of the century had begun to marry into *le gratin*, the upper crust of French society. From the 1880s onward this group played a key role in French cultural life as patrons, collectors, *salonnières*, artistic dilettantes, and supporters of innovative artistic trends.[15] Here, in a nutshell was *le tout Paris* mined by Astruc for Diaghilev's audience.

For artists *le tout Paris* represented a liberal source of patronage, an alternative to the institutions of France's official, subsidized culture. Its salons were not merely brilliant, but in contrast to the conservatism of general public taste, broadminded and receptive to new ideas. "They . . . helped to create a new society of talents in which the painter, the scientist, the philosopher, the politician, the novelist and the musician could meet on equal terms in a sympathetic atmosphere and into which newcomers might make their way."[16] The *salonnières* of the Belle Epoque generously supported artists, taking them into their homes for long periods, encouraging their work, and introducing them to potential buyers or patrons. In the performing arts, especially, salons held the key to success, acting as way stations on the road to a professional career. Isadora Duncan's rise to stardom illustrates their influence. Arriving in Paris in 1900, she made friends with Jacques Baugnies, whose mother, Madame de Saint-Marceaux, invited her to perform at a soiree, with no less an accompanist than Ravel. The audience was "appreciative," and as a result Comtesse Greffuhle and Madeleine Lemaire invited her to dance at their homes. Although these performances established Duncan's reputation among a select society public, she had yet to achieve general acclaim. At this point the Princesse de Polignac stepped into the breach, opening the doors of her home to influential theatergoers, critics, and producers. The hugely successful concert was followed by a subscription series, organized with the Princesse's assistance, at the Duncan studio. Professional engagements soon followed.[17]

Duncan's story was not unique. Mata Hari, too, danced at the salons of the rich and well connected before making her public debut at the Musée Guimet in 1905, as did Marie Rambert and Natalia Trouhanova. In both 1907 and 1908 friendly *salonnières* were pressed into Diaghilev's service. At Princesse Murat's reception honoring Grand Dukes Cyril and Paul, high musical society heard Camille Bellaigue lecture on *Boris Godunov* a week before the opera's premiere; a few days later, Madame de Bénardaky introduced leading *Boris* singers to the diplomatic community. Performances such as these created more than a flurry of publicity represented by a notice in the *Figaro* society columns. They conjured into being a miniature public even before the debut of a new performer or the premiere of a new work, oiling the rumor mills of society that far more than reviews brought the cultured sophisticates of *le tout Paris* to the theater. And when such performances occurred at the end of seasons, as did two exceptionally brilliant fêtes given by Madame de Bénardaky in 1907 and 1908 (the later event even included an appearance by Mathilde Kchessinska), they conferred a society seal of approval on individuals and the larger artistic enterprise of which they were part.[18]

If the art encouraged by these salons was "new," it was rarely avant-garde. Rather, it stood at a social and artistic midpoint between the academic culture of France's subsidized institutions and undertakings of purely commercial intent. Progressive by contrast with the subsidized product, this "new" art represented something akin to an "alternative mainstream," where technical innovation and an ethos of cosmopolitan individualism might be integrated into the traditional purposes of high art.

By profession, inclination, and religion, Astruc stood at the business hub of this "alternative mainstream," which, through his numerous ventures, he actively promoted. Thus, it comes as no surprise to find among the bankers and financiers in the *Boris* audience a generous sprinkling of individuals and institutions associated with modern trends in music. The composers alone form an impressive list: Debussy, Ravel, Fauré, Vincent d'Indy, Paul Dukas, Albert Roussel, Edouard Kann, Georges Hüe, several of whom had attended the reception organized the previous year by Saint-Saëns in honor of Russia's visiting artists.[19] Debussy, Fauré, d'Indy, and Dukas also sat on the *Boris* patronage committee, as did Camille Chevillard, the Slavophile director of the Concerts Lamoureux who conducted one of Diaghilev's 1907 concerts; Paul Vidal, the Opéra's principal conductor; composer André Messager and L. Broussan, the Opéra's newly-appointed codirectors; and M.D. Calvocoressi, Diaghilev's assistant and the French biographer of Mussorgsky. *Boris* drew powerful impresarios to the theater as well: Otto Kahn, who brought the Ballets Russes to the United States in 1916–1917; Emile and Vincent Isola, who presented it in Paris in the 1920s; Raoul Gunsbourg, who sponsored its debut in Monte Carlo. At every performance, moreover, multiple bookings were taken by firms that controlled the music business: Durand, the publishing company that handled Saint-Saëns, Debussy, Fauré, Ravel, and numerous other French composers; Gaveau, the French piano-making firm that opened the prestigious concert hall that bears its name; and Pleyel, Gaveau's manufacturing rival.

No less important than the makers and purveyors of music were the critics who sat in Diaghilev's audience. Although scarcely unknown, Russian music in Paris before 1907 was a cognoscente taste, restricted to patrons of the Concerts Colonne and Lamoureux and those like Ravel with entree to the few salons where lieder and keyboard snippets were performed. In bringing large-scale Russian masterworks and, especially, the little known dramatic repertory before a broad, influential public—Diaghilev's momentous accomplishment of 1907–1909—critics played a key role both as publicists and reviewers.

In 1906 *Figaro* music critic Robert Brussel wrote his first Diaghilev notice, a glowing account of the Russian concert given in tandem with the exhibition at the Grand Palais. Three months later from St. Petersburg, the future ballet enthusiast datelined the first installment of an eight-part series that traced the history of Russian music from its popular and ecclesiastic origins to the triumphant nationalism of the "Five." With the final article appearing a fortnight before Diaghilev's first concert, the series not only alerted *Figaro*'s readership to the "stars" of the coming season (Glinka, Tchaikovsky, and Rimsky-Korsakov, in particular), but lent the overall enterprise an air of artistic importance.[20]

As Brussel lobbied social tastemakers, others readied the intelligentsia. Among these were Calvocoressi, whose monographs on Russian music in *Le Correspondent* and *Mercure de France* appeared only days before Diaghilev's 1907 and 1909 opening events, and critic Pierre Laloy, who wrote at length on Mussorgsky and Borodin for *La Grande Revue.* Such articles did more than acquaint the general public with an unfamiliar body of work. Because of the place of their publication and the stature of their authors, they conferred intellectual standing on their subject, a standing the Ballets Russes would soon inherit. Apart from specialist critics, *Boris* also drew to the theater that larger Parisian brotherhood of men of letters. Like their musical counterparts, Jacques Rivière, future editor of the *Nouvelle Revue Française,* novelist/journalist Abel Hermant, and poet Jean-Louis Vaudoyer would subsequently write, comment upon, and collaborate with the Ballets Russes. Along with bodies, music brought the company intellectual respectability.[21]

In its fin-de-siècle avatar, *le tout Paris* was a meeting ground for bankers and aristocrats sharing a common interest in the arts. It also included many first- and second-generation Jews who found in its relatively tolerant atmosphere an outlet for their cultural aspirations and a means of assimilating into French high society. In noting Bakst's death for the *Dial* in June 1925, novelist Paul Morand suggested that the designer's Jewishness held the key to the "great Israelite audiences that established the success of the Russian Ballet."[22] ("Catholic" painter and art critic Maurice Denis made a similar "racial" connection in a 1910 journal entry: "Saison russe: les ballets juifs.")[23] Jews did, indeed, champion the Ballets Russes, but they supported with equal fervor the production of *Boris Godunov* that anticipated by nearly a year Bakst's triumphant acclaim with *Cléopâtre.* They came to Diaghilev's seasons, not as Jews, but as patrons, music lovers, and an integral part of the era's *tout Paris.* Nor were they alone. Other groups shared the social and aesthetic values that guided the Jews of Paris to Diaghilev's audience. As a means of social mobility, an affirmation of cosmopolitan identity, and gesture of support for artistic innovation, identification with the Russian "movement" in art expressed the bourgeois aspirations that had crystallized in the formation of *le tout Paris.*[24]

In *Remembrance of Things Past,* Marcel Proust, who himself embodied the many worlds that met in Diaghilev's audience, found a logical connection in Madame Verdurin's evolution from a Dreyfusard hostess to a champion of the Russian dancers:

> Just as she had been seen by the side of Mme. Zola . . . during the trial in the Assize Court, so when the new generation of humanity, in their enthusiasm for the Russian ballet, thronged to the Opera, crowned with the latest novelty in aigrettes, they invariably saw in a stage box Mme. Verdurin by the side of Princess Yourbeletief. And just as, after the emotions of the law courts, people used to go in the evening to Mme. Verdurin . . . so now, little inclined

for sleep after the enthusiasm aroused by the *Scheherazade* or *Prince Igor,* they repaired to Mme. Verdurin's, where . . . an exquisite supper brought together every night the dancers . . . their director, their designers, the great composers Igor Stravinski and Richard Strauss, a permanent little nucleus, around which . . . the greatest ladies in Paris were not too proud to gather.[25]

Wealthy foreigners added a distinctive note to this cosmopolitan milieu. By the late nineteenth century Americans like the Princesse de Polignac and her sister the Duchesse Decazes (*née* Isabelle Singer), Comtesse Boni de Castellane (*née* Anna Gould, the railroad heiress), and Princesse Joseph de Caraman-Chimay (*née* Clara Ward of Detroit) had penetrated the barriers of the French aristocracy, restoring with their millions its threadbare facade. Other English-speaking millionaires like Mrs. Bertha Potter Palmer, the Chicago biscuit manufacturer's wife, W. K. Vanderbilt, a New York railroad magnate, and James Hennessy of champagne and cognac fame, took to spending long periods in Paris, where they frequented such glamorous events as *Boris,* high points of the city's *grande saison.* This Anglo-Saxon presence, which came at a time of intense Anglophilia among the Parisian upper classes, was not the only national strain embellishing *le tout Paris.* In the decades immediately preceding World War I, the French capital became an international pleasure ground, the haunt of Argentine playboys and Indian rajahs, and a mecca for nobilities from Europe's southern and eastern periphery. All these cosmopolitans entered the lore of their adopted city, just as they left a mark on Diaghilev's early audiences.

For a work so intensely Russian, the ardent support of the city's Polish colony seems at odds with patriotic fervor. Little love was lost between the Godebskis, Potockis, and Czartoryskis, Polish nationalist families long resident in France, and the Russian colossus occupying their homeland. (Count Nicholas Potocki, doyen of the Polish aristocratic community, came to Paris via his parents' Siberian exile, punishment for their role in Poland's uprising of 1863.)[26] For the Poles, however, Mussorgsky transcended politics: his work sprang from the Slavic East, that cauldron of festering nationalism. This "Eastern" note struck a familiar chord among others than the Poles and Jews of Diaghilev's audience. *Boris* drew Brancovans and Bibescos, the foremost Rumanian clans of Paris, erstwhile devotees of Wagner who, like Comtesse Anna de Noailles's mother, championed Rumanian musical talent in their salons. (The daughter, for her part, served on Diaghilev's 1910 committee, along with Count Nicholas Potocki.)[27] In the stateless cosmopolitans who figured so prominently in Diaghilev's public, one finds an analogue to the supranationalist sensibility of his exotic fare.

These slightly *déclassé* aristocrats turned out in force for *Boris,* as they would in subsequent years for the ballet. For them, as for the other wealthy foreigners in the audience, the exoticism and social cachet of Diaghilev's productions mirrored the ambiguities of their own position, the assimilationist aspirations and distinctive tastes that set them apart from the upper-class French mainstream. At the same time *Boris,* like the greater part of Diaghilev's early ballet repertory, presented a "racial" and even political counterpoint to Wagnerism. As Bayreuth became increasingly identified with the extremist ideology of propagandists like Houston Stewart Chamberlain,[28] Diaghilev's annual *Festspiele* celebrated within the context of Latin "cosmopolitanism" the Slavic and "oriental" legacy of the non-Teutonic East.

The ethnic, national, and cultural interests of Astruc's brilliantly fabricated audience made it particularly susceptible to both the exoticism and musical sophistication of Diaghilev's earliest dance productions. Not only did the move from opera to ballet demand relatively minor artistic shuffling, but exoticism—or more properly speaking, orientalism—was a thread woven into the high and popular art of the fin de siècle even if theatrical fashion and design awaited the inspiration of Bakst, Golovin, and Roerich to discover it. The late nineteenth century witnessed a resurgence of interest in Far Eastern art with entrepreneurs such as Camondo, Henri Cernuschi, and Emile Guimet amassing great collections of Chinese, Japanese, and Indian antiquities.[29] Notwithstanding the influence of *japonisme* on painters and decorative designers, the substance of French orientalism derived from the ancient Biblical and Islamic lands that stretched from north Africa to Iran, following the course of French imperialism. Beginning in mid-century, writers, painters, and interior designers found in these new spheres of European influence a rich vein of exotica that provided both motifs and thematic material for their work. With the dawn of the new century, orientalism made its appearance in dance, thanks in large part to occidental foreigners on the French stage who extended the familiar pale of exotica eastward to India. The most famous—or infamous—of these performers was Mata Hari (alias Margaretha Zelle MacLeod) who made her Paris debut at the Musée Guimet of Asiatic Arts in 1905 and subsequently appeared as Salomé and Cleopatra on the international opera house circuit. Her spectacular success (a horseback performance au naturel before a Sapphist gathering attended by Colette is legendary) induced other "Hindu" dancers to try their luck in the French capital. Among these was Ruth St. Denis, whose engagement at the Théâtre Marigny in the autumn of 1906 led one critic to compare her "sinister" *Cobra* dance to Baudelaire's "poison." Meanwhile, at the Olympia Theater a rival "danseuse hindique" entertained audiences with an imitation of Miss Ruth's *Radha* ballet.[30]

Despite the widespread interest in orientalia, the fashionable craze for "oriental" color and costume on the eve of World War I dated from Diaghilev's first ballet performances. Almost overnight, the highly coloristic and sensual vein of orientalism identified with the Ballets Russes became decorative and fashion commodities. "The taste for oriental art came to Paris as a Russian import, through ballet, music, and decoration," commented *Figaro* in 1913. "Russian artists have acted as intermediaries between the East and us, and they have given us a rather greater taste for oriental color than a taste for their own art."[31]

In subtle ways the audience that followed Diaghilev through the by-ways of Ballets Russes orientalia shifted the aesthetic emphasis of the company's repertory, narrowing, by virtue of its taste, the field of artistic possibilities. Exoticism wove a vivid thread in Fokine's early work, but it was only one of several coloring his imagination. Hellenism and neoromanticism were equally vivid, and in the ballets conceived outside Diaghilev's purview, these other themes and styles held their ground. Paris, however, remained cool to them. What thrilled Diaghilev's audience was the exoticism of *Cléopâtre*, *Schéhérazade*, and *Firebird*, whose visual opulence, luxurious costuming, and flamboyant effects mirrored, as Paul Morand later observed, "the boldness of the audience's dress, its immodesties, extravagant coiffures, depilated bodies, cosmetics."[32] Such opulence had been second only to music in the impression created by *Boris*, and it remained the single most important production value up to the war. The proliferation of orientalia on Diaghilev's stage between 1909 and 1914 is more than a sign of Fokine's spent imagination. Rather, it betrayed a willingness on Diaghilev's part to cater to the tastes of his public and transform a genre of limited possibilities into a commercially exploitable formula. As early as 1910 the charge of pandering to the demands of a sensation-seeking Paris audience was raised in the St. Petersburg press by Vladimir Telyakovsky, Director of the Imperial Theaters.[33] Although scarcely an unbiased source, given the history of his relations with Diaghilev and the inevitable competition between the latter's seasons and the Imperial Ballet, Telyakovsky's barbed remarks underscore a central paradox of artistic endeavor in the marketplace. For if removal of institutional constraints opens the field of artistic choices, the loss of financial security imposes its own set of imperatives.

In the *Nouvelle Revue Française*, Henri Ghéon echoed Telyakovsky's criticism, although he ascribed the cause to snobbery. The latter had made the success of the Ballets Russes, he asserted; now (the year is 1911) a work like *Narcisse* simply exploited the snob's uncritical adulation of the star ingredients of Diaghilev's formula:

> Over Tcherepnine's mediocre music [the snob] willingly passes; enough for him that the decor is signed by Bakst and is, moreover, splendid, that the swarming little green fauns amuse him, and that Nijinsky is the center. For Nijinsky the dancer is his idol, the object of a cult that in another era he would have dedicated to the *première danseuse* of the Paris Opéra . . . Once again, ballet becomes a pretext to give importance to a "star"; without sufficient dramatic or poetic motive, without unity, it resembles the incoherent divertissements of the National Academy of Music. That the Russians have lost sight of their initial goal—the transposition of action into spectacle—is of no concern to our snob. But why seek to please him, when he is ready to take pleasure in everything, even the beautiful?[34]

Commercialization of artists and key repertory trends was not the only sphere where *le tout Paris* made its presence felt. Diaghilev's first Western collaborative choices also reflected its influence, dramatizing the role of salons in setting artistic fashion. As early as the summer of 1909 Diaghilev approached Debussy, Fauré, and Ravel in the hope of securing their collaboration.[35] Although Fauré declined, pleading other commitments, and Debussy's ballet *Masques et Bergamasques* never materialized, both the timing of Diaghilev's pourparlers and the list of proposed collaborators reveal how quickly he had taken the pulse of Parisian life. Fauré, Ravel, and Debussy certainly figured among the era's leading musical lights. But unlike Satie, shuttling from suburban Auteuil to the studios and cafes of Montmartre, all three were reigning favorites of salons. Debussy's wife Emma Bardac, who had divorced a Jewish financier to marry the composer, was a prominent musical hostess. Ravel was the "lion" of Cipa Godebski's salon, while Fauré, who had once taught socialites like Misia Sert, counted sundry princesses among his patrons.

No work revealed salon influence quite so transparently as *Le Dieu Bleu,* which teamed composer Reynaldo Hahn with librettists Frédéric de Madrazo and Jean Cocteau, the reigning "prince frivole" of fashionable life. "Diaghilev needed [Hahn]," Stravinsky later wrote, "and therefore staged his Dieu Bleu; he was the salon idol of Paris, and salon support was very useful to Diaghilev at that time. After the war, however, Diaghilev dropped him for the very reason that he had once found him important—his salon reputation."[36] Indeed, Hahn traveled in very high circles. Grand Duke Paul and Princess Paley took him up, and at their home, where Diaghilev and the Princesse de Polignac regularly dined, he often entertained. "Tante Winnie" also opened her doors to him, as did the Otto

Kahns, Mrs. Potter Palmer, and Comtesse de Trédern, while Madeleine Lemaire, a watercolorist better known for her huge "crushes," invited him to lecture at her "University of Arts." These engagements bore professional fruit. His *Le Bal de Béatrice d'Este,* given in April 1907 at the Princesse de Polignac's, received a public performance the following month; less than three years later, the Paris Opéra mounted his *La Fête chez Thérèse,* a ballet evoking the romantic era that had a libretto by Catulle Mendès. Jewish like his intimate Proust, Hahn was a musical conservative, a "Mozartian classicist" who showed in the "delicate, traditional refinement" of his compositions his "indifference to innovators such as Fauré and Debussy, and his antipathy to Wagner." Known as "Coco" to his friends, Madrazo was another salon favorite, a dilettante who "composed a little and sang a little, both very badly, and painted, rather better a good deal."[37] Like Hahn, to whom he was related, Madrazo was a wealthy South American and a friend of Proust, who used him as one of the originals for the sculptor Ski, his novel's dabbler in all the arts. At a time when cubists and fauves were redrawing the landscape of modern art, Diaghilev plucked his collaborators from the Proustian world of the 1890s.

Diaghilev's imaginative reworking of Art Nouveau and especially the designs of Bakst drew many artists to performances. But like the Ballets Russes itself, the painters, photographers, and illustrators most closely associated with the company moved in the privileged world of Diaghilev's patrons and collaborators. If Rodin's bearded figure cast a spell of national genius over the theater, minor players in the era's artistic chronicle set the prevailing tone: Baron de Meyer, the photographer par excellence of high society; cartoonist Georges Coursat, who as Sem caricatured events and personalities of *le tout Paris* for *Figaro;* fashion illustrators George Barbier, Paul Iribe (who doubled as an interior decorator), Georges Lepape, and Erté; Cocteau, the salon darling who so wickedly chronicled Diaghilev's inner court, and his friend Valentine (Gross) Hugo, an up-and-coming illustrator; Jacques-Emile Blanche, the "smartest artist of his day, who painted in and dined out only at the most fashionable houses," as Janet Flanner slyly described the Belle Epoque's favorite portraitist.[38] These were the artists Diaghilev esteemed, and it was through their eyes that the characteristic images of his prewar performers and art works were filtered. Writing in the Christmas 1920 issue of the fashion magazine *Femina,* Barbier recalled the "new thrill" that swept the first-night audience before "those chords at once sumptuous and sharp, where marigold yellows and nasturtium reds sang among Prussian blues and Veronese greens."[39] His prose, as colorful as the scene he invokes, locates Diaghilev's newness within the fin-de-siècle context of symbolism, a symbolism prolonged by the Ballets Russes and redefined as an aesthetic of decorative luxury. The presence of such artists in the theater, like the visual record of their impressions, linked the Ballets Russes with a retrograde aesthetic nestling in the bosom of high society.

This image suggests the reasons for one of the most puzzling phenomena of these years: the almost total absence of the avant-garde at Diaghilev's repasts. Only Henri Matisse and Fernand Léger seem to have made appearances at the theater, and in the case of the first one suspects these visits had rather more to do with Sergei Shchukin, the great Moscow patron for whom Matisse was completing his murals of "Music" and "The Dance," than a fascination with Diaghilev's art.[40] Otherwise, none of the host of talents employed by Diaghilev and his competitors in the 1920s seems to have ventured to the fashionable halls of the Ballets Russes. (Or if they did, none seem to have bothered to record their impressions.) Only in 1914, the year of Léger's cubo-futurist "Exit the Ballets Russes," does Apollinaire even allude to the Ballets Russes, and tellingly, he does so in anticipation of *Le Coq d'Or,* the first of Diaghilev's ballets to employ a designer from the avant-garde. "Far from aping the ways of the public and people in high places toward young French painters, the Russians . . . have made Mme. Goncharova a real success . . . And so it is that Russian futurism will display all its pomp at the Opéra, while the new French painting . . . still meets only mockery here." (Elsewhere the same week, however, Apollinaire referred to two ballets commissioned from his friend, composer Alberto Savinio, by "Monsieur Fokine himself . . . that will probably be performed in one of the future Russian seasons.")[41] One also suspects that to artists who shunned society the opulence of Diaghilev's audience proved as disturbing as its philistinism. "There was the evening we went to see Nijinsky in the Russian Ballet," recalled American writer John Cournos who visited Paris with his fiancée in 1912. "After the marvelous performance that left me intoxicated and exultant, I became suddenly aware, without a word being said, of Dorothy's thoughts as she scrutinized the well-dressed, well-to-do, self-assured men and handsome modishly attired women issuing from the ground-floor tiers and boxes . . . and a pall settled on my exuberantly happy mood."[42]

Fashion was indeed a keynote of Diaghilev's public, as it would remain throughout his company's life. Always in his audience sat key purveyors of the glamorous lifestyle of his successive elites. Like the Belle Epoque tastemakers they gowned, the *grands couturiers* who went to *Boris* belonged to an era drawing rapidly to a close. Clustered along and just off the Rue de la Paix, the "Sacred Street" of fashion running from the Opéra to the Comédie Française, establishments like Doucet, Caron, and Worth were slowly yielding power to the less staid houses moving westward toward the Champs-Elysées.

Typical of this newer element among Diaghilev's audience was couturier Paul Poiret, whose name, with Bakst's, invokes the "oriental" invasion in women's dress before the war and whose meteoric rise to fashion stardom paralleled that of the Ballets Russes. Like Diaghilev, Poiret was a master of packaging, a marketing wizard who combined artistic flair with business acumen. He was the first couturier to develop subsidiary product lines and market them internationally, and the first to advertise his styles in limited edition publications.[43] At his lavish costume balls, celebrities of the demimonde mingled with personalities drawn from the financial and artistic elite. Like his marketing techniques, Poiret's "audiences" foreshadowed important changes in the Ballets Russes.

The first modern couturier to become a social celebrity, Poiret was also the first to design regularly for the stage. Other houses, including Doucet, where Poiret received his start, had previously "dressed" theater personalities, thus lending costume a touch of high-fashion elegance and the creations of less well-known designers the cachet of theatrical exposure. Poiret, however, extended the couturier's traditional role to include not only full-scale productions but, in a major break with the past, the supervision of decor and overall visual effect. Almost always, his designs mirrored the exotic opulence of the ballet stage: *Nabuchodonozor* was Assyrian in inspiration, *Aphrodite* Egyptian, *Eightpence a Mile* Persian.[44] Commercial undertakings of this kind not only popularized Poiret's own fashion signature; equally, they marketed the decorative aesthetic of the Ballets Russes.

Poiret's shuttling between theater and couture suggests the blurring of traditional distinctions between style and stage. Advertisements for a "Parfum Prince Igor" in the official Ballets Russes program for the 1911 season and the tendency of illustrators George Barbier and Paul Iribe to transform Diaghilev's prewar dancers into the eroticized mannequins of exotic fashion plates point to a similar phenomenon. Bakst's secondary career as a dress designer offers still another example of the conflation of categories that ended by fetishizing onstage costume as an object of private consumption for the Ballets Russes audience. Between 1910 and 1914, when color reproductions of his designs dominated company programs and special inserts in *Comoedia Illustré*, Diaghilev's star artist signed his name to a whole range of fashion plates that duplicated the bold colors and patterns, Grecian draperies, and exotic headdresses of his stage creations. During this period as well, he acquired a following among Europe's new-style international celebrities whose taste in clothing was outré rather than refined and who used dress to create a theatrically conceived persona. Tall, green-eyed Marchesa Luisa Casati was the most fascinating and extravagant of these clients. The daughter of a Milanese industrialist, she had married into the Venetian nobility, and between stays in Paris, lived off the Grand Canal at the Palazzo Non Infinito, later the home and museum of Peggy Guggenheim. The Marchesa gave immense parties, orgies of conspicuous consumption, where serpents, panthers, and ocelots—draped around her body or accompanying her—added a bizarre note to her toilette. For Casati, Bakst created numerous costumes for fancy dress and private wear that rivaled in effect the designs for bayadères and odalisques of his exotic ballets.[45] Like Poiret's theatrical and product sidelines, commissions of this kind revealed both the impact of Diaghilev's prewar art on fashion and that of fashion on artistic packaging and promotion. At the same time they illustrated the intersection of ballet with a celebrity-seeking, consumption-minded public.

The *Boris* audience remained the foundation of Diaghilev's Parisian public. But as years went on, the Ballets Russes began to attract other elements as well. Reviewing the 1912 season, critic Louis Laloy described these newcomers to Diaghilev's audience:

> Finally, four consecutive seasons of ballets have brought out the noisy mob of the fashionable public who arrive late, whose chatter serves to drown out the orchestra the moment the curtain has fallen, who know neither the titles of the works nor the names of their creators, but who glory in stuffing with their diamonds and their pearls the hall of the Châtelet which becomes even more sparkling than the Opéra for a few evenings, in spite of its ineffaceable dust and its moldy smell of the stable.[46]

A master publicist, Diaghilev used every means possible to create an artistic and social "splash," pressing salons, newspapers, and embassy contacts into service for *Boris* and his early dance seasons. With each succeeding year, however, the need to surpass previous successes became more urgent. With the formation of a permanent company, it became an economic necessity. Diaghilev now set out to entice the merely fashionable to grand "celebrity" events.

Charity galas and other special performances were among the ways Diaghilev created that aura of social-cum-artistic uniqueness that became his company's trademark. The first *répétition générale* of the 1910 season marked the occasion of an extremely fashionable charity event, although because of a mishap to the scenery en route from Berlin, it had to be canceled.[47] Two weeks later, however, the company gave *The Polovtsian Dances* and *Le Festin* on a gala Opéra program that also included Richard Strauss's *Salomé* (with Mary Garden singing the title role) and a *Coppélia* in which the Opéra's Mlle. Léa Piron *en travesti* partnered Carlotta Zambelli as Swanilda. On July 1 Russians and French again pooled their talents. For this unique event, *Cléopâtre* shared a bill with *Rigoletto* and the ballet divertissement from *Thaïs*.[48] Events of this kind, duly reported in the society columns of *Figaro*, added immeasurably to the cachet of Diaghilev's enterprise.

Open rehearsals were another device calculated to bring fashionable Paris to the theater. In June 1910 *Figaro* carried notices of three *Firebird* rehearsals, reporting the ballet's "most considerable effect" upon the audience and anticipating the work's future success.[49] These "sneak previews" served many purposes. Diaghilev's practice of inviting friendly critics like Robert Brussel and Raoul Brevanne of *Figaro*, Ricciardo Canudo of *Montjoie!*, and Jean-Louis Vaudoyer to observe new works in the final stage of preparation ensured favorably disposed articles up to the day of the actual premiere. (Another way of accomplishing this was to "plant" commissioned texts—like Cocteau's 1911 panegyric "Le Ballet russe"—in influential newspapers and magazines. Here, Astruc's connections proved invaluable.)[50] In addition to creating advance press, rehearsals fueled the gossip mills. Diaghilev distributed vast numbers of free tickets, recalled Stravinsky, to the hand-picked audience of "actors, painters, musicians, writers, and the most cultured representatives of society" that attended his *répétitions générales*. In the case of *Giselle* only 203 of the 1,967 spectators who attended the *répétition générale* actually paid for tickets. With their access to salons, these unofficial publicists sent news of company events rippling among Diaghilev's target audience,[51] while preparing the ground for works that might otherwise have risked financial failure.

Under Diaghilev's aegis, the rehearsal itself became an event where the offstage antics of a celebrity public rivaled those of the dancers onstage. In his journal entry for July 1, 1910, André Gide described one such occasion:

> . . . a month ago, upon the insistent urging of Mme de Noailles and Mme Mühlfeld, I . . . [joined] them in their box at a rehearsal of the Russian Ballet at the Opéra. In my whole life I [have] never felt more numb, more out of place, more mute. Mme de Regnier and her sister-in-law, Henri de Regnier, who was being witty, and Vaudoyer, with a dark and fatal look, were also there . . .
>
> "M. Gide," exclaimed Mme de Regnier, "come and help us calm Mme de Noailles." (The latter was talking so loud and so animatedly that she was attracting the attention of half the audience on the floor.)[52]

Let us identify the poetasters and socialites of whom Gide speaks: Franco-Rumanian Comtesse Anna de Noailles, famed for her languors even more than her verse; journalist Jean-Louis Vaudoyer, who wrote poetic garlands to Karsavina and the libretto of *Le Spectre de la Rose;* Marie de Regnier, daughter of Parnassian poet José María de Heredia, who wrote lackluster poetry under the pseudonym Gérard d'Houville; Madame Mühlfeld, a powerful hostess in whose drawing room congregated everybody who was anybody among critics.[53] This was not the first time society had intruded on Gide's pleasure in ballet. Reviewing Diaghilev's 1909 season for the *Nouvelle Revue Française,* the novelist prefaced his remarks with criticism of the propagandist on whose enthusiasm, social cachet—and pen—Diaghilev relied well into the 1920s:

> In *Figaro* at the end of the month of May, Jacques-Emile Blanche expressed his admiration for the mise-en-scène and decors of the Russian performances offered us at the Châtelet. Doubtless, a little less wonderment would have been revealed in the course of his eloquent article had Monsieur Blanche been acquainted with the efforts in this area by Reinhardt, Martersteig, and Valentin in Berlin, Cologne, Vienna, etc. and their often felicitous results. The Prince Igor backdrop would not have appeared any less admirable, but assuredly the decor for *Pavillon d'Armide* would have.[54]

The conduct of Diaghilev's society following may have disgruntled Gide and enraged Fokine.[55] Diaghilev, however, both condoned and encouraged it, establishing a precedent for audience decorum that foreshadowed the tumultuous reception of Nijinsky's works in 1912 and 1913. The memorable premiere of *Le Sacre du Printemps* again found Madame Mühlfeld in the audience, and when composer Florent Schmitt bellowed, "Down with the sluts of the sixteenth!," she set the tone for high society by uttering loud peals of laughter.[56] Not surprisingly, the artistic and social values of Diaghilev's key Paris audience condemned all but the most innocuous forms of innovation.

With the advent of ballet, another new element was added to the audience, one that sent a whiff of notoriety across the theater. Beginning in 1909 and accelerating as the war approached, the demimonde, that glamorous half-world of courtesans, actresses, rakes, and tabloid journalists, whose amorous intrigues and tragic suicides so fascinated the Belle Epoque, found a place alongside the connoisseurs and collectors of high society. Like actresses, dancers gravitated almost automatically to the demimonde: no amount of artistry could wipe the stigma of low class origins and sexual impropriety from the followers of Terpsichore. With the exception of Rosita Mauri, a former *étoile* teaching at the Opéra school, and Mathilde Kchessinska, St. Petersburg's *prima ballerina assoluta,* dancers had shied from *Boris.* In 1909, by contrast, they occupied a place of honor, with such celebrated personalities on hand as Carlotta Zambelli, the Opéra's reigning *étoile,* Madame Mariquita, ballet mistress of the Opéra-Comique, Isadora Duncan, and Natalia Trouhanova. But Astruc's efforts to introduce a specifically dance element into the audience did not stop with notables. From the Opéra and Comédie Française, he commandeered a "frieze" of "bediamonded" beauties, a *corbeille* of alternating blondes and brunettes, whom he sat in the front of the dress circle. "Never," wrote a susceptible critic, "has a gala hall been more agreeable to contemplate."[57] Nor was this the only means by which Astruc reiterated ballet's traditional association with sexual impropriety. Among the other celebrities in the audience were actresses such as Louise de Mornand and Madeleine Carlier, who doubled offstage as demimondaines.

The popularity of the Ballets Russes among Paris pleasure-seekers also reflected the renaissance of dance as a public social pastime. In 1911 and 1912 the tango invaded fashionable tearooms, "revolutionizing the manners and mores of the salons and the habits of society,"[58] while at chic supper clubs exhibition dancers like Vernon and Irene Castle entertained a cosmopolitan mélange of Argentine millionaires, Russian Grand Dukes, French aristocrats, and New York's "Four Hundred." Among the pleasure-minded habitués of the Café de Paris, the audience for ballet and social dancing overlapped, as it did at the races and across the footlights. But there were other connections as well. At one of Anthony Drexel's parties in London, the Castles shared the limelight with Nijinsky, while at Deauville, the Casino engaged both the star couple and the Ballets Russes to headline the resort's inaugural season. Leaving no stone unturned in its quest for elegance and cachet, the Casino had Gabriel Astruc prepare the guest list for Deauville's official opening.[59]

In private entertaining, too, ballet overlapped with fashions in recreation. In June 1913 the cream of Paris society turned out for the "leçon de danse" organized by Princesse Amédée de Broglie. That same month the Marquise de Ganay, a longtime Diaghilev supporter, gave a brilliant fete that featured lords and titled ladies in a program of "dances of yesteryear." With backgrounds that ranged from Byzantine to Empire (Josephine's rose garden at Malmaison was the setting for a tableau to the music of *Le Spectre de la Rose*), the event was styled a *répétition générale.* Still another entertainment that June drew inspiration from ballet. At Comte Aynard de Chabrillan's, guests in romantic-era tarlatans à la *Les Sylphides* performed a "Fantaisie sur des valses de Schubert" staged by Opéra ballet master Léo Staats.[60] All these events coincided with Diaghilev's most brilliant prewar season.

Isadora Duncan's success, moreover, spawned a host of "interpretative" imitators, who, like the fashionable converts to eurhythmics, added to the heterogeneity of Diaghilev's audience. The dancer Caryathis was among the growing number of Paris teachers who catered to this new clientele of amateurs and the figure-conscious. A former dressmaking apprentice with a studio in Montmartre, she taught an unorthodox blend of eurhythmics and ballet and gave recitals of dances choreographed to Ravel and Satie. In a poster for one such event, Bakst drew a tunic-clad figure weaving Duncanesque movements among serpentine lengths of exotic cloth.[61]

Unlike the painters who were her neighbors, Caryathis did not confine her activities to Montmartre. A part-time demimondaine, she ventured into the limelight of fashionable Paris, and with another "kept" woman, her pupil Gabrielle Chanel, and two of her lovers, attended the premiere of *Sacre*. Caryathis's appearance that night added still another sensation to that sensation-filled occasion: the fringe across her forehead, all that was left of tresses clipped off in a fit of romantic pique, gave Paris its first sight of bobbed hair.[62]

By 1913 Diaghilev had certainly put ballet on the artistic map of fashionable Paris. His mixed dance and opera season that spring at Astruc's recently inaugurated Théâtre des Champs-Elysées was a "stupendous success," with the public, even before the opening gala, "literally [taking] the box office . . . by assault to carry off the last seats." Receipts for the first two ballet nights totaled Frs. 62,000, while takings for the third performance alone exceeded Frs. 100,000, Frs. 35,000 more than the highest figure of Astruc's record-breaking Metropolitan Opera season at the Châtelet in 1910. On the morning of the fourth performance, not a seat was to be had, and on June 11 Astruc announced that seven performances had been added to the season in view of its "enormous success."[63]

Despite the glowing record of triumphs, dance itself remained the least appreciated ingredient of Diaghilev's recipe. Indeed, among the outpouring of press reports and articles, Jacques Rivière's attempts to analyze choreographic form, particularly in his impassioned articles about *Le Sacre du Printemps,* stand out as unique. Critics lavished attention on composers and designers who awoke on the morrow of a premiere to find themselves instant celebrities, while stars like Nijinsky and Karsavina inspired the passion of company devotees. Under the pressure of financial necessity, Diaghilev eschewed the task of educating his Parisian public. Instead, he sought to dazzle and tantalize it, counting on the allure of fashion and scandal to establish a niche for his enterprise on the Parisian firmament.

Diaghilev's early seasons held a special appeal for Slavic, Jewish, and other notables of foreign descent living in the French capital. By 1913, however, this relatively assimilated group was overshadowed as fresh arrivals from abroad crowded Diaghilev's seasons. Not all these foreigners were as sophisticated as Carl Van Vechten, who shared a loge with Gertrude Stein at a performance of *Sacre*. Many critics decried the enormous influx of tourists ("knot-headed foreigners," Roland-Manuel called them), who flocked to the Ballets Russes and other "cosmopolitan spectacles" during the *Grande Saison de Paris*. To this status- and pleasure-seeking public, which descended, as Astruc wrote, "upon our caravansaries, our restaurants, our theaters, and our racetracks" and willingly paid "three times the normal price for the same hotel room, the same mutton chop, the same orchestra stalls which are offered at a saving—but to no avail during the rest of the year,"[64] reviewers sought to lay the blame for the outrageous behavior of the *Sacre* audience.

"A good half of the so-called Parisian audience," wrote Léon Vallas in *La Revue française de musique*:

> is made up of people who are as foreign to France as they are to art, and that more than a quarter of the remainder are socialites who are incapable of being moved by a daring artistic venture. We are constrained to believe that the audience which ordinarily frequented the *théâtres lyriques* and concerts was not heavily represented in the shocking racket that has been heard throughout all the performances of *Le Sacre du Printemps*.[65]

Vallas and his confrères undoubtedly exaggerated the role of foreigners. Certainly, at the premiere, some of the noisiest spectators—Madame Mühlfeld, Comtesse René de Pourtalès, the woman who called Ravel "a dirty Jew"—were French. But critics were right in discerning a connection between the riotous events of 1913 and the changing composition of Diaghilev's audience.

By 1913 the Diaghilev enterprise inevitably prompted thoughts of fashion and scandal, along with artistic daring. A web of similar associations also figured in the public mind about Astruc's Théâtre des Champs-Elysées, which stirred controversy even prior to opening in early 1913. Located on one of the most fashionable triangles of the city's most luxurious quarter, the theater epitomized cosmopolitan opulence. A striking example of the Modern Style in architecture and the first public building in Paris to use reinforced concrete, it drew charges of "industrial rigidity" and foreign—meaning German—influence in its design. To finance his triple theater complex, Astruc set up international patronage committees. He approached the city's foreign communities, flattering wealthy expatriates like Count Nicholas Potocki (who eventually donated Frs. 100,000) with the assurance that contributing to the project would validate their status as Parisians. Astruc's programming also came under fire on nationalist grounds, and he was accused again and again of promoting German, Italian, and Russian art at the expense of the home-grown product. Similar charges had been raised in April 1911, when various theatrical unions threatened to strike in protest of Astruc's engagement of Italian musicians for a "saison russe" at the Théâtre Sarah-Bernhardt that featured Julie Sedova, a Maryinsky ballerina, and Ivan Clustine, a one-time Bolshoi ballet master. The prevailing xenophobia carried racial overtones as well. A caricature of the era depicted Astruc as a long-nosed pasha complete with turban and oversized rings, another as a ticket-salesman-cum-moneychanger.[66]

By 1913 the noisy, untutored mob of fashionable and demimonde Paris had largely overshadowed the musically sophisticated community of Diaghilev's early seasons. That community had been one of connoisseurs bred in the habits of aristocracy, even if they were not bluebloods themselves. The Rothschilds, Camondos, Doucets, Singers, and Reinachs, names enshrined as the "grands donateurs" of the Louvre and Jeu de Paume, allied the collector's instinct with the spirit of the connoisseur. Their superb collections of eighteenth-century and impressionist art found their way not into the marketplace but to the halls of museums.

Diaghilev's newly crystallizing public, by contrast, was one of consumers. The keynote of the connoisseur is disinterested appreciation and taste; that of the consumer "good value." The first seeks beauty; the second judges quality by rarity and price. Indeed, provisions for artistic and social *rarité* were written in 1911 into Diaghilev's contract with the Société des Casinos de Deauville. Here he agreed to stage "a ballet not yet performed in Paris" for the opening season of the fashionable resort in August 1912 and also promised not to accept engagements at any other resort on the Norman coast that summer.[67] Where repetition might offer the connoisseur further occasion for contemplation, for the consumer it merely lessens the value of the original. By 1913 the company's de luxe programs had become collector's items, and as bibliographic rarities, these beautifully illustrated publications were sold independently of performances. With the emergence of the ballet consumer, the props, programs, costumes, designs, and even performances of the Ballets Russes were transformed from objets d'art to articles whose value was determined by their scarcity in the marketplace.

With its high-sounding titles and unexpected connections, Diaghilev's French public certainly makes for lively reading. But antiquarian interest aside, it has an importance that far transcends historical chitchat. The cultivated audience coaxed into being from 1906 to 1914 elucidates two longstanding puzzles. It explains the speed with which the Ballets Russes put down roots in Western Europe and the obsession with exoticism and luxury that became Diaghilev trademarks. That ballet reentered the cultural consciousness of the West via the French upper class is equally a matter of import. The idea of privilege synonymous with the Ballets Russes in its most legendary era remains, even today, branded into the identity of classical dancing.

11 ✎

LONDON: LORDS, LADIES,

AND LITERATI

IT IS WITH A CERTAIN trepidation that one approaches the subject of Diaghilev in England. For here, in the country Diaghilev regarded with mingled condescension and distrust, his company left a mark whose traces are perceptible even today. Nowhere else has the Ballets Russes become a part of the cultural inheritance of so many educated people or inspired so many knowledgeable tomes; in no other country has the company been so mythologized.

Like the art of translation, memory betrays as often as it reveals, reconstructing the past through a prism of later perceptions and experiences. For British memoirists of the early Ballets Russes, this is especially true. Diaghilev's lengthy sojourns in postwar London, together with the revival of interest in the Ballets Russes spurred by Richard Buckle's 1954 Diaghilev Exhibition, inevitably colored memories of the troupe's initial seasons—even those of participants. Consider Marie Rambert's rhapsodic recollection of Diaghilev's Georgian public. "It was not at all the fashionable Covent Garden audience of the Ring, or even the fashionable Drury Lane audience of the autumn melodrama of those days," she wrote after seeing the Diaghilev Exhibition, "but . . . an *intelligentsia* of the theatre, such as assembled in the same years for the *Sumurun* of Max Reinhardt and the best productions of Granville-Barker of the Savoy."[1]

Here, as with so many recollections of the Diaghilev era, contemporary evidence tells a different story. Intellectuals did indeed give their allegiance to the Ballets Russes, but only after the war. Between 1911 and 1914 Diaghilev's public resembled nothing so much as an exclusive club where the British ruling class displayed its brilliant plumage.

Even more so than in Paris, the core of Diaghilev's ballet audience in London came from the city's traditional opera-going public. Of his six prewar seasons, no fewer than four took place at Covent Garden, then as now England's premier musical showplace. Venue, however, only partly explains the distinctive cast of his public. Ironically, the city over which the Ballets Russes exerted its greatest long-term influence failed in the pre-war era to offer a single independent season of this immensely popular attraction. From 1911–1914 Russian ballet appeared on the London stage exclusively within the context of regular opera seasons and even, occasionally, on the same bill with its sister art.[2] With evenings of Russian ballet alternating with programs of German, French, Italian, and Russian opera and subscription plans that covered both lyrical and choreographic events, Diaghilev raised before London's admiring audiences the standard of music drama in yet another of its many contemporary guises.

London's opera-going audience was far from uniform. It encompassed Society, serious music-lovers, and people of modest means, all of whom patronized at least some of Diaghilev's ventures between 1911 and 1914. In launching the Ballets Russes, however, Diaghilev ignored the last two categories of patrons. He swept into the English capital on the crest of an imperial wave that brought royalties, dignitaries, high government officials, and the flower of the nation's peerage to the coronation of George V. At the dazzling gala that formed part of the festivities, his troupe danced its most courtly work, *Le Pavillon d'Armide,* and found its prewar public.

In 1911–1912 the secessionist stood silently by as the *barin* in Diaghilev enlisted the most conservative institution in London to ensure his company's triumph. "I have purposely omitted any mention of the Covent Garden Grand Opera Season," wrote Francis Toye in a 1911 survey of "Opera in England," "because that stands and will always stand apart":

> It is frankly exotic, a flower carefully nurtured to capture the fancy of a few rich people. Without wishing to echo the conventional . . . sneer at the subscribers who regard it mainly as a parade-ground for their best clothes and their most expensive jewels—which is and always has been one of the functions of an Opera House in a metropolis—it were idle to pretend that Covent Garden is primarily concerned with opera as an art. The audience demands first-rate singers, and cares very little what they sing; the Syndicate expects a profit, and cares almost as little how it is earned . . . There the matter ends.[3]

For this Covent Garden audience Puccini was god. Verdi stood high among the angels, Rossini, Leoncavallo, and Wolf-Ferrari in the lesser orders. Their works dominated the repertory in 1911 and 1912, prompting outbursts far less temperate than Toye's measured critique. Henry Hardinge urged Oscar Hammerstein, proprietor of the short-lived, popularly priced London Opera House, "to sweep away the old operas and conventions, above all the horrible old scenery which is one of Covent Garden's most cherished traditions, and . . . lift [your] eyes towards the dawn of that new era for opera which rose with the coming of [Gordon] Craig."[4] It is indeed ironic that the Ballets Russes found its earliest supporters, not among partisans of the "new art" or even Wagner's ardent enthusiasts, but among the tiara-ed admirers of "second-rate Italians."[5]

If critics and highbrows railed at this state of affairs, Society was content with things as they were. "We are often reproached," wrote "The Woman About Town," a *Sketch* society column that regularly noted doings at Covent Garden, "for not being musical, and the Opera people are accused of not giving us new works":

> The Truth is that our Opera is characteristic of ourselves; we do not care to take our musical pleasures too seriously . . . we have works we know which we can enjoy, usually as a respite between social engagements. Occasionally, we have a novelty to discuss and decide upon, by way of a little sensation . . . The Russian ballet came, was seen, conquered, comes again . . . The Opera Syndicate . . . have tried us with new works with great reputations many a time, to their great cost—only a very limited number were approved.[6]

A greater contrast with Diaghilev's novelty-hungry Paris audience can scarcely be imagined.

"Opera and Society function combined," to quote the same columnist, sums up the Diaghilev ballet in its earliest London avatar. Hence, the silence of the era's intellectual journals, scarcely broken until Diaghilev's magnificent productions of Russian opera in 1913–1914, and the equally telling clamor of the society weeklies, which brimmed with details of costume, headdress, and jewelry of ballet boxholders during their sojourns in town for the Season.[7] The aura of privileged frivolity that surrounded the troupe is evoked by other artifacts: the advertisements for Paquin gowns, J. Duvelleroy fans, Madame Rubinstein's Maison de Beauté Valaze, and Austin "Pullman Limousines" in the Coronation season souvenir program;[8] and more prosaically, by the schedule of ticket prices—the highest in London—that kept Diaghilev's repasts from all but the very few.[9]

Fashion, too, reflected the company's welcome by Society. "All nights have been Arabian nights since 'Sumurun' and 'Kismet' came to town," quipped a *Sketch* columnist in 1911, referring to the exotic spectacles that invaded the West End at the time of Diaghilev's first appearances at Covent Garden. From Bakst, however, came the bright new color schemes of fashionable drawing rooms and the turbans that swathed the heads of stylish tastemakers.[10] His *Schéhérazade* inspired the "Arabian Nights Ball" that crowned with "Oriental splendor" the end of Diaghilev's autumn 1911 season and enjoyed the blessing of four of the troupe's most prominent supporters—Mrs. Margot Asquith (the Prime Minister's wife), the Duchess of Sutherland, Mrs. Alfred Lyttelton, and Lady Horner.[11] In its wake a "craze" for fancy-dress extravaganzas swept London, spawning a minor industry in houri garb and fur-trimmed peasant wear and a rash of tableaux vivants evoking ballet themes and opulence. At the 1912 Pantomime Ball, Mrs. Asquith shone in a "Russian Fairy Tale"; for the "Russian Court" pageant at the 1913 "Fête de Versailles," the wife of the British Ambassador sent dresses over from St. Petersburg; society girls like Lady Diana Manners—better known as Diana Cooper—donned ballet shoes and learned to glide like Russian peasants, and found their wide-eyed devotion to Diaghilev spoofed in the intellectual pages of the *English Review*.[12] Yes, fashion guided Diaghilev's star to the center of the theatrical and social firmament.

Privilege, however, has many faces, and in the anonymous throng of turbans and stiff shirt fronts, the analytic eye discerns subtle differences of feature. From society columns, tacked-on paragraphs of reviews noting who attended such-and-such a premiere, published subscription lists, and memoirs emerges a composite portrait of the Diaghilev audience. " 'I've thought of three subjects to talk about,' " chitchats Martin to a society girl in Virginia Woolf's novel *The Years,* " 'Racing; the Russian ballet; and . . . Ireland.' "[13] With disarming brevity, the novelist evokes the preoccupations of Court, Society, and Parliament, those pillars of Britain's Establishment and Diaghilev's Georgian public.

Diaghilev's Paris audience did not lack for titles, but Covent Garden brought royalty to the ballet. Over the years Victoria's far-flung clan of descendants made numerous appearances in the Royal Box, lending a touch of Maryinsky glamor to Diaghilev performances. The visitors, duly noted in the "Court Circular" column of the *Times,* were many: King George, various members of his immediate family, and sundry German, Greek, and Russian cousins. In Queen Alexandra, Princess Henry of Battenberg, Princess Louise Duchess of Argyle, and King Manoel of Portugal, the "Imperial Russian Ballet," as Diaghilev initially styled his company in England, had a following of royal devotees. All, remarked the *Dancing Times,* "are constant visitors at Covent Garden just now," now being winter 1913 when "scarcely a vacant place" was to be had on ballet nights.[14] The recently deposed King Manoel, a familiar figure of the social scene, headed the list of subscribers to Beecham's three seasons of Grand Opera and Russian Ballet in 1913–1914. Other royal subscribers in summer 1913 were the Grand Duke of Mecklenburg-Strelitz and Prince Paul of Serbia, and the following year, Princess Arthur of Connaught and Grand Duke Michael of Russia.[15]

In England's constitutional monarchy, royalty reigned but did not rule.

But the elite that actually governed the country was also heavily represented among Diaghilev's public, constituting a political world that was itself an adjunct of Society. Abroad, as a *Bystander* columnist opined in 1911, "politics is *bourgeois,* middle-class . . . Here politics cannot exist without Society, Society without politics." [16] Over one hundred names turn up on the subscription lists and press reports of Diaghilev events. [17] Many are familiar. Others stir to life only in the telegraphic entries of *Who's Who.* Together, they form a roll call of the elite that over the previous thirty-five years had governed the British polity at home and abroad.

Rarely, in modern times, has the audience for any cultural phenomenon assumed so completely the air of a government club. Even in the heyday of the Kennedy administration, when "eggheads" smiled benevolently on the arts, how many Cabinet members or Congressmen, high-level policymakers or former military heroes spent evening after evening in the company of the Muses? Between 1911 and 1914, by contrast, consider the ministers alone who figured at Diaghilev events: H. H. Asquith, Prime Minister; the Marquess of Ripon, Lord Privy Seal; D. Lloyd George, Chancellor of the Exchequer; Winston Churchill, First Lord of the Admiralty; Walter Runciman, President of the Board of Agriculture; Sir Rufus Isaacs, Attorney-General. [18] (The Earl of Plymouth, Marquess of Londonderry, and A.J. Balfour, meanwhile, represented previous Tory Cabinets.) Ambassadors of the Great Powers and other diplomats lent an equally official air to the assemblage, as did the presence of many other high-ranking officials: the Marquess of Dufferin and Ava, a Senior Foreign Office Clerk; Sir Charles Mathews, Director of Public Prosecutions; Lord Mersey, Commissioner of the Titanic inquiry; Lord Murray, Parliamentary Secretary to the Treasury, Comptroller of His Majesty's Household, and Scottish Liberal Whip. And in names such as Lord Beresford, Major John Brinton, Sir John French, the Earl of Minto, and Sir George Warrender, veterans of Khartoum, India, Turkey, and South Africa, one finds the warriors and administrators of Victoria's Raj. [19]

To be sure, not all Diaghilev's subscribers belonged to such high political circles. A number came from the great banking and manufacturing clans on which late nineteenth-century British financial and industrial might rested. These dynasties—Rothschilds, Barings, Behrens, Coats, Cunards, Speyers, Monds, Neumanns, Petos, Nobles, Sassoons, Schusters, and Sterns—joined by Northcliffe and Astor press barons and entitled American millionairesses, brought an air of trade, a whiff of the City and particularly its small Jewish contingent, to first nights. But it was an aroma already sanitized by the public schools, country seats, and outdoor pursuits that were the essential accouterments of an upper-class lifestyle. And the baronies, titles, and initials appended to the names of descendants of the original empire builders chronicle the passage of these clans from money-making to the genteel professions of politics, law, and the army.

Diaghilev by no means lacked a following among the Unionists, as members of the Conservative Party styled themselves because of their opposition to Irish independence. But, with the move to the Theatre Royal, Drury Lane, in the summer of 1913, the roll call of his first night audiences displayed an increasingly Liberal cast. The rival Covent Garden "Grand Season," by contrast, was a bastion of Conservatism. "In all the three or four hundred names of the first [Covent Garden] list of subscribers," noted the *Sketch* in April 1914, "Lord Crewe and Mr. Walter Runciman are the sole representatives of official Liberalism."[20] As Liberals affirmed their allegiance to the Beecham-Diaghilev enterprise, King and Queen pledged fealty to Covent Garden. By 1914 the royal component of the Diaghilev audience had markedly diminished with only the Princess Royal and Princess Maud, among the sovereign's closest family, venturing to the theater in Drury Lane.[21] As Diaghilev's enterprise, thanks to the publicity surrounding its association with Beecham, assumed more and more the air of a commercial venture, it became, so to speak, a cultural extension of the party of Town, Gown, and Industry.

The guest list for a Downing Street "At Home" given by Mrs. Asquith in 1914[22] reveals the core of this Liberal audience with startling clarity; it was nothing less than a descendant of the social set of the 1880s known as the "Souls." In this grouping of Asquiths, Balfours, Tennants, Churchills, Horners, Trees, Mannerses, Charterises, Lytteltons, Ripons, Grenfells, Rothschilds, and Custs, one discerns the same tangled pattern of friendship, family, and political alliances, the same combination of moral uplift, fashion, and art revealed in Diaghilev's audience. The group had its poet (George Wyndham), and its ladies of culture: Lady de Grey (Marchioness of Ripon), who was devoted to opera; Lady Horner, at whose feet sat Ruskin and Burne-Jones; Lady Granby (Duchess of Rutland), who painted and sculpted; and Lady Tree, who gave after-theater supper parties with an elegant Bohemian touch.[23]

All four ladies subscribed to Beecham's seasons, and at least two of them entertained Diaghilev and his dancers in their homes. Along with Lady Cunard, who indefatigably promoted Beecham and his enterprises ("There appeared to be no limit to the number of boxes she could fill," wrote Osbert Sitwell)[24] from the Cavendish Square home she had leased from Mrs. Asquith, they wove Liberal politics, fashion, aristocracy, and art into the distinctive pattern of Diaghilev's audience. "Soulful" children followed in their mothers' footsteps, and society columns often noted Lady Juliet Duff (daughter of the Marchioness of Ripon), Lady Diana Manners, Lady Marjorie Manners, and Lady Violet Charteris (daughters of the

Duchess of Rutland), Miss Iris Tree and Mrs. Alan Parsons (daughters of Lady Tree), and others at Diaghilev events. The youngsters, known as the "Corrupt Coterie," incorporated into their circle still other Diaghilev familiars—Nancy Cunard and Prince Felix Yusupov, then a student at Oxford. From this group came the brightest of the twenties "Bright Young Things." But like so many who took their pleasure in the Georgian twilight, these young tastemakers showed little interest in the new art coming to life in Kensington or Montmartre. Their taste was geared resolutely to the past. "There was among us," Diana Cooper (née Lady Diana Manners) subsequently wrote, "a reverberation of the *Yellow Book* and Aubrey Beardsley, Ernest Dowson, Baudelaire and Max Beerbohm. Swinburne often got recited. Our pride was to be unafraid of words, unshocked by drink and unashamed of 'decadence'."[25]

The "Souls" were not Diaghilev's only audience link with the fin de siècle. Mrs. Charles Hunter, a favorite Sargent subject and subscriber to all three Beecham seasons, "represented," wrote Osbert Sitwell, "the Edwardian generation, the Edwardian hostess, *in excelsis*." "She belonged," he added, "to the world that . . . 'dined out for art'."[26] Sir Ernest Cassel, Sir Philip Sassoon, and Mrs. George Keppel, all former intimates of Edward VII and Beecham subscribers, evoked the racier side of the 1890s. Diaghilev, Nijinsky, and Karsavina often dined at Mrs. Keppel's home in Grosvenor Street, and on one occasion her vast drawing-room did service as a rehearsal hall. Upstairs, in a studio draped with Bakst-inspired cushions, her daughter Violet (Vita Sackville-West's future *inamorata*) entertained Lady Juliet Duff and the Alington younger set, Lady Alington being yet another Diaghilev hostess and subscriber. In 1912 Vita's mother, Lady Sackville, purchased two Baksts: an oil of *Schéhérazade* for herself and a sketch of *Cléopâtre* for her daughter.[27]

Diaghilev's London audience did not lack for collectors. But in the Duke of Manchester, Duke of Rutland, Earl of Kilmorey, Earl of Craven, and Viscount Massereene and Ferrard, who inherited along with their ancestral seats priceless galleries of Old Masters, one finds no connoisseurs of the modern. The same applies to Margot Asquith's brother, Lord Glenconner, whose "charming . . . picture gallery" in Queen Anne's Gate housed masterpieces by Reynolds, Romney, Fragonard, and Watteau.[28] If the American-born millionairess Mrs. Bradley Martin, whose daughter acquired the Coombe Collection on her marriage to the Earl of Craven, offered dinner guests a recital by the divine Karsavina in 1911, the Marchioness of Ripon commissioned portraits of Diaghilev stars by John Singer Sargent, and Saxton Noble, who haunted Karsavina's dressing room, ordered a set of murals from José-María Sert, these very acts of patronage betrayed the innate conservatism of their taste.[29] By summer 1914 futurists drew the intrepid to the Doré Galleries and Coliseum. Chez Beecham, however, the arts establishment held sway: curators and trustees of Britain's leading museums, long-established art publishers and writers, and artists whose work in no way violated canons of good taste.[30]

The very presence of these artists (with the exception of Sargent) on the 1914 subscription list does suggest, however, a change in the coloring of Diaghilev's audience. For the first time, one discerns an artistic spark in the general Society blaze, the presence of a community of professionals: playwrights Clifford Bax and Alfred Sutro; novelist Somerset Maugham; Lord Howard de Walden, composer of the operas *The Children of Don* and *Dylan;* M. Montague Nathan, who had just published the first of several works on Russian music. Reviews, society columns, and memoirs add detail to the tapestry: the photographer Baron de Meyer; opera superstars Nellie Melba, Enrico Caruso, and Luisa Tetrazzini; the Sitwell trio; Muriel Draper, who, with her husband Paul, was the "friend and guardian of all visiting foreign musicians"; George Bernard Shaw, who wrote a spirited defense of *Legend of Joseph* in the *Nation*.[31]

To be sure, Diaghilev's Russians had long since seduced the Sitwell siblings, and earlier seasons had found Duncan-style dancer Lady Constance Stewart-Richardson and actresses Ellen Terry and Mrs. Patrick Campbell among the impresario's following. But it could be argued that Society as much as Art propelled them to Covent Garden: by reason of birth in the case of the fledgling poets and Lady Constance or by marrying into the aristocracy, as Mrs. Campbell had.[32] In 1914, by contrast, one reads for the first time of "serious music lovers" flocking "by the score, by the hundred, perhaps by the thousand" to Drury Lane.[33] Significantly, it was opera rather than ballet that drew this more "serious" audience to Diaghilev's enterprise.

Diaghilev's career as an opera producer is an unwritten page in the London history of his company. Ballet writers occasionally allude to it, but they do not discuss it, and they certainly do not regard it as molding the distinctive shape of particular seasons or influencing public expectations. Yet from the time Beecham embarked on independent programming in winter 1913, opera gradually usurped the role of dance as the center of Diaghilev's repasts. By 1914, when rumor had it that Sir Joseph Beecham had "acquired something in the nature of a permanent interest in Mr. de Diaghilew's company,"[34] Terpsichore basked in the reflected glory of opera.

"The chief object of the spring season which Mr. Thomas Beecham has undertaken at Covent Garden," wrote the *Times* on January 30, 1913, "was achieved last night at the opening performance, when Strauss's opera *Der Rosenkavalier* was given in England for the first time."[35] The opera,

Strauss's third to premiere under the conductor's proselytizing baton in as many years, was sung no fewer than eight times in succeeding weeks, and with the addition of three performances of *Elektra* and four of *Salomé*, marked this "Season of Grand Opera and Russian Ballet" as a homage to the Viennese composer.[36]

Of the season's thirty-six performances, fewer than half were devoted exclusively to ballet, and of these, only Nijinsky's *L'Après-midi d'un Faune* ventured into unfamiliar terrain. *Petrouchka*, noted the *Times* was "very favourably received" by the first night audience: its "riotous colour and tingling vitality," so "refreshingly new and refreshingly Russian,"[37] marked the ballet as yet another of Diaghilev's brilliantly exotic tapestries. *Faune*, however, was a different matter. Here, Bakst's exquisite Grecian setting evoked a contemplative mood, Nijinsky's choreography a private world of awakening desire and solitary pleasure, where neither charm nor virtuosity intruded. In dispensing with exoticism, the convention that made the portrayal of lust in *Schéhérazade*, *Thamar* or *Cléopâtre* at once exciting and morally innocuous, Nijinsky stripped the veil of ritualized fantasy from the representation of sexuality. In France the work had inspired one of Diaghilev's great succès de scandale. Across the Channel audiences clapped politely, clucked disparagingly, and went the next night to *Salomé* or *Der Rosenkavalier*, where distant locale and grandiloquence of gesture safely consigned the erotic to the realm of theatrical fantasy.

More than any other work presented that season, *Der Rosenkavalier* caught the spirit of the Beecham-Diaghilev audience, so cosmopolitan in its pleasures, so bourgeois in its tastes. The famous waltz "formed the background to every dance," wrote Osbert Sitwell, "so that if I . . . ever catch the rhythm of it today, the world is again for the moment peopled with a legion of the young, enjoying themselves, who have long ceased to exist . . ."[38] His statement echoes a "curious feature" noted by music critic Ernest Newman when *Elektra* premiered in 1910: "that while many advanced musicians . . . have been chilled by the work, the general public has been enthusiastic," a phenomenon he ascribed in part to the number of "friendly and . . . commonplace" tunes in the supposedly "advanced and recondite" idiom of the composer.[39] In 1914 *Der Rosenkavalier* opened Beecham's most ambitious season yet—his "Grand Season of German Opera, Russian Opera, English Opera, and Russian Ballet" at Drury Lane. In another of those ironies that mesh so curiously the history of art with that of enterprise, the opera that criticized bourgeois social-climbing and materialism became the talisman of an enterprise founded on both.

Strauss was present in other ways during that 1914 season. His *Legend of Joseph* was the linchpin of Diaghilev's new choreographic offerings: it linked the balletic side of the program, not only with *Der Rosenkavalier*, but also with *The Magic Flute,* Strauss's eighteenth-century model that was a major event of the season, being then virtually unknown in London.[40]

Strauss and the other Germans who figured in Beecham's repertory, however, do not explain the perceptible change in the 1914 audience remarked again and again by contemporary critics. The force that conjured the semblance of a national audience into being was neither Strauss nor the triumvirate of *monstres sacrés*—Pavlova, Nijinsky, Karsavina—that presides over memories of Diaghilev's initial conquest. Rather, it was the majestic figure of Feodor Chaliapin, who, as Boris Godunov, Ivan the Terrible, and the other epic heroes of Russian opera, revealed an art and a repertory completely unknown to London. "Who can forget the face of Chaliapine as the Mogul King in *Prince Igor?*" rhapsodized W.B. Yeats in 1916.[41] Few could or would. "In the history of grand opera in England," wrote the *Sketch* reviewer by way of summing up his impressions of Beecham's "Season of Russian Opera and Ballet," "the summer of 1913 will be set down as *annus mirabilis.*"[42]

The overwhelming success of *Boris Godunov, Khovanshchina,* and *Prince Igor* in 1913 did more than whet a taste for Russian opera. It perceptibly altered the course of the Diaghilev enterprise, steering it away from choreographic experiment toward the infinitely calmer straits of operatic production. Ballet writers have generally attributed the relative coolness of London audiences toward Nijinsky's *Jeux* and *Le Sacre du Printemps* to British stodginess and conservatism. Such accounts ignore the unbounded enthusiasm for Diaghilev's operatic works, and how the contrast between the twin faces of the repertory influenced the reception of Nijinsky's new choreography. "Of the ballets," wrote one reviewer, "there is little to be said":

> They remain attractive and are presented with all the old skill and enthusiasm. If they suffer . . . it is by reason of the fact that they cannot make an impression to compare with that of the operas. Moussorgsky and Rimsky-Korsakov interpreted by Mr. Chaliapine and his . . . compatriots have created such a profound impression that everything else, however good, seems to stand upon a lower plane.[43]

This critic had yet to see *Sacre.* But not even Nijinsky's "bewildering," "disgusting" ballet, so crude in its dismissal of "grace," so oblivious of "beauty" and "charm,"[44] could efface the overwhelming impression of *Boris.* By popular demand, an extra performance of the opera was scheduled, while reviewers waxed eloquent in praise of Chaliapin's vocal and dramatic gifts, the conviction of the chorus, whose acting surpassed anything on the contemporary stage, the realism that in Mussorgsky's work broke with opera's romantic conventions. Above all, critics sounded the theme of a new dawn in the history of the musical stage. "We live in changing times; one after another the old conventions disappear . . . The revolution has been a long time in coming, and it may be that the short season of Russian Opera at Drury Lane will take a well-defined place in this country's operatic annals."[45] Ironically, the revolution that so shook London's theatrical world in 1913 had Mussorgsky rather than Stravinsky at the helm.

Diaghilev did not find this unappealing. In 1914 he willingly sacrificed the Nijinsky repertory, and with Sir Joseph Beecham's millions as backing, showered London with an embarrassment of operatic riches—*Prince Igor, May Night, Le Rossignol, Le Coq d'Or, Boris Godunov, Khovanshchina,* and *Ivan the Terrible.* "For the next week, as well as at the time of writing," a reviewer noted on June 17, "Drury Lane monopolises the public attention; not because Covent Garden is failing to present good operas to large houses, but because Drury Lane is pouring out one novelty after another. Opera-goers have never known such largess, and, in addition to opera, there is the ballet."[46]

With *Midas, Papillons, Daphnis and Chloë,* and *Legend of Joseph* as the season's novelties, no wonder ballet seemed an afterthought. The *Times* pronounced *Midas* a failure:

> There is a tawdriness about the whole ballet, the music, the scenery, the grouping, poses and dances of fauns, nymphs, and satyrs, the excessive costumes of Apollo and the judges, . . . the deficient, or at least slender, costumes of the mountain deities and nymphs, all aimed at effects of a very obvious kind. For once the *corps de ballet,* even including Mme. Karsavina and M. Bolm, seemed baffled by their material. They could not disguise the fact that the thing was devoid of all emotional impulse.[47]

Papillons, in Biedermeier style along the lines of *Carnaval,* had a certain charm. But like *Daphnis and Chloë* and the eagerly awaited *Legend of Joseph,* the ballet relied on music (a sparkling score by Robert Schumann) and visual effects (Bakst's Victorian costumes and Mstislav Dobujinsky's setting) to fill an imaginative void. Set against the sonorities of Ravel's score, the dramatic and choreographic action of *Daphnis* seemed almost inconsequential. "The beauty of the scenes," wrote the *Times,* "the poses of the groups of Grecian figures, the dances alike of the individuals, the masses of youths and maidens, and of the pirates, seem to take their places in the scheme primarily as illustrations of the symphonic poem played by the orchestra." Another critic noted the paucity of invention that reduced Fokine's choreography "almost to a monochrome."[48]

Of the season's new works, none revealed so spectacularly the aesthetic malaise of the Ballets Russes as Strauss's *Legend of Joseph*. Here, Diaghilev brought together the era's greatest purveyors of theatrical fashion—Strauss, his librettists Hugo von Hofmannsthal and Count Harry Kessler, Bakst and José-María Sert, who designed the costumes and sets, respectively, and Fokine, the choreographer. The result, wrote the *Times*, was "an extraordinarily skilful piece of artifice" that sacrificed dramatic development and metaphysical contrast to the achievement of spectacular effects. Strauss conducted the premiere before an "auditorium crowded to its utmost capacity,"[49] and in the fashionable throng whose ballrooms waltzed to *Der Rosenkavalier*, in whose closets hung Bakst's "fantasies" in modern dress,[50] and on whose walls were to be seen murals by Sert, one finds the ideal consumer of Diaghilev's spurious product. For how else can this marketing man's dream be described? With its celebrity names and proven formulas, *Legend of Joseph* came to life not from any genuine artistic impulse, but as a "concept." Collaboration was now a matter of business, and the business of ballet, it seemed, was the making and marketing of spectacular, saleable commodities.

At what point box office considerations tip the scales of art in the direction of enterprise is always difficult to ascertain. But it seems that by 1914 a combination of indebtedness and Beecham largess had pushed Diaghilev in the direction of opera, while at the same time pressuring him to produce the kind of works for which a market already existed. The former accounts for the overall content of the repertory; the latter for the "shock and colour" effects that assumed an all-important place in the new works. The theater critic of the *English Review* hinted at this when he decried the "Parisian preciosity" and "Semitic glitter" of recent productions, "the attempt . . . to astonish" that yielded a work like *Le Rossignol*, "clotted and sicklied-o'er with extraordinariness." In none of the new ballets was to be felt the "awe of *Cleopatra*, the ferocity of . . . *Scheherazade*," only a "Byzantinism, an art groping from no standards," in danger of "self-destruction":

The spectacle tends to dethrone the dance; the music to defeat human gesture. One would very seriously like to know what the Ballet Master said when the new scores came in; what the composers thought when they saw the Ballet, so discordant do they sometimes seem, like the cacophonies and rugosities which inspire them.[51]

As market values sapped imaginative energy from ballet, London feasted on the aesthetic vitality of Diaghilev's first love. "Drury Lane under the Beecham régime has made operatic history," wrote the *Sketch*,[52] and even today the reviews of *Prince Igor, Khovanshchina, Boris Godunov, Le Coq d'Or, Ivan the Terrible, May Night,* and *Le Rossignol* vibrate with excitement. In opera, now, was to be found what had once animated the Ballets Russes—Slavic intensity, collective feeling, and a profound belief in the meaning of art. "The Russian opera," concluded the *English Review:*

> has not come under the influence of Reinhardt or Münich. Nothing finer than the Choral March in *Ivan,* the acting and singing of the crowd in *Boris,* has been seen. This, and Chaliapine, are unalloyed Russian, pure as the steppes, blasts out of the soul of Russia. So Drury Lane has become the Mecca of London.[53]

The man who climbed from Russia's lower depths, bankrolled Gorky and Social Revolutionaries with the notes, redeemable in gold, commanded by his appearances, nestled, paradoxically, in the bosom of Society. Lady Diana Manners flung herself at Chaliapin, as did other hopelessly enamored ladies, and no one grumbled at the high prices that went into effect when he trod the boards. By 1914, defaulting guests, tempted by last-minute invitations to a "Chaliapine night," were the bane of many a fashionable hostess.[54]

The "Lane" had indeed become *grand chic.* Night after night its hall was crowded with pleasure-seekers, who did not "as a rule patronize musical entertainments."[55] Their misbehavior—late arrivals, early departures, loud conversation, continual twittering—angered listeners in the audience, who gave vent to their indignation in the letter columns of the *Times.*[56] "Another Sufferer" complained about "the great nuisance of conversation at the Russian Opera":

> I was in the stalls at the performance of *Le Coq d'Or* and *Narcisse* last night, and the talk round me was incessant. The quaint humour of the former . . . excited as much laughter and comment as if it had been a harlequinade in a pantomime . . . and much of the beautiful music of *Narcisse* was inaudible. When will people who go to the Opera to talk have some consideration for those who wish to listen to music?[57]

Celebrity-seekers added appreciably to Beecham's public, so that despite the rivalry with Covent Garden, where Caruso and Melba held the stage, empty seats at Drury Lane were few. But the stalls were not the only part of the house where new faces could be discerned. For the first time the gallery seems to have emerged from anonymity, and it revealed a spectacle "as wonderful" as Diaghilev's stage. "People mount the stairs to see them," wrote the *English Review:*

the Henry Arthur Jones villain sombreros, the Egyptian coiffures of the ladies, the waistcoats of poets, the side-whiskers *à la* Café Royal, the shawls and kissing curls, the nightly kaleidoscopic assembly of 'creators' from Vorticists upwards, such as only Ta-ra-ra-bom-de-ay ever succeeded in attracting in a British auditorium."[58]

Just who made up this colorful throng is hard to say, but it was in these upper reaches that Sir Joseph's alliance of business and art was applauded loudest and longest. On July 24, when Chaliapin sang his last, magnificent *Boris,* nearly a thousand people crowded the gallery, many of whom, noted the *Times,* "had waited for places since early morning."[59] Ovation followed ovation. Even when the stalls and dress circle had emptied, flowers and applause continued to bombard Chaliapin and Sir Joseph from the gallery. The following evening, when *Legend of Joseph, Carnaval,* and *Papillons* rang down the curtain on Diaghilev's prewar enterprise, Sir Joseph again stepped forward, this time to accept a gilded laurel wreath from the dancers and to thank the gallery for the wreath sent to him the night before. He also promised another season.[60] How self-effacing Diaghilev appears, his hand everywhere, his face nowhere, with the name of the Maecenas writ large on his achievement. Did the ego that drove him from Perm to Petersburg to Paris chafe at this anonymity? Did it feel the odd twinge of jealousy, the fear that it might have lost the upper hand? Here, as on so many occasions when one would like to probe Diaghilev's motives, the man behind the public figure remains inscrutable.

The Beecham-Diaghilev enterprise of 1914 sensibly broadened the public for opera. In so doing, it laid the foundation for the relatively democratized audience that today supports two resident companies in the British capital. Beecham's undertakings in these immediate prewar years proposed to do more than simply upgrade the style and quality of offerings at Covent Garden. They sought to transform the character of the public, to weld music-lovers, socialites, theatergoers, and artistic enthusiasts of modest means into an audience more closely attuned to Britain's middle-class social order. Neither the provincial troupes, which played at most a brief and occasional London season, nor Covent Garden, which catered almost exclusively to the haut monde, managed to make the necessary social and artistic adjustments. Beecham was able to do so, only in part because of his family's pharmaceutical empire. Thanks to Diaghilev and the revelation of Chaliapin and Russia's lyric theater, Beecham found an artist and a repertory whose appeal transcended divisions of class and differences in taste. In the sophistication of his programming and perceptible broadening of his audience, Beecham laid the cornerstone for British national opera. In the 1920s Diaghilev would perform a similar service for British ballet.

Between 1911 and 1914 Diaghilev's audience revealed the many faces of Establishment privilege. It marked ballet as a pastime, at once fashionable and frivolous, and more than anything else, enforced the ban against choreographic art as a subject of intellectual discourse. Yet writers, artists, and intellectuals did not shun the Ballets Russes. Many went regularly, even frequently, to Diaghilev events, although few wrote at length about them, and fewer still revealed how they touched the imagination. In no way, however, did their presence alter the character of the audience. Indeed, in the case of that circle of critics, writers, and painters, collectively known as Bloomsbury, habits of class and social background linked the most assiduous of Diaghilev's intellectual followers with the world of his fashionable devotees.

In his memoir *Beginning Again* Leonard Woolf recalled his excitement at returning to London in 1911, after nearly seven years as a civil servant in the colonial backwaters of Ceylon:

> Profound changes were taking place . . . Freud and Rutherford and Einstein were at work beginning to revolutionize our knowledge of our own minds and of the universe . . . In literature one seemed to feel the ominous lull before the storm which was to produce in a few years *A la Recherche du Temps Perdu*, *Ulysses*, Prufrock and *The Waste Land*, *Jacob's Room* and *Mrs. Dalloway*. In painting we were in the middle of the profound revolution of Cézanne, Matisse, and Picasso . . . And to crown all, night after night we flocked to Covent Garden, entranced by a new art, a revelation to us benighted British, the Russian Ballet in the greatest days of Diaghilev and Nijinsky.[61]

Time and again, Diaghilev's Russians weave through the "kaleidoscopic dream" of Woolf's first six months in London. At Covent Garden, "the pleasures of London life and old friendships met";[62] here, Bloomsbury gathered and romance flowered to the strains of Schumann and Rimsky-Korsakov:

> The Russian Ballet became for a time a curious centre for both fashionable and intellectual London . . . night after night one could go to Covent Garden and find . . . the people whom one liked best in the world, moved and excited as one was oneself. In all my long life in London this is the only instance in which I can remember the intellectuals going night after night to a theatre, opera, concert, or other performance as, I suppose, they have and do in . . . Bayreuth or Paris.[63]

In the autumn of 1911 *Schéhérazade*, *Carnaval*, and *Swan Lake* were not the only seductions to be found at Covent Garden. That season Russian ballet alternated with Wagner's *Ring,* and Woolf took a box in October for *Das Rheingold, Siegfried, Götterdämmerung,* and *Die Walküre.* At his side sat Rupert Brooke, Adrian and Virginia Stephen, and Saxon Sydney-Turner, Bloomsbury's resident Wagnerian. As occurred with Diaghilev's fashionable audience and among his following of established writers,[64] opera led Bloomsbury to the ballet.

Although her biographer Quentin Bell minimizes the writer's passion for the Bayreuth master, Virginia Woolf shared the vogue for Wagner that Leonard found so disconcerting among the "frequenters of the Russian Ballet."[65] In May 1908 she was "so miserably involved in opera and the German language" that she had barely a free afternoon for tea with Lytton Strachey. The following February a Mr. Ilchester sent her a ticket for the "Wagner opera," and a few days later she returned "half dazed" from "six solid hours" of another performance. In August 1909 she traveled with her brother Adrian to the Master's shrine in Bayreuth.[66] Only in 1913 was the spell broken. "We came up here 10 days ago to attend the Ring," she wrote to Katherine Cox on May 16, 1913, "and I hereby state that I will never go again . . . My eyes are bruised, my ears dulled, my brain a mere pudding of pulp—O the noise and the heat, and the bawling sentimentality, which used once to carry me away, and now leaves me sitting perfectly still. Everyone seems to have come to this opinion, though some pretend to believe still."[67]

Maestros other than Wagner drew the young writer to Covent Garden. In 1909 her brother Adrian recorded that in a space of six weeks she went twice to *Don Giovanni,* twice to *Louise,* to the first performance of *The Wreckers,* to *Aïda, Orpheus and Eurydice, Madame Butterfly,* and *Faust.*[68] That summer, too, she paid a visit to the troupe of Russian dancers headed by Karsavina performing at the Coliseum, a foretaste of the rich fare Diaghilev brought to Covent Garden two years later. In 1911, 1912, and 1913 ballet added a new texture to the pleasures of "spectacle" and "social event" she associated with opera-going. Striking a Russian chord after her immersion in Wagner, on November 6, 1911, she invited Lytton Strachey to "the dancers"—a performance of *Le Pavillon d'Armide, Les Sylphides,* and *Carnaval,* all with Pavlova. The tickets were "only amphitheatre this time," she wrote, "but when they do the other thing we will go to the stalls." Another invitation followed for the twenty-first: the program again was *Le Pavillon d'Armide* and *Carnaval,* this time with Mathilde Kchessinska, and *Schéhérazade,* doubtless the reason Woolf "hoped to get stalls."[69] The years 1912 and 1913 were crowded with event, but wedding plans, social engagements, and illness notwithstanding, Woolf still found time for performances at Covent Garden and Drury Lane.[70]

Bloomsbury did indeed "assist" at some great ballet moments: "Nijinsky's leap in *Le Spectre de la Rose*, the first London performance of *Le Sacre du Printemps*, the drop-curtain of *Schéhérazade* and the scene revealed when it rose" were the ones E. M. Forster, a fellow traveler of the circle, remembered forty years later.[71] In 1911 alone Rupert Brooke saw no fewer than fifteen performances. "All the summer," he wrote in September, "I alternated between seeing the Russian Ballet at Covent Garden and writing sonnets on the lawn" at Cambridge. The ballet reappears on his social calendar in February and March 1913, and the following year he attended the premieres of *Le Rossignol* and *Legend of Joseph* and the performance of *Le Coq d'Or*, where the final rupture of his friendship with Lytton Strachey took place.[72] That last prewar season remained in Clive Bell's mind for other reasons. "We all remembered how Madame Karsavina danced in 1914," he wrote five years later, "she had seemed to us miraculous almost. And if we remembered her better in one ballet than another that ballet was Petroushka." John Maynard Keynes was another early devotee of the Russians. He spent the summer of 1911 writing his *Treatise on Probability*, but when statistics palled, the economist slipped down from Cambridge to "view Mr Nijinsky's legs." Two years later, Keynes saw *Boris Godunov* as well as *Le Sacre du Printemps*.[73] Among Bloomsbury, Diaghilev acquired a small, but loyal, following of intellectuals.

Only Lytton Strachey seems to have recorded firsthand impressions of Nijinsky's ballet. *Sacre*, he wrote, was "one of the most painful experiences of my life. I couldn't have imagined that boredom and sheer anguish could have been combined together at such a pitch."[74] How accurately his confession of pain and confusion mirrored the feeling of Bloomsbury is impossible to judge. Yet there is evidence that Nijinsky's ballet occupied a rung apart from Diaghilev's other works; that it conveyed something akin to "significant form" in choreography. In the howl of derision provoked by *Sacre*, only the *Nation* and *New Statesman* voiced minority opinions, and these, tellingly, were journals with more than a casual relationship to Bloomsbury. Roger Fry wrote regularly on art for the *Nation*, while the *New Statesman*, a Fabian weekly launched in April 1913, published Clive Bell, Leonard Woolf, Lytton Strachey, Roger Fry, Rupert Brooke, and Desmond MacCarthy in the first fifteen months of its existence. More pragmatic than its rival in politics, more openminded in its coverage of the arts, the *New Statesman* wove together the leftward leaning politics, feminism, and aesthetic concerns that formed Bloomsbury's loosely defined "ideology."[75]

In July 1913 the *New Statesman* published no fewer than three articles about the Russian Ballet, and two of these spoke directly to the issue of Nijinsky's choreography.[76] Here, at last, Nijinsky found a London critic who appreciated both the artistic intent of his work and the central place of choreography in the composition of a ballet:

In the three "revolutionary" ballets we find a passionate endeavour towards the ballet as a unity . . . In *Jeux* and *L'Après-midi* Nijinsky's work . . . has been at pains to put choreography itself on a true artistic level; he has put his own vigour into pattern; we have seen him working to express an idea through moving forms . . . In *Jeux* Nijinsky uses the toe-dancing of marionettes, the gestures of French dolls dressed in white, a magnified tennis ball, conventionalised flower-beds and grass-plots . . . and with the motives of quarrel, reconciliation, childish impulsiveness and restlessness, weaves his poem of pattern . . . In *Le Sacre du Printemps* you may see the barbaric Russian gestures and dances not, as in *Schéhérazade* and *Prince Igor,* used for their own natural oddness and barbarity . . . but used to build up a synthesis in movement of a barbaric idea, the sacrifice of a young girl to Spring. The literalness of plot has gone; we do not rely on an unforeseen dénouement to excite us; we look for the unfolding of an idea . . . Here there was much more nearly a synthesis of [music and choreography], neither in service to the other, but both expressing one idea.[77]

Who was this anonymous critic who eyed Nijinsky's work with such understanding? Surely, he must have been close to Bloomsbury. The concern for pattern, structure, organic union, draws on Roger Fry's ideas about the coherence and expressive function of design; implies, with Clive Bell, that art is significant form. The history of the journal's first fifty years skips over this choreographic episode.[78] But even if all trace of the critic has been lost, is it idle to suggest that Strachey's remarks, penned within hours of hearing Stravinsky's troubling cacophonies, may have been less fully considered than those of this reviewer? In the circles around the *New Statesman* (for which Rambert's future husband, playwright Ashley Dukes, also wrote), one discerns the enlightened intelligentsia Rambert claimed for the Ballets Russes.[79]

Sacre, however, was only one ballet, and with *Jeux* and *Faune* made up but a fraction of the repertory. In the larger context of the prewar Ballets Russes, sensory thrill, not structure, was the pivot on which the company's aesthetic turned, and Diaghilev's refined stimulants provoked complaints of cheap and flashy spectacle even as they drew Bloomsbury again and again to the theater. In an address to the Cambridge Heretics' Society in early 1913, Rupert Brooke paid a resounding tribute to Gordon Craig, then went on to damn in a single breath the "tawdry and inharmonious" designs "of a Russian Jew called Bakst" and "that energetic fraud Max Reinhardt." A year earlier, Clive Bell had also coupled the names of Bakst and Reinhardt, "wizards of 'the new art' [who] claim to express the most profound and subtle emotions," but, in reality, produce "imitation art," "physical reactions . . . subtle enough to do duty for aesthetic emotions." Like the best music-hall pageants and ballets, their work made for a "good show," but it was a "faux bon," not a work of art.[80] In the references to Gordon Craig and Max Reinhardt, harbingers in very different ways of the new stagecraft, one glimpses the intellectual scaffolding of Bloomsbury's critique of Diaghilev.

Just weeks after the close of the Coronation season, Roger Fry's long and laudatory article on an exhibition of Craig's designs appeared in the *Nation*. Diaghilev is not mentioned nor is his enterprise, but Fry's praise of the spare and abstract models on display implied a criticism of both. In contrast to the opulent materiality of the Ballets Russes, Craig's was:

> an art concerned with the imaginative approach to things of higher import, not with their final consummation. It is like the narthex of a cathedral, the frame of a picture, the avenue to a great palace, and, as in all these things, something must be left out, its perfection depends upon its incompleteness.[81]

Again and again, Fry made the point that Craig had rid his designs of the "imitative" and "picturesque."

In its appreciation of contemporary painting, Bloomsbury stood far ahead of Diaghilev. Only a year before this review, Fry's first Post-Impressionist Exhibition had introduced Cézanne, Van Gogh, and Gauguin, then virtually unknown in England, to a public that heaped scorn, ridicule, and abuse on both their works and their sponsors.[82] In 1912, long before Diaghilev awarded either artist a commission, paintings by Larionov and Gontcharova hung in the Russian section of Fry's Second Post-Impressionist Exhibition. Ranged against the moderns, the *Mir iskusstva* aesthetic, of which no one more than Bakst was the apotheosis, seemed stale and second-rate. "For a long time," wrote Fry in 1919, "the Russian Ballet was content with a *décor* which, though it could not be called old-fashioned or reactionary, was by no means on a level with the conceptions of the great original designers of Europe":

> M. Bakst was a most effective and ingenious designer, sufficiently alert to pick up ideas from all sides, but he did not himself stand in the front rank of creative designers. Probably the exact note of compromise on which M. Bakst fixed . . . was nearly exactly suited to M. Fokine's habitual methods of choreography. But when M. Fokine . . . created Petrushka, it became apparent that the choreographic conception was far ahead of the *décor*, and the same dissidence was even more apparent between the extremely original and formal

design of the dance in 'Le Sacre du Printemps' and the rather fusty romanticism of M. Ruhrich's [sic] scenery.[83]

In early twentieth-century England, Puritanism was still a force to be
reckoned with. Temperance leagues fought the evils of drink; "purity" drives
the immorality of sex; to many the theater remained the apogee of sin. As
late as 1907 the *Spectator* printed no dramatic reviews for fear of putting
off the clerics in its audience.[84] Ballet before Diaghilev meant pretty girls
and glittering accompaniments: the difference between a guardsman and a
ballet girl, it was said, was that the first sins on two legs, the other on
one.[85] Even in Bloomsbury, asceticism ran deep, deeper at times than the
impulse toward hedonism. It bred a mistrust of the stage to the extent that
theater was spectacle: the Word was sacred, the Flesh that dressed it pro-
fane. In an essay on stage setting, Roger Fry alluded to this dichotomy,
ascribing it to an upbringing where theater was forbidden. Now he cared
only for drama. "My attitude to the stage, then, is mainly negative. I ask
of it not to interfere unduly with the drama, not to destroy the imaginative
conviction which spoken words and gestures can create."[86]

Like Bell, who drew on many of his ideas, Fry linked spectacle to the
music-hall. "There I like the plaster Caryatids, the rollicking Cupids, and
all the gingerbread magnificence, just as there I can appreciate the sham
oriental scenery before which the serio-comic lady declaims. Nor do I mind
in that atmosphere how many sensations I receive, since I know that I may
neglect any number without missing the point."[87] Fry's allusion to sham
oriental scenery and magnificent settings strikes a critical note echoed by
other partisans of new art. "BLAST . . . Naively seductive Houri salon-
picture Cocottes," declared a Vorticist manifesto in 1914.[88] In *The Cal-
iph's Dream*, published in 1919, *Blast* editor Wyndham Lewis contrasted
the primitivism of the avant-garde moderns with the pseudo-savagery of
ballets like *Prince Igor*—clashing cymbals, howling clansmen, voluptuous
belly-dances, Caucasian vendettas. "That is about as far as a respectable
Public-school fancy takes you. It is like a scene from the more boring of
the Russian ballets or a Victory Ball."[89] Fry ends his article with what
sounds like an admonition to Diaghilev. "Striking or brilliant oppositions
of colour, even if they are beautiful, should be avoided as making too
distracting an appeal to the eye."[90]

One of the more curious aspects of Diaghilev's reception in England
is the way perceptions among intellectuals were colored by the popular
stage. Reinhardt's "new art," in particular, offered a compendium of theatrical effects—"opulent sensuousness," "unity of effect," "dumb show,"
"idea of ensemble," and "Eastern romance"[91]—which approximated Diaghilev's contribution to the operatic stage. Although the *Nation* published

nothing about the Ballets Russes in 1911 and 1912, its coverage of Rein-hardt's "wordless plays" sketches the intellectual context of those years, the feeling among London highbrows at the time of Diaghilev's second and third seasons that little of what was seemingly innovative was really new. "There is . . . a curiously sporadic activity about our theatres now," be-gan an essay on Reinhardt's "new art" in October 1911:

> It is an activity that seems to excite everybody and satisfy nobody—new wine in old bottles, concentrations upon side-issues, large efforts loudly heralded to small ends . . . ideas flying this way and that, like meteors on a November night . . . Written in large and flaming letters across the full arc of heaven, one perceives the legend—Reinhardt![92]

The *Nation* found much to praise in the man who brought scholar and mechanic to the theater. In *The Miracle,* wrote editor H. W. Mas-singham, Reinhardt's orchestration of color and crowd, movement and mass, was "a brilliant feat of management"; the production marked a "real epoch in the development of spectacular art in this country."[93] But, he added, it was not "poetic drama." Nor was it new. The sentimental reli-gious appeal, the setting of medieval romance were as familiar as the "old store-house of Eastern fantasy" of Reinhardt's *Sumurun*.[94] Or, one might add, of *Schéhérazade* or *Cléopâtre,* then drawing crowds at Covent Gar-den. Spurious novelty aside, the very notion of a spectacle that dispensed with speech troubled the *Nation;* in Reinhardt's "wordless play" drama vanished into stagecraft; the result was a human and intellectual void. In another review, Massingham linked the appeal to eye and ear in these productions to the influence of film. "The great London theatre," he wrote in September 1912, "becomes more and more of a 'cinema,' with vocal accompaniments. Large numbers of actors and actresses are made to go through much expressive and rapidly changing pantomime, culminating in clashing moments and vivid scenic groups . . . This is the essential stuff of the spectacular play."[95] It was the stuff, too, of Fokine's exotic ballets, of which no fewer than four—*Firebird, Thamar, The Polovtsian Dances,* and *Schéhérazade*—were presented that summer at Covent Garden. To the intellectual mind, it seems, Diaghilev stood close to Reinhardt on the "new art" continuum, offering via the opera house the refined stimulants and thrills of the "Professor's" wordless spectacles in the West End.

No wonder Bakst was so disparaged in Bloomsbury's Georgian squares; his style tagged as vulgar; his effects demoted to the level of the music-hall. But sensuousness, like the theater generally, works in strange ways upon the repressed sensibility: as much as it repels, so it fascinates; it opens an arena for the free play of fantasy, a space where the unconscious can take pleasure in the ritualized representation of the forbidden. In Blooms-bury's response to the Ballets Russes, rational and liberatory impulses warred.

In *Beginning Again* Leonard Woolf insisted that it was the classicism of Diaghilev's earliest ballets that Bloomsbury found so appealing, a state-ment that raises as many questions as it claims to answer:

> I have never seen anything more perfect nor more exciting, on any stage, than Scheherazade, Carnaval, Lac des Cygnes [Swan Lake], and the other famous classics. There develops in nearly all the arts . . . a classical style which com-bines great power and freedom and beauty with a kind of self-imposed aus-terity and restraint. In the hands of a great master, like Sophocles, Thucydides, Virgil, Swift, La Fontaine, La Bruyère, this combination of originality and freedom with formal purity and restraint is tremendously moving and exciting, and it was this element of classicism in the ballets of 1911 which made them so entrancing.[96]

But can one really speak of "classicism" in the context of Diaghilev's early seasons, if we take this term to mean the gradual unfolding of a tradition, until, like the Balanchine repertory for the audience of the New York City Ballet, the individual work becomes both a familiar pleasure and a form resonating between past and present? Imagine that *Jeux* and *Sacre* had played more than a handful of performances, that *Giselle* or *Swan Lake* had stayed in the repertory for more than a season, that Lon-don had seen over the years a program more coherent than the hodge-podge of secessionist novelties—Russian, Persian, Greek, Venetian or whatever—on offer from season to season. Then, I think, one could have spoken of classicism and tradition. As it was, between 1911 and 1914 Diaghilev did not help his British viewers to understand the art he was revealing to them.

This is what E.M. Forster alluded to in recalling the ballet high points of his life: that ballet, as presented by Diaghilev, engaged only on the level of sensation, opening no doors to the inheritance of the past. "The mo-ments," he wrote:

> never joined together and built up a tradition for me as opera has: a tradition resident in the mind to be evoked with gratitude. Never, that is to say, until last winter. Last winter I went to the Diaghilev Exhibition. There, the isolated moments coalesced, the scattered impressions of the past fifty years fell into place, and I realised that I had assisted at an attempt of the twentieth century to create civilised pleasure.[97]

Woolf's emphasis on classicism finds no echo in the prewar voices of his contemporaries, and it seems likely that Richard Buckle's *Diaghilev*

Exhibition of 1954, a splendid tribute to the Ballets Russes that coincided with a ground swell of enthusiasm in England for ballet, influenced his thinking, as it did Forster's. The connection that Forster made with "civilised pleasure" does reverberate in earlier writings, as though the totality of the Diaghilev enterprise, rather than any particular work, promised the dawn of a new age. "They, if anything can, redeem our civilisation," rhapsodized Rupert Brooke,[98] echoing a feeling in many quarters that the cultural regeneration of the West would come from the purer spiritual climes of the East. Although he does not explicitly mention the Ballets Russes, Lytton Strachey's ecstatic vision of the "literature of the future" could well be a paean to *Schéhérazade*. "Quelle joie!" he wrote to Virginia Woolf in 1912. "To live in those days, when books will pour out from the press reeking with all the filth of Petronius, all the frenzy of Dostoievsky, all the romance of the Arabian Nights, and all the exquisiteness of Voltaire!"[99]

Literature never quite lived up to these exhilarating vistas, but Bloomsbury parties tried to, and in the style of fancy dress and the themes of after-dinner charades, one perceives both the inspiration and liberating impact of the ballet stage. At one 1913 party the young painter Mark Gertler met "a very graceful girl, who made me dance a ballet with her. I took the part of Nijinsky; I had on a jersey and a belt." Oliver Strachey and Karin Costelloe went as Karsavina and Nijinsky to another party that year. Strachey wore "a red ballet costume," his partner "a piece of purple satin," and they "enacted Spectre de la Rose with much success." In 1914, Lady Ottoline Morrell opened her wardrobes of Oriental clothing to Bloomsbury friends and art students from the Slade who danced pianola versions of *The Polovtsian Dances* and *Schéhérazade* at her Thursday evening parties.[100]

On the level of play, Diaghilev touched the Bloomsbury imagination, animating its fantasies with movement, dressing them in the hedonist imagery of his stage. " 'Schéhérazade,' " wrote artist Anne Estelle Rice in *Rhythm*, a journal identified with the modern movement in painting and literature, "obviously expresses the sensuous note":

> In this Arabian Nights' orgy of voluptuous fullness, where designs, drapery, arms, legs, bodies, groups have a circular movement, the luxuriant overhanging emerald green curtain, the undulating movement of the dancers, the immense trousers of the supple almées, the rich flowing music of Rimsky-Korsakow—harem and spectator are caught up in a maddening whirl of sound, colour and curve to the point of exhaustion."[101]

As a painter, Rice was allied with the Fauves. Her gods were Gauguin and Van Gogh, and in the many drawings of ballet scenes and dancers published in *Rhythm,* one detects the bold line and sensuous primitivism of her mentors. Bloomsbury, however, preferred the conceptual architecture and impersonality of Cézanne; it valued composition over the kaleidoscope of vibrating color Rice found teeming with life in Bakst. Yet in the dancers, acrobats, and bright colors that figured in products of the Omega Workshop (with which many Bloomsbury artists were associated), one again discerns a ballet presence. Vanessa Bell's panels for the Omega room at the Ideal Home Exhibition in 1913 "were based on the Russian ballet, largely inspired by Matisse's first version of *The Dance* (which had been included in the Second Post-Impressionist Exhibition)."[102] Duncan Grant's *Queen of Sheba,* painted in 1912, is another instance of the ballet acting as a catalyst on the Bloomsbury imagination.

With age, the bonhomie and good times added up to something more. In her biography of Roger Fry, published in 1940 when German armies occupied Europe for the second time in living memory, Virginia Woolf evoked the optimism and sense of possibility that so many felt during that Indian summer before World War I, and that Diaghilev with hindsight seemed to represent. Fry's "excitement," she wrote, "was not confined to the Omega . . . There were parties; there were plays; there were operas and exhibitions. London was full of new enterprises. He went to see the Russian dancers, and they, of course, suggested all kind of fresh possibilities, and new combinations of music, dancing, and decoration. He went to the Opera with Arthur Balfour. It was *Ariadne,* by Strauss, and he was enthusiastic."[103]

Woolf continues her sketch of that last summer of peace. Like Balfour, the friends who gathered around Fry were Diaghilev familiars—Princess Lichnowsky, the literary wife of the German Ambassador, a regular subscriber; Lady Ottoline Morrell, at whose home in Bedford Square Duncan Grant, Lytton Strachey, and other Bloomsbury figures had met Nijinsky. "Many of the things that he had worked for seemed to be coming within reach. Civilisation, a desire for the things of the spirit, seemed to be taking hold not merely of a small group, but to be breaking through among the poor, among the rich . . . 'We are at last', he summed it up, 'becoming a little civilised.' And then of course the war came."[104] Surely, Woolf was also talking about herself.

If Diaghilev's art seemed to bode a civilized future, Nijinsky's persona augured a new age of sexual freedom. His physique alone provoked the desire of Bloomsbury's homosexual fraternity: Keynes came down from Cambridge for a look at his "legs," Lytton Strachey daydreamed about him and sent "magnissime flowers" to Drury Lane. (George Bernard Shaw, by contrast, "consoled himself with Karsavina," as he wrote to Mrs. Patrick Campbell.)[105] But Nijinsky was more than a siren; his range of parts—

the Golden Slave in *Schéhérazade,* the rose-petaled spirit of *Le Spectre de la Rose,* Harlequin in *Carnaval,* the title role of *Petrouchka,* the Faun in *L'Après-midi d'un Faune*—traced a spectrum of male role possibilities that transcended conventions of gender. The attraction of the Ballets Russes for Bloomsbury rested, in part, on the image of sexual heterodoxy projected by Nijinsky, a subject, however, that memories of Oscar Wilde confined to the hush of private discourse.[106]

Interest in Russian literature, and Dostoievsky, particularly, coincided with the arrival of the Ballets Russes.[107] Indeed, one senses that both novelist and dancer inhabited similar compartments of the mind; that Bloomsbury dressed Nijinsky in the guise of a spiritual, sexual, and emotional primitive. For E. M. Forster, Nijinsky's faun was "a humorous and alarming animal, free from the sentimentality of my stories." Rupert Brooke recalled the dancer in letters from Samoa describing a "thrilling and tropical and savage" siva-siva performance.[108] Virginia Woolf never wrote about Nijinsky, but in the twenties, when Lydia Lopokova took up lodgings in Bloomsbury, she observed her closely, fascinated by her differentness, imagining her as a "parrokeet" on one occasion, on another, as a "poor sparrow turning into a discreet, silent, serious, motherly, respectable fowl, with eggs, feathers, cluck cluck clucking all complete."[109] The mere mention of Lydia sent Woolf rummaging the animal kingdom for images. "A rare bird would really suit Maynard better," she complained to her sister Vanessa Bell. "However she [Lydia] caught a frog and was very charming about the crows she rhymes to Cows, and her armpits, which are called mouseholes in Russia; and I see I should rather like her as a mistress myself."[110] In human guise, Lydia was a tempestuous exotic or naif. Her scenes "shook the rafters—rage, tears, despair, outrage, horror, retribution, reconciliation"; her "contribution" to tea consisted of "one shriek, two dances; then silence, like a submissive child, with her hands crossed."[111] She was deliciously and exasperatingly primitive—emotional, infantile, and irrational.

The future Lady Keynes obviously charmed the novelist. Her flashes of temperament, quick changes of feeling, and apparent spontaneity spoke to Woolf's intuitive sense; they touched an emotional chord while leaving her intellect cold. One suspects that Nijinsky exerted a similar power and awoke a similar ambivalence in Bloomsbury: instinct counted for only so much in that haven of intellect. Telling in this regard is Lytton Strachey's courting of the "gorgeous" dancer: the purple suit he bought anticipating an introduction, and his eventual disenchantment with "that cretinous lackey."[112] Nijinsky "was very nice," he wrote, after meeting his idol in 1913, "and much more attractive than I'd expected—in fact very much so . . . Otherwise he did not seem particularly interesting—as the poor fellow cannot speak more than 2 words of any human language it's difficult to get very far with him. As it was, there was another Russian who acted as interpreter and the conversation was mainly conducted by Granville Barker."[113] Strachey's linguistic chauvinism speaks for itself.

Of all the "Bloomsburies," only Lady Ottoline Morrell discerned the "soul" in the beast. Alone among the sophisticates of her circle, she offered "understanding and appreciation of his serious work." Nijinsky gave her a photograph of himself as Petrouchka—"the mythical outcast," he told her, "in whom is concentrated the pathos and suffering of life, one who beats his hands against the walls, but always is cheated and despised and left outside alone"—a figure she likened to Dostoievsky's Idiot.[114] She admired his unworldliness, dislike of possessions, and singleminded devotion to art, and saw his reaction to the lavish trappings of Ballets Russes exotica as a sign of his conversion to Tolstoyism. At her home in Bedford Square he stepped out briefly from under Diaghilev's shadow; here, he met Boris Anrep, with whom he spent hours talking about Russian myths and religion; Duncan Grant, Strachey, Simon Bussy, and Granville Barker.[115] Her garden was immortalized: an afternoon tennis match inspired the setting of *Jeux*. To Strachey's amusement, Nijinsky continued to enthrall her, and even after his marriage she plied him with sentimental attentions. "On one occasion," writes Strachey's biographer, "the two of them were sitting together in a tiny inner room when Lytton entered the house. As he advanced down the drawing-room he overheard Ottoline's husky voice . . . utter the words: 'Quand vous dansez, vous n'êtes pas un homme—vous êtes une idée. C'est ça, n'est-ce pas, qui est l'Art? . . . Vous avez lu Platon, sans doute?'—The reply was a grunt."[116] Was Strachey jealous perhaps that "Lady Ott" had penetrated the dancer's reserve? Or was this, like so many of Strachey's letters, merely another flirtatious performance?

London's avant-garde took far less heed of Diaghilev than Bloomsbury. The ban was never absolute as among the artists of Montmartre, but it was strong, nonetheless, and for essentially the same reason: the social character of the Ballets Russes, as much as its aesthetic, clashed with those of the avant-garde. In a 1913 poem "Les Millwin," Ezra Pound expressed his contempt for both. At the time the Slade was a haven for "arty" types, girls like Dora Carrington and Iris Tree who traveled in Bloomsbury circles and even Society:

> The little Millwins attend the Russian Ballet.
> The Mauve and greenish souls of the little Millwins
> Were seen lying along the upper seats
> Like so many unused boas.

The turbulent and undisciplined host of art students—
The rigorous deputation from "Slade"—
Was before them.

With arms exalted, with fore-arms
Crossed in great futuristic X's, the art students
Exulted, they beheld the splendours of *Cleopatra*.

And the little Millwins beheld these things;
With their large and anaemic eyes they looked out upon
   this configuration.[117]

Few personalities of the time were so full of paradox as the transplanted Pennsylvanian, and here, as elsewhere in his writings, Pound reveals more about his bêtes noires of the moment than his response to a
particular phenomenon. According to John Gould Fletcher, an acquaintance of Pound's in 1913–1914, the guru of the avant-garde passed up the
French premiere of *Sacre*. Pound did see the work when it came to London, and after the war even reviewed ballet pseudonymously as music critic
for the *New Age*. (Consistency not being one of his stronger suits, Pound
now sang the praises of *The Polovtsian Dances*—to the detriment, ironically, of *Le Tricorne*.) The image of Serafima Astafieva stayed with him
long after she appeared with Diaghilev: the dancer, who became an important London teacher, is mentioned twice in the Pisan Cantos.[118]
   Just how the avant-garde took initially to Diaghilev is hard to say.
The only statement we have comes from a friend of T. E. Hulme, the critic
and philosopher, whose Tuesday evening gatherings in 1912 attracted many
writers and artists, including Pound, Fletcher, Ford Madox Ford, Richard
Aldington, John Cournos, Wyndham Lewis, Henri Gaudier-Brzeska, Rupert Brooke, John Middleton Murry, Edward Marsh, Jacob Epstein, Edwin Evans, and Ashley Dukes.[119] "I count my acquaintance with Hulme,"
D. L. Murray told his biographer, "as really beginning in the autumn of
1911 where we met in the gallery at Covent Garden during a performance
of the Diaghilev Ballet":

   I think we each expressed surprise at seeing each other there, for in those days
   ballet was still generally reckoned . . . a "low-brow" form of art associated
   with music halls. We soon discovered . . . that our enthusiasm for the Diaghilev enterprise concealed a deep difference of appreciation. I admired in it
   the classical elements it still retained from the traditional Franco-Italian . . .
   school, while Hulme was only impressed by the endeavors being made by
   Nijinsky and others . . . to bring the *plastique* of ballet into line with the
   non-humanistic ideals that inspired Egyptian, archaic Greek and Polynesian
   art.[120]

Apart from professionals like Evans, who as a music critic and occasional Diaghilev employee, wrote frequent notices of the company, and Ashley Dukes, a young drama reviewer and playwright, who called Diaghilev's first season "the event of the century," [121] the constellation of talents in Hulme's salon wrote little about the ballet. Aldington, it has been said, counted London's first *Schéhérazade* among the highlights of his youth, but neither he nor imagist poet Hilda Doolittle, whom he married in 1913, recorded impressions of performances. [122] Nor did John Middleton Murry or Katherine Mansfield comment publicly about the ballet, although the literary couple attended performances in 1912 and 1913 and published articles about the Ballets Russes in *Rhythm*. (Only in 1921 did Murry break this silence. Reviewing W.A. Propert's *The Russian Ballet in Western Europe 1909–1920*, he ranked the contributions of Gontcharova, Benois, Roerich, and "even Bakst" far above the designs of Picasso, Matisse, and Derain.) [123] Only Fletcher, an imagist with a pictorial imagination, responded wholeheartedly to the ballet. In 1911 he "sat spellbound through the barbaric splendor of *Scheherazade* and the Polovtsian dances from *Prince Igor*," an encounter that provoked such early experiments as "The Vowels," a poem synthesizing sound with the exotically colored imagery of Bakst—to whom it was dedicated. [124]

Sacre, however, was to be remembered by Fletcher long after the Paris premiere, which he attended with the painters Anne Estelle Rice and John Duncan Fergusson, the former art editor of *Rhythm*. For it was this performance, "more than anything else" that confirmed him in his dedication "to risk everything in order to become a modern artist": "a determination to make and accept every kind of experiment, and not flinch from any novelty, however strange and uncouth it might seem, or however deeply it aroused the hatred of the mob." [125] During her sojourn in London that summer, Amy Lowell went regularly to Drury Lane, as she would do the following year. Like Fletcher, she accepted *Sacre* "instantly as a masterpiece and eventually came to consider Stravinsky as the greatest living composer. For years afterward," wrote S. Foster Damon, "she used to describe with gusto the effect of her first hearing" of the ballet. [126]

Balletomanes aside, Nijinsky's work did, it seems, bring the London avant-garde en masse to the theater. John Cournos, a Pound protégé who later translated many Russian literary works, recalled the controversy that raged in Harold Monro's attic—a gathering place for imagist and Georgian poets—on the night of the first London performance. To Jacob Epstein's strange new vision had been added Stravinsky's, and a copy of Epstein's *Christ* in Monro's living room downstairs "had to be rescued hastily and indiscriminately from his opponents and exponents alike, and I from the sister of an eminent British novelist . . . who was threatening Stravinsky in my unworthy person with her umbrella."[127] In an essay on the composer in *The Egoist,* a journal that published many imagists and articles about the new art, Leigh Henry summed up what we may assume to be the avant-garde position:

> The latest and greatest of Stravinsky's dance-creations, the tremendous dance tragedy, "Le Sacre du Printemps" . . . surpasses even his own earlier work and gives us the first perfect and unified conception of synthetic choreography. Here we have the veritable essence of Dionysian ecstasy, the sensitivism and nervous power present in the new consciousness of the world expressed with a perfect mastery which transcends almost everything which we have hitherto understood by the term "dramatic".[128]

In the work of Wyndham Lewis, Gaudier-Brzeska, and David Bomberg, dance images appear with increasing frequency in the years 1912–1914. Of course, dance was both an integral part of the futurist agenda and a concern of many artists interested in primitivism. Yet in certain items dating from the years of Nijinsky's ascendancy as a choreographer, Diaghilev's hand is undeniable: Lewis's 1914 drawings of Nijinsky, his depiction of a dancer in arabesque en pointe in a 1912 mural painted for Madame Strindberg's Cabaret Theatre Club and his design of dancers in a classical lift for one of its brochures; Gaudier-Brzeska's 1912 bronzes of Karsavina and Bolm in *Firebird,* a lost statuette of Nijinsky, and drawings of dancers; David Bomberg's 1913–1914 watercolors of the "Dancer" series and the artist's commemorative volume of abstract lithographs published under the title *Russian Ballet.* But one is tempted to venture further afield, and draw analogies between Nijinsky's rugged musculature, displayed in revealing body stockings in *Spectre* and *Faune,* and Lewis's dancing figures of 1912, two of which the painter entitled "Faunesque" and "Seraglio." Similarly, one cannot help but think that the "Red Stone Dancer" sculpted by Gaudier-Brzeska in 1914, bore some connection with the primitivist idiom of *Sacre.*[129]

Sacre quickened the imagination of London's avant-garde. Like Chaliapin, the only Diaghilev figure "blessed" rather than "blasted" by the vorticists in 1914, *Sacre* breathed that "extraordinary acuity of feeling and intelligence" Lewis so admired in the Slav.[130] But this response was an isolated phenomenon, a tribute to the uniqueness of Nijinsky's primitivist vision, rather than a response to the art and enterprise of ballet at large. For between these modernist pioneers, who "despised politics and the civil service and the middle classes,"[131] and the prewar Ballets Russes yawned a nearly insurmountable divide, one founded as much on social claims as on differences in aesthetic program. Among the imagists and vorticists circulated few Establishment insiders, few graduates of the public schools and Oxbridge, few descendants of the Victorian intelligentsia, few who enjoyed the comforts of a private income. Many were foreigners; several were poor; nearly all were excluded from the drawing-rooms of Diaghilev's followers in Society. When *Blast* rhetorically asked in a manifesto signed by Aldington, Pound, Lewis, Gaudier-Brzeska, and others, "MAY WE HOPE FOR ART FROM LADY MOND?" or declared its "violent boredom with that feeble Europeanism, abasement of the miserable 'intellectual' before anything coming from Paris, cosmopolitan sentimentality, which prevails in so many quarters,"[132] can one doubt the alliance of social and aesthetic factors in the modernist critique of the Ballets Russes?

Like the Kensington avant-garde, Bloomsbury parted ways with Society in its assessment of Diaghilev's aesthetic. But it differed from the scruffy Bohemia across the city in that Covent Garden was familiar terrain. By schooling, class, breeding, and profession, Bloomsbury belonged to the larger social world of Diaghilev's audience; it fringed the haut monde of Asquiths and Cunards, at whose weekend homes and dinner tables Keynes, Lytton Strachey, and even, on occasion, Virginia Woolf held forth. That Bloomsbury elected to distance itself from this milieu testifies to the strength of its convictions and non-conformity. But it did so as dissenters standing on the radical wing-tip of prewar Liberalism, not as outsiders marginalized by Society.

Ultimately, not even Bloomsbury counted for much in the overall picture of Diaghilev's audience. After the war things would be different; the pundits and makers of art would step to the fore of ballet's democratized public. Between 1911 and 1914, however, the company wore a badge of social and economic privilege. To later generations Diaghilev's six prewar seasons spun a tale of glamor, elegance, and aristocracy; evoked a society untrammeled by the usages of democracy and the greyness of the welfare state; wove a saga of Imperial succession that led from the Maryinsky to Britain's Royal Ballet. Diaghilev, of course, built his empire on the shifting sands of credit and the box office. But that is not the only irony in the myth. As Diaghilev's audience nightly preened itself during the Coronation Season in 1911, the foundations of its privilege were being shaken. Two years earlier Lloyd George's "People's Budget" had raised the spectre of jacquerie, or, at least, the prospect of higher taxes. Now, in August 1911, the Lords at Parliament Square surrendered the vestiges of their feudal power to the Commons: they had "decided to die in the dark."[133] From 1911 until 1914 aristocratic prerogative, ironically, took a last, public stand in the theatrical ritual of Diaghilev's audience.

12 🖋

THE POSTWAR AUDIENCE

IN 1919 AN ASTONISHED Cecil Beaton discovered in the gallery of the Alhambra Theatre the "new disciples" of Diaghilev's Ballets Russes. Scanning the uppermost reaches of the house, his society eye registered "gaunt, angular women with lank, untidy bobbed hair and shapeless clothes, and red-bearded ballet-maniacs who would think nothing of waiting ten to fifteen hours in the rain for a seat in the 'gods'."[1] Beaton was not the only spectator to note the remarkable change that had come over Diaghilev's London audience. "I am so glad," Charles Ricketts wrote the impresario in 1918, "that the big common public adores the Ballet like the old elite of Covent Garden before these tragic days."[2]

No less protean than the aesthetic face of the Ballets Russes was the changing configuration of its audience between 1918 and 1929. To chronicle Diaghilev's public before World War I is a relatively easy task; *le tout Londres* and *le tout Paris,* different as they were, rested on similar touchstones of class and plutocratic privilege. The war impoverished Diaghilev even as it opened new artistic vistas, and both prompted far-reaching changes within his audience. The brief appearance of a truly popular following in London and the gradual narrowing of his public on both sides of the Channel to the circles of High Bohemia were phenomena that added to the complex identity of the postwar Ballets Russes.

At no time in the history of his enterprise did Diaghilev actively solicit a popular following. By taste and inclination, he viewed the masses as alien, and one finds no parallel in his twenty-year round of touring to Pavlova's popular-priced marathons in bullrings. His ideal remained constant: a select public dressed in the aristocratic state of the Maryinsky and the sophistication of *le tout Paris.* In the years 1918–1922, however, by dint of circumstance and force majeure, he won a British following that swept across the social spectrum. By promoting modernism through the music-halls, he added to the old elite an audience of impassioned intellectuals and modest pleasure-seekers. Never again would Diaghilev be so thoroughly lionized by the British public or exert so great an influence on public taste as during these years when he laid the foundation for Britain's modern ballet audience.

For the historian, nothing is so difficult as tracing the features of an anonymous public. Only the illustrious keep journals for publication, pen memoirs of their lives, will scrapbooks, letters, and miscellanea to libraries and family archives. But even if the faces of Diaghilev's new audience are blurred, their presence in the theater is not. The "tolerant good tempered public" that appeared so "incongruous" to Virginia Woolf,[3] so "common" to Ricketts, and so gauche to Beaton, was precisely the audience that "saved" the Ballets Russes.

As flagships of national entertainment combines, the Coliseum, Alhambra, and Empire stood among the music-hall elect. Yet compared to Drury Lane and Covent Garden, the ticket schedule when the "Russian Ballet" opened as the Coliseum's headliner in September 1918 slashed admission prices by almost ninefold. With balcony seats a penny less than a quart of milk and four times less than a pound of butter, Stoll's variety palace brought Diaghilev's art within reach of a popular audience.[4]

Ballet, of course, was only one of eight or nine items on the typical variety program, and many of the Coliseum's faithful no doubt preferred ventriloquists and elephant comedians, lady jugglers and gymnasts to the "posing and springing" of Diaghilev's dancers. This, at any rate, was Virginia Woolf's impression of the folk "who had been bellowing like bulls over the efforts of a man to nail a carpet down"—Will Evans in "Laying the Carpet"—but seemed "a little bit contemptuous" of *Carnaval.*[5] (Clive Bell, for his part, thought the audience "seemed to like [the ballet] rather better than the performing dogs and distinctly less than the ventriloquist.")[6]

But impressions can deceive, especially in construing behavior alien to the observing eye. Despite appearances, ballet did strike a chord in the bellowing vulgarians, and a responsive one. Diaghilev's record-breaking run at the Coliseum whetted a taste that altered the character of programming at the theater long after his troupe had departed. "Since Sir Oswald Stoll revived the glories of the Russian ballet at the Coliseum," noted the *Times* in August 1919, "the weekly programme has rarely been without a dancing entertainment."[7]

Over the next several years, dance artists from the concert stage found a warm welcome at the house, justifying Sir Oswald's faith in the willingness of the British public to "go and see ballet if they are given the real thing."[8] Many were newcomers to London: Jenny Hasselquist, a principal

at Stockholm's Royal Opera House; Bolshoi dancers Tamara Gamsakour-
dia and Alexander Demidoff; Julie Sedova, a former Maryinsky ballerina;
the Danes Elena Jorgen-Jenssen and John Andersen, who performed excerpts from Bournonville's *La Sylphide* and *Flower Festival in Genzano*.
Others like Tamara Karsavina (a frequent headliner), Alexander Gavrilov,
Lubov Egorova, Ludmilla Schollar, Anatole Vilzak, María Dalbaicín, Lydia Lopokova, Lydia Sokolova, Leon Woizikovsky, and Vera Savina were
Diaghilev familiars. Still other attractions evoked themes and styles popularized by the Ballets Russes: Jean Cocteau's *Le Boeuf sur le Toit* (translated as *The Nothing-Doing Bar*), Nikita Balieff's Chauve-Souris, the
"Cuadro Flamenco" troupe of Spanish dancers, even the "dancing sylphs"
of Loie Fuller's "ballet fantastique." By no means is this a complete listing
of all the dance artists and attractions that followed in Diaghilev's wake
at the Coliseum. Nor does it include the many ballet dancers who performed at other theaters or participated in matinées and special events that
featured dancing prominently. And it does not take into account Anna
Pavlova's lengthy seasons, which in both 1920 and 1921 partially overlapped Diaghilev's summer appearances in the British capital.

Ballet had indeed taken root in London, winning a popular following
that stood by Diaghilev when older aesthetes like Charles Ricketts cold-
shouldered the troupe's new modernist repertory. It became a familiar
pleasure, an art to be savored in the congenial surroundings of the music-
hall, on a stage shared with England's most cherished variety artists. In
the years when, as one columnist put it, "London took to [Russian ballet]
like a duck to water," this new audience also grew increasingly sophisticated; it acquired knowledge along with favorites, turning the gallery queue
for Diaghilev performances into a gathering of student dancers and balletomanes.[9]

Here, one suspects, was the public tapped by the *Dancing Times* as it
entered its most glorious decade. Shedding its Edwardian guise, the magazine became a chunky treasure-trove of contemporary dance, an invaluable guide to performers and performances of all kinds. Month after month
it published cast lists, photographs, and reviews of Diaghilev productions,
musings about his artists, ruminations on ballet style, choreography, and
technique. With its pedestrian writing and unattractive layout, the *Dancing Times* was neither a collectible aimed at an audience of connoisseurs
nor a journal laying claim to a readership of intellectuals. It aspired, rather,
to instill an intelligent appreciation of dancing among the self-educated
newcomers to ballet. At sixpence a copy the *Dancing Times* found its ideal
public among the growing ranks of music-hall balletomanes.[10]

Diaghilev's sojourn in the West End did more than create a popular
following for his Russians. The venues in which his troupe appeared, like

the company it kept on stage, gradually dulled ballet's exotic, Society patina. Little by little the art was "Englished," acquiring an identity that mirrored the features of its indigenous public. Before the war ballet had been a hothouse bloom, a rare and cosseted species. Now it took root among the pinks and primroses, naturalizing itself as a perennial of the English landscape. No less remarkable than Diaghilev's other post-Armistice achievements was his "anglicizing" of Russian ballet for the era's public.

The public Diaghilev created for his post-Armistice enterprise laid the foundation for Britain's modern ballet audience. For Diaghilev, however, democracy at the theater was simply an accident of fate, an accommodation with economic necessity. Indeed, throughout the years survival of the Ballets Russes hung on the thread of popular approval, Diaghilev labored to very different purpose: to regain his company's lost cachet and its erstwhile society public. Advertising ballet curtain times, a practice that began only weeks after the troupe settled at the Coliseum, was the first sign of a two-tier audience in the making. Another came the following January at a charity gala when boxholders paid as much as five guineas a ticket for a Diaghilev triple bill.[11] This performance, organized in aid of the Russian Relief Fund and other Slavic charities, rallied to the troupe the prestige of London's highborn émigré community—Obolenskys, Bariatinskys, even Romanovs. In the past Diaghilev had viewed Russia's aristocrats with a mixture of diffidence and contempt. Now he publicly identified himself with their cause. Declining an invitation to attend a public banquet honoring the Russian ballet, he wrote:

> While our country is in its present tragic condition, we Russians naturally feel . . . unable to accept the offer of a public festivity, even on artistic grounds. Especially now, when the Dowager Empress has arrived in England a fugitive, and when we hear daily that people are dying of hunger in Petrograd, we feel it behooves us to abstain from public functions of this kind . . .[12]

One cannot doubt the anguish that lies behind this statement, the pain of recent exile. But in the mention of Queen Alexandra's sister and the organizing committee's request that subscriptions be donated to Russian charities, one suspects that Diaghilev was also catering to the émigré brokers of society influence.

Before the war high society had formed the backbone of Diaghilev's audience. It had filled the theaters his company played and lionized his artists, while dressing his offerings in the ideology of the Establishment. As we have seen, this society audience did not abandon the postwar enterprise. The old Liberal network stood firm, even if the party itself had disintegrated. In 1919 the cream of society crowded Lady Cunard's box at the Alhambra, while for her daughter Nancy a "perfect" evening that summer wedged a visit to the ballet between dinner and late-night champagne. Mrs. Asquith was also very much in evidence, courting Diaghilev and his stars with luncheons and tea parties, and dashing off first-night impressions in vigorous, if idiosyncratic prose. Arthur Rubinstein recalled an evening when he found "the entire Diaghilev Ballet . . . leaping about [her] drawing-room," and the irrepressible Margot as well.[13]

However chummy the relationship between Diaghilev and his elite devotees, Society itself contributed little more in these years than an occasional touch of first-night glamor. The bedrock of the audience had passed upward from the boxes to those modest reaches of the house where the new enthusiasts clambered. But society was not merely outnumbered: its role in tastemaking was also largely usurped. Between 1918 and 1922 intellectuals adopted the Ballets Russes as their own.

In these post-Armistice years, plenty rather than scarcity rewards the ballet detective. Before the war, only an occasional line in a column of music notes, a cryptic aside in a lecture, a reference here and there in diaries, letters or reviews disclosed the company's standing among the intelligentsia. Now, weeklies such as the *Nation, Athenaeum, New Statesman,* and *New Age* carried regular notices of company premieres, while articles and commentaries appeared in many other intellectual journals— the *Fortnightly Review, Burlington Magazine, Drama, London Mercury, English Review,* and even the American *Dial* and *New Republic.*

Bloomsbury, of course, was no stranger to the Ballets Russes. From 1911–1914 it had formed a Bohemian covey among Diaghilev's society flock. By and large, however, it had kept the impresario and his works at arm's length, a distance reflecting its critical view of Diaghilev's aesthetic.

Beginning in 1918 a new era opened in Bloomsbury's relationship with the company. Only days after the troupe's maiden turn at the Coliseum, Keynes paid the first of many visits to the ballet, and in the ensuing months other Bloomsburies followed suit.[14] Lady Ottoline, meanwhile, had risen in Diaghilev's esteem to the position of confidante. They took tea together in the afternoons; ballerinas cluttered her sitting-room between shows; painter and writer friends ventured backstage in her company. But this remarkable woman, a "Spanish Armada in full sail," as Virginia Woolf described her appearance at this time, was not the circle's only connection with Diaghilev. Among the newcomers that swam into its life in autumn 1918 was Osbert Sitwell, whose parties became the ground where the "Junta"—one of his many disparaging terms for Bloomsbury—and its "subrout of high-mathematicians and low-psychologists" crossed paths with the ballet's new stars. (At one such event, Keynes met his future wife, the effervescent Lydia Lopokova, whose dressing room he took to visiting.)[15] But it was Armistice night 1918 that sealed the bond between intellectual London and the Ballets Russes. As crowds surged through Piccadilly and Leicester Square, singing snatches of popular songs, cheering into the wee hours soldiers, sailors, and King, the city's intelligentsia danced in the peace under Diaghilev's watchful eye—Augustus John, Roger Fry, Clive Bell, Keynes, Lytton Strachey, Lady Ottoline, Duncan Grant, Mark Gertler, Dora Carrington, David Garnett, St. John and Mary Hutchinson, Francis Birrell, Nina Hammett, D.H. Lawrence, Osbert and Sacheverell Sitwell. Lopokova and Léonide Massine, one imagines, added a touch of professional grace to the rejoicing.[16]

A newcomer to the Bloomsbury circle, Aldous Huxley waxed eloquent in praise of Diaghilev's Coliseum entertainment. "The only thing which brightens the general darkness," he wrote in September 1918, "is the Russian Ballet, which is pure beauty, like a glimpse into another world." Old Bloomsbury was less sanguine. Although it welcomed the troupe, it did so "without wild excitement," Clive Bell told readers of the *New Republic*. Virginia Woolf noted in her diary after a first view of *Schéhérazade* that she "remembered it better done at Covent Garden." In these early months only Roger Fry seems to have detected the modernist elements of Diaghilev's newer repertory.[17]

With the company's move to the Alhambra in spring 1919, reticence yielded to passion. This was the season when Virginia Woolf scribbled a breathless "must now rush up to the Alhambra," at the end of a letter to Saxon Sydney-Turner and wrote of having "an afternoon's gaiety at the Ballet" in her diary; when Vanessa Bell lent André Derain her flat in Regent Square; when Clive Bell took to dining in Picasso's shadow at the Savoy and attending smart ballet suppers; when Roger Fry entertained the designers of *La Boutique Fantasque* and *Le Tricorne* at his home; when John Maynard Keynes gave a "grand party" where Picasso, Ansermet, Lopokova, and Derain mingled with dozens of painters, writers, and students of the host's Bohemian acquaintance.[18]

The year was remarkable on still another count. For the first time in the annals of the company in England, intellectuals hastened to record their enthusiasm for Diaghilev's new repertory and style. Clive Bell, Roger Fry, and James Strachey wrote major articles about the company; Ezra Pound, Richard Aldington, and Rebecca West penned reviews; Arthur Symons published the first of a spate of essays on Diaghilev and related dance subjects. In 1919, too, Harold Monro devoted an entire issue of his poetry journal *The Monthly Chapbook* to Albert Rutherston's "Decoration in the Art of the Theatre," which examined at some length Diaghilev's prewar artists and included reproductions of costume designs by the author for

Pavlova. *Drama,* the reform-minded publication of the British Drama League, organized a ballet "symposium" in its December issue, with contributions by Massine, Karsavina, Diaghilev's English conductor Adrian Boult, and James Strachey, who compiled a bibliography of dance books in the collection of the British Museum. If 1913 was Diaghilev's annus mirabilis in the history of British opera, surely 1919 holds a similar place in that of British ballet.[19]

What delighted Bloomsbury, above all, was the visual modernism of the troupe's newest productions. For the first time, Diaghilev used his proscenium to frame genuine works of art; he turned the stage into a magnificent gallery serving the artists Bloomsbury had championed for a decade. Analyzing Larionov's designs for *Children's Tales* (as *Contes Russes* was titled at the Coliseum), Roger Fry spoke at length of the vivid illustrational value of the artist's abstract method and the uniform quality of form such a method imposed on every part of the design:

> M. Larionow . . . gives us only slight suggestions of the actual appearance of a peacock, but out of certain geometrical forms, the suggestions for which are given by nature, he builds us a figure which has almost ridiculously the character Renard describes. It is, indeed, curious, how convincing an idea of mood and character these abstract forms convey, how exactly the movements suggested might stand either for the peacock or the Indian prince . . . the colour is also at once non-natural and intensely suggestive of the character. It is in tones of intense ultramarine, vermilion, deep maroon, intense green, and as the intensest accent of all, white in spots and half-circles. It is largely by the intensity of the accents that the whole movement is given.[20]

What pleasure irradiates these lines, what delight in the revelation of form. One imagines that Fry was not alone in experiencing the epiphany of design on the stage of the Coliseum, that the friends who accompanied him to the theater shared it too, that at this turning point in her development as an artist, Virginia Woolf may have sensed in ballet the design, rhythm, and texture Bloomsbury sought in literature no less than painting.

Larionov was only an hors d'oeuvre. Derain was the entree on which Bloomsbury feasted. He stood, as Clive Bell wrote, "for what [was] . . . vital and valid in France—a passionate love of the great tradition, a longing for order and the will to win it, and that mysterious thing which . . . schoolmasters call 'high seriousness'."[21] In his review of *La Boutique Fantasque,* Fry, too, spoke of Derain's "purest French classicism," his "precise accent of high civilisation," his "profound appreciation of all the artistic expressions of the past." Here was an artist "who [gathered] up all the radiations of past art and [focussed] them exactly on the present." But

Fry devoted nearly a full *Athenaeum* column to another issue entirely: Diaghilev's role as a publicist of modernism, his "genius for putting genuine works of art upon the British public":

> In the case of "Children's Tales," for instance, a large British public was coaxed into rapturous delight, while at the same moment cultured people were being infuriated at the "ridiculous" and "preposterous monstrosities" of M. Larionov's drawings. This was done . . . by the atmosphere of exotic fantasy set up by the story and its perfect expression in the dance. And here again in "La Boutique Fantasque" the uproarious fun of the whole thing, its entire subversion of all standards of verisimilitude and probability, actually prevent people from even for a moment noticing the outrage on their dignity and commonsense which is implied in the exhibition of a work of art.[22]

Diaghilev had indeed helped England to see. Thanks to Larionov, Picasso, and Derain he had initiated his public into the practices of modernism—pure color, intellectual form, expression stripped of sentimentality. But the works of this period educated the eye in still another way. "Dancing [is] a more significant speech than words," Arthur Symons has written,[23] and in these years British audiences learned to appreciate the choreographic element in ballet, its role in articulating and unifying the larger scheme. In variants reflecting the term's French origins, "choreography" now entered common parlance. Massine's billing at the Coliseum in 1918 identified him simultaneously as "choregraphe" and "premier danseur"; programs attributed to him the "choregraphy" of a work. By June 1919 no less a bastion of linguistic conservatism than the *Times* was employing the neologism between inverted commas. Five months later the commas disappeared, and Massine's title was further anglicized as "choregrapher."[24] Usage, in this case, was more than a linguistic fashion. It implied a new way of looking at dance, an awareness of movement as design.

Even at the Coliseum the choreographic modernism of *The Good-Humoured Ladies* and *Children's Tales* had claimed Fry's attention. He noted with approval that "the formal relations of movement in all the different parts of the ballet have become more and more distinct and evident—the whole pattern is keyed up to an intenser unity and the intellectual quality of the design is further intensified." Bell echoed his mentor. Massine's "idea of a ballet," he wrote some months later, "is an organized whole, detached from circumstance, and significant in itself." Few could articulate how choreography worked as lucidly as Bloomsbury's aestheticians. But thanks to lengthy seasons and the chance to view again and again the offerings of the repertory, all sensed that it did work and that it brought both substance and meaning to a ballet. When Massine left the troupe in 1921, the loss of his dancemaking talent brought home the value of his choreography. As Raymond Mortimer told readers of the *Dial*, "We soon realized that it was not so much the dancer as the choreographer who was irreplaceable. For when Chout was produced, with music by Prokofieff, the choreography [by Larionov and Thadée Slavinsky] was neither dramatically nor plastically interesting." [25]

Something else arrested Bloomsbury's eye. For the first time intellectuals were presented with a performing style—objective, impersonal, abstract—that mirrored the qualities they esteemed most in the other arts. When Karsavina rejoined the Ballets Russes in 1919 after a five-year absence, Clive Bell noted that "she was playing a different game and a poorer one" compared with Diaghilev's younger stars; he drew a distinction "between an actress and a pure artist," between the expression of personality and the transmuting of that personality into art:

> Madame Karsavina communicates her gracious and attractive personality direct to the audience . . . she is apt to express herself, not through the work of art she is interpreting, but immediately, as in conversation . . . Madame Lopokova is different . . . [She] has been called "the greatest comedienne of the age"; what is more, her deliciously gay temperament is reckoned one of her main instruments. So it is; and the same might be said of Mozart or Fra Angelico. The point is that neither Mozart, nor Fra Angelico, nor Lopokova express themselves directly to the public. They transmute personality into something more precious. The public gets no raw material from them. They pour themselves into works of art from which the public may deduce what it can . . .
>
> It is because she sometimes crosses to [our side of the curtain] that Madame Karsavina is not perfectly in key with the new ballet: whereas little Lopokova, bouncing in her box, making vivid contacts with every line and color on the stage, impressing her personality on each gesture of her own, and so helping to build up an organic whole, is the choreographer's first violin. [26]

Between late 1920 and early 1923 another major writer at least partially connected with Bloomsbury observed with fascination this revolution in performing style. Allusions to the Ballets Russes appear in many of T.S. Eliot's writings; as revealed in his London letters for the *Dial,* the troupe occupied a key place in his meditations on theater. "Two years ago," he wrote in 1921:

> M. Diaghileff's ballet arrived . . . we greeted the Good-humoured Ladies, and the Boutique Fantasque, and the Three-Cornered Hat, as the dawn of an art of the theatre. And although there has been nothing since that could be called a further development, the ballet will probably be one of the influences

forming a new drama, if a new drama ever comes. I mean of course the later ballet which has just been mentioned; for the earlier ballet, if it had greater dancers—Nijinsky and Pavlowa—had far less significance or substantiality. The later ballet is more sophisticated, but also more simplified, and simplifies more; and what is needed of art is a simplification of current life into something rich and strange.[27]

Like Bell, Eliot admired the aloofness and detachment of performers who played for themselves rather than for the audience. In "Dramatis Personae," a short essay of theatrical criticism published in his recently founded *Criterion,* Eliot expostulated on the virtues of Massine, "the greatest actor . . . in London . . . the most completely unhuman, impersonal, abstract." Taking Bell's distinction between the expression and transmuting of personality one step further, Eliot contrasted the "conventional gesture of the ordinary stage, which is supposed to *express* emotion, and the abstract gesture of Massine, which *symbolises* emotion."[28] Most astonishing, perhaps, was the occasion prompting these remarks: George Robey's *You'd Be Surprised,* a revue that by all accounts displayed neither Massine's performing nor choreographic talents to great advantage. Well before George Balanchine emigrated to the West the "impersonality" many would credit him with inventing had become a trademark of the Diaghilev company's performing style.

As Bloomsbury aged, it grew more conservative; it joined the swim of Society and began to extoll the virtues of civilization. In Clive Bell's writings for the *New Republic* between 1918 and 1922, ballet appears as a marker of this rightward path; in the theater Diaghilev alone upheld standards of taste and critical intelligence, order and excellence. At the end of his essay "The Creed of an Aesthete," Bell imagines a perfect day: lunch, sunshine, Proust, ballet, a gay supper in a house full of beautiful objects with Arthur Rubinstein at the piano[29]—allusions in which the pleasures of art are nearly identical to those of Society. Bell was not alone in linking the demise of high culture with the demise of Edwardian privilege. "Opera," wrote Eliot in July 1921, referring to the collapse of the Beecham organization, "was one of the last reminders of a former excellence of life, a sustaining symbol even for those who seldom went." For both Eliot and Bell, the disease wasting the critical spirit was the "emporium malady." "Our tastes," wrote Bell, "are imposed on us by our tradesmen, under which respectable title I include newspaper owners, book-sellers' touts, bookstall keepers, music-hall kings, opera syndicates, picture dealers and honest bagmen."[30]

Where Bell the Englishman was apt to blame the collapse of standards on a leisured class that had abjured its role as cultural leaders, Eliot the transplanted American took umbrage with democracy: the "decent middle-class mob" and its works, particularly the "cheap and rapid breeding cinema," threatened culture both high and low.[31] In the depressing scene of post-Armistice London, the Ballets Russes appeared a lone bastion of civilization, the miraculous survival of another era. But as *The Sleeping Princess* revealed, not even Diaghilev was immune to the demands of trade. To salvage for an elite some semblance of cultural control was an idea that took root in post-Armistice Bloomsbury, and one that yielded strange fruit. "Much as I disliked the idea of a Ministry of Fine Arts," Bell confessed in his memoirs, "the creation of such a ministry would be when private patronage had been destroyed by economic egalitarianism, the only means of saving the arts from extinction."[32] Ironically, the preservation of high theatrical art in Britain—opera, drama, and ballet—became possible only when the populist ground swell of World War II voted Labour into office in 1945.

Important as Bloomsbury was in championing the Ballets Russes, it comprised only a fraction of the "artistic" public remarked upon in the press with increasing frequency and pique as the war decade drew to a close. From these post-Armistice years dated the cult following that remained an attribute of the troupe to the end: the "highly sensitized beings" and "small-talk aesthetes" who gushed over Diaghilev's "newest Parisian modes" as a matter of snobbery.[33] Reviewing a new play in the *London Mercury*, W.J. Turner decried these self-appointed arbiters of theatrical taste and the power they exercised by 1920:

> If The Young Visitors had been produced by the Russian Society called Zahda, or by the Russian Miniature Theatre, it would have been hailed as a wonderful masterpiece of bizarre and original art, and all the young freaks of London who frequent the Russian Ballet and sneer at Gilbert and Sullivan would have flocked to see it and talked of nothing else for months. As it is a product, however, of the despised English . . . and as . . . it has had the misfortune to have been in its book form enormously popular, there is little likelihood of its being adequately appreciated.[34]

Sentiments of this kind were by no means rare. Nor were they restricted to the theatrical columns. As taste in both music and painting leaned toward the Continent, observers lamented again and again the "too ready assimilation of foreign ideas"—like those put into circulation by Diaghilev.[35]

Leigh Henry ascribed the "antagonism" to Diaghilev in "certain 'cultured' and journalistic circles" to the "ooze of cult pretention" and the "indiscriminate vogue [that had] welled up about the . . . company" and its artists.[36] There was more to it, however. Diaghilev's tactic of using journalists to publicize his artistic line did not sit well with London's critical brotherhood; it smelled of compromise and venality, while implying that Englishmen needed experts to tell them what to think. (The "Diaghilevite" of the music columns, Edwin Evans, just happened to be on the company's payroll.)[37] Matters came to a head in 1921 when Stravinsky, in London for the revival of *Le Sacre du Printemps,* delivered a barrage of musical-cum-theoretical pronouncements that stirred a furor in the press. The British lion was roused, and much to his chagrin, the composer found himself its victim.[38]

Diaghilev overplayed his hand in 1921 not only because he had miscalculated the psychology of the players, but because the cards themselves had partly changed. No art form exists in a social vacuum, and when Turner noted the "curious affinity between Stravinsky's music and the smart hats and frocks of society,"[39] he was taking to task not the aesthetics of modernism but its cult among a segment of Diaghilev's public. For what critics in these years were attending was the birth of High Bohemia—that alliance of modern art and fashion that framed Diaghilev's efforts in the 1920s. Like Turner, Edward J. Dent, music critic of the *Athenaeum,* looked askance at this phenomenon. He also sketched its countenance:

> The Diaghilev audience (I must call it by his name, for it is his creation) consisted of or was at any rate dominated by the "intellectual-smart"—musicians who know all about painting, painters who know all about music, poets who like to be men about town, men about town who like to be poets, up-to-date scholars, antiquarian modernists—all those in fact who, whatever class they may belong to, like to flatter themselves that they at any rate stand outside it. They may not understand themselves, but M. Diaghilev understands them as if he were himself the *maestro* whose immortal hand had framed their sawdust and tinsel anatomies.[40]

By 1920 this "intellectual-smart" audience had become the ideological center of Diaghilev's public, the salon, so to speak, where rumors flew and gossips buzzed. But this small world, a London outpost of *le tout Paris* in its taste and social style, could never rule English cultural life with quite the iron hand of similar coteries across the Channel. Again and again, the pecking order of class notwithstanding, one encounters in Britain a phenomenon largely absent in France—an impulse to democratize high culture, to bring opera, music, Shakespeare, and the classics to ordinary people at popular prices. Compared to such efforts, a Stravinsky first night at Covent Garden, no matter how gala the occasion or rhapsodic the small talk, was apt to lose something of its importance. As Turner wrote in 1920:

It strikes one very strongly when coming from abroad how much less such idols of the intelligentsia as Stravinsky count in England than on the Continent. Here the chief musical interest of the past season has not been the first performance of Stravinsky's *Nightingale* in its ballet form, or the concert of his chamber music, nor, in fact, anything that has happened at Covent Garden or in the London concert halls. It has been the performance of Blow and Mozart at the "Old Vic," the Purcell *Dido and Aeneas* at Hyde Park, where thousands of people stood listening for hours, and almost tore the officials to pieces in their eagerness to learn more about it, the Cambridge undergraduates' production of *The Fairy Queen* and the coming Glastonbury Festival . . . These are examples of the true musical life of the country.[41]

The ballets Diaghilev staged in 1920–1921 may have polarized the critical brotherhood, but they continued to draw intellectuals to the theater. With the production of *The Sleeping Princess,* however, a rift appeared within the audience itself: the ballet drove a wedge between aesthetes, who applauded the work, and modernists, who cold-shouldered it. Between the critical intellectuals of Bloomsbury and the style-minded dandies of the Sitwell circle differences in outlook had long simmered, even if both shared a taste for ballet and an interest in contemporary painting. (The 1919 exhibition of French moderns that launched the Sitwell brothers as fine art impresarios prominently featured Bloomsbury's idols—Picasso, Derain, and Matisse.) *The Sleeping Princess* brought these differences to the surface. "After *Boutique Fantasque* and *Le Tricorne,*" reminisced Sacheverell Sitwell:

> the old masterpiece of Tchaikowsky and Petipa was looked forward to with mixed feelings by the 'advance guard' . . . the prospect of five scenes and three hundred dresses by Léon Bakst was in thrilling anticipation for myself. During the first interval, many conflicting points of view were expressed. Lytton Strachey, poor thing, told me that it made him feel sick, it was so degraded, especially the music. A person, now eminent on the "Nation and New Statesman" concurred with this . . . But, to someone like myself, who had loved the music of Casse-noisette since childhood, the matter was not even in dispute. And I only repeat those hostile animadversions because it is curious that often the "intelligentsia" can be utterly and entirely wrong.[42]

But was the intellectual press so utterly wrong in condemning the ballet, the antithesis of everything Diaghilev had taught it to esteem? The modernist felt betrayed and sharpened his scalpel accordingly. "What was M Diaghileff to do?" asked Raymond Mortimer in the *Dial* with ill-concealed ire:

"What *do* the English like?" he asked. "Clothes! Clothes! Clothes!" came the reverberating answer to the tune of Chu Chin Chow. "What music?" A thousand provincial orchestras answered with the strains of Casse Noisette . . . Tchaikovsky was dead, but his music was obtainable . . . M. Bakst was alive, just. And so *he* set about designing hundreds of dresses, the dancers set about learning a thirty-year-old ballet, The Sleeping Princess, and the press set about informing us that the dresses were to cost two million francs and that Tchaikovsky's music was all that music should be. Stravinsky himself proclaimed this in every news-sheet . . .

The result is what you can imagine—a ballet of the early Nineties, a ballet in which even such artists as Madame Lopokova and Monsieur Idzikovsky can make no effect, a ballet all clothes and three hours long, a ballet that delighted those who hated the Sacre.[43]

Few reviewers expressed themselves with Mortimer's gusto. But the objections raised against the ballet—Tchaikovsky's suburban tunefulness, Bakst's vulgar dress parade (Turner compared the costumes to "Bank Holiday dresses on Hampstead Heath"[44]), and Petipa's old-fashioned choreography—reverberated throughout the intellectual press. For the advance guard of the intelligentsia, *The Sleeping Princess* was a sort of superior Pantomime.

Such cavils reflected more than a sense of betrayal. They stemmed from a critical attitude toward the past. The modernist looked at history with a contemporary eye; he analyzed it through a prism of new forms and ideas: Rossini recast by Massine and Derain was the balletic analogue of those eminent Victorians reinterpreted by Strachey. The dandy-aesthete, on the other hand, exulted in the resurrection of the past; he took pleasure in the evocation of its rituals and conceits, icons that opened the corridors of the imagination. For Sacheverell Sitwell, *The Sleeping Princess* marked the start of a journey through the byways of theatrical history—Victorian pantomime, commedia dell'arte, juvenile drama, as well as romantic ballet—a journey informed by "a sense of nostalgia bordering on despair for the vanished past, particularly for the arts that blossomed in a lost, golden age and are dead in the present time."[45] We are far from Bloomsbury revisionism and experiment.

Preciousness was never entirely absent from the Ballets Russes. But in the period following Diaghilev's return to London in late 1924 the dandy element would come to the fore among his cultivated public. The schoolboy *Sonnenkinder* of post-Armistice years, treading in the Sitwells' footsteps, would displace Bloomsbury's critical intellectuals from the ideological center of the audience. In part, this change reflected a natural passing of the generations. But the company that returned to London in 1924 itself differed from its predecessor: the whiff of artistic fashion and aristocratic pretense that hung about its repertory appealed to a different clientele than the catholic works of high modernism. With the failure of *The Sleeping Princess,* Diaghilev cast his lot with High Bohemia.

For the man of St. Petersburg, Paris remained a spiritual and artistic home. He cursed its fickleness and derided its costliness, but it was to its studios and salons that Diaghilev returned again and again for new ideas and critical validation, and where, finally, he made a home for his priceless collection of musical scores, books, and art works.

From 1917 to 1929, however, Paris was rarely home to the Ballets Russes. Premieres might continue to take place there, but with first London and then Monte Carlo established as the company's headquarters, it became only a brief stopover in the troupe's annual migrations. But time alone does not determine quality of feeling. In 1909 Paris had capitulated to the art of Diaghilev's Russians in a matter of weeks, and did so every spring up to the war. After 1917, however, the city stinted its affections: *le tout Paris social et artistique,* so courted by Diaghilev, found other enterprises, including many that owed inspiration and personnel to the Ballets Russes, on which to lavish time, money, and interest. Never again would Diaghilev recover his prewar standing in the French capital.

World War I may have redrawn the map of Europe, but it had relatively little effect on Diaghilev's Parisian audience. Crossing the Channel from England, where populism eddied throughout the post-Armistice years against the current of chic, one touches familiar ground. The artifacts themselves speak of continuity with the past: there are the same charity galas and patronage committees, society page columns and souvenir programs, elegant magazine spreads and top-of-the-scale ticket prices at top-of-the-line theaters, the same combination, in short, of elegance and art. New faces were to be seen, of course, and lean postwar silhouettes, but the names, like the haute couture fashions, bore a striking resemblance to those of audiences past. Nor does one find much evidence of the artists Diaghilev claimed to have cultivated so assiduously or the kind of intellectual support he garnered in England. Indeed, compared to London, the changes in the company's Paris audience were neither profound nor far-reaching.

Throughout these years Diaghilev's public remained what it had always been—*le tout Paris.* But this motley collection of cosmopolitan tastemakers had itself subtly changed: it had acquired a democratized facade along with a style of deluxe modernity, and it now cultivated the avant-garde as once it had taken up the exotic and the Slav. In its latest avatar, *le tout Paris* was no less heterogeneous a group than before; now, however, instead of banking family scions and Proustian figures, high society jostled with High Bohemia, Café Society celebrities, fashion moguls, titled émigrés, and the artists—dilettante and serious—who trundled in their wake. In the years 1917–1929 Diaghilev's Paris audience, like the Ballets Russes itself, did more than dictate taste from a Right Bank Olympus. It acted, now, as a broker of contemporary art, promoting the wares of a market that extended as far as America. Diaghilev's public may have included some of the makers of modernism, but it contained far more of its promoters, proselytizers, and collectors. In that quarter of *le tout Paris* where art was the coin defining a modern style of luxury and a new aristocracy of taste, Diaghilev found the ideal audience for ballet's commerce in the avant-garde.

In December 1919 Diaghilev made his "triumphal return" to the Paris Opéra, a six-week season marred only by a strike of the theater's backstage and performing personnel. For a time, it seems, Diaghilev harbored the idea of making this theater, the apogee of the French subsidized system, his Paris base. As early as January 1919, he was writing to Misia Sert, an intermediary in the negotiations, that the season would be a "very brilliant" one and "not too *objectionable*," a reference to the *scandale* occasioned by *Parade* two years before. Jacques Rouché, director of the Opéra since 1914, need not have worried: the receipts at certain performances, noted the *Mercure de France*, exceeded Frs. 100,000.[46] But the season was more than a financial coup for the under-subsidized Opéra. With a repertory of Fokine favorites, plus three of Massine's newer ballets, Diaghilev established his supremacy as a purveyor of balletic entertainment among the *grand public* of theatergoing Paris.

Competition took many forms in postwar Paris, quite apart from the challenge from Rolf de Maré's newly formed Ballets Suédois. The artists and aesthetics of Diaghilev's past now became the stuff of mainstream theatrical ventures that whittled away the base of his audience. The seasons organized by Maria Kuznetsova, Ida Rubinstein, and Nikita Balieff, not to mention revues at such tourist meccas as the Folies-Bergère, appropriated the Russian and Orientalist themes of the company's prewar repertory. At the same time, Paris was awash in a new cult of primitivism, one that had roots in Africa rather than the Middle East. Jazz, Josephine Baker, and the *Revue Nègre* cast the sensual spell once worked by Rimsky-Korsakov and Diaghilev's dancers in *Schéhérazade*. In 1921, at Rouché's invitation, Fokine mounted Ravel's *Daphnis and Chloë* as part of the Opéra's first all-dance evening in decades. This was not the only occasion when Rouché intruded upon Diaghilev's traditional bailiwick. Beginning in 1918 Ida Rubinstein appeared in the first of the sumptuous spectacles that became a nearly annual feature of Opéra programming and drew on the talents of such prewar luminaries as Bakst, Gabriele d'Annunzio, Vincent d'Indy, and Florent Schmitt.

As Rouché partly recast the Opéra in an earlier image of the Ballets Russes, Diaghilev was expurgating the fin de siècle from his repertory. In spring 1920 no fewer than nine of the season's fourteen works at the Opéra had choreography by Massine, and of the remaining Fokine ballets two had music by Stravinsky. The composer figured prominently the following December at the Théâtre des Champs-Elysées, where an all-Stravinsky program was given on Christmas night, and in May 1921, when the brief season at the Gaîté-Lyrique ended with a "Stravinsky Festival" at which prices for the most expensive seats were doubled. In December 1920 all-Picasso evenings further underscored the rupture with the World of Art aesthetic.

Only in October 1921 did Rouché open his theater again to the Ballets Russes.[47] With its stars, magnificent settings, and spectacular costumes, *The Sleeping Princess* promised the kind of brilliance that translated into box office success. Diaghilev's proposal in April 1922 to stage the one-act *Aurora's Wedding*, along with revivals of *L'Après-midi d'un Faune* and *Le Spectre de la Rose*, and two new Stravinsky productions, *Mavra* and *Le Renard*, infuriated Rouché. "Who, pray tell, will be doing the scenery and costumes for 'Aurora's Wedding'? You propose reviving *L'Après-midi d'un Faune* and *Le Spectre de la Rose*. With the same scenery and costumes or in versions by new painters? If the latter, by whom? Apart from *Petrouchka*, we have no grand ballet: neither *Schéhérazade* nor *Firebird*, only very short works demanding numerous rehearsals and appealing solely to an audience of artists."[48]

From Rouché's incensed remarks one gathers that a dramatic change had come over Diaghilev's audience. Between 1920 and 1922 the promotion of modernism, and Stravinsky's newest works in particular, had alienated the more conservative elements of the fashionable public. At the same time, a cult had grown up around the troupe; it had acquired a following of artistic sophisticates. (One hesitates to take Rouché's "artists" at face value; only a minority of working artists could have afforded the ticket prices he himself described as "very high.")

Cult audiences serve many purposes. At their best, they bring a loyalty and recognition to unpopular art or the unknown artist. At their worst, and this was the case of Diaghilev's Paris audience in the 1920s, they set themselves up as arbiters, self-serving proselytizers of an exclusive code. Cult followings are always select, because by definition they are self-selected. But Diaghilev wanted his public to be select in a worldly sense as well—a central paradox of his behavior in the twenties. He wanted a cult following with all the powers of *le tout Paris*. Thus, he never abjured the stages of the *grand public* for the venues of the avant-garde: always he deemed Covent Garden or the Opéra, those Western analogues of the Maryinsky, the settings appropriate to his company. But if he wanted their aura of history, along with the distinction and glamor of their clientele, he wanted no part of the boxholders themselves. Diaghilev's willingness to slight this influential majority of the fashionable audience explains in part the brevity of his seasons in the French capital. No matter how loyal or diligent in promoting his cause, friends alone could not fill a theater. Indeed, by June 1923, rumors of the company's imminent disbandment had surfaced in the press.[49]

Diaghilev never completely abjured the broad fashionable audience: he still mined its cachet and publicity value. For the *répétition générale* of *Les Noces*—ironically, the most sober of Diaghilev's twenties ballets—a dazzling house assembled in the cause of Russian charities in France: the old prewar public echoes momentarily in the society palaver of *Le Gaulois* and *Figaro*, where Jacques-Emile Blanche, that portraitist par excellence of the Belle Epoque, even wrote an encomium of the impresario.[50] But time is inexorable, even in Paris. However ringing, Imperial titles carried only memories of power and vast estates, and one notes with surprise subscriptions taken out in the names of banks—perhaps the first instance of corporate patronage of ballet.[51]

A more general aura of aristocracy adhered to the Ballets Russes in Diaghilev's other major Continental venue, Monte Carlo, for if the Blue Train sped artists to Diaghilev's side, it also discharged in Cannes and Menton, Nice, Cap d'Antibes, and Monte Carlo, Europe's wintering royalties and titled cosmopolitans, and the "special correspondents" who relayed their doings home. In these years Riviera sunshine captured the imagination of the grey-clouded north. On the new photograph page of the *Times,* Londoners might vicariously warm themselves with a sight of outdoor idlers sipping apéritifs, strollers and pets on the Promenade, a ladies' doubles match with Suzanne Lenglen in Cannes. From November onwards they might scan the column of "Riviera Notes" that related at least twice and sometimes as often as four times a week news of arrivals, dinner parties, and concerts. And throughout the winter they would find regular features on such edifying subjects as Riviera flowers, golf, weather, prices, fashions, its calendar of social and sporting events, and, of course, its increasing vulgarization.[52]

Figaro was as prodigal as the *Times* in covering the Riviera, even if it eschewed photography. Nearly every day during the winter of 1922–1923, "Le Figaro aux pays du soleil," as the newspaper's half-page feature was called, published calendars of events, lists of arrivals, and even tennis scores from the southern resortland. Diaghilev's name is seldom mentioned—as always he shied from personal publicity—but his dancers frequently are: notices of ballets, including the names of their principal interpreters, appeared in *Figaro*'s columns the day before a Monte Carlo performance. Unlike the *Times*, *Figaro* ignored the crowds of pleasure-seekers despoiling once select locales; rather, it stressed the distinction of Riviera society. "The Christmas and New Year festivities that traditionally mark the opening of the Riviera's grand social season have been particularly brilliant this year," noted the front page "Echos" column on January 9, 1923. "Every day, Europe's high aristocracy meets at concerts . . . or at ballet and operetta performances, or at the social gatherings of the Hôtel de Paris. A real whirl of elegance anytime and everywhere."[53] Here was the "elegant public" that acclaimed Diaghilev's stars on the opening night of his April season.[54]

Proximity to the royal family—and with the dethroning of Austria's Hapsburgs the Grimaldis were Europe's oldest ruling house—enhanced the aura of privilege surrounding the Ballets Russes. The company danced at birthday galas for the reigning Prince and other national *fêtes,* entertained at palace dinners, while its seasons enjoyed the patronage of Princess Charlotte, an ardent balletomane who had lessons with Lubov Tchernicheva and sat in on the company's daily class.[55] Monte Carlo may have been a stone's throw from France, but in these years it resembled a winter outpost of Mayfair. ("The Tower of London has replaced the Tower of Babel," jested a Riviera correspondent in *Figaro*.)[56] At dinner parties and galas sat many of Diaghilev's prewar subscribers—King Manoel, the Duke of Westminster, the Princess of Pless, Lady Michelham, to name only a few—as well as the patrons who would smooth his company's return to England. Indeed, Monte Carlo cemented relationships between Diaghilev and that triumvirate of Britishers—the Duke of Connaught, Viscount Rothermere, and Lady Cunard—who stood behind his London seasons in the middle and late twenties.

Amid the chatter of English, another tongue could be heard: the courtly Russian of émigrés who had settled along the Côte d'Azur and on whose behalf the cream of Riviera society assembled for one glamorous benefit after another. "The Franco-Russian ball at the [Cannes] Municipal Casino last night attracted society *en masse*," reported the *Times* in March 1923. "More than six hundred people attended, and the profit for the Russian refugees on the Riviera amounted to about 75,000f." The *Times* went on to list the most distinguished personalities of this "brilliant assemblage"— Grand Duke and Grand Duchess Cyril, Grand Duke Michael, Countess Torby, Prince and Princess Dolgorouky, Prince and Princess Christian of Hesse, Princess Karageorgevitch, the Princess of Pless, and several dozen titled British guests. Less than three weeks later, charity again summoned the resortland's elite—this time for a brilliant affair in Monte Carlo where Diaghilev's stars danced for Russian refugees in France. Yet another high point of the Riviera social calendar was the "magnificent" 1925 performance by the Ballets Russes in Cannes on behalf of the Franco-Russian Children's Home, one of the many émigré benefits to which the Princesse Héritière gave her blessing.[57]

Even as Diaghilev each winter made over his repertory for Paris, the Théâtre de Monte-Carlo added a jarring note to the image of artistic experimentation he cultivated in its studios. Little is known of the day-to-day performing life of the troupe outside Diaghilev's own seasons: a list of the operas and ballets in which his dancers appeared has yet to be compiled. But, surely, the *Coppélias, Korriganes,* and *Deux Pigeons* of the Monte Carlo repertory, like the variety matinees at the Palais des Beaux-Arts in 1923 (which teamed Diaghilev's dancers with singers, jugglers, and "burlesque" comedians), altered perceptions of the troupe, adding to its image the tastes and habits of its Riviera public. For what was the real Ballets Russes in these years? The company that performed *Les Noces* in Paris during a season that made a clean "sweep . . . of the repertory associated with its early years," or the troupe that danced *Coppélia, Au Temps Jadis* and *Fleurs et Papillons* in Monte Carlo?[58] Throughout the 1920s Diaghilev's alliance with fashion weakened his credibility as an experimentalist. The repasts he served in Monte Carlo, like the audience ("subtle, suburban, and subconscious" in Satie's caustic phrase[59]), eroded still further his claim to the vanguard. In the gilded world of royalty and idle pleasure, Diaghilev entwined the mystique of the Ballets Russes with the last idyll of the nineteenth century's aristocracy.

Throughout his career Diaghilev insisted that artists were his true following. Yet in these years, when Paris was a mecca for creative spirits from the four corners of the globe, the Ballets Russes rarely impassioned Montparnasse or became the hub of a community of artists, as did the Ballets Suédois or the short-lived Soirées de Paris. From the galleries and ateliers of the city came the ideas that remade the Ballets Russes in the image of modernity, but the audience itself only occasionally reflected this. In Paris, circles and cénacles dotted the cultural horizon; they spanned a social territory that reached from the Hotel Meurice to unheated rooms on the Left Bank. As before the war, Diaghilev's artists stood at the upper end of the scale; the others visited his theater more rarely. Never in these postwar years would Diaghilev excite the imagination of Paris as he had quickened the artistic and intellectual pulse of post-Armistice London.

Paris in the 1920s is a subject of enduring interest to Americans, and recent years have added to its romance with a spate of biographies, reissued memoirs, and gossipy books about that charmed decade of the Lost

Generation. The Anglo-American colony embraced talents as diverse as the home towns left behind; it comprised sons and daughters of millionaires and writers on the edge of poverty; it included those who traveled in high society, others who lived among the surrealists, and a few who penetrated the outer reaches of Diaghilev's circle. America's expatriate community gazed on Paris with very different eyes from its European counterparts, and it interpreted what it saw by the light of quite different assumptions. For this reason, the picture it drew of Diaghilev's artists and personalities, like its presence or absence from the theater itself, offers a judicious corrective to mythologies about his "artistic" audience.

In those days, reminisced poet/publisher Robert McAlmon in his memoir *Being Geniuses Together,* "people moved en masse from performance to performance,"[60] and, indeed, a book remains to be written about the impact of the Paris theatrical scene on the expatriate community. Commenting in his October 1926 "Paris Letter" for the *Dial* on the "colonization" of Paris by Greenwich Village and Hollywood, Paul Morand noted that "one of the rare points of contact" between the "travellers and the country in which they are travelling" was the Russian Ballet.[61] But if the company became an obligatory stop on the American grand summer tour, the magic of earlier days had dimmed. For artists and writers of the avant-garde, Diaghilev's stock was highest in the late teens and early twenties, when Stravinsky and Prokofiev sounded the call to experiment and high modernism dominated the repertory.

Of all the writers who passed through Paris in those years, none succumbed to the spell of the Ballets Russes so completely as e.e. cummings and John Dos Passos. Both had seen the company on the Boston leg of its 1916 tours; discovered it again on visits to Paris; both would testify in their work to its passage across the imagination.

A "genuine balletomane"—this is cummings's biographer speaking— ever since "his youthful rapture at seeing Pavlova and Nijinsky in Boston and *Petrouchka* and *Parade* in Paris," cummings waited nearly twenty years to write the ballet scenario based on *Uncle Tom's Cabin* intended to pay homage to Diaghilev.[62] But long before, in an essay written shortly after his discovery of free verse in the late teens, this poet who also painted, revealed the impact of the company on his speculations about modern art. Not only did cummings identify *Parade, Till Eulenspiegel, L'Après-midi d'un Faune,* and *Petrouchka* with the modernist renaissance; he also borrowed from Diaghilev's stage such concepts as gesture and synaesthesia to define the vital new art that so thrilled him.[63]

For Dos Passos, too, the Ballets Russes belonged to modernism's heroic moment—"the creative tidal wave that spread over the world from the Paris of before the last European war":

Under various tags: futurism, cubism, vorticism, modernism, most of the best work in the arts in our time has been the direct product of this explosion . . . Cendrars and Apollinaire, poets, were on the first cubist barricades with the group that included Picasso, Modigliani, Marinetti, Chagall; that profoundly influenced Maiakovsky, Meyerhold, Eisenstein, whose ideas carom through Joyce, Gertrude Stein, T.S. Eliot . . . The music of Stravinski and Prokofieff and Diageleff's Ballet hail from this same Paris . . . as do the windows of Saks Fifth Avenue, skyscraper furniture . . . and the newritz styles of advertizing in American magazines.[64]

In 1923 Dos Passos met Gerald and Sara Murphy, a wealthy expatriate couple, whose friendship would have important consequences for the young painter/novelist. Of all the Americans in Paris the Murphys alone enjoyed entree to the Ballets Russes.[65] They had studied painting with Natalia Gontcharova; helped refurbish damaged Diaghilev sets; come to know Picasso, Braque, Derain, and Bakst. "In addition to being the focal center of the whole modern movement in the arts," Gerald told Calvin Tompkins, "the Diaghilev ballet was a kind of movement in itself. Anybody who was interested in the company became a member automatically. You knew everybody, you knew all the dancers, and everybody asked your opinion on things."[66] Renegades from stuffy American privilege—Sara was the daughter of an ink manufacturer, Gerald the son of the president of Mark Cross—they lived at the crossroads of High Franco-American Bohemia.

In 1923, when Dos Passos saw them almost daily, the Murphys took an active part in the life of their adopted family. They attended rehearsals for *Les Noces* and even helped paint Gontcharova's sets, and on some of these visits Dos Passos and cummings joined them. Excitement over *Les Noces* ran high, and to celebrate its premiere, the Murphys hired a barge moored in the Seine for a champagne supper that lasted till dawn. Diaghilev, who stilled his fear of water on this occasion, was among the forty-odd guests, as were a handful of his principal dancers, and his artistic cabinet—Picasso, Cocteau, Larionov, Gontcharova, Stravinsky, Ansermet, Kochno—and others who had taken a hand in the production. Only the choreographer and corps de ballet were missing.[67]

By and large, however, the American colony did not take to the Ballets Russes. The little magazines devoted few pages to its novelties, while the notices written by Janet Flanner for the *New Yorker* amounted at most to three or four paragraphs. In March 1924 *Theatre Arts Monthly* published the only important article about the company written by an American expatriate. The author, Florence Gilliam, was a theater critic for the Paris *Tribune*, contributor to American theater magazines, and with her husband Arthur Moss, copublisher of *Gargoyle*, the first English-language journal of arts and letters on the Continent. Reviewing the 1923 season, which included the premiere of *Les Noces* and a revival of Massine's *Le Sacre du Printemps*, Gilliam marveled at Diaghilev's uncompromising modernism. For the choreography of Nijinska's new ballet, she had nothing but admiration. And in a city where Russian cabarets and music-hall acts were commonplace, she welcomed the sobriety of Gontcharova's sets, "the most complete reaction of the modern artist from the violent and ubiquitous color which has been exploited, particularly by the Russians, to the point of . . . losing its artistic verity." Doubtless many Americans shared her view that "the biggest thing . . . the Ballet has ever given in any season or on any program is Stravinsky's brutally magnificent *Sacre du Printemps*" and that with *Les Noces*, "it brought [the] year's program up to a standard not previously surpassed."[68]

At no time in the course of the 1920s did the repertory tread so uncompromising a path; never again would it shed its veneer of frivolity. The contrast between the worldliness of the Ballets Russes and the cloistered existence of the dancer is one of the themes of Zelda Fitzgerald's *Save Me the Waltz*. In this thinly veiled autobiographical fiction, the studio ruled by "Madame"—retired Maryinsky ballerina Lubov Egorova in real life—offered a disciplined escape from the aimless hedonism of sophisticated high life. That Zelda found her way to Egorova's studio, where over the decades Anton Dolin, Alexandra Danilova, George Skibine, Roland Petit, and Marjorie Tallchief hastened whenever they were in Paris, is a tribute to her dedication as much as a sign of the social milieu in which she moved: her entree there was smoothed by Gerald Murphy.

Zelda was not the only troubled woman of the expatriate literati to take up dance. Between 1926 and 1929 Lucia Joyce, the novelist's daughter, also flung herself into the studio, but although she, too, studied briefly with Egorova, her training reflected the more eclectic interests of the avant-garde: Dalcroze eurhythmics, Swedish gymnastics, and Duncan-style "interpretative" dancing.[69] (Among the more eccentric of her teachers was Isadora's brother, Raymond Duncan, who wandered around Paris in long robes, had a "colony" at Neuilly, and ran profitable tunic-cum-sandal emporia on the Rue du Faubourg St. Honoré and Boulevard St. Germain.) As a doting parent, Joyce was in the audience for Lucia's recitals—the kind that brought an eclectic flavor to the Paris dance scene. Like many expatriates, Joyce preferred other forms of dance to ballet. Indeed, the only evidence that he actually saw the Ballets Russes appears in a letter praising the Indian dancer Uday Shankar. "If he ever performs at Geneva," Joyce wrote his daughter in 1934, "don't miss going there. He leaves the best of the Russians far behind. I have never seen anything like it."[70] In the mid-1930s Joyce offered to collaborate with Virgil Thomson on a ballet based on the children's games chapter of *Finnegan's Wake*. The proposal, which included designs by Picasso, choreography by Massine, and a production at the Paris Opéra,[71] harked back to Diaghilev's earliest postwar seasons— the probable era of Joyce's first encounter with the troupe and the one that obviously touched him most deeply.

Joyce stood at the avant-garde hub of expatriate Paris—a world bounded by the cafés of Montparnasse, the bookstores of the Rue de l'Odéon, and the little magazines that catered to the "Quarter's" Bohemians. In this heartland of Anglo-American experiment, the Ballets Russes made few inroads during the years when Diaghilev cultivated the pose of a vanguardist. If Sylvia Beach and Adrienne Monnier, proprietors of Shakespeare and Company and La Maison des Amis des Livres, attended "several" performances in December 1920,[72] balletgoing never stuck, nor was it a habit acquired by their friends. Unlike Ezra Pound's opera *Le Testament*, George Antheil's *Ballet Mécanique,* and Cocteau's *Roméo et Juliette,* no Diaghilev event entered the pantheon of expatriate myth.

In these years the community gave its heart to George Antheil, the Trenton-born "bad boy" of American composers in Paris. The little magazines sang his praises: *transition* published no fewer than five articles by or about him in 1927–1928, while the musical supplements of the *Transatlantic Review* existed solely as a platform to advance his opinions. And he had many opinions, particularly on the subject of Stravinsky, against whom he railed continually:

> Do we necessarily need to link all new rhythmic experimentation with Stravinsky's "Sacre," or Rimsky-Korsakoff's "Scheherazade"? At the least sign of a break from the four Gods of music; 3/4, 2/4, 6/8, or 4/4, do we need to run to Stravinsky like little cry-babies, and call Father? . . .
>
> Aha! Igor Stravinsky, you Rimsky-Korsakoffist! Aha Rimsky-Korsakoff, you Moussorgskyist! Aha Moussorgsky, you swiper from the Russian peasants. What about the music from the campfires of a thousand, no! a million years! What about the tom-toms. What about the neggers down in Africa. What about the Mongols sweeping over Europe in the middle ages. Do we have to track everything back to the courts of Louis and Napoleon? Do you forever have to stilt about in court dress to 4/4 time, or waltz in the evenings to 3/4? Is there nothing else to your measely little European culture of the last few centuries?[73]

Like his mentor Ezra Pound, the composer was longer on self-promotion than analysis: the cult of Stravinsky naturally detracted from his own genius. But one suspects other grounds for Antheil's disgruntlement: a feeling that something was fundamentally amiss in Diaghilev's latest turn, that neither his revivals or musical pastiches nor the commissions he had awarded *Les Six* boded well for the continued vitality of modernism. One also suspects that many expatriates shared his scorn for Diaghilev's pastiche classics. In the *Little Review*'s special theater issue published in 1926, the Ballets Russes did not even warrant a mention.[74]

Although many Americans kept to the expatriate world, others ventured beyond its ghetto. In his memoir *Life Among the Surrealists,* Matthew Josephson describes with warmth friendships with Philippe Soupault, Louis Aragon, André Breton, and Tristan Tzara and their "Dadaist excursions." At one, the future biographer of Zola, Rousseau, and Sidney Hillman mounted a table and read a German tract on socialism to a restaurant full of Russian émigrés, who pelted him with bread.[75] Here, among the habitués of Dada-Surrealist Paris was the home of the expatriate avant-garde: the younger painters reproduced in *transition* and the *Little Review* and the writers who formed the majority of their French contributors. Here, too, were to be found collaborators of Rolf de Maré and Comte Etienne de Beaumont—Francis Picabia, who designed the scenery of *Relâche,* produced by the Ballets Suédois in 1924; Tristan Tzara, whose "tragedy in fifteen acts," *Mouchoir de Nuages,* was mounted by the Soirées de Paris the same year; Man Ray, the Philadelphia-born painter and photographer whose avant-garde films enjoyed the collaboration and backing of Beaumont; Antheil, whose Paris debut at a Ballets Suédois gala in October 1923 provoked a legendary, if not wholly spontaneous, *scandale.* (A riot was needed for Georgette Le Blanc's film *L'Inhumaine,* and with the connivance of Margaret Anderson, coeditor of the *Little Review,* who invited Antheil to perform, one was engineered.)[76] And among the adopted fathers of Dada-Surrealist Paris were artists like Picasso, Léger, and Derain, whose work figured prominently in both the little magazines and the repertory of Diaghilev's ballet rivals.

Only rarely did this Montparnasse confraternity stray across Diaghilev's path, even if the impresario attended its stellar events. A short note from Blaise Cendrars in May 1922 asking for tickets to a performance of *Le Renard* at the Paris Opéra[77] is one of the few documented instances of contact between the impresario and an avant-garde artist who was neither a Diaghilev employee nor a habitué of his social circle. (Oddly, Cendrars, who composed the scenario for the Swedish Ballet's *La Création du Monde,* seemed genuinely fond of Diaghilev's older works. Nina Hammett, an English painter and Montparnasse familiar, recalled a dinner with Cendrars and Fernand Léger at which the Frenchmen sang snatches of *Petrouchka* and *Schéhérazade.*)[78] In March 1923 the Kamerny Theater, performing at the Théâtre des Champs-Elysées, brought Diaghilev briefly in touch with Left Bank Paris. Coming up from Monte Carlo, he attended performances by the troupe—very likely his first glimpse of Soviet stagecraft—and possibly a banquet honoring its director Alexander Tairov.[79] In subsequent years the *Little Review* and *Theatre Arts Monthly* published a number of articles about the Soviet theater, a sign of the avant-garde's fascination with Soviet constructivism and experimental stagecraft. The émigré theater cast no such spell.

A rather noisier encounter between Left and Right Bank Paris took place in 1926, when surrealists staged a demonstration at the Paris premiere of Diaghilev's *Romeo and Juliet:* two errant artists of the group, Max Ernst and Joan Miró, had contributed designs for the ballet. When the curtain rose to reveal Miró's decor, an "indescribable hubbub" broke out, and from the upper balconies a shower of leaflets printed in red ink fell on the audience in the stalls. The manifesto was signed by Louis Aragon and André Breton:

> PROTEST! It is inadmissable that thought should be at the beck and call of money . . . Those . . . who capitulate to the point of disregarding social conditions are of no importance, for the ideal to which they paid allegiance before their abdication survives without them . . . [The Surrealist] ideal is essentially subversive; it cannot compromise with such enterprises, whose aim has always been to tame the dreams and rebellions engendered by physical and intellectual starvation for the benefit of an international aristocracy.
>
> It may have seemed to Ernst and Miró that their collaboration with M. de Diaghilev, legitimized by the example of Picasso, would not have such serious consequences. However, it forces us whose main concern is to keep the outposts of the intellect beyond the grasp of slave traders of every kind . . . to denounce an attitude that supplies weapons to the worst partisans of moral equivocation.[80]

Who then were the artists of Diaghilev's "unique" public, those "admirers" and "enthusiasts" who came again and again to the theater and "belonged to the best society of Paris"? An item published in *Le Gaulois* during the 1924 Olympics season offers a clue:

> These performances, which breed cordiality and even a kind of intimacy, unite again and again the friends of the Ballets Russes, who do not part once the show is over. Not far from the [Théâtre des] Champs-Elysées is a little cafe that has been done over and modernized. Here, people meet after the theater . . . On Sunday, Mlle. Cécile Sorel, very beautiful and still excited by the performance, could be seen, along with Mlle. Marthe Davelli, M. Madrazzo [sic] and others . . . And when M. Serge Diaghilev entered the room with Picasso, there was a little demonstration of sympathy, accompanied by discreet bravos.[81]

Actress Cécile Sorel was a reigning idol of the Comédie Française; Marthe Davelli an opera singer at the peak of her career; Frédéric de Madrazo, a nephew of the dress designer Fortuny and the original for Proust's artistic dabbler Ski. All three belonged to the Right Bank Establishment of high art, the milieu of Diaghilev's prewar *tout Paris*. The guest list for a tea-dance at Sorel's "museum" on the Quai Voltaire evokes this cultured Establishment world: amidst the *chinoiserie* crowded an ex-President of the Republic, a Bourbon duchess, British admirals, French generals, Russian princesses, the couturière Lucille (Lady Duff Gordon in private life), Hubert Stowitts, the American-born partner of Anna Pavlova, and Harry Pilcer, a popular exhibition dancer who owned one of the most exclusive dance clubs in Paris.[82] And when Sorel attended a gala first night, *le tout Paris* in miniature seemed to accompany her: André de Fouquières, the Beau Brummel of contemporary fashion, Francis Picabia, the millionaire Cuban dadaist, and George Barbier, the Beardsley-esque fashion illustrator and author of prewar albums about Nijinsky and Karsavina.[83]

In 1924 the "ghosts of the 'Tout-Proust'," in Edmonde Charles-Roux's picturesque phrase—flickered among the icons of Establishment culture in the audience of the Théâtre des Champs-Elysées. But neither of these groups stood at the center of Diaghilev's thoughts, even if they represented an important segment of his public. Rather it was the salons of the new that Diaghilev now regarded as his ideal audience, those power circles of the modernist Establishment that revolved around the Princesse de Polignac, Misia Sert, and Comte Etienne de Beaumont. Both Virgil Thomson and George Antheil have stressed the importance of salons in Paris artistic life of the twenties. For Diaghilev and other entrepreneurs of modernism, these crossroads of Right Bank fashion and contemporary art defined the narrow world of their ventures: here, reputations were launched, commissions awarded, and audiences mustered for a theatrical debut. Throughout the decade Diaghilev relied on salons to promote the Ballets Russes, to create that disturbing aura of an enterprise at once chic and "advanced." Thus, even before their official premieres, *Mavra, Renard,* and *Les Noces* were heard by a select public in the music-room of Stravinsky's patron Madame de Polignac, while from Misia Sert's apartment in the Hotel Meurice, word of Diaghilev's annual "finds" whipped through fashionable Paris with the speed of a *petit bleu.*

The artists who set the tone in this milieu—Cocteau, Les Six, and the other painters, musicians, and writers of the poet's "Mutual Admiration Society"—formed the core of Diaghilev's artistic following. They and their friends provided the majority of his French collaborators, and included several personal, even intimate, friends of the impresario. For Diaghilev, the social "packaging" of his artists was always important. He dressed his "favorites" in the tailoring of Saville Row, and of the many painters and composers who worked for him over the years, remarkably few came to his attention without society backing. In Cocteau and his band, art and social standing neatly fused. "Well-to-do and upper-class," these youthful aesthetes circulated among the salons, promoting, as Virgil Thomson wrote, "a conversation about the arts among people well-off enough to be making them or rich enough to buy."[84] "Conversation," however, is too mild a word to describe the group's activities, even if it captures the informal flavor of salon relationships. For a great deal more than talk was going on in the drawing rooms of this alternative Establishment, developments in which Cocteau, especially, in his multiple roles as talent scout, publicist, and go-between, played a major part.

In these years modernism was redefined, transformed under the aegis of Cocteau, his acolytes, and patrons from a radical statement into a socially palatable style. At the same time, through enterprises like the Ballets Suédois, Soirées de Paris, and to a somewhat lesser extent the Ballets Russes, the private promoters of modernism acquired something akin to a public arm—one that extended their tastes into a larger arena. Theatrical exposure secured at least in part the hegemony of salon-promoted modernism. But it did something more as well. The commercial setting in which performances took place added luster to their component parts: the artwork itself became a prestige commodity. What occurred, therefore, was a twofold phenomenon: the consecration of key patronage choices as modernist chic and the rapid commercialization of these tastes through balletic enterprise.

The promptness with which modernism triumphed as the artistic style of the 1920s reflects the marketplace setting of its diffusion. But the ballet stage was only one arena where this took place. The new art promoted by Cocteau and his group was a look, a style, a tone that could be adapted with equal ease to the walls of a nightclub, costumes for a fancy dress ball, and score of a ballet. Even before the Exposition des Arts Décoratifs in 1925, chic gathering spots had assumed a modernist guise. At Le Boeuf sur le Toit, a bar where Cocteau received on almost any evening in the early twenties, Picassos and Picabias hung on the walls. Here, clients "drank champagne for luxury, whisky for style" and rubbed shoulders with celebrities—Picasso, Les Six, Arthur Rubinstein, Nancy Cunard, Clive Bell, Yvonne Printemps, Misia Sert, Count Harry Kessler, Chanel, Diaghilev, Comte Etienne de Beaumont, Princesse Violette Murat, and the Prince of Wales—while the best dancers in Paris capered to American jazz.[85] "The Boeuf," Cocteau said later, "became not a bar at all, but a kind of club, the meeting place of all the best people in Paris, from all spheres of life, the prettiest women, poets, musicians, businessmen, publishers—everybody met everybody at the Boeuf."[86] Paul Poiret's Oasis was another nightspot with an air of avant-garde chic; in step with the times, the erstwhile purveyor of orientalia had commissioned art work from Cocteau, Derain, Serge Soudeikine, and others. Count Harry Kessler, colibrettist of *Legend of Joseph* and an intimate of Diaghilev and his circle recorded in his diary yet another of these ventures: a dance-bar on a launch in the Seine where young Polish artists under the wing of Misia Sert made up the band and where the "fantastically expensive" price of a hundred and fifty francs was charged for a bottle of champagne.[87] In these settings modernism became the coin of an international pleasure style, the background against which Tout Londres and Tout Paris and Tout New York relaxed and "recreated." As much as it dressed the stage of the Ballets Russes, modernism framed the chic lifestyle of Diaghilev's smart, international public.

Unlike London, where a dance boom cutting across the lines of class lent a touch of democracy to the company's social aura, in Paris the Ballets Russes retained the plumage of social elitism throughout the twenties. Yet the character of Diaghilev's audience had changed, and not only in style. The tightly knit world of aristocrats and "aristocratizing" bourgeois that had assembled for his prewar rituals now yielded to a motley crowd of smart cosmopolitans—a beau monde where money, art, and fashion were blurring older distinctions of class. Before the war Diaghilev's stars had danced at the fetes of the most exclusive society. Now wealth alone seemed to fuel such events. In her memoirs *R.S.V.P.* Elsa Maxwell recalled a birthday party she gave herself in the 1920s at the Paris Ritz, a gift from Jay O'Brien, the ex-husband of movie star Mae Murray, and his wife, the ex-Mrs. Julius Fleischmann of the yeast-making family. "Jay asked Cole Porter what he could give me for my birthday and Cole told him there was nothing I adored more than a party . . . Serge Diaghilev was then in Paris and that meant, of course, that I must have his ballet company perform at the party. I had the Ritz build a stage in the garden and sent out 300 invitations to a buffet supper."[88] This was not the only time Diaghilev crossed paths with Café Society's most famous hostess. The two had met before the war in London, and they saw each other often in the following decade, particularly at Monte Carlo, which Maxwell was paid to promote as a summer resort. Indeed, the "famous impresario," whom she regarded as a "friend," celebrated her fortieth birthday in Monte Carlo in May 1923 "by staging the *premières* of two new ballets," while as an added treat Vladimir Horowitz played Lizst's "Mephisto Waltz" during the interval, his first performance in the West.[89] (At Venice, another of the resorts she launched as a Café Society playground, Maxwell paid an unusual tribute to Diaghilev: in the Russian Ballet tableau that was the "hit" of the 1928 Robillant fancy-dress ball, she appeared as the impresario and "made an introductory speech which nearly sent everyone into hysterics.")[90]

Paris of the twenties was the capital of fashion as much as it was the capital of art. Ballet, as we have seen, played an important part in advertising the city's artistic wares; it played a similar role in promoting its haute couture. In 1924 Diaghilev soloists gave a program of divertissements at one of many gala fashion shows sponsored by the magazine *Femina;* another the previous year had featured the troupe of Ballets Russes alumnus Alexander Gavrilov.[91] The opening of the Galeries Lafayette was another occasion where Diaghilev's dancers placed their art at the service of fashion. (They did so, as usual, without compensation, and at Ninette de Valois's instigation, staged a mild protest, walking off with the soap and towels provided by the department store.)[92] Nor were private troupes the only ones drawn into such promotions. At a "brilliant fête" organized by France's silk merchants attended by several government officials, including the Minister of Commerce, the Paris Opéra Ballet performed a *pièce d'occasion* that displayed the famous Lyons silks while illustrating their manufacture in pantomime. At the same time mannequins from Redfern, Worth, and other couture houses modeled dresses—silk ones, of course.[93]

By no means was ballet the only kind of dancing on which fashion smiled. At *Femina* events, eclecticism was the rule, as it was at charity galas: both reflected the pluralism of the Paris dance scene.[94] Indeed, at every turn, dancing in Paris intersected with the makers and purveyors of fashion—from the couturiers who designed for the stage to the champagne prices of the era's "dancings"[95]—dance clubs—to the glamorous settings for the "negro revues" imported from America. (At the Ambassadeurs, where Florence Mills performed in 1926, Count Harry Kessler "saw '*Tout Paris*' together in its full glory," "the first time . . . since the first night of the Russian Ballet," while Josephine Baker's *Revue Nègre,* a sensation at the Théâtre des Champs-Elysées, represented "modern jazz" at the Opéra's 1925 ball "Dancing Throughout the Ages.")[96]

The alliance of modernity in dancing with the luxury marketplace was only one of many signs of a larger cultural phenomenon—the containment of modernism's potentially disruptive force within a milieu of social privilege. Both modernism and its practitioners hovered close to the center of society. As at Comte Etienne de Beaumont's balls, they brought an artistic theme to the charades of the privileged, the outré note snapped by Man Ray's camera.[97] But even in less exalted quarters, links between the makers and buyers of modernism are not hard to find. André Breton, that uncompromising theorist of surrealism, not only conducted a gallery devoted to the art of his followers, but also served as an artistic adviser to couturier Jacques Doucet, who collected modern manuscripts and paintings.[98]

The containment of modernism through the ballet and artistic marketplace had a number of consequences. It shortened the path for the unknown to fame, making the promise of success immanent in the very act of creation. With the dynamic of the market now intruding on the imaginative process itself, the very concept of the avant-garde was jeopardized: the quest for the new was no more than an economic imperative. From the wedding of modernism to the luxury art world, moreover, came a new and perturbing myth: a belief in the primacy of talent and taste in defining the function of a modern aristocracy. In an age when birth counted for little and wealth had squandered its claim to leadership through public displays of hedonism, art alone seemed to justify the continued existence of older forms of social privilege. Within this redefined aristocracy, however, noblesse oblige counted for little. Indeed, apart from the series of performances given by striking Paris Opéra dancers in 1920, the masses never impinged on ballet in the French capital as they did in post-Armistice Britain. Like the other high arts in France, ballet remained throughout the decade within the traditional framework of salon and State, and neither the makers nor purveyors of modernism showed any inclination to change this. The paradox of the Ballets Russes—and modernism generally in France—lay in its alliance of radical form with an older social ideology.

When Diaghilev returned to the Coliseum in November 1924, an enraptured house welcomed him. But even if many names on the program were familiar, the company itself had changed. Along with trunks of costumes and scenery, another form of baggage made the Channel crossing: the aura of aristocracy and salon modernism acquired during the company's years abroad. The works conceived under the aegis of Monte Carlo and the Paris art market appealed to only a segment of Diaghilev's once broad London public, above all, to that part of the audience that espoused the snobbery, aesthetic chic, and francophilia they proclaimed. In its final years 1925–1929 the Ballets Russes became a public embodiment of the values and lifestyle of England's dandy-aesthetes.

In 1924 and 1925 Diaghilev presented three seasons at the Coliseum, discharging a portion of his *Sleeping Princess* debt to Sir Oswald Stoll and the Alhambra Company. As in the post-Armistice years, one ballet was given at each of the music-hall's two daily shows, and again the troupe was a headliner, with artists like Noble Sissle and Eubie Blake—two of many black musicians to desert America for the comparatively unpreju-

diced shores of Europe—sandwiched in small print between announcements of repertory, cast lists, and critical blurbs.[99]

In 1918 and 1919 the gallery had edged the stalls from the limelight
in Diaghilev's audience, a sign of ballet's new, popular public. Now, however, the spotlight rarely panned the gods. It flooded, instead, the boxes
and stalls, illuminating the antics and outfits of their smart occupants. Between 1924 and 1929 Diaghilev spurned the general public he had once
seduced. In its place he cultivated the decade's latest trendsetting elite, sophisticates who took their style from Paris and aesthetic cues from the
Sitwells. As British ballet struggled valiantly to establish a native beachhead, Diaghilev created his distinctive audience from the gallery aficionados of Bond Street and the pleasure seekers of High Bohemia.

"The whole high-brow and snob world were there," remarked Arnold
Bennett about the first-night crowd jamming the Lyceum Theatre where
Diaghilev's popular-priced season opened in November 1926.[100] But even
before the move earlier that year from the music-hall to the legitimate
stage, the "snob world" occupied a prominent place at Diaghilev events.
"How much better suited to a fashionable audience the Coliseum is than
any of our fashionable theatres," commented the *Evening Standard* on the
morrow of Diaghilev's return to the house in November 1924. "One noticed this last night, when there was a throng of white waist-coated men
and sleek-headed and pearly ladies to greet the Russian Ballet, who wandered about and paid calls in the interval in the manner of grand opera
days at Covent Garden."[101]

In this last half-decade, the Bright Young Things made Diaghilev their
own. They trailed his company from theater to theater, their prattle and
their gowns providing grist for the gossip columns and the frivolous setting
that appeared inseparable from Diaghilev's newest art. In these years the
Sketch published numerous photographs of the company's dancers, half-a-
dozen profiles of its outstanding personalities, and reams of reportage about
its first nights.[102] Thanks to "Mariegold," the weekly's pseudonymous,
untiring chronicler of parties and premieres, we glimpse the "special and
very sophisticated audience" that "haunt[ed] the Russian Ballet" in the
middle and late 1920s.[103] Here is her description of opening night at His
Majesty's Theatre in 1926:

"Going on" from one entertainment to another was the order of Monday
night, and music-lovers had a perfect feast offered to them that evening . . .
Those who plumped for the Ballet included a very distinguished company,
headed by Lord Balfour and his clever niece, Mrs. Edward Lascelles . . . What
an amusing variety of costume was brought out by this first night! There were
women in the latest and smartest of evening frocks, and young men in the

gayest of coloured shirts and softest of soft collars—the latter, of course, drawn from the camp of the highbrows. Some of the Intelligentsia, however, conform to regulation evening dress, including young "Puffin" Asquith, who was in the upper circle . . . Violet Duchess of Rutland . . . had a long wait in the foyer before she was joined by Lady Diana Cooper, wearing a gold-spangled frock, and Mrs. Alan Parsons (Viola Tree), in a dress of the new pale-green. When they took their seats in the second row of the stalls, I saw Lady Colefax seated just in front of them. Lady Juliet Duff, in bright scarlet, was a little further along in the front row.[104]

Asquiths, Duffs, Coopers, Balfours, Trees—the names alone evoke the family, social, and political web of Diaghilev's Georgian public. The war ended Liberal rule over England's body politic, but "Souls" still reigned in Society. Their children were the decade's new elect, setting the tone for its high life. Like Lady Diana Cooper, some took to the stage. Others, like Nancy Cunard and Anthony "Puffin" Asquith, became writers, publishers, and filmmakers. The faces of this bright young crowd vied with filmland celebrities in the illustrated press, and the beauties of the group lent their names and looks to product endorsements. (Read one 1933 advertisement: "Lady Diana Manners, famed as the most beautiful woman of the English aristocracy, said 'I know that every woman can effectively accomplish loveliness by using Pond's Two Creams'.")[105] Little wonder *New Statesman* critic W.J. Turner described balletgoers as "less middle-class and respectable, better looking and more amusing" than the "army of successful wholesale grocers" that invaded Covent Garden on opera nights.[106]

In these years style became a battleground of Society, a field where Hearties and Arties warred over ruling class values, and, especially, the definition of masculinity. "The Athletes," wrote Jessica Mitford, whose sisters Nancy and Diana led the pack of Bright Young Things, "were direct ideological descendants of past patriots, winners of wars on the playing fields of Eton, Old School Tie men and their horsey-set women":

> The Aesthetes laid claim to a more exotic heritage . . . the Romantics, the England of Oscar Wilde, the France of Baudelaire and Verlaine. Most of the Aesthetes were vaguely pro-Socialist, pro-pacifist, and (horrors!) opposed to shooting, hunting, and fishing . . . They gaily toppled the old, uncomplicated household gods—England, Home and Glory . . . the axiomatic superiority of the English over all other races; they sacrilegiously called the Boer War . . . "the Bore War".[107]

One such dandy was poet Harold Acton, who exemplified the combination of aestheticism, frivolity, and social privilege of Diaghilev's "highbrow" following in the 1920s. Even before the war Acton had succumbed to the voluptuous thrills of *Schéhérazade:* "the heavy calm before the storm in the harem: the thunder and lightning of negroes in rose and amber; the fierce orgy of clamorous caresses . . . death in long-drawn spasms to piercing violins."[108] In Florence, where his American-born mother and painter/art dealer father lived among Berensons, Dodges, and expatriated Grand Duchesses, he had glimpsed Diaghilev reciting Pushkin in the Boboli Gardens and shied from the "autocratic Russian bear" who with Bakst called at the magnificent family villa La Pietra.

From 1918 to 1922 Acton attended Eton. Here, among the school's art-minded collegians, a minority group that included Acton, Brian Howard, Oliver Messel, Cyril Connolly, Peter Quennell, Robert Gathorne-Hardy, and Anthony Powell, the web of interests that surrounded the Ballets Russes in mid-decade was spun. "What they stood for at Eton," Martin Green has written:

> was modernism in general, understood as the movement against the consensus culture of Victorian and Edwardian England. They stood for French poetry—Mallarmé, Rimbaud, Verlaine, and Laforgue—and for French fiction—Proust, Huysmans, and Cocteau—and for France in general—Paris and Poiret and Charvet (maker of the most exquisite ties) . . . They stood for American poetry—Eliot and Amy Lowell, and some Pound—and for cocktails and jazz. They stood for modern painting—Whistler and John, Picasso and Gauguin. Among English people and things they stood for the Sitwells, above all. And, of course, they stood for Diaghilev and everyone and everything associated with him.[109]

At Eton dandies capered to gramophone recordings of *Petrouchka, Tricorne,* and *Les Sylphides* in the back room of a local jeweler's. They wrote poems like Acton's "La Belle au Bois Dormant," dedicated to Bakst, and Brian Howard's " 'L'Oiseau de Feu,' by Stravinsky," which they published in *The Eton Candle,* a glossy volume filled with advertisements for breeches makers, silversmiths, and cricket bat exporters that sold out on the day of publication and received flattering reviews from the likes of Edith Sitwell.[110] And whenever they could, they entrained for London, where their flamboyant appearance at the ballet raised more than an isolated eyebrow. "One time I happened to be at the Alhambra," recalled a classmate:

> when Brian and Harold walked into the stalls, in full evening dress, with long white gloves draped over one arm, and carrying silver-topped canes and top-hats, looking perhaps like a couple of Oscar Wildes. My step-mother was astonished at the sight of them, and thought they must be foreigners. I was much too nervous, at about fifteen, to say that they were two of my great

friends from Eton. I was very much relieved that we were safely installed out of sight in the dress circle.[111]

Here is an early intimation of the reaction that welled in mid-decade against the dandy-aesthetes in Diaghilev's following.

In a memoir written just after the impresario's death, Jacques-Emile Blanche remarked that "the repercussions [of the Ballets Russes] on Britain's university youth are scarcely to be believed."[112] Blanche spoke from firsthand knowledge, although as a society portraitist who included Acton *père et fils* among his sitters, he doubtless based his observation on a rather limited sample. At Oxford, where Brian Howard and Harold Acton matriculated at Christ Church, the most socially elite of the University's colleges, balletomania did indeed infect the dandy coven. The two planned a Queen Victoria ballet, with Acton improbably cast as Lytton Strachey, an unrealized project that anticipated by three years Diaghilev's own incursion into the Victorian period with Sacheverell Sitwell's *Triumph of Neptune*. Other undergraduate ballets rated at least a passing mention in the press, including the burlesques of *Petrouchka* and *Les Sylphides* staged by the Cambridge Amateur Dramatic Club as part of its 1926 *Christmas Revue*.[113]

Among the all-male university elite, Diaghilev found the ideal public for his mid-twenties repertory, an audience attuned to the new spirit of Gallic, modernist chic. Thanks to their connections, dandies penetrated the Russian's charmed circle, cementing the link between "decadence" and ballet. In *Memoirs of an Aesthete* Acton recalled a flying visit to Paris when he sat for Pedro Pruna and gossiped with Diaghilev's newest find about the "jealousies and intrigues" raging behind the company scenes. Acton was an intimate of Lady Cunard, whom he admired as much as her daughter Nancy, and it was in the company of this remarkable hostess that he supped for a last time with the impresario after witnessing a performance from Covent Garden's royal box with King Fuad of Egypt.[114] During these years when his sketches of smartly dressed first-nighters decorated the gossip pages of British *Vogue,* Cecil Beaton extended his admiration of the Ballets Russes to the person of its director. "Diaghileff became my hero," he later wrote, "it thrilled me to see him, dressed like a dandy, in Monte Carlo, in Venice or at the Savoy Grill, London." On the Piazza San Marco, during a Venetian visit that found the tyro photographer hobnobbing with such Diaghilev devotees as Baroness d'Erlanger, her daughter Princess Faucigny-Lucinge, Lady Diana Cooper, Lady Cunard, and Lady Abdy, Beaton cornered the impresario, spilling an "avalanche" of sketches and photographs before him on a cafe table. Unlike Oliver Messel, an Etonian who at twenty-one designed the golden masks used in the production of *Zéphire et Flore*,

Beaton never received a commission from his hero, although he did gain entree to rehearsals.[115] Brian Howard, whose amateur ballet dancing horrified his father, also established personal ties with the company. A great friend of Anton Dolin, this aesthete and brightest of the bright young things designed the costumes and scenery for one of Dolin's many revue ballets. In 1927, with Edward Gathorne-Hardy, Howard organized a Sailor party at the swimming baths in Buckingham Palace Road, where Lytton Strachey, Tallulah Bankhead, Raymond Mortimer, and London's "fast" crowd celebrated the revival of *Les Matelots* and Serge Lifar appeared in his costume from *The Triumph of Neptune*.[116] Here, in a nutshell, is the smart, sophisticated world of Evelyn Waugh's early novels.

As aristocrats of style, the dandies took their cue from the Sitwells, the gentry triumvirate that embodied the mingling of art, frivolity, and taste that became a generational trademark. In the 1920s, Cyril Connolly has reminisced:

> [the Sitwells] represented the rush towards pleasure and aesthetic enjoyment characteristic of the intelligent young who had come through the war; they were the natural allies of Cocteau and the Ecole de Paris, dandies, impeccably dressed and fed, who indicated to young men down from Oxford and even Cambridge that it was possible to reconcile art and fashion as an alternative to Bloomsbury.[117]

Under Edith's wing nestled Brian Howard and Harold Acton, and they, in turn, introduced other dandy literati into her circle, including novelist Evelyn Waugh, who was among the party Acton shepherded to the second performance of *Façade*.[118]

The Sitwell fame rested on more than purely literary merit. Past masters at courting publicity, they were celebrities, who stood out even in the blaze of a Diaghilev first night. Between 1926 and 1929, when the clan—now enlarged by the addition of Sacheverell's wife, Canadian-born Georgia Doble—rarely missed a premiere, its appearance in the stalls or dress circle was gossip column news:

> A special and very sophisticated audience always haunts the Russian Ballet, and on the first night at the Princes the "regulars" turned up in full force. The Sitwell brothers were accompanied by Mrs. Sacheverell Sitwell, who looked elegant in a gold brocade coat.[119]

So clicked "Mariegold's" shutter in June 1927. In July 1928 it clicked on the "very brilliant house" that packed His Majesty's for the first performance of Stravinsky's newest ballet:

Mrs. Henry McLaren was in red, Lady Juliet Duff in black, and Miss Edith Sitwell was impressive as ever in one of her flowing gowns of blue, rose, and gold brocade. She came with one of her brothers and her sister-in-law, and was telling everyone how much she enjoyed "Apollo Musagetes".[120]

Mariegold's shutter clicked again and again on the Sitwells in the theater and elsewhere. In 1928 we see them at the Claridge Gallery receiving Lady Lavery, Mrs. Henry McLaren, and "the flower of the Intelligentsia," in their campaign to launch Pavel Tchelitchev, the designer of *Ode*. And the following year we sight them en masse at the premieres of *Le Bal* and *Le Renard* and at Diaghilev's "rehearsal party" where Igor Markevitch played his Piano Concerto to "a representative gathering of the Intelligentsia," including Mrs. Asquith (now the Countess of Oxford and Asquith), her son "Puffin" and daughter Princess Bibesco, a writer, in Virginia Woolf's devastating phrase, "without nerves, imagination or sensibility."[121]

As the Diaghilev era drew to a close, Sitwell protégés jostled their mentors in the gossip columns, a sign that they, too, had joined the celebrity elect of Diaghilev's "highbrow" following. But how highbrow was that following really? Where are the Woolfs and Frys and Stracheys and Keyneses and Huxleys and Eliots? In these last postwar years, when society columnists paired "smart" and "intellectual" as coequal halves of Diaghilev's audience, England's foremost intellects deserted the Ballets Russes.

In 1924 the *Nation* and *New Statesman* had greeted the prodigal's return with genuine warmth. "A large number of people believe that M. Diaghileff provides us with one of the very few theatrical entertainments that deserve . . . to be treated as serious works of art; and the return of his ballet to London is likely to carry most of us to the Coliseum in the . . . next few weeks." So opined the *Nation*'s "Omicron" in the first of many capsule reviews of Diaghilev performances published in the next few years. Not even the "baffling heterogeneity" of the Coliseum's other fare could dull the general enthusiasm. On the last night of the season, the "recalls were so frequent and the applause so persistent that the rest of the programme had . . . to be abandoned." Like the *Sketch*, the *New Statesman* commented on the two-tier audience drawn to the Coliseum: house regulars who came for the whole show and balletomanes who sailed in for Diaghilev's half-hour turn. The latter went again and again: in the summer of 1925, "Omicron" predicted a nightly pilgrimage of *Nation* readers to the music-hall in St. Martin's Lane.[122]

In post-Armistice years, commented Turner in 1926, intellectual support for the ballet had made Diaghilev's enterprise a success. Not only had the intelligentsia trooped to the Coliseum—"a world of innocent and light-hearted children and . . . simple savages"—but as the era's new aristocracy of taste, it had led the fashionable world to the company's unfashionable doorstep. Now, with ballet "as popular as . . . Little Tich," intellectuals could rest on their laurels.[123] "Diaghileff has done more than anyone to make the arts popular in a torpid, niggardly, postwar London," summed up Raymond Mortimer:

> He is the Apostle to the Philistines. Thanks to him not only are the airs of Scarlatti, Schumann, Chopin and Rimsky-Korsakov whistled in the bathrooms of thousands who never go to serious concerts, but the idiom of contemporary composers such as Stravinsky receives the appreciation that only familiarity can breed. Thanks to him, too, the crowd has positively enjoyed decorations by the best and most ridiculed living painters. He has given us Modern Music without Tears and Modern Painting without Laughter.[124]

Fifteen years before, crowds of Philistines had jeered the canvases of Picasso, Cézanne, and Matisse at Roger Fry's first Post-Impressionist Exhibition. Then, with peace had come Diaghilev's made-over repertory, which trumpeted the modernist aesthetic from Bloomsbury to London's fashionable and middlebrow quarters.

The very popularity of ballet, however, aroused Bloomsbury's distaste. Already in 1925 Francis Birrell observed in the *Nation* that the troupe "has stopped being a highbrow's holiday," and in subsequent years, the weekly, now under John Maynard Keynes's control and with Leonard Woolf as its literary editor, largely ignored the company, with two important exceptions: Lydia Lopokova's appearances and the production of *Les Noces* in 1926. The ballerina, who had married Keynes the previous year, remained a *Nation* favorite: her performances in *Les Matelots, La Boutique Fantasque,* and *Pulcinella* revived Bloomsbury's erstwhile romance with Diaghilev, emphasizing once again the importance of personal relations in the circle's appreciation of art.[125] Otherwise, only *Les Noces* received the journal's mid-decade plaudits. The ballet, wrote "Omicron," "is by far the most interesting recent addition to M. Diaghileff's repertory":

> It is no slight, "chic" entertainment, as some of these have been: it is a serious and successful attempt to interpret in dancing music which depends entirely on rhythmical and formal qualities of the severest kind. M. Stravinsky's music . . . is . . . without airs and graces, and Mme. Nijinska's choreography follows it with angular, primitive movements which have a great geometrical beauty . . . Mme. Gontcharova's *décor* is fittingly restrained and severe.[126]

That summer the intelligentsia continued to crowd His Majesty's Theatre, although the "excited giggles" that greeted "some of the more bizarre elements of the newer ballets," thought Turner, betrayed "a large sprin-

kling of a less highbrow audience." The following season, which opened
at the Lyceum Theatre in November 1926, brought out an even motlier
public, an "enormous army of admirers, who make up an audience as
unintelligent as any other, and apparently quite incapable of discriminat-
ing between one ballet and another."[127] There is no mistaking in the critic's tone the distance between the *Nation*'s readers and Diaghilev's fashionable herd.

Indeed, in these years old Bloomsbury practically deserted the Ballets
Russes. In vain, one combs the chitchat of Virginia Woolf's letters and
diaries for the offhand allusion to a performance squeezed into the round
of pleasure and work. Nor do Lydia Lopokova's letters mention backstage
visits by the circle: the people who dropped by her dressing room now
were her brother-in-law, Geoffrey Keynes, and his wife, Margaret. Kitty
Lasswade's breezy dismissal of a young danseur—"Ah, but he's not a patch
on Nijinsky"—toward the end of Virginia Woolf's novel *The Years* suggests that a distaste for Diaghilev's frivolous public and memories of a
golden yesteryear clouded Bloomsbury's attitude toward the troupe in these
last years of its existence.[128]

Diaghilev's leaning toward dandy tastes also played its part in this
divorce: the closer he drew to the Sitwells, the farther he drifted from
Bloomsbury. That the *Nation* panned *The Triumph of Neptune* comes as
no great surprise; that it did so without mentioning the name of the ballet's librettist suggests how wide the rift had grown since the coteries had
danced together on Armistice night. In the intervening years the camps had
divided, pitting artist against aesthete, seriousness against fashion, originality against style. Between 1925 and 1929, Diaghilev's British collaborators came exclusively from the dandy fold. Both Constant Lambert, composer of the 1926 "surrealist" *Romeo and Juliet,* and William Walton,
whose music was featured in the symphonic interludes, were Sitwell protégés, while Oliver Messel trod the "primrose path" from Eton to the world
of fashionable photographers and West End success that Evelyn Waugh
retrospectively associated with Diaghilev and decried. In taste as much as
personnel, *Neptune* was a dandy triumph, and one suspects that behind
the *Nation*'s critique of the scenery as being "so strong in tradition and
style, that it quite dwarfed the puny efforts of the world in front of it,"[129]
lurks Bloomsbury's distaste for the art and values of the Victorians.

The Sitwell brothers were not the only dandies to leave their signa-
tures on this English ballet. For the score Diaghilev chose the "rococo
Byron" of British composers, a well-bred amateur who trailed in the prewar wake of that d'Annunzian Muse, Marchesa Casati, lunched with the
brothers Sitwell on their Roman holiday, and traced his friendship with
Stravinsky and Diaghilev at least as far back as 1916. The music Lord

Berners supplied was "throughout adequate," wrote Turner in the *New Statesman,* "although it sounds more like the work of a clever, highly eclectic, than of a truly creative, mind." [130] In part because they were French, Diaghilev's other mid-decade composers fared noticeably worse with Britain's nationally minded musical critics, who abounded in phrases like "strained cleverness" (Auric), "no great consequence" (Sauguet), and "self-contemptuous flippancy" (Auric, Milhaud, Poulenc). [131] In his choice of Lord Berners Diaghilev revealed the dandy network at the core of his new public.

Bloomsbury deserted Diaghilev, but it did not lose its interest in ballet: indeed, from within its extended family came the proposal for a ballet that, although turned down by the impresario, outlived nearly all his "advanced" productions. "I have the honor of sending you the book of William Blake engravings which my sister-in-law has spoken to you about," wrote Geoffrey Keynes in late June 1927, referring to *Illustrations of the Book of Job:*

> Also enclosed is the outline for a ballet based on these engravings. Doubtless you already know the name of this illustrious poet-painter. As the centenary of his death takes place in 1927, a ballet based on his work would evoke the greatest interest in this country . . . and in France as well where his work is being published . . . I also enclose tickets for the exhibition of Blake paintings now on in Saville Row. [132]

The symbolic ballet proposed by Keynes found little favor in Diaghilev's eyes: it was "too English and too old-fashioned," [133] the impresario thought. Ralph Vaughan Williams, the eminent British composer whom Keynes had approached to write the score, had few illusions about the fate of the project. To Keynes's sister-in-law Gwen Raverat, who had made costumed figurines and a miniature theater for the proposed ballet, he wrote:

> I amused myself with making a sketch of *Job*—I never expected Djag wd. look at it—and I'm glad on the whole—the *"réclame"* wd. have been rather amusing—but it really wdnt. have suited the sham serious really decadent and frivolous attitude of the R.B. toward everything—can you imagine *Job* sandwiched between *Les Biches* and *Cimarosiana*—and that dreadful pseudo-cultured audience saying to each other "My dear, have you seen God at the Russian Ballet." No—I think we are well out of it. [134]

In 1931 the Camargo Society, of which John Maynard Keynes was treasurer, staged *Job* at the Savoy Theatre. With choreography by Ninette de Valois, Constant Lambert on the podium, and Anton Dolin in the role of Satan, the production advanced the cause of British ballet as *The Triumph of Neptune* signally failed to. Indeed, after Diaghilev's death the Sitwells by and large lost interest in the art they had previously championed.

The dandy "highbrows" who stepped into the breach left by Bloomsbury found the pages of British *Vogue* more congenial to their tastes than the columns of the *Nation*. In these years, *Vogue* was the beacon of High Bohemia, a London outpost of that cosmopolitan pleasure style which flourished in Paris and the Côte d'Azur and other elite playgrounds of the twenties. Like *Vanity Fair,* another Condé Nast publication, *Vogue* minted fashion, francophilia, and modernism into the coin of international sophistication.

Between 1925 and 1929 no other theatrical venture received the attention lavished by *Vogue* on the Ballets Russes. Sympathetic reviewers covered its seasons in London, Paris correspondents its seasons abroad, while art critics wrote about its designers. Visually, too, the company held the spotlight, with photographs of dancers, reproductions of designs, and portraits of Diaghilev's "masters of décor" appearing whenever the troupe came to town. In June 1925 the magazine published a Picasso drawing of the camera-shy impresario, nominated along with Harold Acton, Georges Braque, and Eugene Goossens for the magazine's "Hall of Fame." The society pages also paid homage to the company in Cecil Beaton's delightful sketches of Lady Wodehouse (in the brocaded cloak she wore to one performance), Mrs. Norman Holden (in the Russian Ballet tutu she donned for the Duchess of Sutherland's fancy dress ball), and "Mrs. Maynard Keynes" (pictured *en décolletage* watching a performance of *Apollon Musagète*).[135]

In 1924–1926, when *Vogue* feted Diaghilev, it also courted Bloomsbury. Indeed, scarcely an issue appeared in these years without an article by one of the lions of the circle—Clive Bell, Virginia Woolf, Leonard Woolf, Roger Fry—or its cubs and friends—Raymond Mortimer, David Garnett, Francis Birrell, Aldous Huxley, George Rylands, Vita Sackville-West, even Lady Ottoline Morrell who contributed a piece entitled "Les Jeunes Filles de Londres."[136] Bloomsbury wrote about books, particularly literature of a modernist bent, contemporary art, French historical figures, and each other, themes that echoed in the work of other contributors like Edith Sitwell and Richard Aldington.

If *Vogue* flattered the worldly side of Bloomsbury, sweeping guineas into the latter's pockets,[137] Bloomsbury, in turn, gave the magazine that air of cultivated sophistication that hovered over twenties fashion. Its presence there testified to more than the tastes of Dorothy Todd, the art-minded editor of *Vogue* dismissed by Condé Nast in 1926. It reflected a larger phenomenon of the period: the appropriation by the trendsetting elite of modernism and Gallic culture, those English bugaboos long championed by Bloomsbury that now became the touchstones of a contemporary life-style.

Compared to the *Times* and the *Sketch, Vogue* paid unwonted attention to Diaghilev's visual artists. Reviews spotlighted their work, while both the art and Paris columns of the magazine alluded to exhibitions at which their theatrical designs and paintings were featured. In *Vogue* Diaghilev's artists received the imprimatur of fashion and their wares the stamp of a commodity. As a sign of this commerce, one remarks the attribution of ownership that accompanied reproductions of Ballets Russes artifacts: a Pruna backcloth for *Les Matelots* "reproduced by courtesy of M. Boris Kochno"; Derain's "original design" for *Jack-in-the-Box* "in the possession of Serge Lifar"; Miró's "rough sketch" for *Romeo and Juliet* published along with a photograph of its owner, Boris Kochno. Attributions were not limited to Diaghilev art works. *Vogue* readers also learned that "La Stylographe," the most important picture at Pruna's first exhibition, was bought by Jean Cocteau, and that Pierre Roy's "Still Life" was in the "Collection de Madame Peignat." And in singling out the activities of Comte Etienne de Beaumont, that Maecenas of the moderns who had deserted ballet for the cause of avant-garde film, *Vogue* drove home the theme that modern art was an elite and eminently desirable commodity.[138]

Art was not the only commodity linking Diaghilev's audience and the stage. Fashion also meshed the two, and caption writers were quick to note the overlaps between costume and couture in *Le Train Bleu, Les Biches,* and *La Pastorale.* But even in ballets with period themes, contemporary allusions abounded. In *Romeo and Juliet* a modish pink dressing gown hung from a peg in the rehearsal scene. Alicia Markova's white "pyjamas" in the 1927 revival of *Le Chant du Rossignol* also struck a contemporary note: by 1926 the rage for these trouser fashions had christened the Lido the "plage du soleil et des pyjamas." Indeed, in December 1925 Vera Nemchinova, the troupe's star classicist, modeled a Dove "pyjama suit" of black crêpe de Chine in the pages of *Vogue.* Another telltale sign of fashion's impact on ballet was the slim, leggy look of Diaghilev's latest crop of ballerinas, who exemplified the decade's new fashion silhouette and occasionally doubled as mannequins and cover girls.[139] All this cemented the tie between onstage and offstage chic, identifying Diaghilev's art with the consumerist style of his audience.

The blend of fashion, francophilia, and modernism that now characterized Diaghilev's enterprise appealed to only a fraction of his erstwhile public. The theater, wrote dance critic Fernau Hall, was "sometimes half-empty": "people came to see the novelties, but were not much interested in coming to see ballets over and over again."[140] Empty seats were only one repercussion of the polarizing course steered by the impresario in these years. In skimming the cream off his once heterogeneous following, Diaghilev split the ballet audience in two, provoking a reaction by the majority public of dance lovers against the aesthetics and "highbrow" defenders of his newer repertory. In a capsule review of *Le Train Bleu* published in the *Dancing Times,* that middlebrow champion of British ballet, dancer Phyllis Bedells confessed the fear that Diaghilev was "laughing up [his] sleeve at the great British public."[141]

Neither Bedells nor G.E. Fussell, the magazine's resident decor critic, identified themselves with Diaghilev's trendsetting elite. "If I were a highbrow or really intellectual," Fussell prefaced his review of Marie Laurencin's designs for *Les Biches,* "I should designate the drop by one or other of the terms common to the somewhat flatulent art criticism of our time. I should say it was primitive or something of that sort. As it is I do not intend to."[142] Fussell was not the only critic whose response to Diaghilev's artists was swayed by a distaste for their highbrow supporters. Consider Howard Hannay's confession in the *London Mercury:*

> The exhibition of paintings by the French woman artist, Marie Laurencin, at the Leicester Galleries has made at least one convert . . . The pictures I had seen hitherto had impressed me chiefly with certain sophisticated mannerisms and abbreviations which seemed to be devoid of any significance, however slight and trivial. And when Mr. Clive Bell called Marie Laurencin "adorable," this appeared to be merely part of his general flattery of all things Parisian. I was mistaken.[143]

Again and again critics flayed Diaghilev's weakness for Gallic fashions, especially in music. Auric's score for *La Pastorale,* wrote the *Times* in 1926, "is much the same small beer . . . which has been brewed in France for similar occasions in recent years." Only a week later John Bull roared again: the newspaper dismissed Satie's "quips" as "too feeble to last" even if his "little digs" at Chabrier "amused private parties in Paris." Later that month Constant Lambert was taken to task for having "chosen to speak . . . French" in composing *Romeo and Juliet,* even though, like many foreigners, he spoke the language "even better than the Frenchman."[144] The opening lines of its 1927 notice of *La Chatte* dispel all doubt that at the *Times* "Parisian" was anything but a pejorative epithet. The column was entitled "The Russian Ballet":

> It would, perhaps, be more accurate if this notice were headed "The Parisian Ballet." For this new ballet, which was produced at Princes Theatre last night, could have been created nowhere but in cosmopolitan Paris, where fashions, in art as in clothes, are subject to rapid change in the desperate struggle to

achieve originality and the last word. The new ballet, which is called *The Cat*, is certainly the "very latest thing," and lest that be regarded as contemptuous condemnation, it must be added that it has good qualities other than novelty.[145]

In Britain modernism sank shallower roots than elsewhere in Europe, in part, because of its labeling as a frivolous foreign import.

If the course steered by Diaghilev between 1918 and 1922 helped to anglicize ballet, the policy he adopted after 1924 had the opposite effect. No longer did the company seem to dwell in Britain's native "halls": it lounged, now, in the foyers of those expensive hotels mushrooming along the Lido and Côte d'Azur. For the sophisticates who fussed over Diaghilev's periodic descents on London, ballet was not the art taking root in dance studios around the country (which they ignored), but an imported "craze" cementing the cosmopolitan fraternity of Café Society and High Bohemia.

Still another element marked off Diaghilev's audience from the broader public for ballet: the large numbers of male homosexuals who frequented his performances in the late twenties. A review by Philip Page of Anna Pavlova's 1927 season made this point in the *Evening Standard:*

> Mme Pavlova's season of ballet at Covent Garden . . . coming only a few weeks after the close of the Diaghilev troupe's visit to the Princes Theatre, gives an opportunity for studying two opposite types of the ballet entertainment, both of which have a large following. The audiences for each overlap not at all. One does not see at Covent Garden the ecstatic youth with flowing hair who expresses his appreciation of Serge Lifar with a mass of sibilants.[146]

Page was not alone in remarking the presence of many homosexuals in Diaghilev's audience. *Vogue* drama critic Herbert Farjeon devoted the better part of an article in July 1928 to the phenomenon:

> The Russian Ballet has returned to London, and once again in the long intervals . . . the corridors of His Majesty's Theatre are crowded with sweet seasonable young men on whose highly presentable souls the soft down of aesthetic pubescence is just beginning to appear. It takes all sorts to make an audience, but it takes only one sort to make that audience distinguished; and just as the *clientèle* of Collins's Theatre may be distinguished by its partiality for pea-nuts, so the *clientèle* of the Russian Ballet may now be distinguished by the beautiful burgeoning boys who seem to recline on art like Madame Récamier on her couch and to regard the dancers and the *décor* as a kind of personal adornment. Indeed, they might almost be said to wear the Russian Ballet like a carnation in their button-holes.[147]

In these years when the "velvet-voiced youth of twenty [took] possession of the Russian Ballet," flowers ceased to be a tribute paid only to the
ballerina. "I would like to throw bricks at [Serge Lifar] when I see him
receiving bouquets of flowers at the end of the ballet," fulminated P. J. S.
Richardson in August 1926. Later that year Philip Page remarked that
" 'The Triumph of Neptune' was greeted with many floral tributes, even
the female dancers receiving some. Many stall-holders were shrilly enthusiastic, but the booing from the *profanum vulgus* was loud and persistent.
And the uninitiated were not alone in their disapproval."[148] Here in a
nutshell is the class, sexual, and artistic configuration of the dandy-aesthetes.

Homosexuals had long frequented Diaghilev's entertainments. They
had done so, however, as individuals. In his late 1920s incarnation, the
dandy-aesthete was "more formidable" than his fin-de-siècle predecessor,
"not so drooping, so languishing . . . surprisingly unready to go down
like a ninepin." He had emerged, so to speak, from the closet. Indeed, by
1928 His Majesty's Theatre had become a privileged area for "cruising"—
to use a modern idiom—with young men in "strange raiment" crowding
the promenade, now off-limits to women.[149]

From the crowds that flocked to the Coliseum and Paris Opéra just
after the war, Diaghilev might well have fashioned an audience of loyal,
longstanding partisans. He chose, instead, to court a new elite: the era's
consumerist vanguard, tastemakers who created styles of wealth and power
from the products of the modern marketplace and purveyed them through
the media. By the 1920s mass consumption was already a fact of life in
the United States. In Europe, however, this would be true only after the
Second World War. Until then, the accouterments of modern living—cars,
household appliances, telephones—belonged exclusively to the upper strata;
modernity, as a consumerist style, democratized only the elite.

Hence, the cul-de-sac in which Diaghilev found himself by the end of
the decade: the vanguard he had chosen as his ideal public was simply too
small to support his enterprise. But something besides numbers made this
elite a dubious foundation on which to erect an audience. It is the nature
of vanguards to change, particularly a vanguard predicated on the laws of
the marketplace, where the new sweeps away the old as a matter of necessity. Reviewing Diaghilev's last Paris season, a *Times* correspondent noted
just this phenomenon: the very section of the public whom Diaghilev's
novelties were calculated to please had:

decided that Russian *ballet* in whatever form is no longer to be regarded as a
serious manifestation of contemporary art. Thus the true supporters of the
ballet are forced, in order to enjoy their old favourites, to sit through perfor-

mances designed to satisfy a section of the audience which has not turned up.[150]

Between 1918 and 1929 Diaghilev created not one, but several audiences for ballet. This remarkable achievement did more than fill his theaters. It left a deep mark on the very identity of his company, forming its successive public images and influencing the general direction of its repertory. These images and the ideologies associated with them did not vanish with the Ballets Russes in 1929. Even today they remain imprinted on ballet, keys to its very identity.

EPILOGUE

On August 19, 1929, Diaghilev died in Venice. The news made the front pages of nearly every major daily. The company had broken up for vacation a few weeks before, and it was on beaches and movie sets, at beauty parlors and in the homes of friends that the dancers learned the terrible news. The death caught them unawares: although "Big Serge" had looked tired, none of them had imagined he was so ill or that his words of farewell in London were the last they would ever hear from him. Many of the dancers wept. Others went into shock. All felt a keen sense of personal loss, and all knew what his death meant for the Ballets Russes. Soon letters arrived from Serge Grigoriev announcing the demise of the company. For Alicia Markova "life had come to an end." "With Diaghilev's death," Alexandra Danilova later wrote, "the ground collapsed beneath my feet."[1]

The collapse of the Ballets Russes marked the beginning of a long, uncertain journey for its former dancers. In the 1930s most worked at some point with the various "Ballet Russe" touring companies that inherited the repertory and glamor of the Diaghilev organization. Among this group were nearly all of Diaghilev's choreographers—Michel Fokine, Léonide Massine, Bronislava Nijinska, George Balanchine—as well as several former stars, including Danilova, Leon Woizikovsky, Lubov Tchernicheva, Felia Doubrovska, Anton Dolin, and Vera Nemchinova. Other Diaghilev veterans took jobs in music-halls or at established theaters: most notable among these was Serge Lifar, who became artistic director of the Paris Opéra Ballet, a position he held for nearly thirty years. Still others struck out on their own, founding small companies that carried on Diaghilev's experimentalist tradition; George Balanchine's Les Ballets 1933 and Bronislava Nijinska's Théâtre de la Danse were the most important of these adventurous, short-lived undertakings. In England, meanwhile, Diaghilev alumni—Ninette de Valois, Marie Rambert, Alicia Markova, Anton Dolin, Lydia Lopokova, Tamara Karsavina, Ursula Moreton—were busy laying the groundwork for British ballet.

The years following World War I had witnessed the first great scattering of Russian dance talent. As the clouds of war gathered over Europe in the late 1930s, a second diaspora began, and many of those who had spent the interwar years in Europe found their way to the United States. Fokine, Balanchine, Adolph Bolm, Theodore Koslov, Laurent Novikoff, and Mikhail Mordkin had long made homes in America. They were joined now by other Diaghilev alumni—Nijinska, Massine, Danilova, Nemchinova, Boris Romanov, Alexandra Fedorova, Felia Doubrovska, Ludmilla Schollar, Anatole Vilzak. Most settled in New York, where they opened private studios or taught at institutions such as the School of American Ballet, but several—including Nijinska, Schollar, and Vilzak—found their way to the West Coast, and a few to dance backwaters such as Houston, Buffalo, and Miami. As dancers, choreographers, and teachers, these immigrants influenced American ballet for decades. The early history of Ballet Theatre (today, American Ballet Theatre) was partly written by Diaghilev's veterans, that of Balanchine's New York City Ballet almost totally so.

If the Second World War scattered Europe's émigré dance community, it also tarnished the reputation of many former Diaghilev associates. Gabrielle Chanel, Comte Etienne de Beaumont, José-María Sert, Paul Morand, and Serge Lifar were only a few of those who belonged to the collaborationist beau monde of Nazi-occupied Paris. The social ideology embodied in Diaghilev's marriage of art to an aristocracy of taste was also at least partly discredited. This occurred not only in France, where the liberation gave a strong boost to the Left, but also in England, transformed by the new Labour government into a welfare state. The social ideology of postwar ballet had to made some accommodation with populism.

In England, where the Ballets Russes sank its deepest roots, Diaghilev's ballets remained an important part of the repertory. But that repertory was highly selective, with Fokine's works and the classics first brought to the West by Diaghilev being represented disproportionately. Ironically, it was the United States that fell heir to the modernism that had played so central a role in his company's development. This was not so much a question of revivals (apart from *Apollon Musagète* and *Prodigal Son* none of the later works entered the repertory of American companies) as a matter of spirit. Like Diaghilev in the late 1910s, so Balanchine in the 1940s and 1950s was gripped by a frenzy for experiment. He transformed the look and dynamics of classical dancing, redefined the relationship of choreography to narrative and visual design, and extended the boundaries of acceptable music for ballet—all of which Diaghilev had done before him.

And like his mentor, Balanchine created an ensemble that served as an instrument for experiment while also catering to a broad public.

Like Britain's Royal Ballet with regard to Europe, the New York City Ballet has had a seminal influence on classical dancing in the United States. But that influence has rarely extended to the culture at large, despite the genuinely popular audiences both companies enjoy. Among intellectuals, ballet is at best an occasional enjoyment; at worst, a byword for artistic conservatism and privilege, a critique shared by most of today's avant-garde. Since Diaghilev's day, ballet has gradually slipped back to the sidelines from which he rescued it. Significantly, the one occasion in recent years when this isolation was broken was the New York premiere of the Joffrey Ballet's reconstruction of Nijinsky's *Le Sacre du Printemps*. The house was packed with artists, critics, and intellectuals, an audience reminiscent of Diaghilev days. There were many facets to Diaghilev's genius. But the ability, demonstrated time and again, to marshal talent in the creation of an art that touched the consciousness of its era—who today can claim even to aspire to that?

APPENDIX A

Works Created by Michel Fokine, 1905–1917

This chronology is a synthesis of various sources, although it draws heavily on the chronology in the Russian edition of Fokine's memoirs. For works produced in the West, titles are given in their best-known forms. For those staged in Russia, titles have been translated into English, except when the original was in French.

ACIS AND GALATEA

MUSIC: Andrei-Karl Kadletz
LIBRETTO: Michel Fokine, after a story by Vladimir Langammera
PREMIERE: 20 April 1905, Maryinsky Theater, St. Petersburg
PRODUCING ORGANIZATION: Imperial Theatrical School

POLKA WITH A LITTLE BALL

MUSIC: Victor Herbert
PREMIERE: 20 April 1905, Maryinsky Theater, St. Petersburg
PRODUCING ORGANIZATION: Imperial Theatrical School
PRINCIPAL DANCERS: Elena Smirnova, Georgi Rosai

THE DYING SWAN

MUSIC: Camille Saint-Saëns
PREMIERE: [1905], Hall of the Assembly of the Nobility, St. Petersburg
PRINCIPAL DANCER: Anna Pavlova
NOTE: For the performance given on 22 December 1907 at the Maryinsky Theater, St. Petersburg, Pavlova's costume was designed by Léon Bakst.

THE FLIGHT OF THE BUTTERFLIES

MUSIC: Frédéric Chopin
PREMIERE: 12 February 1906, Hall of the Assembly of the Nobility, St. Petersburg
NOTE: This may be the same pas de deux referred to by Bronislava Nijinska in

Early Memoirs as "Vol des Papillons," danced by Elena Smirnova and Vaslav Nijinsky at the Imperial Theatrical School performance on 26 March 1906.

POLKA-PIZZICATO
MUSIC: Johann Strauss
PREMIERE: 12 February 1906, Hall of the Assembly of the Nobility, St. Petersburg

SEVILLANA
MUSIC: Isaac Albéniz
PREMIERE: 12 February 1906, Hall of the Assembly of the Nobility, St. Petersburg

A MIDSUMMER NIGHT'S DREAM
MUSIC: Felix Mendelssohn
PREMIERE: 27 March 1906, Maryinsky Theater, St. Petersburg
PRODUCING ORGANIZATION: Imperial Theatrical School
NOTE: This one-act ballet was first produced by Marius Petipa at the Maryinsky Theater, St. Petersburg in 1876.

DIVERTISSEMENT—THE VALSE FANTASIA
MUSIC: Mikhail Glinka
PREMIERE: 27 March 1906, Maryinsky Theater, St. Petersburg
PRODUCING ORGANIZATION: Imperial Theatrical School
PRINCIPAL DANCERS: Elena Smirnova, Vaslav Nijinsky

LA VIGNE
MUSIC: Anton Rubinstein
PREMIERE: 8 April 1906, Maryinsky Theater, St. Petersburg
PRODUCING ORGANIZATION: Greblovsky National School (benefit in memory of N.V. Gogol)
PRINCIPAL DANCERS: Anna Pavlova, Michel Fokine, Marie Petipa, Tamara Karsavina, Vera Fokina

SPANISH DANCE
MUSIC: Georges Bizet
PREMIERE: 8 April 1906, Maryinsky Theater, St. Petersburg
PRODUCING ORGANIZATION: Greblovsky National School (benefit in memory of N.V. Gogol)

PIERROT'S JEALOUSY
PREMIERE: 8 April 1906

CZARDAS
MUSIC: Johannes Brahms
PREMIERE: 19 July 1906, Summer Theater, Krasnoe Selo

EUNICE

MUSIC: K. N. Shcherbatchev
LIBRETTO: Count Stenbok-Fermor, after Henryk Sienkiewicz's *Quo Vadis?*
PREMIERE: 10 February 1907, Maryinsky Theater, St. Petersburg
PRODUCING ORGANIZATION: Greblovsky National School (benefit in memory of N.V. Gogol)
PRINCIPAL DANCERS: Mathilde Kchessinska, Pavel Gerdt, Anna Pavlova, Alexander Shiryaev

CHOPINIANA

MUSIC: Frédéric Chopin, orchestrated by Alexander Glazunov
LIBRETTO: Michel Fokine
COSTUMES: Léon Bakst (and others)
PREMIERE: 10 February 1907, Maryinsky Theater, St. Petersburg
PRODUCING ORGANIZATION: Greblovsky National School (benefit in memory of N.V. Gogol)
PRINCIPAL DANCERS: Anna Pavlova, Mikhail Oboukhov, Alexis Bulgakov, Julie Sedova, Vera Fokina
NOTE: For subsequent versions of this ballet, see *Danses sur la Musique de Chopin, Rêverie Romantique—Ballet sur la Musique de Chopin,* and *Les Sylphides.*

THE ANIMATED GOBELIN

MUSIC: Nicholas Tcherepnine
LIBRETTO: Alexandre Benois, from Théophile Gautier's story *Omphale*
PREMIERE: 15 April 1907, Maryinsky Theater, St. Petersburg
PRODUCING ORGANIZATION: Imperial Theatrical School
PRINCIPAL DANCERS: Vaslav Nijinsky, Yelizaveta Gerdt, Georgi Rosai
NOTE: This was a scene from the ballet *Le Pavillon d'Armide* (see below).

LE PAVILLON D'ARMIDE

MUSIC: Nicholas Tcherepnine
LIBRETTO: Alexandre Benois, after Théophile Gautier's story *Omphale*
SETS AND COSTUMES: Alexandre Benois
PREMIERE: 25 November 1907, Maryinsky Theater, St. Petersburg
PRODUCING ORGANIZATION: Administration of the Imperial Theaters
PRINCIPAL DANCERS: Anna Pavlova, Pavel Gerdt, Vaslav Nijinsky
NOTE: For the Diaghilev production of this ballet, see below.

LE JEU DE ROBIN ET MARION (DANCES)

AUTHOR: Adam de la Halle
STAGE DIRECTION: Nikolai Evreinov
SETS AND COSTUMES: Mstislav Dobujinsky
PREMIERE: [8] December 1907, New Theater of Nekrasova-Kolginskaya, St. Petersburg
PRODUCING ORGANIZATION: Antique Theater

DANCE WITH A TORCH (DANSE ASSYRIENNE)

MUSIC: Anton Arensky
COSTUME: Léon Bakst
PREMIERE: 22 December 1907, Maryinsky Theater, St. Petersburg (charity performance organized by Michel Fokine)
PRINCIPAL DANCER: Tamara Karsavina

THE NIGHT OF TERPSICHORE

PREMIERE: 26 January 1908, Maryinsky Theater, St. Petersburg

DANSES SUR LA MUSIQUE DE CHOPIN

MUSIC: Frédéric Chopin
COSTUMES: Léon Bakst, Vera Fokina
PREMIERE: 16 February 1908, Maryinsky Theater, St. Petersburg (charity performance organized by Michel Fokine)
PRINCIPAL DANCERS: Anna Pavlova, Tamara Karsavina, Michel Fokine
NOTE: This ballet included solos and ensembles from *Rêverie Romantique—Ballet sur la Musique de Chopin* (see below) and the pas de deux from *Chopiniana* (see above).

UNE NUIT D'EGYPTE (EGYPTIAN NIGHTS)

MUSIC: Anton Arensky
SETS: Oreste Allegri
COSTUMES: Oreste Allegri, Léon Bakst
PREMIERE: 8 March 1908, Maryinsky Theater, St. Petersburg (charity performance organized by Michel Fokine)
PRINCIPAL DANCERS: Anna Pavlova, Michel Fokine, Pavel Gerdt, Vaslav Nijinsky, Olga Preobrajenska, Yelizaveta Timmé
NOTE: *Une Nuit d'Egypte,* with a libretto by Marius Petipa, was choreographed in 1900 by Lev Ivanov for a special performance in Peterhof. Canceled at the last moment, the ballet was never performed. A second version of the Fokine work was produced by the Ballets Russes as *Cléopâtre* (see below).

RÊVERIE ROMANTIQUE—BALLET SUR LA MUSIQUE DE CHOPIN (CHOPINIANA—SECOND VERSION)

MUSIC: Frédéric Chopin, orchestrated by Maurice Keller and Alexander Glazunov
SETS: Ivan Vsevolojsky (forest panorama from *The Sleeping Beauty*)
COSTUMES: Léon Bakst, Vera Fokina
PREMIERE: 8 March 1908, Maryinsky Theater, St. Petersburg (charity performance organized by Michel Fokine)
PRINCIPAL DANCERS: Anna Pavlova, Olga Preobrajenska, Tamara Karsavina, Vaslav Nijinsky
NOTE: This ballet incorporated dances from *Chopiniana* and *Danses sur la Musique de Chopin* (see above). A later version was produced by the Ballets Russes as *Les Sylphides* (see below).

BAL POUDRÉ

MUSIC: Muzio Clementi, orchestrated by Maurice Keller
LIBRETTO: Alexandre Benois
COSTUMES: Léon Bakst
PREMIERE: 11 March 1908, Pavlov Hall, St. Petersburg
PRODUCING ORGANIZATION: Russian Mercantile Society
PRINCIPAL DANCERS: Marie Petipa, Alfred Bekefi, Enrico Cecchetti
NOTE: Bakst's costumes were subsequently used in the original production of *Carnaval* (see below).

THE FOUR SEASONS

MUSIC: Peter Ilitch Tchaikovsky
PREMIERE: 26 March 1908, Maryinsky Theater, St. Petersburg
PRODUCING ORGANIZATION: Imperial Theatrical School

GRAND PAS SUR LA MUSIQUE DE CHOPIN

MUSIC: Frédéric Chopin
PREMIERE: 6 April 1908, Maryinsky Theater, St. Petersburg
PRODUCING ORGANIZATION: Imperial Theatrical School

THE DANCE OF THE SEVEN VEILS (for the play *SALOMÉ*)

AUTHOR: Oscar Wilde
MUSIC: Alexander Glazunov
SETS AND COSTUMES: Léon Bakst
PREMIERE: 3 November 1908, Mikhailovsky Theater, St. Petersburg
PRINCIPAL DANCER: Ida Rubinstein
NOTE: This dance, for Ida Rubinstein's production of the Oscar Wilde play, was subsequently performed on 20 December 1908 at the Conservatory, St. Petersburg. For Rubinstein's Paris production of the play, see below.

PICTURES OF THE ANCIENT WORLD

(Dance at the Feast, The Battle of the Gladiators, After the Example of the Gods, In the Roman Circus)
PREMIERE: 26 February 1909, Theater of the Literary-Artistic Society, St. Petersburg

LE PAVILLON D'ARMIDE

MUSIC: Nicholas Tcherepnine
LIBRETTO: Alexandre Benois, after Théophile Gautier's *Omphale*
SETS AND COSTUMES: Alexandre Benois
SCENE PAINTING: Oreste Allegri, [?] Lockenberg
PREMIERE: 18 May 1909,* Théâtre du Châtelet, Paris

---

*When a *répétition générale* preceded the official premiere, the earlier date is given followed by an asterisk.

PRODUCING ORGANIZATION: Ballets Russes*

PRINCIPAL DANCERS: Vera Karalli, Mikhail Mordkin, Alexis Bulgakov, Tamara Karsavina, Alexandra Baldina, Alexandra Fedorova, Elena Smirnova, Vaslav Nijinsky

NOTE: Based on Fokine's earlier version (see above), this production had new sets and costumes.

PRINCE IGOR

Polovtsian Scenes and Dances (Act II of the opera)

MUSIC: Alexander Borodin, completed and partly orchestrated by Nikolai Rimsky-Korsakov and Alexander Glazunov

LIBRETTO: Alexander Borodin, after a scenario by Vladimir Stasov

CHORUS MASTER: Ulric Avranek

SETS AND COSTUMES: Nicholas Roerich

SCENE PAINTING: Boris Anisfeld

REHEARSAL DIRECTOR: Alexander Sanin

PREMIERE: 18 May 1909,* Théâtre du Châtelet, Paris

PRODUCING ORGANIZATION: Ballets Russes

PRINCIPAL SINGERS: Elisabeth [Elisabeta] Petrenko, Basile [Vasily] Sharonov, Dmitri Smirnov, Kapitan Zaporojetz, Michel d'Arial

PRINCIPAL DANCERS: Adolph Bolm, Sophia Fedorova, Elena Smirnova

NOTE: In later seasons this work was performed without singers under the title of *The Polovtsian Dances*. In 1923 it was partly rechoreographed by Bronislava Nijinska.

LE FESTIN

MUSIC: Alexander Glazunov, Mikhail Glinka, Modest Mussorgsky, Nikolai Rimsky-Korsakov, Peter Ilitch Tchaikovsky

SETS: Konstantin Korovin

COSTUMES: Léon Bakst, Alexandre Benois, Ivan Bilibin, Konstantin Korovin

SCENE PAINTING: Piotr Lambine, Nikolai Charbé

PREMIERE: 18 May 1909,* Théâtre du Châtelet, Paris

PRODUCING ORGANIZATION: Ballets Russes

PRINCIPAL DANCERS: Vera Fokina, Tamara Karsavina, Vaslav Nijinsky, Sophia Fedorova, Mikhail Mordkin, Georgi Rosai, Vera Karalli

NOTE: Fokine choreographed the "Hopak" (Mussorgsky), "Trepak" (Tchaikovsky), and "Finale" (Tchaikovsky). The other dances were "Firebird" (the Blue Bird pas de deux from *The Sleeping Beauty*) and "Grand Pas Classique Hongrois" (from *Raymonda*), both by Marius Petipa, "Czardas" (Glazunov), by Alexander Gorsky, "Mazurka" (Glinka), by Nicolai Goltz and Felix Kchessinsky, and "Lezginka" (Glinka), by Fokine after Petipa. According to Bronislava Nijinska, Fokine's "Finale" was not performed until 1910.

---

*Although the Ballets Russes did not officially come into existence until 1911, the name is used as shorthand for the Diaghilev enterprise.

LES SYLPHIDES

MUSIC: Frédéric Chopin, orchestrated by Alexander Glazunov, Igor Stravinsky, Alexander Taneyev

SETS AND COSTUMES: Alexandre Benois

SCENE PAINTING: Stepan Yaremich

PREMIERE: 2 June 1909,* Théâtre du Châtelet, Paris

PRODUCING ORGANIZATION: Ballets Russes

PRINCIPAL DANCERS: Anna Pavlova, Tamara Karsavina, Alexandra Baldina, Vaslav Nijinsky

NOTE: For earlier versions of this ballet, see *Chopiniana, Danses sur la Musique de Chopin,* and *Rêverie Romantique—Ballet sur la Musique de Chopin.* In 1919, scenery by A. Socrate replaced the Beno's setting.

CLÉOPÂTRE

MUSIC: Anton Arensky, with additional music by Alexander Glazunov, Mikhail Glinka, Modest Mussorgsky, Nikolai Rimsky-Korsakov, Sergei Taneyev, Nicholas Tcherepnine

SETS AND COSTUMES: Léon Bakst

PREMIERE: 2 June 1909,* Théâtre du Châtelet, Paris

PRODUCING ORGANIZATION: Ballets Russes

PRINCIPAL DANCERS: Ida Rubinstein, Anna Pavlova, Tamara Karsavina, Vaslav Nijinsky, Michel Fokine, Alexis Bulgakov

NOTE: *Cléopâtre* was based on Fokine's earlier *Une Nuit d'Egypte* (see above). In 1918 the ballet was restaged with sets by Robert Delaunay, additional costumes by Sonia Delaunay, and a new pas de deux by Léonide Massine.

BACCHANALE

MUSIC: Alexander Glazunov

COSTUMES: Léon Bakst

PREMIERE: 22 January 1910, Hall of the Assembly of the Nobility, St. Petersburg

PRINCIPAL DANCERS: Anna Pavlova, Laurent Novikoff

CARNAVAL

MUSIC: Robert Schumann, orchestrated by Anton Arensky, Alexander Glazunov, Anatol Liadov, Nikolai Rimsky-Korsakov, Nicholas Tcherépnine

LIBRETTO: Léon Bakst, Michel Fokine

COSTUMES: Léon Bakst

PREMIERE: 20 February 1910, Pavlov Hall, St. Petersburg

PRODUCING ORGANIZATION: *Satyricon*

PRINCIPAL DANCERS: Vaslav Nijinsky, Tamara Karsavina, Michel Fokine, Alfred Bekefi, Joseph Kchessinsky, Vsevolod Meyerhold

NOTE: According to Bronislava Nijinska, the costumes for Harlequin, Columbine, Pierrot, and Pantalon were originally created by Bakst for *Bal Poudré* (see above), while the 1840s-style crinoline dresses came from his production of *Puppenfee,* choreographed by Nicolas and Sergei Legat in 1903. For the Ballets Russes production, which received its premiere on 20 May 1910 at the Theater des Westens in Berlin, Bakst created sets and new costumes.

DANSE SIAMOISE

MUSIC: Christian Sinding, orchestrated by Igor Stravinsky
COSTUME: Léon Bakst
PREMIERE: 20 February 1910, Maryinsky Theater, St. Petersburg
Principal dancer: Vaslav Nijinsky
NOTE: This dance was subsequently incorporated into the divertissement *Les Orientales* (see below).

KOBOLD

MUSIC: Edvard Grieg, orchestrated by Igor Stravinsky
COSTUME: Léon Bakst
PREMIERE: 20 February 1910, Maryinsky Theater, St. Petersburg
Principal dancer: Vaslav Nijinsky
NOTE: This dance was subsequently incorporated into the divertissement *Les Orientales* (see below).

GROTTO OF VENUS (Venusberg scene from the opera TANNHÄUSER)

MUSIC: Richard Wagner
PREMIERE: 6 April 1910, Maryinsky Theater, St. Petersburg (benefit performance for the Ladies' Patriotic Society)

SCHÉHÉRAZADE

MUSIC: Nikolai Rimsky-Korsakov
LIBRETTO: Léon Bakst, Alexandre Benois, Michel Fokine, after the first tale of *The Thousand and One Nights*
SETS AND COSTUMES: Léon Bakst
PREMIERE: 4 June 1910, Théâtre National de l'Opéra, Paris
PRODUCING ORGANIZATION: Ballets Russes
PRINCIPAL DANCERS: Ida Rubinstein, Vaslav Nijinsky, Alexis Bulgakov

FIREBIRD

MUSIC: Igor Stravinsky
LIBRETTO: Michel Fokine
SETS: Alexander Golovin
COSTUMES: Alexander Golovin, with additional costumes by Léon Bakst
PREMIERE: 25 June 1910, Théâtre National de l'Opéra, Paris
PRODUCING ORGANIZATION: Ballets Russes
PRINCIPAL DANCERS: Tamara Karsavina, Michel Fokine, Alexis Bulgakov, Vera Fokina
NOTE: *Firebird* was restaged in 1926 with sets and costumes by Natalia Gontcharova.

LES ORIENTALES

MUSIC: Anton Arensky, Alexander Borodin, Alexander Glazunov, Edvard Grieg (orchestrated by Igor Stravinsky), Christian Sinding (orchestrated by Igor Stravinsky)

SETS: Konstantin Korovin

COSTUMES: Konstantin Korovin, Léon Bakst

PREMIERE: 25 June 1910, Théâtre National de l'Opéra, Paris

PRODUCING ORGANIZATION: Ballets Russes

PRINCIPAL DANCERS: Yekaterina Geltzer, Alexander Volinine, Tamara Karsavina, Vaslav Nijinsky, Alexandra Vassilieva, Georgi Rosai, Vera Fokina, Alexander Orlov, Michel Fokine

NOTE: This divertissement included two previously choreographed dances, *Danse Siamoise* and *Kobold* (see above).

THE WOMEN AT THE FOLK MEETING (dances for a play after Aristophanes)

MUSIC: O. Boehm

PREMIERE: 12 November 1910, Tenishev Institute, St. Petersburg

BALL AT THE COURT OF LOUIS XV (dances)

PREIMERE: 11 February 1911, Sporting-Palace, St. Petersburg

LE SPECTRE DE LA ROSE

MUSIC: Carl Maria von Weber, orchestrated by Hector Berlioz

LIBRETTO: Jean-Louis Vaudoyer, after a poem by Théophile Gautier

SETS AND COSTUMES: Léon Bakst

PREMIERE: 19 April 1911, Théâtre de Monte-Carlo, Monte Carlo

PRODUCING ORGANIZATION: Ballets Russes

PRINCIPAL DANCERS: Vaslav Nijinsky, Tamara Karsavina

NARCISSE

MUSIC: Nicholas Tcherepnine

LIBRETTO: Léon Bakst

SETS AND COSTUMES: Léon Bakst

PREMIERE: 26 April 1911, Théâtre de Monte-Carlo, Monte Carlo

PRODUCING ORGANIZATION: Ballets Russes

PRINCIPAL DANCERS: Vaslav Nijinsky, Tamara Karsavina, Bronislava Nijinska, Vera Fokina

LE MARTYRE DU SAINT SÉBASTIEN (dances for the play)

AUTHOR: Gabriele d'Annunzio

MUSIC: Claude Debussy

SETS AND COSTUMES: Léon Bakst

PREMIERE: 22 May 1911, Théâtre du Châtelet, Paris

PRODUCING ORGANIZATION: Ida Rubinstein company

SADKO—AU ROYAUME SOUS-MARIN (scene 6 from the opera SADKO)

MUSIC: Nikolai Rimsky-Korsakov

SETS: Boris Anisfeld

COSTUMES: Boris Anisfeld, Léon Bakst

PREMIERE: 6 June 1911, Théâtre du Châtelet, Paris
PRODUCING ORGANIZATION: Ballets Russes
NOTE: This ballet was restaged in 1916 with choreography by Adolph Bolm and designs by Natalia Gontcharova.

PETROUCHKA

MUSIC: Igor Stravinsky
LIBRETTO: Igor Stravinsky, Alexandre Benois
SETS AND COSTUMES: Alexandre Benois
PREMIERE: 13 June 1911, Théâtre du Châtelet, Paris
PRODUCING ORGANIZATION: Ballets Russes
PRINCIPAL DANCERS: Vaslav Nijinsky, Tamara Karsavina, Alexander Orlov, Enrico Cecchetti

VARIATIONS

MUSIC: Frédéric Chopin
PREMIERE: 1 October 1911, Maryinsky Theater, St. Petersburg

ORPHEUS AND EURYDICE (dances, scenes, and groups in opera)

MUSIC: Christoph Willibald Gluck
STAGE DIRECTION: Vsevolod Meyerhold
SETS AND COSTUMES: Alexander Golovin
PREMIERE: 21 December 1911, Maryinsky Theater, St. Petersburg
PRODUCING ORGANIZATION: Administration of the Imperial Theaters

PAPILLONS

MUSIC: Robert Schumann, orchestrated by Nicholas Tcherepnine
LIBRETTO: Michel Fokine
SETS: Piotr Lambine
COSTUMES: Léon Bakst
PREMIERE: 10 March 1912, Maryinsky Theater, St. Petersburg (Literary Fund benefit)
NOTE: *Papillons* was produced by the Ballets Russes on 16 April 1914 at the Théâtre de Monte-Carlo, Monte Carlo, with sets by Mstislav Dobujinsky.

ISLAMÉ

MUSIC: Mily Balakirev
SETS AND COSTUMES: Boris Anisfeld
PREMIERE: 10 March 1912, Maryinsky Theater, St. Petersburg (Literary Fund benefit)

LE DIEU BLEU

MUSIC: Reynaldo Hahn
LIBRETTO: Jean Cocteau, Frédéric de Madrazo
SETS AND COSTUMES: Léon Bakst
PREMIERE: 13 May 1912, Théâtre du Châtelet, Paris

PRODUCING ORGANIZATION: Ballets Russes
PRINCIPAL DANCERS: Vaslav Nijinsky, Tamara Karsavina, Lydia Nelidova, Bronislava Nijinska, Max Frohman, Michel Fedorov

THAMAR
MUSIC: Mily Balakirev
LIBRETTO: Léon Bakst, after a poem by Mikhail Lermontov
SETS AND COSTUMES: Léon Bakst
PREMIERE: 20 May 1912, Théâtre du Châtelet, Paris
PRODUCING ORGANIZATION: Ballets Russes
PRINCIPAL DANCERS: Tamara Karsavina, Adolph Bolm

DAPHNIS AND CHLOË
MUSIC: Maurice Ravel
LIBRETTO: Michel Fokine, after Longus
SETS AND COSTUMES: Léon Bakst
PREMIERE: 8 June 1912, Théâtre du Châtelet, Paris
PRODUCING ORGANIZATION: Ballets Russes
PRINCIPAL DANCERS: Tamara Karsavina, Vaslav Nijinsky, Adolph Bolm, Margarita Frohman, Enrico Cecchetti

SALOMÉ (dances for the play)
AUTHOR: Oscar Wilde
MUSIC: Alexander Glazunov
STAGE DIRECTION: Alexander Sanin
SETS AND COSTUMES: Léon Bakst
PREMIERE: 10 June 1912, Théâtre du Châtelet, Paris
PRODUCING ORGANIZATION: Ida Rubinstein company

JUDITH (dances in opera)
MUSIC: Alexander Serov
PREMIERE: 13 November 1912, Maryinsky Theater, St. Petersburg
PRODUCING ORGANIZATION: Administration of the Imperial Theaters

THE PEARL DIVERS (dances in opera)
MUSIC: Georges Bizet
PREMIERE: 27 November 1912, Maryinsky Theater, St. Petersburg
PRODUCING ORGANIZATION: Administration of the Imperial Theaters

THE SEVEN DAUGHTERS OF THE MOUNTAIN KING
MUSIC: Alexander Spendiarov
SETS AND COSTUMES: Boris Anisfeld
PREMIERE: 1 January 1913, Neues Operntheater (Kroll), Berlin
PRODUCING ORGANIZATION: Anna Pavlova company

LES PRÉLUDES

MUSIC: Franz Liszt
SETS AND COSTUMES: Boris Anisfeld
PREMIERE: 15 January 1913, Neues Operntheater (Kroll), Berlin
PRODUCING ORGANIZATION: Anna Pavlova company
NOTE: This ballet was first performed at the Maryinsky Theater, St. Petersburg, on 31 March 1913 and at the Palace Theatre, London, on 21 April 1913.

LA PISANELLE OU LA MORT PARFUMÉE (dances in Act III of the play)

AUTHOR: Gabriele d'Annunzio
MUSIC: Ildebrando Pizzetti
SETS AND COSTUMES: Léon Bakst
STAGE DIRECTION: Vsevolod Meyerhold
PREMIERE: 11 June 1913,* Théâtre du Châtelet, Paris
PRODUCING ORGANIZATION: Ida Rubinstein company

LEGEND OF JOSEPH

MUSIC: Richard Strauss
LIBRETTO: Count Harry Kessler, Hugo von Hofmannsthal
SETS: José-María Sert
COSTUMES: Léon Bakst
PREMIERE: 14 May 1914, Théâtre National de l'Opéra, Paris
PRODUCING ORGANIZATION: Ballets Russes
PRINCIPAL DANCERS: Maria Kuznetsova, Vera Fokina, Alexis Bulgakov, Léonide Massine, Serge Grigoriev, Lubov Tchernicheva, Sophie Pflanz, Doris Faithfull, Max Frohman

LE COQ D'OR

MUSIC: Nikolai Rimsky-Korsakov
LIBRETTO: Vladimir Belsky, after Alexander Pushkin, revised by Alexandre Benois
CHORUS MASTER: Nicolas Palitzine
STAGE DIRECTION: Michel Fokine
SETS AND COSTUMES: Natalia Gontcharova
PREMIERE: 24 May 1914, Théâtre National de l'Opéra, Paris
PRODUCING ORGANIZATION: Ballets Russes
PRINCIPAL SINGERS: Jean [Ivan] Altchevsky, Alexandre Belianin, Aurelia Dobrovolska, Elisabeth [Elisabeta] Petrenko, Hélène Nikolaeva, Basile [Vasily] Petrov
PRINCIPAL DANCERS: Tamara Karsavina, Adolph Bolm, Alexis Bulgakov

MIDAS

MUSIC: Maximilian Steinberg
LIBRETTO: Léon Bakst, after Ovid
SETS AND COSTUMES: Mstislav Dobujinsky
PREMIERE: 2 June 1914, Théâtre National de l'Opéra, Paris
PRODUCING ORGANIZATION: Ballets Russes

PRINCIPAL DANCERS: Tamara Karsavina, Adolph Bolm, Max Frohman, Ludmilla Schollar, Sophie Pflanz, Lubov Tchernicheva

THE DREAM
MUSIC: Mikhail Glinka
PREMIERE: 10 January 1915, Maryinsky Theater, Petrograd
NOTE: After the outbreak of World War I, the name of the Russian capital was changed from St. Petersburg to Petrograd.

FRANCESCA DA RIMINI
MUSIC: Peter Ilitch Tchaikovsky
LIBRETTO: Michel Fokine, after Canto V of Dante's *Inferno*
SETS AND COSTUMES: Mikhail Bobyshov (and others)
PREMIERE: 28 November 1915, Maryinsky Theater, Petrograd (charity performance for war orphans)
PRINCIPAL DANCER: Lubov Egorova

STENKA RAZIN
MUSIC: Alexander Glazunov
SETS AND COSTUMES: Mikhail Bobyshov (and others)
PREMIERE: 28 November 1915, Maryinsky Theater, Petrograd (charity performance for war orphans)
PRINCIPAL DANCER: Vera Fokina

EROS
MUSIC: Peter Ilitch Tchaikovsky
LIBRETTO: Michel Fokine, after Valerian Svetlov's *A Fiesole Angel*
SETS AND COSTUMES: Mikhail Bobyshov
PREMIERE: 28 November 1915, Maryinsky Theater, Petrograd (charity performance for war orphans)
PRINCIPAL DANCERS: Mathilde Kchessinska, Pierre Vladimirov

PRELUDE
MUSIC: Frédéric Chopin
PREMIERE: 28 November 1915, Maryinsky Theater, Petrograd (charity performance for war orphans)

ROMANCE
MUSIC: Peter Ilitch Tchaikovsky
PREMIERE: 28 November 1915, Maryinsky Theater, Petrograd (charity performance for war orphans)

BACCHUS
MUSIC: Nicholas Tcherepnine
PREMIERE: 28 November 1915, Maryinsky Theater, Petrograd (charity performance for war orphans)

TARANTELLA
PREMIERE: 28 November 1915, Maryinsky Theater, Petrograd (charity performance for war orphans)

ANDANTINO
MUSIC: Peter Ilitch Tchaikovsky
PREMIERE: 9 January 1916, Maryinsky Theater, Petrograd

KHAITARMA
MUSIC: Alexander Spendiarov
PREMIERE: 12 January 1916, Maryinsky Theater, Petrograd

RUSSIAN SONGS
(a)Joking ("I danced with a little mosquito"); (b)Lullaby; (c)Dancing; (d)Roundelay
PREMIERE: 12 January 1916, Maryinsky Theater, Petrograd

JOTA ARAGONESA
MUSIC: Mikhail Glinka
SETS AND COSTUMES: Alexander Golovin
PREMIERE: 29 January 1916, Maryinsky Theater, Petrograd
PRODUCING ORGANIZATION: Administration of the Imperial Theaters

PRINCESS AVRIZA
MUSIC: Modest Mussorgsky
PREMIERE: 6 February 1916, Maryinsky Theater, Petrograd

THE SORCERER'S APPRENTICE
MUSIC: Paul Dukas
PREMIERE: 12 November 1916, Maryinsky Theater, Petrograd (charity performance for the Ladies' Circle of the Moscow Regiment of Guards)

ABREK
MUSIC: traditional, orchestrated by Boris Asafiev
PREMIERE: 16 February 1917, Maryinsky Theater, Petrograd
NOTE: "Abrek" is the name of an ethnic group living in the Caucasian Mountains.

RUSLAN AND LUDMILLA (dances in opera)
MUSIC: Mikhail Glinka
PREMIERE: 27 November 1917, Maryinsky Theater, Petrograd

APPENDIX B

Operas Produced by Serge Diaghilev

BORIS GODUNOV

MUSIC: Modest Mussorgsky, revised and orchestrated by Nikolai Rimsky-Korsakov
LIBRETTO: Modest Mussorgsky, after Alexander Pushkin
CONDUCTOR: Felix Blumenfeld
CHORUS MASTER: Ulric Avranek
STAGE DIRECTION: Alexander Sanin
SETS: Alexander Golovin, Alexandre Benois, Konstantin Yuon
COSTUMES: Ivan Bilibin, Dmitri Stelletsky, Alexander Golovin, Alexandre Benois, Boris Anisfeld, Eugene Lanceray, Stepan Yaremich, Konstantin Yuon
PREMIERE: 19 May 1908, Théâtre National de l'Opéra, Paris
PRINCIPAL SINGERS: Feodor Chaliapin, Natasha Yermolenko, Vladimir Kastorsky, Elisabeth [Elisabeta] Petrenko, Dagmara Renine, Jean [Ivan] Altchevsky, Basile [Vasily] Sharonov, Dmitri Smirnov, Claudia Tugarinova, Nikolai Kedrov, [?] Tolkatchev, Mitrofan Chuprynnikov, Mikhail Kravchenko
NOTE: The opera, in its original form, was first produced in 1874 in St. Petersburg, and in Rimsky-Korsakov's revised version in 1896.

PRINCE IGOR

Polovtsian Scenes and Dances (Act II of the opera)
MUSIC: Alexander Borodin, completed and partly orchestrated by Nikolai Rimsky-Korsakov and Alexander Glazunov
LIBRETTO: Alexander Borodin, after a scenario by Vladimir Stasov
CONDUCTOR: Emile Cooper
CHORUS MASTER: Ulric Avranek
SETS AND COSTUMES: Nicholas Roerich
SCENE PAINTING: Boris Anisfeld
REHEARSAL DIRECTOR: Alexander Sanin
CHOREOGRAPHY: Michel Fokine
PREMIERE: 18 May 1909,* Théâtre du Châtelet, Paris

*When a *répétition générale* preceded the official premiere, the earlier date is given followed by an asterisk.

PRINCIPAL SINGERS: Elisabeth [Elisabeta] Petrenko, Basile [Vasily] Sharonov, Dmitri Smirnov, Kapitan Zaporojetz, Michel d'Arial
PRINCIPAL DANCERS: Adolph Bolm, Sophia Fedorova, Elena Smirnova
NOTE: This opera was first produced in 1890 in St. Petersburg.

IVAN THE TERRIBLE (THE MAID OF PSKOV)
MUSIC: Nikolai Rimsky-Korsakov
LIBRETTO: Nikolai Rimsky-Korsakov, after Lev Mey
CONDUCTOR: Nicholas Tcherepnine
CHORUS MASTER: Ulric Avranek
STAGE DIRECTION: Alexander Sanin
SETS: Alexander Golovin, Nicholas Roerich
COSTUMES: Dmitri Stelletsky
SCENE PAINTING: [?] Vnoukow (Scene l), Boris Anisfeld (Scenes 2, 4, 5), Nikolai Charbé (Scene 3)
PREMIERE: 24 May 1909,* Théâtre du Châtelet, Paris
PRINCIPAL SINGERS: Feodor Chaliapin, Alexander Davydov, Vladimir Kastorsky, Lydia Lipkowska, Elisabeth [Elisabeta] Petrenko, Basile [Vasily] Sharonov, Basile [Vasily] Damaev, [?] Pavlova
NOTE: The third and final version of this opera was first produced in 1895 in St. Petersburg.

RUSLAN and LUDMILLA (Act I)
MUSIC: Mikhail Glinka
LIBRETTO: Konstantin Bakhturin, Valerian Shirkov, and others, after Pushkin
CONDUCTOR: Emile Cooper
CHORUS MASTER: Ulric Avranek
STAGE DIRECTION: Alexander Sanin
SETS AND COSTUMES: Konstantin Korovin
PREMIERE: 2 June 1909,* Théâtre du Châtelet, Paris
PRINCIPAL SINGERS: Vladimir Kastorsky, Lydia Lipkowska, Basile [Vasily] Sharonov, Dmitri Smirnov, Kapitan Zaporojetz, Yevgenia Zbruyeva
NOTE: This opera was first produced in 1842 in St. Petersburg.

JUDITH (Act III)
MUSIC: Alexander Serov
LIBRETTO: A. Maykov and others, after the Book of Judith
CONDUCTOR: Emile Cooper
CHORUS MASTER: Ulric Avranek
STAGE DIRECTION: Alexander Sanin
SETS: Valentin Serov, Léon Bakst
COSTUMES: Léon Bakst
PREMIERE: 7 June 1909, Théâtre du Châtelet, Paris
PRINCIPAL SINGERS: Feodor Chaliapin, Félia Litvinne, Dmitri Smirnov, Kapitan Zaporojetz, Yevgenia Zbruyeva
NOTE: This opera was first produced in 1863 in St. Petersburg.

BORIS GODUNOV

MUSIC: Modest Mussorgsky, revised and orchestrated by Nikolai Rimsky-Korskov
LIBRETTO: Modest Mussorgsky, after Alexander Pushkin
CONDUCTOR: Emile Cooper
CHORUS MASTER: [?] Pokhitonov
STAGE DIRECTION: Alexander Sanin
SETS: Konstantin Yuon, Léon Bakst (Act II)
COSTUMES: Ivan Bilibin, Léon Bakst, Konstantin Yuon
PREMIERE: 22 May 1913, Théâtre des Champs-Elysées, Paris
PRINCIPAL SINGERS: Feodor Chaliapin, Nicolas Andreyev, Paul [Pavel] Andreyev, Basile [Vasily] Damaev, Hélène Nikolaeva, Elisabeth [Elisabeta] Petrenko, Marie Brian, Alexandre Belianin, Kapitan Zaporojetz, [?] Davidova, Nikolai Bolshakov, [?] Alexandrovitch
NOTE: The opera, in its original form, was first produced in 1874 in St. Petersburg, and in Rimsky-Korsakov's revised version in 1896. The first performance in London of the Diaghilev production was on 24 June 1913 at the Theatre Royal, Drury Lane.

KHOVANSHCHINA

MUSIC: Modest Mussorgsky, completed and orchestrated by Nikolai Rimsky-Korsakov, with additional passages orchestrated by Maurice Ravel and Igor Stravinsky
LIBRETTO: Modest Mussorgsky, Vladimir Stasov
CONDUCTOR: Emile Cooper
STAGE DIRECTION: Alexander Sanin
SETS AND COSTUMES: Feodor Fedorovsky
CHOREOGRAPHY: Adolph Bolm
PREMIERE: 5 June 1913, Théâtre des Champs-Elysées, Paris
PRINCIPAL SINGERS: Feodor Chaliapin, Paul [Pavel] Andreyev, Nicolas Andreyev, Alexandre Belianin, Nikolai Bolshakov, Marie Brian, Basile [Vasily] Damaev, Hélène Nikolaeva, Elisabeth [Elisabeta] Petrenko, Kapitan Zaporojetz, [?] Alexandrovitch, [?] Strobinder
NOTE: This opera was first produced in 1886 in St. Petersburg. The first performance in London of the Diaghilev production was on 1 July 1913 at the Theatre Royal, Drury Lane.

IVAN THE TERRIBLE (THE MAID OF PSKOV)

MUSIC: Nikolai Rimsky-Korsakov
LIBRETTO: Nikolai Rimsky-Korsakov, after Lev Mey
CONDUCTOR: Emile Cooper
SETS AND COSTUMES: Alexander Golovin
PREMIERE: 8 July 1913, Theatre Royal, Drury Lane, London
PRINCIPAL SINGERS: Feodor Chaliapin, Nicolas Andreyev, Paul [Pavel] Andreyev, Marie Brian, Basile [Vasily] Damaev, Hélène Nikolaeva, Elisabeth [Elisabeta] Petrenko, Kapitan Zaporojetz
NOTE: The third and final version of this opera was first produced in 1895 in St. Petersburg.

LE COQ D'OR (THE GOLDEN COCKEREL)

MUSIC: Nikolai Rimsky-Korsakov

LIBRETTO: Vladimir Belsky, after Alexander Pushkin, revised by Alexandre Benois

CONDUCTOR: Pierre Monteux

CHORUS MASTER: Nicolas Palitzine

STAGE DIRECTION: Michel Fokine

CHOREOGRAPHY: Michel Fokine

SETS AND COSTUMES: Natalia Gontcharova

PREMIERE: 24 May 1914, Théâtre National de l'Opéra, Paris

PRINCIPAL SINGERS: Jean [Ivan] Altchevsky, Alexandre Belianin, Aurelia Dobro-volska, Elisabeth [Elisabeta] Petrenko, Hélène Nikolaeva, Basile [Vasily] Petrov

PRINCIPAL DANCERS: Tamara Karsavina, Adolph Bolm, Alexis Bulgakov

NOTE: This opera was first produced in 1909 in Moscow. The first performance in London of the Diaghilev production was on 15 June 1914 at the Theatre Royal, Drury Lane.

LE ROSSIGNOL

MUSIC: Igor Stravinsky

LIBRETTO: Igor Stravinsky and Stepan Mitusov, after Hans Christian Andersen

CONDUCTOR: Pierre Monteux

CHORUS MASTER: Nicolas Palitzine

STAGE DIRECTION: Alexandre Benois, Alexander Sanin

SETS AND COSTUMES: Alexandre Benois

SCENE PAINTING: Nikolai Charbé

CHOREOGRAPHY: Boris Romanov

PREMIERE: 26 May 1914, Théâtre National de l'Opéra, Paris

PRINCIPAL SINGERS: Paul [Pavel] Andreyev, Alexandre Belianin, Marie Brian, Au-relia Dobrovolska, Fedor Ernst, Nicolas Goulaiev, Elisabeth Mamsina, Elisabeth [Elisabeta] Petrenko, Basile [Vasily] Sharonov, Alexandre Varfolomeev

PRINCIPAL DANCERS: Max Frohman, Nicolas Kremnev

NOTE: The first London performance was on 18 June 1914 at the Theatre Royal, Drury Lane.

PRINCE IGOR

MUSIC: Alexander Borodin, completed and partly orchestrated by Nikolai Rimsky-Korsakov and Alexander Glazunov

LIBRETTO: Alexander Borodin, after a scenario by Vladimir Stasov

CONDUCTOR: Leon [Lev] Steinberg

CHOREOGRAPHY: Michel Fokine

PREMIERE: 8 June 1914, Theatre Royal, Drury Lane, London

PRINCIPAL SINGERS: Feodor Chaliapin, Nicolas Andreyev, Paul [Pavel] Andreyev, Marie Brian, Maria Kuznetsova, Elisabeth Mamsina, Elisabeth [Elisabeta] Pe-trenko, Basile [Vasily] Sharonov, Alexandre Varfolomeev

NOTE: This opera was first produced in 1890 in St. Petersburg.

MAY NIGHT

MUSIC: Nikolai Rimsky-Korsakov
LIBRETTO: Nikolai Rimsky-Korsakov, after Nikolai Gogol
CONDUCTOR: Leon [Lev] Steinberg
PREMIERE: 26 June 1914, Theatre Royal, Drury Lane, London
PRINCIPAL SINGERS: Paul [Pavel] Andreyev, Alexandre Belianin, Marie Brian, Fedor Ernst, Elisabeth Mamsina, Elisabeth [Elisabeta] Petrenko, Basile [Vasily] Sharonov, Dmitri Smirnov
NOTE: This opera was first produced in 1880 in St. Petersburg.

MAVRA

MUSIC: Igor Stravinsky
LIBRETTO: Boris Kochno, after Alexander Pushkin
CONDUCTOR: Gregor Fitelberg
STAGE DIRECTION: Bronislava Nijinska
SETS AND COSTUMES: Léopold Survage
PREMIERE: 3 June 1922, Théâtre National de l'Opéra, Paris
PRINCIPAL SINGERS: Zoia Rosovska, Hélène Sadoven, Stephan [Stefan] Belina-Skupevsky, Oda Slobodskaya

LA COLOMBE

MUSIC: Charles Gounod, with new recitatives by Francis Poulenc
LIBRETTO: Jules Barbier and Michel Carré, after Jean de La Fontaine
CONDUCTOR: Edouard Flament
STAGE DIRECTION: Constantin Landau
SETS AND COSTUMES: Juan Gris
SCENE PAINTING: Vladimir and Elizabeth Polunin
PREMIERE: 1 January 1924, Théâtre de Monte-Carlo, Monte Carlo
PRINCIPAL SINGERS: Maria Barrientos, Jeanne Montfort, Théodore Ritch, Daniel Vigneau
NOTE: This opera was first produced in 1860 in Baden-Baden.

LE MÉDECIN MALGRÉ LUI

MUSIC: Charles Gounod, with new recitatives by Erik Satie
LIBRETTO: Jules Barbier and Michel Carré, after Molière
CONDUCTOR: Edouard Flament
CHORUS MASTER: Amédée de Sabata
STAGE DIRECTION: Alexandre Benois
SETS AND COSTUMES: Alexandre Benois
CHOREOGRAPHY: Bronislava Nijinska
PREMIERE: 5 January 1924, Théâtre de Monte-Carlo, Monte Carlo
PRINCIPAL SINGERS: Jacques Arnna, Inès Ferraris, Jeanne Montfort, Théodore Ritch, Daniel Vigneau, Albert Garcia
PRINCIPAL DANCERS: Anton Dolin, Lubov Tchernicheva
NOTE: This opera was first produced in 1858 in Paris.

PHILÉMON ET BAUCIS

MUSIC: Charles Gounod
LIBRETTO: Jules Barbier and Michel Carré
CONDUCTOR: Edouard Flament
CHORUS MASTER: Amédée de Sabata
STAGE DIRECTION: Alexandre Benois
SETS AND COSTUMES: Alexandre Benois
SCENE PAINTING: Vladimir and Elizabeth Polunin
PREMIERE: 10 January 1924, Théâtre de Monte-Carlo, Monte Carlo
PRINCIPAL SINGERS: Maria Barrientos, Nazzareno De Angelis, Alesio De Paolis
NOTE: This opera was first produced in 1860 in Paris.

UNE EDUCATION MANQUÉE

MUSIC: Emmanuel Chabrier, with new recitatives by Darius Milhaud
LIBRETTO: E. Leterrier, A. Vanloo
CONDUCTOR: Edouard Flament
STAGE DIRECTION: Alexandre Benois
SETS AND COSTUMES: Juan Gris
PREMIERE: 17 January 1924, Théâtre de Monte-Carlo, Monte Carlo
PRINCIPAL SINGERS: Inès Ferraris, Théodore Ritch, Daniel Vigneau
NOTE: This opera was first produced in 1879 in Paris.

OEDIPUS REX

MUSIC: Igor Stravinsky
LIBRETTO: Jean Cocteau, after Sophocles, in a Latin translation by Jean Daniélou
CONDUCTOR: Igor Stravinsky
PREMIERE: 30 May 1927, Théâtre Sarah-Bernhardt, Paris
PRINCIPAL SINGERS: Stephan [Stefan] Belina-Skupevsky, Michel d'Arial, Georges Lanskoy, Hélène Sadoven, Kapitan Zaporojetz
NARRATOR: Pierre Brasseur

APPENDIX C

Ballets Produced by Serge Diaghilev

This chronology, drawn chiefly from contemporary programs and reviews, is an expanded version of the chronology by Nancy Van Norman Baer and the author in *The Art of Enchantment: Diaghilev's Ballets Russes 1909–1929.*

LE PAVILLON D'ARMIDE

MUSIC: Nicholas Tcherepnine
LIBRETTO: Alexandre Benois, after Théophile Gautier's *Omphale*
SETS AND COSTUMES: Alexandre Benois
SCENE PAINTING: Oreste Allegri, [?] Lockenberg
CHOREOGRAPHY: Michel Fokine
PREMIERE: 18 May 1909,* Théâtre du Châtelet, Paris
PRINCIPAL DANCERS: Vera Karalli, Mikhail Mordkin, Alexis Bulgakov, Tamara Karsavina, Alexandra Baldina, Alexandra Fedorova, Elena Smirnova, Vaslav Nijinsky
NOTE: This ballet was first produced in 1907 at the Maryinsky Theater, St. Petersburg.

PRINCE IGOR

Polovtsian Scenes and Dances (Act II of the opera)
MUSIC: Alexander Borodin, completed and partly orchestrated by Nikolai Rimsky-Korsakov and Alexander Glazunov
SETS AND COSTUMES: Nicholas Roerich
SCENE PAINTING: Boris Anisfeld
CHOREOGRAPHY: Michel Fokine
PREMIERE: 18 May 1909,* Théâtre du Châtelet, Paris
PRINCIPAL DANCERS: Adolph Bolm, Sophia Fedorova, Elena Smirnova

*When a *répétition générale* preceded the official premiere, the earlier date is given followed by an asterisk.

⟨399⟩

NOTE: In later seasons this work was performed without singers under the title of *The Polovtsian Dances*. In 1923 the opening dance was rechoreographed by Bronislava Nijinska.

LE FESTIN

MUSIC: Alexander Glazunov, Mikhail Glinka, Modest Mussorgsky, Nikolai Rimsky-Korsakov, Peter Ilitch Tchaikovsky

SETS: Konstantin Korovin

COSTUMES: Léon Bakst, Alexandre Benois, Ivan Bilibin, Konstantin Korovin

SCENE PAINTING: Piotr Lambine, Nikolai Charbé

CHOREOGRAPHY: Michel Fokine, Marius Petipa, Alexander Gorsky, Nicolai Goltz, Felix Kchessinsky,

PREMIERE: 18 May 1909,* Théâtre du Châtelet, Paris

PRINCIPAL DANCERS: Vera Fokina, Tamara Karsavina, Vaslav Nijinsky, Sophia Fedorova, Mikhail Mordkin, Georgi Rosai, Vera Karalli

NOTE: Fokine choreographed the "Hopak" (Mussorgsky), "Trepak" (Tchaikovsky), and "Finale" (Tchaikovsky). The other dances were "Firebird" (the Blue Bird pas de deux from *The Sleeping Beauty*) and "Grand Pas Classique Hongrois" (from *Raymonda*), both by Petipa, "Czardas" (Glazunov), by Gorsky, "Mazurka" (Glinka), by Goltz and Kchessinsky, and "Lezginka" (Glinka), by Fokine after Petipa. The Blue Bird pas de deux was revived in 1915 as *La Princesse Enchantée*, with scenery and costumes by Léon Bakst.

LES SYLPHIDES

MUSIC: Frédéric Chopin, orchestrated by Alexander Glazunov, Igor Stravinsky, Alexander Taneyev

SETS AND COSTUMES: Alexandre Benois

SCENE PAINTING: Stepan Yaremich

CHOREOGRAPHY: Michel Fokine

PREMIERE: 2 June 1909,* Théâtre du Châtelet, Paris

PRINCIPAL DANCERS: Anna Pavlova, Tamara Karsavina, Alexandra Baldina, Vaslav Nijinsky

NOTE: *Chopiniana*, the earliest version of this ballet, was produced in 1907 at the Maryinsky Theater, St. Petersburg. In 1919 scenery by A. Socrate replaced the Benois setting.

CLÉOPÂTRE

MUSIC: Anton Arensky, with additional music by Alexander Glazunov, Mikhail Glinka, Modest Mussorgsky, Nikolai Rimsky-Korsakov, Sergei Taneyev, Nicholas Tcherepnine

SETS AND COSTUMES: Léon Bakst

CHOREOGRAPHY: Michel Fokine

PREMIERE: 2 June 1909,* Théâtre du Châtelet, Paris

PRINCIPAL DANCERS: Ida Rubinstein, Anna Pavlova, Tamara Karsavina, Vaslav Nijinsky, Michel Fokine, Alexis Bulgakov

NOTE: *Cléopâtre* was based on Fokine's earlier *Une Nuit d'Egypte*, produced in 1908 at the Maryinsky Theater, St. Petersburg. In 1918 the ballet was restaged with sets by Robert Delaunay, additional costumes by Sonia Delaunay, and a new pas de deux by Léonide Massine.

CARNAVAL

MUSIC: Robert Schumann, orchestrated by Anton Arensky, Alexander Glazunov, Anatol Liadov, Nikolai Rimsky-Korsakov, Nicholas Tcherepnine

LIBRETTO: Léon Bakst, Michel Fokine

SETS AND COSTUMES: Léon Bakst

CHOREOGRAPHY: Michel Fokine

PREMIERE: 20 May 1910, Theater des Westens, Berlin

PRINCIPAL DANCERS: Lydia Lopokova, Vera Fokina, Vaslav Nijinsky, Adolph Bolm, Bronislava Nijinska

NOTE: This ballet was first produced on 20 February 1910 at the Pavlov Hall, St. Petersburg.

SCHÉHÉRAZADE

MUSIC: Nikolai Rimsky-Korsakov

LIBRETTO: Léon Bakst, Alexandre Benois, Michel Fokine, after the first tale of *The Thousand and One Nights*

SETS AND COSTUMES: Léon Bakst

CHOREOGRAPHY: Michel Fokine

PREMIERE: 4 June 1910, Théâtre National de l'Opéra, Paris

PRINCIPAL DANCERS: Ida Rubinstein, Vaslav Nijinsky, Alexis Bulgakov

GISELLE

MUSIC: Adolphe Adam

LIBRETTO: Vernoy de Saint-Georges and Théophile Gautier, after a theme by Heinrich Heine

SETS AND COSTUMES: Alexandre Benois

CHOREOGRAPHY: Jean Coralli, Jules Perrot, Marius Petipa, with revisions by Michel Fokine

PREMIERE: 17 June 1910,* Théâtre National de l'Opéra, Paris

PRINCIPAL DANCERS: Tamara Karsavina, Vaslav Nijinsky, Elena Poliakova, Alexis Bulgakov

NOTE: This ballet was first produced in 1841 at the Académie Royale de Musique, Paris.

FIREBIRD

MUSIC: Igor Stravinsky

LIBRETTO: Michel Fokine

SETS: Alexander Golovin

COSTUMES: Alexander Golovin, with additional costumes by Léon Bakst

CHOREOGRAPHY: Michel Fokine

PREMIERE: 25 June 1910, Théâtre National de l'Opéra, Paris

PRINCIPAL DANCERS: Tamara Karsavina, Michel Fokine, Alexis Bulgakov, Vera Fokina

NOTE: *Firebird* was restaged in 1926 with sets and costumes by Natalia Gontch-arova.

LES ORIENTALES

MUSIC: Anton Arensky, Alexander Borodin, Alexander Glazunov, Edvard Grieg (orchestrated by Igor Stravinsky), Christian Sinding (orchestrated by Igor Stravin-sky)

SETS: Konstantin Korovin

COSTUMES: Konstantin Korovin, Léon Bakst

CHOREOGRAPHY: Michel Fokine

PREMIERE: 25 June 1910, Théâtre National de l'Opéra, Paris

PRINCIPAL DANCERS: Yekaterina Geltzer, Alexander Volinine, Tamara Karsavina, Vaslav Nijinsky, Alexandra Vassilieva, Georgi Rosai, Vera Fokina, Alexander Orlov, Michel Fokine

NOTE: This divertissement included two previously choreographed dances, *Danse Siamoise* and *Kobold,* both presented on 20 February 1910 at the Maryinsky Theater, St. Petersburg.

LE SPECTRE DE LA ROSE

MUSIC: Carl Maria von Weber, orchestrated by Hector Berlioz

LIBRETTO: Jean-Louis Vaudoyer, after a poem by Théophile Gautier

SETS AND COSTUMES: Léon Bakst

CHOREOGRAPHY: Michel Fokine

PREMIERE: 19 April 1911, Théâtre de Monte-Carlo, Monte Carlo

PRINCIPAL DANCERS: Vaslav Nijinsky, Tamara Karsavina

NARCISSE

MUSIC: Nicholas Tcherepnine

LIBRETTO: Léon Bakst

SETS AND COSTUMES: Léon Bakst

CHOREOGRAPHY: Michel Fokine

PREMIERE: 26 April 1911, Théâtre de Monte-Carlo, Monte Carlo

PRINCIPAL DANCERS: Vaslav Nijinsky, Tamara Karsavina, Bronislava Nijinska, Vera Fokina

SADKO—AU ROYAUME SOUS-MARIN (Scene 6 from the opera SADKO)

MUSIC: Nikolai Rimsky-Korsakov

SETS: Boris Anisfeld

COSTUMES: Boris Anisfeld, Léon Bakst

CHOREOGRAPHY: Michel Fokine

PREMIERE: 6 June 1911, Théâtre du Châtelet, Paris

NOTE: This ballet was restaged in 1916 with choreography by Adolph Bolm and designs by Natalia Gontcharova.

PETROUCHKA

MUSIC: Igor Stravinsky
LIBRETTO: Igor Stravinsky, Alexandre Benois
SETS AND COSTUMES: Alexandre Benois
CHOREOGRAPHY: Michel Fokine
PREMIERE: 13 June 1911, Théâtre du Châtelet, Paris
PRINCIPAL DANCERS: Vaslav Nijinsky, Tamara Karsavina, Alexander Orlov, Enrico Cecchetti

SWAN LAKE

MUSIC: Peter Ilitch Tchaikovsky
LIBRETTO: Vladimir Begichev and Vasily Geltzer, adapted by Marius Petipa
SETS: Konstantin Korovin, Alexander Golovin
COSTUMES: Alexander Golovin
CHOREOGRAPHY: Marius Petipa, Lev Ivanov, with revisions by Michel Fokine
PREMIERE: 30 November 1911, Royal Opera House, London
PRINCIPAL DANCERS: Mathilde Kchessinska, Vaslav Nijinsky
NOTE: This production was a two-act condensation of the version first produced in 1895 at the Maryinsky Theater, St. Petersburg. The sets and costumes, purchased by Diaghilev, were created for the 1901 Bolshoi production. In 1923, at the Théâtre de Monte-Carlo, Diaghilev revived the ballet, again in two acts, with scenery by Korovin (Act I) and Golovin (Act II). The principal roles were danced by Vera Trefilova, Anatole Vilzak, Serge Grigoriev, and Jean Jazvinsky.

LE DIEU BLEU

MUSIC: Reynaldo Hahn
LIBRETTO: Jean Cocteau, Frédéric de Madrazo
SETS AND COSTUMES: Léon Bakst
CHOREOGRAPHY: Michel Fokine
PREMIERE: 13 May 1912, Théâtre du Châtelet, Paris
PRINCIPAL DANCERS: Vaslav Nijinsky, Tamara Karsavina, Lydia Nelidova, Bronislava Nijinska, Max Frohman, Michel Fedorov

THAMAR

MUSIC: Mily Balakirev
LIBRETTO: Léon Bakst, after a poem by Mikhail Lermontov
SETS AND COSTUMES: Léon Bakst
CHOREOGRAPHY: Michel Fokine
PREMIERE: 20 May 1912, Théâtre du Châtelet, Paris
PRINCIPAL DANCERS: Tamara Karsavina, Adolph Bolm

L'APRÈS-MIDI D'UN FAUNE

MUSIC: Claude Debussy
LIBRETTO: after the poem by Stéphane Mallarmé
SETS AND COSTUMES: Léon Bakst
CHOREOGRAPHY: Vaslav Nijinsky

PREMIERE: 29 May 1912, Théâtre du Châtelet, Paris
PRINCIPAL DANCERS: Vaslav Nijinsky, Lydia Nelidova
NOTE: In 1922 the ballet was revived with a backdrop by Pablo Picasso.

DAPHNIS AND CHLOË

MUSIC: Maurice Ravel
LIBRETTO: Michel Fokine, after Longus
SETS AND COSTUMES: Léon Bakst
CHOREOGRAPHY: Michel Fokine
PREMIERE: 8 June 1912, Théâtre du Châtelet, Paris
PRINCIPAL DANCERS: Tamara Karsavina, Vaslav Nijinsky, Adolph Bolm, Margarita Frohman, Enrico Cecchetti

JEUX

MUSIC: Claude Debussy
SETS AND COSTUMES: Léon Bakst
CHOREOGRAPHY: Vaslav Nijinsky
PREMIERE: 15 May 1913, Théâtre des Champs-Elysées, Paris
PRINCIPAL DANCERS: Tamara Karsavina, Ludmilla Schollar, Vaslav Nijinsky

LE SACRE DU PRINTEMPS

MUSIC: Igor Stravinsky
LIBRETTO: Igor Stravinsky, Nicholas Roerich
SETS AND COSTUMES: Nicholas Roerich
CHOREOGRAPHY: Vaslav Nijinsky
PREMIERE: 28 May 1913,* Théâtre des Champs-Elysées, Paris
PRINCIPAL DANCERS: Maria Piltz, M.V. Guliuk, [?] Vorontzov
NOTE: This ballet was restaged in 1920 with choreography by Léonide Massine.

LA TRAGÉDIE DE SALOMÉ

MUSIC: Florent Schmitt
SETS AND COSTUMES: Serge Soudeikine
CHOREOGRAPHY: Boris Romanov
PREMIERE: 12 June 1913, Théâtre des Champs-Elysées, Paris
Principal dancer: Tamara Karsavina

PAPILLONS

MUSIC: Robert Schumann, orchestrated by Nicholas Tcherepnine
LIBRETTO: Michel Fokine
SETS: Mstislav Dobujinsky
COSTUMES: Léon Bakst
CHOREOGRAPHY: Michel Fokine
PREMIERE: 16 April 1914, Théâtre de Monte-Carlo, Monte Carlo
PRINCIPAL DANCERS: Tamara Karsavina, Ludmilla Schollar, Michel Fokine

NOTE: *Papillons* was first produced in 1912 at the Maryinsky Theater, St. Petersburg.

LEGEND OF JOSEPH

MUSIC: Richard Strauss
LIBRETTO: Count Harry Kessler, Hugo von Hofmannsthal
SETS: José-María Sert
COSTUMES: Léon Bakst
CHOREOGRAPHY: Michel Fokine
PREMIERE: 14 May 1914, Théâtre National de l'Opéra, Paris
PRINCIPAL DANCERS: Maria Kuznetsova, Vera Fokina, Alexis Bulgakov, Léonide Massine, Serge Grigoriev, Lubov Tchernicheva, Sophie Pflanz, Doris Faithfull, Max Frohman

LE COQ D'OR

MUSIC: Nikolai Rimsky-Korsakov
LIBRETTO: Vladimir Belsky, after Alexander Pushkin, revised by Alexandre Benois
SETS AND COSTUMES: Natalia Gontcharova
STAGE DIRECTION: Michel Fokine
CHOREOGRAPHY: Michel Fokine
PREMIERE: 24 May 1914, Théâtre National de l'Opéra, Paris
PRINCIPAL SINGERS: Jean [Ivan] Altchevsky, Alexandre Belianin, Aurelia Dobrovolska, Elisabeth [Elisabeta] Petrenko, Hélène Nikolaeva, Basile [Vasily] Petrov
PRINCIPAL DANCERS: Tamara Karsavina, Adolph Bolm, Alexis Bulgakov

MIDAS

MUSIC: Maximilian Steinberg
LIBRETTO: Léon Bakst, after Ovid
SETS AND COSTUMES: Mstislav Dobujinsky
CHOREOGRAPHY: Michel Fokine
PREMIERE: 2 June 1914, Théâtre National de l'Opéra, Paris
PRINCIPAL DANCERS: Tamara Karsavina, Adolph Bolm, Max Frohman, Ludmilla Schollar, Sophie Pflanz, Lubov Tchernicheva

SOLEIL DE NUIT (MIDNIGHT SUN)

MUSIC: Nikolai Rimsky-Korsakov
SETS AND COSTUMES: Michel Larionov
CHOREOGRAPHY: Léonide Massine
PREMIERE: 20 December 1915, Grand Théâtre, Geneva
PRINCIPAL DANCERS: Léonide Massine, Nicholas Zverev

LAS MENINAS

MUSIC: Gabriel Fauré
SETS: Carlo Socrate
COSTUMES: José-María Sert
CHOREOGRAPHY: Léonide Massine

PREMIERE: 25 August 1916, Teatro Eugenia-Victoria, San Sebastián
PRINCIPAL DANCERS: Lydia Sokolova, Olga Kokhlova, Léonide Massine, Leon Woizikovsky

KIKIMORA

MUSIC: Anatoly Liadov
SETS AND COSTUMES: Mikhail Larionov
CHOREOGRAPHY: Léonide Massine
PREMIERE: 25 August 1916, Teatro Eugenia-Victoria, San Sebastián
PRINCIPAL DANCERS: Maria Chabelska, Stanislas Idzikowski
NOTE: In 1917 this became part of the ballet *Contes Russes*.

TILL EULENSPIEGEL

MUSIC: Richard Strauss
SETS AND COSTUMES: Robert Edmond Jones
CHOREOGRAPHY: Vaslav Nijinsky
PREMIERE: 23 October 1916, Manhattan Opera House, New York
Principal dancer: Vaslav Nijinsky

FEU D'ARTIFICE (FIREWORKS)

MUSIC: Igor Stravinsky
SETS AND LIGHTING: Giacomo Balla
PREMIERE: 12 April 1917, Teatro Costanzi, Rome

LES FEMMES DE BONNE HUMEUR (THE GOOD-HUMOURED LADIES)

MUSIC: Domenico Scarlatti, orchestrated by Vincenzo Tommasini
LIBRETTO: after Carlo Goldoni
SETS AND COSTUMES: Léon Bakst
CHOREOGRAPHY: Léonide Massine
PREMIERE: 12 April 1917, Teatro Costanzi, Rome
PRINCIPAL DANCERS: Lydia Lopokova, Lubov Tchernicheva, Josephine Cecchetti, Léonide Massine, Enrico Cecchetti, Stanislas Idzikowski, Leon Woizikovsky

CONTES RUSSES

MUSIC: Anatoly Liadov
SETS AND CURTAIN: Michel Larionov
COSTUMES: Michel Larionov, assisted by Natalia Gontcharova
CHOREOGRAPHY: Léonide Massine
PREMIERE: 11 May 1917, Théâtre du Châtelet, Paris
PRINCIPAL DANCERS: Lubov Tchernicheva, Lydia Sokolova, Leon Woizikovsky, Jean Jazvinsky, Stanislas Idzikowski
NOTE: *Contes Russes* consisted of four episodes: (1) Kikimora (first produced in 1916), (2) Bova Korolevitch and the Swan Princess, (3) Baba Yaga, (4) Epilogue and Russian Dances. In 1918 the "Danced Prelude" and "Lament of the Swan Princess" were added, and the music for these sections, also by Liadov, was orchestrated by Arnold Bax.

PARADE

MUSIC: Erik Satie
LIBRETTO: Jean Cocteau
SETS, COSTUMES, AND CURTAIN: Pablo Picasso
CHOREOGRAPHY: Léonide Massine
PREMIERE: 18 May 1917, Théâtre du Châtelet, Paris
PRINCIPAL DANCERS: Léonide Massine, Maria Chabelska, Lydia Lopokova, Nicholas Zverev

LA BOUTIQUE FANTASQUE

MUSIC: Gioacchino Rossini, orchestrated by Ottorino Respighi
SETS, COSTUMES, AND CURTAIN: André Derain
SCENE PAINTING: André Derain, Vladimir and Elizabeth Polunin
CHOREOGRAPHY: Léonide Massine
PREMIERE: 5 June 1919, Alhambra Theatre, London
PRINCIPAL DANCERS: Lydia Lopokova, Léonide Massine, Enrico Cecchetti, Serge Grigoriev, Josephine Cecchetti, Lydia Sokolova, Leon Woizikovsky, Nicholas Zverev, Vera Savina, Nicolas Kremnev

LE TRICORNE

MUSIC: Manuel de Falla
SETS, COSTUMES, AND CURTAIN: Pablo Picasso
SCENE PAINTING: Pablo Picasso, Vladimir and Elizabeth Polunin
CHOREOGRAPHY: Léonide Massine
PREMIERE: 22 July 1919, Alhambra Theatre, London
PRINCIPAL DANCERS: Tamara Karsavina, Léonide Massine, Leon Woizikovsky

LE CHANT DU ROSSIGNOL

MUSIC: Igor Stravinsky
SETS, COSTUMES, AND CURTAIN: Henri Matisse
CHOREOGRAPHY: Léonide Massine
PREMIERE: 2 February 1920, Théâtre National de l'Opéra, Paris
PRINCIPAL DANCERS: Tamara Karsavina, Lydia Sokolova, Serge Grigoriev, Stanislas Idzikowski
NOTE: This one-act ballet was adapted from Stravinsky's opera *Le Rossignol*, produced by Diaghilev in 1914. In 1925 the ballet was restaged with choreography by George Balanchine. The principal roles were danced by Alicia Markova, Lydia Sokolova, Serge Grigoriev, George Balanchine, and Nicolas Kremnev.

PULCINELLA

MUSIC: Igor Stravinsky, after Giambattista Pergolesi
SETS, COSTUMES, AND DROP CURTAIN: Pablo Picasso
SCENE PAINTING: Vladimir and Elizabeth Polunin
CHOREOGRAPHY: Léonide Massine
PREMIERE: 15 May 1920, Théâtre National de l'Opéra, Paris
PRINCIPAL DANCERS: Tamara Karsavina, Lubov Tchernicheva, Vera Nemchinova,

Léonide Massine, Stanislas Idzikowski, Enrico Cecchetti, Nicholas Zverev, Zygmund Novak

LE ASTUZIE FEMMINILI

MUSIC: Domenico Cimarosa, orchestrated and with recitatives by Ottorino Respighi

SETS, COSTUMES, AND CURTAIN: José-María Sert

SCENE PAINTING: Vladimir and Elizabeth Polunin

CHOREOGRAPHY: Léonide Massine

PREMIERE: 27 May 1920, Théâtre National de l'Opéra, Paris

PRINCIPAL DANCERS: Tamara Karsavina, Lubov Tchernicheva, Vera Nemchinova, Lydia Sokolova, Stanislas Idzikowski, Leon Woizikovsky, Zygmund Novak

PRINCIPAL SINGERS: Mafalda de Voltri, Romanitza, Zoia Rosovska, Angelo Masini Pieralli, Aurelio Anglada, Gino de Vecchi

CHOUT

MUSIC: Serge Prokofiev

SETS, COSTUMES, AND CURTAIN: Michel Larionov

CHOREOGRAPHY: Thadée Slavinsky, Michel Larionov

PREMIERE: 17 May 1921, Théâtre de la Gaîté-Lyrique, Paris

PRINCIPAL DANCERS: Catherine Devillier, Thadée Slavinsky, Jean Jazvinsky

CUADRO FLAMENCO

MUSIC: traditional

SETS AND COSTUMES: Pablo Picasso

CHOREOGRAPHY: traditional

PREMIERE: 17 May 1921, Théâtre de la Gaîté-Lyrique, Paris

PRINCIPAL DANCERS: María Dalbaicín, La Rubia de Jérez, La Gabrielita del Gorrotín, La López, El Tejero, El Moreno

THE SLEEPING PRINCESS

MUSIC: Peter Ilitch Tchaikovsky, partly reorchestrated by Igor Stravinsky

LIBRETTO: Ivan Vsevolozhsky and Marius Petipa, after Charles Perrault

SETS AND COSTUMES: Léon Bakst

CHOREOGRAPHY: Marius Petipa, with additional dances by Bronislava Nijinska

PREMIERE: 2 November 1921, Alhambra Theatre, London

PRINCIPAL DANCERS: Olga Spessivtzeva, Pierre Vladimirov, Lydia Lopokova, Carlotta Brianza, Felia Doubrovska, Lydia Sokolova, Bronislava Nijinska, Lubov Egorova, Vera Nemchinova, Lubov Tchernicheva, Ludmilla Schollar, Leon Woizikovsky, Nicholas Zverev, Nicholas Kremnev, Thadée Slavinsky, Anatole Vilzak, Stanislas Idzikowki

NOTE: This was a revival of Petipa's *Sleeping Beauty*, first performed in 1890 at the Maryinsky Theater, St. Petersburg.

LE MARIAGE DE LA BELLE AU BOIS DORMANT (AURORA'S WEDDING)

MUSIC: Peter Ilitch Tchaikovsky, partly reorchestrated by Igor Stravinsky

SETS: Alexandre Benois

COSTUMES: Alexandre Benois, with additional costumes by Natalia Gontcharova

CHOREOGRAPHY: Marius Petipa, arranged and with additional dances by Bronislava Nijinska

PREMIERE: 18 May 1922, Théâtre National de l'Opéra, Paris

PRINCIPAL DANCERS: Vera Trefilova, Pierre Vladimirov, Nina Oghinska, Stanislas Idzikowski

NOTE: Benois's sets and costumes were originally created for *Le Pavillon d'Armide* in 1909. Gontcharova designed the costumes for the fairy tales.

LE RENARD

MUSIC: Igor Stravinsky

SETS AND COSTUMES: Michel Larionov

CHOREOGRAPHY: Bronislava Nijinska

PREMIERE: 18 May 1922, Théâtre National de l'Opéra, Paris

PRINCIPAL DANCERS: Bronislava Nijinska, Stanislas Idzikowski, Jean Jazvinsky, Michel Fedorov

NOTE: In 1929 this ballet was restaged with choreography by Serge Lifar.

DANSES RUSSES

MUSIC: Frédéric Chopin, Peter Ilitch Tchaikovsky, Alexander Borodin

PREMIERE: 19 March 1923, Palais des Beaux-Arts, Monte Carlo

PRINCIPAL DANCERS: Vera Nemchinova, Anatole Vilzak, Nicholas Zverev, Bronislava Nijinska, Nicolas Kremnev

NOTE: This suite of dances, performed at a variety matinee, consisted of "La Valse" (Chopin), "Trepak" (Tchaikovsky), "Polovtsian Dance" (Borodin), and "La Bacchanale." The performance on 11 April 1923 also included "The Swan Princess" to music by Anatoly Liadov.

LES NOCES

MUSIC: Igor Stravinsky

SETS AND COSTUMES: Natalia Gontcharova

CHOREOGRAPHY: Bronislava Nijinska

PREMIERE: 13 June 1923, Théâtre de la Gaîté-Lyrique, Paris

PRINCIPAL DANCERS: Felia Doubrovska, Lubov Tchernicheva, Leon Woizikovsky, Nicholas Semenov

LES TENTATIONS DE LA BERGÈRE, OU L'AMOUR VAINQUEUR

MUSIC: Michel de Montéclair, arranged and orchestrated by Henri Casadesus

SETS, COSTUMES, AND CURTAIN: Juan Gris

SCENE PAINTING: Vladimir and Elizabeth Polunin

CHOREOGRAPHY: Bronislava Nijinska

PREMIERE: 3 January 1924, Théâtre de Monte-Carlo, Monte Carlo

PRINCIPAL DANCERS: Vera Nemchinova, Leon Woizikovsky, Thadée Slavinsky, Nicholas Zverev, Anton Dolin, Jean Jazvinsky, Anatole Vilzak

LES BICHES

MUSIC: Francis Poulenc
SETS, COSTUMES, AND CURTAIN: Marie Laurencin
SCENE PAINTING: Prince Alexander Schervashidze
CHOREOGRAPHY: Bronislava Nijinska
PREMIERE: 6 January 1924, Théâtre de Monte-Carlo, Monte Carlo
PRINCIPAL DANCERS: Leon Woizikovsky, Anatole Vilzak, Nicholas Zverev, Vera Nemchinova, Bronislava Nijinska, Lubov Tchernicheva, Lydia Sokolova
PRINCIPAL SINGERS: Romanitza, [?] Fouquet, [?] Cérésol

BALLET DE L'ASTUCE FÉMININE

MUSIC: Domenico Cimarosa
SETS AND COSTUMES: José-María Sert
SCENE PAINTING: Vladimir and Elizabeth Polunin
CHOREOGRAPHY: Léonide Massine
PREMIERE: 8 January 1924, Théâtre de Monte-Carlo, Monte Carlo
PRINCIPAL DANCERS: Lubov Tchernicheva, Felia Doubrovska, Anatole Vilzak, Lydia Sokolova, Leon Woizikovsky, Vera Nemchinova, Stanislas Idzikowski
NOTE: The title of this ballet was subsequently changed to *Cimarosiana*.

LES FÂCHEUX

MUSIC: Georges Auric
LIBRETTO: Boris Kochno, after Molière
SETS, COSTUMES, AND CURTAIN: Georges Braque
CHOREOGRAPHY: Bronislava Nijinska
PREMIERE: 19 January 1924, Théâtre de Monte-Carlo, Monte Carlo
PRINCIPAL DANCERS: Lubov Tchernicheva, Ludmilla Schollar, Alice Nikitina, Henriette Maikerska, Anatole Vilzak, Nicholas Zverev, Bronislava Nijinska, Leon Woizikovsky, Anton Dolin, Jean Jazvinsky
NOTE: In 1926 the ballet was staged with new choreography by Léonide Massine.

LA NUIT SUR LE MONT CHAUVE (NIGHT ON BALD MOUNTAIN)

MUSIC: Modest Mussorgsky
CHOREOGRAPHY: Bronislava Nijinska
PREMIERE: 6 April 1924, Théâtre de Monte-Carlo, Monte Carlo
PRINCIPAL DANCERS: Lydia Sokolova, Michel Fedorov
NOTE: This was the ballet act of the opera *Sorochintsy Fair*.

LE TRAIN BLEU

MUSIC: Darius Milhaud
LIBRETTO: Jean Cocteau
SETS: Henri Laurens
COSTUMES: Gabrielle Chanel

CURTAIN: Pablo Picasso
CHOREOGRAPHY: Bronislava Nijinska
PREMIERE: 20 June 1924, Théâtre des Champs-Elysées, Paris
PRINCIPAL DANCERS: Lydia Sokolova, Bronislava Nijinska, Anton Dolin, Leon Woizikovsky

LE FESTIN

MUSIC: Alexander Glazunov, Anton Arensky, Modest Mussorgsky, Erik Satie, Léo Delibes, Nicholas Tcherepnine
CHOREOGRAPHY: George Balanchine, Michel Fokine, and others
PREMIERE: 18 February 1925, Nouvelle Salle de Musique, Monte Carlo
PRINCIPAL DANCERS: Vera Nemchinova, Leon Woizikovsky, Alexandra Danilova, Tamara Geva, George Balanchine, Lubov Tchernicheva, Nicolas Kremnev, Lydia Sokolva, Alicia Markova
NOTE: This "suite of dances" consisted of Grand Pas Hongrois (Glazunov); Enigma (Balanchine, Arensky); Hopak (Balanchine, Mussorgsky); Dance of the Little American Girl (Satie), Variation (Balanchine, after Serafima Astafieva; Delibes); Armide's Buffoons (Fokine, Tcherepnine).

LES CONTES DE FÉES

MUSIC: Peter Ilitch Tchaikovsky
CHOREOGRAPHY: Marius Petipa, Bronislava Nijinska
COSTUMES: Natalia Gontcharova
PREMIERE: 25 February 1925, Nouvelle Salle de Musique, Monte Carlo
PRINCIPAL DANCERS: Alice Nikitina, Ninette de Valois, Nicholas Zverev, Alicia Markova, Constantin Tcherkas, Vera Savina, Anton Dolin, [?] Soumarokova, Dorothy Coxon, Nicolas Kremnev, Vera Nemchinova, Leon Woizikovsky, Thadée Slavinsky, Eugene Lapitzky
NOTE: This "suite of dances" consisted of the fairy tales from Act III of *The Sleeping Princess*.

L'ASSEMBLÉE

MUSIC: Charles Gounod, Anatoly Liadov, Alexander Scriabin, Georges Auric, Anton Rubinstein
CHOREOGRAPHY: George Balanchine and others
PREMIERE: 7 March 1925, Nouvelle Salle de Musique, Monte Carlo
PRINCIPAL DANCERS: Lubov Tchernicheva, Anton Dolin, Alexandra Danilova, Leon Woizikovsky, Tamara Geva, George Balanchine, Alicia Markova
NOTE: This "suite of dances" consisted of "Lovers' Dance" (Gounod), "Shepherds' Dance" (Gounod); "Le Moucheron" (Liadov); "Etude" (Balanchine, Scriabin); "Nocturne" (Auric); "Valse Caprice" (Balanchine, after Serafima Astafieva; Rubinstein); "Lezginka" (Rubinstein).

LE BAL DU 'LAC DES CYGNES'

MUSIC: Peter Ilitch Tchaikovsky
CHOREOGRAPHY: Marius Petipa
COSTUMES: Alexander Golovin

PREMIERE: 11 March 1925, Nouvelle Salle de Musique, Monte Carlo

PRINCIPAL DANCERS: Alice Nikitina, Alicia Markova, Nicholas Efimov, Constantin Tcherkas, Lubov Tchernicheva, Leon Woizikovsky, Vera Nemchinova, Anton Dolin, Lydia Sokolova, Nicolas Kremnev

NOTE: This "suite of dances" consisted of the divertissements from Act III of *Swan Lake* plus other dances from the ballet.

ZÉPHIRE ET FLORE

MUSIC: Vladimir Dukelsky [Vernon Duke]

LIBRETTO: Boris Kochno

SETS AND COSTUMES: Georges Braque

SCENE PAINTING: Prince Alexander Schervashidze

CHOREOGRAPHY: Léonide Massine

PREMIERE: 28 April 1925, Théâtre de Monte-Carlo, Monte Carlo

PRINCIPAL DANCERS: Alice Nikitina, Anton Dolin, Serge Lifar

NOTE: Masks and symbols by Oliver Messel were added in November 1925 in London. In 1926 the ballet was partly rechoreographed.

LES MATELOTS

MUSIC: Georges Auric

LIBRETTO: Boris Kochno

SETS, COSTUMES, AND CURTAIN: Pedro Pruna

SCENE PAINTING: Prince Alexander Schervashidze

CHOREOGRAPHY: Léonide Massine

PREMIERE: 17 June 1925, Théâtre de la Gaîté-Lyrique, Paris

PRINCIPAL DANCERS: Vera Nemchinova, Lydia Sokolova, Leon Woizikovsky, Serge Lifar, Thadée Slavinsky

BARABAU

MUSIC: Vittorio Rieti

LIBRETTO: Vittorio Rieti

SETS AND COSTUMES: Maurice Utrillo

SCENE PAINTING: Prince Alexander Schervashidze

CHOREOGRAPHY: George Balanchine

PREMIERE: 11 December 1925, Coliseum Theatre, London

PRINCIPAL DANCERS: Leon Woizikovsky, Serge Lifar, Alice Nikitina, Alexandra Danilova, Tamara Geva

ROMEO AND JULIET

MUSIC: Constant Lambert

DESIGN: Max Ernst, Joan Miró

SCENE PAINTING: Prince Alexander Schervashidze

CHOREOGRAPHY: Bronislava Nijinska, with entr'acte by George Balanchine

PREMIERE: 4 May 1926, Théâtre de Monte-Carlo, Monte Carlo

PRINCIPAL DANCERS: Tamara Karsavina, Serge Lifar, Lydia Sokolova, Leon Woizikovsky, Thadée Slavinsky, Constantin Tcherkas
NOTE: The original title of the ballet was in English.

LA PASTORALE
MUSIC: Georges Auric
LIBRETTO: Boris Kochno
SETS, COSTUMES, AND CURTAIN: Pedro Pruna
SCENE PAINTING: Prince Alexander Schervashidze
CHOREOGRAPHY: George Balanchine
PREMIERE: 29 May 1926, Théâtre Sarah-Bernhardt, Paris
PRINCIPAL DANCERS: Felia Doubrovska, Tamara Geva, Serge Lifar, Thadée Slavinsky

JACK-IN-THE-BOX
MUSIC: Erik Satie
SETS AND COSTUMES: André Derain
SCENE PAINTING: Prince Alexander Schervashidze
PREMIERE: 3 June 1926, Théâtre Sarah-Bernhardt, Paris
PRINCIPAL DANCERS: Stanislas Idzikowski, Alexandra Danilova
NOTE: The first performance of the ballet was dedicated to "the memory of Erik Satie."

THE TRIUMPH OF NEPTUNE
MUSIC: Lord Berners
LIBRETTO: Sacheverell Sitwell
SETS: after George and Robert Cruikshank, Tofts, Honigold, and Webb, collected by B. Pollock and H.J. Webb and adapted by Prince Alexander Schervashidze
COSTUMES: Pedro Pruna, after traditional designs
SCENE PAINTING: Prince Alexander Schervashidze
CHOREOGRAPHY: George Balanchine
PREMIERE: 3 December 1926, Lyceum Theatre, London
PRINCIPAL DANCERS: Alexandra Danilova, Serge Lifar, Michel Fedorov, Lydia Sokolova, Lubov Tchernicheva, Vera Petrova, Tatiana Chamié, George Balanchine, Constantin Tcherkas

LA CHATTE
MUSIC: Henri Sauguet
LIBRETTO: Sobeka [Boris Kochno], after one of Aesop's fables
SETS (ARCHITECTURE AND SCULPTURES) AND COSTUMES: Naum Gabo, Anton Pevsner
CHOREOGRAPHY: George Balanchine
PREMIERE: 30 April 1927, Théâtre de Monte-Carlo, Monte Carlo
PRINCIPAL DANCERS: Olga Spessivtzeva, Serge Lifar

MERCURE

MUSIC: Erik Satie
LIBRETTO: Léonide Massine
SETS AND COSTUMES: Pablo Picasso
SCENE PAINTING: Vladimir and Elizabeth Polunin
CHOREOGRAPHY: Léonide Massine
PREMIERE: 2 June 1927, Théâtre Sarah-Bernhardt, Paris
PRINCIPAL DANCERS: Léonide Massine, Vera Petrova, [?] Lissanevich
NOTE: This ballet was originally produced in 1924 by Comte Etienne de Beaumont's Soirées de Paris.

LE PAS D'ACIER

MUSIC: Serge Prokofiev
LIBRETTO: Serge Prokofiev, Georgi Yakulov
SETS (CONSTRUCTIONS) AND COSTUMES: Georgi Yakulov
CHOREOGRAPHY: Léonide Massine
PREMIERE: 7 June 1927, Théâtre Sarah-Bernhardt, Paris
PRINCIPAL DANCERS: Lubov Tchernicheva, Alexandra Danilova, Vera Petrova, Léonide Massine, Serge Lifar, Leon Woizikovsky

ODE

MUSIC: Nicolas Nabokov
LIBRETTO: Boris Kochno
SETS AND COSTUMES: Pavel Tchelitchev
PROJECTIONS: Pierre Charbonnier
CHOREOGRAPHY: Léonide Massine
PREMIERE: 6 June 1928, Théâtre Sarah-Bernhardt, Paris
PRINCIPAL DANCERS: Ira Belline [Beliankina], Felia Doubrovska, Alice Nikitina, Léonide Massine, Serge Lifar, Nicholas Efimov, Constantin Tcherkas

APOLLON MUSAGÈTE

MUSIC: Igor Stravinsky
SETS AND COSTUMES: André Bauchant
SCENE PAINTING: Prince Alexander Schervashidze
CHOREOGRAPHY: George Balanchine
PREMIERE: 12 June 1928, Théâtre Sarah-Bernhardt, Paris
PRINCIPAL DANCERS: Serge Lifar, Alice Nikitina, Lubov Tchernicheva, Felia Doubrovska, Dora Vadimova, Henriette Maikerska, Sophie Orlova
NOTE: In 1929 the ballet was given with new costumes by Gabrielle Chanel.

THE GODS GO A-BEGGING

MUSIC: George Frederic Handel, arranged by Thomas Beecham
LIBRETTO: Sobeka [Boris Kochno]
SETS: Léon Bakst (from *Daphnis and Chloë*)
COSTUMES: Juan Gris (from *Les Tentations de la Bergère*)

CHOREOGRAPHY: George Balanchine
PREMIERE: 16 July 1928, His Majesty's Theatre, London
PRINCIPAL DANCERS: Alexandra Danilova, Leon Woizikovsky, Lubov Tchernicheva, Felia Doubrovska, Constantin Tcherkas

LE BAL
MUSIC: Vittorio Rieti
LIBRETTO: Boris Kochno, after a story by Count Vladimir Sologub
SETS AND COSTUMES: Giorgio de Chirico
CHOREOGRAPHY: George Balanchine
PREMIERE: 7 May 1929, Théâtre de Monte-Carlo, Monte Carlo
PRINCIPAL DANCERS: Alexandra Danilova, Anton Dolin, André Bobrow, Felia Doubrovska, Leon Woizkovsky, George Balanchine, Eugenia Lipkowska, Serge Lifar

LE FILS PRODIGUE (PRODIGAL SON)
MUSIC: Serge Prokofiev
LIBRETTO: Boris Kochno, after the Biblical parable
SETS AND COSTUMES: Georges Rouault
SCENE PAINTING: Prince Alexander Schervashidze
PREMIERE: 21 May 1929, Théâtre Sarah-Bernhardt, Paris
PRINCIPAL DANCERS: Serge Lifar, Michel Fedorov, Felia Doubrovska, Eleanora Marra, Nathalie Branitska, Leon Woizkovsky, Anton Dolin

NOTES

Chapter 1. The Liberating Aesthetic of Michel Fokine

1. Sidney Harcave, *First Blood: The Russian Revolution of 1905* (New York: Macmillan, 1964), pp. 285–289.

2. Quoted in Serge Prokofiev, *Prokofiev by Prokofiev: A Composer's Memoir*, trans. Guy Daniels (Garden City, N.Y.: Doubleday, 1979), p. 131.

3. *Ibid.*, pp. 136–138. For another account of these events, see V.V. Yastrebtsev, *Reminiscences of Rimsky-Korsakov*, trans. and ed. Florence Jonas, foreword Gerald Abraham (New York: Columbia, 1985), pp. 354–361.

4. Yelena Lukom is quoted in Natalia Roslavleva, *Era of the Russian Ballet 1770–1965*, foreword Ninette de Valois (London: Gollancz, 1966), p. 169; Vladimir Telyakovsky, diary entry, 15 October 1905, quoted *ibid.*, p. 170; Bronislava Nijinska, *Early Memoirs*, trans. and ed. Irina Nijinska and Jean Rawlinson, introd. Anna Kisselgoff (New York: Holt, Rinehart and Winston, 1981), pp. 153–154.

5. Roslavleva, p. 169; Nijinska, *Early Memoirs*, p. 153; Tamara Karsavina, *Theatre Street: The Reminiscences of Tamara Karsavina*, foreword J.M. Barrie (London: Heinemann, 1930), p. 191.

6. Karsavina, *Theatre Street*, p. 194.

7. *Ibid.*, p. 201; Roslavleva, *Era*, p. 168; Yuri Slonimsky, "Fokine and His Time," introd. to Mikhail Fokine, *Against the Tide, Memoirs of a Ballet Master; Articles, Letters,* ed. Yuri Slonimsky (Leningrad/Moscow: Iskusstvo, 1962), p. 27; Keith Money, *Anna Pavlova: Her Life and Art* (New York: Knopf, 1982), p. 88; Nijinska, *Early Memoirs*, p. 155.

8. Adolph Bolm, autobiographical typescript, Part II, p. 9, Adolph Bolm Collection, George Arents Research Library, Syracuse University. See also pp. 1–8 of this typescript and p. 4 of Bolm's autobiographical notes in the same collection; Money, *Anna Pavlova*, pp. 67–69, 75–79; Nijinska, *Early Memoirs*, p. 239; "Ballet and Dancers in London," Diaghilev Scrapbooks, II, n.p., Theater Museum (London); "Courrier des Théâtres," *Figaro*, 20 May 1909, p. 6; Robert Brussel, "La Vie de Paris. Mathilde Kchessinska," *Figaro*, 22 May 1908, p. 1. Russian dancers had previously appeared, although infrequently, on European opera house stages. In 1902, for example, Raoul Gunsbourg, director of the Monte Carlo Opéra, asked conductor R.E. Drigo to compose the music for *La Côte d'Azur,* a ballet

to a subject specially written by the Prince of Monaco for touring Russian artists. The work, presented for the first time in Monte Carlo on 30 March 1902, was staged by Alexander Shiryaev. The dancers included Lyubov Roslavleva, Yekaterina Geltzer, Olga Preobrajenska, and Vera Trefilova. Roland John Wiley, "Memoirs of R.E. Drigo," Part II, *Dancing Times,* June 1982, p. 662. For Preobrajenska, this was a return engagement, as she had appeared in Monte Carlo in 1897 with Alfred Bekefi as her partner, and in 1900, with Bekefi and a group of Maryinsky dancers including George Kyasht, in *Halte de Cavalerie.* "Nouvelles Locales," *Gazette de Monaco,* 30 March 1897, p. 1; 13 April 1897, p. 1. For the information regarding the 1900 engagement, I am indebted to Francis Rosset, former archivist of the Société des Bains de Mer, Monte Carlo.

9. Nijinska, *Early Memoirs,* p. 313; Michel Fokine, *Memoirs of a Ballet Master,* trans. Vitale Fokine, ed. Anatole Chujoy (Boston: Little, Brown, 1961), p. 118.

10. Roslavleva, *Era,* pp. 166–167; Slonimsky, "Fokine and His Time," p. 26.

11. Roslavleva, *Era,* pp. 170–174.

12. Fokine, *Memoirs,* p. 115. It should be noted that the list of ballets appended to the Russian edition of his memoirs is considerably longer than its counterpart in the English-language edition. The pre-Diaghilev works that do *not* appear in the latter are: *Polka With a Small Ball* (20 April 1905; V. Herbert); *The Flight of the Butterflies* (12 February 1906; Chopin); *Polka-Pizzicato* (12 February 1906, J. Strauss); *Sevillana* (12 February 1906, Albéniz); *Spanish Dance* (8 April 1906, Bizet); *Pierrot's Jealousy* (8 April 1906); *Czardas* (19 July 1906, Brahms); *The Night of Terpsichore* (26 January 1908); "The Dance of the Seven Veils" (3 November 1908, Glazunov); *Pictures of the Ancient World* (26 February 1909). Other pre-Diaghilev works, mentioned by Nijinska in *Early Memoirs* and not listed in either the Russian or English version of Fokine's memoirs, include *Divertissement—The Valse Fantasia* (26 March 1906, Glinka), *Danses sur la Musique de Chopin* (16 February 1908, Chopin), and *Grand Pas sur la Musique de Chopin* (6 April 1908, Chopin). Nijinska often gives the names of principal dancers and also indicates those works that were given at charity performances organized by Fokine. For a list of his works choreographed from 1905–1917, see Appendix A.

13. Fokine, *Memoirs,* p. 119.

14. *Ibid.,* p. 125.

15. Tamara Karsavina, "Origins of the Russian Ballet," *Dancing Times,* September 1966, pp. 624, 636.

16. Fokine, *Memoirs,* pp. 49–50.

17. Quoted in Roslavleva, *Era,* p. 175.

18. Quoted in Cyril W. Beaumont, *Michel Fokine and His Ballets* (London, 1935; rpt. New York: Dance Horizons, 1981), pp. 23–24.

19. Fokine, *Memoirs,* p. 53.

20. *Ibid.,* p. 58.

21. *Ibid.,* p. 62.

22. *Ibid.,* p. 60.

23. André Levinson, "A Crisis in the Ballets Russes," *Theatre Arts Monthly,* November 1926, p. 786.

24. Quoted in Vera Krasovskaya, "Marius Petipa and 'The Sleeping Beauty,' " trans. Cynthia Read, *Dance Perspectives,* 49 (Spring 1972), p. 10.

25. Fokine, *Memoirs,* p. 104.

26. That the term enjoyed wide currency is indicated by the fact that when Serge Oukrainsky joined the Pavlova company just prior to World War I, his contract specified that he was to dance principally in works of the "genre nouveau," such as the Persian dance he had performed at his audition. Serge Oukrainsky, *My Two Years With the Dancing Genius of the Age: Anna Pavlova* (Hollywood: Suttonhouse, [1940]), p. 56.

27. Fokine, *Memoirs*, p. 102.

28. *Ibid.*, p. 103.

29. *Ibid.*, p. 104.

30. *Ibid.*, p. 119.

31. *Pictures of the Ancient World*, choreographed in February 1909 for the Literary-Artistic Society, seems to have drawn on *Quo Vadis?* as well. The titles of the four parts—Dance at the Feast, The Battle of the Gladiators, After the Example of the Gods, and In the Roman Circus—invoke major episodes of the novel.

32. Fokine, *Memoirs*, p. 155.

33. *Ibid.*, p. 150; Roslavleva, *Era*, pp. 127–128. *Acis and Galatea*, Fokine's first choreographic work, was also a restaging of a ballet originally mounted by Ivanov and dropped from the Maryinsky repertory. Nijinska, *Early Memoirs*, p. 140. For Roerich, see Prince Peter Lieven, *The Birth of Ballets-Russes*, trans. L. Zarine (London: Allen and Unwin, 1936), p. 82.

34. Alexandre Benois, *Memoirs*, I, trans. Moura Budberg (London: Chatto and Windus, 1960), p. 136.

35. *Ibid.*, p. 137.

36. Nikolai Volkov, *Meyerhold* (Moscow: Academia, 1929), I, p. 163.

37. Joan Ross Acocella, "The Reception of Diaghilev's Ballets Russes by Artists and Intellectuals in Paris and London, 1904–1914," Diss. Rutgers 1984, p. 138.

38. For a list of the operas produced by Diaghilev in Western Europe, see Appendix B.

39. Mikhail Vrubel was another painter/designer discovered by Mamontov and lionized by *Mir iskusstva*. Mental illness, however, precluded his participation in Diaghilev's theatrical enterprise.

40. For Mamontov's activities, see Stuart Ralph Grover, "Savva Mamontov and the Mamontov Circle: 1870–1905 Art Patronage and the Rise of Nationalism in Russian Art," Diss. Wisconsin 1971, chaps. 3 and 4; John E. Bowlt, *The Silver Age: Russian Art of the Early Twentieth Century and the "World of Art" Group* (Newtonville, Mass.: Oriental Research Partners, 1979), pp. 30–39. For Princess Tenisheva, see Bowlt, pp. 39–46, 180 (for Benois's curatorship of her collection), and 234 (for Bilibin's tenure at her school). For some idea of Russia's multiethnic character, see Chloe Obolensky, *The Russian Empire: A Portrait in Photographs*, introd. Max Hayward (New York: Random House, 1979) and *Photographs for the Tsar: The Pioneering Color Photography of Sergei Mikhailovich Prokudin-Gorskii Commissioned by Tsar Nicholas II*, ed. and introd. Robert H. Allshouse (New York: Dial, 1980).

41. For a detailed analysis of Bakst's European, Greek, and Oriental ballets, see Charles Steven Mayer, "The Theatrical Designs of Léon Bakst," Diss. Columbia 1977, chaps. 2–4. The biographical information comes from chapter 1.

42. Among Benois's published volumes, see *Reminiscences of the Russian Ballet*, trans. Mary Britnieva (London: Putnam, 1941); *Memoirs*, I, trans. Moura Budberg

(London: Chatto and Windus, 1960); *Memoirs*, II, trans. Moura Budberg (London: Chatto and Windus, 1964). For a sampling of his journalistic "recollections," see Roland John Wiley, ed. and trans., "Benois and Butter Week Fair," "Benois and Butter Week Fair Part II," "The Diaghilev Exhibition," Parts I, II, and III, *Dancing Times*, April-August 1984. For biographical material, see Chapter 10 of Bowlt's *Silver Age* and his section on Benois in *Russian Stage Design: Scenic Innovation, 1900–1930* (Jackson, Miss.: Mississippi Museum of Art, 1982). Bilibin, Roerich, and Dobujinsky were other Diaghilev associates who designed for the Antique Theater. Alexander Sanin, who staged most of Diaghilev's operas, was one of its directors, and Fokine was in charge of choreography. Among his contributions were the dances for *Le Jeu de Robin et Marion*, Adam de la Halle's thirteenth-century pastorale. Spencer Golub, *Evreinov: The Theatre of Paradox and Transformation* (Ann Arbor, Mich.: UMI Research Press, 1984), pp. 110–120.

43. Fokine, *Memoirs*, pp. 110–111.

44. Marc Slonim, *Russian Theater From the Empire to the Soviets* (Cleveland: World Publishing, 1961), p. 116.

45. Slonimsky, "Fokine and His Time," p. 23.

46. "Miniature" theaters, also known as theaters of "small forms," were a prominent feature of St. Petersburg life in the years before World War I. Inspired by the artistic cabarets of Munich, Berlin, and Paris, most had a strong satirical bent and featured a collection of "turns": poetry readings, "eccentric" acts, parodies, dramatic skits, gypsy romances, etc. Dance figured prominently. At Nikolai Evreinov's "Crooked Mirror," the most famous of these establishments, "audiences [laughed] until they cried" at parodies of *Giselle*, *Swan Lake*, and *Esmeralda*. Isadora Duncan and Maud Allan, impersonated by Nikolai Barabarov, the troupe's "prima ballerina," were other targets of Crooked Mirror satire. Golub, *Evreinov*, pp. 149–151.

47. Vladimir Nemirovitch-Dantchenko, *My Life in the Russian Theatre*, trans. John Cournos, introd. Joshua Logan, foreword Oliver M. Sayler (New York: Theatre Arts Books, 1936), p. 272; Bowlt, *Russian Stage Design*, p. 83; Benois, *Reminiscences*, pp. 348–349, 353. Benois dates the beginning of his association with the troupe from 1912. His role in the *Karamazov* affair lends credence to Bowlt's 1909 date.

48. Fokine, *Memoirs*, p. 91.

49. Unlike their French counterparts, British reviewers tended not to mention the names of opera directors. Hence, it is difficult to establish who staged the 1914 productions of *Ivan the Terrible* and *May Night*, which were presented only in London. Since Sanin had directed the 1909 version of *Ivan*, it seems reasonable to assume that he directed the 1914 one as well. It also seems likely, given his other work for Diaghilev at the time, that Sanin staged *May Night*.

50. Edward Braun, *The Theatre of Meyerhold: Revolution on the Modern Stage* (New York: Drama Book Specialists, 1979), p. 44.

51. Natalia Roslavleva, "Stanislavsky and the Ballet," introd. Robert Lewis, *Dance Perspectives*, 23 (1965), p. 23.

52. Michel Fokine, "The New Russian Ballet. Conventions in Dancing. M. Fokine's Principles and Aims," *Times*, 6 July 1914, p. 6. This letter/manifesto is reprinted in Beaumont, *Fokine*, Appendix A(b), pp. 144–147.

53. Valerian Svetlov, "The Diaghilev Ballet in Paris," *Dancing Times*, December 1929, p. 264.

54. Arnold Bennett, "Russian Imperial Ballet at the Opéra," *Paris Nights and Other Impressions of Places and People* (New York: George H. Doran, 1913), pp. 76–77.

55. André Levinson, *Ballet Old and New,* trans. and introd. Susan Cook Summer (New York: Dance Horizons, 1982), p. 41.

56. *Ibid.*, pp. 7–8.

57. Fokine, *Memoirs,* p. 191.

58. Levinson, *Ballet Old and New,* p. 21.

59. Osip Mandelstam, "The Egyptian Stamp" in *The Prose of Osip Mandelstam: The Noise of Time, Theodosia, The Egyptian Stamp,* trans. and introd. Clarence Brown (Princeton: Princeton Univ. Press, 1965), pp. 174–175.

60. Fokine, "The New Russian Ballet"; *Memoirs,* p. 154.

61. Valerian Svetlov, *Anna Pavlova,* trans. A. Grey (Paris, 1922; rpt. New York: Dover, 1974), p. 156.

62. Fokine, *Memoirs,* pp. 140–141.

63. Benois, *Reminiscences,* p. 246.

64. Acocella, "Reception," pp. 140–141.

65. *Ibid.*, pp. 149–151; for her discussion of Diaghilev's essays, see pp. 140–149.

66. Quoted in Braun, *Meyerhold,* p. 39. The sentence beginning "It is time" is quoted from "Against Naturalism in the Theater," an extensive excerpt from Briusov's essay published in *The Russian Symbolist Theater: An Anthology of Plays and Critical Texts,* ed. and trans. Michael Green (Ann Arbor: Ardis, 1986), p. 28.

67. Braun, *Meyerhold,* p. 37.

68. *Ibid.*, p. 51.

69. Quoted *ibid.*, p. 36.

70. Beaumont, *Fokine,* p. 26.

71. Roland John Wiley, "Benois' Commentaries on the First Saisons Russes," Part VII, *Dancing Times,* April 1981, p. 465. Benois's article was originally published in *Rech'* on 4 August 1911.

72. Both paintings are reproduced in Gabriella Di Mila, *Mir Iskusstva—Il Mondo Dell'Arte: Artisti Russi dal 1898 al 1924* (Naples: Società Editrice Napoletana, 1982), plates 2 and 6. Somov's "Harlequin and Death" is reproduced in Bowlt's *Silver Age,* p. 213. For Bowlt's discussion of the Harlequinade in Somov's work, see pp. 211–215.

73. Quoted Braun, *Meyerhold,* p. 72. It should be noted that one of the four works produced by Fokine for the Greblovsky National School benefit held at the Maryinsky on 8 April 1906 was entitled *Pierrot's Jealousy.* Unfortunately, nothing seems to be known about this piece, which anticipated the premiere of *The Fairground Booth* by eight months.

74. Quoted *ibid.*, p. 70.

75. Fokine, *Memoirs,* p. 136; Nijinska, *Early Memoirs,* p. 284.

76. Quoted in Braun, *Meyerhold,* p. 70.

77. Nijinska, *Early Memoirs,* p. 287.

78. For his reviews of *Death's Victory* (1907), *Tristan and Isolde* (1909), *Dom Juan* (1910), *Boris Godunov* (1911), *Orpheus and Eurydice* (1911), and *Hostages of Life* (1912), see Braun, *Meyerhold,* pp. 83, 98, 109, 111, 113–114, and Konstantin Rudnitsky, *Meyerhold the Director,* trans. George Petrov, ed. Syd-

ney Schultze, introd. Ellendea Proffer (Ann Arbor: Ardis, 1981), pp. 154–155, 158–159, 166, 177.

79. Fokine, *Memoirs*, p. 136.

80. Quoted in Rudnitsky, *Meyerhold*, p. 165. For other accounts of the production, see Beaumont, *Fokine*, pp. 81–83, and Braun, *Meyerhold*, pp. 115–119.

81. Cyril W. Beaumont, *Complete Book of Ballets: A Guide to the Principal Ballets of the Nineteenth and Twentieth Centuries* (London: Putnam, 1937), p. 715.

82. *Ibid.*, p. 725.

83. *Ibid.*, p. 686.

84. Jules Claretie, "La Vie à Paris," *Le Temps*, 21 May 1909, p. 2.

85. Mayer, "The Theatrical Designs of Léon Bakst," p. 182.

86. Quoted *ibid.*

87. Quoted in Beaumont, *Fokine*, p. 23.

88. Nijinska, *Early Memoirs*, p. 363. In 1915, at the Maryinsky, Fokine created his first role for Kchessinska—the Young Girl in *Eros*, a Taglioni-era reverie set to Tchaikovsky's "Serenade in C." The ballet appears to have been a success, although André Levinson suspected Fokine of insincerity: "*Batterie* and . . . complicated *pirouettes* are employed as if made to order for Kchessinska's virtuosic skill." *Eros* remained in repertory at least until 1918–1919, that is, throughout Balanchine's middle years at the Imperial Theatrical School. In 1935 he used the Tchaikovsky music for *Serenade*. Levinson, *Ballet Old and New*, p. 93. For excerpts from other reviews, see Mathilde Kchessinska, *Dancing in Petersburg*, trans. Arnold Haskell (New York, 1961; rpt. New York: DaCapo, 1977), pp. 155–156. For Fokine ballets in the postrevolutionary repertory, see Yuri Slonimsky, "Balanchine: The Early Years," trans. John Andrews, ed. Francis Mason, *Ballet Review*, 5, No. 3 (1975–1976), pp. 25–26.

89. Fokine, *Against the Tide*, p. 64.

90. Quoted in Dawn Lille Horwitz, "A Ballet Class With Michel Fokine," *Dance Chronicle*, 3, No. 1 (1979), p. 42.

91. Francis Steegmuller, *"Your Isadora": The Love Story of Isadora Duncan and Gordon Craig* (New York: Random House and The New York Public Library, 1974), p. 40.

92. Serge Diaghilev, Letter to W.A. Propert, 17 February 1926, in W.A. Propert, *The Russian Ballet 1921–1929*, preface Jacques-Emile Blanche (London: John Lane, 1931), p. 88. For an account of Duncan's first Petersburg concerts, see Steegmuller, *Your Isadora*, chap. 3 and notes.

93. Fokine, *Memoirs*, p. 256.

94. Frederika Blair, *Isadora: Portrait of the Artist As a Woman* (New York: McGraw-Hill, 1986), p. 117.

95. There is a discrepancy between the English and Russian editions in the dates given for the premieres of *Papillons*, *Islamé*, and *The Dream*. In all three instances I have followed the Russian—10 March 1912 instead of 10 March 1913 for *Papillons* and *Islamé*, 10 January 1915 instead of 10 March 1913 for *The Dream*.

96. Quoted in Beaumont, *Fokine*, p. 23.

97. Quoted in Arnold Haskell, *Balletomania Then and Now* (New York: Knopf, 1977), p. 85.

98. Valerian Svetlov, *Le Ballet Contemporain*, trans. M. D. Calvocoressi (Paris:

de Brunoff, 1912), p. 84. For Fokine in class, see Horwitz, "A Ballet Class With Michel Fokine," p. 43.

99. Lopukhov made this claim in *Sixty Years in the Ballet* (1966). I am grateful to Nina Alovert for this information.

100. Beaumont, *Fokine,* p. 102.

101. Levinson, *Ballet Old and New,* p. 90.

102. For Fokine's demands to the administration of the former Maryinsky Theater, see Roslavleva, *Era,* p. 196; for his career in the United States, see Dawn Lille Horwitz, "Michel Fokine in America, 1919–1942," Diss. New York University 1982.

103. Janet Elspeth Kennedy, "The 'Mir Iskusstva' Group and Russian Art 1898–1912," Diss. Columbia 1976, pp. 344–345.

104. Quoted *ibid.,* p. 343.

105. Isadora Duncan, *My Life* (Garden City, N.Y.: Garden City Publishing Company, 1927), pp. 151-152.

106. Levinson, *Ballet Old and New,* pp. 45–46.

107. Comtesse Anna de Noailles, "Adieux aux Ballets russes," *Revue Musicale,* 1 December 1930, pp. 4–5.

108. Levinson, *Ballet Old and New,* p. 33; Denis Bablet, *Esthétique Générale du Décor de Théâtre de 1870 à 1914* (Paris: Editions du C.N.R.S., 1965), p. 190.

109. Robert Brussel, "Théâtre du Châtelet. Grand saison de Paris: *Ballets russes,*" *Figaro,* 8 June 1911. For Blanche, see Truman Campbell Bullard, "The First Performance of Igor Stravinsky's *Sacre du Printemps,* Diss. Eastman School of Music, Rochester 1971, I, pp. 41–42.

110. Nijinska, *Early Memoirs,* pp. 285–286.

Chapter 2. The Vanguard Poetic of Vaslav Nijinsky

1. *The Diary of Vaslav Nijinsky,* ed. Romola Nijinsky (New York, 1936; rpt. Berkeley: Univ. of California Press, 1968).

2. Although there have been several full-length books about Nijinsky, the 1934 biography by his wife, Romola, edited by Lincoln Kirstein and Arnold Haskell, established the factual and interpretative scaffolding for most subsequent studies. The publication of Bronislava Nijinska's *Early Memoirs* in 1981 was the first major challenge to both this framework and its assumptions. The most important books are Romola Nijinsky, *Nijinsky,* foreword Paul Claudel (New York: Simon and Schuster, 1934); ———, *The Last Years of Nijinsky* (London: Gollancz, 1952); Richard Buckle, *Nijinsky* (New York: Simon and Schuster, 1971); Vera Krasovskaya, *Nijinsky,* trans. John E. Bowlt (New York: Schirmer Books, 1979); Lincoln Kirstein, *Nijinsky Dancing,* with essays by Jacques Rivière and Edwin Denby (New York: Knopf, 1975); Bronislava Nijinska, *Early Memoirs,* trans. and ed. Irina Nijinska and Jean Rawlinson, introd. Anna Kisselgoff (New York: Holt, Rinehart and Winston, 1981). Two recent dissertations that examine Nijinsky's work are Shelley Celia Berg, " 'Le Sacre du Printemps': A Comparative Study of Seven Versions of the Ballet," Diss. New York University 1985, and Millicent Kaye Hodson, "Nijinsky's New Dance: Rediscovery of Ritual Design in *Le Sacre du Printemps,*" Diss. California (Berkeley) 1985.

3. Nijinska, *Early Memoirs,* pp. 315–316, 328, 353.

4. Arnold Haskell, *Diaghileff: His Artistic and Private Life* (London: Gollancz, 1935), p. 246.

5. Charles Spencer, *Léon Bakst* (London: Academy Editions, 1973), p. 37. See also Charles Mayer, "The Theatrical Designs of Léon Bakst," Diss. Columbia 1977, I, pp. 42–44, 138–139.

6. For *Masques et Bergamasques*, see Edward Lockspeiser, *Debussy: His Life and Mind* (London, 1965; rpt. Cambidge: Cambridge Univ. Press, 1978), II, p. 9. Debussy's letter to Diaghilev is in the Jean Cocteau Collection, George Arents Research Library, Syracuse University.

7. See, for instance, John Boardman, *Athenian Black Figure Vases* (London: Thames and Hudson, 1974); Martin Robertson, *A Shorter History of Greek Art* (Cambridge: Cambridge Univ. Press, 1981); Ernst Buschor, *Grab eines attischen mädchens* (Munich: F. Bruckmann, 1939).

8. Meyerhold's letter to his wife is quoted in Konstantin Rudnitsky, *Meyerhold the Director*, trans. George Petrov, ed. Sydney Schultze, introd. Ellendea Proffer (Ann Arbor: Ardis, 1981), p. 81. Diaghilev's proposed arrangements for the 1929 season, which was to include Meyerhold's productions of *The Forest, Revisor*, and *The Magnificent Cuckold*, are from a letter to Serge Lifar quoted in Lifar's *Serge Diaghilev: His Life, His Work, His Legend* (New York, 1940; rpt. New York: Da Capo, 1976), p. 338.

9. Rudnitsky, *Meyerhold*, p. 77.

10. Nijinska, *Early Memoirs*, p. 306.

11. Irina Proujan, *Léon Bakst: Esquisses de décors et de costumes, arts graphiques, peintures*, trans. Denis Dabbadie (Leningrad: Editions d'Art Aurora, 1986), p. 219.

12. Quoted in Rudnitsky, *Meyerhold*, p. 58.

13. *Ibid.*, pp. 66–67.

14. "Sister Beatrice," *Meyerhold on Theatre*, trans. and ed. Edward Braun (New York: Hill and Wang, 1969), p. 70.

15. Meyerhold wrote several essays laying out the technical innovations and theoretical premises of his "stylized theater." See, for instance, "The Theatre-Studio," "First Attempts at a Stylized Theatre," and "The Stylized Theatre" in *ibid.*, pp. 39–63. Meyerhold's productions for the Theater-Studio and Komissarzhevskaya Theater are discussed in detail in Rudnitsky, *Meyerhold*, pp. 55–130, and in Edward Braun, *The Theatre of Meyerhold: Revolution on the Modern Stage* (New York: Drama Book Specialists, 1979), pp. 36–84.

16. Nijinska, *Early Memoirs*, p. 199. Nijinska also mentions that the two regularly attended the Saturday evening concerts at the Hall of Nobles.

17. Kirstein, *Nijinsky Dancing*, p. 125. Richard Buckle recounts the Louvre anecdote in *Nijinsky*, p. 163. *La Fille du Pharaon*, created by Petipa in 1862, was revived on numerous occasions in the next forty-five years. In keeping with the spirit of dramatic realism, Alexander Gorsky's version, mounted for the Bolshoi in the early 1900's, employed the profiled stance, although not to the extent that Fokine did in *Cléopâtre*. For photographs of the Moscow production, see Lincoln Kirstein, *Four Centuries of Ballet: Fifty Masterworks* (New York: Dover, 1984), p. 165.

18. "The Stylized Theatre," *Meyerhold on Theatre*, p. 63.

19. Romola Nijinsky, *Nijinsky*, p. 148.

20. Joan Acocella, "Photo Call With Nijinsky: The Circle and the Center," *Ballet Review*, 14, No. 4 (Winter 1987), p. 52.

21. Nijinsky, *Diary*, pp. 21–22.

22. Jacques-Emile Blanche, *Portraits of a Lifetime: The Late Victorian Era, The Edwardian Pageant, 1870–1914*, ed. and trans. Walter Clement, introd. Harley Granville-Barker (London: Dent, 1937), pp. 257–258.

23. Lockspeiser, *Debussy*, II, pp. 174–175.

24. Hector Cahusac, "La Vie de Paris. Debussy et Nijinsky," *Figaro*, 14 May 1913, p. 1.

25. Quoted in Nijinska, *Early Memoirs*, p. 468.

26. *Ibid.*, p. 445.

27. *Ibid.*, pp. 444–445; Buckle, *Nijinsky*, p. 276.

28. Nijinska, *Early Memoirs*, p. 450.

29. Quoted in Lockspeiser, *Debussy*, II, pp. 171–172.

30. Quoted *ibid.*, p. 172.

31. Nijinsky, *Diary*, pp. 140–141.

32. Romola Nijinsky, *Nijinsky*, p. 200.

33. *Ibid.*, p. 185.

34. For details of the first-night *scandale*, see Buckle, *Nijinsky*, pp. 299–301, and Truman Bullard, "The First Performance of Igor Stravinsky's *Sacre du Printemps*," Diss. Rochester (Eastman School of Music) 1971, I, pp. 143–160. Bullard also discusses disturbances at subsequent Paris performances. There are numerous discrepancies in the secondary literature about the number of times the ballet was given. According to newspaper accounts, *Sacre* was danced in Paris on May 28 (*répétition générale*), May 29 (premiere), June 2, 4, 6, and 13; in London, on July 11, 14, and 23.

35. Igor Stravinsky and Robert Craft, *Expositions and Developments* (Berkeley: Univ. of California Press, 1981), p. 140. Excerpts from the composer's letter to Findeizen are quoted in Vera Stravinsky and Robert Craft, *Stravinsky in Pictures and Documents* (London: Hutchinson, 1979), p. 77.

36. Quoted *ibid.*, p. 83. For Roerich, see John E. Bowlt, *Russian Stage Design: Scenic Innovation 1900–1930—From the Collection of Mr. and Mrs. Nikita D. Lobanov-Rostovsky* (Jackson, Miss.: Mississippi Museum of Art, 1982), pp. 250–255, and *The Silver Age: Russian Art of the Early Twentieth Century and the 'World of Art' Group* (Newtonville, Mass.: Oriental Research Partners, 1979), pp. 39–46.

37. Quoted in *Stravinsky in Pictures and Documents*, p. 82.

38. Quoted *ibid.*, p. 92.

39. Richard Taruskin, "From *Firebird* to *The Rite*: Folk Elements in Stravinsky's Scores," *Ballet Review*, 10, No. 2 (Summer 1982), p. 79. The following discussion is based on Professor Taruskin's fascinating article.

40. *Ibid.*, p. 81.

41. *Ibid.*, p. 74.

42. *Ibid.*, p. 80.

43. Millicent Hodson, "Nijinsky's Choreographic Method: Visual Sources from Roerich for *Le Sacre du Printemps*," *Dance Research Journal*, 18, No. 2 (Winter 1986–1987), p. 12.

44. *Ibid.*

45. Nijinska, *Early Memoirs*, p. 449. Because of pregnancy, Nijinska withdrew from the ballet, and the role of the Chosen Maiden was given to Maria Piltz.

46. Roerich referred to his settings in a letter to Diaghilev quoted in Lifar, *Serge Diaghilev*, p. 200.

47. Roger Fry, "M. Larionow and the Russian Ballet," *Burlington Magazine*, March 1919, p. 112.

48. Quoted in *Stravinsky in Pictures and Documents*, p. 94.

49. Lydia Sokolova, *Dancing for Diaghilev*, ed. Richard Buckle (London: John Murray, 1960), p. 43.

50. Kirstein, *Nijinsky Dancing*, p. 145.

51. Jacques Rivière, "Le Sacre du Printemps," *Nouvelle Revue Française*, November 1913, pp. 722, 724. The translation, by Miriam Lassman, comes from a lengthy excerpt of this article in Kirstein, *Nijinsky Dancing*, p. 166.

52. Sokolova, p. 43. For Kirstein, see *Nijinsky Dancing*, p. 143. Romola Nijinsky's description comes from *Nijinsky*, pp. 204–205.

53. Quoted in Kirstein, *Nijinsky Dancing*, p. 168.

54. Quoted in Nikolai Volkov, *Meyerhold* (Moscow: Academia, 1929), I, p. 165.

55. Quoted *ibid.*, I, p. 163. A few pages later, Volkov describes another of the "semi-theatrical and semi-political" sensations of the 1911 season: a speech about the Russian theater delivered by V.M. Purishkevitch to the Duma on February 25. "In that speech, the Tribune of the Black Hundreds, flaunting fantastic statistics about the Jewish overcrowding of the Russian stage and lumping together Lunacharsky, Sologub, Rishkov, Meyerhold, Biely, and Youshkevitch, spoke of the corrupting influence of the Russian theater, its spiritual nihilism and its being the source of antagonism between estates, classes, and societies." Meyerhold, it should be noted, was not Jewish.

56. Nijinska, *Early Memoirs*, p. 450.

57. H.T. Parker, "The Russians in Full Glory," *Boston Evening Transcript*, 7 November 1916, in *Motion Arrested: Dance Reviews of H.T. Parker*, ed. Olive Holmes (Middletown, Conn.: Wesleyan Univ. Press, 1982), pp. 123–124.

58. Only certain Aztec maize rituals specifically called for the sacrifice of a young girl. "The ancient Mexicans," Sir James George Frazer explains in *The Golden Bough*, "sacrificed human beings at all the various stages in the growth of the maize, the age of the victims corresponding to the age of the corn; for they sacrificed new-born babes at sowing, older children when the grain had sprouted, and so on till it was fully ripe, when they sacrificed old men. No doubt the correspondence between the ages of the victims and the state of the corn was supposed to enhance the efficacy of the sacrifice." *The Golden Bough: A Study in Magic and Religion*, 3rd ed. (London: Macmillan, 1913), VII, pp. 237–238. The fullest account of female sacrifice in pre-Columbian Mexico appears in the third edition of Frazer's massive work, specifically in volumes seven (*Spirits of the Corn and of the Wild*) and nine (*The Scapegoat*), both published in 1913. In the second edition, published in 1900, the very brief Mexican section concentrates equally upon the sacrifice of men and women. *The Golden Bough: A Study in Magic and Religion*, 2nd ed. (London: Macmillan, 1900), III, pp. 134–137. Frazer also mentions human sacrifices reported by nineteenth-century travelers, missionaries, and colonial administrators in various parts of the Third World. Only a few of these rituals specifically called for a female victim. Simon Karlinsky, in a study of preliterate

Russian theater, finds no precedent in Slavonic myth for maiden sacrifice, which leads him to speculate that the culminating ceremony of *Sacre* may derive from ancient Mexican mythology. The only evidence, however, that Roerich saw an organic link between ancient Slavic and Mexican rites appears in an essay, unrelated to *Sacre,* published ten years after the production of the ballet. The singling out of a female virgin appears to have its source, not in ancient Slavonic myth, but in Russian symbolist reinterpretations of that myth. At least two Stravinsky scholars have pointed to Sergei Gorodetsky's cycle of poems about Yarilo, written in 1905–1907, as a source of the idea and imagery of *Sacre.* Other possible sources mentioned by scholars are *Follow the Sun,* a 1907 book by Alexei Remizov about seasonal changes and the ancient games associated with them, and Velimir Khlebnikov's series of visionary poems about Stone Age Russia, published in 1911 and 1912, especially "I and Ye," in which a maiden is caught in a competition between two rival tribes and condemned to be sacrificed to pagan gods. For the Roerich reference, see Millicent Hodson, "Nijinsky's New Dance: Rediscovery of Ritual Design in *Le Sacre du Printemps,*" Diss. California (Berkeley), pp. 151–153; for the reinterpretation of Slavonic myth by Russian symbolists, see Simon Karlinsky, "Stravinsky and Russian Pre-Literate Theater," *Nineteenth-Century Music,* 6, No. 3 (Spring 1983), pp. 234–235.

59. Quoted in Katia Samaltanos, *Apollinaire: Catalyst for Primitivism, Picabia, and Duchamp* (Ann Arbor, Mich.: UMI Research Press, 1984), p.3.

60. Nijinska, *Early Memoirs,* p. 482.

61. Romola Nijinsky, *Nijinsky,* pp. 302–304, 404–405.

62. *Lyibov k tryom apelsinam, Zhurnal Doktora Dapertutto,* Nos. 4–5, quoted in *Meyerhold on Theatre,* p. 147.

63. For Meyerhold's biomechanics, see *ibid.,* pp. 197–204; Rudnitsky, *Meyerhold,* pp. 294–305; Braun, *The Theatre of Meyerhold,* pp. 164–168; Mel Gordon, "Meyerhold's Biomechanics," *Drama Review,* September 1974, pp. 73–88. I am grateful to Professor Gordon for identifying Solovyov as a member of the Imperial Ballet.

Chapter 3. The Making of Ballet Modernism

1. Melissa McQuillan, "Painters and the Ballet, 1917–1926: An Aspect of the Relationship Between Art and Theatre," Diss. New York University, 1979; Marianne W. Martin, "The Ballet *Parade:* A Dialogue Between Cubism and Futurism," *Art Quarterly,* 1, No. 2 (Spring 1978), pp. 85–111.

2. A photograph of *Feet (Le Basi,* 1915) appears in Michael Kirby, *Futurist Performance* (New York: Dutton, 1971), p. 57.

3. Francesco Cangiullo, *Le Serate Futuriste: Romanzo Storico Vissuto* (Milan: Ceschina, 1961), pp. 245–249.

4. Quoted in Vera Stravinsky and Robert Craft, *Stravinsky in Pictures and Documents* (London: Hutchinson, 1979), p. 152.

5. Quoted in McQuillan, II, p. 383.

6. Serge Diaghilev, Telegram and Letter to Igor Stravinsky, [late January] and 8 March 1915, in *Stravinsky: Selected Correspondence,* ed. Robert Craft (New York: Knopf, 1984), II, pp. 17, 19.

7. F.T. Marinetti, "The Futurist Dance," trans. Elizabeth Delza, *Dance Observer*, October 1935, pp. 75–76.

8. Filippo Tommaso Marinetti, "The Variety Theatre," trans. R.W. Flint, reproduced in Kirby, *Futurist Performance*, p. 179.

9. Filippo Tommaso Marinetti, Emilio Settimelli, and Bruno Corra, "The Futurist Synthetic Theatre," trans. R.W. Flint, reproduced *ibid.*, p. 197.

10. *Ibid.*, p. 32.

11. Quoted in McQuillan, II, p. 394. Two of Depero's costume designs are reproduced in Kirby, *Futurist Performance*, p. 119. Photographs of the decor appear in Raffaele Carrieri, *La Danza in Italia 1500–1900* (Milan: Domus, 1946), pp. 79–80.

12. The description of Balla's "choreography" comes from Kirby, *Futurist Performance*, p. 95; that of the "rumorist onomatopoeia" from Maurizio Fagiolo dell'Arco, "Balla's Prophecies," *Art International*, 12, No. 6 (Summer 1968), p. 67. Balla's sketches are reproduced in both.

13. *Ibid.* Mikhail Semenov was a former St. Petersburg music critic.

14. *Ibid.* A sketch for the stage set and Balla's handwritten lighting program in fifty *tempi* are reproduced here as well. The piece was reconstructed by Elio Marchegiani at the Exhibition of Light in Rome in 1967.

15. Enrico Prampolini, "Futurist Scenography," trans. Victoria Nes Kirby, reproduced in Kirby, *Futurist Performance*, p. 206.

16. Henri Quittard, "Les Concerts," *Figaro*, 9 May 1914, p. 5.

17. "The Variety Theatre," in Kirby, *Futurist Performance*, pp. 179–180.

18. Cangiullo described the episode: "In Rome in the summer of 1917, Diaghilev asked me for a futurist ballet, and I wrote him something very amusing and original: THE ZOO, which both he and Massine, his premier danseur, liked very much. Who would do the scenes, the costumes, the designs? I, who had seen a fantastic fauna stylized with elegant synthesis by Depero, gave [Diaghilev] his name. But Cocteau, who was influential and very friendly with Diaghilev, had already given him the names of some Parisian designers . . . who eliminated Depero. But the ballet (which Ravel was to compose) was never given, because Ravel went to the front and became ill." Quoted in Leonetta Bentivoglio, "Danza e futurismo in Italia: 1913–1933," *La Danza Italiana*, 1, No. 1 (Autumn 1984), pp. 68–69. Cangiullo seems to have gotten his dates mixed up. Ravel's war service began in September 1914 and ended with a temporary discharge no later than June 1917. The collaboration, moreover, was set in motion at least as early as January of that year, when Ravel wrote to Diaghilev, formally accepting the commission. Because Ravel's letter mentions Cangiullo only, it is possible, although unlikely, that Depero's services were enlisted later. Maurice Ravel, Letter to Serge Diaghilev, 12 January 1917, *Catalogue of Ballet Material and Manuscripts From the Serge Lifar Collection*, Sotheby's (London), 9 May 1984, Lot 203.

19. Martin, "The Ballet *Parade*," p. 85.

20. "Futurist Scenography," in Kirby, *Futurist Performance*, p. 204.

21. Mary Chamot, *Goncharova: Stage Designs and Paintings* (London: Oresko Books, 1979), pp. 9–15, 48.

22. Nathalie Gontcharova, "The Creation of 'Les Noces'," *Ballet and Opera*, 8, No. 3 (September 1949), 23.

23. *L'Illustré*, 24 September 1959, quoted in Chamot, *Goncharova*, p. 15.

24. Nathalie Gontcharova and Michel Larionov, "Serge de Diaghilev et l'év-

olution du décor et du costume de ballet," in Nathalie Gontcharova, Michel Larionov, and Pierre Vorms, *Les Ballets russes: Serge Diaghilew et la décoration théâtrale*, rev. ed. (Belvès Dordogne: Pierre Vorms, 1955), pp. 27–28.

25. Lecture by Professor Simon Karlinsky, "Stravinsky and Russian Pre-literate Theatre," International Stravinsky Symposium, University of California at San Diego, 11 September 1982.

26. Michel Larionov, "Diaghilev and His First Collaborators," *Ballet and Opera*, 8, No. 3 (September 1949), p. 15.

27. Léonide Massine, "On Choreography and A New School of Dancing," *Drama*, 1, No. 3 (December 1919), p. 69.

28. Cyril W. Beaumont, *Bookseller at the Ballet* (London: C.W. Beaumont, 1975), p. 268.

29. Léonide Massine, *My Life in Ballet*, ed. Phyllis Hartnoll and Robert Rubens (London: Macmillan, 1968), p. 70.

30. *Ibid.*, p. 73.

31. *Ibid.*, p. 75.

32. *Ibid.*, pp. 73, 101.

33. Fernand Divoire, *Pour la Danse* (Paris: Editions de la Danse, 1935), p. 266.

34. Valerian Svetlov, "The Diaghileff Ballet in Paris," *Dancing Times*, December 1929, p. 274.

35. Massine, *My Life*, pp. 95–96.

36. Massine, "On Choreography and A New School of Dancing," pp. 69–70.

37. André Levinson, *Serge Lifar: Destin d'un Danseur* (Paris: Grasset, 1934), pp. 26–27.

38. S.L. Grigoriev, *The Diaghilev Ballet 1909–1929*, trans. and ed. Vera Bowen (London: Constable, 1953), pp. 123, 132.

39. *Comoedia*, 15 May 1921, quoted in *Stravinsky in Pictures and Documents*, p. 143.

40. Contracts dated 1 and 2 October 1916 between Serge Diaghilev and Angeles Morillo López and José Rodríguez Martínez, respectively, Fonds Kochno, Pièce 32, Bibliothèque de l'Opéra (Paris); Gregorio Martínez Sierra, *The Cradle Song and Other Plays*, trans. and introd. John Garrrett Underhill (New York: Dutton, 1929), p. XI; Angel Sangardia, *Manuel de Falla* (Madrid: Unión musical española, 1946), pp. 28–29; Jaime Pahissa, *Manuel de Falla: His Life and Works*, trans. Jean Wagstaff (London: Museum Press, 1954), pp. 83–84.

41. Pahissa, *Manuel de Falla*, pp. 96–97; Massine, *My Life*, p. 115.

42. *Ibid.*

43. *Ibid.*, p. 41.

44. *Catalogue of Ballet Materials and Manuscripts from the Serge Lifar Collection*, Sotheby's (London), 9 May 1984, Lot 157. The score for *La Boutique Fantasque* was catalogued separately as Lot 207.

45. *Ibid.*, Lot 157.

46. Igor Stravinsky and Robert Craft, *Expositions and Developments* (Berkeley: Univ. of California Press, 1981), pp. 111–112.

47. Massine, *My Life*, p. 96.

48. Contract between Serge Diaghilev and Ottorino Respighi, 5 September 1919, Fonds Kochno, Pièce 78.

49. I am indebted to Dr. Stephen Roe, staff musicologist of Sotheby's London office, for enabling me to examine the *Boutique* manuscript and offering me his expert comments.

50. Francis Poulenc, Letter to Serge Diaghilev, 28 April 1919, *Catalogue of Ballet Material and Manuscripts from the Serge Lifar Collection,* Lot 186.

51. Quoted in *The Diaghilev Ballet in England,* catalogue for an exhibition organized by David Chadd and John Gage, Sainsbury Centre for Visual Arts, University of East Anglia, 11 October–20 November 1979, and the Fine Arts Society, London, 3 December 1979–11 January 1980, p. 24. In a letter to his friend Thomas Lowinsky, Ricketts added detail: "Diaghilev, the impresario of the Russian Ballet, came over here to try and plant his recent productions on Beecham; one of them to music of Scarlatti is excellent, but none of the stars are there and one of the ballets is staged by Picasso. We quarrelled over German music, which he wants to persecute and suppress; he means to scrap *Carnaval, Papillons,* and the *Spectre of the Rose.* I would hear of nothing of the kind, said that Schumann and Wagner had been the friends of all my life, that modern Germany could go under water for twenty-four hours without my turning a hair, that to ignore it but not the German classics was a better revenge, that . . . I hated nationalism in Art, and that the tables might be turned against Russia. This actually happened. Beecham's excuse not to have a Russian season was that he wished to encourage national British art, so the boomerang returned to roost within a few hours of my lecture." "To Thomas Lowinsky," October 1917, *Charles Ricketts: Self-Portrait,* ed. T. Sturge Moore and Cecil Lewis (London: Peter Davies, 1939), p. 283.

52. Quoted from *La Vie de Rossini,* "Cahier de travail de Serge de Diaghilev avec indications de répertoire, 1915–1916," Fonds Kochno, Pièce 124, n.p. As all the monetary references are in pounds and francs, it seems highly unlikely that the date indicated on the document is correct.

53. Quoted from *Journal d'Eugène Delacroix, ibid.,* n.p.

54. Quoted from *Journal d'Eugène Delacroix, ibid.,* n.p.

55. Lydia Sokolova, *Dancing for Diaghilev,* ed. Richard Buckle (London: John Murray, 1960), pp. 68–69.

56. Natalia Gontcharova, Letters to Serge Diaghilev, 20 September 1918 and undated, Fonds Kochno, Pièce 37.

57. The company also traveled with a hairdresser, prop man, wardrobe master, and chief machinist, all Russians, and the mother of Lubov Tchernicheva. "Liste des Artistes des Ballets Russes," 14 June 1918, Fonds Kochno, Pièce 130.

58. Richard Ellmann, *James Joyce* (New York: Oxford, 1959), pp. 523–524.

Chapter 4. *The Twenties*

1. Quoted in Francis Steegmuller, *Cocteau: A Biography* (Boston: Little, Brown, 1970), p. 87.

2. Kenneth E. Silver, "Jean Cocteau and the *Image d'Epinal:* An Essay on Realism and Naiveté," in *Jean Cocteau and the French Scene,* ed. Alexandra Anderson and Carol Saltus (New York: Abbeville Press, 1984), p. 86.

3. Marianne W. Martin, "The Ballet *Parade:* A Dialogue Between Cubism and Futurism," *Art Quarterly,* 1, No. 2 (Spring 1978), p. 87; Steegmuller, *Cocteau,* p. 94; Filippo Tommaso Marinetti, "The Variety Theatre," trans. R. W. Flint, in

Michael Kirby, *Futurist Performance* (New York: Dutton, 1971), pp. 179–186; Jean Cocteau, *Le Coq et l'Arlequin: Notes autour de la musique 1918*, pref. Georges Auric (Paris: Stock, 1979).

4. Quoted in Martin, "The Ballet *Parade*," pp. 88–89. For Cocteau's relationship with Apollinaire and subsequent mythologizing of that relationship, see Steegmuller, *Cocteau*, chap. 4.

5. Cocteau makes this claim in the preface of *Les Mariés de la Tour Eiffel*. See Jean Cocteau, *The Infernal Machine and Other Plays* (New York: New Directions, 1963), p. 155. The translation is by Dudley Fitts.

6. Steegmuller, *Cocteau*, pp. 170, 245–247, 327–328; Jean Hugo, *Avant d'oublier 1918–1931* (Paris: Fayard, 1976), pp. 57–59, 64–65.

7. *Ibid.*, pp. 65–66; Jean Cocteau, *Carte Blanche* (Paris: Mermod, [1952]), p. 94; Steegmuller, *Cocteau*, p. 201. The Chaplin piece originally appeared in *Paris-Midi* on 28 April 1919.

8. *Carte Blanche*, p. 149. This originally appeared in *Paris-Midi* on 4 August 1919. The translation, by Steegmuller, appears in *Cocteau*, p. 166.

9. Léonide Massine, *My Life in Ballet*, ed. Phyllis Hartnoll and Robert Rubens (London: Macmillan, 1968), p. 104.

10. Jean Cocteau, *Parade*, in *Théâtre de poche* (Monaco: Editions du Rocher, 1955), p. 12, and *Le Boeuf sur le toit ou The Nothing Doing Bar*, in the same collection, p. 16.

11. *Ibid.*, p. 17. This translation, by Margaret Crossland, is from Frank W.D. Ries, "Jean Cocteau and the Ballet," Diss. Indiana 1980, Appendix C1, p. 314.

12. Quoted in Erik Aschengreen, *Jean Cocteau and the Dance*, trans. Patricia McAndrew and Per Avsum (Copenhagen: Gyldendal, 1986), p. 106.

13. Cocteau's interest in slow continuous movement may also reflect the influence of Emile Jaques-Dalcroze, whose technique he began to study with Paul Thévenaz as early as 1911. A painter as well as a dancer, Thévenaz assisted Cocteau in sketching the choreography for *David*. Dalcroze's idea of polyrhythm, especially that formed by counterpoint between the gestures of the individual and those of the crowd, also seems to have influenced Cocteau's conception of stage movement. For Thévenaz, see Aschengreen, *Jean Cocteau*, p. 64, and Steegmuller, *Cocteau*, pp. 94, 103, 114. For Dalcroze's ideas on "collective gesture," see "Rhythm and Gesture in Music Drama and Criticism," in Emile Jaques-Dalcroze, *Rhythm, Music and Education*, trans. Harold F. Rubinstein, rev. ed. (London: The Dalcroze Society, 1980), pp. 124–130. This essay, dated 1910–1916, was probably published in a French journal prior to appearing in book form after the war.

14. Aschengreen, *Jean Cocteau*, p. 79.

15. Steegmuller, *Cocteau*, p. 210. Noble Sissle is quoted in Chris Goddard, *Jazz Away From Home* (London: Paddington Press, 1979), p. 15.

16. *Le Coq et l'Harlequin*, pp. 53–54n. This translation comes from Steegmuller, *Cocteau*, p. 207.

17. *Le Rappel à l'ordre*, p. 141. The article was originally published on 4 August 1919.

18. Cocteau, *Le Coq et l'Harlequin*, p. 63. For the reference to jazz, savagery, and virility, see *Carte Blanche*, p. 151.

19. Silver, "Jean Cocteau and the *Image d'Epinal*," p. 93.

20. *Ibid.*, p. 96.

21. *Ibid.*, p. 99.

22. Madame Cocteau's letter (to Valentine Gross Hugo) is quoted in Steeg-muller, *Cocteau*, p. 240n. For the *Pulcinella* party, see Hugo, *Avant d'oublier*, p. 67; for Diaghilev's appearance at the 1921 "Spectacle Bouffe," see Richard Buckle, *Diaghilev* (London: Weidenfeld and Nicolson, 1979), p. 382. Cocteau's letter to Maré is quoted in Aschengreen, *Jean Cocteau*, p. 232 (note 57). The items per-formed in the symphonic interludes were routinely published in the daily theatrical columns of the *Times*.

23. Jean Cocteau, Letter to Serge Diaghilev, 24 October 1922, Fonds Kochno, Pièce 23, Bibliothèque de l'Opéra (Paris).

24. For some reason, Auric's name does not appear on the program for *Phi-lémon et Baucis*. His participation in the project is confirmed by a 1923 letter to Diaghilev in which the composer discusses his solutions to various musical prob-lems entailed in the commission. Georges Auric, Letter to Serge Diaghilev, [1923], *Ballet Material and Manuscripts From the Serge Lifar Collection*, Sotheby's (Lon-don), 9 May 1984, Lot 142. The Soirées de Paris made its debut at the Théâtre de la Cigale on 17 May 1924 and gave its farewell performance on 30 June. The repertory included *Salade* (Milhaud/Braque), *Mercure* (Satie/Picasso), *Les Roses* (Henri Sauguet/ Laurencin), and *Gigue* (Bach/Handel/Derain), all choreographed by Massine, and Cocteau's theater piece *Roméo et Juliette*. Cocteau's *Antigone* opened at the Théâtre de l'Atelier on 20 December 1922. The music was by Arthur Honegger, the decor by Picasso, and the costumes by Chanel.

25. Erik Aschengreen, who interviewed Auric and Boris Kochno (credited on the program as the librettist of *Les Fâcheux*) in the late 1970s or early 1980s, denies Cocteau's contribution to this ballet as well as to *Les Biches*. Nevertheless, Cocteau's letter of October 1922, partly quoted in the text, strongly suggests that the idea of *Biches*, like the choice of collaborators, originated with him. Not only does he recommend that Diaghilev "give [his] commissions to Poulenc or Lauren-cin," but his query, "Are you pleased with Biches?," indicates that a primitive libretto almost certainly existed. This supports Frank W.D. Ries's contention that Cocteau's sketches (in the Francis Poulenc collection in Paris) "bear a striking re-semblance to the final form" of the ballet. Aschengreen's own study of the *Biches* libretto leads him to the opposite conclusion: "there is no indication that Jean Cocteau should have written the text for *Les Biches*." Neither Ries nor Aschen-green cites the October 1922 letter. Aschengreen, *Jean Cocteau*, pp. 117–118, 232 (note 6); Ries, "Jean Cocteau," pp. 149–150.

26. The libretto of *Le Train Bleu* is reproduced in full (in French) in Aschen-green, *Jean Cocteau*, Appendix V. Scenes I and II appear on p. 270.

27. *Ibid.*, p. 271.

28. *Ibid.*, p. 272.

29. H[oward] H[annay], " 'Zephyr and Flora,' " *Observer*, 15 November 1925, p. 11; "Russian Ballet at the Coliseum. 'Les Facheux,' " *Times*, 4 June 1925, p. 10; "The Russian Ballet. 'The Song of the Nightingale,' " *Times*, 19 July 1927, p. 12; "The Cat Wife in Her Transparent Frock. Dancing in the Highly Stylised Kitchen Décor: M. Serge Lifar and Mlle. Nikitina in the New Ballet," *Sketch*, 22 June 1927, p. 600.

30. Lydia Lopokova, the season's female star, described one of the ballet's three tableaux. "A new choreograph, the Count himself! The ballet called 'Vogue,' our tableau about 3 minutes, with a young man, a young girl, who is like a boy, and I, the woman of the smart set. We lie on the beach in Lido, the man and the

boy are 'getting on,' so that I must produce a vexed face and stand in the middle, showing a costume made up of miroirs (dernier cri, naturally). I do all I am asked except that I cannot look jealous, not in my nature [in] such circumstances. Massin [sic] does not interfere; it is not worthwhile either. A good reclame for Vogue, but perhaps I sound too sarcastic." Lydia Lopokova, Letter to John Maynard Keynes, 5 May 1924, John Maynard Keynes Papers, King's College (Cambridge). The tableau described by Lopokova was "Le Bain de Minuit," performed, according to the program, "with a poem by Paul Morand." The program note describes the scene as follows: "At the end of a ball, a pair of dancers goes to bathe in a stream. The cavalier falls asleep. Another arrives unexpectedly and dances with the girl. The sleeper awakens, gets angry, and ends by joining their dance." The Adolescent, one of the two male roles, was played by a woman. Lopokova withdrew from the piece after the first rehearsals. "I've arrived at the conclusion," she wrote to Beaumont, "that 'jazz' is not truly my style." Lydia Lopokova, Letter to Comte Etienne de Beaumont, 11 May 1924, Keynes Papers.

31. Rolf de Maré, *Les Ballets Suédois dans l'art contemporain* (Paris: Editions du Trianon, 1931), p. 63. *Skating-Rink* premiered on 20 January 1922.

32. Robert Orledge, "Cole Porter's Ballet *Within the Quota*," *Yale University Library Gazette*, 50, No. 1 (July 1975), pp. 19–29. The ballet premiered on 25 October 1923.

33. Quoted in Maré, *Ballets Suédois*, pp. 75–76. *Relâche* premiered on 4 December 1924.

34. *Ibid*, p. 77.

35. *Ibid.*, pp. 77–79.

36. Henrietta Malkiel, "Paris Modernists Rebel Against Outmoded Ballets," *Musical America*, 25 July 1925, p. 3. For Jean Wiener, see Goddard, *Jazz Away From Home*, pp. 116–119.

37. For Nijinska's ballets for Theatre Choréographique, see Nancy Baer, *Bronislava Nijinska: A Dancer's Legacy* (San Francisco: The Fine Arts Museums of San Francisco, 1986), p. 75. Among other things, the critic of *La Prensa*, a Buenos Aires newspaper, wrote: "*At the Seaside*, which has the subtitle 'Sport-Dance,' is a modern work. The occasionally vulgar score by Darius Milhaud plays well, possesses rhythmical richness, and realistically evokes the scenic action, which depicts a series of sports figures and the games—tennis, swimming, acrobatics— played by bathers at a beach. With its recollections of Parisian songs and dances, this music for the open air is fresh and lively, providing a congenial frame for the action. Bronislava Nijinska, Ludmilla Schollar, Leticia de la Vega, Dora del Grande, Blanca Zirmaya, and the corps de ballet brought this sportive vision to life." "Teatro y música. Colón. Segundo espectáculo coreográfico," *La Prensa*, 22 September 1926, p. 14. For *Impressions de Music-Hall*, see Stéphane Wolff, *L'Opéra au Palais Garnier (1875–1962)*, introd. Alain Gueulette (Paris: Slatkine, 1983), p. 288; Ivor Guest, *Le Ballet de l'Opéra de Paris*, trans. Paul Alexandre (Paris: Théâtre National de l'Opéra/Flammarion, n.d.), pp. 166–167. *Touring, Jazz*, and *Holy Etudes* premiered on 3 August 1925 at the Winter Gardens Theatre, Margate (England); *At the Seaside*, on 21 September 1926; *Impressions de Music-Hall*, 6 April 1927.

38. Boris de Schloezer, "Les Ballets Russes. Erik Satie," *Nouvelle Revue Française*, 1 August 1925, p. 248; Emile Vuillermoz, "Russian Ballet, 20 Years After," *Christian Science Monitor*, 25 June 1927, p. 10.

39. Jean Brun-Berty, "22 Juin.-Théâtre des Champs-Elysées. Ballets russes (le Train bleu)," *La Danse*, August-September 1924, n.p.

40. André Levinson, *La Danse d'aujourd'hui: Etudes, Notes, Portraits* (Paris: Duchartre et Van Buggenhoudt, 1929), p. 337.

41. Massine, *My Life*, p. 157; "Sitter Out," *Dancing Times*, March 1923, pp. 600–601; Lydia Sokolova, *Dancing for Diaghilev*, ed. Richard Buckle (London: John Murray, 1960), p. 198; T.S. Eliot, "Dramatis Personae, *The Criterion*, 1, No. 3, p. 305. A program for the show, which opened at the Royal Opera House, Covent Garden in February 1923, and a clipping from *Curtain* are in the Keynes Papers.

42. Massine, *My Life*, p. 165. The *Dancing Times* quotation appeared in "Sitter Out," *Dancing Times*, June 1925, p. 953. The revue opened at the London Pavilion on 30 April 1925.

43. Quoted in "Sitter Out," *Dancing Times*, August 1925, p. 1139. The photograph of *Crescendo* appeared in the *Dancing Times*, June 1925, p. 961.

44. Kenneth E. Silver, "*Esprit de Corps:* The Great War and French Art 1914–1925," Diss. Yale 1981.

45. Quoted in R.B.D., "Historical Review of Music in the Paris Opera Season," *Musical America*, 26 February 1916, p. 38.

46. *Ibid.*

47. Melissa A. McQuillan, "Painters and the Ballet, 1917–1926: An Aspect of the Relationship Between Art and Theatre," Diss. New York Univ. 1979, I, pp. 149–151.

48. Contract between Serge Diaghilev and Jacques Rouché, 8 October 1921, AJ13/1292, Archives Nationales (Paris).

49. Jacques Rouché, Letter to Serge Diaghilev, 26 April 1922, Fonds Kochno, Pièce 86, Bibliothèque de l'Opéra (Paris).

50. Levinson, *La Danse d'aujourd'hui*, pp. 27–28.

51. H[oward] H[annay], "Les Fâcheux," *Observer*, 26 May 1927, p. 15; " 'Zephyr and Flora,' and 'Betty in Mayfair,' " *Sketch*, 18 November 1925, p. 321; H[oward] H[annay], " 'Zephyr and Flora,' " *Observer*, 15 November 1925, p. 11.

52. Sokolova, *Dancing for Diaghilev*, p. 218.

53. *Théâtre Serge de Diaghilew: Les Fâcheux* (Paris: Editions des Quatre Chemins, 1924), p. [6].

54. Maré, *Ballets Suédois*, pp. 70–71; Levinson, *La Danse d'aujourd'hui*, p. 412; *Au Temps du "Boeuf sur le Toit,"* introd. Georges Bernier (Paris: Artcurial, 1981), pp. 76–77.

55. André Levinson, "13 Janvier. 'Cydalise et le Chèvre-pied,' " *La Danse au Théâtre: Esthétique et actualité mêlées* (Paris: Bloud et Gay, 1924), pp. 215, 210, 212–214.

56. For a full list of Opéra productions, including revivals, see Wolff, *L'Opéra au Palais Garnier*.

57. Levinson, *La Danse d'aujourd'hui*, pp. 28, 36. For photographs of *Les Fâcheux*, see Cocteau's volume on the ballet.

58. Jacques Rivière, "La Crise du concept de littérature," *Nouvelle Revue Française*, 1 February 1924, p. 161.

59. Alan Storey, "A Ballet-goer's Causerie (2)," *Ballet Today*, July-August 1949, p. 8.

60. Joan Ross Acocella and Lynn Garafola, introd., Bronislava Nijinska, "On

Movement and the School of Movement," *Ballet Review,* 13, No. 4 (Winter 1986), p. 76. For other material on Nijinska's Russian years, see Baer, *Bronislava Nijinska,* pp. 18–21, and Lynn Garafola, "Bronislava Nijinska: A Legacy Recovered," *Women and Performance,* 3, No. 2 (1987–1988), pp. 78–88.

61. Nijinska, "On Movement and the School of Movement," p. 79. From 1911 until 1922, almost without interruption, Enrico Cecchetti served as the Ballets Russes's principal teacher. In this capacity he conducted daily class and coached the troupe's leading dancers.

62. Bronislava Nijinska, "Reflections About the Production of *Les Biches* and *Hamlet* in Markova-Dolin Ballets," trans. Lydia Lopokova, *Dancing Times,* February 1937, p. 617.

63. Arnold Haskell, "Aurora Truly Wedded: The Choreography of the Sleeping Princess," in Gordon Anthony, *The Sleeping Princess: Camera Studies* (London: Routledge, 1940), p. 38. In "editing" the ballet for production, Diaghilev added chunks of music from *The Nutcracker*—the "Danse Arabe," which became the Sheherazade tale; the "Danse Chinoise," which became "The Porcelain Princesses"; the Dance of the Sugar Plum Fairy, which replaced the Lilac Fairy's variation in the Prologue. He eliminated the coda of the wedding pas de deux, using the music instead for "The Three Ivans," and incorporated two pieces of music omitted from the accepted score—Aurora's solo in the Vision Scene and the interlude between the Panorama scene and Aurora's awakening that he placed between "The Spell" and the Hunting Scene. Among the third-act divertissements that he dropped were Cinderella and Prince Fortuné and Tom Thumb, His Brothers, and the Ogre. Diaghilev also pushed the time of the ballet forward from the reigns of Henri IV/Louis XIV to those of Louis XIV/Louis XV. For the various changes see Buckle, *Diaghilev,* pp. 388–389; Roland John Wiley, *Tchaikovsky's Ballets: Swan Lake, Sleeping Beauty, Nutcracker* (Oxford: Oxford Univ. Press, 1985), pp. 165–188; Cyril W. Beaumont, *Bookseller at the Ballet, Memoirs 1891 to 1929, Incorporating the Diaghilev Ballet in London* (London: C.W. Beaumont, 1975), pp. 273–274; Vera Krasovskaya, "Marius Petipa and 'The Sleeping Beauty,' " trans. Cynthia Read, *Dance Perspectives,* 49 (Spring 1972).

64. Cyril W. Beaumont, *The Sleeping Princess,* Part II (London: C.W. Beaumont, [1921]), p. 15.

65. Bronislava Nijinska, "Creation of 'Les Noces,' " trans. Jean M. Serafetinides and Irina Nijinska, *Dance Magazine,* December 1974, p. 59. Gontcharova's account of the ballet's creation differs substantially from Nijinska's. In fact, Gontcharova takes full credit for the final design of the ballet. Since none of her work before or after *Les Noces* bore the slightest resemblance to this ballet, and given Nijinska's close association with Exter, I have followed the choreographer's version of events. For Gontcharova's account, see Nathalie Gontcharova, "The Creation of 'Les Noces,' " *Ballet,* April 1948, pp. 23–26, and Natalia Goncharova, "The Metamorphoses of the Ballet 'Les Noces,' " *Leonardo,* 12, No. 2 (Spring 1979), pp. 137–143.

66. *Ibid.,* p. 59. Diaghilev's willingness to go ahead with the ballet may well have been a response to the success of Alexander Tairov's Kamerny Theater, which visited Paris in March 1923. Although "panned" in the mainstream press, his *Giroflé-Girofla, Phèdre, Princess Brambilla,* and *Salomé* were much admired by the avant-garde. According to Irina Nijinska, the choreographer's daughter, Nijinska attended the premiere with Diaghilev, who was miffed by the enthusiasm ex-

pressed by Cocteau and other artists for Tairov's modernism—far more radical than Diaghilev's own. What better way for Diaghilev to reassert his "modernity" than by staging *Les Noces*? For mainstream reviews of the Kamerny Theater, see André Messager, "Théâtre des Champs-Elysées: *Giroflé-Girofla*, par la troupe Kamerny, de Moscou," *Figaro*, 8 March 1923, p. 3; Maxime Girard, "Théâtre des Champs-Elysées: *Phèdre* (représentations du théâtre Kamerny, de Moscou)," *Figaro*, 12 March 1923, p. 4; "La Danse à travers le monde," *La Danse*, April 1923, n.p. Alexandra Exter was the designer of *Salomé* (1917), Alexander Vesnin of *Phèdre*(1922), Georgi Yakulov of *Princess Brambilla* (1920) and *Giroflé-Girofla* (1922). Yakulov designed *Le Pas d'Acier* for the Ballets Russes in 1927. For the scenic innovation of these productions, see John E. Bowlt, "Constructivism and Russian Stage Design," *Performing Arts Journal*, 1, No. 3 (Winter 1977), pp. 62–84.

67. Nijinska, "Creation of 'Les Noces,'" p. 61; Goncharova, "The Metamorphoses of the Ballet 'Les Noces,'" p. 142. For the Blue Blouse troupes, see Frantisek Deák, "Blue Blouse," *Drama Review*, 17, No. 1 (March 1973), pp. 35–46; for *The Magnanimous Cuckold*, see Nick Worrall, "Meyerhold's Production of *The Magnificent Cuckold*," *Drama Review*, 17, No. 1 (March 1973), pp. 14–34.

68. André Levinson, "Où sont les 'Ballets russes,'" [*Comoedia*], 18 June 1923, in *Les Noces* clipping book, Bibliothèque de l'Opéra.

69. For a photograph of the pyramid ending one Blue Blouse oratorium, see Deák, "Blue Blouse," p. 35; for a description of Meyerhold's "Building the Pyramid" and a photograph of the complex form used in *Roar China*, see Mel Gordon, "Meyerhold's Biomechanics," *Drama Review*, 18, No. 3 (September 1974), pp. 83–84. The choreographic notebook and diagrams referred to here were exhibited in "Bronislava Nijinska: A Dancer's Legacy" at the Cooper-Hewitt Museum (18 March–6 July 1986) and at the California Palace of the Legion of Honor (13 September 1986–4 January 1987).

70. Nijinska, "Creation of 'Les Noces,'" p. 59.

71. Nijinska, "Reflections," pp. 617–618.

72. Edwin Denby, "Revival of Diaghilev's Noces," in "The Criticism of Edwin Denby," *Dance Index*, January 1946, p. 42.

73. Nijinska, "Creation of 'Les Noces,'" p. 59.

74. "Francis Poulenc on His Ballets," *Ballet*, September 1946, p. 58.

75. Diaghilev used the phrase in a letter to Boris Kochno written late in 1923. Quoted in Boris Kochno, *Diaghilev and the Ballets Russes*, trans. Adrienne Foulke (New York: Harper and Row, 1970), p. 206. The premiere of *Les Biches* took place in Monte Carlo on 6 January 1924.

76. Cocteau, *Le Coq et l'Arlequin*, p. 51. His Barbette essay, written in 1926, is reprinted in *Le Numéro Barbette* (Paris: Jacques Damase, 1980), pp. 5–41.

77. Jean Cocteau, Letter to Serge Diaghilev, 29 February 1924, Fonds Kochno. This translation appears in Kochno, *Diaghilev and the Ballets Russes*, p. 216.

78. For various accounts of what happened, see *ibid.*, p. 219; Ries, "Jean Cocteau," pp. 164–166; Aschengreen, *Jean Cocteau*, pp. 129–131.

79. See *ibid.*, pp. 130–131, and Ries, "Jean Cocteau," p. 166.

80. "The Russian Ballet. 'La Pastorale,'" *Times*, 29 June 1926, p. 14. The Levinson quote appears in *La Danse d'aujourd'hui*, p. 54.

81. *Ibid.*, p. 59.

82. Unident. review, Diaghilev Scrapbook, Theatre Museum (London), V, p. 9; Valerian Svetlov, "The Diaghileff Ballet in Paris," Part II, *Dancing Times,* January 1930, p. 463; Levinson, *La Danse d'aujourd'hui,* pp. 62, 56.

83. Nijinska, "Reflections," p. 617; "The Russian Ballet. 'La Pastorale,' *Times,* 29 June 1926, p. 14; Svetlov, "The Diaghileff Ballet in Paris," Part II, p. 460; Levinson, *La Danse d'aujourd'hui,* p. 67. Diaghilev never produced Carpenter's ballet. As *Skyscrapers,* it received its premiere at the Metropolitan Opera House on 19 February 1926. For a discussion of the ballet, see Verna Arvey, *Choreographic Music: Music for the Dance* (New York: Dutton, 1941), pp. 289–293.

84. "The Russian Ballet. 'The Gods Go A-Begging,' " *Times,* 17 July 1928, p. 14. The choreography of the ballet was by Balanchine, the book by Kochno, and the music by Handel reorchestrated by Sir Thomas Beecham.

85. S.L. Grigoriev, *The Diaghilev Ballet 1909–1929,* trans. and ed. Vera Bowen (London: Constable, 1953), p. 210; H[oward] H[annay], "Coliseum. 'Barabau,' " *The Observer,* 13 December 1925, p. 11; Levinson, *La Danse d'aujourd'hui,* p. 66; Valerian Svetlov, "The Diaghileff Ballet in Paris," Part III, *Dancing Times,* February 1930, p. 569; *The Queen,* 15 December 1926, quoted in Nesta Macdonald, *Diaghilev Observed by Critics in England and the United States 1911-1929* (New York: Dance Horizons, 1975), p. 343.

86. Beaumont, *Bookseller at the Ballet,* pp. 351–352.

87. *Ibid.*, p. 369.

88. The photograph of Lifar's entrance is reproduced in Bernard Taper, *Balanchine: A Biography* (New York: Times Books, 1984), p. 88, and in W.A. Propert, *The Russian Ballet 1921–1929,* preface Jacques-Emile Blanche (London: Bodley Head, 1931), plate 27. Plate 26, in the same volume, gives another, rare view of the ensemble.

89. Taper, *Balanchine,* p. 99.

90. Henry Prunières, "Ballets russes," *Revue Musicale,* 1 July 1928, p. 287.

91. Boris de Schloezer, "A Classic Art," trans. Ezra Pound, *Dial,* July 1929, p. 608. The idiosyncratic spelling is Pound's.

92. Taper, *Balanchine,* p. 99; Levinson, *La Danse d'aujourd'hui,* p. 88; *Les Ballets Russes de Serge de Diaghilev, 1909–1929,* catalogue of the exhibition organized at the Old Customs House, Strasbourg (France), 15 May–15 September 1969, p. 237; W.A. Propert, *The Russian Ballet,* plates XXXI-XXXIII; "The Russian Ballet. M. Diaghilev's Season," *Times,* 26 June 1928, p. 14.

93. Beaumont, *Bookseller at the Ballet,* p. 380.

94. *The Journals of André Gide,* trans. Justin O'Brien (New York: Knopf, 1948), II, pp. 321–322.

Chapter 5. Russian Origins

1. See above, chapter 1.

2. See, for example, Thomas C. Owen, *Capitalism and Politics in Russia: A Social History of the Moscow Merchants, 1855–1905* (Cambridge Univ. Press, 1981); Valentine T. Bill, *The Forgotten Class: The Russian Bourgeoisie From the Earliest Beginnings to 1900* (New York: Praeger, 1959); William L. Blackwell, *The Industrialization of Russia: An Historical Perspective* (New York: Thomas Y.

Crowell, 1970; ———— *The Beginnings of Russian Industrialization, 1800–1860* (Princeton: Princeton Univ. Press, 1968); Beverly Whitney Kean, *All the Empty Palaces: The Merchant Patrons of Modern Art in Pre-Revolutionary Russia* (New York: Universe Books, 1983); Jo Ann Ruckman, "The Business Elite of Moscow: A Social Inquiry," Diss. Northern Illinois 1975. In addition to these studies, the following discussion draws on Stuart Ralph Grover, "Savva Mamontov and the Mamontov Circle: 1870–1905, Art Patronage and the Rise of Nationalism in Russian Art," Diss. Wisconsin 1971; John E. Bowlt, *The Silver Age: Russian Art of the Early Twentieth Century and the "World of Art" Group* (Newtonville, Mass.: Oriental Research Partners, 1979); and Bowlt's "Nikolai Ryabushinsky: Playboy of the Eastern World," *Apollo*, December 1973, pp. 486–493.

3. Quoted in Owen, *Capitalism and Politics*, p. 147.

4. There are various accounts of how the two met. According to Arnold Haskell, this occurred in Moscow, during one of Diaghilev's "frequent visits" to the city. According to Serge Lifar, Mamontov's famous remark on meeting Diaghilev ("Where did this mushroom spring from?") was uttered in 1896, although Lifar does not say where. According to Stuart Grover, who bases his account on Konstantin Korovin's memoir, *Shaliapin. Vstrechi i sovmestnaia zhizn'*, the meeting of the two took place in a restaurant, where, in Korovin's presence, Diaghilev asked Mamontov to help underwrite *Mir iskusstva*, a detail that suggests they met in 1898. I have followed Beverly Whitney Kean's account. Arnold Haskell, *Diaghileff: His Artistic and Private Life*, in collaboration with Walter Nouvel (London: Gollancz, 1935); p. 53; Serge Lifar, *Serge Diaghilev: His Life, His Work, His Legend* (New York, 1940; rpt. New York: Da Capo, 1976), p. 4; Grover, "Savva Mamontov," p. 283; Kean, *Empty Palaces*, p. 38.

5. Haskell, *Diaghileff*, p. 55.

6. See, for instance, Haskell, *Diaghileff*, chap. 2; Lifar, *Serge Diaghilev*, pp. 27–35; Prince Peter Lieven, *The Birth of Ballets-Russes*, trans. L. Zarine (London: Allen and Unwin, 1936), chap. 2; Alexandre Benois, *Reminiscences of the Russian Ballet*, trans. Mary Britnieva (London: Putnam, 1941), chaps. 3–5.

7. Haskell, *Diaghileff*, p. 51. This was not the only event that dampened Diaghilev's musical ambitions. Sometime before, Rimsky-Korsakov had dismissed his compositions as "absurd." V.V. Yastrebtsev, Rimsky's devoted secretary, describes the incident in his diary entry for September 22, 1894. "After this, Nikolai Andreyevich gave an account of a curious visit he had had from some young man named Diaghilev, who fancies himself a great composer but, nevertheless, would like to study theory with Nikolai Andreyevich. His compositions proved to be absurd, and Nikolai Andreyevich told him so bluntly, whereupon he became offended and, on leaving, declared arrogantly that nevertheless he believes in himself and his gifts; that he will never forget this day and that some day Rimsky-Korsakov's opinion will occupy a shameful place in his (Rimsky-Korsakov's) biography and make him regret his rash words, but then it will be too late . . ." V.V. Yastrebtsev, *Reminiscences of Rimsky-Korsakov*, ed. and trans. Florence Jonas, foreword Gerald Abraham (New York: Columbia Univ. Press, 1985), p. 90.

8. Owen, *Capitalism and Politics*, p. 151.

9. Stanislavsky's account of the first-night mishap is summarized in Grover, "Savva Mamontov," pp. 97–98. The quotation is from Constantin Stanislavsky, *My Life in Art*, trans. J.J. Robbins (Boston: Little, Brown, 1924), p. 141.

10. Grover, "Savva Mamontov," pp. 162–163.

11. For an extended discussion of the company's two phases, see *ibid.*, pp. 158–217 and 293–342. For the impression created by the Mamontov troupe on the Diaghilev circle, see Benois, *Reminiscences*, p. 197. The company paid its first visit to St. Petersburg in 1898.

12. David Magarshack, *Stanislavsky: A Life*, foreword Irving Wardle (London: Faber and Faber, 1986), p. 140.

13. Kean, *Empty Palaces*, pp. 105–106.

14. Magarshack, *Stanislavsky*, p. 232; Bill, *Forgotten Class*, p. 29.

15. Serov is quoted in Grover, "Savva Mamontov," pp. 90 and 209; Vasnetsov in Janet Elspeth Kennedy, "The 'Mir Iskusstva' Group and Russian Art 1898–1912," Diss. Columbia 1976, p. 136. The Vrubel reminiscence, told to a Soviet scholar by Alexandra Mamontov, is in Grover, "Savva Mamontov," p. 257.

16. Quoted in Magarshack, *Stanislavsky*, p. 97.

17. Quoted *ibid.*, p. 75.

18. *Chaliapin: An Autobiography As Told to Maxim Gorky*, ed. and trans. Nina Froud and James Hanley (London: MacDonald, 1968), p. 118.

19. *Ibid.*, p. 121.

20. Quoted in Lifar, *Serge Diaghilev*, p. 45.

21. Benois, *Reminiscences*, p. 214.

22. *Ibid.*, p. 203.

23. Quoted in Lifar, *Serge Diaghilev*, p. 130.

24. Benois, *Reminiscences*, pp. 282–283.

25. Bronislava Nijinska, *Early Memoirs*, trans. and ed. Irina Nijinska and Jean Rawlinson, introd. Anna Kisselgoff (New York: Holt, Rinehart, and Winston, 1981), p. 265.

26. Benois, *Reminiscences*, p. 108.

27. Kennedy, "The 'Mir Iskusstva' Group," pp. 38–39.

28. Anton Rubinstein, *Autobiography of Anton Rubinstein, 1829–1889*, trans. Aline Delando (Boston: Little, Brown, 1903), pp. 90–93.

29. Benois, *Reminiscences*, p. 203.

30. Bill, *Forgotten Class*, p. 129.

31. Quoted in Lifar, *Serge Diaghilev*, p. 79.

32. Quoted *ibid.*, p. 81.

33. Quoted in Magarshack, *Stanislavsky*, p. 71.

34. Serge Diaghilev, Letter to Ilya S. Ostrukhov, 13 April 1900, Manuscript Department, Tretiakov Gallery, Moscow; D. Filosofov, "S.S. Botkin," *Moscow*, 31 January 1910. I am grateful to Professor Ilya Zilberstein of Moscow for this and the references below to material in Soviet archives.

35. Walter Nouvel, Letter to Alexandre Benois, 30 July/12 August 1906, Manuscript Department, State Russian Museum; Alexandre Benois, *Memoirs*, trans. Moura Budberg (London: Chatto and Windus, 1964), II, p. 232n; Andrei Bely (for the description of Hirschmann), quoted in Kean, p. 64; *Salon d'Automne: Exposition de l'Art Russe* [exhibition catalogue] (Paris: Moreau Frères, 1906), p. 6; Comtesse Elisabeth Greffuhle, Draft letter, 6 October 1906, GA103–12, Gabriel Astruc Papers, Dance Collection, New York Public Library; Benois, *Reminiscences*, p. 195; Charles Spencer, *Léon Bakst* (London: Academy Editions, 1973), p. 18; Bowlt, *Silver Age*, pp. 97–99. I am grateful to Joan Acocella for permitting me to see her photocopy of the 1906 exhibition catalogue.

36. Unfortunately, the *Boris Godunov* patronage list (GA123–7, Astruc Pa-

pers) does not give first names, so there is no way of knowing which Morozov was involved. No fewer than four Morozovs lent to the 1906 exhibition. The information about the 1909 loan was provided by Professor Zilberstein. The 1910 rescue by Argutinsky and Ratkoff-Rognoff, and the latter's relationship to Diaghilev, appear in Lieven, *Birth*, pp. 116 and 248.

37. Kennedy, "The 'Mir Iskusstva' Group," p. 182.

38. Alexandre Benois, *The Russian School of Painting* (St. Petersburg: L. Golike and A. Wilborg, 1904). Among the other collections represented are those of the Tretiakov Gallery, Alexander III Museum, Prince P. Galitzine, and E. Schwartz. I am indebted to Asya Yefimova Kounina of Moscow for allowing me to see this priceless volume.

39. Alexander Siloti, *Vospominaniia i pis'ma* (Leningrad, 1963), p. 419; Haskell, *Diaghileff*, p. 150n; Yastrebtsev, *Reminiscences of Rimsky-Korsakov*, p. 473; *Peterburgskaia Gazeta*, 22 June 1908; Nikolai van Gilse van der Pals, *N.A. Rimsky-Korssakow* (Leipzig, 1914); ——— *N.A. Rimsky-Korssakow. Opernschaffen nebst Skizze über Leben und Wirken* (Leipzig, 1929). A list of the 1907 patronage committee appears in A.V. Lunacharsky, *V mire muzyki*, ed. G.B. Bernandt and I.S. Sats (Moscow, 1958), p. 507. In addition to Gilse van der Pals, the members were: Alexis de Hitroff, Alexander Taneyev, Pedro Gailhard, André Messager, L. Broussan, Camille Chevillard, Arthur Nikisch, Felix Blumenfeld, Nikolai Rimsky-Korsakov, Alexander Glazunov, Sergei Rachmaninov, Aristide Briand, Comtesse Greffuhle, and a Mr. Reineke. I am grateful to Professor Zilberstein for the Siloti and *Peterburgskaia Gazeta* references.

40. Siloti, *Vospominaniia*, p. 419; *Peterburgskaia Gazeta*, 22 June 1908.

41. Gabriel Astruc, "Rapport Confidentiel sur la Saison Russe," 19 November 1909, GA25–17, Astruc Papers; Haskell, *Diaghileff*, p. 182; Benois, *Reminiscences*, p. 279. The identity of "D" is another mystery.

42. For Morozov, see Bill, *Forgotten Class*, pp. 28–29. For Mamontov's "education" of Chaliapin, see Grover, "Savva Mamontov," pp. 297–305.

43. Benois, *Reminiscences*, p. 283.

44. Stanislavsky and Mamontov are quoted in Kennedy, "The 'Mir Iskusstva' Group," p. 138. For *Orpheus*, see Grover, "Savva Mamontov," p. 318.

45. Lionel Kochan, *Russia in Revolution, 1890–1918* (London: Granada, 1970), p. 67.

46. Kennedy, "The 'Mir Iskusstva' Group," pp. 244, 214, 38; "Autobiographie de Serge de Diaghilev," trans. Boris Kochno, Fonds Kochno, Pièce 122, Bibliothèque de l'Opéra (Paris); Haskell, *Diaghileff*, pp. 10, 36; Benois, *Reminiscences*, p. 117; V.I. Gurko, *Features and Figures of the Past* (Stanford: Stanford Univ. Press, 1939), pp. 608–609.

47. Benois, *Reminiscences*, p. 164.

48. Quoted in Richard Buckle, *Homage to the Designers of Diaghilev (1909–1929). An Exhibition Made on Behalf of the Theatre Museum, London* (Palazzo Grassi-Venice, 15 June–14 September 1975), n.p.

49. Anatole Chujoy, "Russian Balletomania," *Dance Index*, March 1948, pp. 49–50.

50. Benois, *Reminiscences*, p. 208. In addition to Benois, this account draws on Lifar, *Serge Diaghilev*, pp. 92–94.

51. Benois, *Reminiscences*, p. 209.

52. For a list of Bakst's various assignments, see Charles Steven Mayer, "The Theatrical Designs of Léon Bakst," Diss. Columbia 1977, pp. 286–290.

53. Benois, *Reminiscences*, pp. 211-212.

54. *Ibid.*, pp. 213–224.

55. *Ibid.*, pp. 214–218; Lifar, *Serge Diaghilev*, pp. 94–98; Bowlt, *Silver Age*, p. 160.

56. "Valentin Serov v vospominaniiakh, dnevnikakh i perepiske sovremenni-kov," T.I.L., 1971, p. 675; Bowlt, *Silver Age*, p. 160; Alex de Jonge, *The Life and Times of Grigorii Rasputin* (New York: Coward, McCann, and Geoghegan, 1982), pp. 158–159; Alexander Scriabin, *Pis'ma* (Moscow, 1965), pp. 471–472; Serge Diaghilev, Telegram to Gabriel Astruc, 22 April 1907, Astruc Papers.

57. "Around the World With the Russian Ballet: A Previously Unpublished Interview with Serge Diaghilev," trans. and ed. Parmenia Migel Ekstrom, *Dance Magazine*, September 1979, p. 48. A substantial portion of this interview, although not the section quoted, was published in "About the Russian Ballet," *Graphic*, 20 July 1929, p. 133.

58. "Notes autobiographiques de Serge de Diaghilev," trans. and introd. Boris Kochno, Fonds Kochno, Pièce 122, p. 9.

59. *Ibid.*, p. 14.

60. Haskell, *Diaghileff*, p. 93; "Notes autobiographiques de Serge de Di-aghilev," p. 10; Alexander, Grand Duke of Russia, *Once a Grand Duke* (New York: Farrar and Rinehart, 1932), p. 137.

61. Quoted in Lifar, *Serge Diaghilev*, p. 115.

62. Quoted *ibid.*, p. 114.

63. Quoted in Kennedy, "The 'Mir Iskusstva' Group," p. 349.

64. Quoted *ibid.*, p. 45.

65. For Telyakovsky, see Haskell, *Diaghileff*, p. 119; for Fredericks, see Gurko, *Features and Figures*, p. 649. The allusion to Telyakovsky being Fredericks's "adopted nephew" appears in miscellaneous notes in Folder 8, Box 8 of the Joseph Paget-Fredericks Collection, University of California, Berkeley. Paget-Fredericks was a great-nephew of Baron Fredericks and allegedly the recipient of ministerial documents that were brought out of Russia by Lady Muriel Paget who organized relief work after the 1917 Revolution. The original documents, on which Paget-Fredericks's surviving manuscripts were based, disappeared after his death in 1963.

66. "Notes autobiographiques de Serge de Diaghilev," p. 15; Lieven, *Birth*, p. 220; M.D. Calvocoressi, *Musicians Gallery: Music and Ballet in Paris and London* (London: Faber and Faber, 1933), p. 191; "Saison russe (mai-juin 1909)," GA26–6, Astruc Papers; H.S.H. Princess Romanovsky-Krassinsky, *Dancing in Petersburg: The Memoirs of Kschessinska*, trans. Arnold Haskell (1961; rpt. New York: Da Capo, 1977), p. 111. The exchange rate at the time was 2.6 francs to the ruble and 25.2 francs to the pound. William Tate, *Tate's Modern Cambist*, 25th ed. (London: Effingham, Wilson, 1912), p. 108.

67. Nikoly Andreyevich Rimsky-Korsakov, *My Musical Life*, trans. Judah A. Joffe, ed. Carl van Vechten (New York: Alfred A. Knopf, 1942), p. 436.

68. "Notes autobiographiques de Serge de Diaghilev," p. 11.

69. "Around the World With the Russian Ballet," p. 48; Benois, *Reminiscences*, pp. 280–281; Alexander, *Once a Grand Duke*, pp. 159–160.

70. Olga Crisp, "The Russian Liberals and the 1906 Anglo-French Loan to

Russia," *The Slavonic and East European Review,* 39 (1960–1961), pp. 497–501; René Girault, "Sur Quelques Aspects financiers de l'alliance franco-russe," *Revue d'Histoire Moderne et Contemporaine,* 8 (1961), p. 76.

71. Benois, *Memoirs,* II, p. 230. For the Embassy's role in Diaghilev's audiences, see chapter 10.

72. Gabriel Astruc, Letter to Serge Diaghilev, 22 April 1909, Astruc Papers.

73. Pierre Michaut, "Souvenir de Serge de Diaghilew," *L'Opinion,* 1 September 1934; "Bénac, André," *Dictionnaire de Biographie française,* 1951 ed.; *The Memoirs of Count Witte,* trans. and ed. Abraham Yarmolinsky (London: Heinemann, 1921), pp. 293–294; Gurko, *Features and Figures,* p. 618; Lieven, *Birth,* p. 116; Gabriel Astruc, "Rapport Confidentiel sur la Saison Russe," 19 November 1909, GA25–17, Astruc Papers. For Camondo and Deutsch de la Meurthe, see chapter 10, below.

74. Pierre Gheusi, Letter to Misia Sert, 27 June 1909, Stravinsky-Diaghilev Foundation (New York); Lieven, *Birth,* p. 116.

75. Keith Money, *Anna Pavlova: Her Life and Art* (New York: Knopf, 1982), pp. 75–84.

76. Joseph Paget-Fredericks, "Russia's Last First Minister and Russian Arts, 1896–1917," TS, n.p.; Resumé of documentation for "Russia's Last First Minister and Russian Arts, 1896–1917" and "The Unforgettable Anna Pavlova," Paget-Fredericks Papers. The Fredericks family was known as "the lumber barons of the Baltic."

77. Paget-Fredericks, "Pavlova Dances: Impressions and Drawings," TS, pp. 5–6, 15–17b, 22, Paget-Fredericks Papers; Lifar, *Serge Diaghilev,* p. 98; Haskell, *Diaghileff,* pp. 110–114, 182; Benois, *Reminiscences,* pp. 205–207, 279–280; Wolkonsky, *My Reminiscences,* II, pp. 69–74.

78. Alexander, *Once a Grand Duke,* pp. 146–148; Gurko, pp. 408, 667; Haskell, *Diaghileff,* p. 125; Count Ivan Tolstoi, Letter to Serge Diaghilev, 8 August 1906, Archives of the Academy of Arts. I am grateful to Professor Zilberstein for the Tolstoi reference.

79. Paget-Fredericks, "Pavlova Dances," p. 21.

80. "Courrier des Théâtres," *Figaro,* 11 June 1909, p. 6; 15 June 1909, p. 6; 19 June 1909, p. 4.

81. Paget-Fredericks, "Pavlova Dances," p. 22.

82. The statement issued to the *New York Times* came from Prince Peter Lieven, whose memoir has been quoted extensively in these pages. At the time, he was in the United States "representing the Russian Government in financial matters connected with the war and war supplies." "Pavlova May Gain an Ally. Hopes for Co-operation of Russian Imperial Opera House," *New York Times,* 1 November 1915, p. 11, col. 3. For Rabinoff, see Money, p. 112.

83. Yuri Slonimsky, "Fokine and His Time," introd. to Mikhail Fokine, *Against the Tide: Memoirs of a Ballet Master; Articles, Letters,* ed. Yuri Slonimsky (Leningrad/Moscow: Iskusstvo, 1962), p. 38. Bypassing Telyakovsky, Diaghilev asked Baron Fredericks for permission to organize a Paris-style season on the Imperial stage. Slonimsky does not give a date for this proposal, which was turned down, but it may well have been for the winter of 1911–1912, when Diaghilev did in fact organize a season at St. Petersburg's Narodny Dom theater. The season, scheduled to begin in February 1912, was canceled when the "People's Palace" burned to the ground. The following year the Maryinsky presented a special "Fokine

Month." By that time Diaghilev had broken with his erstwhile choreographer. For Dandré's legal difficulties, see Lifar, *Serge Diaghilev,* p. 136, and Paget-Fredericks, "Pavlova Dances," p. 20.

Chapter 6. Into the Marketplace

1. *Gabriel Astruc: A Register of His Papers in the Dance Collection of the New York Public Library: Biographical Note;* "Papiers Gabriel Astruc" [Guide to Astruc Collection], Archives Nationales (Paris); Gabriel Astruc, *Le Pavillon des fantômes* (Paris: Grasset, 1929). "Astruc Papers" refers to the Astruc holdings in the Dance Collection, New York Public Library.

2. Contract between Serge de Diaghilev/Gabriel Astruc and Raoul Guns-bourg, 7 July 1909, GA28–10; Contract between Serge de Diaghilev and Gabriel Astruc, 29 June 1909, GA27–5; Gabriel Astruc, "Rapport Confidentiel sur la Saison Russe" to Baron Fredericks, Minister of the Imperial Court, [19 November 1909], GA25–17, Astruc Papers. For the *Ivan the Terrible* first performed in Monte Carlo on 2 March 1911, Gunsbourg composed both the libretto and the music. Chaliapin sang the title role, and members of the Ballets Russes performed the "Tartars' Dance." I am grateful to Francis Rosset, former archivist of the Société des Bains de Mer (Monte Carlo), for confirming that the sets and costumes were indeed those acquired from Diaghilev in the 1909 sale and for providing me with a copy of the 1911 program.

3. Gabriel Astruc, Letter to Mathilde Kchessinska, 2 August 1909, GA13–10, Astruc Papers.

4. Gabriel Astruc, Letter to Emile Enoch, 14 December 1909, GA15–12; F. de Coube, Letter to Gabriel Astruc, 17 November 1909, GA15–3; A. Mossoloff, Letter to Gabriel Astruc, 17/30 November 1909, GA20–5; "Rapport Confidentiel sur la Saison Russe," GA25–17, Astruc Papers. For drafts of letters written in October and November advising potential backers of the 1909 financial disaster at the Châtelet, see GA14, Astruc Papers.

5. Boris Schidlovsky, Letters to Gabriel Astruc, 1 and 24 November 1909, GA23–12; 28 December 1909, GA23–14; 11 February 1910, GA38–8, Astruc Papers.

6. Nicholas Wilenkin-Minsky, Letter to Gabriel Astruc, 14 December 1909, GA21–4, Astruc Papers; Messrs. Messager and Broussan, Letter to Baron de Gunzburg, 2 June 1910, AJ13/1292, Archives Nationales (Paris); Liquidation document signed by Gabriel Astruc, 14 February 1910, AJ13/1292, Archives Nationales; Serge Diaghilev, Telegram to Gabriel Astruc, 7 February 1910, GA35–3, Astruc Papers.

7. Confidential Statement of Expenditures, GA28–1, Astruc Papers. Receipts for the 1910 season are in AJ13/1292, Archives Nationales. The season estimate appears in Diaghilev's "Black Notebook," pp. 65–66, at the Dance Collection.

8. "Black Notebook," p. 14; Jules Martin, Letter to Gabriel Astruc, 8 December 1909; Telegram, n.d., GA36–32, Astruc Papers. The description of Bezobrazov comes from Bronislava Nijinska, *Early Memoirs,* trans. and ed. Irina Nijinska and Jean Rawlinson, introd. Anna Kisselgoff (New York: Holt, Rinehart and Winston, 1981), p. 259.

9. Draft contracts with the Thomas Beecham Opera Company, 3 August

1910, GA40–1; the Metropolitan Opera, 28 July 1910, GA40–7; and Teatro Colón, December 1910, GA40–13, Astruc Papers. See folders GA34–GA36 for correspondence and other material relating to these negotiations.

　10. Nijinska, *Early Memoirs,* p. 315–319; Claude Debussy, Letter to Serge Diaghilev, 26 October 1910, Jean Cocteau Papers, George Arents Research Library, Syracuse University; Draft contract between Serge Diaghilev and Reynaldo Hahn, 9 December 1910, GA39–4; Serge Diaghilev, Telegram to Gabriel Astruc, 30 December 1910, GA36–7, Astruc Papers.

　11. Direzione Generale, Teatro alla Scala, Letter to Gabriel Astruc, 14 July 1910, GA37–2, Astruc Papers.

　12. A Russian-born Jew, Max Rabinoff turned to producing after making his first million in the music business in Chicago. Although he did not bring Pavlova to the United States, he sponsored her most critically acclaimed tours. In 1915–1916 he organized the joint tour by the Boston Grand Opera and Pavlowa Ballet Russe that won high praise throughout the country. In the late 1930s he was among the founders of New York's City Center. Max Rabinoff Papers, Manuscript Division, Columbia University.

　Oscar Hammerstein's Manhattan Opera House, said to be more beautiful than the Metropolitan, also presented high art attractions. The Pavlova company danced on numerous occasions at the house, and it was here, in 1917, that the Ballets Russes opened its second American tour. In 1910 there was talk that Hammerstein would bring over the Diaghilev company in a coup aimed at upstaging the Metropolitan. Serge Diaghilev, Telegram to Gabriel Astruc, 24 January 1911, GA36–8, Astruc Papers.

　13. Sir Thomas Beecham, *A Mingled Chime: An Autobiography* (New York: Putnam, 1943), p. 174.

　14. *Ibid.,* p. 295.

　15. "The Russian Imperial Ballet Which Enraptured Our Royalties Last Week," Diaghilev Scrapbook, I, p. 95, Theatre Museum (London).

　16. List of income and liabilities—1913, GA96–1, Astruc Papers.

　17. "Benois' Commentaries," Part VI, trans. Roland John Wiley, *Dancing Times,* March 1981, p. 390.

　18. "Nijinski," *El Día,* 13 September 1913, p. 8.

　19. Beecham, *Mingled Chime,* p. 185; "Extrait du Contrat Diaghilew-Beecham," GA82–9, Astruc Papers.

　20. Beecham, *Mingled Chime,* p. 193.

　21. Astruc, *Le Pavillon des fantômes,* p. 258; Contract between Serge Diaghilev and Gabriel Astruc, 19 June 1913, GA94–1, Astruc Papers.

　22. Contract between Serge Diaghilev/Baron Dmitri de Gunzburg and Sir Joseph Beecham, 13 March 1914, Fonds Kochno, Pièce 129, Bibliothèque de l'Opéra (Paris).

　23. S.L. Grigoriev, *The Diaghilev Ballet 1909–1929,* trans. and ed. Vera Bowen (London: Constable, 1953), pp. 104, 110.

　24. Beecham, *Mingled Chime,* pp. 249, 268, 285–286, 292; Donald Bayliss, Letter to Jacques Rouché, 23 June 1917, AJ13/1205, Archives Nationales; Eugene Goossens, *Overture and Beginners: A Musical Autobiography* (London: Methuen, 1951), chaps. 22, 25–26. Goossens, a future Diaghilev conductor, was at this time employed by the Beecham Opera Company.

　25. Michael de Cossart, *The Food of Love: Princesse Edmond de Polignac*

(1865–1943) and Her Salon (London: Hamish Hamilton, 1978), p. 102; Misia Sert, *Two or Three Muses*, trans. Moura Budberg (London: Museum Press, 1953), pp. 128–129.

26. Richard Buckle, "Lady Juliet Duff," obit., September 1965, Diaghilev Scrapbook, III, p. 115, Theatre Museum (London); Astruc, *Le Pavillon des fantômes*, p. 257; *Who's Who* (1914); Serge Diaghilev, Telegram to Gabriel Astruc, 24 January 1911, GA36–8, Astruc Papers.

27. William L. Blackwell, *The Beginning of Russian Industrialization, 1800–1860* (Princeton: Princeton Univ. Press, 1968), p. 235; "The Black Notebook of Serge Diaghilev", p. 14; List of company liabilities, GA96–19, Astruc Papers. The draft contract of 3 August 1910 with the Beecham organization provided for payment of a Frs. 30,000 cash advance on or before August 12, 1910, to be reimbursed or deducted from receipts at the rate of Frs. 2,000 per performance until the full Frs. 30,000 was repaid. "It is understood that Baron Dimitri de Gunzbourg promises with respect to the management to guarantee reimbursement of the full amount of this advance in the event of noncompliance with this contract on the part of M. Serge de Diaghilew." GA40–1, Astruc Papers.

28. "Procès verbal de saisie conservatoire," 5 June 1914, AJ13/1292, Archives Nationales; Dmitri Gunzburg and Serge Diaghilev, Letter to G. Astruc et Cie., 20 July 1912, GA73–1, and G. Astruc et Cie., Letter to Gabriel Astruc, 16 August 1912, GA70–19, Astruc Papers.

29. List of income and liabilities—1913, GA96–1; Statement of daily expenditures—1913, GA96–6, Astruc Papers; "Procès verbal de saisie conservatoire," 5 June 1914, and attachment authorizations of 2 June 1914, 3 June 1914, and 5 June 1914 and supporting documentation, AJ13/1292, Archives Nationales.

30. Addie Kahn, Cables to Otto Kahn, 18 July 1914 and 19 August 1914, Otto Kahn Papers, Box 34, Princeton University.

31. Nijinska, *Early Memoirs*, p. 334. For Pavlova's salary, see Keith Money, *Anna Pavlova: Her Life and Art* (New York: Knopf, 1982), p. 63.

32. Ercole's letters and Geltzer's salary are quoted in Ivor Guest, "The Alhambra Ballet," *Dance Perspectives*, 4 (Autumn 1959), pp. 51–52. See also Lydia Kyasht, *Romantic Recollections* (London: Brentano, 1929), p. 150. Alexandra Balashova, who replaced Geltzer after eight weeks, received £40 a week as did the leading man Vasily Tikhomirov; Vera Mossolova, who followed Balashova as the ensemble's ballerina, earned £50 a week. Calculated at an exchange rate of Frs. 25.2 to the pound, their salaries were equivalent to Frs. 2,268, Frs. 1,008, and Frs. 1,260 respectively. James Robertson, *Dictionary for International Commercial Quotations* (London: Oxford Univ. Press, 1918). In Russian currency, this came to 855, 380, and 475 rubles a week. Until 1914, £1 equaled 9.5 rubles.

33. Lydia Lopokova, Letter to A.D. Krupensky, 9/22 July 1910, Fond 497, Opis' 5, Conservation No. 1866, Central State Historical Archive (Leningrad). I am grateful to Elizabeth Souritz for providing me with the Lopokova material.

34. Fond 497, Opis' 5, Conservation No. 1866, Central State Historical Archive (Leningrad); "Theatrical Echo," *Petersburg Gazette*, 18 August 1910, p. 4.

35. For details of these companies and tours, see Barbara Naomi Cohen, "The Borrowed Art of Gertrude Hoffmann," and Oliver M. Sayler and Marjorie Barkentin, "On Your Toes—America! The Story of the First Ballet Russe," in *Dance Data*, 2 (n.d.); Money, *Anna Pavlova*, pp. 96–140. For clippings and other material about the "Saison russe" presented at the Théâtre Sarah-Bernhardt in Paris in

April 1911 with Julie Sedova as principal dancer and Ivan Clustine as choreographer, see GA121–122, Astruc Papers.

36. Contract between Serge Diaghilev and Dmitri Molotzoff, n.d., GA64–11; "Nom et Prénom de la troupe Molotzoff," GA66–3; André Aron, Letter to Serge Diaghilev, 13 October 1913, GA84–2; Receipts dated 29 and 30 October 1913, GA95–11; List of income and liabilities—1913, GA96–1; List of liabilities as of 25 May 1913, GA96–19; Astruc Papers. The original contract covered the period 1 April 1911–1 April 1912. As for the Frs. 60,000 payable during the 1913 season, Diaghilev's failure to abide by the terms of the contract resulted in legal suit being brought by Molotzoff and partial settlement of the debt in October 1913.

37. The one and only contract Diaghilev signed with Nijinsky, dated 10 October 1908, is a case in point. Sold at Sotheby's (London) on 15 October 1963, it provided for a season salary of Frs. 2,500. Richard Buckle, *Diaghilev* (London: Weidenfeld and Nicolson, 1979), pp. 136 and 551 (note 87).

38. Nijinska, *Early Memoirs*, p. 259.

39. Sources: For the 1910 Diaghilev season, "The Black Notebook of Serge Diaghilev," p. 1. In Nijinska's category, both the Frs. 2,200 and Frs. 2,500 figures appear. Lopokova received 600 rubles a year when she entered the Maryinsky corps de ballet in 1909. On 28 April 1910, she was promoted to coryphée, and in early August her salary was raised to 720 rubles. Fond 497, Opis' 5, Conservation No. 1866, Central State Historical Archive (Leningrad). I am indebted to Elizabeth Souritz for this information as well as for the salary figures of the other Imperial Ballet artists. The exchange rate in 1910 was 2.6 francs to the ruble. William Tate, *Tate's Modern Cambist*, 25th ed. (London: Effingham Wilson, 1912), p. 108.

40. Contract between Serge Diaghilev and M.V. Guliuk, 10 February 1911, Max Rabinoff Papers, Manuscript Division, Columbia University; Direction du Ballet Russe, Letter to Hilda Bewicke, 15 December 1912, GA76–3, Astruc Papers; Lydia Sokolova, *Dancing for Diaghilev*, ed. Richard Buckle (London: John Murray, 1960), p. 31. Sokolova gives her salary as thirty pounds a month, equivalent to Frs. 756. For Paris Opéra salaries, see "Our Paris Letter," *Dancing Times*, February 1920, p. 369; "Opera Strike Threat; Dancers' Miserable Wages," *Times* (London), 1 January 1920, p. 12; "Menaces de grève à l'Opéra," *Le Temps*, 1 January 1920, p. 3.

41. "In Indiana during the long [1911] tour," writes Pavlova's biographer, Keith Money, the ballerina "had been interviewed by a cub reporter . . . After referring to her mother and grandmother as a reason for her to return to Russia, Pavlova added: 'But I have seen freedom in the outside world. I shall not spend so much time there [in Russia] as before. How would you feel toward a country where it is possible for a Grand Duke to come backstage and order the *maitre de ballet* to line up the ballet corps for his inspection? Then, as he strolls down the line, he points with his cane. "There. That one! Put her in my carriage. I will take that one for tonight." ' Pavlova made it quite clear that she had equivocal feelings toward her homeland and its class system wherein she had had to struggle to be accepted and promoted." Money, *Anna Pavlova*, p. 140n.

42. "The Black Notebook of Serge Diaghilev," pp. 1, 9, 61.

43. Feodor Chaliapin, Telegram to Gabriel Astruc, 22 March 1906, GA1–2; Confidential Statement of Expenditures, GA28–1; "Extrait du Contrat Diaghilew-Beecham," GA82–9, Astruc Papers; Truman C. Bullard, "The First Performance

of Igor Stravinsky's *Sacre du Printemps,*" Diss. Rochester (Eastman School of Music) 1971, I, Appendix A, pp. 228–230.

44. Serge Diaghilev, Telegram to Gabriel Astruc, 15 June 1912, GA74–26, Astruc Papers.

45. This contract, negotiated through the H.B. Marinelli, Ltd., theatrical agency and dated May 31, 1914, obviously became void with the outbreak of World War I. I am indebted to Dr. Mikaly Cenner of Budapest for a copy of this and other documents relating to the efforts of Oscar Pardany of Budapest to negotiate various engagements for Nijinsky in June 1914. The originals are in Dr. Cenner's possession.

46. Serge Diaghilev, Telegram to Carlotta Zambelli, 21 September 1911, GA54–21; Draft contract between Serge Diaghilev and Carlotta Zambelli, n.d., GA82–10; Draft contract between Serge Diaghilev and Maria Kuznetsova, 8 October 1912, GA82–3, Astruc Papers. Kuznetsova's engagement was for June 8–July 7, 1913. Although she did not appear in either of Diaghilev's 1913 productions, the following year she sang in his *Prince Igor* and appeared in a mime role in *Legend of Joseph.*

47. Guest, "The Alhambra Ballet," p. 51; Otto Kahn, Letter to Max Rabinoff, 30 July 1912, Max Rabinoff Papers; Dawn Lille Horwitz, *Michel Fokine,* foreword Don McDonagh (Boston: Twayne, 1985), p. 184 (note 10). For the Pavlova company Fokine choreographed *The Seven Daughters of the Mountain King* and *Les Préludes;* for Rubinstein, the dances in *La Pisanelle.*

48. Guest, "The Alhambra Ballet," p. 51; Direzione Generale, Teatro alla Scala, Letter to Gabriel Astruc, 14 July 1910, GA37–2, Astruc Papers; "The Black Notebook of Serge Diaghilev," p. 61; Grigoriev, *The Diaghilev Ballet,* p. 55. La Scala paid Bakst Frs. 5,000 for the designs, and Rubinstein Frs. 3,000 to repeat the roles she had created in Paris. Direzione Generale, Teatro alla Scala, Letter to Gabriel Astruc, 23 July 1910, GA37–3, Astruc Papers.

49. Giulio Gatti-Casazza, Telegram to Serge Diaghilev, 26 November 1910, GA36–11; Gabriel Astruc, Telegram to Metropolitan Opera, 14 December 1910, GA36–6; Direzione Generale, Teatro alla Scala, Letter to Gabriel Astruc, 23 July 1910, GA37–3, Astruc Papers; Konstantin Rudnitsky, *Meyerhold the Director,* trans. George Petrov, ed. Sydney Schultze, introd. Ellendea Proffer (Ann Arbor: Ardis, 1981), pp. 165–166. Until Fokine lowered his demand to $20,000, Gatti-Casazza was prepared to dispense with him altogether, and at one very sticky point in the negotiations, Diaghilev indicated his willingness to oblige. Serge Diaghilev, Telegram to Metropolitan Opera, 26 November 1910, GA36–10, Astruc Papers. Fokine's "money-mindedness" continued in emigration. "When Fokine came to America in 1919 at the invitation of the American impresario Morris Gest, rumor had it that his salary for choreographing the Broadway musical *Aphrodite* was higher than that paid to any other balletmaster in the world." Dawn Lille Horwitz, "Michel Fokine in America, 1919–1942," Diss. New York University 1982, p. 8. The following year Gest paid Fokine $1,000 a day for his work on the exotic extravaganza *Mecca. Ibid.,* p. 17.

50. Astruc et Cie., Letter to Serge Diaghilev, 4 November 1912, GA71–25, Astruc Papers. In a 1972 lawsuit filed against Stravinsky's publishers Boosey and Hawkes, Romola Nijinsky claimed that a contract signed in mid-1913 stipulated that one-third of the royalties for *Le Sacre du Printemps* were to be divided be-

tween Nijinsky and the ballet's designer, Nicholas Roerich. According to the choreographer's widow, Stravinsky failed to mention this contract when he registered the copyright of *Sacre* with the Society of Music Publishers in Paris, thus depriving his collaborators from ever receiving British or American royalties. Jack Kindred, "Charge Nijinsky Left Out of 'Rites'," *Variety*, 6 December 1972, p. 2.

51. Serge Diaghilev, Letter to Jacques Rouché, 5 December 1923, AJ13/1207, Archives Nationales. The one Fokine ballet that Diaghilev did tamper with was *The Polovtsian Dances*. According to a program note for the matinee given in Monte Carlo on 22 April 1923, the "choreography of the first two dances" was by Nijinska and that of the "grand final ensemble" by Fokine. The choreographic credits for the full opera staged at the same house on March 11, 1924, read: "Chorégraphie de la première danse de La Nijinska. Chorégraphie du Grand Ensemble final de M. Michel Fokine." In subsequent years, the work appears to have been given in the 1924 version. Diaghilev also tampered a bit with the choreography of *Cléopâtre*, for which Massine created a new pas de deux in 1918.

Chapter 7. Underwriting Modernism: American Intermezzo

1. Henry Russell, Cable to Otto Kahn, 26 December 1915, "Diaghilev Correspondence 1915–1916," Metropolitan Opera Archives. The cable reads in part: "Diaghilev begs me to explain to you that owing to the suspension of all communication from Russia, not even with the aid of the Embassy, can he obtain money for himself and company." Hereinafter, MOA will be used for Metropolitan Opera Archives.

2. Contract between Serge Diaghilev and the Metropolitan Opera Company, 10 October 1914; Otto Kahn, Cable to Serge Diaghilev, 14 May 1915, "Diaghilev Correspondence, 1915–1916," MOA.

3. Giulio Gatti-Casazza, Letter to Serge Diaghilev, 28 August 1915; Henry Russell, Cables to John Brown, 15 December 1915; Metropolitan Opera, 25 December 1915; Otto Kahn, 28 December 1915; and John Brown, 21 February 1916, "Diaghilev Correspondence, 1915–1916," MOA. As it turned out, a balance of Frs. 40,000 remained in the form of eight promissory notes, the payment of which Russell apparently guaranteed, and in September 1916, "at the request of [his creditor] Mademoiselle Muelle" and on her own stationery, Diaghilev wrote to the Metropolitan's cashier, demanding that the opera house pay the Frs. 12,673 still outstanding. Serge Diaghilev, Letter to "Monsieur le Caissier," 6 September 1916, "Diaghilev Ballet Russe, 1916–1917," Box 2, MOA. According to the program notes for the Century Theatre season that began in mid-January, *Prince Igor* and *La Princesse Enchantée* (the Blue Bird pas de deux from *The Sleeping Beauty*) had new costumes and decors as well. For an extended account of the two American tours, see Nesta Macdonald, *Diaghilev Observed* (New York: Dance Horizons, 1975), pp. 128–213, and Lynn Garafola, "The Ballets Russes in America," in *The Art of Enchantment: Diaghilev's Ballets Russes, 1909–1929*, ed. Nancy Van Norman Baer (San Francisco: Fine Arts Museums of San Francisco, 1988), pp. 122–137.

4. Henry Russell, Cable to Otto Kahn, 27 November 1915; Robert Lansing, Telegram to Otto Kahn, 7 February 1916; John Brown, Cable to Henry Russell, 28 February 1916, "Diaghilev Correspondence, 1915–1916," MOA. For an ac-

count of Kahn's remarkable career as a financier and Maecenas, see Mary Jane Matz, *The Many Lives of Otto Kahn* (New York: Macmillan, 1963).

5. Henry Russell, Cable to John Brown, 3 March 1916; John Brown, Cable to Henry Russell, 4 March 1916; Henry Russell, Cable to John Brown, 5 March 1916; John Brown, Cable to Henry Russell, 6 March 1916; Otto Kahn, Cable to Henry Russell, 15 March 1916; Henry Russell, Cable to Otto Kahn, 16 March 1916, "Diaghilev Correspondence, 1915–1916," MOA.

6. Letter contract between Serge Diaghilev and Vaslav Nijinsky, 11 April 1916, MOA.

7. Edward L. Bernays, *Biography of an Idea: Memoirs of Public Relations Counsel Edward L. Bernays* (New York: Simon and Schuster, 1965), p. 102.

8. Adella Prentiss Hughes, *Music is My Life* (New York: World Publishing Co., 1947), p. 203.

9. Bernays, *Biography*, pp. 105–106, 108.

10. *Ibid.*, p. 108.

11. "The Russian Imperial Ballet Which Enraptured Our Royalties Last Week," Diaghilev Scrapbook, I, p. 95, Theatre Museum (London); Tableau de la troupe, GA123–10, Gabriel Astruc Papers, Dance Collection, New York Public Library.

12. Baron de Meyer, "The Ballet Russe—Then and Now," *Vanity Fair,* January 1917, p. 120.

13. Draft contract between Serge Diaghilev and the Metropolitan Opera Company, n.d., MOA.

14. "Minutes of a Meeting of the Incorporators and Subscribers to the Capital Stock of Metropolitan Ballet Company, Inc., 6 April 1915; Metropolitan Opera, Letter to F.D. Edsal, 11 September 1916, "Diaghilev Ballet Russe 1916," MOA.

15. S.L. Grigoriev, *The Diaghilev Ballet 1909–1929*, trans. and ed. Vera Bowen (London: Constable, 1953), p. 121.

16. Draft contract between Serge Diaghilev and Metropolitan Opera Company, n.d.; Contract between Vaslav Nijinsky and Metropolitan Opera Company, 2 August 1916; Metropolitan Opera, Cable to Serge Diaghilev, 4 August 1916, "Diaghilev Ballet Russe 1916," MOA.

17. Ernest Henkel, Letter to Alwynn Briggs, 22 May 1917; Metropolitan Opera, Letter to J.S. Morissey, 14 September 1916, "Diaghilev Ballet Russe 1916"; Ernest Henkel, Letter to Otto Kahn, 11 December 1916, "Diaghilev Ballet Russe 1916–1917," Box 2; Ben Franklin, Letter to Ernest Henkel, 30 January 1917, "Diaghilev Ballet Russe 1916"; Ben Stern, Memorandum [to Ernest Henkel], 16 December 1916, "Diaghilev Ballet Russe 1916–1917," Box 2; Ernest Henkel, Letter to L.A. Steinhardt, 27 February 1917, "Diaghilev Ballet Russe 1916"; Will L. Greenbaum, Letter to Maximillian Elser Jr., 28 December 1916; R.G. Herndon, Telegram to Ernest Henkel, 22 November 1916, "Diaghilev Ballet Russe 1916–1917," Box 2, MOA. For a partial selection of reviews see Nesta Macdonald's chapter on "The Nijinsky Tour" in *Diaghilev Observed,* pp. 198–213.

18. The following unsigned letter exemplifies this attitude: "I do not know whether you have suggested the engagement of Lopokowa, but I do know that the public will not accept her with this company as a five dollar artist and if we must have someone to replace Karsavina it must absolutely be someone from abroad. I can feature a new name and get the public to accept it, but please, I beg of you, do not attempt it with Lopokowa who has appeared not only at Keith's Palace and other theatres charging dollar and a half prices, but at . . . theatres far below

the standard set for the Ballet. Even taking her as one of the ensemble would be most inadvisable. We have advertised a complete organization from Abroad—and the public will accept nothing less." Unsigned letter to Otto Kahn, 26 December 1915, "Diaghilev Correspondence 1915–1916," MOA.

19. "Lydig Sues on War Orders; Demands Share of Profits on an $8,100,000 Shell Contract," *New York Times,* 23 June 1916, Sec. 1, p. 17; "Col. P.M. Lydig Dies in Nice at 61," *New York Times,* 17 February 1929, Sec. 1, p. 28; Metropolitan Opera, Cables to Artemieff, 25 July 1916 and 7 August 1916, and to American Embassy, Petrograd, 7 August 1916 and 13 September 1916; Capt. Philip Lydig, Cable to Metropolitan Opera, 13 September 1916, "Diaghilev Ballet Russe 1916," MOA; Dept. of State, Cable to American Embassy, Petrograd, 31 May 1916, 124.613/52a; Philip Lydig, Telegram to Robert Lansing, 2 May 1917, 763.72/4387–1/2, Diplomatic Section, National Archives. The Metropolitan categorically turned down Diaghilev's suggestion that Nijinsky's sister Bronislava be engaged for the tour. Metropolitan Opera, Cables to Serge Diaghilev, 8 August and 12 August 1916, "Diaghilev Ballet Russe 1916," MOA.

20. Ernest Henkel, Letter to R.G. Herndon, 8 December 1916, "Diaghilev Ballet Russe 1916–1917"; R.G. Herndon, Cable to Ernest Henkel, 22 November 1916; Ernest Henkel, Letter to R.G. Herndon, 8 December 1916, "Diaghilev Ballet Russe 1916–1917," Box 2, MOA.

21. Stanislaw Drobecki and Randolfo Barocchi, Telegram to Ernest Henkel, 7 January 1917, "Diaghilev Ballet Russes 1916–1917," Box 2, Serge Diaghilev, Cables to Rawlins Cottenet and Ernest Henkel, 11 February 1917, "Diaghilev Ballet Russe 1916"; M. Oustinoff, Letter to Metropolitan Opera House, 24 February 1917, "Diaghilev Ballet Russe 1916–1917," Box 2, MOA.

22. For the Metropolitan's remittances, see Metropolitan Ballet Company, Letters to National City Bank, 22 and 28 December 1916, 4, 11, 24, and 25 January 1917, 10 and 19 February 1917, Box 2, MOA. For the Depero commission, see Leonetta Bentivoglio, "Danza e futurismo in Italia 1913–1933," *La Danza Italiana,* 1, No. 1 (Autumn 1984), p. 66; for the Balla commission, see Melissa A. McQuillan, "Painters and the Ballet, 1917–1926: An Aspect of the Relationship Between Art and Theatre," Diss. New York University 1979, II, pp. 383–384; for *Parade,* see Richard Buckle, *In Search of Diaghilev* (New York: Thomas Nelson and Sons, 1956), pp. 93–94; for the Ravel-Cangiullo project, see *Catalogue of Ballet Material and Manuscripts from the Serge Lifar Collection,* Sotheby's (London), 9 May 1984, Lot 203.

23. R.G. Herndon, Letter to Ernest Henkel, 4 December 1916, "Diaghilev Ballet Russe 1916–1917," Box 2, MOA.

24. R.G. Herndon, Letter to Ernest Henkel, 11 December 1916, "Diaghilev Ballet Russe 1916–1917," Box 2, MOA.

25. Doris Faithfull, Letter to Otto Kahn, 11 November 1916, Box 57, Otto Kahn Papers, Princeton University. She was writing on behalf of Anna and Lubov Samarokoff [Soumarokova], Mechkovska, Galina Chabelska, Stas Paerska, and Lila [Valentina] Kachouba. Kahn's reply, if any, has not survived.

26. Leigh Henry, unidentified review, Diaghilev Scrapbook, IV, p. 158, Theatre Museum (London).

27. Lydia Sokolova, *Dancing for Diaghilev,* ed. Richard Buckle (London: John Murray, 1960), pp. 116, 124.

Chapter 8. Era of the Dance Boom

1. Robert Craft, "Stravinsky, Diaghilev, and Misia Sert," *Ballet Review,* 6, No. 4 (1977–1978), p. 76. This article appears as Appendix B in Vera Stravinsky and Robert Craft, *Stravinsky in Pictures and Documents* (London: Hutchinson, 1979), pp. 514–522.

2. Raymond Mortimer, "London Letter," *Dial,* March 1922, p. 295.

3. Felix Barker, *The House That Stoll Built: The Story of the Coliseum Theatre* (London: Frederick Muller, 1957), p. 70.

4. "New Alhambra Ballet. 'La Boutique Fantasque'," *Times,* 16 June 1919, p. 14. *Le Tricorne,* too, "received a tremendous ovation from a house packed from stalls to galleries," with admirers showering choreographer Léonide Massine with flowers, wreaths, and even a large cake. " 'The Three-Cornered Hat.' Russian Ballet at the Alhambra," *Times,* 23 July 1919, p. 10.

5. Paul Thompson, *The Edwardians: The Remaking of British Society* (St. Albans, Herts.: Paladin, 1977), p. 277.

6. Charles S. Maier, *Recasting Bourgeois Europe: Stabilization in France, Germany, and Italy in the Decade After World War I* (Princeton: Princeton Univ. Press, 1975), p. 43.

7. Craft, "Stravinsky, Diaghilev, and Misia Sert," p. 76.

8. Gabriel Astruc, Letters to Otto Kahn, 10 and 17 May 1921, 7 and 31 December 1921, Otto Kahn Papers, Box 146, Princeton University; Gabriel Astruc, Letters to Jacques Rouché, 1 July 1921 and 17 September 1921, AJ13/1207, Archives Nationales (Paris).

9. "Co-operative Opera. Future of the Beecham Company," *Times,* 2 July 1921, p. 10.

10. For a discussion of the Ballets Suédois, see Sally Banes, "An Introduction to the Ballets Suédois," *Ballet Review,* 7, Nos. 2–3 (1978–1979), pp. 28–59; for the Soirées de Paris, see Lynn Garafola, "Les Soirées de Paris," in *Lydia Lopokova,* ed. Milo Keynes (London: Weidenfeld and Nicolson, 1983), pp. 97–105; for Cocteau's *Le Boeuf sur le Toit,* see Francis Steegmuller, *Cocteau: A Biography* (Boston: Little, Brown, 1970), pp. 238–245.

11. Patrick George Friel, "Theater and Revolution: The Struggle for Theatrical Autonomy in Soviet Russia (1917–1920)," Diss. North Carolina 1977, p. 195n; Naoum Mitnik, Letters to Jacques Rouché, spring/summer 1920, AJ13/1208, Archives Nationales; N.D. Lobanov,"Russian Painters and the Stage," *Transactions,* 2 (1968), p. 137; André Levinson, "Les Ballets romantiques russes," *La Danse,* April 1924, n.p. Among Rubinstein's postwar productions at the Paris Opéra were *La Tragédie de Salomé* (1919), *Antoine et Cléopâtre* (1920), *Artemis Troublée* (1922), *Phaedre* (1923), *Istar* (1924), and *Orphée* (1926). Nijinska's Theatre Chorégraphique toured English resort towns in the summer and early autumn of 1925 and subsequently gave a few performances in Paris. Nancy Van Norman Baer, *Bronislava Nijinska: A Dancer's Legacy* (San Francisco: The Fine Arts Museums of San Francisco, 1986), pp. 49–57.

12. For a brief summary of activity on the English side of the Channel, see "A Chronology of the Ballet in England 1910–1935," *Dancing Times,* October 1935, pp. 3–11. This is substantially reproduced in Philip J.S. Richardson, "A Chronology of the Ballet in England 1910–1945," *The Ballet Annual: A Record*

and Yearbook of the Ballet, ed. Arnold Haskell (London: Adam and Charles Black, 1947), pp. 117–124. Richardson edited the *Dancing Times* from 1910–1951.

13. "Paris Notes," *Dancing Times,* July 1922, p. 857.

14. "Sitter Out," *Dancing Times,* January 1925, p. 400.

15. For a discussion of Rouché's reforms, see Ivor Guest, *Le Ballet de l'Opéra de Paris: Trois siècles d'histoire et de tradition,* trans. Paul Alexandre (Paris: Théâtre National de l'Opéra, n.d.), pp. 157–169.

16. Notices of Levinson's lectures and reviews of Théâtre des Champs-Elysées concerts regularly appeared in the French monthly *La Danse* as well as in the "Paris Notes" column of the *Dancing Times.* For the Gaîté-Lyrique, see "Paris Notes," *Dancing Times,* April 1924, p. 701. Levinson's *La Danse d'aujourd'hui. Etudes, Notes, Portraits* (Paris: Editions Duchârtre et Van Buggenhoudt, 1929) reproduces (with minor changes) essays and reviews written by the author in the middle and late 1920s.

17. "Paris Notes," *Dancing Times,* April 1921, p. 567.

18. Eugene Goossens, *Overture and Beginners: A Musical Autobiography* (London: Methuen, 1951), pp. 182–186; "Paris Notes. Troubles of the Opera," *Dancing Times,* April 1921, pp. 567–569; Josephine Baker and Jo Bouillon, *Josephine,* trans. Mariana Fitzgerald (New York: Harper and Row, 1977), pp. 48–53.

19. Contracts between Serge Diaghilev and Messrs. Messager and Broussan, 22 October 1913; Jacques Rouché and Serge Diaghilev, 10 April 1919, 5 July 1919, and 8 October 1921, Bibliothèque de l'Opéra (Paris); T.E. Gregory, *Foreign Exchange Before, During, and After the War* (London: Oxford Univ. Press, 1922), pp. 110–113.

20. Letter-contract between Loie Fuller and the Paris Opéra, 8 July 1922, AJ13/1208, Archives Nationales.

21. Jacques Rouché, Letter to Serge Diaghilev, 26 April 1922, Fonds Kochno, Pièce 86, Bibliothèque de l'Opéra (Paris).

22. "Recettes des Ballets Russes. Théâtre de la Gaîté—Mai 1921," Bibliothèque de l'Opéra. The 1914 figure is calculated from the Opéra's daily "Recette de ce jour," AJ13/1292, Archives Nationales.

23. Theatre Directory, *Times,* 1 June 1921, p. 8; 29 June 1921, p. 8.

24. "Serge Diaghileff's Russian Ballet, Princes Theatre, House Receipts," Stravinsky-Diaghilev Foundation (New York); C[harles] B. Cochran, *Secrets of a Showman* (London: Heinemann, 1925), p. 372. By 1921, the exchange rate was sixty-one francs to the pound. William F. Spalding, *Tate's Modern Cambist,* 28th ed. (London: Effingham Wilson, 1929), p. 117.

25. Boris Kochno, *Diaghilev and the Ballets Russes,* trans. Adrienne Foulke (New York: Harper and Row, 1970), p. 89; Richard Buckle, *Diaghilev* (London: Weidenfeld and Nicolson, 1979), p. 368. Buckle gives as his source Paul Morand, *L'Allure de Chanel* (Paris: Hermann, 1976).

26. S.L. Grigoriev, *The Diaghilev Ballet 1909–1929,* trans. and ed. Vera Bowen (London: Constable, 1953), p. 176; " 'Chu Chin Chow' Ended. Last Scenes at His Majesty's. 2,238 Performances in Five Years," *Times,* 23 July 1921, p. 8. For Adeline Genée's *Coppélia,* see Ivor Guest, *The Empire Ballet* (London: Society for Theatre Research, 1962), pp. 66–67. In addition to the Cochran version staged at the Trocadero Grill Room in late 1924, an excerpt was presented by Nicolas Legat and his wife Nadejda Nicolaeva in January 1925 at the Coliseum. "Sitter Out," *Dancing Times,* January 1925, p. 400; "Another 'Coppelia'," *Dancing Times,* Feb-

ruary 1925, p. 512. Some months earlier, Pavlova had presented a two-act version of the ballet with Hilda Butsova in the title role. "Sitter Out," *Dancing Times,* October 1924, pp. 3–4. In June 1926 the French dancer Camille Bos gave "a short series of dances" from *Coppélia* during a one-week engagement at the Victoria Palace. "Sitter Out," *Dancing Times,* July 1926, p. 344. Although the Diaghilev literature makes no mention of it, in April 1920 Pavlova presented the Vision Scene from *The Sleeping Beauty* during her London season. Four years earlier she had staged a more complete version of the ballet at the New York Hippodrome. The 1916 production had sets and costumes by Bakst.

27. Cyril W. Beaumont, *Bookseller at the Ballet, Memoirs 1891 to 1929, Incorporating the Diaghilev Ballet in London* (London: C.W. Beaumont, 1975), pp. 275n and 273; Léon Bakst, Letter to Jacques Rouché, 29 December 1921, AJ13/1207, Archives Nationales.

28. Beaumont, *Bookseller at the Ballet,* pp. 276–277.

29. Unidentified review, Diaghilev Scrapbook, VI, p. 13, Theatre Museum (London); "London Theatres Hard Hit by Slump," *New York Times,* 2 February 1922, p. 5; Grigoriev, *The Diaghilev Ballet,* pp. 181–182. Citing conversations with Marie Rambert as his source, Richard Buckle gives the amount borrowed by Diaghilev from Mrs. Bewicke as £300. Buckle, *Diaghilev,* p. 397. This is contradicted by a letter from Mrs. Bewicke's solicitors in May 1925 demanding repayment of the £500 loan plus interest. Messrs. Le Brasseur and Oakley, Letter to Serge Diaghilev, 19 May 1925, C-20–12.1, Serge Diaghilev Papers, Dance Collection, New York Public Library. See also Messrs. Le Brasseur and Oakley, Letter to Eric Wollheim, 21 November 1925, 10–1.3, Serge Diaghilev Correspondence, Dance Collection, New York Public Library.

30. "La Société des Ballets Russes," Fonds Kochno, Pièce 138.

31. Arnold Haskell, *Diaghileff: His Artistic and Private Life,* in collaboration with Walter Nouvel (London: Gollancz, 1935), p. 299. Eugene Goossens, who had been Diaghilev's principal conductor throughout *The Sleeping Princess* engagement, took a different view of the results of her generosity. The Princesse's "good sized cheque," he wrote, arrived "just in time to give him [Diaghilev] enough pocket money to enable him to eat at his favourite restaurant instead of a cheap *bistro,* but too late to save his favourite black pearl studs . . ." Goossens, *Overture and Beginners,* p. 180.

32. "A Successful Teacher," *Dancing Times,* February 1912, p. 123; Ruby Ginner, Letter, *Dancing Times,* October 1917, p. 25; "Sitter Out," *Dancing Times,* January 1918, p. 125.

33. Mark E. Perugini, "The Four Schools. Have We the Material for a British Royal Academy of Dance and Ballet?," *Dancing Times,* September 1920, p. 906.

34. Many articles in the *Dancing Times* sought to remedy this professional inexperience. In "The Novice and the Theatre," a series that began in April 1919, Rachel Verney dispensed advice on make-up and other practical matters. A number of Russian émigré ballerinas opened studios in Paris as did Alexandre Volinine in the mid-twenties. These studios, however, like the five-year dance course added to the curriculum of the Paris Conservatoire in 1926, were geared to professional training. "Paris Notes," *Dancing Times,* February 1926, p. 585.

35. Perugini, "The Four Schools," p. 906.

36. *Dancing Times,* October 1922, p. 20.

37. Henry Mayhew, *London Labour and the London Poor,* III (London, 1861;

rpt. New York: Dover, 1968), p. 144. For a mid-nineteenth century view of music-halls as a "social evil," see "Social Characteristics of London Life. No. I. The 'Music-halls'," *The Beehive,* 25 October 1862, p. 1.

38. Audrey MacMahon, "Oh, What a Past: Revealing a Number of Dark Secrets As to the Cause of Certain Famous Careers," *The Dance Magazine,* December 1926, p. 18. See also Keith Money, *Anna Pavlova: Her Life and Art* (New York: Knopf, 1982), pp. 137–138. In an interview with the author in April 1981, Madge Abercrombie, who joined the Pavlova company in 1911, emphasized the point about the girls coming from "good families."

39. Ellen Terry, *The Russian Ballet* (London: Sidgwick and Jackson, 1913), pp. 9–10; Leonard Rees, *Russian Ballet, Containing the Story of the Russian Dancing and Dances and the Plots of the Ballets. Royal Opera—Covent Garden Season—1912* (London: John Long, 1912), pp. 14–15.

40. *Ibid.,* p. 17.

41. "Sitter Out," *Dancing Times,* June 1915, pp. 298–300; July 1915, pp. 331–332; August 1915, pp. 356–358.

42. Rees, p. 12; "Sitter Out," *Dancing Times,* June 1915, p. 300, and August 1915, pp. 356–357.

43. Thompson, *Edwardians,* p. 267; Mark E. Perugini, "Where Are We Going?," Part I, *Dancing Times,* August 1925, pp. 1173–1175. The Dean of Manchester and the "orgy" headline are quoted in "Sitter Out," *Dancing Times,* March 1919, p. 190.

44. "Button Box," "Chats With Young Dancers," *Dancing Times,* March 1923, p. 685.

45. "Button Box," "Chats With Young Dancers," *Dancing Times,* June 1923, p. 967.

46. "Button Box," "Chats With Young Dancers," *Dancing Times,* March 1923, p. 685.

47. Mark E. Perugini, "Where are We Going?," Part III, *Dancing Times,* October 1925, p. 39.

48. Contracts between Yvonne André and Serge Diaghilev, 20 October 1918; Vera Clark and Serge Diaghilev, 3 December 1919; Anatole Bourman and Serge Diaghilev, 3 August 1921; C.L. Lucas, Receipt, 17 August [n.y.], Stravinsky-Diaghilev Foundation.

49. Gregory, *Foreign Exchange,* p. 113; Spalding, *Tate's Modern Cambist,* 28th ed., p. 117; "La Vie trop chère," *Le Gaulois,* 10 March 1924.

50. Ninette de Valois, *Come Dance With Me: A Memoir 1898–1956* (London: Dance Books, 1973), p. 62.

51. H.G., "Lopokova's Ambition. To Be a 'Comedy Actress.' The Ballet Today in Russia," *Observer,* 26 March 1933, Lopokova Clipping File, Harvard Theatre Collection.

52. Lydia Sokolova, *Dancing for Diaghilev,* ed. Richard Buckle (London: John Murray, 1960), pp. 250, 264–265.

53. Nouvel is quoted in Haskell, *Diaghileff,* pp. 298–299. For the lawsuits filed by the four dancers, see Gabriel Joubier's judgments on behalf of Leon Woizikovsky and Lydia Sokolova, 10 March 1922, and Messrs. T[hadée] Slavinsky and Jalmuzynski, 26 May 1922, C-20–21.1, C-20–21.2, C-20–21.3, Serge Diaghilev Papers.

54. "Actors' Minimum Salary; Valentine Contract Upheld," *Times,* 12 Janu-

ary 1922, p. 8; "Actors' 'Closed Shop.' A Meeting to Discuss Boycott Proposal," *Times*, 10 March 1922, p. 10; "Moneyed Amateurs and the Stage. Entrance Examinations Suggested," *Times*, 21 March 1922, p. 10.

55. Buckle, *Diaghilev*, p. 387; Lydia Lopokova, Letter to Comte Etienne de Beaumont, 8 February 1924, John Maynard Keynes Papers, King's College (Cambridge); H.J. Bruce, *Thirty Dozen Moons* (London: Constable, 1949), p. 36.

56. Lydia Lopokova, Letters to John Maynard Keynes, 1 March 1924, 25 October 1924, 29 April 1923, Keynes Papers.

57. Lydia Lopokova, Letter to John Maynard Keynes, 2 November 1923, Keynes Papers.

58. de Valois, *Come Dance*, p. 66.

59. Bronislava Nijinska, Telegram to Serge Diaghilev, 25 July 1921, Fonds Kochno, Pièce 65; Serge Lifar, *Ma Vie: From Kiev to Kiev*, trans. James Holman Mason (New York: World Publishing, 1970), p. 28.

60. Serge Diaghilev, Letter to Charles B. Cochran, 30 March 1926, Fonds Kochno, Pièce 22.

Chapter 9. *Protean Identities*

1. Pièce 128, Fonds Kochno, Biblothèque de l'Opéra (Paris).

2. Cyril W. Beaumont, *The Ballet Called Swan Lake* (London, 1952; rpt. New York: Dance Horizons, 1982), p. 151.

3. S.L. Grigoriev, *The Diaghilev Ballet 1909–1929*, trans. and ed. Vera Bowen (London: Constable, 1953), p. 188.

4. Contracts (2), April 1924, Bibliothèque de l'Opéra; 18 April 1924, C-20–22.1, Serge Diaghilev Papers, Dance Collection, New York Public Library.

5. Philippe Saint-Germain and Francis Rosset, *La Grande Dame de Monte-Carlo* (n.p.: Editions Stock, 1981), p. 366.

6. The programs may be found in the archives of the Société des Bains de Mer (Monte Carlo).

7. René Léon, Letters to Serge Diaghilev, 11 November 1924, 25 October 1924, 4 December 1924, 18 February 1925 (2), 19 February 1925; Serge Diaghilev, Letter to René Léon, 6 November 1924, Palace Archives (Monaco).

8. Francis Poulenc, *Moi et mes amis* (Paris: La Palatine, 1963), p. 179.

9. Gaston Davenay, "Les Concerts de danse de Mlle N. Trouhanowa," *Figaro*, 18 April 1912, p. 1; Robert Brussel, "Au Châtelet: Spectacle de danse de Mlle Trouhanowa," *Figaro*, 24 April 1912, p. 4; Henri Quittard, "Courrier des Théâtres," *Figaro*, 25 April 1917, p. 3.

10. René Léon, Letter to Serge Diaghilev, 13 March 1925, Palace Archives.

11. René Léon, Letter to Serge Diaghilev, 14 March 1925, Palace Archives.

12. Raoul Gunsbourg, Letter to René Léon, 27 March 1925; René Léon, Letter to Serge Diaghilev, 30 March 1925, Palace Archives.

13. Draft contract between Serge Diaghilev and René Léon, 30 April 1925, Pièce 136, Fonds Kochno.

14. Contracts (2) between Serge Diaghilev and René Léon, 17 July 1926, Pièce 136, Fonds Kochno. These contracts included provisions for 1927–1928 as well.

15. Contracts between Serge Diaghilev and Juan Mestres, 9 March 1925; Guido

Gatti, 16 July 1926; Angelo Scandiani, 15 November 1926, Stravinsky-Diaghilev Foundation (New York).

16. Grigoriev, *The Diaghilev Ballet*, p. 219. "Berlin is the one capital he has been unable to conquer," noted Count Harry Kessler in 1928. "He has enjoyed triumphs in all other great cities of the world, but *'devant Berlin, je suis comme un collégien qui est amoureux d'une grande dame et qui ne trouve pas le mot pour la conquérir.'* His Berlin efforts had always proved a material disaster, involving deficits of a hundred to a hundred and fifty thousand francs." *The Twenties: The Diaries of Count Harry Kessler*, trans. Charles Kessler, introd. Otto Friedrich (New York: Holt, Rinehart and Winston, 1971), p. 357.

17. Arnold Haskell, *Diaghileff: His Artistic and Private Life*, in collaboration with Walter Nouvel (London: Gollancz, 1935), p. 308.

18. Receipt, 28 December 1927, AJ13/1292, Archives Nationales (Paris); Contract between Serge Diaghilev and Jacques Rouché, 9 November 1928, Bibliothèque de l'Opéra. In 1927 the house skimmed Frs. 25,000 "off the top" for each of the company's two Christmas season performances and ten percent of the remainder. Contract between Serge Diaghilev and Jacques Rouché, 5 November 1927, Bibliothèque de l'Opéra.

19. Contract between Serge Diaghilev and Sir Oswald Stoll, 9 January 1925, Theatre Museum (London); Grigoriev, *The Diaghilev Ballet*, p. 217.

20. For Bewicke, see Le Brasseur and Oakley, Solicitors, Letter to Serge Diaghilev, 19 May 1925, C-20–12.1, Serge Diaghilev Papers, and Le Braseur and Oakley, Solicitors, Letter to Eric Wollheim, 21 November 1925, 10–1.3, Serge Diaghilev Correspondence; for Gulbenkian, see R. Pioche, Telegram to Serge Diaghilev, 10 July 1925, Stravinsky-Diaghilev Foundation; L. Durand-Villette and R. Pioche, Solicitors, Letter to Serge Diaghilev, 16 July 1925, C-20–12.5, and Letters to Walter Nouvel, 30 October 1925, C-20–13.3, and 11 December 1925, C-20–13.8; for Polignac, see L. Durand-Villette and R. Pioche, Letters to Walter Nouvel, 30 November 1925, C-20–13.5, 13 March 1926, C-20–14.1, and 15 March 1926, C-20–14.2; for Nijinsky, see L. Durand-Villette and R. Pioche, Letter to Serge Diaghilev, 15 July 1925, C-20–12.4, Serge Diaghilev Papers, Dance Collection, New York Public Library.

21. Grigoriev, *The Diaghilev Ballet*, p. 223.

22. Lydia Lopokova, Letter to John Maynard Keynes, 18 November 1926, John Maynard Keynes Papers, King's College (Cambridge); Lilian Rothermere, Letter to Serge Diaghilev, [December 1924], 10–16.7, Serge Diaghilev Correspondence; Eric Wollheim, Telegram to Serge Diaghilev, 11 June 1925, Stravinsky-Diaghilev Foundation; Loretta Lucido Johnson, "T.S. Eliot's *Criterion*: 1922–1939," Diss. Columbia 1980, pp. 44–46, 61, 121–123.

23. Serge Diaghilev, Letter to Lord Rothermere, 18 March [1926]; Pièce 84, Fonds Kochno; Eric Wollheim, Telegram to Serge Diaghilev, 11 April 1927, Stravinsky-Diaghilev Foundation; Serge Diaghilev, Letter to Lady Juliet Duff, 4 May 1928, C-20–6.5, Serge Diaghilev Papers; "Russian Ballet Disbanded. Company's Financial Need. Leader's Influence Missed," *Daily Telegraph*, 20 September 1929.

24. Walter Nouvel, Telegram to Serge Diaghilev, 21 February 1928, Stravinsky-Diaghilev Foundation.

25. Paul Rosenberg, Telegram to Serge Diaghilev, 4 May 1928; Dr. G.-F.

Reber, Telegrams to Serge Diaghilev, 7 May and 10 May 1928, Stravinsky-Diaghilev Foundation. The art dealer Daniel-Henry Kahnweiler has described Reber as a great supporter of cubism. Daniel-Henry Kahnweiler, *Juan Gris: His Life and Work*, trans. Douglas Cooper (New York: Abrams, 1969), p. 53.

26. Diaghilev was far more serious about a mid-decade American tour than has been previously thought. Among the Boris Kochno papers at the Bibliothèque de l'Opéra is a document on the letterhead of the Excelsior Palace Hotel where Diaghilev vacationed in 1924, listing ballets for an American tour. Included among the works "never performed in America" is the untitled ballet by John Alden Carpenter commissioned in the summer of 1924, at the behest, so Kochno claims, of Otto Kahn, who "stipulated that Diaghilev stage an American ballet." Carpenter was the composer of *Krazy Kat*, a "jazz pantomime" that had been recently staged in New York by Adolph Bolm. Diaghilev did not completely jettison the production until the winter of 1925. In February 1926 the Metropolitan Opera produced the ballet as *Skyscrapers: A Ballet of Modern American Life*. "Répertoire des Ballet Russes, Activités de Diaghilev," Pièce 125, Fonds Kochno; John Alden Carpenter, Letters to Serge Diaghilev, 5 September 1924 and 15 November 1924, Pièces 17 and 109, Fonds Kochno; John Alden Carpenter, Telegram to Serge Diaghilev, 1 January 1925, and Gerald Murphy, Telegram to Serge Diaghilev, 6 March 1925, Stravinsky-Diaghilev Foundation; Boris Kochno, *Diaghilev and the Ballets Russes*, trans. Adrienne Foulke (New York: Harper and Row, 1970), p. 222. For background material on the composer, see Verna Arvey, *Choreographic Music: Music For the Dance* (New York: Dutton, 1941), pp. 286–294. In 1925 Diaghilev granted an option to Harry Block and Max Endicoff for a fifteen-week American tour beginning the following October. Although Diaghilev failed to exercise the option, rumors of a forthcoming tour were bruited about the American community. Agreement between Harry Block/Max Endicoff and Serge Diaghilev, 10 October 1925; Serge Diaghilev, Letter to Harry Block, 27 October 1925, Stravinsky-Diaghilev Foundation; Gilbert Seldes, "The Theatre Abroad," *Dial*, September 1926, p. 325.

27. E. Ray Goetz, Telegram to Serge Diaghilev, 16 August 1927, Stravinsky-Diaghilev Foundation; Charles Schwartz, *Cole Porter: A Biography* (New York: Dial, 1977), pp. 94–95; draft contract between Serge Diaghilev and E. Ray Goetz, [November-December 1927], Serge Diaghilev Papers; Serge Diaghilev, Telegram to [?] Seligsberg, 25 April 1928, Stravinsky-Diaghilev Foundation; [?] Seligsberg, Letter to Serge Diaghilev, [May 1928], 10–17.3, Serge Diaghilev Correspondence; Walter Nouvel, Telegram to Serge Diaghilev, 2 May 1928; [?] Seligsberg, Telegram to Walter Nouvel, 20 May 1928; E. Ray Goetz, Telegram to Serge Diaghilev, 23 May 1928; [?] Seligsberg, Telegram to Serge Diaghilev, 27 May 1928, Stravinsky-Diaghilev Foundation; Oliver Sayler, Letter to Serge Diaghilev, 8 June 1928, 10–17.1, Serge Diaghilev Correspondence.

28. E. Ray Goetz, Letter to Serge Diaghilev, [June-July 1928], Stravinsky-Diaghilev Foundation.

29. E. Ray Goetz, Letter to Otto Kahn, 25 October 1928, Box 347, Otto Kahn Papers, Princeton University.

30. Serge Diaghilev, Letter to Lady Juliet Duff, 7 May 1928, C-20–6.6, Serge Diaghilev Papers.

31. Lady Juliet Duff, Letter to Serge Diaghilev, 5 May 1929, 10–14.12, Serge Diaghilev Correspondence; Peter Heyworth, *Otto Klemperer: His Life and Times*,

I (New York: Cambridge Univ. Press, 1983), p. 319; "The Donor of £5000 A Year for Imperial Opera," *Sketch*, 10 July 1929, p. 61; Ernest Outhwaite, Letter to Serge Diaghilev, 18 May 1929, 10–16.4, Serge Diaghilev Correspondence.

32. "Carnet de Serge de Diaghilev, 1922–1923," Pièce 133, Fonds Kochno.

33. "Cahier de travail de Serge de Diaghilev avec indications de répertoire 1915–16," Pièce 124, Fonds Kochno. As all the references to casting, currency, and repertory belong to the immediate postwar period, the dating of this workbook is obviously incorrect.

34. In late 1927 the French foreign affairs ministry approached Maxim Litvinov, the Soviet Commissar of Foreign Affairs, for information about the whereabouts of Diaghilev's half-brother Valentin and sister-in-law, both of whom had disappeared. An enquiry was made, but the results were doubtless what the impresario feared: the secret police "found no trace of an arrest." Jean Herbette, Letters to Philippe Berthelot, 15 January, 24 January 1928, C-20–16.2, Serge Diaghilev Papers.

35. Richard Buckle, *Diaghilev* (London: Weidenfeld and Nicolson, 1979), p. 441. Buckle erroneously dates this encounter as taking place in 1924. For the couple's month-long stay at the Italian resort, see Gordon McVay, *Esenin: A Life* (Ann Arbor: Ardis, 1976), p. 190.

36. Buckle, *Diaghilev*, p. 408; I. S. Zilberstein and V. A. Samkov, eds., *Serge Diaghilev and Russian Art* (Moscow: Izobrazitelnoe Iskusstvo, 1982), I, p. 33; Robert C. Williams, *Culture in Exile: Russian Emigres in Germany, 1881–1941* (Ithaca: Cornell Univ. Press, 1972), pp. 111, 133–134.

37. N.A. Iavorskaia, "Les relations artistiques entre Paris et Moscou dans les années 1917–1930," in *Paris-Moscou, 1900–1930*, Catalogue of the exhibition held at the Centre National d'Art et de Culture Georges Pompidou, Paris, 21 May–5 November 1979, pp. 49–51. With Tristan Tzara, Larionov was host of a banquet given in honor of the Kamerny Theater that Diaghilev was invited to attend. D. O. Widhopff, Tristan Tzara, and Michel Larionov, Letter to Serge Diaghilev, [March 1923], Stravinsky-Diaghilev Foundation. During the season Tairov wrote to Diaghilev asking that he "express in the form of a letter or an article" his "views on the Kamerny Theatre's performances, both for the information of the troupe and its numerous friends and admirers in Moscow, for whom your opinion will be of the greatest interest." Alexander Tairov, Letter to Serge Diaghilev, 14 March 1923, Pièce 98, Fonds Kochno.

38. Buckle, *Diaghilev*, p. 444. Lunacharsky's interview was republished in 1958 in a collection of his writings on music. A.V. Lunacharsky, "Diaghilev's New Season," *V mire muzyki*, ed. G. B. Bernandt and I.A. Sats (Moscow: Sovetski'i Kompozitor, 1958), pp. 347–350. Diaghilev's acquaintance with Lunacharsky dated to at least the turn-of-the-century. Beverly Whitney Kean, *All the Empty Palaces: The Merchant Patrons of Modern Art in Pre-Revolutionary Russia* (New York: Universe Books, 1983), p. 143.

39. Israel V. Nestyev, *Sergei Prokofiev: His Musical Life*, trans. Rose Prokofieva, introd. Sergei Eisenstein (New York: Knopf, 1946), p. 101. The Soviet writer Ilya Ehrenburg, who, like Prokofiev, spent much of the 1920s in Europe, was also considered as a librettist. Victor Serov, *Sergei Prokofiev* (London: Leslie Frewin, 1969), pp. 154–156.

40. Nestyev, *Sergei Prokofiev*, p. 104; Lawrence and Elisabeth Hanson, *Pro-*

kofiev: A Biography in Three Movements (New York: Random House, 1964), p. 198.

41. Grigoriev, *The Diaghilev Ballet*, p. 241; Hanson, *Prokofiev*, p. 214.

42. Kochno, *Diaghilev and the Ballets Russes*, p. 264; Grigoriev, *The Diaghilev Ballet*, p. 237; Yuri Slonimsky, "Balanchine: The Early Years," trans. John Andrews, *Ballet Review*, 5, No. 3 (1975–1976), pp. 37–38.

43. Quoted in Serge Lifar, *Serge Diaghilev: His Life, His Work, His Legend* (1940; rpt. New York: Da Capo, 1976), p. 338.

44. Serge Diaghilev, Letter to Lady Juliet Duff, 7 May 1928, C-20–6.6, Serge Diaghilev Papers.

45. Quoted in Nesta Macdonald, *Diaghilev Observed by Critics in the United States and England 1911–1929* (New York: Dance Horizons, 1975), pp. 348–349; Elizabeth T.F. Courtauld, Letter to Serge Diaghilev, 29 October 1927, 10–20.8, Serge Diaghilev Correspondence.

46. Lady Cunard, Letter to Serge Diaghilev [1926], 10–20.12, Serge Diaghilev Correspondence. The underscoring is Lady Cunard's.

47. Philip Ziegler, *Diana Cooper: A Biography* (New York: Knopf, 1982), p. 146.

48. Lady Diana Cooper, Letter to Serge Diaghilev, [1928], 10–4.1, Serge Diaghilev Correspondence.

49. Eric Wollheim, Telegram to Serge Diaghilev, 4 March 1927, Stravinsky-Diaghilev Foundation; "Sitter Out," *Dancing Times*, January 1926, p. 449. In England *Les Biches* was retitled *The House Party*.

50. "Sitter Out," *Dancing Times*, July 1926, p. 339.

51. *Ibid.*, p. 340.

52. In keeping with the British theme, Diaghilev asked Christopher Wood, a young English expatriate with influential connections in Paris, to do the designs. In April 1926, however, he dismissed Wood and reassigned the ballet to the newly fashionable surrealists Max Ernst and Joán Miró.

53. Edwin Evans, "Serge Diaghilev," *Musical Times*, 1 October 1929, p. 894.

54. "Sitter Out," "Modernism in the Dance," *Dancing Times*, July 1929, p. 320.

55. Eric Wollheim, Telegram to Serge Diaghilev, 1 October 1926, Stravinsky-Diaghilev Foundation; Lord Rothermere, Letter to Serge Diaghilev, [1926], Pièce 84, Fonds Kochno.

56. For a description of the Blue Train, see Paul Fussell, *Abroad: British Literary Traveling Between the Wars* (New York: Oxford Univ. Press, 1980), pp. 132–133.

57. Frank W.D. Ries, "Jean Cocteau and the Ballet," Diss. Indiana 1980, p. 167.

58. Nigel Wilkins, *The Writings of Erik Satie* (London: Eulenberg, 1981), p. 91; Darius Milhaud, *Notes Without Music: An Autobiography* (New York: Knopf, 1953), pp. 153–156.

59. Henri Matisse, Telegram to Serge Diaghilev, 30 January 1929; Michel Georges-Michel, Letter to Serge Diaghilev, [1929], Stravinsky-Diaghilev Foundation. Apparently, the decision to use Derain in *Jack-in-the-Box* rested with Comte Etienne de Beaumont, not Diaghilev. As owner of the musical performance rights, Beaumont authorized Diaghilev "to stage the ballet with decors and costumes by

Derain and in the orchestration of Darius Milhaud" during the Erik Satie Festival. Comte Etienne de Beaumont, Letter to Serge Diaghilev, 29 April 1926, Pièce 10, Fonds Kochno.

60. Wyndham Lewis, "The Russian Ballet the Most Perfect Expression of the High Bohemia," in *Time and Western Man* (New York: Harcourt, Brace, 1928), p. 32.

61. Arthur Gold and Robert Fizdale, *Misia: The Life of Misia Sert* (New York: Knopf, 1980), pp. 238, 245; Ries, "Jean Cocteau and the Ballet," p. 167.

62. Walter Nouvel, Telegram to Serge Diaghilev, 9 April 1925, Stravinsky-Diaghilev Foundation.

63. For a reminiscence of the group's Saturday night dinners after the war, see Jean Hugo, *Avant d'oublier 1918–1931* (Paris: Fayard, 1976), chap. 3.

64. Buckle, *Diaghilev*, p. 382.

65. Jean Cocteau, Letter to Serge Diaghilev, 24 October 1922, Pièce 23, Fonds Kochno.

66. Cocteau's scenario, published with the piano score of the ballet in 1924, is reproduced in English translation in Ries, "Jean Cocteau and the Ballet," Appendix D1, pp. 323–330.

67. Marie Laurencin, Jean Cocteau, Darius Milhaud, and Francis Poulenc, *Théâtre Serge de Diaghilew: Les Biches* (Paris: Editions des Quatre Chemins, 1924); Jean Cocteau, Georges Auric, Georges Braque, and Louis Laloy, *Théâtre Serge de Diaghilew: Les Fâcheux* (Paris: Editions des Quatre Chemins, 1924).

68. The articles in *Paris-Journal* and *Création* are reproduced in English translation in Nigel Wilkins, *The Writings of Erik Satie* (London: Eulenberg, 1981), pp. 73–74 and 111. Erik Satie, "Cahiers d'un mammifère," *Transatlantic Review*, 2, No. 2, p. 218.

69. Francis Steegmuller, *Cocteau: A Biography* (Boston: Little, Brown, 1970), pp. 321–323. Obviously, conflict of interest was not an issue for French critics of that era. The previous year, Laloy wrote the "French Festival" piece in the Monte Carlo season brochure.

70. Paul Morand, "Paris Letter. June 1924," *Dial*, July 1924, p. 67.

71. Haskell, *Diaghileff*, p. 312.

72. Typical is a letter from Milhaud's music publisher Heugel. "For the thirteenth time we confirm our claim and ask you, in conformity with your agreement of May 21, 1924, contract No. 13,786, to send us the sum of royalties payable for the performances of Darius Milhaud's "Train Bleu" given in London and Monte Carlo." Heugel, Editeurs de Musique, Letter to Serge Diaghilev, 17 March 1925, C-20–11.3, Serge Diaghilev Papers. In April 1928 the Society of Authors, Playwrights and Composers threatened legal action to force Diaghilev to pay Constant Lambert royalties for *Romeo and Juliet*. Herbert Thring, Letters to Walter Nouvel, 11 April and 20 April 1928, 10–10.3a and 10–10.3, Serge Diaghilev Correspondence.

73. Richard Buckle, *In Search of Diaghilev* (New York: Thomas Nelson, 1956), p. 94. According to Bakst, Picasso's "going rate" by 1921 was Frs. 6,000 per act even "when there were at most ten or twelve costume designs." Léon Bakst, Letter to Jacques Rouché, 29 December 1921, AJ13/1207, Archives Nationales.

74. Contract between Serge Diaghilev and Henri Matisse, 13 September 1919, Pièce 59, Fonds Kochno; contract between Serge Diaghilev and Michel Larionov, 15 March 1921, Pièce 51, Fonds Kochno; Serge Diaghilev, Letter to Comte Etienne

de Beaumont, 2 June 1926, in *Au Temps du Boeuf sur le Toit 1918–1928,* introd. Georges Bernier (Paris: Artcurial, 1981), p. 75; Serge Diaghilev, Letter to René Léon, 3 April 1924, Stravinsky-Diaghilev Foundation; contract between Serge Diaghilev and Pedro Pruna, 18 November 1924, Pièce 76; Maurice Utrillo, Letters to Serge Diaghilev, 18 March and 13 April 1926, Pièce 102; Georges Auric, Letter to Serge Diaghilev, 7 April 1924, Pièce 3; Henri Sauguet, Receipt, 2 May 1927, Pièce 88, Fonds Kochno.

75. Georges Auric, Letters to Serge Diaghilev, 7 April 1924 and 10 July 1925, Pièce 3, Fonds Kochno.

76. Boris Kochno, Letter to Georges Auric, 9 July 1925, Pièce 3, Fonds Kochno.

77. Georges Auric, Letter to Serge Diaghilev, 10 July 1925, Pièce 3, Fonds Kochno.

78. Universal-Edition A.G., Letter to Vittorio Rieti, 24 September 1925, C-20–13.2, Serge Diaghilev Papers. Gris's letter of 14 April 1921 is quoted in Kahnweiler, *Juan Gris,* p. 38.

79. Jacob, quoted in Douglas Cooper, *Picasso Theatre* (New York: Abrams, 1968), p. 35; Patrick O'Brian, *Picasso: A Biography* (New York: Putnam, 1976), p. 56.

80. Daniel-Henry Kahnweiler and Francis Crémieux, *My Galleries and Painters,* trans. Helen Weaver, introd. John Russell (New York: Viking Press, 1971), pp. 68, 71.

81. Wood is quoted in David Chadd and John Cage, *The Diaghilev Ballet in England,* foreword Richard Buckle, catalogue for an exhibition at the Sainsbury Centre for Visual Arts, University of East Anglia, 11 October–20 November 1979, p. 52; Paul Morand, "Paris Letter. July 1924," *Dial,* September 1924, p. 241. The Boeuf sur le Toit and the Jockey were popular watering spots among the denizens of High Bohemia.

82. Quoted in Virginia Woolf, *Roger Fry: A Biography* (New York: Harcourt, Brace, Jovanovich, 1976), p. 237.

83. For a partial listing of London exhibitions of Diaghilev's designers, see Frances Baldwin, "Critical Response in England to the Work of Designers for Diaghilev's Russian Ballet, 1911–1929," M.A. Thesis, Courtauld Institute of Art (London) 1980, Appendix 3; for Bakst, see Irina Proujan, *Léon Bakst: Esquisses de décors et de costumes, arts graphiques, peintures,* trans. Denis Dabbadie (Leningrad: Editions d'Art Aurora, 1986), pp. 227–230; for Gontcharova, see Mary Chamot, *Goncharova: Stage Designs and Paintings* (London: Oresko Books, 1979), p. 23.

84. In addition to the above, see G.E. Fussell, "The International Theatre Exhibition," *Dancing Times,* August 1922, pp. 937–939; G.E.F., "Russian and Other Pictures at the Redfern Gallery," *Dancing Times,* December 1925, p. 339.

85. I am grateful to Mary Ann de Vlieg for showing me the catalogue for this exhibition. The dates suggest that Diaghilev began collecting cubist and contemporary French work around in 1916.

86. During the 1926 summer season in London, Chelsea's New Chenil Galleries organized an exhibition of Lifar's collection. Macdonald, *Diaghilev Observed,* p. 337. A show was also planned for the 1928 American tour. Oliver Sayler, Letter to Serge Diaghilev, 8 June 1928, 10–17.1, Serge Diaghilev Correspondence.

87. Contracts between Serge Diaghilev and Henri Matisse, 13 September 1919,

Pièce 59; Michel Larionov, 15 March 1921, Pièce 51; and Pedro Pruna, 18 November 1924, Pièce 76, Fonds Kochno; Paul Rosenberg, Telegram to Serge Diaghilev, 4 May 1928, Stravinsky-Diaghilev Foundation.

88. Nikita D. Lobanov, Nina Lobanov, and Aimée Troyen, *Russian Theatre and Costume Designs From the Fine Arts Museums of San Francisco, January 19–March 9, 1980*, introd. John Bowlt, p. 45; *Le Tricorne: Ballet d'après les dessins en couleurs de Picasso* (Paris: Editions Paul Rosenberg, 1920); Juan Gris, Letters to Serge Diaghilev, 29 April 1921 and 9 December 1923, Pièce 39, Fonds Kochno.

89. The following full-page announcement appeared in the program for the 1921 Gaîté-Lyrique season: "Ballets Russes programs, published by *Comoedia Illustré* . . . are sought by all lovers of this admirable company, by all those interested in theatrical decoration, and by all lovers of fine books. Composed always of unpublished material, they form, together with the collection of *Comoedia Illustré* the most complete documentation of the work of Serge Diaghilev. Today, many programs are no longer to be found. Copies of others may be acquired from Comoedia Illustré, 32, rue Louis-le-Grand, Paris."

90. *La Danse*, April 1921, n.p.

91. "Sitter Out," *Dancing Times*, April 1922, p. 586.

92. *Collection des plus beaux programmes des Ballets russes de Serge de Diaghilew de 1909 à 1921* (Paris: M. de Brunoff, 1921); *L'Oeuvre de Léon Bakst pour la Belle au Bois Dormant*, introd. André Levinson (Paris, M. de Brunoff, 1922); Valerian Svetlov, *Anna Pavlova*, trans. W. Petroff (Paris: M. de Brunoff, 1922).

93. Between 1917 and 1931 the Beaumont Press brought out no fewer than twenty-six volumes of poems and letters. *A Bibliography of the Dance Collection of Doris Niles and Serge Leslie*, IV, annotated Serge Leslie, introd. Sir Sacheverell Sitwell (London: Dance Books, 1981), p. 13. For Beaumont's dance publishing activities, see his autobiographical *Bookseller at the Ballet, Memoirs Incorporating The Diaghilev Ballet in London, A Record of Bookselling, Ballet Going, Publishing, and Writing* (London: C.W. Beaumont, 1975).

94. The volumes on *Le Tricorne*, *Les Biches*, and *Les Fâcheux* have already been noted. Other examples are Valentin Parnakh, *Gontcharova et Larionow: l'art décoratif théâtral moderne* (Paris: Edition La Cible, 1919); W.A. Propert, *The Russian Ballet in Western Europe 1909–1920* (London: John Lane, 1921); Michel Georges-Michel, *Ballets russes, histoire anecdotique* (Paris: Editions du Monde nouveau, 1923); André Levinson, *Histoire de Léon Bakst* (Paris: Société d'Editions et de Librairie, 1924) and *La Danse d'aujourd'hui: Etudes, Notes, Portraits* (Paris: Duchartre et Van Buggenhoudt, 1929); Arnold Haskell, *Some Studies in Ballet* (London: Lanley, 1928).

95. Paul Morand, "Paris Letter. February 1927," *Dial*, March 1927, p. 234.

96. Grigoriev, *The Diaghilev Ballet*, p. 188.

97. *Ibid.*, p. 231.

98. Alice Nikitina, *Nikitina By Herself*, trans. Baroness Budberg (London: Alan Wingate, 1959), p. 33; Ninette de Valois, *Invitation to the Ballet* (London: John Lane, 1937), p. 46; "Paris Notes," *Dancing Times*, September 1926, p. 557.

99. Salaries in the music-halls, wrote René Bizet, "are inverse to the amount of clothing worn." "The *grand nu* who earns twenty-five francs a day has her physical charms to thank for such generosity . . . On the average, these women

are paid between five and six hundred francs a month." René Bizet, *L'Epoque du Music-Hall* (Paris: Editions du Capitole, 1927), pp. 45–46.

100. "Paris Notes," *Dancing Times*, September 1926, p. 557.

101. "Paris Notes," *Dancing Times*, January 1926, p. 465; de Valois, *Invitation to the Ballet*, p. 54.

102. Serge Diaghilev, Letter to René Léon, 3 April 1924, Stravinsky-Diaghilev Foundation.

103. de Valois, *Invitation to the Ballet*, p. 40.

104. Cited in *Catalogue of Decor and Costume Designs, Portraits, Manuscripts and Posters Principally for Ballet*, Sotheby's (London), 21 June 1973, Lot 48.

105. Grigoriev, *The Diaghilev Ballet*, pp. 208–209.

106. Grigoriev says they did not while in recent interviews Vilzak insists that they did. Carol H. Denny, "Viva Vilzak: On His Toes at Eighty-Six," *San Francisco Sunday Examiner and Chronicle*, 31 January 1982, p. 13; George Heymont, "A Real Charmer," *Ballet News*, February 1983, p. 16.

107. Grigoriev, *The Diaghilev Ballet*, p. 209; de Valois, *Invitation to the Ballet*, p. 68.

108. *Ibid.*, p. 58.

109. Dorothy Coxon, Letter to Serge Diaghilev, 29 July [1925], 10–4.2, Serge Diaghilev Correspondence.

110. Dorothy Coxon, Letter to Serge Diaghilev, [1926], 10–4.3, Serge Diaghilev Correspondence.

111. "Conversation with Karsavina," *Dancing Times*, June 1965, p. 460.

112. Tamara Karsavina, Letter to Serge Diaghilev, 30 April 1926, Pièce 43, Fonds Kochno; Payroll Sheet, 1 April–1 June 1926, Stravinsky-Diaghilev Foundation.

113. Solomon Volkov, *Balanchine's Tchaikovsky: Interviews with George Balanchine*, trans. Antonina W. Bouis (New York: Simon and Schuster, 1985), p. 211.

114. Quoted in John Martin, *Ruth Page: An Intimate Biography*, foreword Margot Fonteyn (New York: Marcel Dekker, 1977), p. 60.

115. de Valois, *Invitation to the Ballet*, pp. 59–60.

116. *Ibid.*, p. 46; Ninette de Valois, *Come Dance With Me: A Memoir* (London: Dance Books, 1973), p. 69.

117. *Ibid*; Jean Hugo, *Avant d'oublier 1918–1931* (Paris: Fayard, 1976), p. 63.

118. Quoted in Buckle, *Diaghilev*, p. 537.

Chapter 10. Paris: The Cultivated Audience

1. Arnold Bennett, "Russian Imperial Ballet at the Opera," *Paris Nights and Other Impressions of Places and People* (New York: George H. Doran, 1913), p. 67.

2. A[natole] Nekludoff, *Diplomatic Reminiscences Before and During the World War, 1911–1917*, 2nd ed., trans. Alexandra Paget (London: John Murray, 1920), p. 292. Comtesse Greffuhle also chaired the 1910 patronage committee.

3. "Un Monsieur de l'Orchestre," "La Soirée. La Saison russe au Châtelet," *Figaro,* 20 May 1909, p. 5; Regina, "Le Vernissage à l'exposition russe," *Figaro,* 16 October 1906, p. 2; Robert Brussel, "Concert de l'Exposition de l'Art Russe," *Figaro,* 7 November 1906, p. 3; Ch. D., "Rimsky-Korsakow à l'Opéra," *Figaro,* 15 May 1907, p. 5; C. D., "Dans la salle," *Figaro,* 17 May 1907, p. 5; Le Masque de Fer," "Echos," *Figaro,* 6 May 1909, p. 1, and 10 May 1909, p. 1; Raoul Brévannes, "Le Gala russe," *Figaro,* 19 May 1909, p. 4; Raoul Brévannes, "Le Second Gala russe," *Figaro,* 25 May 1909, p. 4; A.V. Lunacharsky, *V mire muzyki,* ed. G.B. Bernandt and I.S. Sats (Moscow, 1958), p. 507 (for 1907 patronage committee); *Boris Godunov* flyer, GA123–7, Gabriel Astruc Papers, Dance Collection, New York Public Library (for 1908 patronage committee); *"feuilles de location,"* AJ13/1292, Archives Nationales (Paris).

4. "Le Monde et la Ville," *Figaro,* 23 May 1909, p. 2.

5. For a list of French visitors to Bayreuth between 1876 and 1902, see Albert Lavignac, *Le Voyage Artistique à Bayreuth,* 5th ed. (Paris: Charles Delagrave, 1903), pp. 548–578, 601–617.

6. See, for instance, [Comte] Robert de Montesquiou, "Aubrey Beardsley," *Figaro,* 21 February 1907, p. 1; Georges Claretie, "L'auteur de 'Salomé'," *Figaro,* 1 April 1907, p. 1; Robert Brussel, "Avant 'Salomé'," *Figaro,* 6 May 1907, p. 4; "Un Monsieur de l'Orchestre," "La Soirée. Salomé au Châtelet," *Figaro,* 7 May 1907, p. 4; Gabriel Fauré, "Les Théâtres. Salomé," *Figaro,* 9 May 1907, p. 4; René Lara, "Notre Page Musicale," *Figaro,* 11 May 1907, p. 2; Emile Berr, "Salomé en fuite," *Figaro,* 15 May 1907, p. 4; Foemina, "Salomé," *Figaro,* 16 May 1907, p. 1.

7. Nicolas de Bénardaky was an ennobled Polish Jew who was "said to have gained his wealth as a tea-merchant. He had once been master of ceremonies at the court of the Tsar, and was still entitled to be called 'Your Excellency'." His daughter Marie was Proust's first schoolboy love. George D. Painter, *Marcel Proust: A Biography* (Harmondsmith, Middlesex: Penguin, 1977), I, p. 42. Bénardaky's 1909 visiting card, preserved in the Astruc Papers, identified him as "Conseiller d'Etat Actuel de Russie." Tereshchenko was a leading member of the Cadet Party, who served as Kerensky's Finance Minister after the February Revolution. Olga Crisp, "The Russian Liberals and the 1906 Anglo-French Loan to Russia," *Slavonic and East European Review,* 39 (1960–61), pp. 497–511; Lionel Kochan, *Russia in Revolution, 1890–1918* (London: Granada, 1970), pp. 118–119. Count Nostitz was Russia's military agent in France. "Le Monde et la Ville," *Figaro,* 8 May 1909, p. 2.

8. Debussy's second wife, Emma Bardac, *née* Moyse, had been the wife of a prominent Jewish financier, Sigismund Bardac, before marrying the composer. The Lyon family was in the piano business (Pleyel Lyon et Cie.), and Max Lyon's stepfather had been a Rothschild. A Gramont-Rothschild alliance gave Elisabeth Gramont, Duchesse de Clermont-Tonnerre, the writer and friend of Proust, a Rothschild stepfather as well. The family of the Marquise de Ganay, *née* Haber, was also prominent in the financial community. The Marquis de Ganay owned magnificent paintings by Reynolds, Goya, and Watteau, and at the couple's lavish receptions, the greatest singers of the day entertained. Alice Heine, a distant cousin of the poet, married the Duc de Richelieu and subsequently the Prince of Monaco. Edward Lockspeiser, *Debussy,* rev. ed. (London: J.M. Dent, 1963), p. 37; Philippe Jullian, *Robert de Montesquiou: A Fin-de-Siècle Prince,* trans. John Haylock and

Francis King (London: Secker and Warburg, 1965), pp. 73, 174, 186; Mina Curtiss, *Other People's Letters: A Memoir* (Boston: Houghton Mifflin, 1978), p. 44; Arsène Alexandre, "La Collection Camondo au Louvre," *Figaro*, 4 June 1914, p. 2; Courrier des Théatres," *Figaro*, 16 May 1908, p. 4; "Henri Deutsch de la Meurthe," *El Sol* (Madrid), 26 November 1919, p. 10; "Marquise de Ganay," *Femina*, 1 May 1922, p. 40; "Le Monde et la Ville," *Figaro*, 4 June 1908, p. 2; Gabriel Astruc, *Le Pavillon des fantômes* (Paris: Grasset, 1929), p. 5; *The Universal Jewish Encyclopedia* (1942); *Encyclopaedia Judaica* (New York: Macmillan, 1971); *Grosse Jüdische National-Biographie; Dictionnaire de Biographie Française* (Paris: Librairie Letouzey, 1951). Astruc's notes of possible contributors are in GA26–1/2/3, Astruc Papers.

9. See, for example, the list of boxholders for the *bals masqués* he organized on behalf of the Association des Directeurs de Théâtres de Paris at the Opéra in April 1914. AJ13/1286, Archives Nationales. In his memoirs Astruc singles out Camondo, that "most generous of Maecenas", for his unstinting generosity and support of all Astruc's many projects, including the Théâtre des Champs-Elysées. Astruc, *Le Pavillon des fantômes*, pp. 5, 264, 266.

10. "Feuilles de location," AJ13/1292, Archives Nationales.

11. Misia Sert, *Two or Three Muses* (London: Museum Press, 1953), p. 111. In addition to her memoirs, this account is drawn from Arthur Gold and Robert Fizdale, *Misia: The Life of Misia Sert* (New York: Knopf, 1980).

12. "Memoirs of the Late Princesse Edmond de Polignac," *Horizon*, August 1945, pp. 110–141; Michael de Cossart, *The Food of Love: Princesse Edmond de Polignac (1865–1953) and Her Salon* (London: Hamish Hamilton, 1978); [Comte] Alexandre de Gabriac, "La Vie de Paris. Un spectacle d'art," *Figaro*, 1 June 1908, p. 1; "Le Monde et la Ville," *Figaro*, 4 June 1908, p. 2; 13 April 1907, p. 2; 6 April 1908, p. 2; 6 May 1909, p. 2; Gabriel Astruc, "Rapport Confidentiel sur la Saison Russe," 19 November 1909, GA25–17, Astruc Papers.

13. *Dictionnaire de Biographie Française; Encyclopaedia Judaica;* Jullian, *Robert de Montesquiou*, p. 37; Painter, *Proust*, I, pp. 118–119; "Le Monde et la Ville," *Figaro*, 20 May 1907, p. 2; 25 May 1907, p. 2; 12 June 1909, p. 2; Serge Diaghilev, Telegram to Gabriel Astruc, 15 June 1912, GA74–26, Astruc Papers.

14. *The Memoirs of Count Witte*, trans. Abraham Yarmolinsky (London: Heinemann, 1921), p. 381; Jullian, *Robert de Montesquiou*, pp. 41, 223; *The Jewish Encyclopedia* (New York: Funk and Wagnalls, 1942).

15. In addition to the sources indicated above, see Paul H. Emden, *Money Powers of Europe in the Nineteenth and Twentieth Centuries* (London: Sampson Low, Marston, 1937), pp. 259–261.

16. Raymond Rudorff, *The Belle Epoque* (New York: Saturday Review Press, 1972), p. 245.

17. de Cossart, *The Food of Love*, pp. 65–67.

18. Erika Ostrovsky, *Eyes of Dawn: The Rise and Fall of Mata Hari* (New York: Macmillan, 1978), pp. 68–79; Marie Rambert, *Quicksilver: An Autobiography* (London: Macmillan, 1972), pp. 41–42; "Le Monde et la Ville," *Figaro*, 31 May 1907, p. 2; 13 May 1908, p. 2; 18 May 1908, p. 2; 10 June 1908, p. 2.

19. "Le Monde et la Ville," *Figaro*, 28 May 1907, p. 2; Arbie Orenstein, *Ravel: Man and Musician* (New York: Columbia Univ. Press, 1968), p. 54.

20. Robert Brussel, "Concert de l'Exposition de l'Art Russe," *Figaro*, 7 November 1906, p. 3; "L'Evolution musicale en Russie," *Figaro*, 28 February 1907,

p. 4; 11 March 1907, p. 4; 20 March 1907, p. 5; 26 March 1907, p. 5; 31 March 1907, p. 4; 1 April 1907, p. 4; 2 April 1907, p. 5; 1 May 1907, p. 6.

21. M.-D. Calvocoressi, "La Musique Russe," *Le Correspondant*, 10 May 1907, pp. 462–488, and "L'Avenir de la musique russe," *Mercure de France*, 16 May 1909, pp. 262–274; Louis Laloy, "La Musique russe," *La Grande Revue*, 10 June 1908, pp. 597–606, "Le Dit de la bande d'Igor et le prince Igor de Borodine," *La Grande Revue*, 25 May 1909, pp. 397–403, and "La Musique. La saison russe.— La *Flute enchantée*," *La Grande Revue*, 10 June 1909, pp. 607–610.

22. Paul Morand, "Paris Letter. May 1925," *Dial*, June 1925, p. 499.

23. Maurice Denis, *Journal*, II (Paris: La Colombe, 1957), p. 133.

24. Gold and Fizdale, *Misia*, pp. 231–232; Arthur Rubinstein, *My Young Years* (London: Cape, 1973), pp. 231–232.

25. Marcel Proust, *The Captive*, trans. C.K. Scott Moncrieff (New York: Vintage, 1970), pp. 164–165.

26. Gold and Fizdale, *Misia*, p. 23; Rubinstein, *My Young Years*, pp. 214, 230. Potocki was a member of Diaghilev's 1910 patronage committee. "Courrier des Théâtres," *Figaro*, 2 June 1910.

27. "Courrier des Théâtres," *Figaro*, 2 June 1910; Program, 23 June 1910, Stravinsky-Diaghilev Foundation (New York).

28. Geoffrey G. Field, *Evangelist of Race: The Germanic Vision of Houston Stewart Chamberlain* (New York: Columbia Univ. Press, 1981), chap. 7.

29. Albert Boime, "Entrepreneurial Patronage in Nineteenth-Century France," *Enterprise and Entrepreneurs in Nineteenth and Twentieth-Century France*, ed. Edward C. Carter II, Robert Forster, and Joseph N. Moody (Baltimore: Johns Hopkins Univ. Press, 1976), pp. 151–152.

30. Ostrovsky, *Eyes of Dawn*, ch. 10; Suzanne Sheldon, *Divine Dancer: A Biography of Ruth St. Denis* (Garden City, N.Y.: Doubleday, 1981), pp. 73–75.

31. Delhi, "La Vie de Paris. Le Goût Oriental," *Figaro*, 4 June 1913, p. 1.

32. Paul Morand, "Paris Letter. May 1925," *Dial*, June 1925, p. 154.

33. V. Serov, Letter to the Editor, *Rech'*, 22 September 1910. Serov's letter is an attack on the position articulated by Telyakovsky in an interview published in *Birzhvye vedomosti* (Stock Exchange Bulletin) a short time before. I am grateful to Professor Ilya Zilberstein for providing me with a copy of Serov's text.

34. H[enri] G[héon], "La Saison russe au Châtelet," *Nouvelle Revue Française*, September 1911, pp. 250–251.

35. Richard Buckle, *Diaghilev* (London: Weidenfeld and Nicolson, 1979), p. 154.

36. Igor Stravinsky and Robert Craft, *Memories and Commentaries* (Garden City, N.Y.: Doubleday, 1960), p. 77.

37. Painter, *Proust*, I, pp. 162–163, 101; "Memoirs of the Late Princesse de Polignac," pp. 132–133; "Le Monde et la Ville," *Figaro*, 13 April 1907, p. 2; "Courrier des Théâtres," *Figaro*, 11 May 1907, p. 4; "Le Monde et la Ville," *Figaro*, 13 May 1907, p. 2; 23 April 1909, p. 2; 1 May 1909, p. 2; "A Travers Paris," *Figaro*, 2 June 1912, p. 1; Ivor Guest, *Le Ballet de l'Opéra de Paris: Trois Siècles d'histoire et de tradition*, trans. Paul Alexandre (Paris: Théâtre National de l'Opéra, n.d.), p. 152.

38. Janet Flanner, *Paris Was Yesterday, 1925–1939*, ed. Irving Drutman (New York: Viking, 1972), p. 54.

39. George Barbier, "Le Vestiaire de Thalie," *Femina*, 1 December 1920, p. 8.

40. Serov, *Rech'*, 22 September 1910; Alfred H. Barr, *Matisse: His Art and His Public* (New York: Museum of Modern Art, 1951), pp. 132–135. Léger's 1914 "Exit the Ballets Russes" is reproduced in Magdalena Dabrowski, *Contrasts of Form: Geometric Abstract Art 1910–1980*, introd. John Elderfield (New York: Museum of Modern Art, 1985), p. 37.

41. Guillaume Apollinaire, "Futurisme et Ballets russes," *Chroniques d'art 1902–1918*, ed. L.-C. Breunig (Paris: Gallimard, 1960), p. 479, and in the same volume, "Nouvelle Musique," p. 476.

42. John Cournos, *Autobiography* (New York: Putnam, 1935), p. 212.

43. Charles Spencer, *Erté* (New York: Clarkson Potter, 1970), p. 23.

44. Paul Poiret, *My First Fifty Years* (London: Gollancz, 1931), pp. 90–91, 102–103, 176; Martin Battersby, "Diaghilev's Influence on Fashion and Decoration," in Charles Spencer and Philip Dyer, *The World of Serge Diaghilev* (Chicago: Henry Regnery, 1974), pp. 150–151.

45. Charles Spencer, *Léon Bakst* (London: Academy Editions, 1973), pp. 170–183; Virginia Cowles, *1913: The Defiant Swan Song* (London: Weidenfeld and Nicolson, 1967), pp. 165–167.

46. Louis Laloy, "La Musique: Les Ballets Russes. Igor Stravinski," quoted in Truman C. Bullard, "The First Performance of Igor Stravinsky's *Sacre du Printemps*," Diss. Rochester (Eastman School of Music) 1971, I, p. 26.

47. "Courrier des Théâtres," *Figaro*, 2 June 1910.

48. "Courrier des Théâtres," *Figaro*, 1 July 1910.

49. "Courrier des Théâtres," *Figaro*, 19, 23, and 25 June 1910.

50. Francis Steegmuller, *Cocteau: A Biography* (Boston: Little, Brown, 1970), pp. 74–75. The article in question was commissioned as a publicity text by Astruc and subsequently published in *Comoedia Illustré*. For his services, Cocteau billed Astruc's Société Musicale 100 francs. Diaghilev exploited Cocteau's writing skills on other occasions. His front-page letter to the editor of *Figaro* protesting the newspaper's scurrilous attack on *L'Après-midi d'un Faune* was actually drafted by Cocteau. Gaston Calmette, "A propos d'un faune," *Figaro*, 31 May 1912, p. 1. Cocteau's handwritten draft is in the Jean Cocteau Collection, George Arents Research Library, Syracuse University.

51. Igor Stravinsky, *Stravinsky: An Autobiography* (New York: Simon and Schuster, 1936), p. 47. The Opéra records for the *Giselle* preview, which took place on 17 June 1910, are in AJ13/1292, Archives Nationales. Astruc exploited this technique for non-Diaghilev events as well. On 9 June 1913 *Figaro* reported a "most interesting private recital of a new opera" by the Italian composer Ildebrando da Parma, author of the music for Ida Rubinstein's *La Pisanelle*, which opened at the Théâtre du Châtelet two days later. The singer was Madame Golouboff, a well-known figure in the Paris Russian colony, and the guests included Misia Edwards (Sert), Princesse de Polignac, Claude Debussy and his wife, Chaliapin, Gabriele d'Annunzio, Count Harry Kessler, Jean Cocteau, José-María Sert, and the Russian Ambassador. "Le Monde et la Ville," *Figaro*, 9 June 1913, p. 3, col. 6.

52. *The Journals of Andre Gide*, ed. and trans. Justin O'Brien (New York: Knopf, 1947), I, pp. 265–266.

53. Edmonde Charles-Roux, *Chanel—Her Life, Her World and the Woman Behind the Legend She Herself Created*, trans. Nancy Amphoux (New York: Knopf, 1975), p. 125; Gold and Fizdale, *Misia*, pp. 42–51; Painter, *Proust*, I, p. 132.

54. A[ndré] G[ide], "Les représentations russes au Châtelet," *Nouvelle Revue Française*, I, No. 1, p. 546; Jacques-Emile Blanche, "Les Décors de l'Opéra russe," *Figaro*, 29 May 1909, p. 1.

55. S.L. Grigoriev, *The Diaghilev Ballet 1909–1929*, trans. and ed. Vera Bowen (London: Constable, 1953), pp. 28–29.

56. Doris J. Monteux, *It's All in the Music* (New York: Farrar, Straus and Giroux, 1965), p. 90; Bullard, "First Performance," I, p. 152; Charles-Roux, *Chanel—Her Life*, p. 125.

57. Jules Claretie, "La Vie à Paris," *Le Temps*, 21 May 1909, p. 2, col. 5. See also Raoul Brévannes, "Le Gala russe," *Figaro*, 19 May 1909, p. 4.

58. Miguel Zamacoïs, "Lettre à mon neveu sur la Danse," *Figaro*, 12 June 1913, p. 1.

59. Irene Castle, *Castles in the Air*, as told to Bob and Wanda Duncan (Garden City, N.Y.: Doubleday, 1958), pp. 56–58, 79–80; E. Cornuche, Letters to Gabriel Astruc, 22 June 1912 and 1 July 1912, GA115–7, GA115–8, Astruc Papers. The Casino selected and contracted entertainment for the resort.

60. "Le Monde et la Ville," *Figaro*, 9 June 1913, p. 3; Ververt, "La Vie de Paris. Danses d'autrefois. Une Fête chez la comtesse de Béarn," *Figaro*, 8 June 1913, p. 1; Régina, "La Nuit Blanche," *Figaro*, 2 June 1913, p. 3.

61. Charles-Roux, *Chanel—Her Life*, pp. 118–120. The Bakst poster is reproduced in illustration 60.

62. *Ibid.*, pp. 122–126.

63. "The New Lawn Tennis Ballet," *Dancing Times*, June 1913, p. 579; "Courrier des Théâtres," *Figaro*, 14 May 1913, p. 5; 19 May 1913, p. 7; 1 July 1910; 23 May 1913, p. 6; 11 June 1913, p. 5.

64. Carl Van Vechten, *Fragments From an Unwritten Autobiography* (New Haven: Yale Univ. Library, 1955), II, p. 20; Roland-Manuel, "Le Sacre du Printemps," quoted in Bullard, "First Performance," I, p. 107; Gabriel Astruc, "A Propos d'un temple enseveli," quoted *ibid.*, I, p. 105.

65. Léon Vallas, "*Le Sacre du Printemps*," quoted *ibid.*, I, p. 108.

66. *Ibid.*, I, p. 72; Astruc, *Le Pavillon des fantômes*, pp. 274–275; Rubinstein, *My Young Years*, pp. 231–232; Paul Bochin, "Le Conflit des Musiciens," *Le Journal*, 28 April 1911, GA122–2, Astruc Papers. The first caricature, by Jean Gast, was reproduced in the London *Bystander*. Gabriel Astruc, Clipping File, Dance Collection. The second, "La Saison italienne à Paris," by Sem, appeared in *Figaro*, 17 May 1910, p. 3.

67. Contract between M. Cornuche and Serge Diaghilev, 30 December 1911, GA64–16, Astruc Papers.

Chapter 11. London: Lords, Ladies, and Literati

1. Dame Marie Rambert, "What the Diaghileff Ballet Meant to Us," in *Ballet Decade*, ed. Arnold Haskell (London: Adam and Charles Black, 1956), p. 203.

2. During the company's 1911 and 1912 summer seasons, for instance, Diaghilev's works were frequently paired with the one-act operas *Pagliacci* and *Il*

Segreto di Susanna. In winter 1913 *Carnaval* and Richard Strauss's *Salomé* made up an unlikely bill. Diaghilev's last prewar season teamed *Le Rossignol*, in its original operatic version, with *Midas* and *Schéhérazade, Le Coq d'Or* with *Schéhérazade* or *Narcisse*, and *May Night* with *Petrouchka*.

3. Francis Toye, "Opera in England," *English Review*, December 1911, p. 159. *Saturday Review* critic John Runciman echoed this view. "What has Covent Garden to do with opera?" he asked in 1913. "Nominally, of course, a very great deal: in practice next to nothing. The centre of interest is the auditorium, not the stage. The success of the season is not Melba, Caruso or another, but the lady who appears in the boxes with the smallest amount of clothing above the waist and whose headgear and the rest represent the vastest sum of money." John F. Runciman, "Opera of To-day and Yesterday," *Saturday Review*, 26 July 1913, p. 107.

4. Henry Hardinge, "A Word on the Hammerstein Opera," *English Review*, March 1912, p. 724. In summer 1912 Puccini's *Madama Butterfly, La Bohème, La Fanciulla del West*, and *Tosca* claimed fully a quarter of the "Grand Season's" offerings. Verdi was represented by *Aïda, Rigoletto*, and *La Traviata*, Rossini by *The Barber of Seville*, Leoncavallo by *I Pagliacci*, and Wolf-Ferrari by *Il Segreto di Susanna* and *I Giogelli della Madonna*. The other works produced that season were Charpentier's *Louise*, Meyerbeer's *Les Huguenots* (italianized as *Gli Ugonotti*), Massenet's *Manon*, and Zandonai's *Conchita*.

5. "It is overwhelmingly a sign of the times, is it not," began a *Bystander* article in the autumn of 1911, when Diaghilev shared the stage at the Royal Opera House with Wagner's *Ring*, "this rage for Russian Ballet, this craze for dancing at Covent Garden, which has put mere opera into quite suburban shade (compare clothes, also jewels on 'Ring' nights with clothes, also jewels, when the Russian Ballet dances) . . ." O.M.D., "Society's Love of the Wordless Play," *Bystander*, 15 November 1911, p. 332. For "second-rate Italians," see the review of the books *The Russian Opera* by Rosa Newmarch and *History of Russian Music* by H. Montague Nathan, *English Review*, June 1914, p. 568.

6. "The Woman About Town," *Sketch*, 17 April 1912, p. 63.

7. The intellectual periodicals include the *Fortnightly Review, Edinburgh Review*, and *English Review* as well as weeklies such as the *New Age, Athenaeum, Nation, Saturday Review, Outlook*, and *New Statesman*. The *Athenaeum* "noted" Diaghilev premieres, usually in brief items in its "Musical Gossip" column. The *Outlook* gave more extended coverage to Ballets Russes productions, but as its reviews were usually written by Edwin Evans, they focused almost exclusively on the music. Only the *New Statesman*, which began publication in the spring of 1913, gave regular coverage to Diaghilev's ballet works. By contrast, the society-oriented *Sketch* and *Bystander* referred repeatedly to Diaghilev events, while also publishing photographs and reviews of productions.

8. H. Saxe Wyndham, *Royal Opera and Imperial Russian Ballet. Coronation Season Covent Garden 1911. Containing the Plots of the Operas and Ballets and Biographical Sketches with Portraits of the Singers and Dancers* (London: John Long, 1911).

9. In 1914 a West End theatergoer could expect to pay half a guinea for a seat in the stalls, nearly £13 at 1981 prices. (Tom Sutcliffe, "Has the Arts Council Outlived its Usefulness?" *Guardian*, 27 January 1981, p. 9.) At Diaghilev's performances, by contrast, a guinea was the prevailing rate, and there were even programs for which orchestra tickets rose to twenty-five and thirty shillings. A shilling

bought a gallery bench in the West End, but at Drury Lane in 1913, places in the amphitheater cost four and even five times as much. Orchestra stalls were by no means the most expensive seats in the house. In autumn 1911 the price for a single ticket in a pit or grand tier box cost four guineas, while at Drury Lane in 1913 and 1914 an individual place in the most expensive boxes sold for twice that sum. For the first time in many decades, ballet in London commanded the prices of opera.

10. "Covent Garden audiences have not wanted for the excuses of a fancy-dress gathering to seize upon the garments that most snugly fit the aesthetics of the moment. Mrs. Brown Potter's turban, when, not many nights ago, she entered a box in the picturesque company of Baroness de Meyer, twisted all eyes from the stage." "Crowns, Coronets, Courtiers," *Sketch,* 15 November 1911, p. 172.

11. "Sitter Out," *Dancing Times,* September 1913, p. 730; "Crowns, Coronets, Courtiers," *Sketch,* 15 November 1911, p. 172.

12. "The Fancy Dress Ball Craze," *Dancing Times,* February 1913, p. 412; "My Lady Fair. Debenham and Freebody," *ibid.,* p. 405; "My Lady Fair. At the Pantomime Ball," *Dancing Times,* January 1913, p. 267; "My Lady Fair. The Versailles Ball," *Dancing Times,* June 1913, p. 595; Diana Cooper, *The Rainbow Comes and Goes* (Boston: Houghton Mifflin, 1958), p. 83; "Lady Diana Goes to the Ballet," *English Review,* August 1911, pp. 167–169. This piece is attributed to Gordon Craig and reprinted in *Gordon Craig on Movement and Dance,* ed. and introd. Arnold Rood (New York: Dance Horizons, 1977), pp. 77–79.

13. Virginia Woolf, *The Years* (New York: Harcourt, Brace and World, 1965), p. 254.

14. "Russian Ballet at Covent Garden," *Dancing Times,* February 1913, p. 379.

15. "The Beecham Opera Season. List of Subscribers," *Times,* 20 January 1913, p. 9; "Russian Opera at Drury Lane. Subscribers to Sir J. Beecham's Season," *Times,* 20 June 1913, p. 10; "Opera at Drury Lane. Subscribers for Beecham Season," *Times,* 8 May 1914, p. 11.

16. O.M.D., "Parliament as the Stepping Stone to Society," *Bystander,* 27 December 1911, p. 686.

17. Except where otherwise noted, my sources are the *Sketch* (especially, the columns "The Woman About Town," "Crowns, Coronets, Courtiers," "Small Talk," and Ella Hepworth Dixon's "Woman's Ways"), and the *Bystander* ("At Court and in Society"), the "Court Circular" column of the *Times,* reviews of Diaghilev events in that newspaper from 1913–1914, and the published subscription lists cited in note 15 above.

18. Affairs of state rarely kept Asquith from a night out at the ballet. A bit of verse written to his *petite amie* Venetia Stanley in July 1913 records his devotion: "A hasty rubber: off I hie/Where Beecham rules the scene:/And sample for the 20th time/Nijinsky, Chaliapine." H. H. Asquith, *Letters to Venetia Stanley,* ed. Michael and Eleanor Brock (New York: Oxford Univ. Press, 1982), p. 32. Other references to Diaghilev productions appear in his letters of 24 June and 22 July 1914. Asquith's granddaughters Helena and Perdita, along with the children of several other Cabinet ministers, had private dance classes in 1914 with Marie Rambert. Marie Rambert, *Quicksilver: An Autobiography* (London: Macmillan, 1972), p. 85.

19. R. C. K. Ensor, *England 1870–1914* (Oxford: Clarendon Press, 1936),

pp. 610–614; *Who's Who* (1914); *Almanach de Gotha* (1914), pp. 855–860. Other high officials and empire-builders in Diaghilev's audience were Lord Lucas, Parliamentary Secretary to the Board of Agriculture; Earl Howe, Lord Chamberlain to Queen Alexandra; Baron Sandhurst, Lord Chamberlain; Harold Tennant (brother-in-law of Prime Minister Asquith), Under-Secretary to the War Office; Sir Frank Swettenham; the Hon. Charles Fortescue and his brother Sir Seymour Fortescue.

20. "Small Talk," *Sketch*, 15 April 1914, p. 60.

21. "The King and Queen," announced the *Times* in March 1913, "have granted their patronage to the Royal Opera, Covent Garden for the forthcoming season." "Court Circular," *Times*, 4 March 1913, p. 11. Their Majesties' presence at Covent Garden was frequently noted that season as well as the following summer. In July 1913 they paid only one visit to the rival house in Drury Lane—for a performance of *Boris Godunov*. "Court Circular," *Times*, 22 July 1913, p. 11. For the Princess Royal and Princess Maud, see "Court Circular," *Times*, 27 May 1914, p. 11.

22. "Mrs. Asquith's 'At Home'," *Times*, 16 July 1914, p. 11.

23. Margot Asquith, *The Autobiography of Margot Asquith* (London: Thornton Butterworth, 1920), pp. 173–200; Daphne Fielding, *The Rainbow Picnic: A Portrait of Iris Tree* (London: Methuen, 1974), pp. 28–32.

24. Osbert Sitwell, *Great Morning: An Autobiography* (London: Reprint Society, 1948), p. 250.

25. Cooper, *Rainbow*, p. 77.

26. Sitwell, *Great Morning*, pp. 252–253.

27. Philippe Jullian and John Phillips, *Violet Trefusis: Life and Letters* (London: Hamish Hamilton, 1976), pp. 32–33; *Catalogue of Dance, Theatre, Opera, Music Hall and Film*, Sotheby's (New York), 21 November 1984, Lot 42.

28. "Lorgnette," *Bystander*, 15 November 1911, pp. 328–330. The Tennant wealth derived from great chemical works in Glasgow. Both Lord Glenconner and his brother Harold John Tennant entered politics under the Liberal banner. *Who's Who* entries for 1914 often indicate the existence and location of major collections as well as the artists represented.

29. "Small Talk," *Sketch*, 12 July 1911, p. 8; Tamara Karsavina, *Theatre Street: The Reminiscences of Tamara Karsavina*, foreword J.M. Barrie (London: Heinemann, 1930), p. 279; Arthur Gold and Robert Fizdale, *Misia: The Life of Misia Sert* (New York: Knopf, 1980), p. 218. Mrs. Bradley Martin was the daughter of Isaac Sherman, a New York railroad financier and confidant of Abraham Lincoln. A lavish dinner party given by her husband at Delmonico's during the depression of the 1890s was the subject of a famous caricature of the period.

30. Among these were the Marquess of Ripon, a trustee of the Wallace Collection and longstanding member of the board of Covent Garden; Baron Weardale, a trustee of the National Portrait Gallery; Sir Claude Phillips, keeper of the Wallace Collection, 1897–1911; Sir Sidney Colvin, former Slade Professor and keeper of prints and drawings, British Museum, 1884–1912; stage designer Charles Ricketts, coeditor of the *Dial*, 1889–1897, publisher of Vale Books and publications, 1896–1904, and author of books on Titian and the Prado; Robert Cust, who wrote extensively on Italian Renaissance art; artists John Singer Sargent, Sir George Frampton, Sir William Goscombe John, James Shepherd, Edmund Dulac, and Glyn Philpot. Sargent drew Nijinsky (at the request of Lady Ripon) and made several drawings of Karsavina.

31. For Baron and Baroness de Meyer, "Chaliapin's Farewell. End of the Drury Lane Opera Season," *Times*, 25 July 1914, p. 6; for Melba, " 'Die Zauberflöte'. Mozart's Opera at Drury Lane. Mr. T. Beecham's Conducting," *Times*, 22 May 1914, p. 10; for Caruso and Tetrazzini, "Notes From the Opera Houses," *Sketch*, 10 June 1914, p. "I"; for the Sitwells, Osbert Sitwell, *Great Morning*, pp. 236, 243 *et seq.*; for the Drapers, Muriel Draper, *Music at Midnight* (New York: Harper, 1929), pp. 135 *et seq.*; for George Bernard Shaw, Letter to the Editor, *Nation*, 18 July 1914; rpt. *Shaw's Music: The Complete Musical Criticism*, ed. Dan H. Laurence (New York: Dodd, Mead, 1981), II, p. 661.

32. For Osbert Sitwell, *Great Morning*, pp. 136–140; for Lady Constance Stewart-Richardson, "Court Circular," *Times*, 15 November 1911, p. 11. Mrs. Patrick Campell subscribed to the winter 1913 season under her married name, Mrs. George Cornwallis West. Ellen Terry's book *The Russian Ballet* was published in 1913. Osbert, a member of the elite Grenadier Guards from 1913–1919, hobnobbed with both the elder and younger generations of "Souls." Lady Constance's defiance of convention by taking to the professional stage invited no little ridicule in the press.

33. "Notes From the Opera Houses," *Sketch*, 10 June 1914, p. "I."

34. "Notes From the Opera Houses," *Sketch*, 8 July 1914, p. XII.

35. "Der Rosenkavalier. First Production in England. Opening of Mr. Beecham's Spring Season," *Times*, 30 January 1913, p. 6.

36. Also in the repertory were Wagner's *Tristan* (two performances) and *Die Meistersinger* (four performances).

37. "The Russian Ballet. Triple Bill at Covent Garden," *Times*, 5 February 1913, p. 8.

38. Sitwell, *Great Morning*, p. 256.

39. Ernest Newman, Letter to the Editor, *Nation*, 26 March 1910; rpt. in *Shaw's Music*, III, p. 612.

40. "There is no need of a missioner in the cause of the moderns now, for are we not all panting to hear *The Legend of Joseph?* But Mozart—yes, there is certainly room for a Mozart mission when one hears people in the stalls informing their neighbours that probably *Die Zauberflöte* has been heard some time between the eighteenth century and this, but that this is practically its first performance." " 'Die Zauberflöte'. Mozart's Opera at Drury Lane. Mr. T. Beecham Conducting," *Times*, 22 May 1914, p. 10. In fact, the opera had been produced at Cambridge in 1911 and, not long before the Drury Lane production, in Leeds. W. Denis Browne, "Die Zauberflöte," *New Statesman*, 30 May 1914, p. 245. The drop curtain for the work was painted by Vladimir Polunin, identified in the *Times* review as a "disciple" of Bakst. After the war Polunin became Diaghilev's chief scene painter.

41. William Butler Yeats, "Introduction to *Certain Noble Plays of Japan* by Pound and Feneollosa," in Ezra Pound and Ernest Fenollosa, *The Classic Noh Theatre of Japan* (New York: New Directions, 1959), p. 155.

42. S.L.B., "Notes From the Opera Houses," *Sketch*, 30 July 1913, p. 128.

43. S.L.B., "Notes From the Opera Houses," *Sketch*, 16 July 1913, p. XII.

44. S.L.B., "Notes From the Opera Houses," *Sketch*, 30 July 1913, p. 128. "We Take Off Our Hats To . . . M. Nijinsky—for so amply proving how he hates the word 'grace' by his production of 'Sacre du Printemps' . . . Discussing his production of the Cubist dance 'Le Sacre du Printemps,' M. Nijinsky said, 'I am accused of a crime against "grace." ' . . . Really, I begin to have a horror of the

very word; "grace" and "charm" make me feel seasick.' " *Sketch*, 23 July 1913, p. 68. As its cover that week, the *Sketch* had a drawing by W. Heath Robinson of a ballerina in a tutu flanked by cherubim with a caption reading: "Exiled by Order of Nijinsky: The Spirit of the Old Regime." Another caption linked *Sacre* to one of the most controversial prewar art events: Roger Fry's first Post-Impressionist Exhibition. "Nijinsky's Revolution in Choreography: The Post-Impressionist and Prehistoric Dance 'Sacre du Printemps'." "The Twitching, Bobbing Turn-Your-Toes-In Cubist Dance," *Sketch* [Supplement], 23 July 1913, p. 5.

45. S.L.B., "Notes From the Opera Houses," *Sketch*, 23 July 1913, p. XII.

46. "At the Opera Houses," *Sketch*, 17 June 1914, p. "h."

47. " 'The Nightingale.' New Opera and Ballet at Drury Lane," *Times*, 19 June 1914, p. 10.

48. "Return of the Russian Ballet. Ravel's 'Daphnis and Chloé'," *Times*, 10 June 1914, p. 11; S.O., "The Russians at Drury Lane," *English Review*, June 1914, p. 562.

49. "A Medieval Joseph. Strauss's New Ballet and Its Music. Spectacular Splendours," *Times*, 24 June 1914, p. 11.

50. Bakst's line of offstage gowns, inspired, so he claimed, by the contemporary setting of *Jeux*, was very much in the news in 1913, as was his Fine Arts Society Exhibition and Arsène Alexandre's *The Decorative Art of Léon Bakst*, the publication of which coincided, as did these other activities, with Diaghilev's summer season. The tennis setting and movement style of Nijinsky's ballet gave rise to numerous sallies in the society press, including the series of caricatures "Jeux d'Esprit: Suggestions For the Russian Ballet," published in the *Sketch* on 2 July 1913 (pp. 408–409).

51. S.O., "The Russians at Drury Lane," pp. 562–564.

52. "London's Opera Seasons," *Sketch*, 5 August 1914, p. 162.

53. *Ibid.*, p. 164.

54. "Defaulting Guests. The Hostess's Permanent Dilemma," *Times*, 30 June 1914, p. 11. In 1914 Chaliapin received £100 a performance, the reason no doubt that four and five shillings were added to the cost of a ticket in the orchestra or grand circle on "Special Chaliapine Nights." "Opera in London. The Competition of the Old and New. Sir Joseph Beecham's Plans," *Times*, 13 May 1914, p. 6. See also Cooper, *Rainbow*, p. 84, and S.L.B., "Notes From the Opera Houses," *Sketch*, 30 July 1913, p. 128.

55. "Last Night at Drury Lane. Sir Joseph Beecham and Another Season," *Times*, 27 July 1914, p. 11.

56. Edward Speyer, Letter to the Editor, *Times*, 18 July 1914, p. 6; William de Morgan, Letter to the Editor, *Times*, 20 July 1914, p. 10; G. N. Sutton, Letter to the Editor, *Times*, 21 July 1914, p. 11; Edith Lyttelton and "Sufferer," Letters to the Editor, *Times*, 22 July 1914, p. 10.

57. "Another Sufferer," Letter to the Editor, *Times*, 25 July 1914, p. 6. Arnold Bennett also deplored the musical bad manners of Diaghilev's audience. "The mere social behaviour of the moneyed seatholders," he wrote in April 1913, "was as atrocious as it is during the regular season. Wishing to see and hear well some of the Russian ballets, I committed the imprudence of taking a box on the grand tier. I saw the ballet. What I heard was the boisterous antics of a party of picnickers in the box on my left, and the boisterous antics of another party of picnickers in the box on my right. Similar phenomena, I willingly admit, are to be observed

at the Paris Opera, and worse at the Scala at Milan. But the Brussels Monnaie is better, and the New York Opera House is much better." Arnold Bennett, "Music and Art at Covent Garden," *New Statesman,* 19 April 1913, pp. 51–52.

58. S.O., "The Russians at Drury Lane," p. 561.

59. "Chaliapin's Farewell. End of the Drury Lane Opera Season," *Times,* 25 July 1914, p. 6.

60. "Last Night of Drury Lane. Sir Joseph Beecham and Another Season," *Times,* 27 July 1914, p. 11.

61. Leonard Woolf, *Beginning Again: An Autobiography of the Years 1911 to 1918* (New York: Harcourt Brace Jovanovich, 1963), p. 37.

62. *Ibid.,* p. 20.

63. *Ibid.,* pp. 48–49.

64. Shaw, of course, was a music critic of long standing, a fervent admirer of both Wagner and Strauss. During his sojourn in Paris, Bennett became good friends with M.D. Calvocoressi, the musicologist who assisted Diaghilev in 1907–1908 and introduced Bennett to Cipa Godebski's musical salon. In January 1911 the *English Review* published Bennett's backstage impressions of the Ballets Russes in Paris, which later appeared in *Paris Nights and Other Impressions of Places and People.* Bennett's screed against Diaghilev's ill-mannered audience, written for the banner issue of the *New Statesman,* opened with a similar complaint about the first night audience for *Rosenkavalier.* There are also passing mentions of Diaghilev artists and productions in Bennett's diaries and letters. Margaret Drabble, *Arnold Bennett* (London: Weidenfeld and Nicolson, 1974), p. 150; Arnold Bennett, "Paris Nights," *English Review,* January 1911, pp. 243–257; *Paris Nights and Other Impressions of Places and People* (New York: George H. Doran, 1913); "Music and Art at Covent Garden," *New Statesman,* 19 April 1913, pp. 51–52; Arnold Bennett, Letter to Cedric Sharpe, 13 September 1913, *Letters of Arnold Bennett,* ed. James Hepburn (London: Oxford Univ. Press, 1966), II, p. 335; *The Journals of Arnold Bennett, 1911–1921,* ed. Newman Flower (London: Cassell, 1932), pp. 12, 177. Only Compton MacKenzie, a popular novelist from a distinguished theatrical family, seems to have "moved on" to the Ballets Russes from music-hall ballet rather than opera. Compton MacKenzie, *My Life and Times, Octave 4* (London: Chatto and Windus, 1965), pp. 130–132.

65. Leonard Woolf, *Beginning Again,* p. 49; Quentin Bell, *Virginia Woolf: A Biography* (New York: Harcourt Brace Jovanovich, 1972), I, p. 149.

66. Virginia Woolf, Letters to Lytton Strachey, 18 May 1908, 1 and 9 February 1909, *Virginia Woolf and Lytton Strachey Letters,* ed. Leonard Woolf and James Strachey (New York: Harcourt Brace, 1956), pp. 11, 34–35; Quentin Bell, *Virginia Woolf,* I, p. 149.

67. Virginia Woolf, Letter to Katherine Cox, 16 May 1913, *The Letters of Virginia Woolf,* ed. Nigel Nicolson and Joanne Trautmann (New York: Harcourt Brace Jovanovich, 1976), II, p. 26.

68. Quentin Bell, *Virginia Woolf,* I, p. 149n.

69. Virginia Woolf, Letters to Lytton Strachey, 6 and 20 November 1911, *Virginia Woolf and Lytton Strachey Letters,* pp. 45–46.

70. Quentin Bell, *Virginia Woolf,* II, pp. 4, 12.

71. E. M. Forster, "A Shrine for Diaghilev," *Observer,* 25 December 1955, p. 4. The recent edition of Forster's letters contains three references to the prewar Ballets Russes. On July 28, 1911, the novelist attended a matinee of *Le Pavillon*

d'Armide, Les Sylphides, and *Schéhérazade.* The following summer he was "lucky to get a seat" for a performance of *Les Sylphides, Firebird,* and *Carnaval* on June 20. Writing of a Mystery Play he saw in India, Forster described the performance as "[working] up to a real crisis, like the Russian Ballet." "To Malcolm Darling," 29 July 1911, Letter 94; "To Forrest Reid," 19 June 1912, Letter 104; "To Alice Clara Forster, 1 December 1912, Letter 113, *Selected Letters of E. M. Forster,* ed. Mary Lago and P. N. Furbank (Cambridge: Harvard Univ. Press, 1983), I, pp. 122, 136, 165.

72. Christopher Hassall, *Rupert Brooke: A Biography* (New York: Harcourt, Brace and World, 1964), pp. 265, 380, 449; Rupert Brooke, Letters to Erica Cotterill and Jacques Raverat, 18 September 1911 and July 1914, *The Letters of Rupert Brooke,* ed. Geoffrey Keynes (London: Faber and Faber, 1968), pp. 314, 595; Michael Holroyd, *Lytton Strachey: A Critical Biography* (New York: Holt, Rinehart and Winston, 1968), II, p. 28n. Also present on the dramatic occasion in the Drury Lane foyer was Lytton's brother James, the future pyschoanalyst who published a bibliography of dancing in 1919. James Strachey, "Bibliography of the Ballet," *Drama,* 1, No. 3 (December 1919), 71–73.

73. Clive Bell, "The New Ballet," *New Republic,* 30 July 1919, p. 414; John Maynard Keynes, Letter to Lytton Strachey, 17 July 1911, quoted in Robert Skidelsky, *John Maynard Keynes: A Biography* (London: Macmillan, 1983), I, pp. 259, 279.

74. Holroyd, *Lytton Strachey,* II, pp. 94–95.

75. Leonard Woolf, *Beginning Again,* pp. 127–131; Desmond MacCarthy, *Experience* (New York: Oxford Univ. Press, 1935), pp. x–xv. Desmond MacCarthy joined the staff of the *New Statesman* as drama critic in 1913 and became literary editor in 1920. In 1913–1914 Woolf attended the journal's weekly lunches and contributed unsigned as well as signed articles. In early 1914 Rupert Brooke wrote that while the *Nation* was better written, the *New Statesman* "represents my views more." Rupert Brooke, Letter to Mrs. Brooke, 7 January 1914, *Letters,* p. 560. The minority opinion voiced by the *Nation* was written by Francis Toye ("The Newer Russian Ballets," 2 August 1913, pp. 675–676).

76. I., "The Russian Ballet. I," *New Statesman,* 5 July 1913, pp. 406–407; I., "The Russian Ballet. II," *New Statesman,* 19 July 1913, pp. 469–470; I., "The Russian Ballet: A Postscript," *New Statesman,* 26 July 1913, p. 501. An article on Mussorgsky and Rimsky-Korsakov by the same critic appeared in the July 12 issue (p. 438). Most unusually, the journal took no notice of the rival season at Covent Garden.

77. "The Russian Ballet. II," p. 470. Edward Marsh, a friend of Rupert Brooke's who described *Jeux* as a "Post-Impressionist picture put in motion," reversed his initial opinion of *Sacre,* thanks to W. Denis Browne, another close friend of Brooke's, who wrote music reviews for the *New Statesman* in 1914. "I told you in my last letter," Marsh reported to Brooke in July 1913, "how he loved it and I hated it the first time. He gave me a lecture, and said my mistake had been to listen too much to the music—and that just as oxygen and hydrogen, tho' disgusting separately, made a delicious compound . . . so the cacophonous music and the ungracious gestures melted into a perfectly harmonious whole . . . I went again, followed his instructions, and succeeded in being ravished with delight." Edward Marsh, Letter to Rupert Brooke, [July 1913], quoted in Christopher Hassall, *Edward March: Patron of the Arts, A Biography* (London: Longmans, 1959), pp. 238–239.

78. Edward Hyams, *The New Statesman: The History of the First Fifty Years,* introd. John Freeman (London: Longmans, 1963), chaps. 2–3.

79. The music critic Edwin Evans (who addressed "a few preliminary remarks to the audience" before the curtain went up on *Sacre*) may well have been referring to the *Nation* and *New Statesman* milieux when he wrote in his own review of the ballet: "M. Nijinsky's new principles of choreography have found acceptance in some influential quarters, and rejection in some others, but there is an increasing tendency to treat them with the respect they deserve, as representing a courageous effort to free the ballet from its perennial taint of mere conventional prettiness." E[dwin] E[vans], "Saison Russe," *Outlook,* 26 July 1913, p. 128. In May and June 1913 the *Outlook* serialized "Stage, Music, and Movement" by Prince Serge Volkonsky, Diaghilev's one-time nemesis at the Imperial Theaters. Earlier that year the journal reviewed Loie Fuller's *Fifteen Years of a Dancer's Life* and Ellen Terry's *Russian Ballet.*

80. Hassall, *Rupert Brooke,* p. 377; Clive Bell, " 'Oedipus Rex' at Covent Garden," *Athenaeum,* 20 January 1912, pp. 75–76. This was not the only time Brooke tacked a Semitic label to the visual style of Diaghilev productions. Inviting a friend to *Legend of Joseph,* he noted that as Strauss "isn't a Jew," he "may be patronized." "The Bally is going in more and more for decorations by Bennois (Benois?) and other decent people, and less and less for Bakst the Jew; so it's improving in that way." Rupert Brooke, Letter to Jacques Raverat, July 1914, *Letters,* p. 595.

81. Roger Fry, "Gordon Craig's Stage Designs," *Nation,* 16 September 1911, p. 871.

82. Frances Spaulding, *Roger Fry: Art and Life* (Berkeley: Univ. of California Press, 1980), p. 133.

83. Roger Fry, "M. Larionow and the Russian Ballet," *Burlington Magazine,* March 1919, p. 112.

84. Holroyd, *Lytton Strachey,* I, p. 381. Lytton Strachey was the *Spectator's* first drama critic.

85. I., "The Russian Ballet. I," p. 406.

86. Roger Fry, "Stage Setting," *New Statesman* [Dramatic Supplement], 27 June 1914, p. 2.

87. *Ibid.,* p. 3.

88. "Great Preliminary Vortex. Manifesto II," *Blast,* No. 1 (20 June 1914; rpt. New York: Krauss Publishing, 1967), p. 13.

89. *Wyndham Lewis on Art: Collected Writings 1913–1956,* ed. Walter Michel and C. J. Fox (New York: Funk and Wagnalls, 1969), p. 155.

90. Fry, "Stage Setting," p. 3.

91. "Reinhardt and His 'New Art'," *Nation,* 14 October 1911, pp. 90–91; H. W. M[assingham], "Signs of Change," *Nation,* 30 December 1911, p. 549. Massingham was the *Nation's* editor.

92. "Reinhardt and His 'New Art'," p. 90.

93. In his review of Reinhardt's *Oedipus* originally published in the *Athenaeum,* Clive Bell closely followed Massingham's argument. "In Prof. Reinhardt's productions there are dramatic pauses and suspensions, effects of light and sound, combinations of movement and mass, line and colour, which . . . provoke, in the right kind of spectator, precisely those trains of thought and feeling that are provoked by real works of art . . . It is hard to believe that these refined stimulants

are precisely the same in kind as the collisions and avalanches of melodrama; but they are." Clive Bell, "Sophocles in London," *Pot-Boilers* (London: Chatto and Windus, 1918), p. 130.

94. H. W. M[assingham], "The Wordless Play. Sumurun—The Honey-moon," *Nation*, 21 October 1911, p. 128.

95. H. W. M[assingham], " 'Kinemacolor' at His Majesty's," *Nation*, 14 September 1912, p. 863.

96. Leonard Woolf, *Beginning Again*, pp 48–49.

97. Forster, "A Shrine for Diaghilev," p. 4.

98. Rupert Brooke, Letter to Edward Marsh, quoted in Skidelsky, *Keynes*, I, p. 284.

99. Lytton Strachey, Letter to Virginia Woolf, 8 November 1912, *Virginia Woolf and Lytton Strachey Letters*, p. 55.

100. Mark Gertler, Letter to Dora Carrington, quoted in Joan Ross Acocella, "The Reception of Diaghilev's Ballets Russes by Artists and Intellectuals in Paris and London, 1909–1914," Diss. Rutgers 1984, p. 399; Karin Costelloe, Letter to Mary Berenson, [June 1913], quoted in Barbara Strachey, *Remarkable Relations: The Story of the Pearsall Smith Women* (New York: Universe Books, 1982), p. 269; Frances Baldwin, "Critical Response in England to the Work of Designers for Diaghilev's Russian Ballet, 1911–1929," M.A. Thesis, Courtauld Institute of Art (London) 1980, pp. 22–23.

101. Anne Estelle Rice, "Les Ballets Russes," *Rhythm*, 2, No. 2 (August 1912), p. 108. *Rhythm* was edited by J. Middleton Murry and Katherine Mansfield. Rice was one of the short-lived journal's two Paris-based theater editors, the other being Georges Banks. In addition to Rice's article, *Rhythm* also published articles by Banks on "Petrouchka" (2, No. 2 [July 1912], pp. 57–63), and Ida Rubinstein's production of *Salomé* (2, No. 4 [September 1912], pp. 169–172).

102. Frances Spalding, *Vanessa Bell* (London: Weidenfeld and Nicolson, 1983), p. 123.

103. Virginia Woolf, *Roger Fry: A Biography* (New York: Harcourt Brace Jovanovich, 1976), pp. 198–199.

104. *Ibid.*, p. 199. Clive Bell said much the same thing in "Before the War," an essay published in May 1917 in the *Cambridge Magazine* and reprinted the following year in his collection *Pot-Boilers*, pp. 247–256.

105. Holroyd, *Lytton Strachey*, II, p. 95; George Bernard Shaw, Letter to Mrs. Patrick Campbell, 18 July 1913, *Bernard Shaw and Mrs. Patrick Campbell: Their Correspondence*, ed. Alan Dent (New York: Knopf, 1952), p. 148.

106. Although Forster's *Maurice*, written in 1913–1914, was circulated in manuscript among the author's friends, the explicitly homosexual novel was only published in 1971.

107. Lytton Strachey read Dostoievsky in late 1909, at a time when few in the West knew his work. The first Dostoievsky novel to appear in English was *The Brothers Karamazov*, published in 1912 in a translation by Constance Garnett (mother of David Garnett, a younger Bloomsbury figure). The Woolfs collaborated with S.S. Koteliansky on a translation of *Stavrogin's Confession*, unpublished chapters of *The Possessed*, which the Hogarth Press brought out in 1922. Other Russian authors published by the Woolfs in 1920–1923 were Gorky, Bunin, and Tolstoy. Holroyd, *Lytton Strachey*, II, p. 12n; Leonard Woolf, *Downhill All the Way: An Autobiography of the Years 1919 to 1939* (New York: Harcourt Brace Jovanovich,

1967), pp. 65–67, 74. For Dostoievsky's emotional appeal and influence on Strachey, see Holroyd, *Lytton Strachey*, II, pp. 113–114. The first performance of a Chekhov play in London took place in 1911, when the Stage Society produced *The Cherry Orchard*. Ashley Dukes, *The Scene is Changed* (London: Macmillan, 1942), p. 35.

108. P. N. Furbank, *E. M. Forster* (New York: Harcourt Brace Jovanovich, 1978), p. 255; Rupert Brooke, Letter to Cathleen Nesbitt, 28 October 1913, *Letters*, p. 521; also his letter to W. Denis Browne, 20 November 1913, *ibid.*, p. 532.

109. Virginia Woolf, Letters to Vanessa Bell and Jacques Raverat, 24 May 1923 and 26 December 1924, *The Letters of Virginia Woolf*, ed. Nigel Nicolson and Joanne Trautmann (New York: Harcourt Brace Jovanovich, 1977), III, pp. 43, 149.

110. Virginia Woolf, Letter to Vanessa Bell, 25 April 1924, *Letters*, III, p. 101.

111. Virginia Woolf, Letters to Jacques Raverat, 4 November 1923 and 4 September 1924, *Letters*, III, pp. 76, 129.

112. Holroyd, *Lytton Strachey*, II, pp. 94–95, 109.

113. Lytton Strachey, Letter to Henry Lamb, 24 July 1913, quoted Holroyd, *Lytton Strachey*, II, p. 94.

114. Lady Ottoline Morrell, *Memoirs of Lady Ottoline Morrell: A Study in Friendship, 1873–1915*, ed. Robert Gathorne-Hardy (New York: Knopf, 1964), p. 215.

115. *Ibid.*, p. 231.

116. Holroyd, *Lytton Strachey*, II, p. 109. Throughout this period Lady Ottoline took parties of friends to the ballet, and notwithstanding Nijinsky's break with Diaghilev, subscribed, like so many Liberal ladies, to Beecham's 1914 season. Sir Paul Vinogradoff, the Russian born Corpus Professor of Jurisprudence at Oxford, who counted Virginia Woolf's brother Adrian Stephen among his medieval law students, was another 1914 subscriber with a link to Bloomsbury. In the 1920s Lady Ottoline's daughter Julian became enamored of Vinogradoff's son Igor, a brilliant Oxford undergraduate. She married him in 1942. *Who's Who, 1914*; Leonard Woolf, *Downhill All the Way*, p. 164; Sandra Jobson Darroch, *Ottoline: The Life of Lady Ottoline Morrell* (New York: Coward, McCann and Geoghegan, 1975), p. 238.

117. *The Selected Poems of Ezra Pound* (New York: New Directions, 1957), p. 30.

118. John Gould Fletcher, *Life Is My Song* (New York: Farrar and Rinehart, 1937), p. 71; Ezra Pound, "Tibor Serly, Composer," *New English Review*, 28 March 1935, p. 495; "William Atheling," "At the Ballet," *New Age*, 16 October 1919, p. 412; rpt. *Ezra Pound and Music: The Complete Criticism*, ed. R. Murray Schafer (New York: New Directions, 1977), pp. 188–191; Canto LXXIX, *The Cantos of Ezra Pound* (New York: New Directions, 1948), pp. 62, 67.

119. Alun R. Jones, *The Life and Opinions of T. E. Hulme* (London: Gollancz, 1960), pp. 94–95; Hassall, *Edward Marsh*, pp. 186–187.

120. Jones, *Hulme*, p. 92.

121. Dukes, *The Scene is Changed*, p. 36.

122. Thomas McGreevy, *Richard Aldington: An Englishman* (London: Chatto and Windus, 1931), p. 11. After the war Cyril W. Beaumont published a limited edition of Aldington's translation of *The Good-Humoured Ladies*, the Goldoni

play on which Diaghilev had based his very popular ballet. Carlo Goldoni, *The Good-Humoured Ladies,* trans. Richard Aldington, pref. Arthur Symons (London: C. W. Beaumont, 1922).

123. F.A. Lea, *The Life of John Middleton Murry* (New York: Oxford Univ. Press, 1960), p. 33; J. Middleton Murry, "The Art of the Russian Ballet," *Nation and Athenaeum,* 10 September 1921, p. 834.

124. Fletcher, *Life is My Song,* p. 65. The poem was first published in John Gould Fletcher, *Fire and Wine* (London: Grant Richards, 1913), pp. 42–43.

125. Fletcher, *Life is My Song,* p. 68.

126. S. Foster Damon, *Amy Lowell: A Chronicle With Extracts From Her Correspondence* (New York, 1935; rpt. Hamden, Conn.: Archon Books, 1966), p. 229.

127. Stanley Weintraub, *The London Yankees: Portraits of American Writers and Artists in England 1894–1914* (New York: Harcourt Brace Jovanovich, 1979), p. 290.

128. Leigh Henry, "Liberations: Studies of Individuality in Contemporary Music. IV.—Igor Stravinsky and the Dionysian Spirit," *Egoist,* 1 June 1914, p. 214. The journal was heavily influenced by Pound at this time.

129. Walter Michel, *Wyndham Lewis: Paintings and Drawings,* introd. Hugh Kenner (Berkeley: Univ. of California Press, 1971), Plates 5–16; H. S. Ede, *Savage Messiah: Gaudier-Brzeska* (New York: Literary Guild, 1931), pp. 175, 180; Hassall, *Edward Marsh,* p. 286; *David Bomberg 1890–1957: Paintings and Drawings* (London: Arts Council, 1967), pp. 8, 24–25; John Rodker, "Russian Ballet," *Little Review,* 6, No. 6 (October 1919), pp. 35–36; Baldwin, "Critical Response in England," pp. 23, 86–87; Acocella, "Reception of Diaghilev's Ballets Russes," pp. 18–22.

130. "Great Preliminary Vortex. Manifesto II," *Blast,* No. 1 (20 June 1914), pp. 28, 33. "Beecham (pills, opera, Thomas)," on the other hand, was soundly blasted. *Ibid.,* p. 21.

131. McGreevy, *Richard Aldington,* p. 10.

132. "Long Live the Vortex!" and "Great Preliminary Vortex. Manifesto II," *Blast,* No. 1 (20 June 1914), n.p., p. 34. Lady Mond was married to the head of one of England's biggest chemical empires. Sir Alfred Mond had bought the *English Review* in late 1909 and promptly ejected Ford Madox Ford from the editor's chair because he was not a Liberal. Mond's father, Ludwig, assembled a priceless collection of Italian paintings that was subsequently given to the National Gallery. Lady Mond was a Beecham subscriber in 1913. Ford Madox Ford, Letter to R. A. Scott-James, [January 1910], *Letters of Ford Madox Ford,* ed. Richard M. Ludwig (Princeton, N.J.: Princeton Univ. Press, 1965), pp. 39–40; "Mond, Ludwig," *Universal Jewish Encyclopedia* (1942).

133. George Dangerfield, *The Strange Death of Liberal England* (New York: Capricorn Books, 1961), p. 65.

Chapter 12. The Postwar Audience

1. Cecil Beaton, *Ballet* (Garden City, N.Y.: Doubleday, 1951), p. 19.

2. Charles Ricketts, Letter to Serge Diaghilev, [1918], 10–22.8, Serge Diaghilev Correspondence, Dance Collection, New York Public Library.

3. *The Diary of Virginia Woolf,* I, ed. Anne Oliver Bell, introd. Quentin Bell (New York: Harcourt Brace Jovanovich, 1977), p. 222.

4. "Food Prices at Home and Abroad. Comparisons with 1914," *Times,* 5 March 1920, p. 13.

5. *The Diary of Virginia Woolf,* I, p. 222.

6. Clive Bell, "Standards," *New Republic,* 14 June 1919, p. 208.

7. "New Dancers at the Coliseum. Mr. Graves in 'After the Ball,' " *Times,* 6 August 1919, p. 8.

8. "The Russian Ballet," *Dancing Times,* May 1919, p. 229.

9. "The Russians at the Alhambra," *Dancing Times,* July 1919, p. 431; Anton Dolin, *Autobiography: A Volume of Autobiography and Reminiscence* (London: Oldbourne, 1960), pp. 21–22.

10. It is no coincidence that Philip J.S. Richardson, the magazine's editor, served as Diaghilev's assistant press representative in 1918–1919. *British Ballet,* ed. Peter Noble (London: Skelton Robinson, 1949), p. 338.

11. "The Russian Ballet Gala," *Times,* 24 January 1919, p. 11.

12. "The Russian Ballet. No Public Festivity," *Times,* 14 May 1919, p. 14.

13. Anne Chisholm, *Nancy Cunard: A Biography* (Harmondsworth, Middlesex: Penguin, 1981), pp. 74, 79; R.J. Minney, *"Puffin" Asquith: A Biography of the Hon. Anthony Asquith, Aesthete, Aristocrat, Prime Minister's Son, and Film Maker* (London: Leslie Frewin, 1973), p. 69. For Margot Asquith's "review" of *Tricorne* (including suggestions about the unison work and Karsavina's hairdo), see her letter to Diaghilev, 23 [July] 1919], 10–20.1, Serge Diaghilev Correspondence. This was not the only occasion this remarkable—and energetic—woman offered Diaghilev unsolicited advice. At a luncheon arranged by Florence Grenfell in December 1924, wrote Lydia Lopokova, Margot announced that "there was too much movement in his ballet and posed herself as it should be done. Serge laughed and asked about Puffin and that way changed conversation." Lydia Lopokova, Letter to John Maynard Keynes, 5 December 1924, John Maynard Keynes Papers, King's College (Cambridge).

14. Robert Skidelsky, *John Maynard Keynes: A Biography* (London: Macmillan, 1983), I, p. 352; Roger Fry, "M. Larionow and the Russian Ballet," *Burlington Magazine,* March 1919, pp. 112–113; Virginia Woolf, Letter to Lytton Strachey, 12 October 1918, *The Letters of Virginia Woolf,* ed. Nigel Nicolson and Joanne Trautmann (New York: Harcourt Brace Jovanovich, 1975), I, pp. 201, 222; Clive Bell, "Standards," *New Republic,* 14 June 1919, p. 208, and "The New Ballet," *New Republic,* 30 July 1919, p. 414; Frances Spalding, *Vanessa Bell* (London: Weidenfeld and Nicolson, 1983), p. 176; Nina Hammett, *Laughing Torso* (London: Constable, 1932), p. 176.

15. Osbert Sitwell, *Laughter in the Next Room* (London: Reprint Society, 1950), pp. 16–18; Spalding, *Vanessa Bell,* p. 184; Aldous Huxley, Letter to Juliette Baillot, 14 September 1918, in *Letters of Aldous Huxley,* ed. Grover Smith (London: Chatto and Windus, 1969), p. 163; Virginia Woolf, Letter to Lytton Strachey, 12 October 1918, *The Letters of Virginia Woolf,* ed. Nigel Nicolson and Joanne Trautmann (New York: Harcourt Brace Jovanovich, 1976), II, p. 282; R.F. Harrod, *The Life of John Maynard Keynes* (Harmondsworth, Middlesex: Penguin, 1972), p. 266; Skidelsky, *Keynes,* I, pp. 352–353.

16. "The Lights of London. Scenes of Rejoicing at Night," *Times,* 12 November 1918, p. 10; Frances Spalding, *Roger Fry: Art and Life* (Berkeley, Univ. of

California Press, 1980), p. 222; Hammett, *Laughing Torso*, p. 114; Sitwell, *Laughter in the Next Room*, pp. 16–23; Michael Holroyd, *Lytton Strachey: A Critical Biography* (New York: Holt, Rinehart and Winston, 1968), II, p. 343. The party was given by Montague Shearman, a barrister and collector of modern paintings, who was one of Mark Gertler's most loyal friends and patrons.

17. Aldous Huxley, Letter to Juliette Baillot, 14 September 1918, *Letters*, p. 163; Clive Bell, "The New Ballet," p. 414; *The Diary of Virginia Woolf*, I, p. 201; Roger Fry, "M. Larionow and the Russian Ballet," p. 112.

18. Virginia Woolf, Letter to Saxon Sydney-Turner, 11 June 1919, *Letters*, II, p. 367; *The Diary of Virginia Woolf*, I, pp. 287, 290; Spalding, *Vanessa Bell*, p. 184; Clive Bell, *Old Friends: Personal Recollections* (London: Chatto and Windus, 1956), pp. 171–172; Spalding, *Roger Fry*, p. 225; Skidelsky, *Keynes*, I, p. 380.

19. Clive Bell, "The New Ballet"; Roger Fry, "M. Larionow and the Russian Ballet"; "The Scenery of 'La Boutique Fantasque,'" *Athenaeum*, 13 June 1919, p. 466; James Strachey, "The Russian Ballet," *Athenaeum*, 30 May 1919, pp. 406–407; Ezra Pound, "At the Ballet," 16 October 1919, and "Music," 18 December 1919, *New Age*, reprinted in *Ezra Pound and Music: The Complete Criticism*, ed. R. Murray Schafer (New York: New Directions, 1977), pp. 188–191, 200–203; Richard Aldington, "The Russian Ballet," *Sphere*, 16 August 1919, p. 160; Rebecca West, "The Russian Ballet," *Outlook*, 7 June 1919, pp. 568–568; Arthur Symons, "The Russian Ballets," *Fortnightly Review*, January 1919, pp. 89–99, "Notes on the Sensations of a Lady of the Ballet," *English Review*, February 1920, pp. 104–120, and "Dancing as Soul Expression," *Forum*, October 1921, pp. 308–317; Albert Rutherston, "Decoration in the Art of the Theatre," *Monthly Chapbook*, August 1919; "Some Aspects of the Ballet," *Drama*, December 1919, pp. 68–73.

20. Roger Fry, "M. Larionow and the Russian Ballet," p. 118.

21. Clive Bell, "The Authority of M. Derain," *New Republic*, 16 March 1921, p. 66.

22. Roger Fry, "The Scenery of 'La Boutique Fantasque,'" p. 466.

23. Symons, "The Russian Ballets," p. 97.

24. "New Alhambra Ballet," *Times*, 6 June 1919, p. 14; "New Russian Ballet. 'Parade' at the Empire," *Times*, 15 November 1919, p. 10.

25. Roger Fry, "M. Larionow and the Russian Ballet," p. 117; Clive Bell, "The New Ballet," p. 415; Raymond Mortimer, "London Letter," *Dial*, March 1922, p. 295.

26. Clive Bell, "The New Ballet," pp. 414–415.

27. T.S. Eliot, "London Letter, July 1921," *Dial*, August 1921, p. 214.

28. T.S. Eliot, "Dramatis Personae," *Criterion*, April 1923, pp. 305–306. Eliot also addressed the issues of performance and impersonality in "The Possibility of Poetic Drama," *Dial*, November 1920, pp. 446–447, and "London Letter, May 1921," *Dial*, June 1921, p. 688.

29. Clive Bell, "The Creed of an Aesthete," *New Republic*, 25 January 1922, p. 242.

30. T.S. Eliot, "London Letter, July 1921," p. 213; Clive Bell, "Standards," p. 208. The "heavy losses sustained during the . . . grand [Covent Garden] season of foreign opera and Russian ballet" in the summer of 1920 drove the Sir Thomas Beecham Opera Company, Ltd., out of business. "Co-operative Opera. Future of the Beecham Company," *Times*, 2 July 1921, p. 10.

31. T.S. Eliot, "London Letter, April 1922," *Dial*, May 1922, p. 511; "In Memoriam: Marie Lloyd," *Criterion*, January 1923, p. 194.

32. Clive Bell, *Old Friends: Personal Recollections* (London: Chatto and Windus, 1956), p. 57.

33. "The Russian Ballet. 'Le Sacre du Printemps,' " *Times*, 29 June 1921, p. 8; Simon Pure, "The Londoner," *Bookman*, August 1921, p. 539; Edward J. Dent, "Music," *London Mercury*, August 1920, p. 491.

34. W.J. Turner, "Drama," *London Mercury*, April 1920, p. 756.

35. Julius M. Price, "The Transition in Modern British Art," *Fortnightly Review*, July 1921, p. 107.

36. Leigh Henry, unidentified review of *Parade;* quoted in Diaghilev Scrapbook, IV, p. 158, Theatre Museum (London).

37. Statements of account submitted by Edwin Evans to Serge Diaghilev, 8 and 24 November 1919, Stravinsky-Diaghilev Foundation (New York).

38. See, for instance, W.J. Turner, "The Rite of Spring," *New Statesman*, 2 July 1921, p. 358; Edward J. Dent, "Le Sacre du Printemps," *Nation and Athenaeum*, 18 June 1921, pp. 445–446; Charles Henry Meltzer, "Stravinsky—The Enigma," *Forum*, September 1921, pp. 241–248; Leigh Henry, "Stravinsky and the Pragmatic Criterion in Modern Music," *English Review*, July 1921, pp. 67–73.

39. W.J. Turner, "Stravinsky in London and Paris," *New Statesman*, 31 July 1920, p. 475.

40. Edward J. Dent, "Covent Garden: 'Pulcinella,' " *Athenaeum*, 18 June 1920, p. 807.

41. W.J. Turner, "Stravinsky in London and Paris," p. 475.

42. Sacheverell Sitwell, "The Sleeping Beauty at the London Alhambra, 1921," *Ballet—To Poland*, ed. Arnold Haskell (New York: Macmillan, 1940), pp. 17–18.

43. Raymond Mortimer, "London Letter, February 1922," *Dial*, March 1922, pp. 295–296.

44. W.J. Turner, "The Sleeping Princess," *New Statesman*, 12 November 1921, p. 169.

45. Edward Ricco, "The Sitwells at the Ballet," *Ballet Review*, 6, No. 1 (1977–1978), p. 101.

46. Antoine Banès, "Théâtre National de l'Opéra. Ballets Russes. *Petrouchka, Prince Igor, la Boutique fantasque,*" *Figaro*, 29 December 1919, p. 3; Serge Diaghilev, Letter to Misia Sert, 23 January 1919, quoted in *Catalogue of Ballet Material and Manuscripts from the Serge Lifar Collection*, Sotheby's (London) 9 May 1984, Lot 161; Jean Marnold, "Musique," *Mercure de France*, 1 April 1920, p. 223.

47. Contract between Serge Diaghilev and Jacques Rouché, 8 October 1921, AJ13/1292, Archives Nationales (Paris).

48. Jacques Rouché, Letter to Serge Diaghilev, 26 April 1922, Pièce 86, Fonds Kochno, Bibliothèque de l'Opéra (Paris).

49. Arthur Moss, "The Passing of the Ballet Russe," *Freeman*, 27 June 1923, pp. 375–376. Arthur Moss was an American expatriate writer, copublisher of the little magazine *Gargoyle,* and occasional contributor to *The Dance Magazine.*

50. Jacques-Emile Blanche, "L'oeuvre d'un Russe," *Figaro*, 7 June 1923, p. 1. See, also, Louis Laloy, "Le Gala des Ballets Russes," *Figaro*, 5 June 1923; "Le Grand Gala des Ballets Russes," *Le Gaulois*, 8 June 1923; "Le Gala de la Gaîté,"

Le Gaulois, 14 June 1923, in Theater Pressbook, *Les Noces,* Bibliothèque de la Opéra.

51. "Carnet de la charité," 10 June 1923, *ibid.*

52. See, for instance, "Riviera Flowers. Antibes and Its Gardens," *Times,* 4 February 1922, p. 13; "Gaiety at Monte Carlo. Golf and Society. The Value of Money," *Times,* 13 January 1921, p. 8, col. 1; "Riviera Weather. Effects of the Early Frosts," *Times,* 24 January 1921, p. 13, col 5; "Cheap Francs. Gambling in the Exchange," *Times,* 1 December 1919, p. 17; "Riviera Prices. The Season's Prospects," *Times,* 23 December 1921, p. 11; "Riviera Finance. Francs and the Cost of Living," *Times,* 3 March 1924, p. 15; "London Fashions. Varieties for the Riviera," *Times,* 9 January 1924, p. 15; "Riviera Season. Calendar of Social and Sporting Events," *Times,* 11 December 1922, p. 15; "Riviera Notes. The British Invasion," *Times,* 2 March 1920, p. 19; "The Woman's View. Winter on the Riviera," *Times,* 6 January 1922, p. 13; "Riviera Crowds. Beaulieu Villas and Gardens," *Times,* 21 January 1924, p. 13.

53. "Le Masque de Fer," "Echos," *Figaro,* 9 January 1923, p. 1.

54. Untitled clipping, *Figaro,* 23 April 1923; Dance Clipping File (Stanislas Idzikowski), Dance Collection.

55. "The Riviera," *Times,* 17 January 1924, p. 15; Untitled clipping, *Figaro,* 23 April 1923, Dance Clipping File (Stanislas Idzikowski), Dance Collection; Anton Dolin, *Autobiography,* p. 34; S.L. Grigoriev, *The Diaghilev Ballet 1909–1929,* trans. and ed. Vera Bowen (London: Constable, 1953), pp. 200, 208–210.

56. Carlo Monte, "Petit bleu de la Côte d'Azur," *Figaro,* 26 December 1919, p. 3.

57. "Riviera Notes," *Times,* 6 March 1923, p. 17; "Figaro aux pays du soleil," *Figaro,* 23 March 1923, p. 6; "Le Monde et la ville," *Figaro,* 2 April 1925, p. 2.

58. Florence Gilliam, "The Russian Ballet of 1923," *Theatre Arts Monthly,* March 1924, p. 191. *Coppélia* and *Le Spectre de la Rose* were given at the Théâtre de Monte-Carlo on January 10. On January 22, at the same theater, *Spectre* appeared on a triple bill with *Hagoromo,* danced by Sonia Pavloff of the Opéra Comique, and *Au temps jadis,* a Monégasque national ballet, with Lubov Tchernicheva, Vera Nemchinova, Serge Grigoriev, and Anatole Vilzak. On February 6 Nemchinova and Vilzak appeared in Belloni's *Fleurs et Papillons* at the Palais des Beaux-Arts. "Le Figaro aux pays du soleil," *Figaro,* 9 January 1923, p. 6; 21 January 1923, p. 7; 5 February 1923, p. 5. For variety programs at the Palais des Beaux-Arts, see "Le Figaro aux pays du soleil," *Figaro,* 5 February 1923, p. 5; 20 March 1923, p. 7; 26 March 1923, p. 5.

59. "The 'Ballets Russes' at Monte-Carlo: Souvenirs (1923)," *Paris-Journal,* 15 February 1924; reprinted in Nigel Wilkins, *The Writings of Erik Satie* (London: Eulenberg, 1981), p. 111.

60. Robert McAlmon, *Being Geniuses Together 1920–1930,* rev. with supplementary chapters by Kay Boyle (Garden City, N.Y.: Doubleday, 1968), p. 218.

61. Paul Morand, "Paris Letter. October 1926," *Dial,* November 1926, p. 428.

62. Richard S. Kennedy, *Dreams in the Mirror: A Biography of E.E. Cummings* (New York: Liveright, 1980), pp. 373–374. *Tom,* which had music by David Diamond, was never produced.

63. *Ibid.,* p. 179. The essay has been lost.

64. Quoted in *The Fourteenth Chronicle: Letters and Diaries of John Dos Passos*, ed. Townsend Luddington (Boston: Gambit, 1973), p. 378.

65. During the war years an American circle that included Alice Garrett (a Baltimore patron of Bakst married to a diplomat in the American legation in Paris), Bernard Berenson, Walter Berry, and Edith Wharton had crystallized around Diaghilev. As might be expected in view of the age and standing of this expatriate elite, its ties with Diaghilev were largely social. Mrs. Garrett's name appears on the list of "Dames Patronesses" for the 1917 Paris season when *Parade* received its first tumultuous performance, an early sign of the hiatus between Diaghilev's postwar repertory and his Paris audience of the 1920s. Susan B. Tripp, "Bakst," *Johns Hopkins Magazine*, June 1984, p. 21.

66. Calvin Tompkins, *Living Well is the Best Revenge* (New York: Dutton, 1982), pp. 8–9.

67. Townsend Luddington, *John Dos Passos: A Twentieth Century Odyssey* (New York: Dutton, 1980), pp. 225–227; Tompkins, pp. 30–31.

68. Gilliam, "The Russian Ballet of 1923," pp. 191–192.

69. Richard Ellmann, *James Joyce* (New York: Oxford Univ. Press, 1959), p. 625.

70. Quoted *ibid.*, p. 686.

71. Virgil Thomson, *Virgil Thomson* (New York: Knopf, 1966), pp. 77–78.

72. Noel Riley Fitch, *Sylvia Beach and the Lost Generation: A History of Literary Paris in the Twenties and Thirties* (New York: Norton, 1983), p. 74.

73. George Antheil, "Mother of the Earth," *Transatlantic Review* [Musical Supplement], 2, No. 2, p. 227.

74. Both Rolf de Maré and Comte Etienne de Beaumont, however, contributed articles about their respective enterprises. See "The Swedish Ballet and the Modern Aesthetic" and "The Soirées de Paris," *Little Review*, 11, No. 2 (Winter 1926), pp. 24–28, 55–57.

75. Matthew Josephson, *Life Among the Surrealists: A Memoir* (New York: Holt, Rinehart and Winston, 1962), p. 132.

76. George Antheil, *Bad Boy of Music* (London: Hurst and Blackett, [1947]), pp. 107–111. Antheil ingenuously pleaded ignorance at the purpose of this "premiere," which took place three weeks before the opening of Maré's three-performance season and the aim of which was announced in the paid and very public columns of *Figaro*. "Courrier des Théâtres," *Figaro*, 2 October 1923, p. 6.

77. Blaise Cendrars, Letter to Serge Diaghilev, 16 May 1922, Stravinsky-Diaghilev Foundation.

78. Hammett, *Laughing Torso*, p. 135.

79. D.O. Widhopff, Tristan Tzara, M. Larionov, Letter to Serge Diaghilev, [March 1923], Stravinsky-Diaghilev Foundation. The designs for the production of *Giroflé-Girofla*, which premiered on March 10, were by Georgi Yakulov, who designed the 1927 production of *Le Pas d'Acier*. As indicated in chapter 7, Tairov approached Diaghilev for a letter or article containing his views of the season.

80. Quoted in Boris Kochno, *Diaghilev and the Ballets Russes*, trans. Adrienne Foulke (New York: Harper and Row, 1970), p. 237.

81. J.B.-O., "Les Théâtres," *Le Gaulois*, 21 June 1924.

82. Howard Greer, "In the Salon of a Great Parisian Coquette," *Theatre Magazine*, September 1920, p. 128 *et seq.*

83. Howard Greer, "Causons de la Mode!" *Theatre Magazine*, February 1920, p. 128.

84. Thomson, *Virgil Thomson*, p. 57.

85. *Ibid;* Hammett, *Laughing Torso*, p. 198; Bell, *Old Friends: Personal Reminiscences*, pp. 184–186; Count Harry Kessler, *In the Twenties: The Diaries of Count Harry Kessler*, trans. Charles Kessler, introd. Otto Friedrich (New York: Holt, Rinehart and Winston, 1971), p. 209; McAlmon, *Being Geniuses Together*, pp. 123–125; Arthur Gold and Robert Fizdale, *Misia: The Life of Misia Sert* (New York: Knopf, 1980), p. 216; Francis Steegmuller, *Cocteau: A Biography* (Boston: Little, Brown, 1970), pp. 281–283.

86. Quoted in Steegmuller, *Cocteau*, p. 281.

87. Kessler, *Diaries*, pp. 298–299. A design by Soudeikine for the Oasis was sold at Sotheby's, New York, on 6 December 1977, Lot 82.

88. Elsa Maxwell, *R.S.V.P. Elsa Maxwell's Own Story* (Boston: Little Brown, 1954), p. 14.

89. *Ibid.*, p. 8. Maxwell must have gotten her dates confused (or pared a few years off her age) as the pianist did not leave the Soviet Union until autumn 1925. This is not to say that Diaghilev did not at some time arrange such a recital. Indeed, given the importance of the émigré world in Horowitz's early career in the West, the absence of all mention of Diaghilev in the pianist's biography is certainly odd. See Glenn Plaskin, *Horowitz: A Biography of Vladimir Horowitz* (New York: Morrow, 1983), chaps. 5–6.

90. "Mariegold in Society," *Sketch*, 19 September 1928, p. 557. One wonders what she said.

91. "Fêtes par-ci, fêtes par-là," *Femina*, August 1924, p. 14; "Courrier des Théâtres," *Figaro*, 25 April 1923, p. 3.

92. Ninette de Valois, *Come Dance With Me: A Memoir 1898–1956* (London: Dance Books, 1973), pp. 69–70.

93. "Paris Notes," *Dancing Times*, January 1921, pp. 343–345.

94. Among the dance artists featured at *Femina* events were Nina Payne, a popular American "excentric" dancer from the Folies-Bergère, Sakaë Ashida and Toshi Komori, Japanese concert dancers, and the exhibition team of Misguett and Maxly. "Courrier des Théâtres," *Figaro*, 25 April 1923, p. 3; 19 October 1923, p. 6. In 1923 the talent line-up for three well-publicized charity affairs evoked the gamut of French theatrical dance—Carlotta Zambelli, Albert Aveline, Tamara Swirskaya, Natalia Trouhanova, Rahna, Harry Pilcer, Anna, Lisa, and Margo Duncan, Yevgenia Nikitina, and Jeanne Ronsay. "Gala à Exposition de la Musique et de la Danse," *Figaro*, 16 January 1923, p. 2, cols 4–5; "Pour les Veuves et Orphelins des Associations des Jornalistes parisiens et des Nouvellistes parisiens," *Figaro*, 29 May 1923, p. 2; for the "Fête de l'Enfance et des Jeux," see "Le Monde et la Ville," *Figaro*, 3 June 1923, p. 2.

95. Chanel, Erté, Jeanne Lanvin, Paul Poiret, and Worth all designed for the stage. "Dancing" was the fashionable name for a Paris dance establishment, and the very use of an English term suggests the elitist character of a majority of the establishments where "jazz" was danced. Throughout the 1920s the *Dancing Times* published many articles about Paris "dancings" that noted cover prices, attire, manners, and the cost of drinks in addition to commenting on the style of dancing. See, for instance, George Cecil, "Paris 'Dancings,'" *Dancing Times*, September

1920, pp. 955–957; "Sitter Out," *Dancing Times*, May 1921, pp. 630–636; George Cecil, "Paris Open-Air Dancing," *Dancing Times*, May 1921, pp. 641–642; Len Chaloner, "Dancing in the Quartier Latin," *Dancing Times*, March 1922, pp. 535–537; Jack Carlton, "Where One Dances in Paris," *Dancing Times*, December 1922, pp. 275–277; George Cecil, "Parisian Partners," *Dancing Times*, February 1923, pp. 507–509.

96. Kessler, *Diaries*, p. 302; "Paris Notes," *Dancing Times*, January 1926, p. 463.

97. " 'To-morrow's Fashions': Paris Prophecies at a Ball. An English Poet and Her Dress Prophecy," *Sketch*, 15 April 1925, pp. 50–51. Among the revelers photographed by Man Ray were Nancy Cunard, Tristan Tzara, the Picassos, Baron and Baroness de Meyer, the Marquise de Jaucourt, Madame Errazuriz, and the hosts. For the program and principal protagonists of Beaumont's 1923 baroque ball, see "Le Monde et la Ville," *Figaro*, 1 June 1923, p. 2.

98. Josephson, *Life Among the Surrealists*, pp. 141, 255.

99. These black Americans shared the Coliseum bill with the Ballets Russes in November 1925.

100. *The Journals of Arnold Bennett, 1921–1928*, ed. Newman Flower (London: Cassell, 1933), p. 133.

101. *Evening Standard*, [25] November 1924; quoted in "Theatre Directory," *Times*, 26 November 1924, p. 12.

102. Among the celebrities profiled were Anton Dolin, Eugene Goossens, Stravinsky, and Diaghilev. Martin Lane, "The Irish Russian-Dancer: Anton Dolin," *Sketch*, 24 December 1924, p. 657; Beverley Nichols, "Celebrities in Undress: Diaghileff," *Sketch*, 30 June 1926, p. 526; "Celebrities in Undress: Eugene Goossens," *Sketch*, 4 August 1926, p. 210; "Celebrities in Undress: Stravinsky," *Sketch*, 6 July 1927, p. 14. These and other *Sketch* profiles by dandy novelist Beverley Nichols were reprinted in Beverley Nichols, *Are They the Same at Home? Being a Series of Bouquets Diffidently Distributed* (London: Jonathan Cape, 1927).

103. "Mariegold in Society," *Sketch*, 22 June 1927, p. 579.

104. "Mariegold in Society," *Sketch*, 23 June 1926, p. 469.

105. Quoted in Raphael Samuel, "The Middle Class Between the Wars," Part II, *New Socialist*, March/April 1983, p. 30.

106. W.J. Turner, "*Mercury* and *The Nightingale*," *New Statesman*, 23 July 1927, p. 479.

107. Jessica Mitford, *Hons and Rebels* (London: Quartet Books, 1978), p. 33.

108. Harold Acton, *Memoirs of an Aesthete* (London: Methuen, 1948), p. 113.

109. Martin Green, *Children of the Sun: A Narrative of "Decadence" in England After 1918* (New York: Basic Books, 1976), pp. 125–126.

110. *The Eton Candle*, ed. Brian Howard (Eton: Saville Press, 1922), pp. 30–31 and 81–82; Acton, *Memoirs*, pp. 81–82, 108; Green, *Children of the Sun*, p. 140.

111. Quoted in Green, *Children of the Sun*, p. 86.

112. Jacques-Emile Blanche, "Souvenirs sur Serge de Diaghilew," *L'Art Vivant*, 15 September 1929, p. 714.

113. Green, *Children of the Sun*, pp. 90, 154; Acton, *Memoirs*, p. 127; "Undergraduates as Ballerinas," *Sketch*, 15 December 1926, p. 542.

114. Acton, *Memoirs*, pp. 152, 221–222. Egypt was in high favor that season. Apart from the Royal performance, there was a "splendid party" given by the Egyptian legation, at which Lubov Tchernicheva, Felia Doubrovska, Alexandra Danilova, and Serge Lifar danced. "Mariegold in Society," *Sketch*, 31 July 1929, p. 208.

115. Cecil Beaton, "Designing for the Ballet," *Dance Index*, August 1946, pp. 195–196, and *Diaries 1922–1939: The Wandering Years* (London: Weidenfeld and Nicolson, 1961), pp. 127–128. *Zéphire et Flore* was Messel's first professional assignment. In the summer of 1925 some of Messel's masks for the theater were exhibited with Pedro Pruna's designs and sketches for *Les Matelots* at the Claridge Gallery, and it was here, presumably, that Diaghilev first became acquainted with Messel's work. Cyril W. Beaumont, *Bookseller at the Ballet, Incorporating the Diaghilev Ballet in London* (London: C.W. Beaumont, 1975), p. 337; "Omicron," "From Alpha to Omega," *Nation and Athenaeum*, August 1925, p. 544.

116. Green, *Children of the Sun*, pp. 208, 210; Nesta Macdonald, *Diaghilev Observed by Critics in England and the United States 1911–1929* (New York: Dance Horizons, 1975), p. 352; "How One Lives From Day to Day," *Vogue*, Early August 1927, p. 31.

117. Quoted in Green, *Children of the Sun*, p. 140.

118. Acton, *Memoirs*, pp. 128–130.

119. "Mariegold in Society," *Sketch*, 22 June 1927, p. 579.

120. "Mariegold in Society," *Sketch*, 4 July 1928, p. 10.

121. "Mariegold in Society," *Sketch*, 18 July 1928, p. 110; 17 July 1929, p. 107; 24 July 1929, pp. 156–157; *The Diary of Virginia Woolf*, III, ed. Anne Olivier Bell (New York: Harcourt Brace Jovanovich, 1980), p. 27.

122. "Omicron," "From Alpha to Omega," *Nation and Athenaeum*, 6 December 1924, p. 361; W.J. Turner, "The Diaghileff Ballet," *New Statesman*, 6 December 1924, p. 264; and "The Popularity of the Ballet," *New Statesman*, 24 January 1925, p. 446; "Mariegold in Society," *Sketch*, 10 June 1925, p. 477; "Omicron," "From Alpha to Omega," *Nation and Athenaeum*, 30 May 1925, p. 268.

123. W.J. Turner, "Something for the Sightseer," *New Statesman*, 17 July 1926, p. 385; Francis Birrell, "The Last Theatrical Season," *Nation and Athenaeum*, 25 July 1925, p. 514.

124. Raymond Mortimer, "Les Matelots," *New Statesman*, 4 July 1925, p. 338. In 1928 Mortimer returned to the theme of Diaghilev's "educative influence" in a review of the season at His Majesty's Theatre. Raymond Mortimer, "The Russian Ballet," *Nation and Athenaeum*, 30 June 1928, p. 424.

125. Birrell, "The Last Theatrical Season," p. 514; "Omicron," "From Alpha to Omega," *Nation and Athenaeum*, 7 November 1925, p. 209; "From Plays to Pictures," *Nation and Athenaeum*, 26 June 1926, p. 444. In 1929 Lopokova, in search of new horizons, tried her hand at ballet writing for the journal. See her articles "Enrico Cecchetti," *Nation and Athenaeum*, 29 June 1929, p. 438; "The Russian Ballet at Covent Garden," *Nation and Athenaeum*, 6 July 1929, p. 476; "The Russian Ballet at Covent Garden," *Nation and Athenaeum*, 13 July 1929, p. 507; "The Russian Ballet at Covent Garden," *Nation and Athenaeum*, 20 July 1929, p. 536; "Serge Diaghileff 1872–1929," *Nation and Athenaeum*, 31 August 1929, pp. 706–707.

126. "Omicron," "Plays and Pictures," *Nation and Athenaeum,* 26 June 1926, p. 353.

127. Turner, "Something for the Sightseer," p. 384; "Omicron," "Plays and Pictures," *Nation and Athenaeum,* 27 November 1926, p. 301.

128. Lydia Lopokova, Letters to John Maynard Keynes, 28 November and 29 November 1926, Keynes Papers; Geoffrey Keynes, *The Gates of Memory* (New York: Oxford Univ. Press, 1983), pp. 198–203; Virginia Woolf, *The Years* (New York: Harcourt Brace Jovanovich), p. 393.

129. "Omicron," "Plays and Pictures," *Nation and Athenaeum,* 18 December 1926, p. 422. The Waugh allusion appears in *Put Out More Flags* (Boston: Little Brown, 1948), p. 48.

130. W.J. Turner, "An English Ballet," *New Statesman,* 11 December 1926, p. 275. For Berners, see Nichols, "Lord Berners or A Rococo Byron," *Are They the Same at Home?,* p. 59; Acton, *Memoirs,* p. 37; *Stravinsky: Selected Correspondence,* ed. Robert Craft (New York: Knopf, 1984), II, pp. 135–159.

131. "C.," "Russian Ballet," *Musical Times,* 1 August 1926, p. 738; E[dwin] E[vans], "The Russian Ballet," *Musical Times,* 1 August 1927, p. 744; "C.," "Russian Ballet Season," *Musical Times,* 1 August 1925, p. 742.

132. Geoffrey Keynes, Letter to Serge Diaghilev, 29 June 1927, 10–12.6, Serge Diaghilev Correspondence. Keynes's letter was written in French. For his account of these events, see *The Gates of Memory,* pp. 203–205.

133. Quoted *ibid.,* p. 204.

134. Quoted in Macdonald, *Diaghilev Observed,* p. 353.

135. See, for instance, Edwin Evans, "The Russian Ballet," *Vogue,* Early June 1925, p. 52, and "The Truth About the Russian Ballet," Early July 1926, p. 49; Nancy Cunard, "Paris To-day As I See It," Late May 1926, p. 75, and Early July 1926, p. 50; "Pruna and the Ballet," Late July 1925, pp. 54–55; Clive Bell, "A Tour of Summer Shows," Late August 1925, p. 42, and "Round About Surréalisme," Early July 1926, p. 54–55; "We Nominate for the Hall of Fame," Early June 1925, p. 62. Featured as Diaghilev's "Masters of Décor" in early July 1926 (p. 51) were his Paris-based stars: Picasso, Braque, Derain, Larionov, Gontcharova, Laurencin, Matisse, and Miró. For Beaton's sketches, see "How One Lives From Day to Day," Early August 1927, p. 30, "Seen At Mayfair's Latest Parties," Late July 1927, p. 27, and "Our Lives From Day to Day," 11 July 1928, p. 43.

136. Lady Ottoline Morrell, "Les Jeunes Filles de Londres," *Vogue,* Late November 1924, p. 41. In addition to Lady Ottoline's article, the November issues of *Vogue* included articles by David Garnett, Clive Bell, and Virginia Woolf as well as a story on the decorative work of Duncan Grant and Vanessa Bell, with photographs of their panels for the Woolf house in Tavistock Square.

137. Virginia Woolf received £20 an article from *Vogue* editor Dorothy Todd, a tidy sum in those days. *The Diary of Virginia Woolf,* III, p. 31. Not everyone approved of her writing for Mayfair. "I've been engaged in a great wrangle with an old American called [Logan] Pearsall Smith on the ethics of writing articles at high rates for fashion papers like Vogue," she wrote to Jacques Raverat in January 1925. "He says it demeans one. He says one must write only for the Lit. Supplement and the Nation and Robert Bridges and prestige and posterity and to set a high example. I say Bunkum. Ladies' clothes and aristocrats playing golf don't affect my style; and they would do his a world of good. Oh these Americans! How

they always muddle everything up! What he wants is prestige: what I want, money."
Virginia Woolf, Letter to Jacques Raverat, 24 January 1925, *Letters,* III, p. 154.

138. *Vogue,* Late July 1925, pp. 44, 54; Late July 1926, p. 36; Early July 1926, p. 55. In late January 1926, for instance, the magazine published a full-page portrait of Beaumont and, on the following page, four of Man Ray's "rayographs" used in *A quoi rêvent les jeunes filles?,* the Count's "new 'surréaliste' picture" (pp. 58–59). *Vogue* reproduced several Man Ray photographs of Ballets Russes figures, including portraits of company designers (Early June 1925, p. 62; Early July 1926, p. 51), a portrait of Serge Lifar in *Zéphire et Flore* (Late November 1925, p. 83), and portraits of Alexandra Danilova, Tamara Geva, and Stanislas Idzikowski in *Jack-in-the-Box* (Early July 1926, p. 78; Early August 1926, p. 48).

139. " 'Zephyr and Flora,' and 'Betty in Mayfair,' " *Sketch,* 18 November 1925, p. 321; H[oward] H[annay], " 'Zephyr and Flora,' " *Observer,* 15 November 1925, p. 11; H[oward] H[annay], " 'Les Facheux,' " *Observer,* 26 June 1927, p. 15; "The Russian Ballet, 'The Song of the Nightingale,' " *Times,* 19 July 1927, p. 12; "At the Grotto Restaurant on the Lido: Lady Abdy and Her Peke," *Sketch,* 4 August 1926, p. 206; *Vogue,* Late December 1925, p. 57. For the 13 July 1927 *Sketch* cover, Nikitina modeled "one of the latest hats—a dainty affair of feathers . . . with ear pieces." The following year in Monte Carlo, both she and Danilova posed in elegant fox skins for a *Sketch* photographer. *Sketch,* 25 April 1928, p. 160.

140. Fernau Hall, *An Anatomy of Ballet* (London: Andrew Melrose, 1953), p. 80.

141. "Sitter Out," *Dancing Times,* January 1925, p. 400.

142. G.E. Fussell, "Notes on Decor. The Diaghileff Ballet," *Dancing Times,* July 1925, p. 1129.

143. Howard Hannay, "The Fine Arts," *London Mercury,* January 1925, p. 313.

144. "The Russian Ballet. 'La Pastorale,' " *Times,* 29 June 1926, p. 14; "The Russian Ballet. Works by Erik Satie," *Times,* 6 July 1926, p. 14; "The Russian Ballet, 'Romeo et Juliet,' " *Times,* 22 July 1926, p. 14.

145. "The Russian Ballet. Production of 'The Cat,' " *Times,* 15 June 1927, p. 14.

146. Quoted in Oleg Kerensky, *Anna Pavlova* (New York: Dutton, 1973), p. 99.

147. Herbert Farjeon, "Seen on the Stage," *Vogue,* 11 July 1928, p. 48.

148. *Ibid.,* p. 80; "Sitter Out," *Dancing Times,* August 1926, p. 436; P[hilip] P[age], unidentified review, Diaghilev Scrapbook, V, p. 51, Theatre Museum (London).

149. Farjeon, "Seen on the Stage," p. 80; "Dress Reform at the Ballet," *Daily Telegraph,* 19 July 1929; Douglas McClean, Letter to the Editor, *Times,* 25 July 1928, p. 12.

150. "Russian Ballet in Paris. Stravinsky's 'Renard,' " *Times,* 31 May 1929, p. 10.

Epilogue

1. Alicia Markova, *Markova Remembers* (Boston: Little, Brown, 1986), p. 25; Alexandra Danilova, *Choura: The Memoirs of Alexandra Danilova* (New York: Knopf, 1986), p. 107.

SELECTED BIBLIOGRAPHY

Archives

Archives Nationales (Paris)
Gabriel Astruc Papers, Dance Collection, New York Public Library
Adolph Bolm Papers, George Arents Research Library, Syracuse University
Dr. Mikaly Cenner, Private Collection (Budapest)
Central State Historical Archives (Leningrad)
Jean Cocteau Papers, George Arents Research Library, Syracuse University
Covent Garden Archives (London)
Serge Diaghilev Correspondence, Dance Collection, New York Public Library
Serge Diaghilev Papers, Dance Collection, New York Public Library
Otto Kahn Papers, Princeton University
John Maynard Keynes Papers, King's College (Cambridge)
Boris Kochno Papers [Fonds Kochno], Bibliothèque de l'Opéra (Paris)
Metropolitan Opera Archives (New York)
Ruth Page Collection, Dance Collection, New York Public Library
Joseph Paget-Fredericks Collection, Bancroft Library, University of California, Berkeley
Palace Archives (Monaco)
Max Rabinoff Papers, Manuscript Division, Columbia University
Société des Bains de Mer (Monte Carlo)
Stravinsky-Diaghilev Foundation (New York)
Theatre Collection, Harvard University
Theatre Museum (London)

Books

Alexandre, Arsène, and Jean Cocteau. *The Decorative Art of Léon Bakst*. Trans. Harry Melvill. London, 1913; rpt. New York: Dover, 1972.
Anderson, Jack. *The One and Only: The Ballet Russe de Monte Carlo*. New York: Dance Horizons, 1981.

⟨491⟩

Antheil, George. *Bad Boy of Music*. London: Hurst and Blackett, 1947.

Armitage, Merle. *Dance Memoranda*. Ed. Edwin Corle. New York: Duell, Sloan and Pearce, 1947.

Arvey, Verna. *Choreographic Music: Music for the Dance*. New York: Dutton, 1941.

Aschengreen, Erik. *Jean Cocteau and the Dance*. Trans. Patricia McAndrew and Per Avsum. Copenhagen: Gyldendal, 1986.

Astruc, Gabriel. *Le Pavillon des fantômes*. Paris: Grasset, 1929.

Au Temps du Boeuf sur le Toit 1918–1928. Introd. Georges Bernier. Paris: Artcurial, 1981.

Axsom, Richard H. *"Parade": Cubism as Theater*. New York: Garland, 1979.

Bablet, Denis. *Esthétique générale du décor de théâtre de 1870 à 1914*. Paris: Centre national de la recherche scientifique, 1965.

Baer, Nancy Van Norman, ed. *The Art of Enchantment: Diaghilev's Ballets Russes, 1909–1929*. San Francisco: Fine Arts Museums of San Francisco, 1988.

—— *Bronislava Nijinska: A Dancer's Legacy*. San Francisco: Fine Arts Museums of San Francisco, 1986.

Barbier, George. *Designs on the Dances of Vaslav Nijinsky*. Foreword Francis de Miomandre. Trans. C.W. Beaumont. London: C.W. Beaumont, 1913.

——, and Jean-Louis Vaudoyer. *Album dédié à Tamara Karsavina*. Paris: Pierre Conrad, 1914.

Barker, Felix. *The House That Stoll Built: The Story of the Coliseum Theatre*. London: Frederick Muller, 1957.

Beaton, Cecil. *Ballet*. Garden City, N.Y.: Doubleday, 1951.

—— *Diaries 1922–1939: The Wandering Years*. London: Weidenfeld and Nicolson, 1961.

Beaumont, Cyril W. *Bookseller at the Ballet, Memoirs 1891 to 1929, Incorporating the Diaghilev Ballet in London*. London: C.W. Beaumont, 1975.

—— *Complete Book of Ballets*. London: Putnam, 1937.

—— *Michel Fokine and His Ballets*. New York: Dance Horizons, 1981.

Bedells, Phyllis. *My Dancing Days*. London: Phoenix House, 1954.

Beecham, Sir Thomas. *A Mingled Chime: An Autobiography*. New York: Putnam, 1943.

Bell, Quentin. *Virginia Woolf: A Biography*. 2 vols. New York: Harcourt, Brace, Jovanovich, 1972.

Bennett, Arnold. *Paris Nights and Other Impressions of Places and People*. New York: George H. Doran, 1913.

Benois, Alexandre. *Memoirs*. 2 vols. Trans. Moura Budberg. London: Chatto and Windus, 1964.

—— *Reminiscences of the Russian Ballet*. Trans. Mary Britnieva. London: Putnam, 1941.

—— *Russian School of Painting*. St. Petersburg: L. Golicke and A. Willborg, 1904.

Bernays, Edward L. *Biography of an Idea: Memoirs of Public Relations Counsel Edward L. Bernays*. New York: Simon and Schuster, 1965.

Bizet, René. *L'Epoque du Music-Hall*. Paris: Editions du Capitole, 1927.

Blanche, Jacques-Emile. *Portraits of a Lifetime: The Late Victorian Era, The Edwardian Pageant, 1870–1914*. Ed. and trans. Walter Clement. Introd. Harley Granville-Barker. London: Dent, 1937.

Bourman, Anatole. *The Tragedy of Nijinsky.* In collaboration with D. Lyman. London: Robert Hall, 1937.

Bowlt, John E. *Russian Stage Design: Scenic Innovation, 1900–1930—From the Collection of Mr. and Mrs. Nikita D. Lobanov-Rostovsky.* Jackson, Miss.: Mississippi Museum of Art, 1982.

——— *The Silver Age: Russian Art of the Early Twentieth Century and the "World of Art" Group.* Newtonville, Mass.: Oriental Research Partners, 1979.

Braun, Edward. *The Theatre of Meyerhold: Revolution on the Modern Stage.* New York: Drama Book Specialists, 1979.

Brody, Elaine. *Paris: The Musical Kaleidoscope 1870–1925.* New York: George Braziller, 1987.

Bruce, Henry James. *Thirty Dozen Moons.* London: Constable, 1949.

Buckle, Richard. *Diaghilev.* London: Weidenfeld and Nicolson, 1979.

——— *George Balanchine, Ballet Master.* In collaboration with John Taras. New York: Random House, 1988.

——— *In Search of Diaghilev.* New York: Thomas Nelson, 1956.

——— *Nijinsky.* New York: Simon and Schuster, 1971.

——— *Nijinsky on Stage.* London: Studio Vista, 1971.

Calvocoressi, M.D. *Musicians Gallery: Music and Ballet in Paris and London.* London: Faber and Faber, 1933.

Castle, Irene. *Castles in the Air.* As told to Bob and Wanda Duncan. Garden City, N.Y.: Doubleday, 1958.

Chadd, David, and John Cage. *The Diaghilev Ballet in England.* Foreword Richard Buckle. Catalogue for an exhibition at the Sainsbury Centre for Visual Arts, University of East Anglia, 11 October–20 November 1979.

Chaliapin, Fyodor. *Chaliapin: An Autobiography As Told to Maxim Gorky.* Trans. and ed. Nina Froud and James Hanley. London: MacDonald, 1968.

Chamot, Mary. *Gontcharova.* Trans. Helen Gerebzow. Paris: Bibliothèque des Arts, 1972.

——— *Goncharova: Stage Designs and Paintings.* London: Oresko Books, 1979.

Charles-Roux, Edmonde. *Chanel—Her Life, Her World and the Woman Behind the Legend She Herself Created.* Trans. Nancy Amphoux. New York: Knopf, 1975.

Chisholm, Anne. *Nancy Cunard: A Biography.* Harmondsworth, Middlesex: Penguin, 1981.

Choreography by George Balanchine: A Catalogue of Works. Ed. Leslie George Katz, Nancy Lassalle, and Harvey Simmonds. New York: Eakins Press, 1983.

Cochran, Charles B. *I Had Almost Forgotten.* Preface A.P. Herbert. London: Hutchinson, 1932.

Cocteau, Jean. *A Call to Order.* Trans. Rollo H. Myers. London: Faber and Faber, 1926.

——— *Carte Blanche.* Paris: Mermod, [1952].

——— *Le Coq et l'Arlequin: Notes autour de la musique 1918.* Preface Georges Auric. Paris: Stock, 1979.

——— *Dessins.* Paris: Stock, 1923.

——— *The Infernal Machine and Other Plays.* Trans. Dudley Fitts. New York: New Directions, 1967.

——— *Nouveau Théâtre de poche.* Monaco: Editions du Rocher, 1960.

——— *Le Numéro Barbette.* Paris: Jacques Damase, 1980.

————, Georges Auric, Georges Braque, and Louis Laloy. *Théâtre Serge de Diaghilew: Les Fâcheux*. Paris: Editions des Quatre Chemins, 1924.

————, Marie Laurencin, Darius Milhaud, and Francis Poulenc. *Théâtre Serge de Diaghilew: Les Biches*. Paris: Editions des Quatre Chemins, 1924.

Cogniat, Raymond. *Cinquante Ans de spectacles en France: Les Décorateurs de théâtre*. Paris: Librairie Théâtrale, 1955.

Collection des plus beaux programmes des Ballets russes de Serge de Diaghilew de 1909 à 1921. Paris: de Brunoff, 1922.

Cooper, Diana. *The Rainbow Comes and Goes*. Boston: Houghton Mifflin, 1958.

Cooper, Douglas. *Picasso Theatre*. New York: Abrams, 1968.

Cossart, Michael de. *The Food of Love: Princesse Edmond de Polignac (1865–1943) and Her Salon*. London: Hamish Hamilton, 1978.

Craig, Gordon. *Gordon Craig on Movement and Dance*. Ed. and introd. Arnold Rood. New York: Dance Horizons, 1977.

The Dance Encyclopedia. Ed. Anatole Chujoy and P.W. Manchester. New York: Simon and Schuster, 1967.

Danilova, Alexandra. *Choura: The Memoirs of Alexandra Danilova*. New York: Knopf, 1986.

The Designs of Léon Bakst for The Sleeping Princess. Preface André Levinson. London: Benn Brothers, 1923.

di Milia, Gabriella. *Mir Iskusstva—Il Mondo dell'Arte: Artisti Russi dal 1898 al 1924*. Naples: Società Napoletana, 1982.

Dolin, Anton. *Autobiography: A Volume of Autobiography and Reminiscence*. London: Oldbourne, 1960.

———— *The Sleeping Ballerina: The Story of Olga Spessivtzeva*. Foreword Dame Marie Rambert. London: Frederick Muller, 1966.

Draper, Muriel. *Music at Midnight*. New York: Harper, 1929.

Dukes, Ashley. *The Scene is Changed*. London: Macmillan, 1942.

Duncan, Isadora. *My Life*. New York: Boni and Liveright, 1927.

Espinosa, Edward. *And Then He Danced: The Life of Espinosa by Himself*. Ed. Rachel Ferguson. London: Sampson Low, Marston, 1948.

Fitch, Noel Riley. *Sylvia Beach and the Lost Generation: A History of Literary Paris in the Twenties and Thirties*. New York: Norton, 1983.

Fitzgerald, Zelda. *Save Me the Waltz*. Introd. Harry T. Moore. London: Jonathan Cape, 1968.

Flanner, Janet. *Paris Was Yesterday, 1925–1939*. Ed. Irving Drutman. New York: Popular Library, n.d.

Fokine, Michel. *Memoirs of a Ballet Master*. Trans. Vitale Fokine. Ed. Anatole Chujoy. Boston: Little, Brown, 1961

———— *Against the Tide: Memoirs of a Ballet Master, Articles, and Letters*. Introd. Yuri Slonimsky. Leningrad: Iskusstvo, 1962.

Gale, Joseph. *I Sang for Diaghilev: Michel Pavloff's Merry Life*. New York: Dance Horizons, 1982.

Georges-Michel, Michel. *Ballets Russes: Histoire anecdotique suivie du Poème de Shéhérazade*. Paris: Editions du Monde Nouveau, 1923.

Geva, Tamara. *Split Seconds: A Remembrance by Tamara Geva*. New York: Harper and Row, 1972.

Goddard, Chris. *Jazz Away From Home*. London: Paddington Press, 1979.

Gofman, I. *Alexander Golovin*. Moscow: Izobrazitelnoye Iskusstvo, 1981.

Gold, Arthur, and Robert Fizdale. *Misia: The Life of Misia Sert.* New York: Knopf, 1980.

Golub, Spencer. *Evreinof: The Theatre of Paradox and Transformation.* Ann Arbor: UMI Research Press, 1984.

Gontcharova, Nathalie, Michel Larionov, and Pierre Vorms. *Les Ballets russes: Serge Diaghilew et la décoration théâtrale.* Rev. ed. Belvès Dordogne: Pierre Vorms, 1955.

Goossens, Eugene. *Overture and Beginners: A Musical Autobiography.* London: Methuen, 1951.

Green, Martin. *Children of the Sun: A Narrative of "Decadence" in England After 1918.* New York: Basic Books, 1976.

Grigoriev, S.L. *The Diaghilev Ballet 1909–1929.* Trans. and ed. Vera Bowen. London: Constable, 1953.

Guest, Ivor. *Adeline Genée: A Lifetime of Ballet Under Six Reigns.* London: Adam and Charles Black, 1958.

———— *Le Ballet de l'Opéra de Paris: Trois Siècles d'histoire et de tradition.* Trans. Paul Alexandre. Paris: Théâtre National de l'Opéra, n.d.

Hanson, Lawrence, and Elisabeth Hanson. *Prokofiev: A Biography in Three Movements.* New York: Random House, 1964.

Haskell, Arnold. *Balletomania: The Story of an Obsession.* London: Gollancz, 1934.

———— *Diaghileff: His Artistic and Private Life.* In collaboration with Walter Nouvel. London: Gollancz, 1935.

Holroyd, Michael. *Lytton Strachey: A Critical Biography.* 2 vols. New York: Holt, Rinehart and Winston, 1968.

Horwitz, Dawn Lille. *Michel Fokine.* Foreword Don McDonaugh. Boston: Twayne, 1985.

Hugo, Jean. *Avant d'Oublier 1918–1931.* Paris: Fayard, 1976.

Jullian, Philippe. *Robert de Montesquiou: A Fin-de-Siècle Prince.* Trans. John Haylock and Francis King. London: Secker and Warburg, 1965.

Kahnweiler, Daniel-Henry. *Juan Gris: His Life and Work.* London, 1969.

Karsavina, Tamara. *Theatre Street: The Reminiscences of Tamara Karsavina.* Foreword J.M. Barrie. London: Heinemann, 1930.

Kean, Beverly Whitney. *All the Empty Palaces: The Merchant Patrons of Modern Art in Pre-Revolutionary Russia.* New York: Universe Books, 1983.

Kendall, Elizabeth. *Where She Danced.* New York: Knopf, 1979.

Kerensky, Oleg. *Anna Pavlova.* New York: Dutton, 1973.

Kessler, Count Harry. *In the Twenties: The Diaries of Count Harry Kessler.* Trans. Charles Kessler. Introd. Otto Friendrich. New York: Holt, Rinehart and Winston, 1971.

Keynes, Geoffrey. *The Gates of Memory.* London: Oxford University Press, 1983.

Keynes, Milo, ed. *Lydia Lopokova.* London: Weidenfeld and Nicolson, 1983.

Kirstein, Lincoln. *Nijinsky Dancing.* New York: Knopf, 1975.

Kochno, Boris. *Diaghilev and the Ballets Russes.* Trans. Adrienne Foulke. New York: Harper and Row, 1970.

Krasovskaya, Vera. *Nijinsky.* Trans. John E. Bowlt. New York: Schmirner, 1979.

Kschessinska, Mathilde (Princess Romanovsky-Krassinsky). *Dancing in Petersburg: The Memoirs of Kschessinska.* Trans. Arnold Haskell. Garden City, 1961; rpt. New York: Da Capo, 1977.

Kyasht, Lydia. *Romantic Recollections.* Ed. Erica Beale. London: Brentano, 1929.

Lambert, Constant. *Music Ho! A Study of Music in Decline.* Introd. Arthur Hutchings. New York: October House, 1967.

Levinson, André. *Bakst: The Story of the Artist's Life.* 1923; rpt. New York: Blom, 1971.

—— *Ballet Old and New.* Trans. Susan Cook Summer. New York: Dance Horizons, 1982.

—— *La Danse au Théâtre: Esthétique et actualité mêlées.* Paris: Bloud et Gay, 1924.

—— *La Danse d'aujourd'hui: Etudes, Notes, Portraits.* Paris: Duchartre et Van Buggenhoudt, 1929.

Lieven, Prince Peter. *The Birth of Ballets-Russes.* Trans. L. Zarine. London: George Allen and Unwin, 1936.

Lifar, Serge. *Ma Vie: From Kiev to Kiev.* Trans. James Holman Mason. New York: World Publishing, 1970.

—— *Serge Diaghilev: His Life, His Work, His Legend. An Intimate Biography.* 1940; rpt. New York: Da Capo, 1976.

Lockspeiser, Edward. *Debussy: His Life and Mind.* 2 vols. Cambridge: Cambridge University Press, 1978.

Macdonald, Nesta. *Diaghilev Observed by Critics in England and the United States 1911–1929.* New York: Dance Horizons, 1975.

Maré, Rolf de. *Les Ballets Suédois dans l'art contemporain.* Paris: Editions du Trianon, 1931.

Markevitch, Igor. *Etre et avoir été: Mémoires.* Paris: Gallimard, 1980.

Markova, Alicia. *Markova Remembers.* Boston: Little, Brown, 1986.

Massine, Léonide. *My Life in Ballet.* Ed. Phyllis Hartnoll and Robert Rubens. London: Macmillan, 1968.

Materials for the History of Russian Ballet. Ed. M. Borisoglebsky. Vol. 2. Leningrad, 1939.

Matz, Mary Jane. *The Many Lives of Otto Kahn.* New York: Macmillan, 1963.

Maxwell, Elsa. *R.S.V.P.: Elsa Maxwell's Own Story.* Boston: Little, Brown, 1954.

Mayer, Charles S. *Bakst: Centenary 1876–1976.* London: Fine Art Society, 1976.

Melba, Nellie. *Melodies and Memoires.* London: Butterworth, 1925.

Mérode, Cléo de. *Le Ballet de ma vie.* Preface Françoise Ducout. Paris: Pierre Horay, 1985.

Oliver Messel. Ed. Roger Pinkham. London: Victoria and Albert Museum, 1983.

Meyerhold on Theatre. Trans. and ed. Edward Braun. New York: Hill and Wang, 1969.

Migel, Parmenia. *Pablo Picasso: Designs for "The Three-Cornered Hat" (Le Tricorne).* New York: Dover/Stravinsky-Diaghilev Foundation, 1978.

Milhaud, Darius. *Notes Without Music: An Autobiography.* New York: Knopf, 1953.

Mirsky, D.S. *A History of Russian Literature.* Ed. Francis J. Whitfield. New York: Knopf, 1949.

Money, Keith. *Anna Pavlova: Her Life and Art.* New York: Knopf, 1982.

Montenegro, Robert. *Vaslav Nijinsky: An Artistic Interpretation of His Work in Black, White and Gold.* Introd. C.W. Beaumont. London: C.W. Beaumont, 1913.

Monteux, Doris G. *It's All in the Music.* New York: Farrar, Straus and Giroux, 1965.

Morrell, Lady Ottoline. *Memoirs of Lady Ottoline Morrell: A Study in Friendship, 1873–1915.* Ed. Robert Gathorne-Hardy. New York: Knopf, 1964.

Nabokov, Nicolas. *Old Friends and New Music.* London: Hamish Hamilton, 1951.

Nichols, Beverley. *Are They the Same at Home? Being a Series of Bouquets Diffidently Distributed.* London: Jonathan Cape, 1927.

Nijinska, Bronislava. *Early Memoirs.* Trans. and ed. Irina Nijinska and Jean Rawlinson. Introd. Anna Kisselgoff. New York: Holt, Rinehart and Winston, 1981.

Nijinsky, Romola. *Nijinsky.* Foreword Paul Claudel. New York: Simon and Schuster, 1934.

Nijinsky, Vaslav. *The Diary of Vaslav Nijinsky.* Ed. Romola Nijinsky. Berkeley: University of California Press, 1968.

Nikitina, Alice. *Nikitina By Herself.* Trans. Baroness Budberg. London: Alan Wingate, 1959.

Ostrovsky, Erika. *Eyes of Dawn: The Rise and Fall of Mata Hari.* New York: Macmillan, 1978.

Oukrainsky, Serge. *My Two Years With the Dancing Genius of the Age: Anna Pavlowa.* Hollywood: Suttonhouse, [1940].

Painter, George D. *Marcel Proust: A Biography.* 2 vols. Harmondsmith, Middlesex: Penguin, 1977.

Parnakh, Valentin. *Gontcharova et Larionow: l'art décoratif théâtral moderne.* Paris: La Cible, 1919.

Poiret, Paul. *My First Fifty Years.* London: Gollancz, 1931.

Ezra Pound and Music: The Complete Criticism. Ed. R. Murray Schafer. New York: New Directions, 1977.

Proujan, Irina. *Léon Bakst: Esquisses de décor et de costumes, arts graphiques, peintures.* Trans. Denis Dabbadie. Leningrad: Editions d'Art Aurora, 1986.

Priddin, Deirdre. *The Art of the Dance in French Literature from Théophile Gautier to Paul Valéry.* Foreword Arnold L. Haskell. Preface Cyril W. Beaumont. London: Adam and Charles Black, 1952.

Prokofiev, Serge. *Prokofiev by Prokofiev: A Composer's Memoir.* Trans. Guy Daniels. Garden City, N.Y.: Doubleday, 1979.

Propert, W.A. *The Russian Ballet in Western Europe 1909–1920.* London: John Lane, 1921.

——— *The Russian Ballet 1921–1929.* Preface Jacques-Emile Blanche. London: John Lane, 1931.

Racster, Olga. *The Master of the Russian Ballet: The Memoirs of Cav. Enrico Cecchetti.* Introd. Anna Pavlova. London: Hutchinson, [1922].

Rambert, Marie. *Quicksilver: An Autobiography.* London: Macmillan, 1972.

Ricketts, Charles. *Self-Portrait.* Ed. T. Sturge Moore and Cecil Lewis. London: Peter Davies, 1939.

Ries, Frank W.D. *The Dance Theatre of Jean Cocteau.* Ann Arbor: UMI Research Press, 1986.

Rimsky-Korsakov, Nikolai. *My Musical Life.* Trans. J.A. Joffe. Ed. Carl van Vechten. London: Secker, 1924.

Roslavleva, Natalia. *Era of the Russian Ballet 1770–1965.* Foreword Ninette de Valois. London: Gollancz, 1966.

Rubinstein, Arthur. *My Young Years.* London: Cape, 1973.

Rudnitsky, Konstantin. *Meyerhold the Director.* Trans. George Petrov. Ed. Sydney Schultze. Introd. Ellendea Proffer. Ann Arbor: Ardis, 1981.

The Russian Symbolist Theater: An Anthology of Plays and Critical Texts. Ed. and trans. Michael Green. Ann Arbor: Ardis, 1986.

Saint Germain, Philippe, and Francis Rosset. *La Grande Dame de Monte-Carlo.* Paris: Stock, 1981.

Schouvaloff, Alexander, and Victor Borovsky. *Stravinsky on Stage.* London: Stainer and Bell, 1982.

The Serge Lifar Collection of Ballet Set and Costume Designs. Hartford, Conn.: Wadsworth Atheneum, 1965.

Sert, Misia. *Two or Three Muses: The Memoirs of Misia Sert.* Trans. Moura Budberg. London: Museum Press, 1953.

Shaw, Bernard. *Shaw's Music: The Complete Musical Criticism.* New York: Dodd, Mead, 1981. Vol. 3.

Shead, Richard. *Music in the Twenties.* London: Duckworth, 1976.

Sitwell, Edith. *Children's Tales From the Russian Ballet.* London: Leonard Parsons, 1920.

Sitwell, Osbert. *Great Morning: An Autobiography.* London: Reprint Society, 1948.

——— *Laughter in the Next Room.* London: Reprint Society, 1950.

Skidelsky, Robert. *John Maynard Keynes: A Biography.* London: Macmillan, 1983. Vol. 1.

Slonim, Marc. *Russian Theatre From the Empire to the Soviets.* Cleveland: World Publishing, 1961.

Sokolova, Lydia. *Dancing for Diaghilev.* Ed. Richard Buckle. London: John Murray, 1960.

Spalding, Frances. *Roger Fry: Art and Life.* Berkeley: University of California Press, 1980.

Spencer, Charles. *Léon Bakst.* London: Academy, 1973.

———, and Philip Dyer. *The World of Serge Diaghilev.* Chicago: Henry Regnery, 1974.

Stanislavsky, Constantin. *My Life in Art.* Trans. J.J. Robbins. Boston: Little, Brown, 1924.

Steegmuller, Francis. *Cocteau: A Biography.* Boston: Little, Brown, 1970.

Stravinsky, Igor. *Stravinsky: An Autobiography.* New York: Simon and Schuster, 1936.

——— *Stravinsky: Selected Correspondence.* Ed. Robert Craft. New York: Knopf, 1982. Vol. 1.

——— *Stravinsky: Selected Correspondence.* Ed. Robert Craft. New York: Knopf, 1984. Vol. 2.

———, and Robert Craft. *Conversations with Igor Stravinsky.* London: Faber and Faber, 1959.

——— *Expositions and Developments.* Berkeley: University of California Press, 1981.

——— *Memories and Commentaries.* Garden City, N.Y.: Doubleday, 1960.

Stravinsky, Vera, and Robert Craft. *Stravinsky in Pictures and Documents.* London: Hutchinson, 1979.

Svetlov, Valerian. *Anna Pavlova.* Trans. A. Grey. Paris, 1922; rpt. New York: Dover, 1974.

———— *Le Ballet Contemporain*. With the collaboration of Léon Bakst. Trans. M.D. Calvocoressi. Paris: de Brunoff, 1912.

Taper, Bernard. *Balanchine: A Biography*. Rev. ed. New York: Times Books, 1984.

Terry, Ellen. *The Russian Ballet*. London: Sidgwick and Jackson, 1913.

Thomson, Virgil. *Virgil Thomson*. New York: Knopf, 1966.

Tompkins, Calvin. *Living Well is the Best Revenge*. New York: Dutton, 1982.

Tyler, Parker. *The Divine Comedy of Pavel Tchelitchew*. New York: Fleet Publishing, 1967.

Valois, Ninette de. *Come Dance With Me: A Memoir 1898–1956*. London: Dance Books, 1973.

———— *Invitation to the Ballet*. London: John Lane, 1937.

Volkov, Solomon. *Balanchine's Tchaikovsky*. Trans. Antonina W. Bouis. New York: Simon and Schuster, 1985.

Walker, Kathrine Sorley. *De Basil's Ballets Russes*. London: Hutchinson, 1982.

White, Eric Walter. *Stravinsky: The Composer and His Works*. Berkeley: University of California Press, 1979.

Whitworth, Geoffrey. *The Art of Nijinsky*. London, 1913; rpt. New York: Benjamin Blom, 1972.

Wiley, Roland John. *Tchaikovsky's Ballets: Swan Lake, Sleeping Beauty, Nutcracker*. London: Oxford University Press, 1985.

Wilkins, Nigel. *The Writings of Erik Satie*. London: Eulenberg, 1981.

Wolff, Stéphane. *L'Opéra au Palais Garnier (1875–1962)*. Introd. Alain Gueullette. Paris: Slatkine, 1983.

Yastrebtsev, V.V. *Reminiscences of Rimsky-Korsakov*. Ed. and trans. Florence Jonas. Introd. Gerald Abraham. New York: Columbia University Press, 1985.

Zilberstein, I.S., and V.A. Samkov, eds. *Serge Diaghilev and Russian Art*. 2 vols. Moscow: Izobrazitelnoe Iskusstvo, 1982.

Articles

Acocella, Joan. "Photo Call With Nijinsky: The Circle and the Center." *Ballet Review*, 14, No. 4 (Winter 1987), pp. 49–71.

Banes, Sally. "An Introduction to the Ballets Suédois." *Ballet Review*, 7, Nos. 2–3 (1978–1979), pp. 28–59.

Bowlt, John E. "Constructivism and Russian Stage Design." *Performing Arts Journal*, 1, No. 3 (Winter 1977), pp. 62–84.

———— "Nikolai Ryabushinsky: Playboy of the Eastern World." *Apollo*, December 1973, pp. 486–493.

Celli, Vincenzo. "Enrico Cecchetti." *Dance Index*, 5, No. 7 (1946), pp. 158–179.

Chujoy, Anatole. "Russian Balletomania." *Dance Index*, 7, No. 3 (March 1948), pp. 45–71.

Cohen, Barbara Naomi. "The Borrowed Art of Gertrude Hoffmann." *Dance Data*, No. 2 (n.d.), pp. 2–11.

Fry, Roger. "M. Larionow and the Russian Ballet." *Burlington Magazine*, March 1919, pp. 112–118.

Goldman, Debra. "Mothers and Fathers: A View of Isadora and Fokine." *Ballet Review*, 6, No. 4 (1977–1978), pp. 33–43.

Goncharova, Natalia. "The Creation of 'Les Noces.' " *Ballet and Opera*, September 1949, pp. 23–26.

——— "The Metamorphoses of the Ballet 'Les Noces.' " *Leonardo*, 12, No. 2 (Spring 1979), pp. 137–143.

Gordon, Mel. "Meyerhold's Biomechanics." *Drama Review*, 18, No. 3 (September 1974), pp. 73–88.

Guest, Ivor. "The Alhambra Ballet." *Dance Perspectives*, 4 (Autumn 1959), pp. 5–70.

Hodson, Millicent. "Nijinsky's Choreographic Method: Visual Sources from Roerich for *Le Sacre du Printemps*." *Dance Research Journal*, 18, No. 2 (Winter 1986–1987), pp. 7–15.

Horwitz, Dawn Lille. "A Ballet Class With Michel Fokine." *Dance Chronicle*, 3, No. 1 (1979), pp. 36–45.

Iavorskaïa, N.A. "Les relations artistiques entre Paris et Moscou dans les années 1917–1930." In *Paris-Moscou, 1900–1930*. Paris: Centre National d'Art et de Culture Georges Pompidou, 1979.

Jones, Robert Edmond. "Nijinsky and Til Eulenspiegel." *Dance Index*, 4, No. 4 (April 1945), pp. 44–54.

Karlinsky, Simon. "Stravinsky and Russian Pre-literate Theater." *Nineteenth-Century Russian Music*, 6, No. 3 (Spring 1983), pp. 232–240.

Krasovskaya, Vera. "Marius Petipa and 'The Sleeping Princess.' " Trans. Cynthia Read. *Dance Perspectives*, 49 (Spring 1972), pp. 6–45.

Levinson, André. "A Crisis in the Ballets Russes." *Theatre Arts Monthly*, November 1926, pp. 785–792.

Lobanov, N.D. "Russian Painters and the Stage." *Transactions*, 2 (1968), pp. 133–210.

Nijinska, Bronislava. "Creation of 'Les Noces.' " Trans. and introd. Jean M. Serafetinides and Irina Nijinska. *Dance Magazine*, December 1974, pp. 58–61.

——— "On Movement and the School of Movement." Introd. Joan Ross Acocella and Lynn Garafola. *Ballet Review*, 13, No. 4 (Winter 1986), pp. 75–81.

——— "Reflections About the Production of *Les Biches* and *Hamlet* in Markova-Dolin Ballets." Trans. Lydia Lopokova. *Dancing Times*, Feb. 1937, pp. 617–620.

Orledge, Robert. "Cole Porter's Ballet *Within the Quota*." *Yale University Library Gazette*, 50, No. 1 (July 1975), pp. 19–29.

Polignac, Princesse Edmond de. "Memoirs of the Late Princess Edmond de Polignac." *Horizon*, August 1945, pp. 110–141.

Ricco, Edward. "The Sitwells at the Ballet." *Ballet Review*, 6, No. 1 (1977–1978), pp. 58–117.

Richardson, Philip J.S. "A Chronology of the Ballet in England 1910–1945." In *The Ballet Annual: A Record and Yearbook of the Ballet*. London: Adam and Charles Black, 1947, pp. 115–131.

Ries, Frank W.D. "Acrobats, Burlesque, and Cocteau." *Dance Scope*, 11, No. 1 (Fall/Winter 1976–1977), pp. 52–67.

Rivière, Jacques. "Des Ballets russes et de Fokine." *Nouvelle Revue Française*, July 1912, pp. 174–180.

——— "La Crise du concept de littérature." *Nouvelle Revue Française*, 1 February 1924, pp. 159–170.

———— "Le Sacre du Printemps." *Nouvelle Revue Française,* November 1913, pp. 706–730.

Silver, Kenneth E. "Jean Cocteau and the *Image d'Epinal:* An Essay on Realism and Naiveté." In *Jean Cocteau and the French Scene.* Ed. Alexandra Anderson and Carol Saltus. New York: Abbeville Press, 1984.

Slonimsky, Yuri. "Balanchine: The Early Years." Trans. John Andrews. Ed. Francis Mason. *Ballet Review,* 5, No. 3 (1975–1976), pp. 1–64.

———— "Marius Petipa." Trans. Anatole Chujoy. *Dance Index,* 6, Nos. 5–6 (May-June 1947), pp. 100–144.

Souritz, Elizabeth. "Fedor Lopukhov: A Soviet Choreographer in the 1920s." *Dance Research Journal,* 17, No. 2 (Fall 1985/Spring 1986), pp. 3–20.

———— "Soviet Ballet of the 1920s and the Influence of Constructivism." *Soviet Union/Union Soviétique,* Parts 1–2 (1980), pp. 112–137.

Svetlov, Valerian. "The Diaghileff Ballet in Paris." *Dancing Times,* December 1929, pp. 263–274.

———— "The Diaghileff Ballet in Paris." Part II. *Dancing Times,* January 1930, pp. 460–463.

———— "The Diaghileff Ballet in Paris." Part III. *Dancing Times,* February 1930, pp. 569–574.

———— "The Old and the New." *Dancing Times,* July 1929, pp. 326–331.

Taruskin, Richard. "From *Firebird* to *The Rite:* Folk Elements in Stravinsky's Scores." *Ballet Review,* 10, No. 2 (Summer 1982), pp. 72–87.

Tripp, Susan B. "Bakst." *Johns Hopkins Magazine,* June 1984, pp. 12–22.

Wiley, Roland John. "Alexandre Benois' Commentaries." Parts I-VII. *Dancing Times,* October 1980-April 1981.

Unpublished Theses and Dissertations

Acocella, Joan Ross. "The Reception of Diaghilev's Ballets Russes by Artists and Intellectuals in Paris and London, 1909–1914." Diss. Rutgers 1984.

Baldwin, Frances. "Critical Response in England to the Work of Designers for Diaghilev's Russian Ballet, 1911–1929." M.S. Thesis, Courtauld Institute of Art (London) 1980.

Berg, Shelley Celia. " 'Le Sacre du Printemps': A Comparative Study of Seven Versions of the Ballet." Diss. New York University 1985.

Bullard, Truman C. "The First Performance of Igor Stravinsky's *Sacre du Printemps.*" Diss. Eastman School of Music (Rochester) 1971.

DeBold II, Conrad. "*Parade* and '*Le Spectacle Intérieur*': The Role of Jean Cocteau in an Avant-garde Ballet." Diss. Emory 1982.

Grover, Stuart R. "Savva Mamontov and the Mamontov Circle: 1870–1905; Art Patronage and the Rise of Nationalism in Russian Art." Diss. Wisconsin 1971.

Hodson, Millicent Kaye. "Nijinsky's New Dance: Rediscovery of Ritual Design in *Le Sacre du Printemps.*" Diss. California (Berkeley) 1985.

Horwitz, Dawn Lille. "Michel Fokine in America, 1919–1942." Diss. New York University 1982.

Kennedy, Janet Elspeth. "The 'Mir Iskusstva' Group and Russian Art 1898–1912." Diss. Columbia 1976.

McQuillan, Melissa A. "Painters and the Ballet, 1917–1926: An Aspect of the Relationship Between Art and Theatre." Diss. New York University 1979.

Mayer, Charles Steven. "The Theatrical Designs of Léon Bakst." Diss. Columbia 1977.

Pasler, Jann Corinne. "Debussy, Stravinsky, and the Ballets Russes: The Emergence of a New Musical Logic." Diss. Chicago 1981.

Ries, Frank W.D. "Jean Cocteau and the Ballet." Diss. Indiana 1980.

Silver, Kenneth Eric. "*Esprit de Corps:* The Great War and French Art." Diss. Yale 1981.

Sommer, Sally R. "Loie Fuller: From the Theatre of Popular Entertainment to the Parisian Avant-garde." Diss. New York University 1979.

Weinstock, Stephen Jay. "Independence Versus Interdependence in Stravinsky's Theatrical Collaborations: The Evolution of the Original Production of *The Wedding.*" Diss. California (Berkeley) 1981.

PHOTO CREDITS

Photographers or sources of photographs used in this book are listed below in alphabetical order.

Reproduced from the Ballets Russes souvenir program, 1919–1920, 24.
Ballet Society Archives, 40 (photograph by Henri Manuel), 41 (photograph by Sasha), 44 (photograph by Sasha), 45 (performance photograph by the *Times*), 47 (photograph by Numa Blanc).
Bibliothèque Nationale (Opéra), 22, 32, 63, 65, 66.
Photograph by Saul Bransburg (reproduced from the *Sketch*, 15 July 1914), 3.
Photograph by Bulla (reproduced from the *Sketch* [Supplement], 2 July 1913), 64.
Copyright © The Condé Nast Publications Ltd., 57.
Courtesy of Robert Craft, 62.
Courtesy of Dance Books Ltd., 59, 60.
Dance Collection, The New York Public Library at Lincoln Center, frontispiece (photograph by Jan de Strelecki), 4 (photograph by Baron de Meyer—Roger Pryor Dodge Collection), 5 (photograph by Elliot and Fry—Roger Pryor Dodge Collection), 6 (photograph by Baron de Meyer—Robert Pryor Dodge Collection), 13, 16 (photograph by Baron de Meyer—Roger Pryor Dodge Collection), 17 (photograph by Gerschel—Roger Pryor Dodge Collection), 19 (Roger Pryor Dodge Collection), 30 (performance photograph by the *Times*—Tatiana Chamié Collection), 50, 68 (Tatiana Chamié Collection), 69 (Tatiana Chamié Collection), 70.
Reproduced from *The Designs of Léon Bakst for The Sleeping Princess*, 28.
The Fine Arts Museums of San Francisco (Achenbach Foundation for Graphic Arts), 21, 53.
Reproduced from Michel Fokine, *Against the Tide*, 10.
Photographs by Lipnitzki, copyright © Lipnitzki-Violett, 42, 43, 71.
Reproduced from *Materials for the History of Russian Ballet*, 48, 49.
Music Collection, The New York Public Library at Lincoln Center, 2.
Copyright © 1989 Sotheby's, Inc., 14, 23.
Courtesy of Sotheby's (London), 20, 61 (photograph by Cecil Beaton).
Rare Book and Manuscript Library, Columbia University, 15.
Reproduced from the *Sketch* [Supplement], 23 July 1913, 18.

Photographs by Stage Photo Company (reproduced from the *Dancing Times,* December 1921), 29.

Stravinsky-Diaghilev Foundation, 7 (photograph by Bertram Park), 9 (photograph by Hoppé), 11, 25, 26 (photograph by Rehbinder, 27, 31, 33 (rehearsal photograph by J. Enrietty), 35 (performance photograph by the *Times*), 36, 37 (photograph by Man Ray), 38, 39 (photograph by Man Ray), 56, 67.

Reproduced from Valerian Svetlov, *Le Ballet Contemporain,* 12.

Performance photograph by the *Times* (reproduced from W. A. Propert, *The Russian Ballet 1921–1929*), 34.

George Verdak Collection, 1.

Wadsworth Atheneum, Hartford (from the Serge Lifar Collection and The Ella Gallup Sumner and Mary Catlin Sumner Collection), 46.

Reproduced from I. S. Zilberstein and V. A. Samkov, eds., *Serge Diaghilev and Russian Art,* 8.

INDEX